SOCIAL STUDIES FOR THE TWENTY-FIRST CENTURY

Methods and Materials for Teaching in Middle and Secondary Schools, Second Edition

SOCIAL STUDIES FOR THE TWENTY-FIRST CENTURY

Methods and Materials for Teaching in Middle and Secondary Schools, Second Edition

by Jack Zevin
Queens College, City University of New York

2000

LAWRENCE ERLBAUM ASSOCIATES, PUBLISHERS
Mahwah, New Jersey   London

Lawrence Erlbaum Associates, Inc., Publishers
10 Industrial Avenue
Mahwah, NJ 07430

Cover design by Kathryn Houghtaling Lacey

Library of Congress Cataloging-in-Publication Data

Zevin, Jack.
Social studies for the twenty-first century : methods and materials for teaching
in middle and secondary schools / Jack Zevin. — 2nd ed.
        p. cm.
Includes bibliographical references and index.
ISBN 0-8058-2465-0 (cloth : alk. paper)
1. Social sciences—Study and teaching (Secondary)—United States.   I. Title.
H62.5.U5Z48   1999
300'.71'273—dc21   98-12977
CIP

Books published by Lawrence Erlbaum Associates are printed on acid-free paper,
and their bindings are chosen for strength and durability.

Printed in the United States of America
10 9 8 7 6 5 4 3 2 1

Contents

Preface   vii
Acknowledgments   xi
Personal Prologue   xiii

PART ONE
Philosophy and History of Social Studies: What Is (Are) the Social Studies?

1. The Social Studies: Definition, Organization, and Philosophy   3
2. The Fields of Social Studies: How They Relate   21

PART TWO
Teachers and Students: A Context for Social Studies Instruction

3. Teacher Roles and Student Audiences   39
4. Organizing for Instruction   60

PART THREE
Strategies for Social Studies Instruction

A General Overview of Chapters 5 and 6: Teaching Strategies for Lower and Higher Level Skills   95
5. Teaching Strategies for Lower Level Skills   97
6. Teaching Strategies for Higher Level Skills   115
7. Planning a Unit From Start to Finish   140
8. Evaluation in Social Studies   160

PART FOUR
Teaching the Social Studies Curriculum

9. Teaching World/Global Studies   199
10. Teaching U.S. History and American Studies   225
11. Teaching U.S. Government and Civics   253
12. Old Concerns, New Directions   282

PART FIVE
Textbooks and Media in the Social Studies

13.   The Role of Textbooks in Social Studies Education   317
14.   The "New Age" of Multimedia: Part I. Reading Words and Images: 334
      Print Media and the Fine Arts
15.   The "New Age" of Multimedia: Part II. Interpreting Moving Images   365
      and Sounds

PART SIX
Beyond the Social Studies Classroom:
Professional Issues and Trends

16.   The Complete Professional   383
17.   The Future of Social Studies Education   396

Appendix A: Resources for Instruction   409
Appendix B: Social Studies Education, Social Science, and History   425
              "Good Reads for Big Ideas"
Index   427

Preface

In the sky there is no East or West
We make these distinctions in the mind
Then believe them to be true
Everything in the world comes from the
mind, like objects appearing from the
sleeve of a magician
　　　—The Buddha, Lankavatara Sutra

You are invited to use this book as a guide for teaching social studies at the middle and secondary levels. As much as possible, I provide you with a fair and balanced review of the field using up-to-date curriculum, research, and theory. Social studies is a large and complex field, seeming so fragmented at times that its essence is difficult to grasp. Therefore, throughout the sixteen chapters, social studies theory, goals, curriculum, and everyday practice are viewed in terms of three components: the didactic, reflective, and affective.

　　Didactic refers to all teaching and learning activities that revolve around gathering knowledge from memorizing dates to matching tests. *Reflective* concerns all activities that focus on analyzing and thinking about data, research, or issues for which more than one answer is possible. *Affective* deals with all those facets of classroom life in which feelings, opinions, values, ethics, and morality dominate. Thus each component has a different, though not exclusive, focus: didactic on the what, reflective on the why, and affective on the should or ought. Each component is discussed as contributing to and complementing the others; each enriches classroom discussion and learning. In addition to basic philosophy, there will be informative boxes scattered throughout with information for you to think about. These include tidbits about research (Research Reports), items to stimulate ideas (Let's Decide), instructional gimmicks (Sample Lessons), and places for you to get involved with activities that grow out of each section (To Do).

　　This text is organized into six parts. Part One, "Philosophy and History of the Social Studies," includes two chapters that lay out the underlying arguments of the book, including the tripartite structure of instruction in the social studies (didactic, reflective, and affective), and the view that social studies is a single field of study that incorporates history and the social sciences, as well as borrowing now and then from the humanities and the sciences.

　　Part Two, "Teachers and Students," provides a context for understanding the ways in which teachers plan instruction for middle and secondary social studies classrooms. We look at the roles teachers play to promote knowledge goals, provoke imaginative thinking, and stimulate the examination of values. Then we also look at the student population you will teach—both the typical developmental characteristics of young adults and the instructional adaptations you can make to meet the needs of both regular and special students.

　　Part Three, "Strategies for Social Studies Instruction," and Part Four, "Teaching the Social Studies Curriculum," provide specific guidance for the social studies classroom teacher. Part Three contains information about organizing for instruction, including guidance about group dynamics and about questioning techniques. Chapters 5 and 6 lay out specific teaching strategies designed to encourage lower and higher level thinking skills in the social studies, including data gathering, comparison and contrast, drama building, frame of reference, mystery, and controversy. Each offers a creative way to interest students in social studies instruction with examples that you are free to try out in your own classrooms. Chapter 7 takes you through the planning of a whole unit from start to finish. And, finally, chapter 8 examines the sometimes difficult issue of evaluation, describing the theory and practical construction of diagnostic and assessment tools. The chapter provides guidance for designing tests and examples of effective test items, including an introduction to the concept of authentic assessment or portfolio preparation.

Part Four, "Teaching the Social Studies Curriculum" (chapters 9, 10, and 11), presents detailed analyses of how to teach the most commonly required social studies courses: world or global history, U.S. history, and U.S. government. Information about goals, roles, group dynamics, and evaluation from previous chapters is applied to the preparation of actual instructional plans and outlines for these courses. Chapter 12, New Directions, Old Concerns, looks at important but less widely taught courses and topics—including economics, geography, globalism or international studies, multicultural studies, law-related studies, and courses in other social science disciplines. For each topic, suggestions about teaching techniques and materials are provided.

In Part Five, "Textbooks and Media in Social Studies," chapter 13 offers wide-ranging possibilities for using the ubiquitous textbooks common to the social studies classroom. This includes a discussion of the advantages and disadvantages of relying on texts as major teaching tools. Chapter 14 provides an overview of the burgeoning multimedia field, from print and photography through sound, with a special focus on words and images. Chapter 15 extends the discussion of media to moving images and electronic forums for presenting or obtaining ideas, including film, Internet/World Wide Web sources, and interactive computer simulations and databases, including suggestions for classroom applications and innovations.

Finally, Part Six, "Beyond the Social Studies Classroom: Professional Issues and Trends," deals with your role as a professional in social studies education. Chapter 16 provides an overview of the major organizations in which you may participate and the journals and publications you can turn to for assistance in thinking about your goals, resources, and philosophy of education. Chapter 17, The Future of Social Studies Education, provides a glimpse, however imperfect, into the future of the field completes this book.

Throughout, you are encouraged to read, analyze, and debate my views and consider those issues that are embedded in social studies education. You need not take any statement made here as conclusive or any teaching suggestion as definitive. Try out the suggestions; argue with the assertions. For further help in defining your own views, turn to the "For Further Study" section at the end of each chapter, and to Appendix A for "Resources for Instruction" as well as Appendix B on "Social Studies Edcation, Socal Science, and History 'Good Reads for Big Ideas.'" Taken together, these references provide places to look for some great lessons, as well as organizations that will send you interesting and informative materials to work with or offer you a chance for extended in-service education.

True professionals are always seeking to enhance their knowledge and understanding of our complex world and to share the depth and breadth of their experience with students. Therefore, you are cordially directed to make full use of this book as a guide to the field of social studies, as a course of classroom experimentation with methods and materials for instruction, and as a resource for extended learning. In particular, apply the material in the two new chapters on the media to your classroom so we can all take a step toward moving along with the computer and electronic "revolution." As the Internet and Web TV and other related developments are moving very fast, I invite you to update and revise the new chapters as you develop new uses for the media with your students. You are also invited to use new material in the chapter on evaluation to create an authentic assessment portfolio for your students as part of your overall testing and evaluation program. Keep up with the flow of developments in the social sciences and history, and develop your own philosophy of teaching and learning social studies—one that suits your needs and style, and serves your students effectively.

Acknowledgments

I acknowledge some debts, old and new, in the writing of the second edition of my book for social studies teachers. In particular, I thank my wife, Iris, a front-line secondary social studies teacher, for her confidence in me and for her many suggestions that sprang from a realistic sense of what can be achieved with young people in the classroom. I also owe a debt to my mentor and teacher, Byron G. Massialas, who set me on the path of social studies education some years ago. My students deserve special thanks and an honorable mention because they taught me a great deal about clarity, specificity, and meaning in creating lessons for secondary students. Their valuable suggestions, and recognition of errors helped shape the new edition. There are also many colleagues, scholars, and experts from whom I borrowed or adapted ideas and to whom I owe a deep sense of intellectual gratitude. Finally, my editor, Naomi Silverman, deserves kudos for the encouragement and personal assistance given me during the development of *Social Studies for the Twenty-First Century*, and toward the rewriting of this, our second edition.

Personal Prologue

This book presents the field of social studies with an up-to-date discussion of its most important developments and persisting issues. Like many other fields, social studies is a vast and complicated subject full of problems and inconsistencies to which experience alone can give full meaning. To the new teacher and the uninitiated, social studies may seem confusing and fragmented, leaving teachers rudderless in steering a course through its reefs and shoals.

This volume offers an overall framework that can act as a guide for setting objectives, devising lessons, and choosing classroom strategies. I have also offered assistance in constructing tests and planning lessons, units, and courses for some of the field's most popular and widespread programs. Throughout, all aspects of curriculum and instruction are viewed from a tripartite perspective that divides the world of social studies into didactic, reflective, and affective components. I have used didactic, reflective, and affective to stand for the lower (factual), middle (analytical), and upper (judgmental) ranges of thinking, decision making, and feeling, allowing each about a third of classroom time. The three levels are seen as supporting one another rather than acting in opposition. At no time do I subscribe to interest groups in the field who want their goals stressed at the expense of any others. In my view, the greatest need is for social studies professionals who can balance goals so that students obtain necessary knowledge, are given time for adequate discussions of data, and are asked to probe their own feelings and those of others on the important issues of our time, ultimately taking a stand that they are willing and able to defend. It is the teacher's job to give students the knowledge and skills needed to prepare a solid defense for their views, decisions, and actions.

Of course, giving equal emphasis to each of the three components of teaching is deeply optimistic. We know that social studies teachers are pressed from myriad directions to cover the "facts," finish the textbook, teach thinking skills, complete special projects, use cooperative learning techniques, add authentic assessment to their testing repertory, keep up-to-date with research and curriculum in the field, join and become active in professional organizations, meet national standards in many subjects, and on and on. On top of this, many schools provide a work experience for the teacher that can be characterized only as bureaucratic, demanding, and overstuffed with nonteaching responsibilities. Some schools are repressive and authoritarian as well, giving teachers little or no leeway for creativity or even time to breathe freely for a few moments.

Naturally, such highly pressured situations make excellence in teaching social studies nearly impossible. Valiant effort is necessary to overcome professional demands and personal development problems. Certainly, stoic qualities of endurance have served teachers and teachers-to-be better than Epicurean, fun-loving characteristics!

Nevertheless, I believe that this frequently grim picture must be resisted or we will all lose sight of the joys of teaching, of working with young adults and future citizens, of experimenting with new and exciting methods and materials, and of learning new ideas and improving our own knowledge and understanding of the subject we teach. Teachers and students need to recapture a sense of play as well as meet the goals of work.

Part of the reason social studies is disliked by so many secondary students is that it holds out the promise of democracy, of vibrant discussion and debate, without delivering much in actual practice. Didactic or knowledge aims nearly always triumph over reflective reasoning and ethical arguments. The "sexy stuff," as one of my students put it, caves in to the "laundry list" of purportedly vital knowledge of dates, names, places, and books. Oddly enough, the famous "great books" are almost never experienced firsthand by young adults even though reports and studies decry this group's lack of familiarity with the classics that give history and the social sciences its conceptual and philosophical direction.

To my mind, the only topics in the social studies worth teaching and talking about are those that contain or suggest questions with more than one answer. As a beginning high school teacher in Chicago, I remember very vividly how bored my urban, inner-city classes were with the facts they had to know and how lively they would become when we did anything together that gave them an active role and a chance to "spout off." Many were so unused to speaking in public that they would at first slump down into their desks to avoid a question from their overly zealous teacher. Others found the experience of free speech in a social studies classroom utterly exhilarating and shone immediately. However, after a period of frustration and struggle with their new roles, most found that they not only had something to say but also were getting better at saying it!

I still recall having to teach these young people the dynasties of ancient Egypt—a really useful topic for them! The class session was awful until we got around to discussing death, a grim but fascinating topic to which nearly everyone suddenly had something to contribute. The class divided along the lines of those who judged the ancient Egyptians "nuts" for their practices and others who empathized with their fears about death and their need to soften its blow. The dynasties were quickly forgotten but the conversation on death and how humans cope with it carried on throughout the year. This and other experiences taught me a lesson in ideas, how to motivate student inquiry, and what goals are important to creating an exciting social studies classroom.

Clearly, didactic information is not enough! There must be analysis, synthesis, and an examination of values or the whole teaching enterprise dies a slow death from information overkill. My second job, teaching younger middle school students in Michigan, only served to confirm this principle. The young teens were, if anything, even more restless and impatient than the senior high school students. They, too, had plenty to say, even though much of it was relatively uninformed and immature. Nevertheless, the teacher must start where the students are if some measure of success is to be achieved. The opposite path seems to lead mainly to college-style lecturing and the worst kind of pedantic demands—that students need great amounts and sophisticated types of background data to think adequately about any topic in history and the social sciences.

Overlooked is the fact that it takes a lifetime truly to master a field! Thus, full background knowledge is a goal that is not only impossible for young adults but one that also prevents them and their teacher from going beyond the data given to the realms of understanding and making choices.

So, you might ask, where is this treatise going? It is moving toward this point: The very heart and soul of social studies instruction, perhaps all teaching, in my conception, lies in stimulating the production of ideas, looking at knowledge from others' viewpoints, and formulating for oneself a set of goals, values, and beliefs that can be explained and justified in open discussion.

Thus, you are asked to read this book as a set of optimistic suggestions for goals, lesson planning, curriculum design, and testing. You are free to choose from its resources what you need and can handle. You are also free to reject ideas and opinions that you see as unsuitable. You may say, "You're kidding, I can't do this!" You are also invited to accept and experiment with ideas and judge the outcomes yourself. This book is constructed to represent an ideal for the social studies classroom and is probably inherently impractical for many classrooms. But what can I do as a teacher who has devoted more than 30 years to our field? Should I bemoan its problems and restrictions? Should I fall into the trap of cynicism and apathy? It seems to me we must all struggle with our local work situations, redefining teaching in terms that suit ourselves and provide the deepest and most exciting instruction we can offer our pupils. One way of doing this is to keep our minds open to new ideas and keep a wary eye on those administrators, bureaucrats, and social problems that hem us in and sap our energies.

Just as I am advocating a balance between social studies goals and techniques, so I am advising teachers to juggle subjects, students, and school life until a satisfactory equilibrium is achieved among competing forces. Any classroom session I observe in which the social studies teacher and the students divide their time equally among acquiring knowledge, thinking about motives, and making choices amid competing values, in my book, rates as a wonderful experience.

PART ONE

Philosophy and History of Social Studies: What Is (Are) the Social Studies?

CHAPTER 1

The Social Studies: Definition, Organization, and Philosophy

When a superior man knows the causes which make instruction successful, and those which make it of no effect, he can become a teacher of others. Thus in his teaching, he leads and does not drag; he strengthens and does not discourage: he opens the way but does not conduct to the end without the learner's own efforts. Leading and not dragging produces harmony. Strengthening and not discouraging makes attainment easy. Opening the way and not conducting to the end makes the learner thoughtful. He who produces such harmony, easy attainment, and thoughtfulness may be pronounced a skillful teacher.

—*Confucius*

OVERVIEW OF CONTENTS

Main Ideas —————————————————————————————

What Is (Are) the Social Studies?: Defining Discipline —————————————

      Organizing Principles
      The Origins of Differing Social Studies Perspectives
      Fusion or Fission Approach?

Goals as a Bridge Between Theory and Practice —————————————————

      Theory
      Practice

Recapping the Three Dimensions of Social Studies Instruction ——————————

Summary ——————————————————————————————————

Notes ————————————————————————————————————

For Further Study: Definition, Organization, and Philosophy ——————————

MAIN IDEAS

Educators have never agreed on a common definition of social studies. We have not yet decided whether the subject is singular or plural, a unity or a collection.

We have experienced considerable conflict over goals. As a result, all social studies teachers confront certain dilemmas at the outset: what to teach, how to teach, and why to teach it. To some extent, of course, these questions are answered by the curriculum of your state, district, or school. But, in a larger sense, you must come to certain decisions yourself.

Many argue that the main goal of social studies is to transmit knowledge about the past. This is called a *didactic goal*, which is one that emphasizes telling. Others protest strongly that information as a goal in and of itself is not enough. These critics point out that information must be digested, analyzed, and applied in order to be useful. This view is termed a *reflective goal*. There is also a strong lobby for social studies to serve as an agent of social change and citizenship education. These educators worry about the need for activists and participants in the democratic system, in other words, those who pursue an ethical lifestyle. This is described as an *affective goal* because it encompasses feelings, emotions, and values. These dimensions—the didactic, reflective, and affective—grow out of both everyday school practices and disputes about educational theory and philosophy.

In addition to debating goals, some educators define the social studies largely as the study of history; others see it primarily as the study of the social sciences (i.e., anthropology, economics, political science, psychology, and sociology). Still others suggest that social studies is a field unto itself, offering an interpretation of society, and a minority views it as mainly the building of student self-confidence. At the secondary school level the field is usually defined by its mandated course content: world and U.S. history, economics, and civics or American democracy with a smattering of social science and special electives. Classroom realities (e.g., too much work, public pressures, budgets, restricted classroom time, and sometimes limited teacher skills or knowledge) further narrow the range of what is actually offered and how the subject is taught. In addition to the usual pressures, there are newer ones calling for national standards, a common curriculum, and uniform testing in teaching social studies and its allied fields.

Theoretically, social studies may include any topics or issues that concern human behavior—past, present, or future. Content is most typically organized around one of the three dimensions or goals already identified. Some educators would add at least two other organizing principles to this list: a philosophy of social action, and a person-oriented humanism that encourages self-growth, confidence building, and personal enhancement. Each of these organizing principles has its own goals, methods, and curriculum recommendations, that have grown out of those schools of philosophy that influenced educators over the last hundred years or so.

WHAT DO YOU THINK?

Which subjects have you studied that ought to be included in social studies? Which should be excluded: Sociology, Driver Training, Marketing, Media, Ancient History?

As an organizational tool for this text, social studies is viewed as divisible into three major, interrelated, dimensions: (a) the *didactic*, which concerns lessons and curriculum with a predominantly information-processing orientation that promotes the acquisition of data and the transmission of knowledge; (b) the *reflective*, which encompasses lessons and curriculum with a predominantly problem-finding and problem-solving orientation that fosters reasoning skills and the formation and checking of hypotheses; and (c) the *affective*, which includes lessons and curriculum with a predominantly ethical and policymaking orientation that encourages the examination of values and the testing of beliefs and belief systems. As shown in Fig. 1.1, these three dimensions should be thought of as complementary ways of understanding social studies.

Offered as a set of categories for choosing classroom goals, lesson plans, questions, texts, group dynamics, and tests, this model allows a choice in dealing with the disparate schools of thought about social studies. For instance, some educators say that social studies can and/or should be integrated into a unified, coherent whole. Others maintain that the conflicts and disagreements about goals and definition cannot or should not be blended together. Why? Because they are incompatible and because the differences lend a vitality to the field by offering a system of checks and balances so that no single viewpoint is dominant.

RESEARCH REPORT

Anderson et al. examined the attitudes and views of several small local and national samples of social studies teachers in 1993 to learn more about their "principal conceptions" of the field as a prelude to collecting a larger national sample of opinions that would extend and corroborate preliminary findings. Using an analytical technique known as a Q-sort, or Q-method, researchers surveyed teacher beliefs in the national sample of 361 respondents using a forty-item form with questions like, "issues which are politically controversial should generally not be raised in a classroom" and "the schools exist to uphold and transmit the values of American civilization." Such questions were sorted out according to philosophical groupings, ranging from critical thinking, legalism, and cultural pluralism to assimilationism. Each, the authors argue, represents a "strain," or viewpoint, in social studies that is a fairly consistent point of view among different segments of the social studies teaching population.

For example, teachers who viewed citizenship education from a critical thinking view (47 percent of the sample) tend to be Democrats, liberals (self-identified), and to teach high school rather than elementary or middle school. Teachers who view citizenship from a cultural pluralism view (26 percent of the sample) tend to lack identification with religion, and tend to inhabit the West South-Central United States. Teachers expressing an assimilationist (8 percent of the sample) view are reported as perhaps the most unusual group, hailing mainly from small towns and cities and they are much more conservative and Republican than liberal or Democrat. Teachers reporting a legalist or "authoritarian" view (13 percent of the sample) tend to be the most varied, cutting across all demographic groups in about equal proportions and did not seem correlated with any of the other views or groups. The researchers argue that their survey supports observations that social studies teachers hold widely varying beliefs in terms of educational objectives and civic goals and tend to fall into fairly consistent philosophical groups, of which the critical thinking and cultural pluralism perspectives are dominant, when approaching both subject matter and teaching methods.

SOURCE: Anderson, C., P. G. Avery, P. V. Pederson, E. S. Smith, and J. L. Sullivan, "Divergent Perspectives on Citizenship Education: A Q-Method Study and Survey of Social Studies Teachers," *American Educational Research Journal* 34, no. 2 (Summer 1997): 333–64.

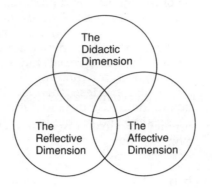

Figure 1.1   The dimensions of social studies.

This chapter invites you to study different definitions of social studies, different ways of organizing goals, and how competing schools of philosophy have influenced this field. Throughout the book, you will be invited to apply the three dimensions to help you decide what, how, and why to teach every day in your social studies classroom.

WHAT IS (ARE) THE SOCIAL STUDIES?: DEFINING A DISCIPLINE

The title of this section hints at major conflict in the definition of social studies: Is the social studies a single, integrated field, or are the social studies a series of related disciplines? Educators have not yet been able to settle this question. The social studies is a relatively new subject area in the world of academic disciplines, a product of public school expansion in the late nineteenth and early twentieth centuries. The field of study was originally designed to meet a number of needs, including the preservation of democratic life, the upgrading of skills for an increasingly industrialized, technological economy, and the socialization of vast numbers of new immigrants into the general population.[1] Given these diverse purposes, it comes as no surprise that the social studies represent a fusion of several different strands, including history (a classical academic discipline), the social sciences (with roots in the empirical, scientific tradition), citizenship training (derived from both nationalism and social criticism), and self-enhancement (with roots in psychological and pluralistic or multicultural traditions).

Edgar B. Wesley's famous definition, "the social studies are the social sciences simplified for pedagogical purposes,"[2] suggests that social sciences form the heart of the discipline—a notion that many would dispute and that does not typically represent the practices of secondary teachers. More fairly, secondary school social studies can be defined as the study of those data, analyses, and ethical issues that deal with human history, human behavior, and human values in relation to technology and ecology. In short, social studies in the classroom is about how and why people act, what they believe, and where and how they live and have lived. It is about actions, ideas, values, time, and place—a series of topics that covers an immense range and is somewhat amorphous but that allows tremendous latitude in the selection of both materials and methods for teachers.[3]

Although there is and will continue to be considerable debate on a theoretical level about what social studies is and ought to be, most secondary instruction on a practical level is defined by content and courses mandated by state or local requirements and teaching techniques that are basically similar from district to district. Your style and philosophy, however, are your own. As a social studies teacher, you must understand the different schools of thought and the rationales behind them, and from this understanding, you must slowly and carefully evolve a philosophy that suits your own view of the subject and the audience for which it is intended. A key issue here is the choice between eclecticism, an attempt to include many viewpoints, or a commitment to one viewpoint as the major guide to action. An eclectic approach that collects many topics, views, and techniques may be practical and seem fairer in the classroom, but it may also lead to confusion about goals, to inconsistency, and to a disorganized approach to content. A single-minded approach, on the other hand, may produce clear, consistent results, but also may leave you with narrow, conflicting choices.

Different conceptions of the social studies exist on both a theoretical and a practical classroom level from which alternative definitions of the field have grown. The social sciences, history, citizenship, social action, and personal development advocates each want to give social studies a different "heart" to supply its body with the sustenance of life, to set its goals, and to direct the action that will take place. Each position derives from different philosophic grounds and tends to stress widely varying criteria for the content, methods, and outcomes of instruction.

For example, in a reflective social science lesson, students might be asked to analyze the reasons for the rise of dictators rather than to focus on any single example such as Mussolini or Hitler. A didactic history lesson might list the political causes and consequences of the American Revolution during a narrow time period. Citizenship-centered material could be represented by a debate focusing on voting rights and responsibilities. A social action approach might typically ask students to study an issue such as world hunger, take a position on how to address it, and implement a plan for action. A lesson stressing personal development could call on students to review the contributions in their own heritage as a step toward building personal self-confidence. Thus, there is a dilemma not only of definition but also of choice: Should you attempt to resolve conflicting conceptions, integrating and fusing them into a united whole? Or, should you accept and utilize one of the competing conceptions to guide all classroom decisions? In sum, how can we organize our thinking about this diverse and fragmented field?

LET'S DECIDE

Form a group with at least three colleagues or classmates, write your own definition of social studies, and then share your views with the others. Is everyone's view more or less alike or different? Why?

Organizing Principles

A Three-Part Approach.   A number of organizing conceptions of social studies have been presented that can serve as an aid to understanding its dynamics and pressures. Barr, Barth, and Shermis, for example, favor a tripartite scheme that views social studies as divisible into three traditions: one to promote social science, a second to promote reflective inquiry, and a third to promote citizenship transmission.[4]

The *social science tradition* offers the findings, concepts, and rules of the different social sciences, centering on the steps of the scientific method. Organizing ideas in this approach could be class, culture, location, power, or market system. This tradition seeks to give secondary students a sample of the ideas, skills, and data available to social scientists, "reduced to manageable terms for young people."[5] Ultimately, Barr, Barth, and Shermis see the social sciences as supporting citizenship education by encouraging analysis of and generalization about human behavior.

The *citizenship transmission approach* basically stresses the teaching of goals and expectations about U.S. society, seeking to develop the ideal participant in a democratic society. The desired product is someone who knows and understands the culture and its values and is able to function effectively within it. The intent of the transmitters is to inculcate within students those democratic beliefs and convictions that will be supportive yet critical of social and political institutions while providing them assistance in career decision making and personal development. Barr, Barth, and Shermis view the purpose of the citizenship transmission tradition as being "to raise up a future generation of citizens who will guarantee cultural survival."[6]

The third tradition, *social studies taught as reflective inquiry*, proposes analysis and decision making as the heart or vital element in a student's classroom life, applied to both the content and process of knowing and valuing. Method and content are closely interrelated with a critical view toward all conclusions, theories, and summary judgments. Problem solving and critical thinking are integral to the reflective inquiry tradition; students are placed in a situation in which they must deal with ambiguities and unknowns in order to make sense of the world. The inquiry process, according to Barr, Barth, and Shermis, is one "that involves all of the techniques and strategies that lend themselves to improving the students' ability *to ask important questions and find satisfactory answers*" (emphasis added).[7]

The scheme as a whole can be summarized using the three traditions to correlate purpose, method, and content:

Tradition I   Citizenship/Cultural Transmission/National Values and
                Heritage
Tradition II   Reflective Thinking/Inquiry-Problem Solving/Social
                Criticism
Tradition III   Social Science/Scientific Method and Empiricism/Search
                for Truth.[8]

A Five-Part Approach.   Brubaker, Simon, and Williams suggest a similar organizing scheme for the social studies. Their model includes a citizenship area, a social science area, and a reflective inquiry area, but adds two more dimensions: a student-oriented tradition and a sociopolitical "involvement," or participatory tradition.[9] The purpose of the student-oriented tradition is self-enhancement and the building of self-confidence; it includes ethnic awareness. These authors view social studies as a vehicle to build identity and strengthen psychological perceptions of the self, aiming at successful social and family relationships. Sociopolitical involvement is a label for what some would call *social criticism* or *political activism*. In this view, a major purpose of the social studies would be to promote the values of political activism. This would include daily participation in working for such goals as social justice, freedom of speech and assembly, international peace, and so forth.

Whichever organizing schema is used to define the social studies—that of Barr and his associates or Brubaker and his colleagues—both seem to share strong commonalties and to contain the three major dimensions termed here as the *didactic, reflective,* and *affective*. Social science and history, particularly when promoting content knowledge, have a didactic purpose. Reflective inquiry and critical thinking are, of course, most like our reflective dimension because in them reasoning is primary to these processes. Citizenship clearly involves values, social criticism, self-analysis, and public controversy, which are all aspects of judgment that fit the affective dimension. We view almost all social studies theory, curriculum, and instructional methodology as generally fitting into these three dimensions.

The Origins of Differing Social Studies Perspectives

Most social studies goals, definitions, categories, research, curricula, and pedagogy can be traced wholly or in part to several influential philosophical movements that have had widespread impact on education content and method. Almost every teacher's pattern of behavior, self-concept, and curriculum decisions reflects one or more of the philosophic conceptions that have molded educational thought and institutions over the past two centuries. Sometimes conflicting, sometimes overlapping, often evolving one from another, some of these systems of thought have had almost universal impact on educators, whereas others have remained the province of theoreticians and researchers. The major organization for social studies education, the National Council for the Social Studies (NCSS), itself reflects the many competing philosophies of education trying to influence the field, with some members advocating citizenship as its center and others claiming history as its center and some viewing it only as a "theory of instruction" and others as a real "education program."[10] Many have directly affected thought about social studies education and classroom practice. Several of these philosophies are discussed later.

RESEARCH REPORT

A five-dimensional view of the social studies was bolstered by a survey of teachers' philosophic preferences conducted in 1977 by Irving Morrissett for the Social Science Education Consortium. In this study, most teachers surveyed chose one or more of five principal areas with which they identified social studies. These five definitions for social studies included the following:

1. The transmission of culture and history.
2. The life experiences of personal development.
3. Reflective or critical thinking and inquiry.
4. Social sciences processes and subject matter.
5. The study of social and political controversies with the aim of promoting political activism.

History is seen as a main link in providing students with knowledge of the past and with citizenship values. The social sciences are viewed as providing a scientific/analytic framework of concepts, hypotheses, and theories through the study of the different disciplines. Reflective inquiry promotes students' thought processes through the investigation of social issues and problem solving. The action approach promotes involvement in real political processes and leadership in taking action in the world outside as well as in school. Last, the student oriented approach is defined as using the social studies to enhance an appreciation and understanding of the self, especially in relation to others in society through shared ideas and open-ended discussion of personal beliefs and deeply held values.

SOURCE: Irving Morrissett, "Preferred Approaches to the Teaching of Social Studies," *Social Education*, 41 (March 1977): 206–209.

Perennialism and Essentialism.   Advocates of an old and influential philosophy labeled *perennialism* argue that absolute and unchanging truths exist in human history. Social studies educators who adhere to this tenet believe that students need to understand and apply these truths in their daily lives and that the study of them will produce competent, culturally literate individuals who know and understand their own historical milieu and are capable of transmitting this understanding to others. Perennialists support the study of history with an emphasis on skill development; their curriculum centers on the study of Western civilization's classic books, typified by Mortimer Adler's Great Books program.[11] The liveliness and current appeal of the perennialist perspective is attested to by the popularity of E. D. Hirsch's work, including *Cultural Literacy*, and the more recent educational bestsellers suggesting that a school curriculum should consist of two complementary parts: an intensive and an extensive curriculum. "The extensive curriculum is traditional literate knowledge, the information, attitudes, and assumptions that literate Americans share—cultural literacy," a "network of associations ... that has to be known by every child and must be common to all the schools of the nation." The intensive curriculum "encourages a fully developed understanding of a subject, making one's knowledge of it integrated and coherent."[12] Hirsch extends his argument for common goals and curriculum, arguing in favor of a standard national curriculum as a key to improving student learning.[13]

A second school of thought closely allied to perennialism is often referred to as *essentialism*. One advocate, William Bagley, argues that students must know the basics or essentials of knowledge to be truly educated, and these essentials include a strong dose of skills, concepts, and values arising primarily from the study of history, government, and economics.[14] Essentialism has a classical bent, usually emphasizing rigorous training in traditional disciplines of study. Theodore Sizer is one of the more organized modern exponents of essentialism, directing a movement for school reform through a "coalition of essential schools" that aims to solve both elite and urban educational problems.[15]

A wide variety of applications derive from these philosophical beliefs, ranging from a relatively didactic chronological approach to the social studies to a more humanistic stress on issues and problems. Above all, however, perennialism and essentialism share a primary commitment to the transmission of knowledge in as effective a manner as possible. In his most recent work, Sizer makes clear that the essential schools movement seeks a school with a "focus on helping adolescents learn to use their minds well," and learning to use what they know rather than simply memorizing it by rote methods.[16] Through the years, the transmission or cultural literacy advocates have probably had the greatest impact in terms of what and how secondary school social studies teachers actually teach on a day-to-day basis.

Scientific Empiricism and the New Criticism.   A second approach to social studies education derives from the principles of scientific inquiry. Social scientists have built the content and methodologies of their disciplines on the techniques and tools of the scientific method in an effort to derive laws, principles, theories, and rules of human thought and behavior. They have studied people on an individual, group, social sample, or cross-cultural basis. In the 1950s, this approach was characterized by a demand for value-free observation analysis.[17] In the secondary schools, educators sought to involve students in the scientific method by creating projects based on experimentation, survey research techniques, case studies, and other analytical tools. Students were encouraged to think in terms of probabilities rather than absolute truths, were offered different frames of reference with which to interpret evidence, and were exhorted to be fair, objective, and unbiased in drawing conclusions. This search for solidly grounded data was an all-consuming passion in the social science approach of the 1950s, 1960s, and early 1970s.

Toward the end of the 1970s, however, many attacks were mounted against the attempt to define social science through the scientific method, and especially against the notion that conclusions and theories could ever be entirely value free. Strongly influenced by the work of Jurgen Habermas and Thomas Kuhn, many social scientists turned to a philosophy of "new criticism."[18] New critical ideas, sometimes termed *phenomenology*, abandoned (wholly or in part) the concept of objectivity and suggested that science can never (and should never) be free of value claims.[19] The critics in social studies, as elsewhere, expressed deep suspicion not only about many of the empiricists' conclusions but also about the research designs and methods themselves, arguing that values form the basis of all human investigation and that the values themselves must be examined and assumptions made explicit if communication is to be effective and meaningful. As Richard Bernstein points out:

> When we examine those empirical theories that have been advanced, we discover again and again that they are not value-neutral, but reflect deep ideological biases and underlying controversial value positions. It is a fiction to think that we can neatly distinguish the descriptive from the evaluative components of these theories, for tacit evaluations are built into their very framework.[20]

Scientific empiricism greatly influenced the social studies curriculum in both content and method throughout the middle decades of this century. As an attack on essentialist dominance and citizenship education, the new criticism has wielded less influence through daily lessons at the practical level, but has had a considerable impact on academics and administrators who seek to promote student activism and decision making. Advocates of criticism suggest that an awareness of and willingness to examine policy and value claims or critical-mindedness, should be the fundamental element of social studies education.[21]

Pragmatism and Progressivism.   *Pragmatism* is a term often applied to the work of John Dewey, the eminent educational philosopher, and other educational "progressives" who emphasize the development of students' reasoning and judgment capabilities, particularly as applied to everyday life. Other terms associated with this philosophy include *problem solving, problem finding, reasoning, reflective thinking, inquiry, critical thinking,* and *creative thinking.* Dewey stresses the importance of building linkages between school, community, and student experience.

> Relationships are recognized, ideas analyzed, and decisions made through a thinking process that works from a grounding in evidence and logic through inductive and/or deductive approaches to a culminating conclusion. This conclusion or decision will then presumably lead to taking action in terms of social commitments, political decisions, and personal growth.[22]

If perennialists tend to be preoccupied with content, then pragmatists and progressives tend to emphasize process.[23] They see the curriculum as an open and flexible system capable of absorbing new ideas rather than as a short list of universal or eternal classics. As might be expected, progressives advocate the building of critical thinking and decision-making skills in the social studies classroom. The product of a progressive social studies education might well be a shrewd consumer, an intelligent and well-informed voter, an active participant in community life, and a lifelong seeker of new ideas and new skills.

Another important movement derived at least in part from Dewey's principles is that which sees social studies education as primarily a vehicle to foster the personal growth of the student. This movement, sometimes termed *ethical humanism* or *values clarification* has been a popular approach to social studies in recent decades; terms associated with it include *self-actualization, self-fulfillment,* and *identity.*[24] Multiculturalism often draws on this philosophical base because minority or disadvantaged students are often seen as needing reinforcement of their own worth and cultural identity in order to approach the dominant culture around them with confidence. Some recent work on "character education" also draws from Dewey and from essentialists at the same time.

Reconstructionism and Public Issues.   Social justice is a cherished value in Western tradition. For those to whom social justice is a primary goal, social studies education provides a perfect vehicle for encouraging students to take an active role in the affairs of the community, the nation, and the world, and to raise their voices in objection to moral lapses, political chicanery, and the destruction of the earth for economic gain. George S. Counts, who christened this philosophy "reconstructionism," argues that the schools must take an active role in changing or reconstructing society.[25] Count's work has been eagerly adopted by many,[26] some of whom see schools not only as sites for discussion of controversial issues but also as active participants in social action projects.[27] The critical pedagogy developed by scholars such as Michael Apple, Henry Giroux, and Peter McLaren provides a thorough analysis of the relation between schooling and society rooted in the argument that social injustice results in part from the unequal distribution of skills and knowledge in the public schools.[28]

Reconstructionism has had a wide-ranging impact on social studies education (especially in the 1930s and later in the 1960s and 1970s), which is reflected in the kind of curriculum that includes discussion of current events, mock trials and debates, and simulations that raise questions about equality, the distribution of goods and services in the economy, international peace, and environmental issues such as famine, the depletion of the ozone layer, the destruction of wetlands, and air and water pollution. The public issues curriculum reflects a primary concern with current or persisting problems and is relatively ahistorical.[29]

Reconstructionists have in common with pragmatists their emphasis on critical thinking and decision making. Adherents teach students to examine their own beliefs in order to decide which ones they would be willing to uphold with action; others frankly seek to indoctrinate students with their own value commitments. Active participation is a major goal.

WHAT DO YOU THINK?

Which of the philosophies or traditions do you find most appealing for a teaching career? What are the reasons for your choices?

Fusion or Fission Approach?

There remains the problem of gaining an overall view of social studies. Should the field be seen from a fusion or a fission perspective? Arguments can be made for both sides, whether directed at practice or theory.[30] Two worlds—one of day-to-day classroom practice and the other of ideological goals, debate, and research—must always be kept in mind if you hope to make sense of the field. Whereas the theoretical is often intensely debated by representatives of the different philosophic schools of thought, practical classroom concerns usually reflect far more preoccupation with mandated content, course sequence, testing, subject matter, and student personalities. Meanwhile, for better or worse, classroom practice tends to be quite stable from decade to decade.[31]

RESEARCH REPORT

Based on a study of over three hundred junior high and five hundred senior high school classrooms, John Goodlad finds that, by and large, teaching, social studies included, is and has been geared to present information as fact in a style closer to old-fashioned recitation than to modern democratic discussion. He concludes:

> What the schools in our sample did not appear to be doing was developing all those abilities commonly listed under "intellectual development": the ability to think rationally, to use and evaluate knowledge, intellectual curiosity, and a desire for further learning. Only rarely did we find evidence to suggest instruction likely to go much beyond mere possession of information to a level of understanding the implication of that information and either applying it or exploring its possible applications. Nor did we see in subjects generally taken by most students (including social studies) activities likely to arouse students' curiosity or to involve them in seeking solutions to some problems not already laid bare by teacher or textbook.

> The traditional image of a teacher possessing the knowledge standing at the front of the classroom imparting it to students in a listening mode accurately portrays the largest portion of what we observed.... And why should we expect teachers to teach otherwise? This is the way they were taught in school and college.*

From your own school experiences and observations, do you agree with Goodlad's findings? Do you see more or less variety than he and his researchers uncovered? What do you believe should be the climate of a secondary social studies classroom?

*John Goodlad, "What Some Schools and Classrooms Teach," *Educational Leadership* 40, no. 7 (1983): 15.

TO DO

Collect two or three social studies textbooks and find passages on the same topic or period—perhaps World War I, or the Progressive Era—or whatever you like, read it over and decide if the lesson represents a fusion of several disciplines or if it is presented pretty much from a single viewpoint: historical, sociological, or geographical.

GOALS AS A BRIDGE BETWEEN THEORY AND PRACTICE

Theory

Is it important for you to understand the kind of philosophical bases from which social studies education derives? I argue that the answer to this question is a clear "Yes". Virtually every choice you will make as a social studies teacher is based on goals or learning objectives that you will set for your students. Objectives and goals, by their very nature, are drawn from a sense of theory and philosophy; they are the bridge between philosophy and practice. Look, for instance, at the following typical objectives for secondary school social studies students:

1. Students will learn the important dates, places, and events of World War II.
2. Students will memorize the definitions of commonly used legal terms.
3. Students will list five issues that divide Israelis and Palestinian Arabs.

These goals share a common thread: data collection. They suggest methods, materials, and questions that derive from a didactic, cultural transmission approach to the social studies.

Now look at a second set of goals:

1. Students will compare and contrast policy positions of the state of Israel and the Palestinian people.
2. Students will discuss some causes and consequences of the rise of dictatorships.
3. Students will use data analysis and generalization to produce a theory of economic development for a given nation.

These goals all suggest a reflective thinking approach to the social studies; they emphasize the social science process in sorting through data and drawing conclusions.

Finally, here is a third set of objectives:

1. Students will study and evaluate U.S. foreign policy as it affects Central America.
2. Students will identify the most urgent environmental problem in their area and propose action to remedy it.
3. Students will debate the ethical and moral ramifications of capital punishment.

These goals share a commitment to the examination of values and represent different elements of social criticism, social action, and citizenship traditions. All reflect controversial themes and an affective approach to social studies education.

Obviously, classroom objectives are not always as clearly derived from one or another of the three major social studies dimensions. The point is, however, that goals almost always reflect these centers or dimensions in some way, and your knowledge of the premises and histories of the centers will enable you to choose your goals more effectively and to support them with appropriate materials, methods, and teaching strategies.

Among the various schools of thought about the social studies, there is considerable agreement (although for different reasons and toward different ends) that the development of high quality reasoning skills is a vital goal. But there is considerable disagreement about how much stress should be placed on teaching controversial and current issues as opposed to teaching the heritage and traditions of the common, dominant culture. Similarly, proponents of virtually all philosophic positions support some matters of content, such as the need for global studies or American history, but argue heatedly about critical thinking versus indoctrination, and value-laden versus value-free teaching.

While the debate rages in scholarly journals, what happens in the classroom is considerably more practical and stable. Classroom teachers tend to be preoccupied with content, sequence and scope, curriculum materials, strategies, and testing. It is important to recognize that the social studies is a fragmented and dynamic field: A level of uncertainty exists ranging from the lack of an acceptable definition through methodology and content. That inherent uncertainty, although problematic, in fact provides the most potent tool: freedom to select your own point of view within the constraints of your particular district's requirements; freedom to set your own goals, design lessons, choose techniques, and build a philosophy of instruction that will guide both short- and long-range decisions.

WHAT DO YOU THINK?

In discussing the national social studies organization, Shirley Engle, then president of the NCSS, notes that the membership and its leaders, who are "held uneasily together by a common concern for the social education of children and youth, ...

> avoid definition of our field of competence, confusing social education with the social sciences ... and afford our members a kind of smorgasbord of educational goodies and services, throughout which no cogent philosophic or pedagogical position runs, and from each, each according to his own interest or bent, may choose to eat whatever he will ... [with] no clear and consistent position on social education and, for that matter, no clear definition of our field.*

Do you think a clear definition of social studies is possible? Is it an advantage or disadvantage to everyday teaching? A serious problem for the future of the field? Think about your views: How do you define the field for yourself?

*S. Engle, "The Future of Social Studies Education and NCSS," *Social Education* 34 (1970): 778–81, 795.

Practice

As has been pointed out, social studies objectives, methods, units, lessons, and courses reflect, consciously or unconsciously, a particular viewpoint or collection of viewpoints about the ultimate goals of the subject. In practice, however, teachers typically offer students an eclectic collection of materials that is often inconsistent and lacks an overall approach. Social studies curriculum is defined more by state, city, or district requirements than by the development of a reasonable, well-planned scope and sequence guided by a philosophy of education. The following is the typical secondary school social studies course plan:

Grade 7:	World culture/world history/world geography/state history
Grade 8:	U.S. history
Grade 9:	World cultures/world history/civics/government/state history
Grade 10:	World cultures/world history
Grade 11:	U.S. history/American studies
Grade 12:	American government/electives: including anthropology, economics, psychology, sociology, problems of American democracy[32]

This sequence of social studies curriculum for middle and secondary schools has not changed substantially since World War II. Courses may vary by grade and subjects may change somewhat, but the general pattern has held for years. Within this often repetitive and illogical sequence, students must frequently contend with lessons derived from conflicting philosophies. They may be asked one day to memorize World War I dates, for instance, and then the next day to analyze the consequences of conflict for Germany, focusing mainly on hypotheses that explain the aggression and its results; and the following day, they may be directed to examine the morality of trench battles of the type portrayed in Erich Remarque's *All Quiet on the Western Front*.

In addition to the curriculum, many other classroom realities are encountered by the social studies teacher. These include pressures to cover an all-too-large number of topics, too many students often packed into too small a space, a sometimes adversarial view of the student audience, insufficient planning and preparation time, and a school culture of isolation from colleagues.[33] As you dash around trying to inform large groups of students—often restless, questioning adolescents—about the entire sweep of American and world studies (including all relevant issues) in an evenhanded and fair manner during precise forty- to sixty-minute periods using textbooks that are one or two decades old, you may lose track of teaching the perfect social studies lesson. In fact, you may lose track of the subject! There is simply too much information to teach, too many skills to practice, and too little time in the day to achieve every goal.[34]

Furthermore, as you try to carry out this mission impossible, many other demands will emanate from the principal, parents, and colleagues, as well as an occasional bid for attention from state, county, or local boards of education. Old or new goals may become prominent, such as the recent surge of interest in national standards or multicultural needs and issues, calls for improved geography instruction, or the clamor for better writing "across the curriculum"—which of course includes social studies. All of this is crammed into an already overstuffed curriculum, where time is at a premium and planning seemingly at a minimum. This set of conditions may very well lead you to believe that there are reasons for less than perfect instruction, and you may wonder why people in the field are still fighting about lofty goals, philosophy, and instructional methodology. You may also understand why teachers band together against critics and outsiders who condemn or criticize them in newspapers, through reports and surveys, or by stereotypical portrayals in films and on television (with the exception of *Mr. Holland's Opus*).

Nevertheless, given all these problems, you must still decide each day what, why, how, and to whom you will offer instruction in social studies. Whether or not a conscious decision, each choice you make and your behavior in the classroom is derived from precedents, traditions, and course requirements laid down over many years. Each of those traditions and topics is itself the product of values and beliefs that rest in an educational theory or philosophy of some kind. Thus, theory has consequences for practice and practice influences theory.[35] If you spend most of your classroom time covering factual material, a transmission or didactic theory is guiding your behavior. If you stress in-depth analysis of original sources, primary documents, and so forth, then a reflective or inquiry theory is influencing your decisions. If you promote the examination of value claims, debate ethical and moral issues, and perhaps foster student involvement in world affairs, then an affective, citizenship, or social activist theory is directing your teaching.[36] Whatever happens, this book argues that there is and must be a link between theory and practice, and offers advice and guidance so that you will have an ideal to strive for even if you cannot always attain it. Given the complexities and problems of teaching social studies, an ideal balance of goals between lower and higher order thinking, or among the didactic, reflective, and affective, may be difficult to achieve, but it will be impossible to reach if there are no ideals, no theory, and no organizing ideas to guide you.

LET'S DECIDE

Get together with at least two or three other classmates or colleagues and write a sample goal that bridges theory and practice for a topic of your choice from a government/civics or economics course.

RECAPPING THE THREE DIMENSIONS OF SOCIAL STUDIES INSTRUCTION

In order to diminish confusion and enhance awareness of educational motives and purposes, this book offers you a view of social studies in didactic, reflective, and affective terms. You may use the scheme to organize daily lessons. You may evaluate both what you intended to happen and student performance outcomes in terms of (a) acquisition of knowledge (didactic goals), (b) development of reasoning skills (reflective goals), and (c) ability to make decisions (affective goals).

Choices for classroom practice are divided throughout this book into three general dimensions: (a) the *didactic*, which concerns lessons and curriculum that have a predominantly information-processing orientation, promoting the acquisition of data and the transmission of knowledge as major goals; (b) the *reflective*, which encompasses lessons and curriculum that have a predominantly problem-finding and problem-solving orientation, fostering reasoning skills with the formation and checking of hypotheses; and (c) the *affective*, which includes lessons and curriculum that have a predominantly ethical and policy-making orientation, encouraging an examination of values and the testing of beliefs and belief systems. These three dimensions should be viewed as related, overlapping parts of a holistic way of understanding the social studies, both theoretically and as taught and experienced in classrooms. Each dimension may be used to generate goals, lesson plans, questioning sequences, textual narratives, group dynamics, lecture subjects, and tests for any given program. Taken as a whole, this three-part conception functions to guide your planning for a particular student audience and to serve as a tool to assess curriculum choices and student productivity. Think about a perfect lesson as achieving a balance among the dimensions such that some attention is given to each within a framework of one or two shared dominant goals.

Our three categories roughly correspond to the tripartite conception of social studies traditions offered by Barr, Barth, and Shermis. The three dimensions are also flexible enough to incorporate all or nearly all of the different philosophic viewpoints that have attained a degree of influence on the field's methods and materials of instruction. Each dimension reflects and may direct lesson planning and classroom performance, serving as a guide in developing both the specific materials you choose and your general style. I will argue that, given the complexities of social studies, its competing interests, and our students' needs, most lessons and interactions contain elements of each dimension. However, every lesson is usually given direction by an overall goal that stresses a didactic purpose, a reflective purpose, or an affective purpose. One of these three goals should be dominant in directing the path of a lesson, whether it is in the form of discussion, lecture, role-play, simulation, or research project. Many other, less specific objectives may be subsumed under the major goals. A lesson that tries to do too much at once or has conflicting goals usually loses direction and confuses students.

Each dimension, therefore, may be viewed as an organizing idea for planning, choosing curriculum content, and evaluating student learning styles and response patterns. For example, a lesson in which students are reviewing the events of African independence may be safely placed in the didactic dimension.

A session in which students are analyzing and comparing Machiavelli's ideas about government with those of Aristotle would undoubtedly be in the reflective dimension. A debate concerning which government welfare policies (and/or actions) should be adopted as best for society would belong, for the most part, in the affective dimension. It is quite conceivable that a lesson, unit, or course could shift in direction and character, combining two or three dimensions in complex ways, perhaps even demonstrating an almost perfect balance among the three categories. This book argues throughout that the very best social studies lessons combine didactic, reflective, and affective purposes to meet an overarching goal that concerns the kind of learning and the type of human being we seek to develop.

TO DO

> If possible, observe several social studies lessons on the same topic. Take notes on the key activities, questions, and answers you observe. Can inquiries and responses be categorized as affective, reflective, or didactic? Is this distinction easy or difficult to determine? Why? Can you improve the distinctions?

SUMMARY

Tensions in social studies have arisen because competing schools of thought seek to implement different goals for the field as a whole. Those who stress mainly didactic goals seek learning in which students acquire a great deal of knowledge about their tradition, culture, and world. They want this transmitted knowledge to be as accurate, reliable, and meaningful as possible to students. Essentialists stress understanding and a sense of what is valuable; they want students who are more than walking encyclopedias. And they must face the problem of dealing with a world in which there is too much, rather than too little, information.

Those who work mainly for reflective thinking goals want students to develop a systematic, scientific way of approaching data, a style for solving problems, and an overall sense of critical-mindedness. Social scientists want skillful analysis, not the following of a series of steps for scientific thinking that move mechanically from problem to conclusion. Finally, those who fervently endorse affective goals want to encourage students to be comfortable dealing with sensitive issues and to be willing to examine their own values and those of others with an open mind. Social activists want students who will make decisions that lead to purposeful political or social action and not simply young people who go through the motions of expressing their opinions as a polite classroom exercise. You must decide how to balance goals and priorities among the didactic, the reflective, and the affective. You have been asked which goal should dominate the others and for what ultimate objective.

Within each of the philosophic approaches, whether viewed as a set of three or five, are recurrent problems of content and concepts, quality and balance. Content without meaning may result in a banal learning, whereas abstract concepts without content may lose touch with reality. Practice without theory tends to reduce every philosophy and tradition to a kind of rote process and rigidly defined content. Theory without practice tends to convey a set of ideas so lofty and out of touch with classroom audiences that most students feel their social studies experience is irrelevant to their lives. To sum up, a balance must be struck among theory and practice, competing philosophies, curriculum depth versus breadth, and the three dimensions of the didactic, reflective, and affective.

LET'S DECIDE

Survey several colleagues and/or classmates on the subject of theory and practice in social studies instruction. Ask what teachers and students see as reasons for requiring young people to complete three or four years of social studies at the secondary level. Can they offer a rationale for the requirements? How do they justify and explain their own methods of instruction? Do they argue primarily for a view? Or do they support all or none of the viewpoints? How can you tell whether and when teachers have taken a position or chosen a philosophy that supports their choices for topics, questions, and tests? How would you judge someone who "just goes along with department plans or district guidelines"? Are guidelines enough for quality instruction in social studies? Do we need a philosophy and goals? Why or why not?

NOTES

1. Hazel Hertzberg, *Social Studies Reform: 1880–1980* (A Project SPAN Report) (Boulder, CO: Social Science Education Consortium, 1981).
2. Edgar B. Wesley and Stanley P. Wronski, *Teaching Social Studies in High School* (Boston: Heath, 1958), p. 3.
3. For examples of how some educators have suggested organizing social studies content, see Dale L. Brubaker, Lawrence H. Simon, and Jo Watts Williams, "A Conceptual Framework for Social Studies Curriculum and Instruction," *Social Education*, 41 (March 1977); Robert D. Barr, James L. Barth, and Samuel S. Shermis, "Defining the Social Studies," in *Bulletin, 51* (Washington, DC: National Council for the Social Studies, 1977); and Irving Morrissett, "Preferred Approaches to the Teaching of Social Studies," *Social Education*, 41 (March 1977).
4. Barr, Barth, and Shermis, "Defining the Social Studies."
5. Ibid., p. 63.
6. Ibid., p. 65.
7. Ibid., p. 67.
8. Ibid., p. 68.
9. Brubaker, Simon, and Williams, "A Conceptual Framework," pp. 201–205.
10. James L. Barth, "NCSS and the Nature of Social Studies," in *NCSS in Retrospect*, ed. O.L. Davis (Washington, DC: National Council for the Social Studies, 1996), pp. 9–19.
11. Mortimer J. Adler, ed., *The Padeaia Program* (New York: Macmillan, 1984).
12. E. D. Hirsch, Jr., *Cultural Literacy* (Boston: Houghton Mifflin, 1987), pp. 127–28.
13. E. D. Hirsch, Jr., *The Schools We Need and Why We Don't Have Them* (New York: Doubleday, 1996).
14. William C. Bagley and Thomas Alexander, *The Teacher of the Social Studies* (New York: Scribner's, 1937).
15. Theodore Sizer, *Horace's School: Redesigning the American High School* (Boston: Houghton Mifflin, 1992).
16. Theodore Sizer, *Horace's Hope: What Works for the American High School* (Boston: Houghton Mifflin, 1996).
17. David Easton, *The Political System: An Inquiry into the State of Political Science* (New York: Knopf, 1953), p. 221.
18. Jurgen Habermas, *On the Logic of the Social Sciences* (Cambridge: MIT Press, 1988); Thomas Kuhn, *Structure of Scientific Revolutions* (Chicago: University of Chicago Press, 1970).
19. Jack Nelson, "New Criticism and Social Education," *Social Education*, 49 (1987): 368–71.
20. Richard Bernstein, *The Restructuring of Social and Political Theory* (New York: Free Press, 1983), p. 228.
21. Ibid.
22. John Dewey, *How We Think* (Boston: Heath, 1933), p. 28.
23. See for example Jerome Bruner, *Toward a Theory of Instruction* (Cambridge, MA: Harvard University Press, 1966); Louis Raths, Merrill Harmon, and Sidney Simon, *Values and Teaching* (Columbus, OH: Merrill, 1966); and Abraham Maslow, *Toward a Psychology of Being* (Princeton: Van Nostrand, 1968).

24. Raths, Harmon, and Simon, *Values and Teaching*.
25. George S. Counts, *Dare the Schools Build a New Social Order?* (Carbondale, IL: Southern Illinois University Press, 1978). Arcturus paperback reissue of 1932 edition.
26. M. P. Hunt and L. E. Metcalf, *Teaching High School Social Studies* (New York: Harper, 1955).
27. See, e.g., Fred Newmann, *Education for Citizen Action* (Berkeley, CA: McCutchan, 1975); and Michael Apple, *Ideology and Curriculum* (London: Routledge & Kegan Paul, 1979).
28. Apple, *Ideology and Curriculum*; Henry Giroux, *Resistance in Education: A Pedagogy for the Opposition* (South Hadley, MA: Bergin & Garcy, 1983); Peter McLaren, *Life in Schools* (White Plains, NY: Longman, 1988). See also Paulo Freire, *Pedagogy of the Oppressed* (New York: Seabury Press, 1973).
29. Donald Oliver and James Shaver, *Teaching Public Issues in the High School* (Boston: Houghton Mifflin, 1966).
30. J. G. Lengel and D. Superka, "Curriculum Organization in Social Studies," *The Current State of Social Studies* (A Project SPAN Report) (Boulder, CO: Social Science Education Consortium, 1982).
31. John Goodlad, "What Some Schools and Classrooms Teach," *Educational Leadership* 40, no. 7 (1983): 8–19.
32. Lengel and Superka, "Curriculum Organization in Social Studies," pp. 11–12.
33. Joseph J. Onosko, "Comparing Teachers' Instruction to Promote Students' Thinking," *Journal of Curriculum Studies*, 22, no. 5 (1990): 443–61.
34. Jane Roland Martin, "There's Too Much To Teach: Cultural Wealth in an Age of Scarcity." *Educational Researcher* 25, no. 2 (March 1996): 4–10.
35. Fred Newmann, "Higher Order Thinking in the Social Studies: Connections Between Theory and Practice," in *Informal Reasoning and Education*, eds. D. Perkins, J. Segal, and J. Voss (Hillsdale, NJ: Lawrence Erlbaum Associates, 1990).
36. Ann Angell, "Practicing Democracy in School," in *Theory and Research in Social Education*, 26, no. 2 (Spring 1992): 149–197.

FOR FURTHER STUDY: DEFINITION, ORGANIZATION, AND PHILOSOPHY

Apple, M. J. *Education and Power*. Boston: Routledge & Kegan Paul, 1982.

Bruner, J. *The Process of Education*. Cambridge: Harvard University Press, 1962.

Davis, O. L., ed. *NCSS in Retrospect*. Bulletin No. 92. Washington, DC: National Council for the Social Studies, 1996.

Dewey, J. *Democracy and Education*. New York: Macmillan, 1922.

Fenton, E. F. *The New Social Studies*. New York: Holt, Rinehart & Winston, 1967.

Giroux, H. A. *Theory and Resistance in Education: A Pedagogy for the Opposition*. South Hadley, MA: Bergin & Garvey, 1983.

Hirsch, E. D. *The Schools We Don't Have and Why We Don't Have Them*. New York: Doubleday, 1996.

Martin, J. R. *Changing the Educational Landscape*. New York: Routledge, 1994.

Massialas, B. G., and B. Cox. *Inquiry in the Social Studies*. New York: McGraw-Hill, 1966.

National Commission on Excellence in Education. *A Nation at Risk: The Imperative for Educational Reform*. Washington, DC: 1983.

National Commission on Social Studies in the Schools. *Charting a Course: Social Studies for the Twenty-first Century: A Report of the National Commission on Social Studies in the Schools*. Washington, DC: National Council for the Social Studies, 1989.

Oliver, D. W., and J. P. Shaver. *Teaching Public Issues in the High School*. Boston: Houghton Mifflin, 1966.

Ravitch, Diane, and Chester Finn. *What Do Our Seventeen-Year-Olds Know?* New York: Harper & Row, 1987.

Saxe, D. W. *Social Studies in Schools: A History of the Early Years*. Albany, NY: State University of New York Press, 1991.

Spring, J. *Wheels in the Head: Educational Philosophies of Authority, Freedom, and Culture from Socrates to Human Rights*. 2nd ed. New York: McGraw-Hill, 1999.

Stanley, W. B. *Curriculum for Utopia: Social Reconstructionism and Critical Pedagogy in the Post-Modern Era*. Albany, NY: State University of New York Press, 1992.

Sternberg, R. J., and T. I. Lubart. *Defying the Crowd: Cultivating Creativity in a Culture of Conformity*. New York: The Free Press, 1995.

CHAPTER 2

The Fields of Social Studies: How They Relate

"We had the best of educations—in fact, we went to school every day—"
"I've been to a day-school, too," said Alice. "You needn't be so proud as all that."
"With extras?" asked the Mock Turtle, a little anxiously.
"Yes," said Alice: "We learned French and music."
"And washing?" said the Mock Turtle.
"Certainly not!" said Alice indignantly.
"Ah! Then yours wasn't a really good school," said the Mock Turtle in a tone of great relief.
"Now, at ours, they had, at the end of the bill, 'French, music, and washing—extra.'"
—Lewis Carroll, The Annotated Alice

OVERVIEW OF CONTENTS

Main Ideas _____

Which Fields Make Up the Social Studies? _____

      History
      The Social Sciences

A Fusion Model _____

Philosophy and Belief Systems _____

Summary _____

Notes _____

For Further Study: Theory and Background _____

MAIN IDEAS

History and the social sciences form a base for social studies theory, but they do not offer a theory of instruction for teachers to follow. In the past, social studies teachers have drawn from many fields as resources, viewing each as independent of the other. More recently, there has been a trend toward seeing unity rather than fragmented subjects. Furthermore, the humanities and sciences, as well as history and the behavioral sciences, are seen as vital elements of the entire social studies curriculum. This opening to other subject areas is based on a recognition that many goals are held in common, the most important of which is the development of students' critical thinking skills.

Underlying the pressure to improve students' reasoning are deep philosophical issues about the nature of knowledge and how decisions are made. An approach to integration is represented by our conception of teaching social studies through incorporating three major dimensions: the *didactic*, transmitting factual information; the *reflective*, fostering analysis and developing reasoning abilities; and the *affective*, examining issues, taking positions, and deciding whether to act. Central to social studies teaching is how we decide to deal with the relation between teaching approaches (e.g., stress one over the others, balance all three, or fuse them into a single system) and subject matter (approach each discipline separately, proportion time among them according to their relative importance, or unite them into a general framework). If we view knowledge as "fixed" truth, then our choice of teaching methods and materials will be very different from a view of knowledge as negotiable and open to revision or as completely subjective and growing out of human perception. What do you think? Can we as social studies teachers teach knowledge as fact, view all information as subjective, or make students aware that conclusions are at best probabilities (i.e., step-by-step approaches subject to human bias and distortion)?

WHICH FIELDS MAKE UP THE SOCIAL STUDIES?

The social studies is a school subject firmly grounded in both history and the social sciences. As a field, social studies also has one foot in the humanities and one in the sciences with all that this implies about content and methodology. Although each camp sometimes seeks to control the content of social studies and alter the curriculum to suit its own interests, neither branch has successfully done so to date. With its deep ethical basis, social studies draws from many sources to achieve its goals. Senesh argues that subject integration and borrowing are a necessity:

> Multidisciplinary awareness must include the humanities in the social science curriculum. The humanities reflect our increasing effort to make moral, philosophical, and ethical sense of the world. A society without ethical standards seriously undermines the values widely regarded as providing the optimum social framework. History, literature, drama, art, philosophy, and music (the traditional humanities) express and preserve the wisdom of courageous men and women. For writers, artists, and spiritual leaders, the humanities represent a landscape in which human potential can be explored. For scientists and social scientists, the humanities provide a structure of accountability for the consequences of the knowledge they create. At this stage of scientific development, when a lack of moral judgment can lead to global destruction, it is imperative that society guide the use of scientific advances by ethical standards so that knowledge may be used for human betterment and not to destroy.[1]

If anything, the social studies is probably more varied in content now and draws on greater resources and tools of study than it has for its entire history prior to the 1960s. Retaining history and the social sciences as dual supports gives social studies educators a great deal of flexibility in selecting content and in promoting different heuristics, or methods of learning. A major contribution of history to the social studies has been its frequent adoption of a humanistic frame of reference focusing strongly on artistic and aesthetic renderings of time and place, as well as portraits of unique people and events. The social sciences have contributed a more empirical frame of mind in which the scientific method is used to guide formation of hypotheses, collection of evidence, and testing of generalizations about human behavior. Social studies is interdisciplinary.

Until quite recently, professional literature for social studies teachers has generally presented the different scholarly traditions it has drawn on as separate entities with their own wholly distinctive concepts and tools, each with its own structure and methods.[2] Sometimes, social studies specialists show a clear bias in favor of one or another field, usually history, as the major foundation for the social studies. Although history has been and still is the mainstay of most social studies educators, there has been extensive borrowing of ideas, materials, and techniques from other fields for many decades, and history itself is far from unified on a theoretical basis.[3] In fact, one can make a persuasive argument that field distinctiveness has eroded significantly over the last several decades because of easier access to and widespread dissemination of knowledge from many fields, which are increasingly viewed as equally capable of contributing to the solution of social, historical, and scientific problems.

For example, how can economic growth be discussed without historical background, political analysis, and an understanding of the role of science in invention and technological change? Assuming that particular disciplines once had distinctive structures (which is questionable), it is hard to defend this separateness now because historians themselves freely borrow from sociology, biology, and psychology for both their hypotheses and their tools of investigation.[4] Furthermore, anthropologists and political scientists are comfortable with techniques drawn from history or even art history and literary criticism.

As we move into the twenty-first century, many scholarly traditions seek more pragmatic or more holistic approaches to their research and curriculum, tending to consider most useful whatever methods and evidence work best in solving problems that have arisen. Historically, this development seems entirely justifiable because intellectual dynamism and liveliness are maintained by the diffusion of ideas from outside sources that serve to enrich a field. Testing and experimentation, rather than ever-narrowing and exclusive traditions that may disintegrate in the face of changing conditions, most often lead to newly developed theories, changing ideas, and innovative solutions to pressing problems.

Given its past history, social studies will change to meet new challenges of historical and social scientific innovation and scholarship. However, there is a serious lag between cutting-edge research and field (classroom) implementation. The room for social studies experimentation is much more limited than are those of its fields of origin because of several built-in constraints: the need to adapt knowledge to the psychology and learning capabilities of children and youth; the need to offer a curriculum and methods based on defensible rationales for the public good; and the need to meet political, social, economic, and cultural demands from various groups and different interests in American society. Despite these constraints, there is space for maneuvering and change, which can be enhanced by examining a wide variety of fields and sources as well as a range of analytical tools. Borrowing generously from the humanities and the social sciences, and from media and the sciences, our field can fulfill common objectives in global studies, U.S. history, civics, economics, and other social science courses.

LET'S DECIDE

Do you believe that each subject in social studies is unique, separate, and special? Or, do you see each subject as borrowing from others?

What makes one subject (e.g., psychology or economics) different from others (e.g., history or anthropology)? What similarities exist?

Along with several colleagues or classmates, choose three traditional topics from American studies and three from world studies. Carefully review the content of each lesson. How many describe only events? How many bring up questions of character or personality? How many mention cultural values or place events in a cultural setting? Which ones point up economic conditions or social factors?

Is it possible to discuss human events in purely descriptive terms? If it is, are we missing anything?

History

History, one major base for the social studies, brings to the field a framework and mind-set of its own drawn largely from literary and humanistic traditions that encourage analysis and discussion of storylines, characters, and context in personalized or particularistic fashion (specific to time and place) that may or may not promote generalizing. Most historians seek to develop carefully drawn descriptions of a time period, event, or personality based primarily on contemporary accounts, statistics, and/or artifacts. In the tradition of the humanities, considerable attention is paid to style, symbol, character, meaning, and message, and the dramatic or emotional side of human art and action is usually a significant part of history. Equally important, historians often express their judgments about the causes and consequences of events covering large or small blocks of time.

However, this description of traditional historical study has been called into question because of the field's growth in many directions, including a more scientific approach to history that has, to a great extent, incorporated social science concerns and methods into its modus operandi.[5] Whereas narrative, descriptive historical writing is still a major part of the discipline, and historians continue to devote a great deal of time and energy to the analysis and reanalysis of documentary evidence, much of this work is animated by theories and investigatory techniques drawn from anthropology, economics, political science, sociology, psychology, law, and philosophy. Underlying all historical and humanities inquiries is philosophy, which guides our views of belief systems and ethical decisions. Any choice of teaching methodology or content is motivated by or fits in with a philosophy, whether consciously expressed or subsumed in the materials. There has been acknowledgment that the field of history itself has changed and is more fragmented theoretically than it once was, and that it is perhaps a dominant but no longer exclusive force in social studies.[6] Whatever the theoretical disputes within the field of history, social studies at its best has drawn from it a mind-set consisting of many or all of the following attitudes and skills, suggested as key elements of any historical inquiry by the Bradley Commission on History in Schools:

Understand the significance of the past to their (students') own lives, both private and public, and to their society.

Distinguish between the important and the inconsequential, to develop the "discriminating memory" needed for a discerning judgment in public and personal life.

Perceive past events and issues as they were experienced by people at the time, to develop historical empathy as opposed to presentmindedness.

Acquire at one and the same time a comprehension of diverse cultures and of shared humanity.

Understand how things happen and how they change, how human intentions matter, but also how their consequences are shaped by the means of carrying them out, in a tangle of purpose and process.

Comprehend the interplay of change and continuity, and avoid assuming that either is somehow more natural, or more to be expected, than the other.

Prepare to live with uncertainties and exasperating—even perilous—unfinished business, realizing that not all problems have solutions.

Grasp the complexity of historical causation, respect particularity, and avoid excessively abstract generalizations.

Appreciate the often tentative nature of judgments about the past, and thereby avoid the temptation to seize upon particular "lessons" of history as cures for present ills.

Recognize the importance of individuals who have made a difference in history, and the significance of personal character for both good and ill.

Appreciate the force of the nonrational, the irrational, the accidental, in history and human affairs.

Understand the relationship between geography and history as a matrix of time and place, and as context for events.

Read widely and critically in order to recognize the difference between fact and conjecture, between evidence and assertion, and thereby to frame useful questions.[7]

TO DO

Develop your own definition of the following:

    history
    philosophy
    culture
    social studies

Do you see history, philosophy, and culture as part of social studies or as outside social studies? Or, do you see social studies as part of history? If you work out a graphic analysis of the relations between history, philosophy, culture, and the social studies, what would it look like: concentric circles, connected circles, tightly interlinked circles? Draw your own conception and explain it to your colleagues. Does it agree or disagree with the one suggested here? Why?

(See Figure 2.1 on following page)

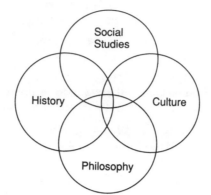

Figure 2.1.

The Social Sciences

The second major base for the social studies is the combined social sciences, which have grown mainly out of the biological sciences and mathematics and share a scientific cast of mind that places a premium on building and testing theories and generalizations through observation and experimentation. Hypotheses are usually defined operationally in the social sciences, and evidence is sampled through a plan or design using research tools that are increasingly statistical. The goal is to validate a theory that explains some aspect of human action or psychology. Social science research follows a model, drawn for the most part from the hard sciences, which seeks objective, replicable, valid, and reliable results.[8] Social scientists are frequently interested in studies that cut across cultures, times, and places, and seek to identify laws or principles that guide human behavior. In fact, the whole concept of empirical laws and provable theories in the biological sciences is repeated in the social sciences (e.g., the law of supply and demand, the theory of cognitive dissonance), with the aim of validating overarching concepts and rules that can be applied to numerous examples and cases, past, present, and future.

Whereas devotion to scientific models varies within the different disciplines, the overall orientation, in a few words, is the attempt to identify universal patterns through the collection and analysis of data acquired by standardized methods that are open to verification and try to control error factors.[9] History and the humanities, as disciplines, emphasize more than the social sciences: particular works, events, and people seen as unique; special phenomena; myths; symbols; and description. However, there is an increasing mixture of theories and methods among and between the fields of study. Differences should not be exaggerated. For instance, there are historians who seek large underlying causes for what happens—that is, the "laws of history." Not all historians focus on the particular; many search the particular for the universal "laws of history." This includes liberal historians such as Wallerstein and his view of the "modern world system."[10] Also counted in the search for the universal may be conservative historians such as MacNeil and his "human condition."[11]

WHAT DO YOU THINK?

> The foundation of the old civic educator was the transmission of unques-
> tioned truths of the fact and of unquestioned consensual values to a passively
> receptive child.... In contrast to the transmission of consensual values, the
> new social studies have been based on Dewey's conception of the valuing
> process [which] postulates the need to focus upon situations which are not
> only problematic but controversial.... These objectives spring from the
> Deweyite recognition of social education as a process with forms of social in-
> teraction as its outcome. A Deweyite concern about action is not represented
> by a bag-of-virtues set of behavioral objectives. It is reflected in an active par-
> ticipation in the social process. This means that the classroom, itself, must be
> seen as an arena in which the social and political process takes place in micro-
> cosm.*
>
> What does the author mean by a "bag-of-virtues set of behavioral objectives"?
> Is this what social studies is all about? Why does the author view "active partic-
> ipation" in the classroom in a positive light as opposed to the "bag of virtues"?
> Which approach do you think is more common in secondary social studies?
> Why?
>
> ---
>
> *Lawrence Kohlberg, "Moral Development and the New Social Studies," *Social Education* (May 1973): p.
> 343.

Economists are frequently engaged in viewing financial decisions or market
trends over time, and psychologists and anthropologists often employ historical
methods to develop case studies of individual people or cultural groups. Whereas
many historians are willing to generalize about history and judge people and decisions, unlike a high proportion of social scientists who seek objective, value-free
generalizations, most in both traditions now view the problem of bias and value
judgment as generic to all discussion and analysis of human behavior patterns.
There is far more consciousness across the fields of study for the need to identify assumptions and control bias in both history and the social sciences, especially as the
pace of exchange grows among fields. At some time or another, most specialists
look to philosophy as a guide for thinking about methods of inquiry.

Just as history has its mind-set, so do the social sciences, with each discipline
stressing different lines of inquiry but with all sharing much the same philosophic base, theoretical structures, and similar investigative approaches. Briefly,
each of the social sciences and law may be characterized as promoting somewhat
different goals and concepts. These are summarized as follows:

Social Science	Major Concepts and Interests
Anthropology	Culture, Family, Kinship, Belief System
Economics	Markets, Resources, Supply and Demand, Opportunity Cost, Productivity, Exchange System
Geography	Landforms, Ecology, Human–Land Interactions, Place, Peoples
Political Science	Power, Government, Interest Groups, Nations
Psychology	Personality, Learning, Individual Psyche, Motivation, Deviance
Sociology	Class and Caste, Social Groups, Social Control, Ethnicity and Race

Jurisprudence   Justice, Order, Equity, Freedom
(Law)

The idea of viewing people in systems, factoring in or out different aspects (such as the political, economic, social, or cultural) and analyzing the roots and consequences of human actions, runs through all of the social sciences.[12] How and why decisions are made and actions are taken is a common thread through nearly all social investigations whether these are on a personal, group, national, or international level. The ways we perceive and know are also very much part of the questions social scientists ask in designing studies and interpreting results.

Thus, the main elements of a social science mind-set would probably be characterized by some or all of the following:

Seek to identify, analyze, and test broad generalizations and theories against experience, data, and logic.

Acquire an understanding of scientific method in which a problem is recognized, evidence collected, alternative theories constructed and tested, and a solution suggested.

Raise questions about the relation of theory to evidence and theory to practice: Does the evidence or theory justify or support an action?

Understand that errors exist in all knowledge; estimate their size, judge their type, and work out means to control for them.

Be ready to admit doubts, ambiguities, and uncertainties, developing a range of probabilities and tests with which to estimate what degree of truthfulness can be accepted.

Evaluate knowledge claims based on explicit public criteria and reliable evidence.

Understand the relations between and among economic, political, cultural, social, environmental, and historical factors for an event or series of events in time and space.

Look into the way in which information was collected and reported, noting the credentials and affiliations of the reporters.

Compare and contrast categories of events and classes of behavior in order to generate an explanatory theory or principle.

Show sensitivity to bias and distortion in reporting about people, places, events, and institutions, separating, as much as possible, prejudices from well-supported conclusions.

Accept and empathize with others' points of view as a step toward coming to grips with unpopular, unusual, and unfamiliar ideas and feelings.

Develop research skills that include such important techniques as observation, questionnaire design and polling, classical experiment, metanalysis, and participation.

WHAT DO YOU THINK?

Which is your favorite social science? Why did you study it? Did the social science contribute anything to your understanding of human behavior that history did not? Did history assist you in learning the social science? Why or why not?

> Compare the historical and the social science mind-sets described in this chapter. What are the similarities and differences? Do the similarities outnumber the differences or vice versa? Do any elements of either or both mind-sets recall aspects of scientific method, for example, "understand that errors exist in all knowledge," or "grasp the complexity of ... causation"?

From the point of view discussed in this chapter, history and the social sciences have a great deal in common in terms of both methods of inquiry and subject matter. There is considerable overlap between disciplines, with social scientists and historians applying each other's theories and techniques to further their research. Some borrowing also occurs from the humanities and the sciences, as well as between and among the social sciences and history, enriching the way in which subject matter is interpreted. From a social studies perspective, if several disciplines can enhance a student's understanding of human behavior, now or in the past, then so much the better for their integration of learning a school subject.

Let's Decide

> Form discussion groups of three to five and decide, after examining both the historical and social science mind-set, if they arise from common or different philosophic concerns. Read and discuss your decision for others, allowing time for questions and answers. What does your decision imply for social studies: a view of the subject as an amalgamation of different fields and problems, or a view of the subject as unified around common themes and questions?

A FUSION MODEL

For the social studies, the methods and ideas of history and the humanities can be merged with those of the social sciences into a single framework from which ideas can be generated for purposes of curriculum and instruction. Rather than viewing each subject as a completely separate discipline to be taught in isolation from the others, you can think about each as complementing the others by providing a rich body of theory and method to apply to both typical and unusual topics in social studies courses.[13]

TO DO

> Write a lesson of your own on any topic of your choice making sure to select data for it that illustrate historical, cultural, social, economic, legal, geographic, philosophic, and psychological factors. Does the event or action you have selected have only a few of these factors present? Does it have them all? Is it theoretically possible to study an event or decision that has only one dimension? Is it possible for an event to incorporate or suggest all dimensions? Which is more likely: for an event to encompass one or all factors? Explain your answer to your peers and colleagues.

Using a unified or holistic approach focuses attention on selecting theories, research methods, and teaching strategies that help us to conceptualize a question or solve a problem. A single-minded approach tends to pigeonhole topics of study—whether Napoleon's character, the teachings of Confucius, the Spanish Civil War, or Chinua Achebe's latest novel about Africa—into neat categories where questions and answers match so nicely that there is little to disturb our thoughts.

The contributions and relations to the social studies of history and the social sciences, and to a lesser extent the humanities and sciences in general, can be conceived as elements or spokes in a wheel that draw on the strength of each to provide "axle power" to a center. All topics are encompassed in broader, underlying questions of philosophy, human motivation, and the expression of ideas. One model that represents a fusion of subjects is shown in Figure 2.2.

LET'S DECIDE

By simplifying events for young people, do we introduce inaccuracies and distortions? By presenting events in all their complexity, do we frustrate and confuse young people? If you and several colleagues or classmates had to choose a best plan for social studies, would it be to stick to one dimension or factor at a time (e.g., historical) or would it be to present many factors or dimensions (e.g., geographical, psychological, economic, and so on)? Defend your decision in a brief written statement.

PHILOSOPHY AND BELIEF SYSTEMS

Ultimately, the social sciences, history, and consequently the social studies depend on and draw from philosophic concepts to select and to justify what is taught, to whom, and by which method. The social studies and its two main pillars of support—history and the social sciences—as discussed in this chapter, are riddled with the most profound questions of meaning and knowledge, any one of which can throw light or engender doubts about nearly every conclusion we hold dear and consider to be true. This is why the deepest educational questions often grow out of and return to philosophies and viewpoints, both ancient and modern, in an appeal for ways to organize our thinking about life, decision making, and the future of the world.

Perhaps the deepest and most difficult of these issues concerns fact or truth. Much of social studies is taught as "received knowledge" that is assumed to be accurate and truthful. Didactic or informational goals reinforce factual acquisition seldom raising questions of bias, perception, honesty, or consistency. Yet from the point of view of modern philosophy, knowledge itself—the very categories, definitions, and ideas we use—is the product of theory. And all theory is suspect or questionable in the sense that it is an interpretation of great quantities of evidence.[14] Logic itself is a socially invented system in this view, which raises problems concerning how knowledge is selected and accumulated. Are we not all the products of a time, place, and culture that has shaped our thinking, our emotions, and our view of the world? Or is there really a universal, objective, verifiable "truth" out there in "reality" that we can rely on in deciding what and how to teach? Perception and theory clearly play a large role in how people absorb and process information.

Sometimes theory helps in organizing and understanding data, but other times it may blind us to what is really happening. For example, what did the much-celebrated Columbus actually discover? What did he really accomplish in the short run or in the view of history? How would the Native Americans Columbus contacted feel about him and his activities? How easy or difficult would it be

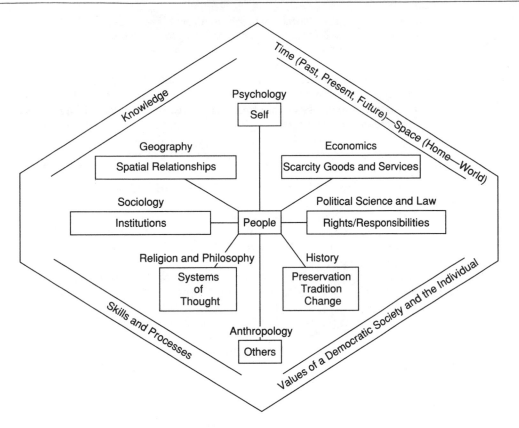

Figure 2.2.   A fusion model. Note that people and their behavior are at the center of this model, whereas history and the social sciences are embedded in broader contexts of time, values, skills, and knowledge.
SOURCE: H. M. Hartoonian, "The Social Studies: Foundation for Citizenship Education in Our Democratic Republic." *The Social Studies*, Volume 76, No. 1, January/February 1985, page 7. Reprinted with permission of the Helen Dwight Reid Educational Foundation. Published by Heldref Publications, 1319 Eighteenth St., N. W., Washington, DC 20036-1802. Copyright © 1985.

to portray Christopher Columbus in a negative light? How about in a positive light? Would our arguments be based on the same "facts"? As you can surmise from this example, the same facts and accounts can be turned upside down depending on your theory of culture contact, your sympathies for different peoples, or your philosophy on issues of freedom and slavery.

For social studies, a reasonable way out of the dilemma of truth and perception, objectivity and subjectivity, is through a critical-mindedness that accepts answers as tentative and open to further examination rather than true for all time. This theory implies that both data and the process of collection can and should be regularly questioned. Yet we should be wary of ruling out universal values entirely or of viewing events as completely dependent on perception alone.

WHAT DO YOU THINK?

The goal of the well-integrated personality is objectionable because it expects the individual to establish an equilibrium between conflicting forces, which does not obtain in existing society. Nor should it, because these forces are not of equal moral merit. People are taught to forget the objective conflicts which necessarily repeat themselves in every individual instead of being helped to grapple with them.*

What does the author mean when he wants people to "grapple" with "objective conflicts"? How would this statement apply to the social studies? Would the author want to see classrooms as mainly repositories of knowledge or as forums for debating social issues?

*Theodore Adorno, "Sociology and Psychology: Part II," *New Left Review* (47): 6.

Deeply embedded in philosophy are also difficult questions of value or meaning that consciously or unconsciously direct the conception we give to disciplines, fields of study, social studies courses, and personal inquiry.[15] The content and methodology behind every social studies classroom presentation reflects and will continue to reflect many layers of choice, from the data that are presented at the surface of a lesson to the most complex issues of universal right and wrong.[16] It is you, the teacher, who must give life to the program and unify it in some meaningful way. Usually, the more universal the concept or value, the more power and interest a program will have for students; conversely, the more specific the issue, the less the chance of application by students. Whether a lesson is derived from history or from a social science, some philosophical questions and problems appear to run throughout the social studies. A suggestive but by no means exhaustive list of questions useful for raising issues on virtually a daily basis is offered next:

Knowledge Questions and Issues

1. What knowledge is most worth knowing and who decides?
2. What is truth? What is falsity? Can we separate the two?
3. Are thought processes objective or subjective? Can language be trusted, or does it beguile us into accepting ideas that are open to question?
4. Is knowledge absolute, probabilistic, or based only on perception?
5. Is human action determined by environment, social values, genetics, free will, or some combination of these factors?
6. What is right and wrong? Can these be defined for universal acceptance or are all ideas culturally bound? How or why not?
7. Can competing values or viewpoints be treated fairly and a reasonable judgment made about what is a best conclusion?
8. Are there universal rules governing human life and development, or are conclusions specific to a time and place?
9. Do all or any human actions/decisions have a value or ideological component?
10. How can we judge fairness and justice: by the goals, the motivation, the process, or the consequences?[17]

The tensions in the social studies between different philosophies—the good citizen, the critical thinker, the expert—affect everyday teaching in important ways. For instance, those who stress mainly didactic goals usually seek learning in which students acquire a great deal of knowledge about their culture and world, but they also want this knowledge to be accurate, reliable, and meaningful. Those who argue mainly for reflective thinking goals want students to develop a systematic way of approaching data, a style for solving problems, an overall sense of critical-mindedness. Finally, those who fervently endorse affective goals want students who can learn to probe sensitive issues, not simply young people who go through the motions of expressing their opinions as a polite classroom exercise. They seek to create in students a willingness to examine their own values and those of others with an open mind, and make decisions that lead to purposeful political or social action.

WHAT DO YOU THINK?

In an overview of the concept of social studies, after expressing a good deal of dissatisfaction with the field's development, Richard Gross describes "the vision … that should have been" as "an inclusive single-subject; … essentially thematic and issue-centered; … offered every year of schooling." He goes on to argue for a social studies that "will have balanced content emphases divided among three sources: societal needs and essentials, student concerns and values, and prime skills, concepts, and generalizations from the social sciences, history, and related subjects."* Is this a vision similar to or different from the fusion approach advocated in chapters 1 and 2? Is it a view of social studies of which you approve or disapprove?

*Richard E. Gross, "In Retrospect—The Concept of the Social Studies," in CUFA NEWS: *Newsletter of the College and University Assembly*, no. 10 (Washington, DC: National Council for the Social Studies, Fall 1996), pp. 1–2.

SUMMARY

In summary, then, the real issue for a theory of social studies is the relation among theory, goals, and practice. Practice without theory tends to reduce every philosophy and tradition to a set of how-to-do-it formulas for content and process in the classroom but with no inkling about the reasons for conclusions. Theory without practice conveys a set of ideas so lofty and out of touch with classroom examples that most students feel their social studies experience is irrelevant to their lives. Ideally, a balance must be struck between theory and practice, philosophy and daily curriculum, to produce a more aware, critical, and sensitive person.

The social studies can be viewed as a secondary school subject in its own right, resting mainly on history and the social sciences for data and theory, drawing to a lesser extent from the humanities and the sciences for its subject matter. A central problem in teaching the social studies, which is as yet unresolved, concerns the nature of knowledge as basically verifiable, as probabilistic, or as perceptual. The tools of social studies analysis can and should be assembled from the wide array of social sciences and historical research that is available. The types of questions we pose as teachers can be informed by more than one discipline. Drawing on the different disciplines is easily accomplished for any event or topic under study. For example, with a slight shift of perspective, Columbus's expedition can be discussed as culture conflict rather than simply exploration; the Buddha's sermons can be discussed as literature and philosophy as well as religion; the Bill of Rights can be viewed as social values, not just laws; and the idea of nationalism can be studied in a long-range historical perspective instead of as a purely nineteenth-century conception.

Thus the different viewpoints and research tools of history and the social sciences, and to a more limited extent the humanities and the sciences, can be used to enrich and extend any lesson you prepare. Combining a unified or integrated view of the disciplines with social studies goals and methods, built from our three-dimensional model of the didactic, reflective, and affective, allows you to approach the curriculum from multiple perspectives. Any topic or lesson that comes along—even one developed on the spot—can be approached as social science only or as history, literature, and social science, leading to the creation of a holistic theory for teaching and learning social studies at the middle and secondary school levels. Subsequent chapters discuss most aspects of goal writing, lesson planning, methodology, and testing in the light of didactic, reflective, and affective points of view, with recognition that the three are closely interrelated so that each influences and shapes the others.

TO DO

Choose two social studies topics that are commonly taught at the middle or secondary level. Develop questions about the materials from the perspectives of at least two of our three dimensions and at least two of the disciplines that form a basis for our field. The following list will assist your thinking and help you to generate different and interesting questions:

1. The Monroe Doctrine
2. The American Revolution
3. Supply and Demand
4. Colonization of the Americas
5. Urbanization
6. The Seneca Falls Declaration
7. The Great Depression
8. The Roman Empire
9. Chivalry
10. Simon Bolivar and Latin American Independence
11. The Songhay Mali Empire
12. The Formation of Modern India

NOTES

1. Lawrence Senesh, "The Four Pillars of the Social Science Curriculum" (paper presented at the 1989 general conference of the Social Science Education Consortium, Boulder, CO, June 1989) p. 20.
2. Irving Morrissett, *Concepts and Structure in the New Social Science Curricula* (New York: Holt, Rinehart & Winston, 1967).
3. David D. Van Tassel, "Trials of CLIO," in *Social Studies and the Social Sciences: A Fifty Year Perspective*, ed. Stanley Wronski and Donald Bragaw (Washington, DC: National Council for the Social Studies, 1986), pp. 1–15.
4. Edwin Fenton, "A Structure of History," in *Concepts and Structure in the New Social Science Curricula*, ed. Irving Morrissett (New York: Holt, Rinehart & Winston, 1966), pp. 38–47.
5. Michael Kammen, ed., *The Past Before Us: Contemporary Historical Writing in the United States* (Ithaca, NY: Cornell University Press, 1980).
6. Paul Robinson and Joseph M. Kirman, "From Monopoly to Dominance," in *Social Studies and the Social Sciences: A Fifty Year Perspective*, pp. 15–27.
7. Bradley Commission on History in Schools, *Building a History Curriculum: Guidelines for Teaching History in Schools* (The Educational Excellence Network, 1988).
8. Karl Lambert and Gordon Brittan, *An Introduction to the Philosophy of Science* (Englewood Cliffs, NJ: Prentice-Hall, 1970).

9. Lawrence Senesh, A. Kuhn, and K. E. Boulding, *Systems Theory and Its Use in the Classroom* (Lafayette, IN: Social Science Education Consortium, 1973).
10. Immanuel Wallerstein, *Rise of the Modern World System*, vols. 1–3 (New York: Academic Press, 1974, 1975, 1976).
11. William MacNeil, *The Human Condition: An Ecological and Historical View* (Princeton, NJ: Princeton University Press, 1980).
12. A. Kuhn, *Unified Social Science* (Homewood, IL: Dorsey Press, 1975).
13. Cleo Cherryholmes, *Power and Criticism: Poststructural Investigations in Education* (New York: Teacher's College Press, 1988).
14. Richard Rorty, *The Consequences of Pragmatism* (Minneapolis: University of Minnesota Press, 1983).
15. John Dewey, *Democracy and Education* (New York: Macmillian, 1916).
16. Senesh, "The Four Pillars."
17. E. R. Emmet, *Learning to Philosophize* (New York: Penguin Books, 1964), p. 68.

FOR FURTHER STUDY: THEORY AND BACKGROUND

Bruner, J. S. *The Culture of Education.* Cambridge, MA: Harvard University Press, 1996.

Cheney, L. *American Memory: A Report on the Humanities in the Nation's Public Schools.* Washington, DC: National Endowment for the Humanities, 1987.

Crabtree, C., and D. Ravitch. *History-Social Science Framework for California Public Schools: K–12:* Sacramento: California State Department of Education, 1988.

Dewey, John. *How We Think.* Chicago: Henry Regnery, 1933.

Egan, K. *The Educated Mind: How Cognitive Tools Shape Our Understanding.* Chicago: The University of Chicago Press, 1999.

Evans, R. W. "Teacher Conceptions of History." *Theory and Research in Social Education,* 17 (1989): 210–40.

Gross, Richard E., and T. L. Dynneson. *Social Science Perspectives on Citizenship Education.* New York: Teacher's College Press, 1991.

Jenness, David. *Making Sense of Social Studies.* New York: Macmillan, 1990.

Massialas, B. G., guest ed. "Essays on the forthcoming Handbook of Research on Social Studies Teaching and Learning." *The Social Studies* 81, no. 6 (Nov./Dec. 1990).

Massialas, B. G., and R. F. Allen, eds. *Critical Issues in Teaching Social Studies, K–12.* Belmont, CA: Wadsworth, 1996.

Muessig, R. H., ed. *The Study and Teaching of Social Science Series* (Economics, Political Science, History, Geography, Sociology, and Anthropology). Columbus, OH: Merrill, 1980.

Shaver, J. P., ed. *Handbook of Research on Social Studies Teaching and Learning.* New York: Macmillian, 1991.

Sizer, T. R. *Horace's School: Redesigning the American High School.* Boston: Houghton Mifflin, 1992.

Weinstein, M. "Critical Thinking: The Great Debate." *Educational Theory,* 43 (1): pp. 99–118.

Wronski, S. P., and D. H. Bragaw, eds. *Social Studies and Social Sciences: A Fifty Year Perspective.* Bulletin No. 78. Washington, DC: National Council for the Social Studies, 1986.

PART TWO

Teachers and Students: A Context for Social Studies Instruction

Chapter 3

Teacher Roles and Student Audiences

It is better to debate a question without settling it than to settle a question without debating it.
—Joseph Joubert

OVERVIEW OF CONTENTS

Main Ideas

Instructional Roles

     Didactic Roles
     Reflective Roles
     Affective Roles

Your Student Audience

     The Adolescent and Young Adult
     Special Students
     Second Language Students and the Multicultural Classroom

Summary

Notes

For Further Study: Teacher Roles and Student Audiences

MAIN IDEAS

This chapter focuses on the *many parts* you will play as a teacher in a social studies classroom and on the students you will encounter there. Your own roles are defined according to the three-part framework laid out in the previous chapters—didactic (authority, resource, guide), reflective (questioner, scientist, artist), and affective (dramatist, socialization agent, devil's advocate). Understanding these different roles allows you to use them appropriately in involving all students in a wide variety of learning activities.

    Suggestions are also offered for adapting instructional approaches to meet the needs of varied student populations. Although the majority of your student audience may consist of students of generally average ability, who are basically assimilated into what we have traditionally called "American culture," more and more frequently you will be teaching individuals with unusual abilities and/or special learning problems. Although excellence in teaching is the foundation on which all adaptations must rest, you will find that you need to emphasize certain instructional roles for students with special gifts and talents, others for students with disabilities, and still others for English as a second language students or those who are at risk for other reasons. The potential social studies audience is examined in terms of the roles that you can play, and a brief summary of adaptations that have been shown to work well with certain learners or that seem to follow logically from the specific needs of your audience is provided. Overall, the focus is on how roles allow you to connect with students, and their particular strengths and weaknesses, and to achieve your goals.

INSTRUCTIONAL ROLES

We, as teachers, play many parts in the classroom. Yet seldom do we consciously choose from among the many acting possibilities open to us to enhance or create a special effect. Instead, we frequently focus on the subject matter of the lesson, limiting our role to the didactic, that is, as surveyor of information to those in need of knowledge. Although knowledge is most certainly a worthy goal of instruction, there are numerous others of equal or greater importance that invite role-play and group dynamics activities.

Each part, or role, has a particular impact on the audience, including getting attention, building self-confidence, reinforcing thinking skills, sparking the imagination, or encouraging participation. As in theater, some roles are more dramatic than others and some are more involving, but all are related to instruction as the spokes of a wheel are related to its core, or hub, or as the parts of an engine are to its energy source.[1] When you take a variety of roles, classroom life becomes more interesting and less predictable than when you play only a few parts in the classroom drama.

In preparing and teaching lessons, units, or courses you can significantly influence student motivation and comprehension by careful selection of those roles, through group dynamics, questions, and materials that most effectively accomplish didactic, reflective, and/or affective goals. Thus, each role may support one or more of the major aims of the social studies, and you should be able to play a wide range of parts to enhance student growth in knowledge, thinking skills, and the examination of values.

Didactic Roles

Didactic roles are designed to convey information. In this case, the teacher's behavior is geared to provide students with the acquisition of data. As much as possible, these data should be accurate and meaningful material from valuable sources. Three roles that come into play to impart knowledge are those of authority, resource, and guide (adviser). Central to all three roles is a didactic concept of the teacher as a source of facts, ideas, and conclusions. You present these to the learner as predigested information based on your considerable study and examination of resources. Lectures, recitations, and consultations are frequently the means by which knowledge is imparted to students. It is usually assumed that the information provided is reliable and will contribute to the students' store of material for tests, future courses, and their roles as citizens.

As an authority figure you play a socializing part by simultaneously disciplining a group and by sharing learning with them.[2] The stress is on facts—giving these to students who will commit them to memory as part of a base for thinking and valuing. You play the role of data provider by pointing out to students the documents, scholarly works, references, research techniques, and library skills that are necessary to respond to assignments, problems, questions, and hypotheses. Bibliographies may be prepared and used in this role, references and footnotes explained, and information assembled and tested against already formulated theories.

Less formal and less directive is your role as a guide or adviser to students. Whereas the authoritative aspect remains, the purpose of a guide is more immediate and personal because you are reacting to individuals' problems and needs, aiding them in the development of questions by challenging statements and through suggesting relevant and significant books and materials. Your word is taken as based on expertise, but the student ought to be expected to check out and reflect on the data collected. Therefore, the role of guide or adviser, although basically didactic in nature, spills over to reinforce reflective purposes as well.

Thus, you may play several basically didactic roles: authoritative resource, guide or adviser, and disciplinarian. Each role presents a somewhat different face to students, more or less formal, more or less aimed at the direct acquisition and testing of knowledge. Overall, however, these didactic roles are central to conveying facts to students who need an information base as a step to more difficult, demanding, and complex social studies problems, questions, and issues.

Figure 3.1   A lecture and recitation in progress. Query: How would you characterize these teacher and student roles?
SOURCE: Riis, Jacob, "Condemned Essex Market School." *The U.S. Department of Labor Bicentennial History of the American Worker*, edited by Richard Morris.

LET'S DECIDE

Discuss the following questions with two or more colleagues:

1. Do didactic roles give you much leeway for creativity?
2. Do didactic roles promote students' critical thinking?
3. Do didactic roles play a part in the classroom that is more positive or more negative?

Reflective Roles

Reflective roles are designed primarily to aid thinking skills and problem solving. In these roles, teachers stress higher order questions and the formation of ideas rather than answers per se, or lower order skills such as memorization and comprehension. The essence of reflective roles is in fostering students' ideas, for example, producing, revising, and testing hypotheses. Reflective roles may be divided into three major types: catalyst or questioner, scientific inquirer, and artistic interpreter of symbols. Central to all three roles is your commitment to raising—but not necessarily answering—problems, questions, mysteries, different viewpoints, and issues that students are asked to deal with and solve.

As much as possible, reflective roles demand that students take a body of evidence, facts, and work with these, and others, they may uncover. It is students who must create their own explanations or theories for an understanding of an event, topic, or problem. Generally, you—as reflective teacher—shape, structure, and stimulate ideas by asking questions, redirecting students' ideas, and challenging hypotheses. Enthusiasm for thinking is a key message to students, perhaps more important than the content itself![3] If you interfere with or help students to discover correct answers, then the mode of inquiry and the role played shift into the didactic realm. Unlike the performance of authority roles in which knowledge is obtained, stored, and accepted as part of a base of accurate information, reflective roles question the evidence itself and its sources. Interpretations are open to attack, revision, and possibly rejection, and demand that meanings or definitions be reformulated and theories or conclusions checked by students against sources and rules of logic.

The role of questioner is perhaps the most central of all reflective roles because it asks that you act as a "philosopher-in-residence."[4] Socrates is still a teaching role model because of his style and ability to ask for clear, unambiguous definitions, present alternative explanations, and call into question hypotheses that most people accept without thinking. You, too, can dig into students' assumptions about any given problem or issue, promoting a good discussion in the process. Questioning in this sense means that you must poke around into reasoning chains, criticize the objectivity or bias in sources, and act as the skeptic who is not satisfied with neat, clean, pat reasons repeated from a book. Students in the hands of such a questioner must produce and defend ideas they themselves have decided are good, correct, "best," or logical in a given situation. This type of questioner role is not aimed at helping students amass knowledge. Rather, the point is to use knowledge for finding and solving problems—"how-to" thinking. Process is the key rather than the product, although product is certainly desirable in this role if students evolve their own responses to a problem based on an examination of the evidence and reasoning that apply.

The scientist role is related to that of questioner but might be thought of as narrower in scope and more closely focused on the method of scientific reason-

Figure 3.2 A discussion in progress. Query: Who is the authority here and how does this class-room compare with the one depicted on page 41? Photograph courtesy of Gerry Gioia, Boys and Girls High School.

ing, inductively or deductively, from the data to a conclusion or, conversely, from a theory to the data.[5] Either way, rules of evidence and logic are followed in an ideal order often characterized as a chain of development. This chain moves from recognizing and defining a problem through finding alternatives to developing and testing conclusions and finally to making a decision. Rules of logic, largely drawn from philosophy, and rules of evidence, largely taken from biological and social science research, are used as standards against which the validity of most conclusions are measured. Throughout, you act as the relatively impartial judge who tests student-initiated ideas in the twin crucibles of logic and empirical veri-fication. Your role is to determine whether claims and assertions are indeed proven true or false in terms of scientific probabilities.

As scientific inquirer, you can role-play in any number of social studies situations. For example, you can assist in evolving and testing a fully developed student generalization such as "Levels of communal violence increase as the differences between rich and poor populations grow larger." For almost any daily lesson, you can react to student ideas with statements like "Can you prove what you say?", "Where's your evidence for ... ?", or "Do we have enough examples to prove our case?" When you ask students to check for proof, to limit their conclusions, to review the clarity of their definitions, to take a second look at a rival theory, or to survey previous conclusions or precedents to a case, they and you are playing the role of scientific investigator.

The artistic role is also related to that of the questioner but is focused on personal and creative approaches to social studies problems.[6] These are problems that require interpretation and discussion of meanings and symbols. As an art-ist-teacher, you can call into question many aspects of events, sources, and personalities from a humanistic viewpoint that seeks articulated feelings about stories, using words, images, and visual representations. Deciding on the meaning of something is a major goal of artistic inquiry that may borrow methods from historiography and legal reasoning or literary and art criticism to meet its goals. An artist-teacher may turn students' attention to the characters, emotions, and plot of novels such as Pearl Buck's *The Good Earth* or Chinua Achebe's *Things Fall Apart*, or such films as *All Quiet on the Western Front, El Norte,* or *Ran.* Seek connections between the images and words in each work with the social or technological changes of the times.

For example, you could bring in official government photographs of Abraham Lincoln, Jawaharlal Nehru, Sun Yat-sen, Adolf Hitler, Francois "Papa Doc" Duvalier, or Saddam Hussein and then ask students to compare and contrast leaders in terms of the state symbols used in the photographs and the manner of presentation. This process would serve as a base toward developing generalizations about leaders and leadership in different times and places. Especially in the middle secondary grades, paintings, music, rock songs, and poetry can also serve for introspection and analysis, with students asked to reflect on the ways in which a time and place may shape culture as well as the ways in which cultural products may influence society.

Questions drawn from historiographical approaches may enrich the teacher-as-artist role by building student awareness of the way in which history is reported and formulated. Eyewitnesses may be evaluated, with discussion of the different values placed on primary and secondary sources. The artist role promotes comparison and collation of sources, particularly the identification of conscious or unconscious feelings, biases, and assumptions in the way a story or document is presented. Questioning and analyzing cultural biases and personal feelings lie at the center of the artistic inquirer role.

Thus, reflective roles tend to stress questioning. Assumptions, feelings, and biases are challenged and the testing of hypotheses against a base of knowledge and philosophical logic is encouraged. The reflective roles discussed here tend to differ in emphasis but are closely related in purpose and structure. The questioner role stresses philosophic logic, a Socratic style of probing ideas and concepts.[7] The scientist role stresses reasoning based on clearly prescribed canons of evidence and logic. And the artist role promotes creative problem finding and problem solving through such varied approaches as literary and artistic criticism, historiographical inquiry, and value examination. Reflective roles demand openness to new and innovative ways of dealing with the study of events, people, and places.

TO DO

1. What do you see as the major aims of the reflective role? Write a statement of this goal in twenty-five or fewer words.
2. Make a list of twenty activities you could invent for a social studies class that encourage reflective dynamics.
3. Which types of activities best promote reflective role development: questioning and answering assignments in a textbook, or playing the parts at the Nuremberg War Trial? Why?

Affective Roles

Affective roles are concerned mainly with the examination of controversies, values, and beliefs on a personal, social, and international level as a step toward decision making. In affective roles, you act to bring values, feelings, and sensitive issues to the forefront of discussion. This should be done in a way that helps students to look at themselves and their own behavior as well as at the values, beliefs, and actions of others. Affective roles such as dramatist, socializer, and devil's advocate seek to awaken students' feelings on a scale that ranges from the beginning of awareness through attitude formation to reasoned judgment.[8] A central goal is the activation and maintenance of decision-making skills that lead students to take and defend positions on a variety of issues.

Affective roles channel emotions into a more rational understanding of the different sides or arguments of a controversy. Students are pressed to discipline and support their own viewpoints by examining the personal and public assumptions offered for each position. Evaluation is, therefore, a strong ultimate component of all affective thinking and role-play.

As a prelude to full-scale judgments, you must present enough information as a base for students to use in decision making. And you must question the reasoning underlying contrasting arguments and probe the quality and quantity of evidence offered to support a position. The overall structure of affective roles is aimed at judgment and decision making, the formation of defensible value choices by students.

To build an awareness of issues and enhance value choices, you may employ a number of roles. First, you can be the dramatic actor or actress. Second, you may perform as a socializing agent who introduces students to new frames of reference. And third, you can be an agent provocateur or devil's advocate who stimulates debate by switching sides or taking unpopular positions.[9] All three roles work to create an atmosphere in the classroom in which the free expression of ideas and beliefs, debate and argument, are normal, legitimate, completely acceptable features of daily discourse. And all three roles channel beliefs and emotions that may be inchoate, ill-formed, or untested into the limelight of public testing and cross-examination. Because public expression of values and criticism can be sensitive and worrisome to adolescents, affective roles require considerably more skill and attention than didactic or reflective roles. You should be honest and open to student opinion and careful about offering authoritative statements on controversies before the students have had an opportunity to form their own views.

In the socializing role, you ought to evolve a structure of orderly, polite, and rational argument and counterargument following some kind of system to guarantee the largest number of students a chance to participate by sharing their ideas with classmates. To build participation you may use an informal set of guidelines: for example, speaking in turn, giving recognition to special spokespersons, or assigning student floor managers. More formal means are also available: debating rules such as Robert's Rules of Order, parliamentary guidelines, panel/committee presentations, or a mix of the aforementioned. Whatever structure becomes central, it is your role to create a positive feeling for participation and free expression in a framework that allows everyone to have a say in the classroom proceedings.[10]

Implicitly, students are also learning to practice democratic methods of participation by involving themselves in the consideration of serious issues that affect them and their world. As a by-product they are developing a commitment to the process of discussion and debate through their secondary school social studies experience. Naturally, great problems and exciting issues will cause some passion and confusion on occasion. Anger, shouting, and a bit of disorder with multiple speakers taking the floor at once should be expected and perhaps even cherished as an expression of real caring and commitment. If you have socialized students sufficiently, then the disorder (which, it should be noted, is still focused on class work) will subside. Students will eventually revert to quieter and more organized discussions that allow thinking and valuing in public so others can listen and evaluate their feelings and views.

RESEARCH REPORT

Teachers should not intervene any more than is absolutely necessary in the groups. Most teachers are geared to jumping in and solving problems for students to get them back on track. With a little patience we would find that cooperative groups can often work their way through their own problems and acquire not only a solution, but also a method of solving similar problems in the future. Choosing when to intervene and when not to is part of the art of teaching and with some restraint, teachers can usually trust their intuition. Even when intervening, teachers can turn the problem back to the group to solve. Many teachers intervene in a group by having members set aside their task, pointing out the problem, and asking the group to come up with an adequate solution.*

1. When should teachers intervene in group activities? When should they refrain from interfering? Why?
2. When would you add your ideas to a group discussion? When might you not?
3. Overall, do you think lecture or group problem solving is more effective in promoting student reasoning?

*David W. Johnson, Roger T. Johnson, and Edythe Johnson Holubec, *Circle of Learning: Cooperation in the Classroom* (Edina, MN: Interaction Book Co., 1986), p. 50.

Complementing your role as a socializer is the acting job that is a common feature of many repertories. The role as actor is delivered through dramatic behaviors borrowed from the theater world. Here you shed a few inhibitions and literally assume a role, perhaps of a famous figure in history, a political leader, or an expert of some kind (e.g., a detective, archaeologist, or foreign diplomat). Props may be part of the plan, with visuals aids, costumes, artifacts, posters, or scenery added to gain attention and make a point. The acting role seeks to motivate students on a topic and to build their awareness of the emotional nuances that might have been part of a situation. For instance, a dramatization, with script, of President Truman's decision to drop the atomic bomb on Nagasaki and Hiroshima could be reenacted with the teacher as director or as president and students playing parts and reacting as a jury to the decision. Nearly all levels of affect would be brought out by a topic such as use of the atomic bomb on Japan. The result is a valuable exercise in critical thinking aimed at an ethical/moral conclusion on the use of force and the value of human life.

Case studies with dramatics attract and hold attention, promote participation, and raise awareness of a host of governmental, political, and sociocultural issues leading eventually to students' reappraisal of their decisions. Case studies also take a great deal of time and preparation and should be treated as special events!

However, you may also dramatize brief cases or issues as these arise on a daily basis in the news, in textbooks, or through other media. Acting can include simply playing the detective and calling attention to an inconsistency in a report or by pointing out a biased remark in a textbook, or portraying another viewpoint. You can perform the actor role to create a new awareness of beliefs and values by directly calling students' emotions into play.

Finally, you can use both socialization and dramatic techniques to develop a third affective role, that of the devil's advocate or agent provocateur, stressing alternative ideas to whatever students suggest. As devil's advocate you may probe, redirect, and cross-examine positions as these are placed on the table during a discussion. In this role, you purposely express unpopular, unpleasant, or even untenable (wacky) theories, judgments, and beliefs as a way of testing students' ideas on an issue or subject. You can use questions and "redirects" to develop this role of provoker, and you may also offer fully prepared positions to counter and disprove students' claims. Students who are unused to their teacher playing the devil's advocate may at first feel disoriented and confused, but will soon come to enjoy the challenge. They feel particularly successful if you are defeated in an argument, which should certainly happen every so often. Plan it that way! As democratic discussion procedures become familiar and comfortable, the number of students who frequently ask and answer questions on their own initiative will rise.[11] As the students grow more experienced with your playing roles, they may take on parts themselves, performing the tasks usually modeled by their instructor.

A provocateur, or devil's advocate, role is probably most useful when controversial issues are debated and discussed, especially if these are clearly organized into camps or sides that can be reviewed and presented by class members. More ambiguous problems or moral dilemmas are better approached through the other roles discussed in this section, although some teacher roles (e.g., guide, questioner, and socializer) can probably cut across the distinctions made here and be useful in many types of classroom activities.

Thus, a wide range of roles (and accompanying behaviors) is available that can have a significant impact on student motivation, thinking, and feeling. A wider variety of roles should lead to more thoughtful consideration of the material under study and to more supportable conclusions and decisions. The various roles—guide, resource, and authority; artist, scientist, and catalyst; actor, socializer, and provocateur—affect students by promoting didactic, reflective, and/or affective learning through different forms of classroom participation. You have the opportunity to consciously choose and apply one or more of the nine roles outlined here for teaching varied goals and topics. Furthermore, if you want to create a more active, thoughtful, and ethically minded classroom, draw on all of these roles at different points during the year to add variety, enjoyment, and challenge to your students' lives.

WHAT DO YOU THINK?

1. Which affective roles do you envision as part of your standard operating procedure in your classroom? Which do you believe will be most effective? Which will you find most comfortable?

2. Plan a dramatization in which you act the role of "Speaker of the House" while the students must consider several bills for passage or rejection. Assign students political parties and districts that resemble those in the United States. Write up at least three different bills, one on trade restriction (autos?), one on gun control, and a third on drug prevention programs. Give these to your "Congress" for debate and discussion. Perhaps you might also dress up for the occasion. Be sure to record student votes for publication.

3. Invent your own role in a class dramatization and write a script for everyone to follow, leaving missing sections for student improvisation.

YOUR STUDENT AUDIENCE

The Adolescent and Young Adult

Adolescence is a period of rapid physical, social, intellectual, and emotional change. Children are becoming young adults. Adulthood entails the experience of physical maturation, including the heightened sexual awareness of puberty. Puberty is not a precise event that occurs all at once, but it is a series of changes that starts and stops, often in unpredictable ways. Our audience of young men and women may have experienced significant physical changes beginning from about age ten, all the way up to age seventeen or eighteen. The average age for the onset of puberty is usually between the twelfth and fourteenth year. Teachers and classmates, especially at the middle or junior high school level, often note the bewildering sizes and shapes of the adolescent community, as well as their frequently peculiar or exaggerated social behaviors. Some are very tall, others short, some hungry all the time, others tired, some in a state of emotional tension, others so relaxed you wonder if they are breathing. Whereas these extremes can be a source of amusement, these behaviors and growth patterns symbolize the dramatic changes of the teen years. An important aspect of your role in dealing with this rapidly but unevenly maturing audience is to assure them that their differences will all even out in the end and that they should try to see themselves in a positive light. Point out that they are also growing more intelligent every day, whether or not they believe it.[12]

Sexuality is a major interest of your adolescent audience, many of whom can switch in one year from an active disregard for the opposite sex to passionate interest and physical experimentation. Sexual activity, according to most studies, is quite common by senior high school—although many schools seem to work at not noticing student involvements unless pregnancy becomes an issue. Other schools offer a variety of sex education programs. More important perhaps than the sexual interest and activity is the development of student identities; as men and women, they may have sexual preferences that become a source of great anxiety and embarrassment. Your role should be to promote discussion of personal identification, particularly on gender and racial issues, demonstrating that these topics belong to social studies and are important social issues rather than taboos or purely personal interests.

The combination of physical changes, intellectual growth, and sexual awareness makes for a potent brew of problems. Preteen students are usually less self-conscious than the teenage group, although both are moving toward building identities for themselves as separate from parents and teachers, more toward peers and the outer world around them. This blend of changes often produces sharp alterations of emotions, with youngsters swinging from almost manic highs to depressed lows. On occasion, you, as teacher, may benefit from a "high" by harnessing student involvement to a lesson that results in sharp insights and quality work. On other occasions, you may suffer from a "low" that produces negative or cynical feelings toward your subject, foul language, and an overall attitude of hostility toward school discipline and authority.

Although a teacher and a student may really be at odds on an issue, most of the control problems at the middle or junior high level are expressions of adolescent difficulties and a desire for freedom from social constraints rather than being personal attacks. As a guide and questioner, you might work to defuse some of this hostility and cynicism by regularly assessing class feelings or by inquiring after individuals' problems, health, and interest. Avoid rushing to judgment on a student's behavior until you have investigated the causes. Of course, this does not mean that immoral, insensitive, rude, or violent behavior should either be overlooked or excused, but you should approach your audience analytically if you can in order to identify the issues and determine whether the event is serious or trivial. Remember that adolescent growth patterns may render these students more emotional, but they may also be more intellectual and sensitive than they were in elementary school. They know a great deal about the world around them and they are attempting to come to terms with their own feelings on a wide range of personal, social, and societal issues.

On the intellectual level, secondary students experience a leap from the concrete to the abstract operational stage in terms of Piaget's descriptive categories for child development.[13] According to Piaget's research, which is widely accepted in education, all children pass through the following major stages as they grow.

1. The *sensorimotor*, which is dominated by the senses of touch, sight, smell, and taste (ages 0–2).
2. The *preoperational*, which is dominated by ability to think in terms of symbols and a beginning one-way logic (ages 2–5).
3. The *concrete*, which is dominated by hands-on approach to the world, and application to new events, and the reversibility of logic (ages 5–11+).
4. The *formal operational*, which is dominated by abstract reasoning and problem solving (ages 11 or 12–adult).

For our purposes, nearly all secondary students have reached the stage of formal operations, although their abilities may be sporadically and unevenly expressed and many may still be more comfortable with the concrete stage, well into the high school years. Although research generally supports Piaget's view of child development, critics have complained about a number of issues. For instance, some see his categories as indistinct and overlapping.[14] Others argue that growth can be accelerated to a much greater extent than Piaget's work implies because the abilities of children and youth were underestimated in his research.[15] In any case, there is little controversy about secondary students' potential for abstract reasoning. It is up to the teacher and the curriculum to take advantage of this potential by involving students in tasks that open up rather than limit imagination, hypothesis formation, and judgment. Thus, in Piaget's terms, all or nearly all young people have moved from the concrete to the abstract levels of reasoning by the time they leave the middle grades and are capable of high levels of inquiry, if given the chance.

Abstract reasoning abilities present great opportunities for the teacher because this is an audience that has the background and conceptual development to verbalize problems, identify causes, and debate issues while taking others' feelings and arguments into consideration. Logical faculties are fully developed for the vast majority of students by the secondary grades, a level at which they can certainly be challenged to engage in sophisticated reasoning activities involving inference, interpolation and extrapolation, induction and deduction, and making decisions and judgments. Secondary students need to be active participants in social studies discussion even if they are a bit immature. And they need their views taken seriously, even if these are not fully developed.

RESEARCH REPORT

M. Gall and colleagues reported that, based on several experiments conducted with small groups of middle school students, recitation was found to be as effective as nonrecitation in promoting learning, especially the acquisition of knowledge. The source of accurate data, either teacher or peers, made no significant difference in increasing achievement scores, nor did recitation seem to inhibit the growth of higher level reasoning skills. Outcomes varied greatly depending on the expertness of the questions and their sequence as well as class size. The smaller groups who were asked relatively sharp, clear questions scored better than larger groups posed with complex, confusing, or illogically sequenced questions.

Do recitation and recall questions harm students? Which goals are best supported by teacher recitation or question and answer methods?

For the best success in building students' knowledge bases, what kind of classroom conditions (class size, textbooks, atmosphere, etc.) would you like to have?

SOURCE: Meredith T. Gall et al., "The Effects of Questioning Techniques and Recitation on Student Learning," *American Educational Research Journal*, 15 (1978): 175–99.

The point is that your students have passed childhood in the sense that they are far more sharply aware of themselves and others than they were before, and they can make decisions based on abstract principles and rules. Unfortunately, growth at this age is uneven and may produce less than perfectly satisfying results for you, the teacher, as well as a good deal of disciplinary problems. Nevertheless, it is still better to deal with the secondary audience as more mature than as less mature because this contributes to their feelings of self-worth that will, in the long run, translate to more positive educational outcomes, greater interest in social studies subject matter, and more productivity in school.

Especially in social studies, there are serious credibility problems for adolescent youngsters in dealing with a good portion of the current curriculum.[16] Remember that these are young people who are in the process of forming individual identities, are changing and growing, are sexually aware and perhaps active, and are undergoing significant intellectual development in knowledge, reasoning ability, and judgmental capacity. They are also people who seek to be independent and wish to place some distance between themselves and the authorities around them. The secondary audience is in the process of seeing others and the world around them in a new light that differs from their trusting childhood beliefs and images. To treat this audience as naive and isolated is a grave error that often leads to cynical attitudes toward subject, teacher, and school. It is better to discuss problems and issues with frankness for adolescent groups than to offer sanitized images of politics and social issues, to promote political adult heroes and heroines uncritically, or to avoid or cover up sexual references. Solid evidence, well presented, followed by serious and intelligent debate should go a long way toward impressing our secondary audience, particularly if students' ideas and beliefs are treated with interest and respect. Although unpleasant remarks may be made by students and the topics may often encourage heavy criticism and angry emotions, in the long run this process will foster the transition of young people from childhood through their adolescent years to a true adulthood in which they will continue to demonstrate an interest and involvement in public affairs.

The following are some general recommendations for the secondary audience as a whole:

Take advantage of their growing intellectual abilities by encouraging problem solving.

Incorporate student feelings and values into everyday discussion.

Regularly bring up current events and ask how students view the issues of the day.

Empathize now and then with students' emotions and worries.

Utilize increasing awareness of self and world to seek decisions on controversial personal and social issues.

Be ready to discuss personal problems openly.

Involve students in planning and active participation in classroom affairs.

Build in opportunities to involve students through panels, debates, games, and sociodrama.

Be humorous, but refrain from embarrassing your audience as a group or as individuals on sensitive growth problems.

Special Students

Different groups exist within any large population, varying in terms of background, ability, and talent. We are all familiar with young people who exhibit significantly greater skills than others, either physical or intellectual, and with those who display serious emotional or learning problems or endure physical disabilities. In addition, in our economically unequal society, many young people have difficulties adjusting to school because of family poverty, negative attitudes, and other social or cultural disadvantages.

Social studies teachers, like all other teachers, must educate students with special problems and special gifts. Unfortunately, our educational system is often underfunded to deal with special groups with costly needs. Also, stereotypic attitudes toward young people who are poor, gifted, non-White, foreign born, or disabled frequently render potentially helpful programs ineffective. Despite these problems, however, social studies can be adapted to the needs of various special groups. I believe firmly that effective instructional techniques can be appropriately adapted for all students, and that your task when teaching students with special needs is to put your effort into those adaptations. Students with special needs may require extra attention from you, but they should be treated as capable of achieving didactic, reflective, and affective goals just like peers—although at different rates and with varying degrees of success.

At-Risk Students.   At-risk students are young people who are likely to drop out of school, usually for emotional and/or economic reasons. Many are urban-based people of color, often from groups in the United States with histories of isolation and impoverishment.[17] Many must work to supplement family income; for some, street life is far more attractive than either work or school—neither of which has provided a satisfying experience. A relatively small proportion suffers from mental, emotional, or physical disorders, or has drug or alcohol habits that dramatically reduce their learning ability and increase their chances of leaving school early. A fair proportion come from cultural backgrounds that may add a language and/or customs barrier to their adjustment.

Often these students seem apathetic or hostile in class and achieve at low levels; teachers may complain that their speaking, reading, and writing abilities are poor. Increased coverage of content and criticism of the students' weaknesses do not appear to be viable solutions to the problems these young people present. Rather, they need instructional approaches and materials with clearer and more immediate application to the world outside school, and they need help in developing skills that will allow them to grow and improve in terms of intellectual competence, job opportunities, and perhaps most important, self-confidence.

Attitudes are an important part of learning for both teachers and students. There is serious confusion in many parents' and teachers' minds between intellectual skills and classroom accomplishments, and between social influences and innate ability. Social prejudices tend to suggest that at-risk students are either lazy or unintelligent; in fact, as a population, at-risk students represent the same normal curve of skills, abilities, and talents as any other group. They frequently perform at lower levels, however, because of low social status, poor self-esteem, or underdeveloped skills in English reading and writing.

Although you cannot personally change the socioeconomic circumstances in which at-risk students typically live, you can adapt teaching approaches in new ways geared to achieving positive changes in self-image, interest, and achievement. In general, didactic approaches like lectures and recitation will be less successful with poorly prepared students who are alienated, restless, and skeptical.[18] A number of projects and resources have been developed for at-risk youth, and several professional organizations offer training for teachers and curriculum materials. (See Appendix A for a list of these resources and organizations.)

There are many instructional adaptations that can be effective with at-risk students.[19] Some are particularly useful in raising self-esteem.[20] Others seek to increase prosocial behavior through group projects and friendships.[21] The following are some suggestions:

An increased attention level and more positive feedback.

Smaller classes, and cooperative learning within larger classes.

Activities like role-playing and simulations, including music and rap.

Frequent evaluation of incremental learning.

Integration of students' interests and traditions into the classroom.

Infusion of everyday examples into instruction, and an emphasis on analogies to real life in history and social science lessons.

Spontaneity—a willingness to drop scheduled work occasionally to discuss students' problems, current events, and social issues.

Frequent feedback—both written and verbal—with strong encouragement for expression of individual views.

A stress on student interaction with the environment outside the school, including field trips.

Students With Physical and Developmental Disabilities.   Students with disabilities are a complex group with an enormous range of problems and talents. Some have learning deficiencies; others have physical or emotional problems but function at high levels intellectually. The behavior of some students indicates multiple learning problems that are difficult to separate and diagnose. There are students who are very bright but achieve at low levels. Poor performance in the social studies may arise from lack of interest in the subject or in the total school experience, from inattention growing out of emotional difficulties or physical deficits such as poor hearing or vision, or from poor language and writing skills.

RESEARCH REPORT

In a study of moderately or mildly disabled students, mainstreaming and peer tutoring in social studies and other regular classrooms was found superior to segregated classes with specialized approaches to different kinds of disabilities. Mainstreaming tends to improve grades and raise self-esteem of these students through enriched programs and contact with "normal" peers, and also to increase prosocial attitudes toward other racial and ethnic minority groups.

SOURCE: Maheady, L., M. K. Sacca, and G. F. Harper, "Classwide Student Tutoring Teams: The Effects of Peer Mediated Instruction on the Academic Performance of Secondary Mainstreamed Students," *Journal of Special Education* 21, no. 3 (1987): 107–121.

Because of federal legislation over the past two decades (in particular, PL 94-142, the Education of All Handicapped Children Act of 1975), young people with disabilities now have many more resources available to them in schools, including more accessible physical arrangements, special curriculum programs, and expert diagnosis.[22] In many schools, special classes are available for nearly every type of disabling condition (retardation, developmental and emotional disabilities, sensory loss, and so on), whereas other schools offer training programs for those who can adapt to the regular classroom (an effort usually referred to as *mainstreaming*).

As with at-risk students, your focus in teaching students with developmental or physical disabilities should be on using instructional opportunities to bolster their self-confidence as well as their skills and intellect.[23] One simple adaptation is to build into coursework, wherever appropriate, examples of people who have dealt with disabilities; such lessons promote self-esteem for students with disabilities, as well as foster tolerant attitudes and respect among their peers. Middle-level students in particular enjoy reading about people who have achieved success over great odds; a large body of young adult literature is available on this topic. More mature students enjoy hands-on activities that involve role-play, map making, and photograph collecting.[24] A teacher must keep in mind that youth disabilities constitute a large and varied group. Those who are physically disabled may be very intelligent and those who are classified as retarded may possess advanced sensorimotor skills.

Several national organizations articulate the needs of students with disabilities. A few are broad based and include all aspects of the exceptional child, whereas others focus on children with particular problems involving sight, hearing, or learning disabilities. Nearly all offer advice to teachers and parents about dealing with the needs of special students, and most provide information about instructional methods and materials that promote learning for them. (See Appendix A for a list of these organizations.)

A number of instructional adaptations have proved effective with students with physical and developmental disabilities.[25] These adaptations include the following:

The use of concrete rather than abstract examples of ideas and concepts (i.e., three-dimensional models rather than maps).

Hands-on activities that students must plan, direct, and produce, like the setting of a model airplane factory, including assembly-line production, production counts, and time limits.

A willingness to vary instructional modes to appeal to students with different cognitive levels and to those who respond to different stimuli (visual, auditory, tactile).

Presenting smaller amounts of information in discrete lessons keyed to one or two major points.

Demonstrations—story-telling, speeches, show-and-tell projects, student-made bulletin boards and posters, songs, plays—rather than lecture.

Frequent evaluation and feedback on incremental learning, with an emphasis on positive feedback.

Students Who Are Gifted, Talented, and Creative

Gifted and talented students are a diverse group who display outstanding abilities, talents, or skills in one or more fields of endeavor. Such students may be all-around academic achievers, may show an astonishing talent in a single field like art or mathematics, may be highly skilled in computer or machine technology, and may also have behavior problems and be bored by school. Some obtain high standardized test scores yet receive low grades from classroom teachers; others perform with ease in some areas but struggle in others. Most students classified as gifted are placed there on the basis of grades, reading scores, teacher recommendations, and/or performances on standardized tests of creativity and intelligence like the Wisconsin Inventory of Skills or the Torrance Test of Creativity.

Given the structure of most secondary schools and the lack of federal or state legislation in support of gifted, talented, and creative programs, many teachers overlook or misdiagnose the needs of these students. Many assume that those who are gifted or talented need little or no special help because they already have advantages conferred on them by birth and/or upbringing. In fact, such assumptions often lead teachers to overlook students from minority or economically disadvantaged backgrounds who are gifted or talented, or to fail to recognize the special needs of students from more advantaged backgrounds.

Students who are gifted and talented may have problems compounded by a relative lack of precise diagnostic tools (as compared with those for other exceptional youth) from which reliable judgments can be made. Creativity in particular is difficult to assess. The definition of creativity is still quite open to debate, and the tests commonly used for evaluation purposes are expensive, time consuming, and cumbersome. Intelligence tests, by contrast, are well organized and well developed but usually measure a narrow spectrum of total ability—specifically, reasoning skills linked to knowledge. These tests may or may not be fair assessments of innate ability for many segments of our population.

Social studies teachers usually view above-average or bright students as candidates for either enrichment activities or acceleration. Most schools provide some enrichment possibilities but tend to avoid acceleration (skipping grades) because of perceived social or developmental problems. Social studies enrichment most often involves an expansion of courses, readings, and coverage, or an in-depth study of one or more topics. Some schools attempt to reach the gifted through research seminars, special projects, minicourses, or subjects that are not part of the regular curriculum, and advanced placement programs in U.S. and/or European history. Many teachers see enrichment as an opportunity to increase the quantity of history or social science offered to students; they overlook the need to build analytical skills. In fact, programs designed to build critical thinking skills or to encourage independent research within the regular social studies classroom are often the most effective and appealing.

Gifted, talented, and creative students can certainly move farther, faster, and deeper than most of their peers, but they are also vulnerable to peer and parental pressures—just as students with handicaps are—for being different. Students with special intellectual or creative gifts may be perceived negatively by their peers out of fear, awe, jealousy, or group bias. Furthermore, they may exhibit maladjustments to their social settings or rebel against controls because of what may be very intense pressure to succeed; this reaction compounds the universal adolescent problems of maturation, self-definition, and self-esteem. An example is test anxiety, which seems to increase at the secondary school level for the brightest students.[26] The result of pressure may be less rather than more productivity, and in the extreme, behavioral problems including drug and alcohol abuse.

High ability students, although a varied group, will generally be better engaged by the social studies teacher who presents a challenge than by one who seeks to cover more ground. The gifted and talented need advanced problem finding and problem solving, which require them to analyze, synthesize, and evaluate data and to compare conflicting viewpoints. They also need the opportunity to use their imaginations in brain storming and similar mind-stretching creative activities.[27] For more extensive information on issues, materials, and methods appropriate to gifted education, you can contact any of a number of organizations that act as advocates for the interests of these students. (A list of these is provided in Appendix A.)

Maker suggests a number of research-based instructional adaptations that have proved effective with gifted and talented students.[28] These include the following:

> Presenting challenges that pique curiosity and provoke imagination: research projects, surveys, student-designed experiments to solve a defined problem.[29]

> Using popular material (e.g., songs, films) to emphasize analytical and judgmental concerns.

> Focusing on problematic, paradoxical, or controversial issues—a juxtaposition of primary and secondary sources, conflicting eyewitness accounts, autobiographies, and biographies.

> Creative reading assignments involving current controversies.

> Student participation in and leadership of panels, debates, simulations, role-playing.

> Use of outside resources—area college professors or other experts, field trips.

> Longer discussion periods, with less emphasis on coverage and more on critical thinking.

> Enrichment through integration of other disciplines (e.g., music, art, literature, current events).

> Inclusion of computer technology, both as potential research tools and for simulation activities.

Second Language Students and the Multicultural Classroom

Over the last two decades, the United States and Canada have again become nations of preference for hundreds of thousands of newcomers. Whereas earlier migrations of the twentieth century came first from Western Europe and then Eastern and Southern Europe, more recent waves have originated in Asia, Latin America, the Middle East, and parts of Africa. These changes are being reflected in our classrooms, particularly those in large urban centers. Most of the new students occupying seats nowadays are from Asia or Latin America. Over all, about 25 percent of the student population of the United States is currently minority, and it is estimated that by the year 2000 over 30 percent will be children and youths of color. Many of these youths do not speak English as their primary language, although many may speak some English and one or more other languages. Spanish speakers are by far the most important of the second language groups considering that 1980 census reports over fourteen million Hispanic residents, old and new, in the United States. As a result of these population changes, many educators are arguing in favor of altering the social studies curriculum in the direction of multicultural education.

Multicultural education usually is taken to mean recognition and respect by American society of all its diverse groups, incorporating their traditions into the general tradition, rejecting both the assimilation of former decades and the development of separate cultures. This approach, which stresses the acceptance and even the celebration of diversity, has been called *cultural pluralism*. Not everyone is happy with this compromise. Some would like to see a return to the view that American traditions are firmly rooted in the Western European tradition and that English should be the major or even sole mode of communication throughout the nation. Others argue that each group should create its own traditions in contradistinction or as a complement to the mainstream culture, for example, an Afrocentric or Hispanocentric education rather than a Eurocentric view of the world.[30]

Although I generally agree with proposals for a multicultural education for social studies students, careful attention should be given to its content and its methods of implementation. Changing ethnic population mixes are alone an insufficient justification for adopting a pluralistic conception of society. Worldwide changes in communication, the emergence of an international economy, and cultural diffusion of ideas, customs, and artifacts are powerful incentives to respect other cultures, even if many fewer representatives of those cultures lived among us. Of course, because the United States and Canada are moving in the direction of great cultural diversity, the importance of understanding other cultures, and migrants from those cultures, has grown to a high order priority in education.

Second language speakers are one aspect of the more general problem of multicultural education. All the newcomers including those lacking English, have brought with them prospects for success and cultural enrichment as well as a variety of social and educational problems. Some are bilingual or multilingual and others are monolingual and sometimes illiterate even in their own tongue. Because English, and to some small extent Spanish and French, are the languages of instruction in North America, a fairly sizable proportion of recent immigrants are at a distinct disadvantage from the very beginning of their educational experience. For such students, many programs have been created. Some focus on teaching and learning English as a second language (ESL), whereas others stress bilingual education (i.e., instruction in two languages simultaneously). Each type of program has its supporters and detractors, and the research on the different programs is so far inconclusive. All agree, however, that the increasingly diverse mix of immigrants requires training in the mainstream language and assistance in understanding and adapting to American customs so these newcomers can be successful in the mainstream.

Many classroom practices have been suggested by research literature to aid second language students.[31] A number of classroom adaptations have been offered, particularly to overcome language deficiency.[32] Proponents argue that success requires daily use of special instructional techniques and approaches. The following are some of these methods:

Motivate interest by using audiovisual materials that are gripping and easy to interpret.

Incorporate key words and phrases from the students' cultures into daily lessons and routines.

Invite all of the students to contribute stories and accounts of their own cultures for the others to discuss.

Encourage students to translate for each other in their native language and then back into English for the rest of the class.

Allow a few minutes of extra preparation time for answers to questions or to tests, and then go over responses in class.

Generally permit longer response and preparation times than usual and correct errors in as supportive a manner as possible.

Show respect for and interest in other cultures, inviting students to share their experiences with you.

SUMMARY

Teacher and student roles were described and discussed in the first half of this chapter. The roles you can play as teacher were conceived as following didactic, reflective, and affective goals. Didactic roles included those of authority, resource, and guide; reflective roles incorporated those of questioner, scientist, and artist; affective roles comprised dramatist, socializing agent, and devil's advocate. It was argued that social studies is an especially inviting field for both teacher and student role-playing in a wide variety of situations, particularly those seeking to motivate and involve your student audience with subject matter.

Just as you will find yourself choosing among a number of instructional roles as you teach middle-level or secondary social studies, you will be faced in the classroom with learners who vary in many ways. Special groups have received more attention in the social studies over recent years than in the past, particularly those students with physical and developmental disabilities. Other students with special needs—particularly at-risk students and those who are gifted and talented—have received less attention, although honors, enrichment, and advanced placement programs are available for the latter group at many schools, and programs that promote career skills have been widely experimented with for the former. Another group—people of color from diverse cultural backgrounds and second language learners—will become more and more of a presence in the classroom in the coming decades.

When we look at the instructional adaptations that seem to have worked with special learners over the past decades, we come to an almost too obvious conclusion: The kinds of adaptations that work for one group tend to work for the other groups as well. And we can go a step farther: Most of these adaptations (including frequent positive feedback, less emphasis on coverage and more on critical thinking, the creative integration of other disciplines and of outside resources) constitute the simple act of good teaching. If you find yourself confronted with a classroom whose occupants vary widely in interest, ability, and skill, then by all means contact any of the numerous professional organizations that provide strategies and materials for teaching those with special needs. But remember that every student in your classroom has a special need, and what you bring to each individual student you bring to all your students.

NOTES

1. Constantin Stanislavski, *An Actor's Handbook* (New York: Methuen, 1963).
2. J. Kounin, *Discipline and Group Management* (New York: Holt, Rinehart & Winston, 1970).
3. Barak Rosenshine and Norma Furst, "Enthusiastic Teaching: A Research Review," *School Review* 78, no. 4 (1979): 23–39.
4. J. T. Dillon, *Questioning and Teaching* (New York: Teacher's College Press, 1988).
5. Arthur Whimbey, "The Key to Higher Order Thinking Is Precise Processing," *Educational Leadership* 42, no. 1 (Sept. 1984): 66-70.
6. Louis Rubin, *Artistry in Teaching* (New York: Random House, 1985).
7. Donald Oliver and James Shaver, *Teaching Public Issues in the High School* (Boston: Houghton Mifflin, 1966).
8. David R. Krathwohl et al., eds., *Taxonomy of Educational Objectives: Handbook II. The Affective Domain* (New York: McKay, 1964).
9. Jack Nelson and John Michaelis, *Secondary Social Studies* (Englewood Cliffs, NJ: Prentice-Hall, 1980), pp. 225–33.
10. Fannie R. Shaftel and George Shaftel, *Role-Playing for Social Values: Decision-Making in the Social Studies* (Englewood Cliffs, NJ: Prentice-Hall, 1967).

11. J. T. Dillon, "Cognitive Complexity and Duration of Classroom Speech," *Instructional Science* 12 (1983): 59–66.
12. D. Rogers, *Adolescents and Youth*, 6th ed. (Englewood Cliffs, NJ: Prentice-Hall, 1989).
13. J. Piaget, *The Origins of Intelligence in Children* (New York: Norton, 1963).
14. R. Gelman and R. Bardlageor, "A Review of Some Piagetian Concepts," in *Carmichael's Manual of Child Psychology*, vol. 3, *Cognitive Development*, ed. P. Mussen (New York: Wiley, 1983).
15. H. and S. Opper, *Piaget's Theory of Intellectual Development*, 3rd ed. (Englewood Cliffs, NJ: Prentice-Hall, 1988).
16. F. Newman, "Reducing Student Alienation in High Schools: Implications of Theory," *Harvard Educational Review,* 51 (1981): 546–64.
17. R. W. , "High School Dropouts: A Review of Issues and Evidence," *Review of Educational Research* 57 (1987): 101–121.
18. D. , "Self-Efficacy Perspective on Achievement Behavior," *Educational Psychologist,* 19 (1984): 48–58.
19. J. D. Hawkins and T. Lam, "Teacher Practices, Social Development, and Delinquency," in *Prevention of Delinquent Behavior*, ed. J. D. Burchard and S. N. Burchard (Beverly Hills, CA: Sage, 1987), pp. 241–324.
20. G. G. , "At-Risk Students and the Need for High School Reform," *Education,* 107 (1988): 18–29.
21. R. E. and N. A. Madden, "Effective Classroom Programs for Students At-Risk" (Center for Research Report, No. 19) (Baltimore: Johns Hopkins University, 1987).
22. Public Law 94-142: The Education of All Handicapped Children Act, 1975, Section 612(5)B.
23. E. Y. Babad, J. Inbar, and R. Rosenthal, "Pygmalion, Galatea and the Golem: Investigations of Biased and Unbiased Teachers," *Journal of Educational Psychology,* 74 (1982): 459–74.
24. B. , *Effective Teaching Behaviors for Successful Mainstreaming* (White Plains, NY: Longman, 1985).
25. D. C. Ferguson, P. M. Ferguson, and R. C. Bogdan, "If Mainstreaming Is the Answer, What Is the Question?" in *Educators' Handbook: A Research Perspective*, ed. V. Richardson-Koehler (White Plains, NY: Longman, 1987).
26. K. T. Hull, "Debilitating Motivation and Testing: A Major Educational Problem," in *Research on Motivation in Education*, vol. 1, ed. R. E. Ames and C. Ames (New York: Academic Press, 1984), pp. 243–49.
27. E. P. Torrance, "Teaching Creative and Gifted Learners," *Handbook of Research on Teaching*, 3rd ed. (New York: Macmillan, 1986), pp. 630–47.
28. C. J. Maker, "Gifted and Talented," in *Educators' Handbook: A Research Perspective*, ed. V. Richardson-Koehler (White Plains, NY: Longman, 1987).
29. The *Concord Review* (Will Fitzhugh, ed., P.O. Box 661, Concord, MA 01742) is a quarterly review of essays by students of history and the social sciences that seeks work by high school students. Accepted essays are generally approximately a thousand words long, with footnotes and references.
30. M. A. , "'Africa-Centered' School Plan Is Rooted in the '60's Struggle," *New York Times*, 5 February 1991, p. B1–20.
31. C. I. Bennett, *Comprehensive Multicultural Education: Theory and Practice*, 2nd ed. (Boston: Allyn & Bacon, 1990).
32. M. Romero, C. Mercado, and J. A. Vazquez-Faria, "Students of Limited English Proficiency," in *Educators' Handbook: A Research Perspective*, ed. V. Richardson-Koehler (White Plains, NY: Longman, 1987), pp. 348–69.

FOR FURTHER STUDY: TEACHER ROLES AND STUDENT AUDIENCES

Adams, R. *Protest by Pupils: Empowerment, Schooling and the State*. Bristol, PA: Falmer Press, 1991.

Allen, Russell et al. *The Geography Learning of High-School Seniors*. Princeton, NJ: Educational Testing Service, National Assessment of Educational Progress, 1990.

Applebee, Arthur N., Judith A. Langer, and Ina V. S. Mullis. *Literature and U.S. History: The Instructional Experience and Factual Knowledge of High-School Juniors*. Princeton, NJ: Educational Testing Service, National Assessment of Educational Progress, 1987.

Ayers, W., J. A. Hunt, and T. Quinn, eds. *Teaching for Social Justice: A Democracy and Education Reader*. New York: Teachers College Press, 1999.

Banks, James. *An Introduction to Multicultural Education*. Boston: Allyn & Bacon, 1994.

Banks, James. *Multiethnic Education*. 3rd ed. Boston: Allyn & Bacon, 1994.

Conant, J. B. *Slums and Suburbs*. New York: McGraw-Hill, 1961.

Davidman, Leonard, with Patricia T. Davidman. *Teaching with a Multicultural Perspective: A Practical Guide*. New York: Longman, 1994.

Diaz, Carlos, ed. *Multicultural Education in the Twenty-First Century*. Washington, DC: National Education Association, 1992.

Finn, J. D. "Withdrawing From School." *Review of Educational Research*, 59 (Summer 1989): 117–143.

Hale-Benson, J. E. *Black Children: Their Roots, Culture, and Learning Styles*. Baltimore: Johns Hopkins University Press, 1986.

Herlihy, J. G., and M. T. Herlihy, eds. *Mainstreaming in the Social Studies*. Bulletin No. 62. Washington, DC: National Council for the Social Studies, 1980.

Heward, William L., and M. D. Orlansky. *Exceptional Children: An Introductory Survey of Special Education*. 2nd ed. Columbus, OH: Merrill, 1984.

McLaughlin, M. W., J. E. Talbert, and N. Bascia, eds. *The Contexts of Teaching in Secondary Schools: Teacher Realities*. New York: Teachers College Press, 1990.

Mercer, C. D., and A. Mercer. *Teaching Students with Learning Problems*. Columbus, OH: Merrill, 1989.

Olson, D. R., and N. Torrance. *Handbook of Education and Human Development: New Models of Learning, Teaching, and Schooling*. Boston, MA: Blackwell Publishers, 1998.

Plowman, P. *Teaching the Gifted and Talented in the Social Studies Classroom*. Washington, DC: National Education Association, 1980.

Pope, Andrew M., and Alvin R. Tarlov, eds. *Disability in America: Toward a National Agenda for Prevention*. Washington, DC: National Academy Press, 1991.

Scarcella, Robin. *Teaching Language Minority Students in a Multicultural Classroom*. Englewood Cliffs, NJ: Prentice-Hall, 1992.

Seelye, H. Ned. *Teaching Culture*. Lincolnwood, IL: National Textbook Co., 1994.

Sisk, D. *Creative Teaching of the Gifted*. New York: McGraw-Hill, 1987.

Wilson, William J. *The Truly Disadvantaged: The Inner City, the Underclass, and Public Policy*. Chicago: University of Chicago Press, 1987.

Chapter 4

Organizing for Instruction

True, reflective attention ... always involves judging, reasoning, deliberation; it means that the child has a question of his own and is actively engaged in seeking and selecting relevant material with which to answer it, considering the bearings and relations of this material—the kind of solution it calls for. The problem is one's own; hence also the impetus, the stimulus to attention, is one's own—it is discipline, or gain in power of control; that is, a habit of considering problems.
—John Dewey, The School and Society

OVERVIEW OF CONTENTS

Main Ideas ————————————————————————————————

Grouping for Instruction: Choosing Group Dynamics ————————————————

    Independent Projects
    Task-Oriented Small Groups/Committee Work: Cooperative Learning ——————
    Role-Play
    Simulations
    Mock Trials

Developing Questions ————————————————————————

    Didactic Questions
    Reflective Questions
    Affective Questions

Summary ———————————————————————————————

Notes ————————————————————————————————

For Further Study: Organizing for Instruction ——————————————————

MAIN IDEAS

The theme of this chapter is organizing for instruction, which deals primarily with selecting roles for students to play and designing the types of questions they will be asked to consider. Just as you can play many parts in the classroom, students can be organized in many ways—as individuals, in small groups, or as members of a gaming team. The organization you choose will strongly influence how students interact with you, each other, and the subject matter. Examples of different dynamics include independent projects, small group discussions, role-play, and simulation games, or mock trials. Each seeks to achieve reflective and affective educational goals through situations involving a high degree of either self-directed or participatory activity. It is argued that varying individual and group interactions during the school year heightens students' interest in the curriculum and provides important prosocial or research experiences for adolescents. Dynamic group processes also offer a valuable change of pace from normal classroom routines.

In addition to selecting an organizing mode for your students, you must make a second vital choice involving the kinds and levels of questions you build into your lessons, units, and courses. The kinds of questions you and your students may pose and answer are discussed.

We also distinguish between two major types of questions: the *cognitive* and the *affective*. The former encompasses data-based inquiries and the latter value or attitude-based inquiries. Cognitive question/answer interactions are described using categories derived from several educational theorists. In one system, for example, questions are classified as ranging in level from low (recall and comprehension) through high (synthesis and judgment). Affective question/answer interactions are discussed using categories that distinguish among feelings, opinions, and values. We offer examples of each kind and level of question, demonstrating how each may be applied to common social studies topics.

GROUPING FOR INSTRUCTION: CHOOSING GROUP DYNAMICS

Just as social studies teachers play a number of roles in the classroom, they may also employ a wide range of individual and group activities to lend variety to daily lessons and to achieve didactic, reflective, and affective goals. Lectures and discussions are, after all, only two ways of many for delivering and comprehending information. Unfortunately, many teachers employ only a few techniques over and over again, ignoring other, more suitable ones that offer a better fit with their intentions and aims for a lesson or unit. As an example, controversial issues with two fairly distinct sides to an argument are well served by a debate format, whereas complex moral or ethical problems can be dealt with effectively by a panel discussion.

Given a modest amount of guidance, students can easily organize and conduct a debate. Conflicts, wars, clashes of interests, and other group interactions are powerfully evoked through a simulation game in which students play roles to solve the problem. Still other problems may be more suitably pursued on an individual basis through library research. Here, facts, assertions, and sources can be cross-referenced and checked. A student investigating the life of a famous person might read and compare two or more biographies with an autobiography to discover whether the same facts and conclusions are presented in all three sources. Agreement or variations in either factual accounts, interpretations, or both can be reported to the whole class.

Thus, a variety of individual or group assignments may be used to involve students in social studies learning activities. Activities may range from simulations in large groups, cooperative problem solving in small teams, and face-to-face debates to historical dramatization or independent research. The choice of activity (i.e., lectures, individual projects, role-play, mock trials, sociodrama, or simulations) depends on your goals, the nature of the lesson, and the students' social and intellectual skills.

Independent Projects

Some tasks in the social studies classroom are best completed on an individual basis in a quiet atmosphere conducive to contemplation. Nevertheless, group research is possible, for example, in those instances when students have collected their own survey data for analysis. If the experiment is real, then group effort becomes much more meaningful. These tasks typically involve students working on research projects, doing independent study, or reading. Generally, individual pursuits are better suited to didactic and reflective goals than to the strongly affective purposes of many role-playing techniques. Intensive reading, the development of footnotes, and the preparation of a bibliography are usually completed in a library setting or a computer center. Research generally requires the compilation of resources and summarization of extensive amounts of data. Students select a problem and document those sources that bear directly on the central idea, theory, person, place, or event to answer one or more questions or test one or more hypotheses that have been identified for review. Unfortunately, many independent study projects or research inquiries at the secondary level fail to stimulate students; too often these involve only the assembling and paraphrasing of large amounts of information. Therefore, many students become bored or overwhelmed by extensive undigested information during their independent inquiry.

A key to a quality project and a way of defeating the information overload syndrome is the care and attention you give to students' research hypotheses. If you, in the role of catalyst and guide, can channel student energies into the investigation of a well-defined research question, with appropriate guidelines or suggestions for reading and study, then the students are far more likely to have a clear sense of purpose and a more enjoyable experience. Usually, the more successful individual projects are those with precise, manageable goals, a testable theory (hypotheses to accept or reject), and a rather narrow subject focus. Huge surveys of war, revolution, the enlightenment philosophies, the works of Freud, or the U.S. Constitution are far too complex and unfocused for most students to deal with and reach a satisfying conclusion. The semester will end first! Much better are projects that stress intensive study, such as (a) a person's life or even one period of a person's life (e.g., the Nixon trip to China), (b) a single work of literature or history (e.g., a critical evaluation of Crane Brinton's *Anatomy of a Revolution*, Dickens's *A Tale of Two Cities*, or Conrad's *Heart of Darkness*), or (c) one event in detail from different viewpoints (e.g., the institution of pre-Civil War slavery from the viewpoints of a slave owner, an abolitionist, and a slave). All of the previous suggestions could be intellectually demanding projects for individualized research requiring didactic, reflective, and affective skills from students. Less demanding examples, for younger or less able students, might include research on the meaning of children's stories like the *Little Red Hen* (economics) or *Jack and the Beanstalk* (law). Or, you might turn to young adult fiction or nonfiction for easier reading material. A good project could involve two accounts of the Lincoln Brigade's role in the Spanish Civil War or two views of the Klondike Gold Rush. For more ambitious students, you might direct them to use databases available in CD-ROM format, or to conduct a search on the World Wide Web for useful information sites. These are more likely to interest than bore, more likely to open minds to new ideas than to close them to the vital questions of content and process inherent in a social science or historiographical inquiry.

LET'S DECIDE

With colleagues or classmates, devise several research projects with relevant sources for middle, junior, or senior high school students and explain why you believe each will be valuable and "do-able" for social studies classrooms.

Task-Oriented Small Groups/Committee Work: Cooperative Learning

In some situations, a task can be completed more effectively by a group effort. This kind of cooperative learning venture suits the social studies well when students have a problem to solve or a project to finish that improves with the sharing of ideas.[1] Cooperative learning can be very effective particularly when goals and concepts are clearly defined, and students understand the roles they are asked to play in their groups.[2]

Teachers are sometimes reluctant to use small group efforts because they fear that discipline will erode or students will waste time. Yet many tasks are better done in groups, particularly those benefiting from peer discussion, requiring a decision or consensus of some kind, or calling for the collation and summarization of material. Keys to avoiding discipline problems while developing good cooperative study efforts lie partly in the task itself and your support. If the task or problem is interesting, permits discussion, and requires a decision by the group, then the chances for solid accomplishment are greater than when a task is dull, already implies an answer, and/or diminishes the role students play in its solution. Your encouragement and excitement for student sharing of ideas and tasks is also crucial to group success.[3]

In committee or face-to-face tasks, students might compare passages on the same events in multiple textbooks in an effort to test accounts for their reliability and validity. Each group would then report its findings to the whole class. Committee analysis of one or more textual treatments of a time period, event, person's life, or ethnic group is an excellent historiographical exercise. A project on the Vietnam War or the treatment of Native Americans is probably better accomplished by group collation of sources than through individual critical analysis. Groups bring out the problems involved in writing historical narrative while holding to standards of objectivity. Finding problems with something presented as "the truth" is a very exciting exercise for students.

Another example of student involvement would be the development, administration, and analysis of results from a survey or opinion poll. This activity could use surveys created by professionals (such as the Gallup Poll), by researchers, or by the students themselves (with appropriate teacher support). Students at the secondary level have the skill to survey their own classes or other classes on such topics as election choices, consumer issues, historical knowledge, attitudes toward politics, and other vital issues of the day. Our society promotes interest in others' opinions and most adolescents love studying peer views on a topic. Students could design a questionnaire based on research precedents or published models, choose a sample, and identify demographic variables such as sex, age, grade, and job status. Then they could administer their questions to a chosen population. Committees would be most appropriate and effective in creating, revising, and refining questionnaire items. Finally, groups in charge of collecting the answers would work together to tabulate the results, a task that might be done laboriously by hand, or easily with the aid of a computer program.

RESEARCH REPORT

Based on a synthesis of several studies, Beebe and Masterson conclude that classroom seating arrangements can expand or inhibit student participation in role-play and small group discussions. They find that, on the whole, a fixed setting where students face the teacher at the head of the room tends to be most inhibiting for discussion. Conversely, placing moveable seats around one or more round tables at which students and teacher face each other tends to promote discussion. Other arrangements, such as rectangular tables, teacher in the middle of a group, or concentric circles, produce immediate improvements in participation and classroom climate. The authors also argue for rotation of class members so that groups do not become fixed and a better social and ideational mix results.

How would you want to arrange your classroom seating?

Would you allow the same students to sit together for the whole semester?

What could you do if your room has fixed seating? Or a desk at the front?

SOURCE: Steven A. Beebe and John T. Masterson, *Communicating in Small Groups: Principles and Practices*, 2nd ed. (Glenview, IL: Scott, Foresman, 1986), pp. 120–29.

In short, you should use small groups, committees, or teams to carry out tasks that are made easier through the efforts of students working together. A positive side effect of tasks done in groups is the reinforcement of social and decision-making skills that are difficult, if not impossible, for a student to practice alone.[4] Furthermore, teams of secondary students have the ability to cross-check and refine each others' writing and ideas in a way that relieves you of the need to be the authority and the critic in a task that is open to creative interpretation.

LET'S DECIDE

Which tasks and lessons in social studies do you see as perfect vehicles for cooperative learning: setting goals, doing reports, completing projects, developing research, debating issues, or constructing tests? Can each of these be reinterpreted as a cooperative venture?

1. Design a plan for a class to write their own examination in, say, world studies.
2. Design a plan for students to create their own newspaper for a time long past; publish and sell it to teachers and classmates.

Role-Play

During role-play students freely enact a part in a problematic situation. The outcome is usually either partially or wholly indeterminate; that is, the players create their own ending. The process of role-play gives students a sense of perspective and what it may have been like to live in a certain situation, be a particular character, or be part of an era. Role-play allows students to get inside a subject or problem rather than look in from the outside through a textbook or lecture. The more latitude offered students in deciding an outcome, the greater is the probability that creativity and higher level thinking will develop.

Role-play often begins with a script of some kind, even if it is just a suggestion of place, event, or character. Students may then fill in the parts as they see fit, according to whatever knowledge, research, or experience they possess. For example, a student might fashion a part as a consumer in a fraud case or a legislator in a simulated parliament. Naturally, those with better information and understanding will create a richer and more interesting script.

Role definition may be easily provided through a setting, a problem, or a biography. More exact roles can be structured by using a partial or full script containing dialogue, scenes, and sets. Such a project is almost a theater piece in which the acting, directing, and interpretation of the part are perhaps more important than improvisation. The reenactment of a Platonic dialogue in class, for instance, dramatizes both the personalities and the arguments. However, it affords players a relatively small degree of leeway to invent, create, or decide the part for themselves. Conversely, an unscripted citizen's council meeting in which each student represents a community interest group (e.g., a homeowner, businessperson, or civil servant) gives students relatively free reign to imagine what characters would say when facing a specific issue, such as permitting a new shopping center on city parkland. Sociodramas are another way in which students perform in a scene from the past using partial scripts based on historical sources and characters. A student playing a roving reporter might interview Napoleon Bonaparte and the Duke of Wellington at Waterloo, calling on each to give his view of the situation before, during, and after the battle.

WHAT DO YOU THINK?

It is clear, therefore, that teachers are constantly on stage. They "act" to bring about the ends they seek. Those who act with greater skill are more likely to accomplish their intent.

Another parallel between teaching and acting lies in the structural similarities of classrooms and theaters. People on stage do things: they function with premeditated intention. Teachers in classrooms also act intentionally: they read, write, talk, solve problems, and stir about, accomplishing various tasks. Their intent is to make learning an active process. Indeed, an old aphorism holds that "we learn by doing." And so we do. The surest sign of a poor classroom is a perverted relationship between the teaching and the learning. When the teacher is perpetually active, and the student forever passive—the results are but a pale facsimile of what could be. Human behavior, on the stage and in the learning hall, must be orchestrated so that maximal effect is obtained.

For all of the parallels, one very important difference separates school and stage. Although a teacher's audience may become intellectually and emotionally involved, they remain observers, witnessing rather than entering into the action. In the classroom, however, the student is a co-performer rather than a vicarious onlooker. Moreover, while the actor follows the script, the teacher continually revises it to fit the learners' response. Teachers need considerable skill in interactive improvisation—the continual refining of the pedagogy to correspond with the situations that evolve.*

What does this author see as similarities between teaching and acting? What are the differences? Do you agree with these distinctions? Would you be comfortable as an "actor"? Why or why not?

*Louis J. Rubin, *Artistry in Teaching* (New York: Random House, 1985), p. 115.

Key elements of any role-play or sociodrama include a setting and problem: jobs and roles, character specifications, scripts, and directions. Your use of role-play may demand more or less student involvement and initiative by diminishing or increasing the amount of scripting and the degree of role definition. Role-plays may be used to increase empathy by requiring greater study in preparation for taking parts—in effect, getting "under the character's skin." This is a way of building historical context and identification with figures and roles.

Role-play can be used for a number of purposes: (a) to create a sense of empathy for an event, person, or issue; (b) to decide on a solution to a problem from different frames of reference; (c) to interpolate or extrapolate characters from fragmentary definitions and accounts; and (d) to develop skills of interaction with other students in creating a scenario for and acting out a dramatic representation. The role-play game or interaction may take several forms: creating a cast of characters who react to an issue and to each other, following a more or less well-defined script or scenario in creating a sociodrama for the classroom, or making decisions as mock representatives of courts, legislatures, rulers, rebels, town councils, or corporations.

TO DO

Plan a series of group activities for a course you plan to teach: in U.S. or global studies.

1. Select a play (published drama) for students to reenact in class or the school auditorium, or show a videotape or film for discussion, such as Lawrence's *Inherit the Wind* or Shakespeare's *Julius Caesar*.
2. Organize student groups to play out a crucial historical event, such as the trial of Socrates, the Salt March of Mahatma Gandhi, or the fall of Constantinople.
3. Have students write their own script dramatizing a recent event of historical importance for the creation of a videotaped docudrama.

Simulations

Simulations are game-like abstractions of events based on a synthesis of case studies that promote problem solving. The role-playing process in simulation is normally aimed at working out a solution to a task given a prescribed set of rules to follow and resources to use. The game of *Monopoly* is an abstraction of many economic rules that players have to follow to reach a goal of financial power based on possession of property and money. Simulations are more elaborate than games because they provide realistic parts for students to play with enough roles to keep a whole class working for several class periods. An exciting problem combined with a desire to win sustains long periods of activity. If the game is interesting and well crafted, then students are often so carried away by their roles that they forget the educational purpose!

Heightened motivation develops because students are free to use their imaginations to solve a mystery. The relatively open-ended nature of most simulations also heightens interest and involvement because students feel free to make their own decisions and to work cooperatively with their peers. Cooperative and competitive simulations are particularly enjoyable for secondary level adolescents who want independence and need participative experiences. Simulations, by their very structure, demand problem solving and critical thinking at high reflective and affective skill levels.

You may want to use simulation games to support larger units of study in the curriculum, bringing alive concepts such as social conflict, compromise, conservation, productivity, special interest lobbying, and political alliances. As a game progresses, students may connect many of the roles they have already studied to more general ideas and classes of events, for example, members of a legislature (representative democracy), participants in arms control talks (negotiations), leaders of a town council (direct democracy), or leaders maintaining their interests while addressing other groups' needs (building alliances).

The game of *War or Peace*, developed several decades ago by a Chicago public school supervisor, is typical of simulation exercises.[5] In this game, a secondary class is first divided into several different groups, each identified with an imaginary country. The groups are presented with a map, military power points, and a morale factor for their country; they are then directed to develop alliances by playing quick negotiating rounds until one country has enough points to defeat or absorb the others. Middle and high school students can learn the game with ease in thirty minutes. Subsequent play may last for a few periods, culminating in a debriefing or analysis of what happened, why it happened, and how the action relates to actual historical events. Because of its alliance concept, this game is particularly suitable before or after the study of a war, such as World War I. Note that the map for War or Peace is a kind of generalized mirror image of Europe with a landlocked powerful Atweena, strong neighbors Andros and Bismania, and an island nation called Galbion. Each student group receives an army and navy plus national morale points (NMFs), which they must use to negotiate peaceful or warlike alliances, as they choose. A crisis, war between Atweena and Nurovia, gets the game underway. After a series of crises and responses, and a good deal of political double-dealing, one of the alliances usually manages to control all the remaining countries and is victorious. The game encourages generalizations about the nature of alliances and the causes of conflicts. The rules for playing it are given here.

War or Peace: A Simulation Game

This is a simple international relations game that can be played by ninth-grade classes in world history. Aside from the enjoyment students derive from playing the game, that activity is designed to provide a genuine learning experience. It may be used to introduce or to strengthen several valuable historical insights.

As a model of international relations, for example, the game can be effectively used to point out the condition of international anarchy that has been an important part of the affairs of people and nations throughout history. A fundamental pattern of international relations, the concept of balance of power, may also emerge clearly as a discovery of the students during their playing of the game. Too, international relations terms come to be better understood in class-room action—such terms as foreign policy, crisis alliance, diplomacy, treaty, neutrality, and peace conference.

The classroom becomes during the game an imaginary world made up of a continent and an island—the arena of interaction of seven sovereign nations. A map of this little world (Figure A) and a chart showing the relative war powers of the nations (Figure B) are all the materials a student needs to play the game. These may be duplicated and given to the students, or they may be drawn on the chalkboard and copied by each student.

The numbers presented in Figure B for army and navy do not correspond to number of men, regiments, divisions or ships of war. They are relative figures that express the comparative war powers of the nations. "NMF" stands for National Morale Factor. All nations are equal in NMF, and these NMF points cannot be taken away from the students who make up the original nations.

Once each student has a copy of the map and chart, three steps are necessary to set up the game:

1. Students may be divided into small groups for the game by counting off by sevens. Number 1's are Androsians; number 2's, Atweenans; number 3's, Bismanians; and so on.
2. The map is oriented to the classroom in the students' minds as it appears to the teacher in front of the class so they may find the relative

position of their nations in the room. Once they have located their respective countries they may form small circles of chairs as their national headquarters.

3. Their first job, when settled, is to pick a ruler for the nation to serve as chairman of the team and to speak out internationally. The ruler may be either a king or a queen—or perhaps a prime minister or a president. The teacher calls the roll of the nations and each ruler responds, introducing himself in a dignified manner by title, name and country: "King Alfred of Bismania!" or "Queen Mary of Atweena!" No suggestion is to be given by the teacher as to the ruler's power. Decision making with the nations is to be left entirely to the students who make up the nation-teams.

Before the game begins the students are given some ideas as to the realities of the international power situation as it exists according to the map and the chart. Atweena, a landlocked nation, has no navy, but it does have the most powerful army. Galbion, an island nation, has the largest navy. The two most powerful nations are Bismania and Galbion. The two weakest are Bontus and Egrama. It is a competitive and hostile world and each nation is faced with a different problem in maintaining its power, security and independence.

The basic rules and pattern of the game should now be explained. In any war the more powerful nation, or alliance of nations, always wins and dictates the terms of the peace settlement. In a war a defeated nation can lose some or all of the power of its army, navy, and its territory on the map to the victorious nation or nations.

Students who belong to a nation that has been wiped out of existence in war and its power and territory lost can continue as a part of the game with their

FIGURE: A
THE CONTINENT AND THE ISLAND

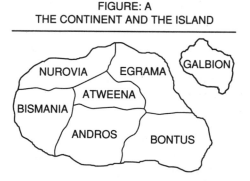

FIGURE: B
RELATIVE WAR POWERS OF THE NATIONS

Nation	Army	Navy	NMF	Total
Andros	700	600	240	1540
Atweena	1000	0	240	1240
Bismania	800	700	240	1740
Bontus	460	400	240	1100
Egrama	520	400	240	1160
Galbion	500	1000	240	1740
Nurovia	500	500	240	1240

Figure 4.1

NMF points. They may stay together as a group without nation status to negotiate for the restoration of their independence in return for the use of their NMF points in another war. As a group, they may join another nation with their NMF points. Or, they may go as individual refugees to join other nations, each taking along his equal share of the NMF points.

The game is played in cycles of well-defined phases, and each cycle begins with an international crisis. The basic four phases for the first cycle are planning foreign policy, negotiations, international declarations, and peace conference. In later cycles, additional phases of planning foreign policy, negotiations, or special international conferences may be called for on the request of the rulers to two or more nations.

> *Crisis.* The game begins in the first cycle with a predetermined international crisis. A state of war exists between Nurovia and Atweena. It must be emphasized to the students that neither side is to be considered the aggressor; there is no right or wrong that can be attached to either; and all possibilities for peace have been thoroughly exhausted. The peace and security of every other nation is threatened. Atweena will conquer Nurovia unless Nurovia is able to bargain successfully to bring other nations into the war on her side. Atweena is, therefore, forced to seek allies. Every nation is faced with the decision to enter the war or remain neutral, on whose side to fight, and what kind of bargain to make for joining one side or the other.
>
> *Planning foreign policy.* This first phase of the first cycle should last about five minutes. Each nation goes into secret conference to decide what to do in the crisis, what its long-term foreign policy ought to be, and what nations its ambassadors should visit for negotiations. No communication with other nations is permitted during this phase.
>
> *Negotiations.* In this phase, lasting about ten minutes, rulers are not allowed to leave their countries. National objectives are to be carried out by sending diplomats to confer secretly—and quietly—with the rulers of other nations. Rulers should generally receive only one diplomat at a time, and they have the right to refuse to confer with any nation's diplomats.
>
> *International declarations.* Diplomats return to their own countries. Rulers stand. The five nations not originally concerned in the war are asked, in order, to declare themselves. The teacher's question is "War or peace?" If the answer is for war the nation must state whether it is joining Atweena or Nurovia. Nothing else can be stated by the rulers. The teacher totals the powers of the belligerent and announces the results of the war.
>
> *Peace conference.* If more than the original two nations were involved in the war, the victorious rulers go to a peace conference to decide what is to be done with the defeated. At the end of a period of from five to ten minutes they must announce whether the defeated are to be wiped out of existence or merely weakened and left alive. The victor, or victors, may revise the map of the world on a chalkboard for all to see, but the changes of national strength need not be given to any nation not involved in the war. Thus ends the first cycle of the game.

The game continues with an intermediate cycle of three phases. The nations meet for planning their postwar foreign policy, and this action is followed by a phase of negotiations. The rulers then stand for international declarations. They are called in alphabetical order and the question is still "War or peace?"

The answer can be "Peace!" Or any nation may declare war on any other nation. No nation can commit any other nation in its declaration.

The first declaration of war precipitates a crisis. When this happens, the declarations stop and the game goes into a new cycle of phases the same as in the first cycle. This is the pattern of the game from then on.

The game can come to an abrupt end during any time of international declarations if all nations declare for peace. Unfortunately, this has never happened in the experience of the writer. If it does happen, perhaps there is real hope for the future of mankind.

From John D. Gearon, "War or Peace: A Simulation Game," *Social Education* (Nov. 1966): 521–22. Reprinted by permission from National Council for the Social Studies, Social Education.

The directions for the game are simple, but the crises, declarations, and peace conferences it engenders stimulate students to reflect on the causes and consequences of conflict. Once the action starts, the students keep the game alive without the teacher's intervention and come to their own conclusions about war and peace. The *War or Peace* game is designed so that settlements can be achieved by either violent or peaceful means, depending on student goals and interpretations, with varied consequences ranging from compromise to bitter feelings.

Many other simulations are available; some are paper-and-pencil exercises, some are in kit form.[6] A growing number are appearing as computer games.[7] The following is a list of simulations for middle and secondary school students:[8]

Printed Format.

Rafa-Rafa/Bafa-Bafa. The former is for more mature students and the latter for those in middle school. This is a game in which cultural misperception and bias are demonstrated by pupils who adopt and promote separate cultures. (Simile II)

Constitution. Students portray representatives at a national convention whose task is to consider revising the U.S. Constitution. (grades 10–12, Interact)

We the Jury. Students play courtroom roles in criminal and civil cases they must decide. (Constitutional Rights Foundation)

Civilization Game. Students reconstruct a culture from finds discovered in ten successive layers of a dig. (McIntyre)

Exchange. Students play all the roles involved in the stock market from directors and brokers to investors buying and selling as events unfold. (grades 8–12, Interact)

American History Recreations. Students reenact famous events, available in scripts such as the following: "The Trial of John Brown," "The Scopes Trial," "The Election of 1800," "The Cuban Missile Crisis," "The Debate at Seneca Fall." These are flexible scripts and include discussion guidelines. (grades 7–12, Interact)

Committee. Students role-play members of congressional committees, listen to lobbyists, bargain, and compromise to get bills passed in Congress. (grades 9–12, TIME)

Computer Format.

The Other Side. Students play leaders of two opposing countries trying to control the outbreak of conflict and solve world problems and deal with each other. (Tom Snyder Productions)

Incomes/Outcomes. Circular flow models are used to create a spaceship, whose economy students must manage. (Joint Council for Economic Education)

Balance of Power. The Great Powers of a generalized time and place vie for supremacy. (grades 9 and up, Mindscape)

Decisions, Decisions. A series of programs on major moral and international issues that students must attempt to solve. (Tom Snyder Productions)

SimCity, SimCity 2000, SimCity 3000. Students design their own present or future cities, or manage historical examples trying to hold budgets in check, fend off catastrophes, and keep their population satisfied in order to be re-elected to public office. (Maxis)

SimEarth. Students guide the evolution of the planet through a series of crises.

Colonial Merchant. Students recreate "mercantilism" in the New/Old World trade. (Educational Activities Corp.)

Where in Europe Is Carmen San Diego? Where in the World Is Carmen San Diego? Where in the U.S.A. Is Carmen San Diego? Students use geographic clues to search Europe or the world for a clever thief. (Broderband Software)

Archeology Search. Students play amateur archaeologists who interpret a seventeenth-century site as a test case. (McGraw-Hill)

Civilization I & II. Build your own empire! History is recreated through trade, diplomacy, and war but cultures and empires interact across times zones as well as places. (grades 7 and up, Microprose)

TO DO

1. Select a computer simulation of your choice—perhaps *Sim City 2000* (Maxis) or *Civilization* (Sid Meier)—and play it through with a group of colleagues. Keep notes on what you see as the game's actual goals and its potential for encouraging reflective or affective goals. Record problems and conclusions. After the simulation, assess the quality and applicability of the game to the secondary classroom.

2. Choose a theme, perhaps based on a recent news item, that involves a clash of ideas on an issue—conservation, political influence, consumer protection, budget choices. Then design a simulation of your own, including goals, format, roles, problem, data, interactions, and conclusion. You might base your game on a local battle to save a town or city historical landmark in which developers are pitted against conservationists. Sketch out roles for city officials, ecological experts, local citizen groups, and business investors, providing skeletal suggestions for students to fill in through their own research and imaginations. Make sure the game has a central issue to resolve.

Mock Trials

Mock trials are usually employed in connection with the study of famous legal decisions, especially those involving the Bill of Rights and the U.S. Constitution. Students may present mock trials that are reduced versions of such well-known cases *as Brown v. Board of Education, State of Georgia v. Southern Christian Leadership Conference,* or *Miranda v. Arizona.* Mock trials may also mimic generic civil cases, such as those involving consumer fraud, landlord–tenant relationships, welfare rights, or public health and safety concerns.

Mock trials often reach back into history, mixing sociodrama, role-play, and historical characters with legal issues. Students can be asked to reenact historically significant cases like the Scopes trial on evolution; the Nuremberg trial of Nazi war criminals; or the Salem, Massachusetts, witch trials (perhaps in conjunction with seeing Arthur Miller's *The Crucible*). In addition, they can hold mock trials that are less structured and more creative in nature, featuring controversial historical figures such as Napoleon Bonaparte, Julius Caesar, Manuel Noriega, Richard Nixon, Ferdinand and Imelda Marcos, Andrew Johnson, or Juan Peron.

Whatever the form and content of the mock trial—whether hypothetical or real, scripted by the students or by experts—students will learn how the process of law works. They will understand what rules are followed and why, and how a decision is made based on precedent, social concerns, and legislative intent as interpreted by judge and/or jury. A major side benefit will be a better sense of the roles involved in the judicial inquiry, including those of judge, jury, attorney, witness, experts, bailiffs, and clerks.

A typical mock trial classroom arrangement appears in Figure 4.4. You can enhance mock trial implementation by providing directions for students to follow. Assign roles:

Clerk of the Court

State's attorney (for criminal cases)

Plaintiff's lawyer (in civil cases)

Defense attorney (for civil or criminal cases)

Defendant

Plaintiff (in civil cases)

Witnesses for state (in criminal cases)

Witnesses for plaintiff (in civil cases)

Witnesses for defense (for criminal or civil cases)

Twelve jurors

Judge

Court reporter

Bailiff

Direct the defense attorney, prosecutor, public defender, or state's attorney to prepare for cross-examining witnesses and making closing arguments.

You can use mock trials to motivate students and to increase their interest in law and other areas of study. Visits to legal institutions can enrich classroom discussion, and visits to classrooms by judges, lawyers, politicians, and police officers can personalize the judicial process. Films and literature can also be drawn into law studies, providing material for extended class discussions. There are so

Figure 4.2   A classroom swearing-in ceremony. Query: How does a ceremony help students get into their roles?
Photograph courtesy of Gerry Gioia, Boys and Girls High School.

many good dramas, television shows, films, and novels about law, justice, and the courtroom that it is hard to choose what to assign to the class, but the films *Judgement at Nuremburg, To Kill a Mockingbird, Gandhi,* and *Breaker Morant,* and the television series *L. A. Law* leap readily to mind. Surely you can choose an even better example. Changing times and new events can regularly be used to update your supply of films, cases, and Supreme Court decisions as you keep your examples current.

TO DO

> Ask students to prepare for two mock trials: one specific and historical and the other generic (perhaps a consumer problem). You prepare a compilation of the facts and assign courtroom roles. Perhaps the trial of the Panamanian dictator, Manuel Noriega, or the leader of Iraq, Saddam Hussein, would be an interesting historical case, and litigation by John Doe, a consumer, who purchases a "lemon" of an automobile, could serve as a civil case.
>
> Role-play, by its very nature, promotes interest in learning through enjoyable interaction that encourages choice. Higher level reasoning (reflection) and judgment (affective) are a natural part of mock trials, sociodramas, and simulations, making this type of activity a potent tool in your repertory.

Figure 4.3   An attorney and client confer with the judge. Query: Which roles are most popular?
Photograph courtesy of Gerry Gioia, Boys and Girls High School.

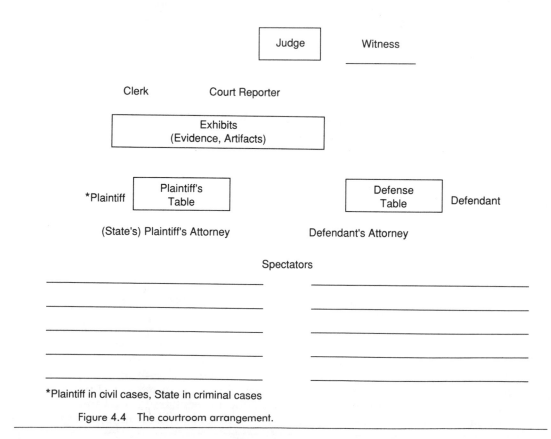

| Judge | | Witness |

Clerk   Court Reporter

Exhibits
(Evidence, Artifacts)

*Plaintiff | Plaintiff's Table | | Defense Table | Defendant

(State's) Plaintiff's Attorney   Defendant's Attorney

Spectators

*Plaintiff in civil cases, State in criminal cases

Figure 4.4   The courtroom arrangement.

You can choose from a wide array of individualized and group learning techniques that are appropriate for social studies. Role-playing methods that stimulate reflective and affective thinking include individualized study and research projects, small group committee work, face-to-face decision making, sociodramas that recreate past or present events, mock trials and legislatures that mimic political and social institutions, and simulations of historical or generalized events that offer students parts to play, problems to solve, and scripts or role descriptions to learn or invent. Role-playing offers participatory experiences for students by imitating life in the world outside the classroom for analytical purposes. In the course of a year, you can use ;nany different options to make your classroom a more varied, exciting, and satisfying place in which to learn social studies.

DEVELOPING QUESTIONS

Questioning is a crucial teaching skill through which you may assess students' knowledge, direct a discussion, stimulate inquiry, promote ideas, and challenge biases and assumptions on controversial issues. Nearly all research on classroom interactions supports the notion that the frequency, type, and level of questions posed to students are important in both the quantity and quality of learning that takes place. Furthermore, the students themselves may ask as well as answer questions. What they ask on their own initiative can be as revealing as their responses to your direct queries. Of particular importance is the complexity or level of question posed because the difficulty or ease of questions has a powerful impact on student expectations and thinking. At one end of the questioning continuum, brief exchanges, if they are nearly all informational, predispose students to view social studies as a "fact" game. At the other end, asking for high-level value judgments without preparing students for this process could lead them to make quick, unsupported opinions, perhaps even breeding a lack of respect for those defending opposing views.

Questions, to be most effective, must match your curriculum goals and begin at a point at which the student audience is comfortable. From this starting point, you should move students toward increasingly deeper and more complex inquiries into any given topic. Ideally, it is probably best to create a balance between lower level, midrange, and higher level questions. But how can you be clear about the category or level of question that is posed?

RESEARCH REPORT

A meta-analysis of dozens of studies on the questioning process in teaching found that consistent and major use of sophisticated, higher level questions in classrooms generally had a positive impact on student achievement measured by a combination of grades, standardized tests, and teacher reports.[*] Others have corroborated this conclusion and supported the use of higher level questions by teachers.[†] However, many studies have demonstrated that, in terms of typical everyday classroom practice, most teachers ask more low level, recall-type questions than they do questions that call on students to understand, apply, analyze, synthesize, or evaluate data.[‡]

[*]D. Redfield and E. Rousseau, "A Metanalysis of Experimental Research on Teacher Questioning Behavior," *Review of Educational Research*, 51 (1981): 237–45.
[†]M. Gall, "Synthesis of Research on Teachers' Questioning," *Educational Leadership* 42 (1984): 40–47.
[‡]V. Hare and C. Pullian, "Teacher Questioning: A Verification and an Extension," *Journal of Reading Behavior*, 12 (1986): 69–72.

A widely used category system for questions and responses was devised by Benjamin Bloom in *Taxonomy of Educational Objectives: Cognitive Domain.*[9] (In our terms, "cognitive" is equated with the knowledge and logic sought by didactic and reflective goals.) Originally, the taxonomy was created to classify educational goals as a basis for writing multiple choice test questions for college examinations. Though not the only system available, Bloom's is probably the most widely used in education as a device to categorize the level and quality of questions. In the cognitive set of categories, Bloom clearly delineates six graduated levels of objectives:

1. *Knowledge.* Knowledge is defined as the remembering of previously learned material. This may involve the recall of a wide range of material, from specific facts to complete theories, but all that is required is the bringing to mind of the appropriate information. Knowledge represents the lowest level of learning outcomes in the cognitive domain.

2. *Comprehension.* Comprehension is defined as the ability to grasp the meaning of material. This may be shown by translating material from one form to another (words to numbers), by interpreting material (explaining or summarizing), and by estimating future trends (predicting consequences or effects). These learning outcomes go one step beyond the simple remembering of material and represent the lowest level of understanding.

3. *Application.* Application refers to the ability to use learned material in new and concrete situations. This may include the application of such things as rules, methods, concepts, principles, laws, and theories. Learning outcomes in this area require a higher level of understanding than those under comprehension.

4. *Analysis.* Analysis refers to the ability to break down material into its component parts so that its organizational structure may be understood. This may include the identification of the parts, analysis of the relations between parts, and recognition of the organizational principles involved. Learning outcomes here represent a higher intellectual level than comprehension and application because they require an understanding of both the content and the structural form of the material.

5. *Synthesis.* Synthesis refers to the ability to put parts together to form a new whole. This may involve the production of a unique communication (theme or speech), a plan of operations (research proposal), or a set of abstract relations (scheme for classifying information). Learning outcomes in this area stress creative behaviors with major emphasis on the formulation of new patterns or structures.

6. *Evaluation.* Evaluation is concerned with the ability to judge the value of material (statement, novel, poem, research report) for a given purpose. The judgments are to be based on definite criteria. These may be internal criteria (organization) or external criteria (relevance to the purpose) and the student may determine the criteria or be given them. Learning outcomes in this area are highest in the cognitive hierarchy because they contain elements of all of the other categories, plus value judgment based on clearly defined criteria.[10]

Questions can be classified in many other ways: by level, as in Benjamin Bloom's taxonomy, or by *type*, as in J. B. Guilford's convergent or divergent distinction shown here:

A. *Memory*

This is simply the ability to remember what has been learned. The best known subtype is rote memory, but this component of intellectual ability also includes visual and auditory memory.

B. *Thinking*

1. *Cognition (discovery)*. This component includes verbal comprehension as well as the ability to discover relationships, patterns, and classes; problems; and implications.

2. *Production (Convergent and divergent thinking)*. The essence of this category is that thinking is used to produce some end result. In the case of convergent thinking, there is usually one unique, correct answer to the question or problem. Thus thinking is channeled or made to converge on the desired answer. By contrast, in divergent thinking there is no single correct answer or solution. "Brainstorming"—in which a large number and variety of responses are the goal—and creative writing are examples of activities that require divergent thinking.

3. *Evaluation*. In this category of abilities, thinking is used to "make decisions concerning the goodness, suitability, or effectiveness of the results of thinking. After a discovery is made, after a product is achieved, is it correct, is it the best that we can do, will it work?" This ability includes making logical evaluations (e.g., determining the soundness of conclusion based on logical consistency) as well as judgments that involve choices between alternatives based on common sense or wisdom.[11]

Note that Guilford's conception is similar to Bloom's in that memory skills are given the lowest rating in difficulty, whereas creative and judgmental skills are characterized as more complex and thought provoking. These classifications may be viewed as aids in planning lessons for any type of material. However, caution must always be exercised in judging the quality (and goal) of a question because almost any form of inquiry can be altered by the context in which it is placed. Even if the word structure of a question seems to call for a reason, the student may not be prepared to answer at that level, or may interpret the query differently from the teacher. In addition, the overall context of a lesson may overpower questions. For instance, if you pose a dozen or more recall questions to a class and suddenly follow these with a sequence of much higher level questions, students may miss the distinction between the two types and offer information-type answers for all responses. A certain amount of "wait-time" must be allowed before you introduce thought questions; waiting creates an atmosphere in which contemplation is encouraged and expected. Asking high-level or divergent questions does not in and of itself guarantee a lesson filled with intelligent discussion, student initiated inquiry, or active participation. Reflection and the examination of values by the students take place best in a context that encourages the free exchange of ideas, where thinking out loud is supported by your praise, your use of students' ideas, and by a well-chosen, stimulating curriculum. In short, there must be a full-fledged system that builds and legitimizes higher level responses to higher level questions.

RESEARCH REPORT

In an early study applying Bloom's taxonomy for the cognitive domain to three popular and typical fifth-grade social studies texts, O. C. Davis, Jr. and Francis P. Hunkins find that all three books predominantly stressed low-level, factual questions, to the exclusion of most higher order questions. The distribution they found was Knowledge, 87 percent; Comprehension, 9 percent; and Application/Analysis/Synthesis and Evaluation, 4 percent. Thus, teachers received little support from these textbooks for building students' thinking skills.

Is this type of textbook still typical?

Are back-of-the-chapter questions still mainly factual?

SOURCE: O. C. Davis, Jr. and Francis P. Hunkins, "Textbook Questions: What Thinking Processes Do They Foster?", *Peabody Journal of Education*, 43 (1966): 285–92.

As you can see, Bloom's six categories and Guilford's three dimensions correspond roughly to the three aspects of teaching that have been discussed: the didactic, the reflective, and the affective. Recall and comprehension are most appropriate to a didactic approach, application and analysis to a reflective approach, and synthesis and judgment to an affective approach. How questions may be used to further each of the three approaches is discussed in the following sections, with examples given for each category using Bloom's cognitive taxonomy or Guilford's structure of intellect as guides.

Didactic Questions

Questions that call on students to recall facts and provide definitions may be placed in the didactic category. According to Bloom, recall questions involve no real thinking activity because storage and retrieval skills are the only ones necessary to provide an answer. If you ask for the capital cities of ten states, students either do or do not have that data at hand. Missing data cannot be used for analysis or synthesis.

Recall Questions.   Typically, informational or recall questions demand a single, correct answer characterized by brevity. Answers usually are short, rapidly paced, and frequently followed by your compliments or criticisms. Recall questions are particularly useful to learn how much knowledge students possess, to review past lessons, and to set up a common database. Usually recall or informational questions begin with a "what," "when," or "which" interrogative, and by directions such as "List all of the important dates of the Russian Revolution."

Here are some examples of typical recall/informational/convergent questions in social studies:

1. Where is Yugoslavia on the world map?
2. How many people live in the nation of Brazil?
3. What are the causes of World War I (if taken directly from a text)?

TO DO

Make up three of your own recall questions. How much time did it take you to invent these, or to answer?

Comprehension Questions.   Comprehension questions require relatively low levels of thinking that call for definition, meaning, and understanding from respondents. When you ask students to define wealth or poverty, they can respond in a number of ways, ranging from the recall of dictionary terms to a paraphrase or elaboration in their own words. When students repeat dictionary terms they add nothing of their own. Paraphrasing and elaborating demonstrate higher levels of understanding because the students have reinterpreted ideas, giving them fresh meaning. Using the language of one's experience indicates more understanding of a definition than does formal recall. If students have only a vague, unclear grasp of common or technical social studies terms, such as social class or gross national product, then this basic lack of understanding will seriously hamper them in any further inquiry in which such concepts are important.

Comprehension questions are especially useful in helping students to clarify ideas and concepts on their own. Typically, these responses are lengthier than recall answers. Comprehension questions are a major tool to help students open up ideas, build language and understanding, and crystallize concepts for further use. Teachers can also employ comprehension questions to diagnose respondents' ability to reinterpret ideas in terms suitable to their level of maturation. Naturally, the clarification and honing of ideas requires more time than recall. You must allow for "searching" behavior, during which terms are defined and redefined several times until there is a general agreement on their meaning among class members. This is a convergent process because the outcomes of comprehension questions are agreed-on definitions or meanings.

Presenting two or more different definitions of the same term can be used to promote discussion until some degree of consensus is reached on the meaning of terms. Overused and abused terms like *revolution, reform, alliance,* or *defensive posture* may form the basis for an excellent comprehension lesson on the problems inherent in creating a new definition that is clearer and more useful than those preceding it.

The greater the time allotted students to define ideas in their own words, the greater will be the level of understanding that is likely to evolve. The following are examples of comprehension questions:

1. How would you define the idea of a *city* in your own words?
2. What are taxes? How do you know when you are paying a tax?
3. When you used the word *leadership*, what did you mean by that?
4. When Henry Kissinger, a former U.S. secretary of state, discussed *defensive posture* on a TV program, what did he mean?
5. Look up the definitions of *liberal* and *conservative* in the dictionary. Does the dictionary description fit your own idea of liberal and conservative? What do you mean by each term? Does everyone agree on this meaning?

TO DO

> Write three questions of your own aimed at eliciting student comprehension. Do you agree with my five choices, or are there any you might challenge?

Reflective Questions

Reflective questions are those that call for some form of explanation, reasoning, or testing of ideas. Reflection can cover a broad range of human reasoning from telling why to creating a theory or generalization that encompasses a whole class of events into one framework, such as a theory of modernization. Included in reflection are processes for testing the explanations and theories presented. Reflective questions move up Bloom's taxonomic levels, requiring more time to formulate and answer because of their increasing depth and complexity. Divergent thinking usually develops when students are faced with reflective questions that require them to weigh alternatives, some of which may conflict.

Application Questions.   Application questions ask students to check their ideas and understandings against new facts, examples, and case studies. New or additional data may support or weaken a conclusion, resulting in its modification, acceptance, or rejection. The process of application in a discussion is cyclical, arising from both the acquisition of new information and the development of explanations. Application questions are a vital part of your repertory for encouraging students to test their ideas through comparison and contrast. Each example added to the students' collection increases their awareness of nuances and subtleties, strengthening reading and reasoning skills. There should be widespread participation in applying ideas to specific cases (deduction) or in using specific cases to build generalizations (induction). Inductive and deductive reasoning both improve a student's ability to distinguish between examples while extracting their commonalities. If students share their conclusions after answering a series of application questions, the overall trend has probably been more convergent, that is, toward agreement. If there is an argument about which examples do or do not fit a theory and rival interpretations emerge, then the overall trend has probably been more divergent.

Application questions are often cast in the form of "how" or "why," but some may be phrased as "what." It is the intent that matters, not so much the form. "Does it fit?" is a commonplace form of application question. So is the familiar *Sesame Street* song, "Which of These Things Go Together; Which Are Really the Same?" Likeness and difference are very much a part of application questions, including these examples:

1. Is the Indian system of government basically like or different from that of the United States?
2. Was slavery in the pre-Civil War South similar to or different from that of other times and places?
3. If you apply Rousseau's idea of the "General Will" to the Chinese Revolution, were leaders like Mao Tse-tung expressing that will or not?
4. Does the Cuban Revolution really fit with the others discussed in Crane Brinton's *Anatomy of Revolution*?

TO DO

Do you agree that these four questions are at the application level? Choose two you think could use improvement and rewrite them. Have you changed the level or are they still aimed at application?

Analysis Questions.   Analytical questions are those that seek the reasons and causes for particular decisions, actions, and events. Analysis usually promotes extended answers in which the respondents dissect information in search of motives, aims, and explanations for an aspect of human nature. Answers may diverge rather than come together when students evolve alternative explanations for the same event. The same student may arrive at more than one explanation and then weigh these against each other in an attempt to settle on the most significant factor.

Analytical questions are perhaps most useful in probing for the underlying reasons and are often added as paraphrases, redirections, or elaborations of student remarks (e.g., "Why do you think that way?").

Analysis presupposes that students should have a knowledge base, comprehension of terms, and a grasp of the process of comparison and contrast. As examples are more carefully scrutinized in class you can ask analytical questions with increasing frequency. Students can also initiate their own "why" questions from a knowledge base. If time is allowed for contemplation, students are usually better able to defend and explain their ideas toward the middle of a lesson. Analytical questions are easy to invent because they arise naturally in the context of discussion.

The following are some examples of analytic questions that challenge assumptions and offer counterarguments:

1. From your studies, what seem to be the causes for the expansion and popularity of Islam in much of the world?
2. What factors do you believe cause economic stagnation or expansion?
3. Which reasons best explain the failure of the League of Nations as a world force?
4. Why do you agree or disagree with the pro- or anti-gun control (or any other issue) viewpoint?
5. How do you explain the high standard of living in the United States or Kuwait and the low standard of living in Congo or Albania?

TO DO

Write two questions of your own that ask students to offer reasons. Can you think of any topics in social studies in which reasons cannot be developed? Can you identify topics that seem particularly well suited to analysis? Explain why.

Synthesis Questions.   Synthesis questions seek to stimulate connections, relations, and combinations between ideas and information. Reasons are gathered, tested, and fused into a generalization or hypothesis. The process of building connections may result in a gestalt, or coming together of many different strands into a whole. The whole is a recognition that a pattern exists in a body of data, or that a theory can draw together many related ideas, events, trends, and observations. Synthesis is a summing up of reasons that is sometimes called hypothesizing, generalizing, concluding, or theorizing, all describing similar levels of thought.

Where analysis seeks to probe and break apart ideas and information, synthesis questions encourage students to develop broad generalizations or principles, pulling together large amounts of data. The particular and specific give way to the general and the universal. Through synthesis questions you can push students to assemble their facts into a coherent hypothesis that makes a whole class of events more understandable and perhaps predictable.

Conclusions can range from a specific hypothesis to universal laws, with many possible answers. Your job is to ask students to support their hypotheses and rules with examples. Conclusions with examples that do not fit very well should be challenged. Exceptions really test a theory, and if one or more of the students do not come up with contrary data, then you should provide these cases or the sources. Generalizations or hypotheses are extremely valuable if developed by the students themselves because they represent practice in systematizing data. Students are likely to remember their own conclusions for a long time, and it is important that the conclusions be sound but not too self-assured. After all, a good theory must be open to new findings and be capable of withstanding attack from competing explanations. As students gather more facts to support their hypotheses, these become stronger, particularly if contrary examples can be explained or accommodated in some way. Hypotheses should be tested and refined throughout a lesson, unit, and course.

Synthesis questions require a good deal of time for discussion, and extended monologues should be welcomed. The following are examples of synthesis:

1. What are the conditions under which an economic recession develops?
2. Which symbols of political power, if any, are universal?
3. Why do open and violent conflicts (such as wars) occur between peoples and nations?
4. Why do some societies develop extremes in social classes while others are relatively equal?
5. After studying a dozen different law codes, can you find any aspects of life that all try to regulate?

TO DO

Synthesis questions are "power" questions that ask students to go beyond the data given to make predictions, formulate theories, and make high order generalizations. To be acceptable, synthesis answers must build on two or more examples or events to make an explanation. One specific case, as in analysis, is not enough. Write three synthesis questions on topics of your choice and formulate answers similar to those you would expect from pupils.

Evaluation and Judgmental Questions.   Evaluation questions ask students to make choices based on more, or objective, criteria between two or more alternatives. Inherent in each choice is a judgment concerning what is better or best. Whether an issue is of an empirical (scientific) nature or of an ethical (moral) nature, judgments can be made about what is best—although everyone may not agree. Proofs can be drawn from experience, public evidence, research, and logic or philosophical reasoning.

The term *snap judgment* typifies a choice made quickly with minimal information, often with poor results. By contrast, *reasoned judgment* is based on commonly understood or agreed-on standards supported by ample facts and logic. Your evaluation questions may produce snap judgments as well as more valuable, better reasoned views. One way of handling overly rapid assessments and poorly supported opinions is to challenge evaluations regularly and invite students to critique their own and others' ideas. Be prepared for heat as well as light, because even debates about the merits of one brand of auto over another can grow quite intense. Judgment, after all, lays bare the underpinnings of students' thinking. When respondents have little or no rationale to offer, they may be embarrassed when asked to defend the choice.

Judgment is a vital part of almost every social studies topic and issue. There is really no escape from evaluation because all of us continually engage in judgment, whether shaky or sound, informed or uninformed. It is your role, through judgmental questions, to bring the rationales behind decisions out into the open for more careful examination. This process of cross-checking judgments demands that a good deal of classroom time be allowed for the give and take of ideas. Determining which answer is best or better, rather than which is correct, is at the heart of discussion. Asking for judgment does not guarantee response on the same level from students who may misunderstand the questions, avoid them, or be unable to answer for lack of facts or reasons. Nevertheless, you and your students should ask tough judgmental questions that call for a choice among alternatives, the establishment of criteria, and decisions about what is best or right.

Clearly, judgmental questions may involve both the affective and reflective realms:

1. On what grounds should someone's views on foreign intervention be accepted or rejected?
2. Who is most convincing in dealing with the slavery issue: historian A, B, or C?
3. Which Supreme Court decision was the most logical: the majority or the minority view?[12]
4. If you are a consumer deciding to buy a new automobile, what are the best criteria on which to base your purchase?
5. How would you define good and evil in the case of leadership? How would you rate Nelson Mandela or Mikhail Gorbachev?

TO DO

Develop several evaluative questions of your own and write predictions of student responses. What will you be willing to accept as full-fledged statements of judgment and what kinds of remarks will you classify as no more than opinions? Can you tell the difference between judgments and opinions?

Affective Questions

Affective questions deal with matters of awareness, personal feeling, choice, imagination, and judgment. As defined in this book, affective questions elicit answers based on a core of values of varying clarity and consistency. At the core of all affective questions are emotional and philosophical issues of right and wrong, from which flow human actions. A second version of Bloom's taxonomy deals with affective levels in much the same way as does the one for the cognitive domain.[13] This taxonomy has five graduated levels:

1. *Receiving* refers to the student's willingness to attend to particular phenomena or stimuli (classroom activities, textbook, music, etc.).
2. *Responding* refers to active participation on the part of the student. At this level he not only attends to a particular phenomenon but also reacts to it in some way.
3. *Valuing* is concerned with the worth or value a student attaches to a particular object, phenomenon, or behavior. This ranges in degree from the simple acceptance of a value (desires to improve group skills) to the more complex level of commitment (assumes responsibility).
4. *Organization* is concerned with bringing together different values, resolving conflicts among them, and beginning to build an internally consistent value system.

5. *Characterization by a Value or Value Complex* means individuals have a value system that has controlled their behavior long enough for them to have developed a characteristic lifestyle.

As defined by the second taxonomy, there are strong parallels between the structure and levels of reflective and affective questions. "What do you mean by wrongdoing in reference to this issue?", or "Why do you feel that way?", or "What ethical principle is guiding you?" are questions that can be part of almost any lesson. Thus, affective questions (and responses) are concerned mainly with feelings, beliefs, mores, and commitments to action.

From Feelings to Values.   Affective questions serve to elicit, examine, and judge decisions based on personal preferences and moral values. At the lowest level, you can ask students for their opinions, preferences, and beliefs on a given topic or issue. Comprehension, analysis, and application questions can be used to ask students what they mean by a preference. At the upper reaches of affective thinking, judgmental questions can encourage students to develop and defend a philosophy or moral code that covers a wide range of economic, social, political, or religious issues.

The higher the level of an affective question, the more imagination, personal probing, and philosophical reasoning is required for a response on a plane of equal sophistication. Affective questions and responses can accommodate divergent feelings, nuances, and ambivalence. The discussions they engender might in time lead you to take an opponent's viewpoint that at first seemed strange and foreign. On the other hand, they could uncover issues that are impossible to settle.

Many affective questions will result in discussion of personal values and beliefs that may be far easier to talk about than the larger social and international issues. Conversely, certain personal topics and feelings may remain hidden while public issues are debated in a safe, formal manner. For example, how we view and feel about others, particularly those unlike us, is a sensitive topic worth discussing in the social studies. Charity, welfare, or aid on a local, national, or foreign scale usually arouse passions and prejudices. Politics come into play when important values are discussed, even when students are wholly or partially unaware they are taking a liberal or conservative position. This is when the real fireworks can begin, but it is also a time when you can call on students to clarify ideas, examine underlying values, and develop and defend positions with examples.

RESEARCH REPORT

A note of caution is in order. Children do enjoy talking about values. They love to deliver themselves of their opinions and to recount their personal experiences. In most instances, there is nothing wrong with this, provided it is seen as the starting point of value inquiry rather than as the terminus of it and provided that the objective is the perfection of skills for reasoning about values rather than the mere unburdening of memories and feelings. So-called brainstorming sessions are alleged to have a therapeutic effect when value questions are at issue; be that as it may, educational goals are best met by educational means and by strengthening the student's character and reasoning skills so as to make therapeutic sessions unnecessary. There are seldom hard data about the impact of such sessions…. Likewise, the use of moral dilemmas in the classroom can be quite problematic. Dilemmas are constructed by arbitrarily ruling out meaningful options and by limiting those that remain to those that contradict either one another or themselves…. Education for values can instead take the form of dialogical inquiry in an atmosphere of intellectual cooperation and mutual respect. The conversation that unfolds in a disciplined fashion in such seminars is then internalized by the children. They become acquainted with the other points of view and the other perspectives in the classroom; they become accustomed to challenging others for reasons and to being challenged for their own; they begin to reflect critically and objectively about their own views; they become more confident as they realize that one may be mediocre in spelling or arithmetic yet very impressive in articulating the perspective one has gained from personal experience. This is so important because so many children who "drop out" in the classroom want desperately to "tell their cause alright," and even more desperately they want to be listened to and respected by their peers. By helping children learn how to reason together, we give them a taste of what community can be. If, then, we fail to reinforce it, they may be stuck for the rest of their lives with this weak, impoverished understanding of the genuine merits and benefits of participatory democracy.*

1. What are some of the "cautions" Lipman refers to in talking about values?
2. How can "affect" change learning for the better? For the worse?
3. What does Lipman see as the proper method for discussing affective or value questions? Do you agree or disagree?

*Matthew Lipman, *Philosophy Goes to School* (Philadelphia: Temple University Press, 1988), pp. 68–69.

Different educational formats and movements have attempted to organize the ways in which teachers deal with affective questions. Some, like Kohlberg and his associates, argue that people move through stages of moral growth as they mature.[14] These stages are much like the stages of moral growth and reasoning ability described by Jean Piaget, who argues that they are an immutable part of growing up. In Kohlberg's view, as young people mature, their ability to deal with increasingly abstract moral questions also increases, within limits, moving from lower to higher stages of sophistication. Kohlberg's six levels of moral growth are summarized in Table 4.1.

Certain questions are appropriate only to certain levels of moral growth (e.g., "responsibility" at stage 4 and "self-chosen principles" at stage 6). Children would probably misunderstand or ignore problems that are far above their level. Kohlberg's stages have been used as the basis for a number of training programs in moral reasoning and had considerable influence in social studies during the 1970s and 1980s.

In contrast to Kohlberg's theory of moral growth, many educators argue that children and youths are completely capable of dealing with moral questions of a philosophical nature at very young ages, depending on how these are broached to them.[15] They contend that philosophical issues can be presented in popular language and appeal to a student's sense of fairness or justice. Most students will show an interest in grappling with moral issues in some way, although at a simple level. Lipman and associates at the Center for the Advancement of Philosophy for Children (CAPFC) argue that children and young people are completely capable of moral and philosophical inquiry at almost any age. They argue that training in logical and syllogistic reasoning is a valuable prelude to and support for future examinations into ideas, beliefs, and feelings. For this training, the CAPFC has developed a series of "novels" through which students learn to philosophize; these books include *Harry Stotelmeyer's Discovery, Lisa,* and *Mark,* the last created specifically for the secondary level to promote critical reasoning.[16]

Regardless of the categories you use, you can foster responding, valuing, and organizing values by asking affective questions at different levels of difficulty. These levels may range from opinions and statements without justification

TABLE 4.1 Kohlberg's Developmental Stages of Moral Reasoning

Level 0

Stage 0	*Social Perspective*
Egocentric viewpoint (ages 3–5)	Child cannot distinguish between thoughts and feeling of another and those of self.
What Is Right	*Reasons for Doing Right*
Whatever child wishes would happen.	To avoid bad consequences or to get rewards. Child is either unable to justify choice or justifies it on some external and arbitrary basis.

Level I: Preconventional

Stage 1	*Social Perspective*
Obedience to authority (ages 5–6)	Child can focus on another's perspective, but viewpoint of an authority overrides.
What Is Right	*Reason for Doing Right*
Avoidance of punishment; literal adherence to rules; not doing physical harm.	Because adults know what's right; to avoid punishment.
Stage 2	*Social Perspective*
Instrumental self-interest (ages 6–9), child is aware of another's point of view and that mutual awareness influences actions of both.	
What Is Right	*Reason for Doing Right*
Whatever is "fair"; equal sharing; "tit for tat."	Self-interest; exchange equally: "Do unto others what they do to you."

Level II: Conventional

Stage 3	*Social Perspective*
Interpersonal conformity (ages 9–12)	Child can step outside own viewpoint and respond to need of another without direct reward.
What Is Right	*Reasons for Doing Right*
Golden rule:"To do unto others as you would have them do unto you."	Need to meet expectations of family or friends and gain social approval; need to think of self as nice person who can do good deeds.
Stage 4	*Social Perspective*
Conformity to social order (ages 12–15)	Child sees individual actions in light of total society and its system of rules and roles.
What Is Right	*Reasons for Doing Right*
Responsibility to follow rules of social system.	To uphold the social order; to do one's duty.

Level III: Postconventional

Stage 5	*Social Perspective*
Social contract (young adulthood)	Person takes "prior to society" perspective; modifications to existing social order may be needed.
What Is Right	*Reasons for Doing Right*
Asserting basic rights, values, and legal contract of society, even when in conflict with existing norms.	To fulfill obligations as part of social contract to family, friends, work and society.
Stage 6	*Social Perspective*
Universal ethical principles (adulthood)	Person takes moral point of view.
What Is Right	*Reasons for Doing Right*
Following self-chosen ethical principles of justice for all.	Responsibility to universal principles of equality of human rights and respect for the dignity of human beings as individuals.

NOTE: Based on Lawrence Kohlberg, *Essays on Moral Development: The Philosophy of Moral Development, Volume 1* (New York: Harper & Row, 1981), pp. 409–12. Copyright © 1981 by Lawrence Kohlberg. Reprinted by permission of HarperCollins Publishers, Inc.

to full-fledged positions based on deeply held philosophical (moral) views. Issues may involve personal questions of justice, fairness, and honesty; they may be questions of social goals, or of public welfare, national security, foreign aid, and international human rights. Whatever the topic or level, you have at hand an arsenal of affective questions, including:

How would you define evil?

How do you feel about homeless people?

Why do you oppose or support the death penalty, increasing the defense budget, and similar issues?

Why would you describe your overall view of politics as liberal or conservative?

Would you agree or disagree that "justice for all" should be a basic value of any society?

SUMMARY

The questioning process represents a "two-way plus" relation in which the questions are posed to an audience or posed by the audience to you. In the heat of discussion, questioning may move in both or many directions, but answers may not always be forthcoming. Sometimes you will meet silence. Students may be unable or unwilling to respond at the level you had intended. Sometimes they will raise new ideas or pose old problems in new forms. Sometimes you may ask yourself questions.

WHAT DO YOU THINK?

A central element in the work of actors and teachers is the ability to judge the audience. The collective mood must be interpreted, receptivity gauged, and timing adjusted. More, both actor and teacher must determine the right level of intensity and the best way to sustain participant involvement. Both must project themselves in a manner that heightens audience involvement. Playgoers quickly recognize an inept performer, much as students (experienced teacher-watchers) readily detect an uncertain or incompetent instructor. There are teachers, for example, who seem to teach as if no one was there. Their behavior is dry, the assignments perfunctory, and there is no effort to fine tune the procedures to situations or to student moods.*

What does the writer mean by "the right level of intensity"? Which audience feature does a teacher-actor have to keep in mind? Why? Do you agree that lessons must be tailored to the audience? Would you do this? Why or why not?

*Louis J. Rubin, *Artistry in Teaching* (New York: Random House, 1985), p. 114.

Context is crucial to the questioning process and much depends on the general atmosphere to which students are accustomed in a classroom. An open climate is usually more conducive to higher level reflective and affective questions and answers, whereas a more closed climate may be more efficient in promoting didactic questions and answers. Other factors also important to consider are audience ability and background, and your style and personality.

If answers and inquiries are on the same level, then it is likely that students were prepared to deal with the materials at hand. However, when students consistently answer your questions at lower levels (e.g., give information when analysis is requested), you should try to learn why. Difficulties can arise if the questions are not phrased clearly, or are too difficult; there can also be problems if students are given insufficient data to develop higher level answers. You may, at this point, decide to ask lower level questions of recall and comprehension, and briefly review the material before trying to raise the level of questioning again, and you might offer additional data and reading to stimulate thinking. If students usually respond at higher levels than those proposed, then you should happily raise the general level of inquiry.

RESEARCH REPORT

In a major review of the role of wait-time in classroom interaction, Kenneth Tobin finds that good questioning technique alone is insufficient to guarantee higher order educational objectives. Teachers must accompany questions with a behavior defined as wait-time, that is, allowing students sufficient time to gather their ideas and develop enough courage to contribute to a discussion or recitation. The concept of wait-time itself is drawn largely from the work of Mary Budd Rowe, in elementary science education, who observes that the teachers she studied were on the whole too worried or impatient to give students time to consider answers or questions of their own. Tobin analyzes fifty research studies covering twenty years of work in all fields, including social studies, focusing on instructional effects with and without wait-time. Overall, Tobin argues that wait-time is a critical element in teacher elicitation of higher levels of student thinking, producing lengthier, more complex responses; increased contributions to discussions; more peer conversation and cross-examination; broader participation within classroom groups; and generally higher scores on average on both teacher-made and standardized achievement tests.

How do you feel about student silence after you have asked a question?

Is meditation time always needed?

Do you need wait-time to recall bits of information or to develop analytical statements or both?

SOURCE: Kenneth Tobin, "The Role of Wait Time in Higher Cognitive Learning," *Review of Educational Research*, 57, no. 1 (Spring 1987): 69–95.

A series of questions may result in no responses or silence. Unresponsiveness may be difficult to interpret, but there are at least three major possibilities to consider. First, the students do not really understand or are unable to answer the question and are embarrassed by their inability to respond. Second, they may be searching their memories for the data requested or may be thinking about the problem. Third, the students may be inventing questions of their own, which they may ask to clarify the problem. Always ask yourself and the students why questions fail to engender a desired response or degree of participation. Perhaps the students need wait-time to think and may be unable to respond rapidly; perhaps you have not provided the right kinds of data; perhaps the class is unprepared. Whatever the reason, diagnose the situation before you decide what to do. Do not jump to conclusions or make decisions until you gain insight into the reasons for poor or missing responses to your questions.

The questioning process is, therefore, a delicate one, involving a number of actors. Questions must be matched to audiences, responses to materials, and topics to goals. Building an environment in which students feel free to express ideas is a key to frequent question–answer interactions. Designing good didactic, reflective, and affective questions that stimulate inquiry is vital to getting the curriculum across and serves as a way of managing discussion.

First, a wide variety of possible student interactions were described, ranging from independent study projects through cooperative group learning to mock trials and simulation games. Mock trials and simulations, including those for the computer, were given special attention because of their capacity to stimulate critical and creative thinking in social studies classrooms. Examples of gaming and mock courtrooms were provided as models for you to follow in creating and/or implementing your own projects.

Second, questioning technique was discussed as a vital tool for you to employ in promoting didactic, reflective, and affective learning goals. Bloom's cognitive domain, with its levels of recall, comprehension, application, analysis, synthesis, and evaluation, was presented as a widely used set of guidelines for classifying questions and answers. Guilford's "Structure of Intellect" model was offered as another way of recognizing lower level convergent and higher level divergent questions. Affective questions were also viewed in the framework of a taxonomy for affective domain objectives as well as through Kohlberg's "Developmental Stages of Moral Reasoning." Each set of categories gives you a way to classify your questions as well as students' questions and answers with the caveat that these are tools of analysis rather than factually "proven" distinctions. Experiment with questioning by using any of the classifications presented in this chapter, or by choosing or inventing one of your own classifications. Incorporate role-playing and group dynamics into your daily lessons through dramatizations and small group cooperation, combining them with graduated sequences of questions that move from gathering information to promoting higher level reasoning.

TO DO

1. Design your own mock trial, including all major roles based on a recent U.S. Supreme Court decision that interests you and ought to engage your middle, junior, or senior high school students.
2. Study a computer simulation game, for example, "Decisions, Decisions" (Tom Snyder Productions) on a political or social topic, and then teach a group of students how to play it. Prepare and administer a survey of students' attitudes toward the game. Did they feel it was fun? Did it promote thinking? Did it result in new ideas?
3. Randomly select at least three textbooks for a course (e.g., world studies, U.S. history, or economics) and classify the end-of-chapter questions for ten lessons. Were most of these seeking divergent or convergent responses? Were the queries predominantly recall or did they seek higher levels of thinking?
4. Draw a chart linking those teacher roles, student dynamics, and questioning techniques that best support didactic, reflective, and affective goals. For example, would the authority role be a good match for a mock trial? Would the devil's advocate role fit well with high-level affective questions? Would the socializing role clash with divergent questions that demand analysis and synthesis?
5. Ask at least five colleagues if they consider teaching to be basically like or different from acting. Do your colleagues believe it is necessary to employ many roles to promote their goals or are a few sufficient? Do you think one,

few, or many roles are needed for your development as a social studies teacher? Why?

6. Is questioning a simple or a complex process? Read at least two studies of questioning to find answers. Can questions be divorced from the classroom climate, from the student audience, from the material and curriculum being studied? How are students' questions and answers related to yours, to the curriculum, and to overall instructional goals? Can there be questions without answers or answers without questions? What is a truly great question, and how do you recognize one when you run across it?

NOTES

1. Robert E. Slavin, "Students Motivating Students to Excel," *The Elementary School Journal*, 85 (1984): 53–64, 349.
2. Ronald L. Van Sickle, "Cooperative Learning, Properly Implemented, Works: Evidence from Research in Classrooms," in *Classroom Learning in the Social Studies Classroom: An Introduction to Social Study*, ed. R. J. Stahl and R. L. Van Sickle (Washington, DC: National Council for the Social Studies, 1992).
3. Jere E. Brophy, "Teacher Praise: A Functional Analysis," *Review of Educational Research* 51 (1981): 5–32.
4. David W. Johnson and Roger T. Johnson, *Leading the Cooperative School* (Edina, MN: Interaction Book Co., 1989).
5. John D. Gearon, "War or Peace: A Simulation Game," *Social Education* (Nov. 1966): 521–22.
6. Ron Stadsklev, *Handbook of Simulation Gaming in Social Education* (Part 2: Noncomputer Materials), 2nd ed. (Tuscaloosa: University of Alabama, Institute of Higher Education, 1979).
7. Howard Budin, Diane S. Kendall, and James Lengel, *Using Computers in the Social Studies* (New York: Teacher's College Press, 1986).
8. James Hodges, "Resources for Teaching with Computers," *Social Education*, 15, no. 1 (Jan. 1987): 54–59.
9. Benjamin S. Bloom, ed., *Taxonomy of Educational Objectives: Book 1. Cognitive Domain* (White Plains, NY: Longman, 1956).
10. Ibid.
11. J. B. Guilford, "The Structure of Intellect," *Psychological Bulletin* no. 4 (1956): 281–82.
12. Two good cases for this are *Memphis Firefighters v. Stotis* heard in 1984, and *U.S.A. v. Paradise*, heard in 1987. In the first, White firefighters with seniority were laid off before Blacks hired under an affirmative action program. The Whites won the case. In the second, the Supreme Court upheld a district court's order that Alabama had to correct historical discrimination against state troopers by promoting according to a strict one-for-one White/Black quota. Both decisions were by a 5-4 vote.
13. David R. Krathwohl, Benjamin S. Bloom, and Bertram B. Masia, *Taxonomy of Educational Objectives: Book 2. Affective Domain* (White Plains, NY: Longman, 1964).
14. Lawrence Kohlberg, *The Philosophy of Moral Development* (New York: Harper & Row, 1981), pp. 409–12.
15. Matthew Lipman, *Philosophy Goes to School* (Philadelphia: Temple University Press, 1988).
16. Ibid.

FOR FURTHER STUDY: ORGANIZING FOR INSTRUCTION

Budin, H., D. S. Kendall, and J. Lengel. *Using Computers in the Social Studies*. New York: Teacher's College Press, 1986.
Byrnes, J. P. *Cognitive Development and Learning in Instructional Contexts*. Boston: Allyn & Bacon, 1996.

Cohen, E. *Designing Groupwork: Stages for the Heterogeneous Classroom.* New York: Teacher's College Press, 1986.

Crocco, M. S., P. Munro, and K. Weiler. *Pedagogies of Resistance.* New York: Teachers College Press, 1999.

Dillon, J. T. *Questioning and Teaching: A Manual of Practice.* New York: Teacher's College Press, 1988.

Gagne, R. M., L. J. Briggs, and W. W. Wager. *Principles of Instructional Design.* New York: Holt, Rinehart & Winston, 1988.

Gardner, H. *Frames of Mind: The Theory of Multiple Intelligences.* New York: Basic Books, 1983.

Holt, T. *Thinking Historically.* New York: The College Board, 1995.

Johnson, D. W., and F. P. Johnson. *Joining Together.* Englewood Cliffs, NJ: Prentice-Hall, 1987.

Joyce, B., and M. Weil. *Models of Teaching.* Englewood Cliffs, NJ: Prentice-Hall, 1985.

Kellough, R. D. et al. *Integrating Language Arts and Social Studies: For Intermediate and Middle School Students.* Englewood Cliffs, NJ: Prentice-Hall, 1995.

Lerner, J. *Learning Disabilities: Theories, Diagnosis, and Teaching Strategies.* 8th ed. Boston: Houghton Mifflin, 1999.

Massialas, B., and J. Zevin. *Teaching Creatively.* Malabar, FL: Kreiger & Sons, 1983.

Pahl, Ronald. "Digital Technology and Social Studies," In *Crucial Issues in Teaching Social Studies*, ed. B. G. Massialas and R. F. Allen. Belmont, CA: Wadsworth Publishing, 1996.

Papert, Seymour. *Mindstorms: Children, Computers, and Powerful Ideas.* New York: Basic Books, 1980.

Perkins, D. *Smart School: From Training Memories to Educating Minds.* New York: Free Press, 1992.

Redfield, D. L., and E. W. Rousseau. "A Metanalysis of Experimental Research on Teacher Questioning Behavior." *Review of Educational Research* 51, no. 2 (1981): 237–45.

Shaftel, F., and G. Shaftel. *Role Playing in the Curriculum.* Englewood Cliffs, NJ: Prentice-Hall, 1982.

Van Sickle, R. L. "The Personal Relevance of the Social Studies." *Social Education,* 54 (1990): 23–27, 59.

PART THREE

Strategies for Social Studies Instruction

A General Overview of Chapters 5 and 6: Teaching Strategies for Lower and Higher Level Skills

Didactic, reflective, and affective goals must be matched with curriculum materials, questions, and teaching strategies that make them attainable for students. For each type and level of goal, research and experience have shown that there are strategies that will motivate students to gather knowledge and achieve high levels of understanding and judgment.[1] Chapters 5 and 6 will introduce six strategies, each offering a way to design lessons that translate educational goals into active teaching. These include the strategies of data gathering, comparison and contrast, drama building, frame of reference, mystery, and controversy.

Some strategies are more philosophically in tune with didactic goals, others with reflective or ethical goals. For the didactic approach, a strategy of comparison and contrast helps students to organize large quantities of data into pigeonholes that make information more approachable. Relating information to a central idea or concept builds more understanding and interest than purely rote methods would be likely to achieve.[2] Thus, a didactic approach may begin by drawing from a rich database but use comparison and contrast to organize the information into categories.

For reflective goals, a frame of reference and mystery approach are good ways to encourage thinking and reasoning by providing students with conflicting accounts to consider, "unknowns" to discover. A frame of reference strategy uses different perspectives on the same event, person, or issue to promote problem solving. An example might be witnesses who disagree on the facts of a case as well as their interpretation, forcing the student to work at resolving or understanding multiple viewpoints. The strategy of an "unknown" or "ill-structured" problem prompts the learner to devise a solution or develop an explanatory generalization that fits the facts, much the way a detective solves a crime.

Affective goals are often united with strategies that employ drama and controversy. The use of dramatic recounting and controversial issues raises emotions and brings out moral, ethical, and value questions. Issues push a student to develop a stand, make a decision, and/or carry out an action, based on either personal or public policy reasons, or both. A controversy strategy is a powerful way of asking students what should be rather than what is, and leads to argument, debate, and critical analysis.

Thus, in the two instructional strategy chapters that follow, knowledge (didactic) goals are allied with data collection and categorization. Reasoning (reflective) lessons are linked to comparison and contrast strategies, frame of reference, and "mystery" strategies that seek commonalties and create puzzles to solve. And the affective dimension is brought out best by the strategies of drama building and controversy. The first two or three strategies tend toward more convergent or closed-ended conclusions whereas the latter three or four tend toward more divergent or open-ended outcomes. We argue that if two or more of the six strategies are built into a lesson or unit, then there is greater likelihood of high student motivation but less certainty of students' conclusions. Conversely, when fewer and less demanding strategies are employed, the excitement level of students will be lower and their conclusions more predictable. Uncertainty can be difficult to deal with in a lesson but you will see that greater certainty or security of knowledge can be obtained only as a trade-off with depth of understanding, richness of ideas, and intellectual excitement. Too high a level of uncertainty may result in student frustration. Too low a level will generate boredom. Thus, your problem is to use one or more of the six strategies to promote interest and excitement without demanding either too much difficulty or too much drudgery.

NOTES

1. Ruth Garner, "When Children and Adults Do Not Use Learning Strategies: Toward a Theory of Settings," *Review of Educational Research,* 60, no. 4 (Winter 1990): 517–29.
2. Suzanne Hidi, "Interest and Its Contribution as a Mental Resource for Learning," *Review of Educational Research,* 60, no. 4 (Winter 1990): 549–71.
3. Kenneth M. Zeichner and Daniel P. Liston, *Reflective Teaching: An Introduction* (Mahwah, NJ: Lawrence Erlbaum Associates, 1996.

CHAPTER 5

Teaching Strategies for Lower Level Skills

Interest is central in determining how we select and persist in processing certain types of infor-mation in preference to others.
—Suzanne Hidi, "Interest and Its Contribution as a Mental Resource for Learning"

OVERVIEW OF CONTENTS

Main Ideas

Data-Gathering Strategy

      Usefulness of Data Gathering
      Problems With Data Gathering
      Data-Gathering Teaching Techniques

Comparison and Contrast Strategy

      Usefulness of Comparison and Contrast
      Problems With Comparison and Contrast
      Comparison and Contrast Teaching Techniques
      An Example of a Comparison and Contrast Strategy
      Drama-Building Strategy
      Usefulness of Drama Building
      Problems With Drama Building

Drama-Building Teaching Techniques

      An Example of a Drama-Building Strategy

Summary

Notes

For Further Study: Teaching Strategies for Lower Level Skills

MAIN IDEAS

This chapter focuses on three teaching strategies that foster the acquisition of knowledge and the less complex reflective and affective skills such as application, comprehension, and an awareness of value differences. The three strategies are *data gathering, comparison and contrast,* and *drama building.* Each strategy increases the problem-solving demands on students. Drama building, which engages the emotions as well as the intellect, generates more thought and feeling than does data gathering. Comparison and contrast requires greater skill at sorting out commonalties and differences than does the acquisition of information. Yet all three strategies are related to and interdependent with one another because higher levels of thinking must rest on a base of knowledge and understanding.

DATA-GATHERING STRATEGY

Data gathering is acquiring information that is assumed to be valid, reliable, and necessary. In this strategy, students memorize the "facts" they need to know through procedures that involve considerable use of mnemonic devices and categories that serve as organizers for large amounts of knowledge. Recent research makes a distinction between *subject matter* knowledge and *strategic,* or *process,* knowledge.[1] Subject matter knowledge, sometimes referred to as domain specific, is composed of "knowing what" and "knowing how" in a field of study (e.g., geography). Defining a peninsula would be "knowing what," and using latitude and longitude to locate a place would be considered "knowing how." Both are specifically related to geography and are usually limited to that particular subject. By contrast, strategic knowledge is more a set of problem-solving skills that can be employed in many fields as guiding principles for working out problems. Strategic knowledge demands more higher order divergent thinking than subject matter knowledge, which asks for more convergent thinking, although this is not a completely accepted division.[2]

Cross-subject strategies are sometimes called *metacognitive strategies* because these are techniques or systems that control other, more specific ways of thinking and acting. The idea of context, time, and place in history can easily be transferred to literature or science as a way of making sense of an issue. As an illustration, Conrad's *Heart of Darkness* can be interpreted in historical context yielding important insights into imperialism and prejudice, whereas President William McKinley's "Manifest Destiny" speech can be analyzed as literature yielding valuable information about the patriotic images and symbols common to his time.

Usefulness of Data Gathering

A data-gathering strategy, then, is useful but limited to the subject at hand, including its tools for research and analysis. However, the data gathered need not remain merely a list but may be subdivided into meaningful classifications for easy retrieval and application. Vast quantities of historical data will be easier to remember in system terms, as related to the concepts of family, gender, government, economy, and culture, than as unrelated bits and pieces. Thus, a data-gathering strategy is a basic element of social studies, encompassing storage of information and tools of organization.

Data must be part of any lesson because theories are built on understanding, analysis, and specifics. Facts—specifics—serve as a base for subsequent conclusions and hypotheses suggesting new paths of inquiry to follow. However, facts or data are all too often presented as the entire lesson, and the data do not always relate to the overall theme or topic. Because data collection nearly always includes the memorization and application of definitions, these should provide a framework for the lesson or unit as a whole. Research has shown that factual learning conforms to well-established psychological principles, one of the most important of which is that facts are more easily remembered for longer periods of time if they are related to each other and to an overall theme. Conversely, data are more easily forgotten if they are unrelated to a question or an idea.[3]

Problems With Data Gathering

A major problem for students in retaining knowledge is the amount, sequence, and interrelatedness of the information collected.[4] If all items are treated as equal in value, students will have difficulty holding onto this information for very long. The strategy of data gathering must, therefore, begin with the recognition that it is impossible to teach all the facts on any topic in the time typically allotted. You should view facts as a sample of what is known. Students should be encouraged to collect, store, and organize those facts that are most reliable and most important. You can bolster students' retention of facts by providing them with points of reference, landmarks, ideas, and labels that will awaken memories and offer you opportunities to give them positive feedback for good performance.[5]

A data-gathering strategy begins with the formulation of clear goals that tell students your expectations of them in class, on tests, and in homework assignments. When they know your requirements, students can plan ahead to reach specific outcomes, adding new information as the program develops. Most important, you should offer students advice on how to organize information using mnemonic devices and how to save it under categories, headings, themes, and topics for future use.

Data-Gathering Teaching Techniques

Lecture is an appropriate and time-honored method for presenting data. If the lecture is well organized around a central topic and the subject matter is divided into clear categories, student absorption will be high. Good lectures require considerable preparation, enhanced by a bit of drama and a solid grounding in the topic. As your lecture proceeds, student memorization takes place naturally and need not be forced if you employ a focal point and a variety of attention-sustaining techniques to enhance student retention.[6]

Students may obtain data from original sources, a textbook, or a lecture; you may also encourage them to acquire information on their own in a research project. They may research a case study, conduct a survey, or seek expert advice. They may also cooperate in groups, collecting and sharing large amounts of data for application to an assigned task. The more interesting the data and the greater its richness or applicability, the higher will be the probability that students will learn and remember them. Even small changes in strategy can make a difference to students, such as limiting your data to the key dates in a big event rather than going through an exhaustive chronology. In the example shown in Figure 5.1, the French Revolution of 1789 provides a set of landmark dates and actions to serve as a base for later questions and discussion.

Using this list, you can cover the dates, names, and places of the French Revolution and relate everything to the concept of revolution and social change. Not too many items are given and nearly all can be viewed as a series of occurrences that has a beginning, middle, and end. You might ask the following questions based on these events:

1. When did the revolution begin and when did it end?
2. What happened during the French Revolution?
3. Is there any pattern to the events? Can they be organized?
4. Which events seem most important? Which seem least important? Why?
5. What additional data would you most like to have?

The Timetable of Revolution

1789

5 May Estates General met for first time since 1614, to rescue France from financial collapse.

20 June Tennis Court Oath by Third Estate (commoners) to remain in session until grievances redressed.

12–17 July Rising tension in Paris: riots against customs barrier and troops, culminating in:

14 July Storming of the Bastille
Mid July–August Spread of the Great Fear—rural riots and provincial revolutions.

5 October March of over 10,000 to Versailles demanding an end to bread shortage. Forced Royal family to return with them to Paris. ,

1790

Consolidation of the revolution. Formation of political clubs including Society of the Friends of the Constitution better known as Jacobins. Formation of provincial "federations" to support the revolution: born from sense of regional autonomy.

19 June Attacks on privilege: Titles declared void; nobles renounced their feudal rights (August 1789)

12 July Clergy "nationalized" via Civil Constitution; church property rights already annexed—November 1789
Reaction: mutinies in navy and army suppressed. Bread riots continued.

27 November Civic oath imposed on the clergy. Many refused to take it.

1791

20 June King and his family flee in secret to join *émigrés* over German border; taken prisoner at Varennes and returned to Paris.
Increasing radical pressure.

17 July "Massacre" of the Champ de Mars: mob out of hand fired on by National Guard. Impatience of *sans-culottes* with slow pace of change.
Rise of more radical party—Girondins—within the assembly, and voices urging war as only solution to threat from royalist *émigrés* and their allies—Austria and Prussia.
Royalists promote counterrevolution in the Vendée in western France, and the Midi to the south.

1792

20 April War declared against Austria. Prussia immediately entered as well. War emergency catalyzed revolution. Volunteer armies arrived from the *fédérations*, notably Marseilles.

17 August Mass action by Parisians and *fédérés* march on Royal Palace of Tuileries, and massacre of Swiss Guards defending it. King universally held to be in league with Austria.

19 August Defection of hero of 1789, Lafayette, to Austrians. Foreign armies entered France. France now under control of revolutionary government.

2 September Fortress of Verdun fell to Prussia; Paris believed open to invasion. Prisoners in Parisian jails slaughtered.

Figure 5.1 An example of a data-gathering strategy: The French Revolution of 1789—Key events, dates, and personalities.

20 September Military tide turned by victory at Valmy. Same morning, National Convention met in Paris, replacing the Assembly, lineal descendant of the National Assembly of 1789. Convention purged of possible royalist sympathizers, and took dictatorial powers. The legislative instrument of revolutionary government.

21 September Monarchy abolished.

6 November Victory at Jemappes. Revolutionary armies carried war to the enemy.

1793

21 January King executed.

10 March Revolutionary tribunal established to apply "revolutionary justice."
War with rebels in the Vendée.

26 March Committee of Public Safety established; with the Committee of General Security, the executive arm of the revolution.
Provincial revolts by *fédérations* against the dictatorship of Paris.
Revolution beset on all sides by enemies. Response: Reign of Terror.

16 October Execution of Queen Marie-Antoinette

31 October Revolution within the revolution; execution of radical Girondins by more radical Jacobins, under Robespierre.
Reign of Terror operative throughout France under control of representatives of the Convention.

1794

5 April Execution of Danton, last threat to Robespierre.

8 April Festival of Supreme Being marked abolition of Christianity.

10 June Abolition of right of defense before revolutionary tribunals.

26 July Robespierre called for mass purges in speech to Convention.

27 July (9 Thermidor). Fearing extent of Robespierre's purge, moderate and largely silent majority in Convention voted him down, and ordered his arrest; summoned loyal militia from *sections* to oppose National Guard led by Robespierrists. Robespierre shot in struggle, jaw shattered.

28 July Robespierre executed, radical revolution put into reverse. Purge of Robespierre faction and abolition of Commune in Paris, power base of radical *sans-culottes*.

12 November Jacobin Club closed.

1795

April and May
Failure of radical elements in Paris to regain position.

22 August Convention approved the Constitution of Year III, reestablishing government in hands of nonradicals and the affluent.

6 October Directory of Five took over executive authority after royalist counter-coup defeated by "a whiff of grapeshot" at the hands of artillery officer Napoleon Bonaparte.

SOURCE: *The World Atlas of Revolutions*, Copyright © 1983 by Andrew Wheatcroft. Reprinted by permission of Simon & Shuster, Inc.

As reinforcement throughout your course, the idea of a revolution and the specifics of the one in France in 1789 may be extended to the Russian, Chinese, or American Revolutions. Because many foreign terms and unusual phrases are used in connection with the dates, call for some reference work. Ask students to identify or define words, events, and phrases such as:

Estates General	Reign of Terror
Tennis Court Oath	Radicals
sans-culottes	*coup d'etat*
Royalists	Revolutionary Tribunal
Monarchy	

TO DO

Select your own list of no more than twenty facts or items that describe the main events and personalities of the Russian Revolution in 1917–18. Do you think you will have trouble selecting the twenty items you want? Will students be able to remember the twenty items? If so, in relation to what ideas? In what way might you change the twenty items if the lesson were intended for a middle or senior high school class? For which group would you be willing to increase the amount of data? For which would you wish to introduce more foreign words and terms? Why?

COMPARISON AND CONTRAST STRATEGY

Comparison and contrast is a strategy based on developing, refining, testing, and redefining a set of categories or classifications.[7] Students spend much of their time applying categories to examples and then deciding how much they are alike or different. It is a familiar and surprisingly effective teaching technique used in many situations. When comprehension is a key goal of learning, students who are able to draw distinctions among phenomena, experiences, ideas, and objects gain an enormously important skill that will be useful throughout their future learning endeavors. Comparison and contrast is basic, then, to both the process of understanding and to the organization of reasoning—whether A and B belong to the same or different sets, or whether all revolutions follow the same or different patterns. When a built-in motivation in data gathering is to know, the primary engine pushing a comparison strategy is the need to understand likenesses and differences.

TO DO

What kind of event is pictured here? What emotions and facts is the artist trying to portray? Why is there violence? Who is attacking whom? Why do the battlements have guns, but the people below only pitchforks and scythes?

Figure 5.2

Usefulness of Comparison and Contrast

Categories and classifications are basic intellectual tools for organizing and analyzing our world. Without agreed-on definitions, which are really categories, communication would be difficult if not impossible. We could not even agree on definitions of simple objects (e.g., a chair or table), much less on complex concepts (e.g., social class, cultural diffusion, or foreign policy). The comparison and contrast process is crucial to building analogies; these, in turn, are critical to analysis and theorizing, which depend on categorization and the recognition of patterns or commonalties. Students almost always jump at the chance to compare and contrast because it is interesting and helps them to make sense of the world. They can separate what belongs from what does not, based on open criteria.[8]

Problems With Comparison and Contrast

Teachers frequently call on students to use categories or classifications but often do not help them toward a complete understanding of the attributes of a category. Even a category as simple and concrete as "peninsula" benefits greatly from additional like and unlike examples. Concrete pictures and photographs also help. For instance, is a long, thin piece of land just barely detached from a shoreline called a peninsula or an island? What terms should we apply if there are periodic floods during which the connecting land disappears? The strategy of comparison and contrast continuously reinforces distinctions, and it encourages students to review their experiences and ideas by building even finer distinctions (identifying more differences), and by formulating better analogies (identifying more shared attributes). Stronger conceptual development in students is one major result of their using the comparison and contrast strategy.

Students are less likely to be bored using the comparison strategy than the data-gathering approach; there is intellectual excitement involved in playing with categories and concepts. However, you and the students must learn to ask questions about comparisons: Are analogies fair to the data? Do the analogies fit the examples? What criteria are used in deciding on likenesses and differences?

Comparison and Contrast Teaching Techniques

Any situation in which two or more examples of evidence, data, or observations are part of a lesson invites a comparison and contrast strategy. You may employ two basic variants of this strategy. First, you may use an inductive approach in which students derive concepts, categories, or definitions on their own, based on a careful examination of evidence. Second, you may use a deductive approach in which you offer a definition to students by giving them a label or term, and have them apply the concept to examples to determine whether they fit the definition.

You may plan a lesson or unit around a series of examples that do or do not fit a concept or category that students must use in a testing process to develop their own conception. For instance, you may show students photographs of "poor" people and photographs of "rich" people, and ask the class to identify the attributes that make the two groups alike and those that make them different. In another approach you might offer students several formal definitions of poverty and wealth—perhaps government guidelines pertaining to these two conditions, a philosophical view of them, and a dictionary definition—and ask the class to discuss these three versions, testing them against one another and outside evidence. The goal is to work toward single, standard definitions of poverty and wealth. Although the outcome of the two procedures is similar, the steps by which conclusions are reached and the degree of learner involvement differ significantly.

Much also depends on the students' degree of sophistication and maturity in dealing with distinctions and analogies. Middle and senior high school students normally have few problems at the lower levels of conceptual development that require classification and formal definitions. Classification demands the ability to generalize from two or more phenomena, behaviors, or objects that seem alike. Formal definition demands the ability to apply accepted social science definitions to new examples, excluding those that are poor fits.

Klausmeier suggests that there are beginner and more mature attempts at comparison and contrast. The less mature approach identifies only one or two major factors and a few examples, whereas the more mature approach juggles multiple factors and a greater variety of examples.[9] We will assume that for secondary school students a more mature deductive or inductive teaching strategy is usually appropriate. Steps for this method are suggested in the following list:

Deductive	*Inductive*
1. Set goals for the concept(s) to be learned and the comparisons to be made.	1. Present examples and non-examples.
2. Name the concept or concepts	2. Ask students to list attributes that examples have in common.
3. Define the concept in full and present the commonly accepted meaning.	3. Ask students to test their list of attributes giving reasons, separating examples from non-examples.

4. Present examples and non-examples simultaneously.

5. List attributes and apply to examples. Ask for reasons in support of the comparisons or contrasts suggested.
6. Develop a systematic way to evaluate new examples.
7. Give positive feedback throughout process.

4. Ask students to develop a systematic way to judge new examples and revise criteria, if necessary.
5. Tentatively define the concept in full and compare with official definition.

6. Name the concept or concepts.

7. Give positive feedback throughout process.

As categories are refined, students will become increasingly aware that concepts are even more of a human invention than "facts." They will begin to use categories or concepts to make sense of the commonalties and variations they discover throughout their studies. Middle or junior high school students who are just beginning to deal with abstract concepts can be asked whether their comparisons or contrasts go too far. You might ask the following questions: Does the word *freedom* mean the same thing to everyone who uses it? Can we define political freedom so the idea separates nations into free and unfree states?

Older, more mature students might be shown that the categories themselves can be called into question if you purposely provide ambiguous examples that require them to test definitions. You could present a selection of real-life examples for consideration, some that fit the concept, some that clearly do not, and some that are in between. It is the ambiguous and borderline examples that drive the comparison and contrast strategy. Historians and social scientists have long used this approach to organize massive sets of data. An example is Crane Brinton's well-known study, *The Anatomy of Revolution*, which compares and contrasts the best-known revolutions of modern times with the American example to develop and test the concept of revolution.[10]

An Example of a Comparison and Contrast Strategy

In the examples provided in Figure 5.3, an inductive problem is posed to students through a series of artifacts representing three societies, identified only as A, B, and C. On examining the exhibits, students will see that each set of artifacts contains examples that probably have much the same function: a weapon, a tool, and a medium of exchange. These are similar in function but quite different in form, character, aesthetic design, and above all, level of technological development.

Lesson themes could be technological development, types of exchange media, or economic systems. Most participants will probably focus on technological development after the data have been submitted to a process of comparison and contrast. You might ask if the beads, coin, and credit card from the three cultures are some form of money? Do the coins represent a much more organized approach than the artistic, unstandardized beads? What does the credit card represent? (It is a still greater level of abstraction in which funds are extended based on the customer's assets and ability to repay a loan.) Ask which of the implements—the stone tools, pot, and washing machine—represents the greatest change in construction and saves the most labor. Do the students view each implement as a radical departure from what went before (contrast)? Do they note that all share similar functions (comparison) in relation to human social needs? Much the same questions and conclusions probably hold true for the weapon set. Thus, the three artifact sets provide a classification game that propels students toward conclusions about social organization and economic history.

Whereas no single line of thought need prevail, the lesson itself is strongly suggestive, through inductive reasoning procedures, of several hypotheses about relations between technology and social organization, and exchange me-

Society A

Society B

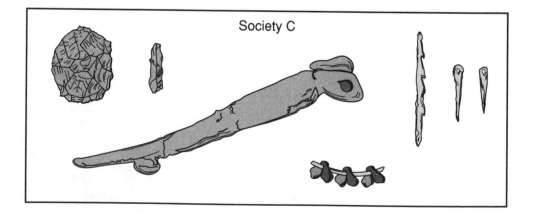

Society C

Figure 5.3
SOURCE: J. Zevin, "Visual Economics: Inquiry Through Art and Artifacts," *Peabody Journal of Education,* 10, no. 3 (April 1980): 183–91. Diagrams are based on the article.

dia. The key ideas of technological invention and economic exchange can be used to organize interpretations of the three charts. Thus, a comparison and contrast strategy, such as the one illustrated earlier, strongly promotes concept formation and encourages students to test categories and definitions. As students become increasingly skillful in dealing with new and more subtle examples, they will develop greater precision in building categories that can be applied to many future questions, cases, and problems.

TO DO

Set up a compare/contrast lesson on race relations in American history. Decide which cases or time periods would present the greatest contrasts for student discussion. Which examples are "musts" for students to know? Would the "Dred Scott Decision" be one of these?

Consider your goals in choosing data: What will the information lead students to conclude about American race relations? Should various problems or facts be hidden, or should there be a frank sharing of historical accounts? Would you include material about views on slavery held by the founding fathers? Would you include slave owners' views abolitionists' opinions, Feminist thinkers' positions, or Visiting foreigners' perceptions?

DRAMA-BUILDING STRATEGY

Drama building is a strategy that examines the emotional impact of a story, person, event, or document and often yields a sense of catharsis and involvement for the learner. The material being studied, whether from primary or secondary sources, attracts students because of excitement generated by the actions described or through the force of the central personalities and events. When students identify, either negatively or positively, with characters and events, their interest is heightened. Social studies topics that elicit a strong emotional involvement and raise awareness of important value questions are major components of the drama-building strategy.[11] The major aims of the drama strategy are to raise student awareness of values and bias, to make more personal or human the people and events of history, and to increase students' identification with roles and situations involving others.

Usefulness of Drama Building

Drama building is particularly effective at attracting and holding student interest in a topic. Students generally enjoy a good story line, especially if it involves adventure, sexual innuendo, or tension among characters. Situations in which people have to deal with crises, characters who are attractive or repulsive, and outcomes that are comic or tragic usually grip our attention.

Drama building is useful for teachers who want students to understand historical figures and events in context, viewing them realistically rather than as abstract phenomena discussed from a second- or thirdhand point of view. Biographies and autobiographies are excellent tools for filling out historical characters. *You Are There*-type television programs, scripted by the class with as much faith to the actual events and sources as possible, also bring history to life. Drama building can be accomplished through role-play by groups in the classroom, by the use of simulation games, mock trials, and sociodramas to help the students recapture a situation. Thus, by stressing the dramatic elements of social studies materials, you may stimulate student interest and help to build a sense of awareness of value issues and a feeling for the personalities and events in history and the social sciences.

Problems With Drama Building

On the positive side, a drama strategy engages students' attention and creates a feeling of association with people and events; on the negative side, there is a danger that their involvement might cause them to suspend critical judgment. Students who feel they have become a part of the events may be overwhelmed by the emotions and values in the drama, whether fact or fiction. As in television docudramas, students may trust the evidence as being totally accurate, even though it is a fictional representation.

The problem of confusing fiction with reality is a serious one. All of us have, at one time or another, been swept away by a drama or film that may be sophisticated propaganda, whether for good or evil, which we accept because of the power of its emotion, the strength of its characters, and the beauty of its images or language.[12] Even when we deal with real-life data (e.g., autobiographies, biographies, diaries, testimony, or political speeches), the element of drama and persuasion is always present. Some educators believe the whole point of most dramatically presented ideas, fictional or nonfictional, is to present a position designed to touch the emotions and play on our sensitivities. Thus, the very strength of the drama-building strategy is also its most serious weakness—a weakness that you and the students have to neutralize or balance with new data and criticism.

Drama-Building Teaching Techniques

Creating a sense of drama in a social studies lesson is easy and effective. There are three major techniques for capturing students' interest: first, through personal play-acting in which you act out a situation with or without props, costumes, and symbols; second, through the selection of primary and secondary sources that are written with flair and style, from a personal point of view that draws the student into the event or issue; and third, through the use of literary, media, and artistic works that use plot, character, images, and language to communicate a viewpoint.

You can bring history to life through preplanned or ad hoc presentations that involve period costumes, symbols, and artifacts, or you may act out the role of a historical figure using the person's ideas as the basis for a monologue of speech. Sometimes the recreation of the past may seem silly, but for many students, the play, however amateurish, is a real attention holder. "Teacher-hams" have performed in classrooms by playing a toga-clad Julius Caesar or by reading the Gettysburg address wearing a Lincoln hat. You might hide artifacts all over a school yard for students to dig up, playing senior archaeologist and adviser to your junior archaeologist assistants. All these activities bring a personal, emotive quality to the classroom that helps students feel special and become more attentive.

Select historical or news readings that have a direct, individual quality in which the author is communicating feelings and values to the reader. For instance, discussing and analyzing a portion of Benjamin Franklin's autobiography is preferable for purposes of building drama to a textbook summary of his life and times. A television interview with Palestinian Arabs and Israelis about their mutual problems will arouse more interest than a bloodless foreign affairs summary of the issues that divide these two peoples. Many novels, short stories, films, paintings, photographs, and theatrical works purposely set out to engage the emotions. Some trivialize an issue and others inflate and distort it, so you must exercise care over classroom choices. You can use distortions and exaggerations to good advantage as springboards for discussing bias and emotion in the presentation of people and issues. Paintings like Picasso's *Guernica* or David's *Death of Socrates* are historically interesting, dramatic, involving, and well worth a classroom discussion. Furthermore, as noted in chapter 4, role-play models build a sense of drama in the social studies classroom through mock trials, staged debates, sociodramas, and simulations.

Of course, we may also encounter the problem of overinvolvement of students in one point of view to the exclusion of a balanced judgment of the evidence. Exercise caution because drama is exciting yet dangerously seductive, sometimes blinding students to other viewpoints.

The problem of students' accepting one point of view because of emotional ties created through involvement in a drama can be counteracted in several ways: (a) switch from one role to another in a play; (b) reverse roles in a debate with the opposition; (c) take the unpopular side on an issue; and (d) play a distasteful character as well as a positive, heroic character. Any one of these techniques will allow students to think about how dramatic language and strong images can alter their conclusions about an issue, person, or event, particularly if they have the chance to see the same event from two or more value positions or viewpoints. Many more questions will arise about the nature of evidence, the problem of subjectivity, and the relation of fact to fiction than would have developed from a single drama-building episode.

An Example of a Drama-Building Strategy

Mao Tse-tung's Long March has been brought to life in a literary recreation by author Jean Fritz, using original sources and diaries as a database.[13] In the following excerpt, the author vividly conveys the feelings and attitudes of the Chinese Communist Red Army as they began their thousand-mile withdrawal in 1937 in an effort to save themselves and their movement from their enemies, the Nationalists. The march, most of it completed on foot, involved millions of people who passed through a vast and dangerous territory to achieve their objectives. The selected excerpt begins with the story of Scout Kong checking out enemy territory for troop movements:

> Long before the army started, scouts had been sneaking into enemy territory to spy out enemy positions. As usual, Scout Kong was in the lead. There was nothing Kong liked better than to be in the thick of danger. In battle his voice would be heard above all others. "Sha!" he would cry—Kill! "Sha! Sha!" But of course as a scout he had to be silent and sly, hiding sometimes for hours in the top branches of a tree, watching enemy movements, estimating enemy strength. He knew all the tricks to use if he was caught. "Act dumb," Zhu De had told him. "Pretend to be a traveling ear-cleaner." Since Chinese loved to have their ears cleaned, there were many professional ear-cleaners who went about with their tiny bamboo cleaning instruments. No one would be suspicious of an ear-cleaner. Or if Kong had a message to deliver, Zhu De said, he should pretend to be a farmer. Write the message on rice paper and hide it in a basket of vegetables.
>
> So far, Scout Kong hadn't needed to resort to these tricks and over the summer he'd returned again and again from the enemy lines with good news. The enemy was taking it easy, Kong reported. Many troops had been withdrawn; none seemed to be on the alert for action. Apparently Chiang Kai-shek had decided that the Red Army was not only trapped but so outnumbered there was no need to worry. Besides, Chiang had another source of trouble on his hands. Japan was attacking China in the north, and once the Communist threat was over he could give his attention to the Japanese. In any case, Kong said, there were weak spots in the enemy barricade which, with luck, might be penetrated.

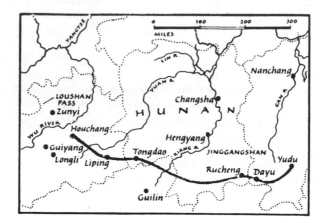

Figure 5.4

Nevertheless, they took no chances. The army left at night, traveled at night, and rested in the day under camphor trees and alders, out of sight as much as possible. Their first obstacle was the Yudu River but it was shallow and narrow. They rattled over the five pontoons that had been thrown across the river and many soldiers simply waded to the other side. Later the army would dread the rivers that lay in their path, but who could foresee that now? No one was thinking of their march in terms of the whole map of China, with its two parent rivers, the Yangtse River and the Yellow River, and all their tributaries spilling across the country like children running away from home.

From end to end the army stretched for sixty miles as it snaked single-file over mountain trails so narrow that the men wore white kerchiefs on their backs to guide those behind them. On rainy nights when the paths became slippery, they had to be especially careful. One misstep could send a man crashing over the side of a cliff. Or a group of men might go together, leaving behind a gap and a silence where they had just been.

But there were good times as well. On a moonlit night a group of men would start to sing and their song would be picked up by another group farther down the line, then again by another, their voices unrolling like a ribbon under the stars. At times like this they all felt warmed by their brotherhood in the revolution, for, though many of the leaders were educated, at heart this was a peasant army, fighting for the peasants of China.

Zhu De himself, who at forty-eight was one of the oldest of the army, had grown up in a peasant family under a landlord so brutal that he was known to his tenants as the King of Hell. As a child Zhu De had never had enough to eat, often not even rice but only a gruel made from a kind of corn fodder. As the family grew, food became scarcer and scarcer, and when there were seven children, Zhu's parents knew they simply could not feed another mouth. To keep them all from starving, his parents drowned their last five children at birth.

Zhu De's wife, Kang Keqing, not only came from a peasant family but also had the bad luck to be born a girl. Every girl from a poor family was a disappointment, hardly worth the trouble of raising since in the end a girl went to live and work in her husband's home while a boy brought his wife home to his parents. Kang Keqing hated so much being a girl that on the night before her wedding she ran away from a marriage that had been arranged for her, from a wedding she didn't want, from a husband she didn't know. At the same time she was running away from being a woman in a society in which women counted for nothing. She joined the Red Army.

And here she was now, a combat soldier! She wasn't marching in the group with the other women; instead she was swinging along with other combat soldiers, a rifle on her shoulder. Like all Communist women, she had cut her hair to show that she was liberated, and when she married Zhu De two years after joining the army, she made it clear that his bodyguards could do the cooking and the sewing. She was through with women's work.

They had common roots, these soldiers, and up and down that long line each one had his or her own story. Somewhere in that line, for instance, was a little red devil who had been twelve years old when he first went to the recruiting office. He said he was thirteen but when he was asked why he wanted to join, he couldn't find any words. How could he tell a recruiting officer that he was an orphan and worked for a cruel landlord? Was that a reason? He hung his head. "I don't know," he said, so he was rejected.

A few months later the boy went back and said he was fourteen.

"Why do you want to join?" he was asked.

Still the boy didn't know, so again he was rejected.

He waited a bit longer, then returned and said he was sixteen.

"And why do you want to join the army?" he was asked.

This time he knew. "I want to overthrow the Nationalists," he replied briskly. "I want to strike down despots." He was accepted.

If the soldiers felt uneasy about the March, the porters, bent double by their heavy loads, groaned, grumbled, spat, and cursed. They had been hired at a dollar a day but they hadn't known how far they'd be going and they hadn't guessed how their poles would rub their shoulders raw, how their backs would strain, their legs knot, their feet stumble and give way. A tiny, four-foot-eleven woman, Liu Ying, had been given the job of trying to keep up the porters' spirits. If anyone could do it, the leaders said, she could. Such a fiery, persuasive woman, she had talked thousands of men in Jiangxi Province into joining the army. Now riding up and down on her small horse, she talked, she praised, she joked, she tried to will revolution into the souls of these suffering porters so their pain would not matter. But these men had moved beyond her reach. From time to time a group would simply drop their burdens, turn around, and head back home.

Slowed down by fifty miles of groaning, baggage-laden porters, the central column did not reach the Xiang until twenty-four hours after the vanguard had crossed. By this time Chiang Kai-shek's troops were ready—300,000 men and several hundred planes. The trap was set. Hiding in forest on either side of the road, Nationalist soldiers fired at the Red soldiers as they passed. Overhead, Nationalist planes, swooping low, strafed the marching columns. Moreover, the blockhouses were fully manned now, and in order to pass them Red soldiers had to climb up the side of each one and throw a hand grenade through a porthole. It was a brutal scene. Although they pressed ahead, fighting every inch, whole companies of men—sometimes in the very act of crying "Sha!"—were cut down and silenced.

When the survivors finally reached the river, they found themselves in the dilemma that military men fear most. The army was cut in two. Part was on one side of the river; the rest was on the other side and the enemy was wedged around them. Yang Chengwu's vanguard regiment, thoroughly aroused, tried to help. Keeping up a steady fire on the enemy, they encouraged the central column to cross. Some did, but there was nothing orderly about what happened. It was shooting, shouting, wading, dying, drowning, scrambling across pontoons, horses rearing, whinnying, and a wholesale scuttling of equipment. Porters simply dumped their loads and disappeared. Cooks threw away pots and pans. Soldiers got rid of anything that they didn't consider essential. Many managed to get across the river safely, including the leaders and the headquarters units, but many lay where they'd been shot down.[14]

The author's account blends humor and drama—for example, Kong's disguise as an ear cleaner and the line of soldiers sixty miles long. Characters have personal problems; all are not heroes, but are described in very human terms, such as the peasant Zhu De's wife Kang Keqing, who joined the Red Army to escape the low status of women in China. Because the army is split in two geographically, it must energetically and creatively try to overcome the problems of coordinating efforts for an eventual union.

The hazards the characters endure and overcome, their wit and humanity, turn what could be an exceedingly dull listing of facts into an account of heroism and adventure. Not only do leaders participate, but common, ordinary people as well. Students who read the account are drawn into the experience of this dramatic event in human history, made all the more interesting because it is not commonly read or understood by Western youth.

You could ask students to read, analyze, and discuss the characters in the story, their motivations and problems, and the problems of China as a whole, using questions such as those suggested here:

What were the reasons for the Long March across thousands of miles?

What was Mao's strategy for survival and victory?

How many problems did the Red Army have to overcome to survive? Why?

Why were the people in the story—men and women, peasants, workers, and intellectuals—all willing to follow their leaders under such trying circumstances?

Why do people believe in a cause and decide to become part of a movement?

Why do people view one side as friends and another as enemies?

As students offer answers to these and related questions, you should also call their attention to the goals, methods, tone, and biases of their reading. In this case, the author has clearly pictured the People's Party sympathetically by presenting their views and their feelings in a positive light. Ordinary people are ennobled and appear heroic at many points in the narrative. To counter previously developed positive feelings, you might ask:

Is the author biased?

Are there other viewpoints?

Should a second version of the Long March be found, read, and compared to this one? Why or why not?

You should conclude this lesson by questioning the trustworthiness of dramatic description, asking when students should be willing to trust dramatic accounts or portrayals as true and when they should challenge them. Do we need several accounts from very different sources for a complete picture of the Long March? Extend the lesson into other topics by introducing at least one or two more frames of reference on the Long March from the Nationalist opposition's viewpoint, or an American view, placing the event in the context of a larger unit or course.

TO DO

Select a primary source, documentary, movie, *The Time-Line Series*,[15] a docu-drama, or Hollywood film on the same subject, if possible, offering students limited portions for analysis and discussion. You might compare a Roman primary source describing the life and death of Julius Caesar with Shakespeare's *Julius Caesar*. You might compare the biblical story of the Jewish exodus from Egypt led by Moses with the Cecil B. de Mille's film *The Ten Commandments*. Design your lesson in a way that gets at both the content and the process of knowing. For example, what does dramatization mean? What does it do for a historical event or character? Can we really ever recapture the past just as it was? Can we really keep our own values and tastes out of a historical recreation? Why or why not? Are dramatizations trustworthy history or not? For that matter, are highly emotional and literary firsthand descriptions from the time period trustworthy? Why or why not?

SUMMARY

This chapter described and discussed teaching strategies that emphasize largely convergent processes: recalling, applying, and defining ideas to reach a conclusion. Data gathering was defined as a principal approach whereby information is collected; comparison and contrast was defined as a process for constructing categories and classification, combining like units and separating those that are different. From this set of categorized and better defined information, students can be engaged in a drama-building strategy that calls for relatively modest affective and analytical skills. These skills are applied to social studies cases and examples that contain exciting reports about events and persons and that may also imply or directly state value judgments about decisions and actions. Thus, the first three strategies suggested for the social studies classroom build a database for students and introduce them to stimulating but not especially demanding intellectual and affective problems. Practice with classification skills and application serve as a series of platforms on which more demanding activities can be constructed, such as frames of reference, mystery, and controversy strategies described and discussed in chapter 6.

NOTES

1. Patricia A. Alexander and Judith E. Judy, "The Interaction of Domain-specific and Strategic Knowledge in Academic Performance," *Review of Educational Research*, 58, no. 4 (Winter 1988): 375–404.
2. M. T. H. Chi, "Interactive Roles of Knowledge and Strategies in the Development of Organized Sorting and Recall," in *Thinking and Learning Skills*, vol. 2, ed. S. F. Chipman et al. (Hillsdale, NJ: Lawrence Erlbaum Associates, 1985), pp. 457–84.
3. A. L. Brown, "Know When and Where and How to Remember: A Problem of Metacognition," in *Advances in Instructional Psychology*, ed. R. Glaser (Hillsdale, NJ: Lawrence Erlbaum Associates, 1978), pp. 319–37.
4. Robert M. Gagne, L. J. Briggs, and W. W. Wager, *Principles of Instructional Design* (New York: Holt, Rinehart & Winston, 1988).
5. N. D. Rohwer and J. W. Thomas, "The Role of Mnemonic Strategies in Study Effectiveness: Theories, Individual Differences, and Applications," in *Imagery and Related Mnemonic Processes*, ed. M. A. McDaniel and M. Pressley (New York: Springer-Verlag, 1987), pp. 428–50.

6. J. MacLeish, *The Lecture Method* (Cambridge: Cambridge Institute of Education, 1968).
7. C. M. Reigluth et al., "The Elaboration Theory of Instruction," *Instructional Science,* 7 (1978): 107–26.
8. Herbert Klausmeier et al., *Conceptual Learning and Development* (Orlando, FL: Academic Press, 1974).
9. Herbert Klausmeier, *Learning and Teaching Concepts: A Strategy for Testing Applications of Theory* (Orlando, FL: Academic Press, 1980).
10. Crane Brinton, *The Anatomy of Revolution* (New York: Prentice-Hall, 1952).
11. B. Weiner, *An Attributional Theory of Motivation and Emotion* (New York: Springer-Verlag, 1986).
12. R. de Charms, "Intrinsic Motivation, Peer Tutoring, and Cooperative Learning," in *Teacher and Student Perceptions: Implications for Learning,* ed. J. M. Levine and M. C. Wang (Hillsdale, NJ: Lawrence Erlbaum Associates, 1983), pp. 391–98.
13. Jean Fritz, *China's Long March: Six Thousand Miles of Danger* (New York: Putnam, 1988), pp. 19–27.
14. From *China's Long March: Six Thousand Miles of Danger* by Jean Fritz, copyright © 1988 by Jean Fritz. Reprinted by permission of G. P. Putnam's Sons.
15. Maryland Public Television (PBS), *The Time-Line Series,* six episodes: "The Vikings," "The Crusades," "The Mongol Empire," "The Black Death," "The Fall of Byzantium," and "Granada, 1492." Available from Zenger Video, 10200 Jefferson Blvd., Culver City, CA 90232-0802.

FOR FURTHER STUDY: TEACHING STRATEGIES FOR LOWER LEVEL SKILLS

Garcia, E. *Student Cultural Diversity: Understanding and Meeting the Challenge.* 2nd ed. Boston: Houghton Mifflin, 1999.

Hidi, Suzanne. "Interest and Its Contribution as a Mental Resource for Learning." *Review of Educational Research,* 60, no. 4 (Winter 1990): 549–73.

Jones, B. F. et al. *Strategic Teaching and Learning: Cognitive Instruction in the Content Areas.* Alexandria, VA: Association for Supervision and Curriculum Development, 1987.

Rubin, L. J. *Artistry in Teaching.* New York: Random House, 1985.

Schneider, W., and M. Pressley. *Memory Development Between Two and Twenty.* New York: Springer-Verlag, 1989.

Tonjes, M. J., and M. V. Zintz. *Teaching Reading, Thinking, and Study Skills in Content Classrooms.* Dubuque, IA: Wm. C. Brown, 1987.

Wade, S. E. "A Synthesis of the Research for Improving Reading in Social Studies." *Review of Educational Research,* 53 (Winter 1983): 461d–97.

Wilen, W. W. *Questioning Skills for Teachers.* 3rd ed. Washington, DC: National Education Association, 1991.

Wilen, W. W. *Teaching and Learning Through Discussion.* New York: Thomas, 1990.

Willis, Scott. *Teaching Thinking.* Curriculum Update. Alexandria, VA: Association for Supervision and Curriculum Development, 1992.

CHAPTER 6

Teaching Strategies
for Higher Level Skills

Thinking is best taught by direct and systematic instruction. Many people assume that if think-
ing is learned, it is learned in the course of ordinary experiences at home and at school and does
not require special instruction. It is true that reading, writing, solving math problems, and other
tasks improve thinking ability. It is also true that walking, running, and playing help youngsters
acquire skills useful in gymnastics, but no one thinks that expertise at gymnastics is the auto-
matic by-product of such activities. To master gymnastics skills, the student must receive formal
training in those skills. To master thinking skills, the student must receive formal instruction in
those skills. The program developers agree that the best way to teach thinking is with a head-on
approach.

—Paul Chance, Thinking in the Classroom: A Survey of Programs

OVERVIEW OF CONTENTS

Main Ideas

Frame-of-Reference Strategy

     Usefulness of a Frame-of-Reference Strategy
     Problems With a Frame-of-Reference Strategy
     Frame-of-Reference Teaching Techniques
     An Example of a Frame-of-Reference Lesson

Mystery Strategy

     Usefulness of a Mystery Strategy
     Problems With a Mystery Strategy
     Mystery Teaching Techniques

Controversy Strategy

     Usefulness of a Controversy Strategy
     Problems With a Controversy Strategy
     Controversy Teaching Techniques
     Examples of Controversy Lessons

Summary

Notes

For Further Study: Teaching Strategies for Higher Level Skills

MAIN IDEAS

Chapter 5 discussed three teaching strategies that foster lower levels of thinking and feeling; this chapter presents three complementary strategies aimed at promoting higher order thinking: frame of reference, mystery, and controversy. All three demand a good deal more of students than comparison or drama building, and each promotes more divergent forms of reasoning. At higher levels, students are encouraged to examine many alternative hypotheses as they work toward a conclusion or decision. Analysis, synthesis, and evaluation, to use Bloom's terms, are more important in the three new strategies than in the previous three. Sometimes, you and the students may find it almost impossible to reach any conclusion at all, such as during the examination of an emotionally charged or very complex controversy. As in the previous chapter, fully developed examples of lessons are provided for the frame-of-reference, mystery, and controversy strategies.

FRAME-OF-REFERENCE STRATEGY

A *frame-of-reference strategy* employs multiple viewpoints of an event, problem, or person to evoke discussion; it requires seeing the same phenomenon through two or more different lenses. This strategy is related to comparison and contrast but pushes beyond that concept to include many perspectives rather than applying categories to similarities and differences. Frame of reference brings to an event, person, or problem a series of accounts that offer complementary, overlapping, and sometimes conflicting versions or provides a range of views for students to consider.

Frames of reference let students see the world through the eyes of others. Literature often employs this technique, for example, when an author describes events as different characters live them. The play *Rashomon* is a classic example of a frame-of-reference view in which each character's account is either self-centered or self-serving in some way and does not agree with the others.[1] Biographies of American presidents frequently give us sharply contrasting viewpoints of the leader's personality and actions, often disagreeing on the facts, the causes, and the evaluation, that is, who was or was not a "great" president. A well-done frame-of-reference lesson immediately causes students to raise questions: "What's the truth?" "Whose word can I believe?" "How do I judge among the different versions?" Historians and social scientists constantly have to deal with the "frame" problem when they evaluate eyewitness accounts or are faced with conflicting reports or theories purporting to explain an action or event.

Usefulness of a Frame-of-Reference Strategy

A frame-of-reference approach is especially powerful in demonstrating how upbringing, politics, social status, and culture can shape one's perception. Employ this approach to teach students how to look for subtle, underlying biases and distortions in the way people think and view one another. Provide practice in interpreting conflicting and debatable viewpoints. Discovering the variety of frames that exist and the way in which values and motives shape worldviews is both a frightening and an enlightening process for most students because it produces a feeling that there is no "truth," only subjectivity.[2]

Like good detectives, students will begin to see the values, theories, and biases embedded in historical and literary accounts. They will increasingly judge sources on logical criteria and by cross-checking other sources. Eventually they will identify a set of working rules for sorting out the more reliable and valid conclusions from those that are on shakier grounds. Students may also purposely adopt others' viewpoints to check the quality and explanatory power of an unfamiliar, perhaps even disturbing, perception. Many anthropological studies employ this method of entering the worldview of other cultures; examples are accounts of General Custer's last stand from U.S. cavalry and Sioux perspectives, or from the outside vantage point of a foreign correspondent.

Problems With a Frame-of-Reference Strategy

A frame-of-reference teaching structure moves students out of a narrow, personal, or ethnocentric pattern of thought and opens up new doors to thinking and decision making. The surprise and subsequent fascination of students who encounter multiple perspectives, a clash of viewpoints, and strikingly different interpretations usually foster vibrant and lengthy discussions. The nature of evidence is called into question, raising issues of objectivity and subjectivity for students in drawing conclusions about human affairs. At first, some students are often shocked with views and arguments that run counter to personal or mainstream traditions, but later they are frequently highly motivated to find answers to help them understand the problem.

In a "frame," or multiple viewpoints, strategy, results sometimes produce a high degree of frustration and cynicism: "There is nothing to believe, and no one to be trusted." Sometimes, adolescents seeking the "right" answers find more problems. This, in turn, leads them to view all data and all values as suspect. To counteract possible student frustration and cynicism, you can direct the discussion toward defining criteria for the interpretation of evidence. Assist students in creating a rationale for their subsequent work. Students may settle on operating principles or rules to follow: Expert testimony is better than that of novices; outsider eyewitnesses to a conflict are more objective than participants; logical accounts are more trustworthy than inconsistent or emotional accounts; and so on. You can recycle these ideas over and over again in many contexts, reinforcing the whole notion of building criteria to test evidence, arguments, and attitudes.

Frame-of-Reference Teaching Techniques

As students become comfortable with evaluating multiple viewpoints, they will be able to decide that some perspectives on a problem are more reliable than others, and more defensible in public debate. Given a set of agreed-on criteria for judgment, students will pick and choose from among many accounts to build the "truest," "best," or "most probably so" picture of an event. Or, if their inquiry bogs down, then they may discard the definition of the problem for a new conception that may be more productive, meaningful, and resolvable.

You could treat matching or contrasting historical documents or different newspaper accounts of an event as a way of building a frame-of-reference strategy. Textbooks, too, may be paired together to illustrate subtle or not so subtle differences in reporting data, characterizing events, and describing personalities. Literary excerpts or films may also serve as examples of sometimes conflicting and sometimes convergent perspectives on a facet of life—such as pro-war and antiwar approaches to famous battles. Some filmmakers could be used as examples of those who glorify human conflict; others could be shown as deriding war. In addition, primary and secondary sources on the same event could be presented together, offering students insight into the way historians and social scientists may draw conclusions different from those of each other and from contemporaries using the same sources. These approaches to questions and problems all require reflective reasoning of a fairly high order, thereby strengthening student critical faculties.

Thus, frames of reference introduce students to the interpretation of multiple perspectives, which may range from the almost mutually exclusive to those that express subtle differences or disagreements about interpretations and judgments. Using a frame of reference ultimately breeds a healthy skepticism in students when they are dealing with data, particularly when loud claims are made by the author of a work for perfect accuracy and truth. Conversely, students will learn to keep their minds open toward views that may be troubling, unusual, or unpopular but that may, in the long run, fit the facts better than other official versions. Thus, a frame-of-reference problem makes a necessity of independent thought and careful decision making by students confronted with many views of an event.

An Example of a Frame-of-Reference Lesson

The American and British Versions of the Battle of Lexington.[3]   The Battle of Lexington, the "shot heard 'round the world," offers a ready-made frame-of-reference strategy because so many witnesses left behind contradictory accounts of both the event and its underlying causes. As might be expected, many of the British versions imply or indicate directly that the Americans provoked the fight, whereas American sources portray the British as having caused the fracas by miscalculated or willful aggression.

In one eyewitness account by an English seaman to a Dr. Rogers on the British warship *Empress of Russia*, the Americans are described as firing the first shots in the battle and as cruelly harassing English troops every step of the way while these soldiers were simply carrying out their orders to "destroy some guns and provisions." Even "weamin" (women) took part in the attack by firing on the English, who of course had to respond in kind. A second witness, the Reverend Jonas Clark, pastor of a church in Lexington, counters the seaman's views in a sermon, reporting that the British troops cried, "Damn them. We will have them!" According to Clark, when the British sighted the patriot soldiers, they charged, although the American militia had been instructed "to disperse" and "not to fire." The English troops are viewed as aggressors who exceeded accepted standards of warfare, behaving brutally toward their American brethren. Which account do you think is the most truthful and how can you decide as you prepare to use these documents with a class?

John Crozier (?) to Dr. Rogers:

Empress of Russia, Boston, April 23, 1775

... On the 18th instant between 11 and 12 o'clock at night I conducted all the boats of the fleet (as well men-o-war as transports) to the back part of Boston, where I received the Grenadiers and Light Infantry amounting to 850 officers and men and landed them on a point of marsh or mudland which is overflowed with the last quarter flood; this service, I presume to say, was performed with secrecy and quietness, having oars muffled and every necessary precaution taken, but the watchful inhabitants whose houses are intermixed with the soldiers barracks heard the troops arms and from thence concluded that something was going on, tho' they could not conceive how or where directed. In consequence of this conception, a light was shown at the top of a church stiple [steeple] directing those in the country to be on their guard.

The intention of this expedition was to destroy some guns and provisions which were collected near Concord, a town 20 miles from where the troops were landed. Colonel Smith, a gallant old officer, commanded this detachment and performed the above service. A firelock was snapt over a wall by one of the country people but did not go off. The next who pulled his trigger wounded one of the Light Infantry company of General Hodgsons of the

Kings Own. The fire then commenced and fell heavy on our troops, the militia having posted them selves behind walls, in houses and woods and had possession of almost every eminence or rising ground which commanded the long vale through which the King's troops were under the disagreeable necessity of passing in their return.

Colonel Smith was wounded early in the action and must have been cut off with all those he commanded had not Earl Percy come to his relief with the First Brigade; on the appearance of it our almost conquered Grenadiers and Light Infantry gave three cheers and renewed the defence with more spirits.

Lord Percy's courage and good conduct on this occasion must do him immortal honor. Upon taking the command he ordered the King's Own to flank on the right, and the 27th on the left, the Royal Welsh Fuseliers to defend the rear, and in this manner retreated for at least 11 miles before he reached Charlestown—for they could not cross at Cambridge where the bridge is, they having tore it up, and filled the town and houses with armed men to prevent his passage; our loss in this small essay amounts to 250 killed, wounded and missing. And we are at present kept up in Boston, they being in possession of Roxbury, a little village just before our lines with the Royal and Rebel centenels [sentinels] within musquet [musket] shot of each other.

The fatigue which our people passed through the day which I have described can hardly be believed, having marched at least 45 miles and the Light Companys perhaps 60. A most amiable young man of General Hodgsons's fell that day, his name Knight, brother to Knight of the 43 who was with us at Jamaica.

The enthusiastic zeal with which those people have behaved must convince every reasonable man what a difficult and unpleasant task General Gage has before him. Even weamin [women] had firelocks. One was seen to fire a blunder bus between her father and husband, from their windows; there they three with an infant child soon suffered the fury of the day. In another house which was long defended by 8 resolute fellows the Grenadiers at last got possession when, after having run their bayonets into 7, the 8th continued to abuse them ... and but a moment before he quitted this world applyed such epethets as I must leave unmentioned. God of his infinite mercy be pleased to restore peace and unanimity to those countrys again, for I never did nor can think that arms will enforce obedience.... The number of the country people who fired on our troops might be about 5 thousand, ranged along from Concord to Charlestown, but not less than 20 thousand were that day under arms and on the march to join the others. Their loss we find to be nearly on a footing with our own.

Three days have now passed without communication with the country; three more will reduce this town to a most unpleasant situation; for there [their] dependence for provision was from day to day on supply from the country; that ceasing you may conceive the consequences. Preparations are now making on both sides the Neck for attacking and defending. The Hampshire and Connecticut Militia have joined so that Rebel army are now numerous. Collins is well and stationed between Charles Town and the end of this town to assist in the defence. The General and Early Percy shall have the perusal of your letter.[4]

From a sermon by the Reverend Jonas Clark, pastor of the church in Lexington:

April 19, 1776

Between the hours of twelve and one, on the morning of the nineteenth of April, we received intelligence, by express, from the Honorable Joseph Warren, Esq., at Boston, "that a large body of the king's troops (supposed to be a brigade of about 12 or 1500) were embarked in boats from Boston, and gone over to land on Lechmere's Point (so called) in Cambridge; and that it was

shrewdly suspected that they were ordered to seize and destroy the stores belonging to the colony, then deposited at Concord." … Upon this intelligence,
as also upon information of the conduct of the officers as above-mentioned,
the militia of this town were alarmed and ordered to meet on the usual place
of parade; not with any design of commencing hostilities upon the king's
troops, but to consult what might be done for our own and the people's safety;
and also to be ready for whatever service providence might call us out to,
upon this alarming occasion, in case overt acts of violence or open hostilities
should be committed by this mercenary band of armed and blood-thirsty op-
pressors.… The militia met according to order and waited the return of the
messengers, that they might order their measures as occasion should require.
Between 3 and 4 o'clock, one of the expresses returned, informing that there
was no appearance of the troops on the roads either from Cambridge or
Charles-town; and that it was supposed that the movements in the army the
evening before were only a feint to alarm the people. Upon this, therefore, the
militia company were dismissed for the present, but with orders to be within
call of the drum—waiting the return of the other messenger, who was expected in about an hour, or sooner, if any discovery should be made of the motions of the troops. But he was prevented by their silent and sudden arrival at
the place where he was waiting for intelligence. So that, after all this precaution, he had no notice of their approach till the brigade was actually in the
town and upon a quick march within about a mile and a quarter of the meeting-house and place of parade.

However, the commanding officer thought best to call the company together;
not with any design of opposing so superior a force, much less of commencing
hostilities, but only with a view to determine what to do, when and where to
meet, and to dismiss and disperse.

Accordingly, about half an hour after four o'clock, alarm guns were fired, and
the drums beat to arms, and the militia were collecting together. Some, to the
number of about 50 or 60, or possibly more, were on the parade, others were
coming towards it. In the mean time, the troops having thus stolen a march
upon us and, to prevent any intelligence of their approach, having seized and
held prisoner several persons whom they met unarmed upon the road
seemed to come determined for murder and bloodshed—and that whether
provoked to it or not! When within about half a quarter of a mile of the meeting-house, they halted, and the command was given to prime and load;
which being done, they marched on till they came up to the east end of said
meeting-house, in sight of our militia (collecting as aforesaid) who were about
12 or 13 rods distant.

Immediately upon their appearing so suddenly and so nigh, Capt. Parker,
who commanded the militia company, ordered the men to disperse and take
care of themselves, and not to fire. Upon this, our men dispersed—but many
of them not so speedily as they might have done, not having the most distant
idea of such brutal barbarity and more than savage cruelty from the troops of
a British king, as they immediately experienced! For, no sooner did they come
in sight of our company, but one of them, supposed to be an officer of rank,
was heard to say to the troops, "Damn them! We will have them!" Upon which
the troops shouted aloud, huzza'd, and rushed furiously towards our men.

About the same time, three officers (supposed to be Col. Smith, Major Pitcanin
and another officer) advanced on horse back to the front of the body, and coming within 5 or 6 rods of the militia, one of them cried out, "Ye Villain Rebels,
disperse! Damn you, disperse!"—or words to this effect. One of them
(whether the same or not is not easily determined) said, "Lay down your
arms! Damn you, why don't you lay down your arms?" The second of these
officers, about this time, fired a pistol towards the militia as they were dispersing. The foremost, who was within a few yards of our men, brandishing his
sword and then pointing towards them, with a loud voice said to the troops
"Fire! By God, fire!"—which was instantly followed by a discharge of arms

from the said troops, succeeded by a very heavy and close fire upon our party, dispersing, so long as any of them were within reach. Eight were left dead upon the ground! Ten were wounded. The rest of the company, through divine goodness, were (to a miracle) preserved unhurt in this murderous action! … One circumstance more before the brigade quitted Lexington, I beg leave to mention, as what may give a further specimen of the spirit and character of the officers and men of this body of troops. After the militia company were dispersed and the firing ceased, the troops drew up and formed in a body on the common, fired a volley and gave three huzzas, by wash of triumph and as expressive of the joy of victory and glory of conquest! Of this transaction, I was a witness, having, at that time, a fair view of their motions and being at the distance of not more than 70 or 80 rods from them.[5]

The two accounts (and there are many others) are contradictory in many respects and contain a good deal of dramatic language as well. The battle raises numerous issues about truth in history and the reliability of evidence. Both accounts used here are firsthand or nearly so, and should in theory at least be more accurate than accounts drawn from memory. However, differences of fact and interpretation make it difficult for students or historians to decide which version would be the most truthful; hence, this problem gives you a marvelous opportunity to ask a wide range of questions about the American Revolution in particular and about the nature of the evidence in general.

You might ask students:

Why do accounts differ and sometimes contradict each other?

Are one-sided views heightened in a conflict?

Are conflicting views deliberately created by opponents as propaganda to justify their own actions?

How can you tell propaganda from genuine differences in perception?

What rules can be followed in judging documents: Should the more emotional story be discounted in favor of the coldly objective view?

Should the more logical story be given greater credence than the confused account?

Should we generally believe the more detailed story? (What if both sides offer equally specific accounts of an event?)

Ought the more consistent stories be believed and those that contradict themselves automatically eliminated?

How can we decide what to believe when faced with different frames of reference?

Which "rules for truth" can we accept as guidelines to follow when considering accounts that conflict with each other?

SAMPLE LESSON PLAN

You just read a really interesting book about manhood, *A Choice of Heroes*,* in which the author attacks a number of male stereotypes and female stereotypes, presenting a series of essays on war, manhood, fatherhood, politics, and so on. What great material for discussion! Which values define "man" and "woman"? What do quotations like Wordsworth's, "The child is father to the man," really say about the relationships between the sexes? What kinds of male heroes do we really want to offer our children and youth? What kinds of heroes do they want for themselves?

*Mark Gerzon, *A Choice of Heroes* (Boston: Houghton Mifflin, 1982).

In response, students might suggest that more eyewitnesses are needed. They might add that rules of logic should apply equally to all stories, causing the least reasonable to be tossed out and the most reasonable to be accepted. Some could argue that motives should be considered in any interpretation, mistrusting those who seem to have produced propaganda for one side or another. Students might also conclude that there may be no conclusions we can believe with 100 percent certainty; the best decision must be made in terms of probabilities or preponderance of the evidence.

LET'S DECIDE

Military actions seem to breed distortion of one contending party by the other. During the 1991 Persian Gulf War, and continuing into the 1990s, the Iraqi leader Saddam Hussein was variously portrayed as a "Hitler" or a "hero," depending on whose interests were at stake. But where is the real Hussein and how can we find out?: from U.S. sources, from Arab or Iraqi sources, from others? Find and compare different sources on the 1991 Iraq conflict and on one previous conflict as well. Are the sources predictably in opposition or are there a few surprises?

Frame-of-reference and historiography problems can be reinforced during the entire year as you return regularly to the same powerful, thought-provoking questions, whether questions arise serendipitously or by design. Issues of truth, method, and interpretation never go away in social studies and are also very much a part of real-world practical problems. Once a frame of reference is adopted, you and your students will begin to see opportunities for discussion in every aspect of the curriculum—from media and current events to historical documents and textbook narratives. Accounts that clash, complement, and contradict are naturals in provoking and sustaining classroom inquiry.

TO DO

Develop a lesson in which perspective plays a vital role. Select one or two cases in which the same event or development is seen from the eyes of observers representing diverse cultures. Would Spanish and Aztec sources describing the conquest of Mexico agree in viewpoint? Would British colonial representatives and Africans agree on what happened during the takeover of African peoples by Europeans? Would Muslims and Christian knights agree on the value and purposes of the Crusades? Research primary and literary sources showing two or more frames of views for an event (e.g., "The Broken Spears" representing Aztec accounts of Mexico and the diaries of Bernal Diaz del Castillo representing a Spanish point of view).

MYSTERY STRATEGY

A "mystery" lesson is driven by the recognition that there are unknowns or missing data needed to solve a problem. The mystery strategy relies on a student's sense of puzzlement and curiosity, pushing the learner to seek a solution by filling in the blanks. Much like a good detective novel, plot, character, and evidence all conspire to drive people to discover the ending, whether by inductive or deductive means, or both.[6] History and the social sciences contain a wide variety of mysteries to draw on, from the classic archaeological find to philosophical disputes with no solution.

You can make ready use of the mystery strategy by choosing open-ended problems that come up quite naturally in the classroom. For example, archaeological reconstructions based on fragments of artifacts or bones have a great many built-in unknowns to hypothesize about, often through either interpolation or extrapolation. Sudden political upsets or reversals, such as Napoleon's defeat at Waterloo, can be presented as causal mysteries. After all, do we really know why the greatest general in Europe, Bonaparte, lost to forces many saw as inferior to his own? Here, the unknowns are internal to the story and require analytical techniques to uncover the true capabilities and values of each party in the battle. Problems can be located with built-in mysteries ripe for student solutions. You may create mysteries by leaving out bits and pieces of information for students to infer or track down. In general, classroom mysteries require students to exercise higher order skills to resolve, however tentatively, puzzling problems.

Usefulness of a Mystery Strategy

A mystery strategy is most powerful when you want to heighten student interest in a topic and promote inference and synthesis. Mysteries are almost inherently successful in arousing interest because the learner is converted into a type of detective relentlessly pursuing the objective of solving the case.[7] The drive to gather knowledge, piece together clues, compare and contrast examples, develop and test hypotheses, and see events from many points of view are all incorporated into the higher goal of completing a puzzle, although the solution itself is elusive. In the social studies, the mystery need not be confined to a simple "whodunnit?" but may also focus on questions of what, when, where, how, and why in much the same fashion as any topnotch example of the mystery genre. Popular computer simulation games such as the *Carmen San Diego* series for social studies play on human curiosity and love of the unknown to teach basic geographical and historical principles.[8] In effect, students are role-playing historian and social scientist as detective.

Solving the elements of a mystery is part of a process in the social studies that aims at reinforcing student confidence in using formal and informal logic to test hypotheses and interpret evidence. When a case is incomplete, information is unavailable, or data have been lost or obliterated, the problem becomes all the more appealing. A case can be both a real mystery and an intellectual puzzle. Science often involves mysteries or unknowns that must be solved by research. The knottier the problem, such as finding the causes of the autoimmune deficiency syndrome (AIDS), the greater is the challenge. Science and social science can combine in studying the reasons for a plane crash: Was it an accident or an act of terrorism? Once students are involved, they willingly throw themselves into the effort to solve a puzzle; going to the library becomes fun when research is applied directly to searching out an unknown.

What is sometimes described as a discovery approach to teaching is quite similar to the mystery approach because both encourage the student to make leaps from limited evidence to hypotheses or generalizations that go beyond the given data.[9] A mystery strategy is, in fact, a research process that may begin with evidence or a set of assumptions and proceed in steps toward a defensible conclusion. Thus, the mystery strategy is useful for teaching students problem-solving skills that will dovetail neatly with research procedures and help them to carry out investigations of their own. A research problem is, in a way, the ultimate type of mystery that a student can attempt. The mystery case develops skills that can be applied to many fields of study or situations in life—from figuring out why the car would not start to identifying the crucial links in a chain of human conflict.

Problems With a Mystery Strategy

Organizing a lesson, unit, or course around a mystery or problem carries with it a number of built-in potential difficulties. Mysteries must be carefully constructed for maximum effect in generating student ideas and in reinforcing reasoning skills, and the mystery must be real in the sense that it admits of at least two or more approaches to its solution. Difficulties develop if the problem is too complex, directions are confusing, or students lack the self-confidence to deal with loosely structured problems.

Like a good game, a mystery should be engaging, not trivial; it should not have an easy solution.[10] If the outcome is clear, or becomes so too early, student interest will flag because a solution will be quickly achieved and the mystery solved. On the other hand, a problem that is too confusing, difficult, or ambiguous will lead to student frustration. Students may surrender their search before even a tentative hypothesis or solution is suggested by their analysis of the evidence. In effect, the level of the mystery must be matched to the ability of the audience to avoid either boredom or frustration.

The way a problem is investigated will shape the students' responses. Suggesting an appropriate problem-solving strategy to assist students is preferable for beginners over asking them to invent their own strategies. Generally, the greater the structure (facts, clues, and strategies) provided by the teacher, the easier it will be for the students to come up with a solution, but at cost to their motivation. On the other side, more interesting and complex problems, which produce the greatest motivation and challenge, may also frustrate or paralyze learning efforts.[11] Your audience brings a mind-set to a lesson that can enhance or retard the learning process. Students that are unfamiliar with problem-solving strategies or lack self-confidence to think independently will need more practice than a group accustomed to the process because they may bring naive or inappropriate strategies to bear on unfamiliar problems or questions.[12] The audience, as well as the problem and the pattern of inquiry, is critical to any mystery strategy.

Because both problems and students may be arranged on a continuum of difficulty and skill, you should design a strategy that is fashioned to challenge a particular group or class enough to involve them in high-level thinking processes but not so much as to overwhelm or defeat them. You need to experiment with the mystery strategy until you discover a level at which your students successfully meet the challenge and grow. With practice, students will build more confidence in their ability to make reasonable and effective decisions.

Mystery Teaching Techniques

The mystery strategy probably requires more planning than either the data gathering or comparison and contrast strategies. You must initially assemble and analyze the data making certain that alternative hypotheses are suggested, but without too many clues. And you need to develop key or central questions at a level of difficulty that matches the skill and experience of your intended audience. You can design your own mystery strategy from available materials or borrow from a body of material that already contains one or more built-in unknowns. Mysteries may range from relatively simple questions, such as "Why didn't Japan surrender before the atomic bomb was dropped?" or "Why was President John F. Kennedy assassinated?" to more complex problems like estimating the age and context of a primary source from clues in the text. You may use a mystery strategy for a particular historical event or for a full-fledged research assignment involving direct observation, survey research and interview techniques, or library detective work.

Throughout, you must follow procedures that encourage investigative behavior and build a gamelike classroom atmosphere. The questions posed should be largely open-ended and thought provoking, divergent rather than convergent, designed to sustain the students' inquiry. The data provided must be rich enough to suggest a problem without intimating a quick, unilinear conclusion. As a rule of thumb, a problem solved within the first half of a class period is probably too easy for the group.

Above all, the whole concept of a mystery strategy, like a game of CLUE, is that students should work out their own (not your) solutions to the questions of who, what, when, how, and why. You may certainly offer advice (but not too quickly!), suggest sources of data or knowledge or references (but not too soon!), and help students define their terms (but not too definitively!). Your true objectives are to arouse students' curiosity and free their imaginations to sustain problem solving through manipulating data and questions, and to develop a sense of pride in reaching a hard-won conclusion.

Perhaps the easiest way to evoke a mystery is through a question that calls on students to identify a cause or test a correlative relation between two or more factors. Examples of strategic questions might include the following:

1. Why did the women's movement develop in the United States?
2. Why is a dictator able to control a nation?
3. Is there really a relation between crime and socioeconomic status?
4. Is industrial pollution causing the hole in the earth's ozone layer?

Challenging mysteries may be designed out of a body of evidence, accompanied by thought-provoking questions. Answers develop slowly because much of the data and resources needed are missing or only suggested. Pressing students to subject the modest data and clues available to them to intense scrutiny usually guarantees much more careful reading and observation than occurs in situations where large portions of the outcome are already known. The "missing pieces" technique may be illustrated by lessons in which students are asked to analyze incomplete primary sources. Students have to piece together available clues to place literature, letters, or speeches in historical context. (Using a sample of archaeological artifacts, students may be asked to construct a reasonable picture of a society by extrapolation.) It is the students who must grapple with the words in documents or the objects in archaeological finds while simultaneously searching for clues that will reveal their function or purpose and historical origins. One such lesson, using the poetry of a well-known seventh-century Chinese poet, Tu Fu, is shown here in a mystery form.

In this poem, issues of war and peace are represented by the story of an old man who deliberately broke his arm to evade a military draft. The elderly survivor explains why he injured himself and what happened during and after the war, while the poet comments on life and politics in the China of his time. Proper names, dates, places, and Chinese phrases are omitted in the reproduction of the poem for students to decontextualize the message and to create a mystery.

The Old Man With the Broken Arm

1   At _____ an old man—four-score and eight;
The hair on his head and the hair of his eyebrows—white as the new snow.
Leaning on the shoulders of his great-grandchildren, he walks in front of the Inn;

4   With his left arm he leans on their shoulders; his right arm is broken.
I asked the old man how many years had passed since he broke his arm;
I also asked the cause of the injury, how and why it happened.

7   The old man said he was born and reared in the District of _____ ;
At the time of his birth—a wise reign; no wars or discords.
"Often I listened in the Pear-Tree Garden to the sound of flute and song;

11   Naught I knew of banner and lance; nothing of arrow or bow.
Then came the wars of T_____ and the great levy of men;
Of three men in each house—one was taken.

13   And those to whom the lot fell, where were they taken to?
Five months' journey, a thousand miles—away to _____.
We heard it said that in _____ there flows the _____ River;

16   As the flowers fall from the pepper-trees, poisonous vapors rise.
When the great army waded across, the water seethed like a cauldron;
When barely ten had entered the water, two of three were dead.

19   To the north of my village, to the south of my village the sound of weeping and wailing,
Children parting from fathers and mothers; husbands parting from wives.

22   Of a million men who are sent out, not one returns. I, that am old, was then twenty-four;
My name and fore-name were written down in the rolls of the Board of War
In the depth of night not daring to let any one know

25   I secretly took a huge stone and dashed it against my arm.
For drawing the bow and waving the banner now wholly unfit;
I knew henceforward I should not be sent to fight in _____.

28   Bones broken and sinews wounded could not fail to hurt;
I was ready enough to bear pain, if only I got back home.
My arm—broken ever since; it was sixty years ago.

31   One limb, although destroyed,—whole body safe!
But even now on winter nights when the wind and rain blow
From evening on till day's dawn I cannot sleep for pain.
Not sleeping for pain is a small thing to bear,

34   Compared with the joy of being alive when all the rest are dead.
For otherwise, years ago, at the ford of _____ River
My body would have died and my soul hovered by the bones that no one gathered.

37   A ghost, I'd have wandered in _____, always looking for home.
Over the graves of ten thousand soldiers, mournfully hovering."
So the old man spoke, And I bid you listen to his words
Have you not heard

40   That the Prime Minister of K_____
Did not reward frontier exploits, lest a spirit of aggression should prevail?
not heard
That the Prime Minister of T_____

43   Desiring to win imperial favor, started a frontier war?
But long before he could win the war, people had lost their temper;
Ask the man with the broken arm in the village of _____![13]

The material presents a triple problem: First, there is a mystery about its origins—time and place; second, there is a problem in interpreting its meaning; and third, there is the potential for controversy over the issue of patriotism. Patriotism, from the old man's viewpoint, may serve as a springboard for discussion of more modern events and values such as antiwar protests and draft evasions that characterized the Vietnam War period, and many others as well.

First, students might be asked to search the poem for clues that could shed light on its origins: Where in the world are pear-tree gardens and pepper trees? Then questions should be posed about the ideas in the poem: Why did the old man break his own arm? Is he happy or sad about his decision? Why? How did he (and does he still) feel about family? What does the old man feel about government exploits at home and at war? Is he for or against wars? All wars? Why or why not? Using the war issue, you may extend the discussion to moral or ethical problems related to support for or rejections of one's government. For example, under what conditions might it be proper to resist a nation's decision to fight another nation: offense, defense, both, or neither? What arguments could be offered to support the old man's views, or to oppose them? What form did his protest take? Are other actions possible? As an extension, students could be asked to write their own poem about war. (Would they glorify or disapprove of it, e.g., the Persian Gulf War?)

Arguments for or against war might include such ideas as love of family over nation, reverence for the elderly, and the wandering of ghosts who died away from their home territory. Concrete items such as "Pear-Tree Garden," "bow and lance," "pepper-trees," "village," "five months journey, a thousand miles," and "rolls of the Board of War" could serve as geographic, cultural, and historical clues. These add up to a picture of a big country with strong family values, widespread village life, and a well-organized central government whose decisions are sometimes contrary to popular opinion. Meanwhile, China of long ago takes on a human face through Tu Fu's story, as students deepen their understanding of its contents.

To discover the precise origins of the poem is a motivation of the mystery strategy, but the real goal is for students to discover meaning on their own. You should guide students to a satisfying conclusion, but only after they have thoroughly exhausted their own resources and analytic powers by debating the old man's ethics and the poet's message, finally arriving at a fairly well-accepted class interpretation. Then you can offer the knowledge that the poet was a Chinese scholar of the seventh century A.D. named Tu Fu, who frequently protested against government decisions and was banished from his home as a result. You might note that in an atmosphere of rule by emperor and ministers that was far from free and open, opposition took a good deal more courage than it would in present-day America.

Research or field studies offer opportunities for a mystery strategy by allowing students to develop and test a hypothesis of their own about an event, person, historical period, or issue of interest to them. Students (with some guidance from teachers, librarians, and scholars) may identify a thesis and collect the data needed to accept or reject it. A good research study should permit alternate theories, allow a fair test of competing interpretations, yet defend the preferred thesis with evidence and logic. Research projects may be suggested by such thesis questions as these:

1. Does history repeat itself? Are the 1980s a reprise of the 1950s?
2. Can parallels be drawn between the rise and decline of empires?
3. Why are some societies economically successful while others are not?
4. Can we trust newspaper reporting? (Examples are a comparison of American and Soviet coverage of the Baltic Republics or U.S. and Iraqi news about the Persian Gulf war.)

5. Who has more trust in our political system: younger students or older students, better students or poorer students, better-off or disadvantaged students?

Thus, there are many ways to build mystery into typical social studies lessons through questions, original documents, literature, and research projects.

TO DO

Create a mystery: Develop a puzzle to solve for your students or offer them a real mystery such as an unsolved controversy to consider. Samples might include topics such as John Brown, the abolitionist who conducted a pre-Civil War raid on Harper's Ferry, Virginia, to free the slaves. For this action, he was sentenced to death and hanged. Southerners portrayed him as a madman and a villain and northern abolitionists portrayed him as a hero. What was the truth? Were his motives noble or evil? Were his methods defensible? Is violence ever reasonable and defensible? If not, why not? If so, when?

Or, you might ask students to conduct their own investigation of the causes of World War I. Do they really think that the assassination of Archduke Ferdinand was enough to set off a worldwide conflict? Have them check on the German, French, and English armament situation at the time. Were these peaceful states who armed at the last minute or had there been a build-up of many years? Which nations really wanted war and which did not? Is there any way of sorting truth from falsehood so the mystery can be cleared up?

CONTROVERSY STRATEGY

A lesson built around a controversy is one that rests on values and philosophies about morality, justice, order, or the "good life." Controversies arise out of clashes between the basic values that provide people with their aspirations, codes of daily behavior, and guides to right and wrong.[14] Because value disputes draw on emotional commitments, they are inherently motivating and take a strong hold on student attention.[15]

Strategies for dealing with controversies range from attempts to hammer out compromises between contending positions, and choosing the better among many evils, to taking a stand based on a universal set of truths. What makes value discussions so interesting is the chance to hear different sides of an issue or debate. What makes value discussions so difficult is the lack of definite answers, sometimes with no resolution possible. Our methods of adjudicating disputes or analyzing values may themselves be called into question from other points of view, challenging our basic notions of truth and method.

For the social studies teacher, however, there is probably no strategy more productive and powerful than that built on a controversy. But there is also no strategy more fraught with pitfalls and problems. A successful discussion of values, issues, or controversies must incorporate both cognitive and affective domains, data and analysis, and theory and practice before well thought-out decisions or recommendations can be formulated. Fairness is difficult to achieve when people are inflamed about a subject, defending beliefs they hold sacred. In addition, you must lead the discussion or debate in a way that is balanced to allow consideration of all student opinions. The free flow of views is sometimes very painful when students express opinions you view, often rightfully so, as crude retrograde, or socially explosive. At these times you desperately want to tell students what is "right"! Yet to do so is often to quash unpleasant or unpopular views, which may crumble in the light of public scrutiny. To favor one position over another is to diminish or destroy the whole strategy, thereby also diminishing freedom of expression and the skills students need to think through a problem on their own. Thus, the social studies teacher's dilemma: how to handle values and value-laden topics in the classroom in a professional manner that is exciting, fair, and civilized.

SAMPLE LESSON PLAN

Why do disputes or protests or differences develop? Why do people hold different beliefs on important topics? How are exchanges of opinions expressed.

Usefulness of a Controversy Strategy

A controversy strategy is most useful in illuminating choices between or among alternative values. These values can be immediate and practical, or long range and theoretical, directed toward such down-to-earth matters as selecting the "best" car on the market based on explicit criteria or toward rethinking gender issues in U.S. or world society based on a philosophy of human relations.

Difficult choices revolve around global or universal values, such as the relation of the rich nations toward the poor ones or the wealthier segments of the nation's population to its disadvantaged. Here, arguments can focus on issues of responsibility, charity, self-help, individualism, need, ability, dignity, and social peace to name but a few appealing values to consider. Even relatively narrow topics (e.g., welfare or tax-reform) affecting economic and social relations can bring out heated value disagreements concerning who deserves help and by what methods aid should be delivered. A serious discussion of poverty and wealth would demand considerable data, careful analysis of policy choices, and a willingness of all to delay judgment until all sides are heard. Tough, you might say, but well worth it in terms of impact on student interest, perspective, growth, and decision-making experience.

Problems With a Controversy Strategy

The great power and interest generated by a controversial issue can also be its downfall. So powerful may the arguments become that passion and heat will overwhelm reason and light in the search to find a defensible solution to a problem. The more sensitive the issue, the greater is the likelihood of the discussion or debate getting out of hand. For instance, students may strongly prefer that only one of the sides in a debate win, creating a hostile climate for minority views, or minority supporters may be so loud and intolerant that they destroy a discussion.

Examination of ideas is difficult to sustain in an atmosphere in which the controversy is seen strictly in terms of win-or-lose goals. Your deepest underlying objective in using a controversy approach is to encourage critical thinking, asking students to judge alternative viewpoints on logical, philosophical, and evidential criteria. More than any other strategy, controversy needs time to develop and deepen through review, debate, and reflection on the major positions. Premature decision making tends to make a mockery of the issues by promoting a rush to judgment rather than a defensible rationale. Although you will probably not have the time to complete a definitive review of a controversy, you must still give a fair representation or sampling of views on an issue, including the basic arguments and key data.

A second problem develops when you or your students are personally affected by an issue. After all, we are all human and have feelings just like our students. Difficulties may arise when your own feelings are very strong on an issue and you wish to condemn or praise a political figure, an act of Congress, or a Supreme Court decision that you may feel has been unfairly attacked. Even more potentially explosive are situations in which students' shock or anger at each others' hostile remarks, racial slurs, or stereotypic thinking is directed at classmates or others. Examples of controversy gone awry might be anti-Jewish remarks that are offered, wittingly or unwittingly, by a student during a discussion of the Holocaust when one or more of the class participants are Jewish, or racial remarks during a discussion of civil rights cases. How, then, can you keep strong personal views under control and limit conflict, prejudice, and bias among students during a debate or argument? The next section on techniques for teaching controversial problems offers methods for training students to deal with potentially nettlesome issues and strong personal beliefs. Your overall aim must be a balanced, thoughtful manner that combines didactive, reflective, and affective components, focusing their power on enlightenment, not necessarily resolution of a controversy.

Controversy Teaching Techniques

Problems generic to a controversy strategy (and its motivational power) may be kept under control by a variety of techniques that harness the energy while producing a balanced understanding of the issues. As much as possible, the discussion of a controversy must provide competing interpretations, accompanied by sufficient data, and a format for analysis and discussion that will give students the time and opportunity to weigh value differences and come to a reasonable decision.[16] For a successful controversy lesson, any issue or difference of opinion must admit to two or more well-developed alternative viewpoints. If the issue is stacked in one direction or another, then students will be involved in a biased effort rather than a philosophical argument.

To promote debate and discussion, a number of techniques may be employed, including research, debates, panels, devil's advocacy, committees, mock trials, journalistic or investigative reporting, and newspaper editorial writing. Debates and panels, if properly prepared for, have the advantage of a two-sided or multifaceted approach to an issue in a structured format that constrains personal emotions and puts a premium on the development of grounds for justifying a position. Well-prepared debaters, for example, support their arguments with detailed data, research findings, expert opinions, and logical arguments against a position. A list of alternative approaches for organizing a controversy strategy follows:

Simulation Games: The class plays general or specific roles that relate directly to a problem or issue through the medium of a game or gamelike series of moves and countermoves, making choices that result in wins, losses, or stalemates.

Debates: Students arrange a formal exchange of ideas in teams who research opposing sides and present their views by offering a defense, cross-examination, rebuttal, and concluding summary.

Panels: Students research a variety of views and solutions for an issue that they present to others as members of an expert panel.

Investigative Reporters: Students role-play newspaper reporters who study the origins, development, and present status of a controversial topic, attempting to write a story that is at once fair to all sides but critical as well.

Devil's Advocates: You or one or more students argue positions that are either unpopular or overlooked by most of the class because you and they believe these should be heard and evaluated in the same way as the accepted viewpoints.

Mock Trials: Students with your aid organize a lengthy role-play or sociodrama in which they reenact either an actual or a fictitious court case playing the parts of lawyers, judges, witnesses, defendants, plaintiffs, and others.

Social Science Researchers: Students are directed to collect, analyze, and evaluate critically the evidence and the arguments used to support different positions on an issue, concluding their studies with a report to the class and a written assessment of the evidence and arguments used by each side.

Poll Takers/Interviewers: Aided by you, a statistician, and/or computer programmer, students will develop, write, and field test a survey of attitudes and opinions on a topic of importance and value to them, their peers, and the community, analyzing, summarizing, and sharing their findings, errors, and problems.

Councils/Committees/Policymakers: Students will be asked to serve as policymakers, role-playing a real group or committee responsible for settling a dispute, problem, or issue based on available information about courses, consequences, and alternative choices.

Role-Reversals: Students are asked to take the position of the "enemy," the opposing side, in an argument or issue, either at the beginning of a controversy lesson or after they have completed the argument for a view they prefer.

After the issues have been thoroughly played out, a discussion of the whole experience is in order. Once a body of data has been acquired in a controversy, reasons heard, and pros and cons thrashed out, the follow-up discussions are usually more focused and hardheaded than freewheeling and emotive. At this point, specifics have been added to general principles, putting flesh on the bones of abstract values. There may, of course, still be students offering ideas that fly in the face of all evidence or reason on an issue, but their problems will become rapidly evident to peers who have given a case careful deliberation.

Thoughtfulness and knowledge puts pressure on everyone to be fairer and more comprehensive than when they were novices. As members of the class offer competing views or point out the poor defenses or illogic of an opinion or statement, you need not intervene. If, however, a majority of students conform to a stand you see as stereotypical, unethical, or indefensible, then you may attempt to battle this stance by offering arguments and evidence in support of alternative views. In this case you must convey to the students that there are positions that run directly counter to theirs, perhaps based on better evidence. If students have had a fairly thorough review of a controversy or value problem and still refuse or are unable to consider the views of others, you must respond strongly and with feeling, even if they find your side of the issue disturbing. Taking a public stand against majority or mainstream values is a time-honored democratic tradition that has been nurtured by both political and cultural leaders. Students may still accept or reject what you see as the better position, but at least they must do so with the understanding that theirs is not an absolute, unchallenged truth! In a context of legitimate disagreement, the psychology of the students certainly permits your opposition without fear of any immediate or premature shift in their thinking.[17]

The doctrine of defensible partiality as described by Massialas and Cox, offers a series of guidelines to employ in classroom situations in which you wish to express an opinion or deeply held belief of your own, need to offer an alternative position that competes with narrow student views, or must counter student views that seem unreasonable or prejudiced.[18] As argued previously, you do not want to be in the position of promoting your personal ideas and views because this will lead to making decisions for the students. Nor do you have to maintain an uncomfortable and unnatural neutrality on all problems, controversial or value oriented. The rationale for defensible partiality is that the imposition of value choices diminishes the learner's independence of thought and reduces decision making to a farce, which is likely to promote political apathy and indifference. Students who are trying to build identities in a complex, democratic social order do not need input that promotes a sense of powerlessness and disrespect for their opinions.[19] Far more preferable are young people who can make up their own minds on clear, publicly stated decisions and policies that they see as either being in their own best interests or as logically and morally correct.

Defensible partiality means that you can express ideas on any issue, case, or controversy, but this must be done with due regard for explaining the basis of the viewpoint to the students. Expression of your views must also be timed in a manner that does not diminish student opportunities to develop and promote their own ideas. Introduce your values and preferences at points in a discussion when students are deadlocked on an issue or too wrapped up in their own emotions to see any other viewpoints. Pedagogically, you must interfere on occasion, but this ought to be accomplished after students already have a grasp of the issues and have been psychologically prepared for a policy position (e.g., while studying the political process during an election campaign or examining a proposition or referendum proposal). As a member of society, you may be for or against someone in the election, or you may decide to abstain or vote for the candidate of a third party. Whatever your views, these can be shared with students at many points in a discussion as a demonstration that you care about election outcomes as shown by your participation. However, if your choice is offered too early or argued too strongly, students may readily agree to an idea that is not really theirs, falling silent out of respect for you, or they may be persuaded by the intensity of your feelings. If you advance your views after students have already argued, or partially argued, about candidates and issues, then the psychological impact will be quite different. Yours will be one among many developing views—a more mature view but not one that will overwhelm the others. You may also seek to play devil's advocate for a position or candidate not popularly received or well understood by the students. Thus, the doctrine of defensible partiality gives you a reasonable plan of action that avoids both a hands-off neutrality and active intervention to teach values to students. Above all, from a defensible partiality viewpoint, it is the students who are expected to identify the issues in a controversy, research the evidence, analyze the alternatives, test the theories, make a judgment, and come to their own decisions to act or not to act.

Examples of Controversy Lessons

Primary or secondary sources can be used to raise moral or ethical issues. Both types allow you to develop multiple viewpoints and alternatives on an issue through the analysis of news accounts, letters, biographies, autobiographies, and public statements. A debate assumes a built-in confrontation of already well-formulated arguments with supporting resources. This usually takes the form of a two-sided argument rather than a continuum of views and invites group dynamics, such as a debate team, panel, committee, or simulation.

Statistics, though sometimes dry and lifeless, can offer the basis for a meaningful discussion of values, particularly if you have identified and prepared for the issues suggested in the materials. For example, the U.S. government, and many other national and world civic bodies, keep records of the distribution of wealth and income among their populations. Allocations of income, or wealth, are often shown in the form of graphs in which the total population is divided into equal units, fifths or tenths, each segment receiving a proportion (in percentages) of the total national income for a given year (Figure 6.2).

Economic concepts, social class structure, and policy issues can be applied to, or drawn from, these bar graphs of income distribution. You can ask students to interpret, analyze, and synthesize the information, inferring economic and social hypotheses to explain the data. After interpretation and analysis, you can ask students to make a bold leap beyond the information given to the realm of policy considerations, by asking a series of analytic and evaluative questions:

Why do some segments (fifths) of the population receive more income than others?

How much does the top 5 percent receive in each time period?

Which fifths receive as much or more than the top 5 percent?

What might this tell you about the top group?

Why do some have less income, others more?

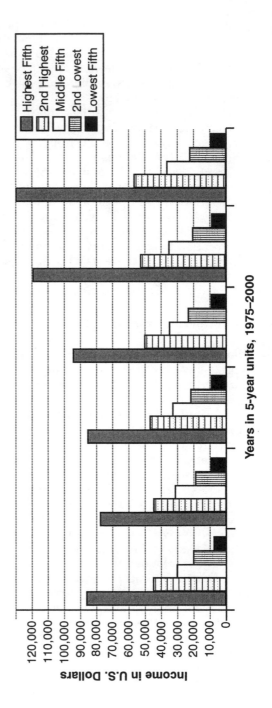

Figure 6.2 Median U.S. annual family income by population fifths. Based on data from U.S. Bureau of Statistics, Statistical Abstract of the United States (Washington, DC: U.S. Government Printing Office, 1998).

How evenly or unevenly is income distributed?

Why are the incomes of the top fifth falling and then rising?

Why are the incomes of the second, third, and fourth fifths rising and then falling?

Why is the percentage of some fifths' incomes hardly growing at all?

Which segments of the population grew better off from 1975 to 1995?

How do trends for this period compare with the period from 1935 to 1955?

Is it morally right or wrong for some to receive more than others? Why?

What conditions or events lie behind different distributions?

Which distribution would you approve of as best for society as a whole—a more or less egalitarian (equal) distribution? Why? For yourself? For your family?

To which fifth would you want to belong? Explain.

After a period of speculation and discussion students may settle on value positions in class. To assist them in thinking about how wealth and income should be allocated in a society, you could present ideas from sources such as Rawls's *Theory of Justice*, Smith's *Wealth of Nations*, or Marx's *Communist Manifesto*. Encourage students to decide what kind of distribution would be fairest: the more equal or the more unequal. As discussion progresses, students will identify and develop alternative positions on social and economic fairness but may not necessarily come to a consensus. Then you could create a formal debate or call a congress to set a policy—laissez-faire, socialist, liberal, or conservative—each one exhibiting a different philosophy, and ask the students to consider these and choose their preference.

LET'S DECIDE

Prepare a controversy for discussion by your present or future students. Develop roles to play for a panel discussion or debate on a highly charged issue. Offer students readings, documents, statistics, resources, and references to use in writing their parts. Design a pre- and post-survey of students' feelings on the issue. Conduct a survey of attitudes just before and at the conclusion of the lesson. Ask students to assist in tabulating the data and in presenting findings to the class. Make sure that everyone develops an initial position on the issue in writing to serve as a basis for argument. Explain that positions may change after the final arguments, and ask students to identify ten to fifteen points in the debate that they think everyone needs to know, regardless of their decision.

Suggested full-scale controversies might focus on international terrorism, socialized medicine in the United States, tax reform, political oppression, women's rights, or economic inequality among the nations of the world. Within these broad areas, more specific issues could be identified, aimed at a particular area, action, or legal decision that would serve as the fulcrum for student arguments. What current events do you see as material ripe for a controversy strategy? How would you try to obtain student cooperation in taking both or all sides of the problem? Are there any issues that you might want to avoid discussing with middle or junior high level students? With senior high school students? With anyone? Give examples and defend your position with reasons and research.

SUMMARY

The three strategies discussed in this chapter—frame of reference, mystery, and controversy—can be used to move a social studies lesson toward higher order thinking levels. Fueled by data, teacher support, thought-provoking questions, and role-playing, student interest and involvement will grow significantly. Whereas the strategies were presented separately for the purpose of describing their uses and limitations, you may certainly mix approaches to suit your goals. The more powerful strategies—those stressing a frame of reference, mystery, or a controversy—demand and encourage somewhat more higher level valuing and thinking (i.e., analysis, synthesis, and judgment). The less powerful strategies—those stressing data gathering, comparison and contrast, or drama—demand and encourage somewhat less complex cognition and affect (i.e., recall, comprehension, and application). Each of the strategies can be combined easily with others to create a more powerful effect than that fostered by any single approach. However, greater power and impact may also yield more student difficulty or frustration. Strategies must be assessed in terms of difficulty for an intended audience and applied accordingly in your classroom. This means that you must prepare students for a thinking process, not absorption of content alone. For example, you might want to hold an informal practice debate before fielding full-scale teams. As students become familiar with the more exacting, complex, and challenging strategic designs, they will increasingly be able to take on greater and more intellectually involving tasks.

The power to build thinking skills in the social studies and to attract student interest is most probably proportional to the intriguing qualities of the problems provided through each strategy. The more curiosity and interest that is aroused, the greater the potential for the growth of rich and varied ideas from students. The relation among the six strategies, which you can look on as parts of your overall repertory, is pictured in Figure 6.3 as a series of overlapping sets or circles.

Each strategy may be conceptualized as both independent and complementary within the overall scheme of didactic, reflective, and affective goals. The six strategies may be viewed as forming a hierarchy in which data gathering and comparison and contrast tend to be associated with didactic goals; drama and controversy are more oriented toward affective goals; and mystery and frame-of-reference strategies are well suited to encourage reflective thinking processes. The choice of a particular strategy will inevitably influence your selection of material and textbooks, questions, style, and behavior. In the chapters that follow, the strategies described here are applied to the most commonly taught middle and secondary social studies courses: world studies, and U.S. history and government.

TO DO

Prepare a list of U.S. history, global studies, civics, and economics topics that are commonly taught. Write these on 3 x 5 cards, one topic to a note card, and re-sort them according to the strategy that would seem most appropriate. For example, would the Civil War lend itself best to a frame-of-reference or a mystery strategy? Would the civil rights movement of the 1960s be most appropriately presented in a comparison and contrast strategy or a controversial issues approach? Might the preparation of a database on Latin America be best suited to a data-gathering or a drama-building strategy?

Are particular topics always suited to a single strategy? Can the same topic be developed in many ways? Is the way you present a topic more dependent on your view of the subject or on the subject itself? Discuss this question in a brief written essay. Purposely choose a topic, such as the Mexican Revolution or British conquest of India or the power of the president in the American system of government and create plans to teach it by each of the six strategies discussed in this chapter: data gathering, drama building, comparison and contrast, frame of reference, mystery, and controversy. Data always seem to be available, but are drama, mystery, and controversial values always a part of human events as well?

Are there any controversies that would be exempt from discussion? Why or why not? Are there any controversies for which you would not follow a defensible partiality approach? Why? How would you approach them?

Figure 6.3   Six strategies for teaching the social studies.

How would you react to the question of knowing "truth"? Do you think that "facts" are always true? Do you think that conclusions are always true? Can facts or conclusions be less than 100 percent true to be acceptable? For example, if more economists, 70 percent, agree on the superiority of a free-market system over traditional or command systems, is the conclusion true? Are high probabilities acceptable as conclusions? Why or why not? Are all conclusions questionable? Are any conclusions fully proven, 100 percent?

When you teach a topic in social studies—any topic—how certain are you that the facts are accurate? How sure are you that the conclusions offered are valid? Will you share with students any doubts or questions you have about the evidence? Or will you teach the knowledge of the texts as factual and proven? Write a brief essay on how you present social studies—as fact, as probability, or as subjective material. Take and defend your position to others. Are there any problems you are willing to recognize in your thinking? Why or why not?

NOTES

1. Ryonosuke Akutagawa, *Rashomon and Other Stories* (New York: Bantam Books, 1959).
2. E. Husserl, *Ideas: General Introduction to Pure Phenomenology*, trans. from the German by W.R.B. Gibson (New York: Macmillan, 1931).
3. Henry Steele Commager and Richard B. Morris, *The Spirit of Seventy-Six* (New York: Harper & Row, 1975), pp. 77–78, 80–82.
4. J. E. Tyler, ed., "Account of Lexington," *William & Mary Quarterly*, 3rd series, 10, no. 1 (1953): 104–7.
5. Charles Hudson, *History of the Town of Lexington*, vol. 1 (Boston: Houghton Mifflin, 1913), pp. 527–29, 530.
6. John Dewey, *Interest and Effort in Education* (New York: Houghton Mifflin, 1913).
7. D. E. Berlyne, *Structure and Direction in Thinking* (New York: Wiley, 1965), pp. 236–76.
8. J. D. Bransford et al., "Computers and Problem-Solving," in *Computer Strategies for Education*, ed. C. Kinzer and J. D. Bransford (Columbus, OH: Merrill, 1986), pp. 147-80; *Where in the World Is Carmen San Diego?*, 1988; *Where in the U.S.A. Is Carmen San Diego?*, 1989; *and Where in Time Is Carmen San Diego?*, 1989 (San Rafael, CA: Broderbund).
9. Jerome Bruner, *On Knowing Essays for the Left Hand* (New York: Atheneum, 1965).
10. A. Iran-Nejad, "Cognitive and Affective Causes of Interest and Liking," *Journal of Educational Psychology*, 79 (1987): 120–30.
11. C. Ames and J. Archer, "Achievement Goals in the Classroom: Students' Learning Strategies and Motivation Processes," *Journal of Educational Psychology*, 80 (1988): 260–67.
12. C. E. Weinstein and R. E. Mayer, "The Teaching of Learning Strategies," in *Handbook of Research on Teaching*, 3rd ed., ed. M. C. Wittrock (New York: Macmillan, 1986), pp. 315–27.
13. Arthur Waley, *Translations from the Chinese* (New York: Knopf, 1964). Missing names include: line 1, Hsin-Feng; line 7, Hsin-Feng; line 11, T'ien Pao; line 14, Yun-Nan; line 15, Yun-Nan, Lu; line 27, Yun-Nan; line 35, Lu; line 37, Yun-Nan; line 40, K'ai-yuan, Sung K'ai fu; line 42, T'ien-Pao; line 45, Yang Kuo-chung.
14. Byron Massialas, "Educating Students for Conflict Resolution and Democratic Decision-Making," *The Social Studies*, 5 (Sept./Oct. 1990): 202–207.
15. L. Festinger, *Conflict, Decision, and Dissonance* (Stanford, CA: Stanford University Press, 1964).
16. Alan Lockwood and David Harris, *Reasoning With Democratic Values: Ethical Problems in United States History* (New York: Teacher's College Press, 1985).
17. J. P. Shaver and W. Strong, *Facing Value Decisions: Rationale-Building for Teachers*, 2nd ed. (New York: Teacher's College Press, 1982).
18. Byron Massialas and Benjamin Cox, *Inquiry in Social Studies* (New York: McGraw-Hill, 1966), pp. 174–77.
19. John Allen Rossi, "In-depth study in an issues-oriented social studies classroom," *Theory and Research in Social Education*, 33, no. 2 (Spring 1995): 88–120.

FOR FURTHER STUDY: TEACHING STRATEGIES FOR HIGHER LEVEL SKILLS

Baron, J. B., and R. J. Sternberg, eds. *Teaching Thinking Skills: Theory and Practice*. New York: W. H. Freeman, 1987.

Beyer, B. K. *Practical Strategies for the Teaching of Thinking*. Boston: Allyn & Bacon, 1987.

Davis, G. A. *Creativity Is Forever*. 3rd ed. Dubuque, IA: Kendall/Hunt, 1992.

Fisher, R., and W. Ury. *Getting to Yes: Negotiating Agreements Without Giving In*. Boston: Houghton Mifflin, 1981.

Germain, M. H. *Worldly Teachers: Cultural Learning and Pedagogy*. Westport, CT: Bergin & Harvey, 1998.

Hartoonian, M. "Social Content and Higher Order Thinking." In *Teaching Complex Thinking in School Subjects*. Alexandria, VA: Association for Supervision and Curriculum Development, 1989.

Laurel, B. *Computer as Theatre: A Dramatic Theory of the Interactive Experience*. Reading, MA: Addison-Wesley, 1991.

Lipman, M. *Thinking in Education*. New York: Cambridge University Press, 1991.

Massialis, B. G., and J. Zevin. *Teaching Creatively*. Malabar, FL: Kreiger and Sons, 1983.

Newmann, F. *Higher Order Thinking in High School Social Studies*. Madison, WI: National Center on Effective Secondary Schools, 1988.

Norman, D. A. *Things That Make Us Smart: Defending Human Attributes in the Age of the Machine*. Reading, MA: Addison-Wesley, 1993.

Paul, R. W. et al. *Critical Thinking Handbook: Grades 6–9, A Guide to Remodelling Lesson Plans in Language Arts, Social Studies, and Science and Critical Thinking Handbook: High School, A Guide for Redesigning Instruction*. Rohnert Park, CA: Center for Critical Thinking and Moral Critique, 1989.

Raths, L. *Teaching for Thinking: Theories, Strategies, and Activities for the Classroom*. 2nd ed. New York: Teacher's College Press, 1986.

Ruggiero, V. *Thinking Across the Curriculum*. New York: Harper & Row, 1988.

Ryan, K., and K. E. Bohlin. *Building Character in Schools: Practical Ways to Bring Moral Instruction to Life*. San Francisco: Jossey-Bass, 1999.

Schmuck, R. A., and P. A. Schmuck. *Group Processes in the Classroom*. 6th ed. Dubuque, IA: Wm. C. Brown, 1992.

Starko, A. J. *Creativity in the Classroom: School of Curious Delight*. White Plains, NY: Longman, 1995.

Winne, P. H. "Experiments Relating to Teachers' Use of Higher Cognitive Questions to Student Achievement." *Review of Educational Research*, 49, no. 1 (Winter 1979): 13–49.

CHAPTER 7

Planning a Unit
From Start to Finish

One general aphorism emerges which ought by logical right to dominate the entire conduct of the teacher in the classroom. "No reception without reaction, no impression without correlative expression,"—this is the great maxim, which the teacher ought never to forget.
—William James, Talks to Teachers

OVERVIEW OF CONTENTS

Main Ideas

Setting Objectives

> Examples of Behavioral Objectives: Didactic, Reflective, Affective
> Conclusions About Objectives

Planning a Civil War Unit

> Setting Objectives
> Choosing a Strategy
> Daily Lessons: A Unit in the Curriculum
> Expectations: Planning for Evaluation
> A Sample Lesson on Civil War Issues
> Some Resources for a Civil War Lesson

Summary

Notes

For Further Study: Planning a Unit from Start to Finish

MAIN IDEAS

Social studies units are the scripts of the profession and include props, dramatis personae, and all the accoutrements of a fine theater piece but with different, though not mutually exclusive, purposes. Central to a unit's impact is the nature of the content, its arrangement and of course the objectives to be pursued. When content is dry and formal, questions pedantic, and goals focused narrowly on imparting information, the unit is unlikely to have a strong effect on students' attention or achievement. When content is varied and dramatic, demands critical

140

thinking, asks students to answer open questions, and stresses goals of a reflective and/or affective nature, the effect is likely to be far more riveting and achievement levels will rise. People go to theater, live drama, and films to have fun and enjoy art, but they may also be searching for intellectual stimulation and an emotional catharsis. This can be carried over into planning a good social studies unit. Scripts for the theater and social studies units share similar dramatic techniques, promote the examination of ethical issues, and foster understanding that commands interest and communicates ideas. However, a teaching unit tends toward a balance of viewpoints based on evidence rather than a playwright's vision of people and ideas.

For most of this book, we have discussed planning the curriculum and organizing for teaching as though this were a rational process. From watching teachers, however, we all know that many lessons are created on the spur of the moment. Something comes up that we see as deserving discussion, the audiovisual presentation suffers mechanical failure, or you forget the materials that were needed to support the lesson. These and a host of other chance occurrences can bring down plans and organization, leaving you with the problem of creating an instant lesson. In general, we advocate careful preparation and a solid grasp of the materials, but the exigencies of daily life often catch up with the best-laid teacher plans. Therefore, although you should view most of this book as laying out an idealized model for organizing and implementing social studies lessons, the reality can be something very different—not necessarily worse, but considerably messier and illogical. On occasion, inspiration may overwhelm you and a brilliant on-the-spot lesson will result—one that you and the students find exciting. On occasion, the doldrums will hit and the muse will desert you, with the outcome that students find dull and directionless. To help inspire you and to demonstrate that last minute, ad hoc lessons can work out, there are inserts throughout the book that are called "Sample Lesson Plans." Each sample presents an idea for a lesson to fit many occasions and fill in for missing materials. Look these over, and come up with some of your own ideas—but not too often, please!

In setting up a unit of study, think through your goals in didactic, reflective, and affective terms. Then write a script, select props, and choose a method from the strategies of data gathering, compare and contrast, drama, frame of reference, mystery, and controversy. In this chapter, the U.S. Civil War is used as the subject for illustrating the process of building a teaching unit. This topic is chosen because of its popularity in the curriculum and its inclusion in every secondary school's course of study. In the following pages, you are invited to look at one way in which the U.S. Civil War could be taught using the ideas discussed in previous chapters. In no way should this sample be construed as either the only or the best way to present these events. Criticism, revision, and extension are welcomed and invited for these two units; remember that units are successful in the degree to which they communicate important ideas to your students. Think about the ways in which you will judge your effectiveness and student accomplishments. Maybe you would like to accumulate a portfolio of their work, or maybe you are too busy and just need a few good examinations. Student feedback will tell you what works and what flops! The last thing we need or hope to see in a unit is one that is so "perfect" that it provides all the answers to all the questions on a subject.

SETTING OBJECTIVES

A well-planned lesson, unit, or course should grow out of a point of view or general aim that is derived from a philosophy of education. From this overall aim should flow a series of objectives that specifically indicate the results you seek in terms of student knowledge, skills, and behavior. Objectives may serve as your guides to deciding what and how to teach, as well as the criteria for judging student achievement. Thus, if goals aim at low knowledge levels, results of the same nature are likely to follow. If goals call for a more demanding progression of student outcomes, then it is likely that more higher order skills will be developed. Most objectives in the social studies represent a compromise between realistic minimum objectives and lofty ideals that represent the highest potential of individual or group accomplishment. This is not to say that student performance will meet a set of objectives, rather it means that the goals set a tone and direction for a social studies lesson. Thus, objectives should be viewed as planning devices and guides that direct your choice of materials toward an end that is both worthwhile and defensible.[1]

In selecting objectives, you should plan for qualitative as well as quantitative outcomes that include didactic, reflective, and affective components. In practice this means that knowledge aims, thinking aims, and value aims should be part of each day's material. Lesser, shorter range objectives may serve as guides for daily routine (e.g., defining and memorizing twenty geographical terms), while your plan as a whole should flow from longer range, more qualitatively complex goals (e.g., "to develop and test generalizations about patterns of human settlement in history"). Many other midrange objectives might fall between these, but overall direction would be set by the higher level objectives rather than the lower ones. A series of steps along the way would move from information and comprehension through application and analysis to synthesis and judgment.[2] In my view, a well-designed knowledge lesson must involve students in an understanding of the material and a sense of the historical and social science sources from which these were drawn: for example, the authorship, value position, if any, and logic of the material being used.

Thus, objectives are useful tools for planning and directing a social studies lesson on a short-, medium-, or long-range basis.[3] Objectives for a unit should incorporate both quantitative (didactic) elements as well as qualitative (reflective and affective) elements within the scope of each day's lesson and the entire course of study. One objective should serve as your overall, organizing goal for student achievement.

TO DO

> Which teaching goals do you think are most vital to a social studies lesson: didactic, reflective, or affective? Why? Can any lesson be taught that is entirely in one goal area (e.g., didactic)?

Examples of Behavioral Objectives: Didactic, Reflective, Affective

Ideally, objectives for any social studies lesson or unit should be behavioral in style, relatively few in number, demand two or more performance levels of students, and accurately reflect what is expected to happen in the classroom. By behavioral we mean that the objective should specify exactly what behaviors and actions you will expect from students based on the input, text, document, questions, and so on, that they receive. Emphasis is placed on what actually happens, what you and students will carry out, rather than on idealized, long-term projections. Furthermore, criteria for assessment should be provided within a rationale or justification that defends the value of the subject. Make a list of all student products you would like to see placed in their unit portfolios: drawings, essays, test scores, projects, and so on. Goals should also be understandable to students and expectations shared with them; they should feel reasonably confident of success.

RESEARCH REPORT

In a metanalysis of twenty-three studies comparing the impact of teacher objectives or lack of objectives on students, Klauer found that learning increased along stated guidelines but decreased for tangential or unrelated material.* In other words, stated guidelines, objectives, or questions tended to narrow but deepen learning of material (covering a wide range from social studies through mathematics) while excluding ideas seen as unrelated. Objectives seem to impact on students by focusing their efforts on achievement that will satisfy the guidelines. This is not particularly surprising but does support the value of objective writing and sharing goals with students in advance of studies. A serious question was raised concerning the possible narrowness of objectives, for example, wholly didactic ones assigned by the teacher. This study showed that more general objectives and more conceptual (i.e., reflective or affective) objectives tend to allow students greater flexibility, giving them the opportunity to absorb data outside of, or marginal to, their lessons while pursuing more directed achievement goals. Another broad study by Hamilton supported these general conclusions.[†]

---

*K. J. Klauer, "Intentional and Incidental Learning with Instructional Tests: A Meta-Analysis, 1970–1980," *American Educational Research Journal,* 21 (1984): 323–39.
[†]R. J. Hamilton, "A Framework for the Evaluation of the Effectiveness of Adjunct Questions and Objectives," *Review of Educational Research,* 55 (1985): 47–86.

Didactic Objectives.   Informational or didactic objectives, as discussed here, are those aimed at increasing students' knowledge, definitions, and ideas. Didactic objectives state how a student will recall certain information. Typically these objectives make use of words like the following:

imitate	review	note
list	repeat	write
recall	tell	separate
recite	label	categorize
identify	arrange	measure
define	present	draw
locate	use	find

The following are examples of information-oriented behavioral objectives:

1. After five lecture presentations on Arab–Israeli relations, students will be able to identify accurately each of the main positions in the dispute.
2. Given three periods for library research on the French Revolution, students will return to class with a chronology of events from 1789 through 1797.
3. As preparation for a panel discussion of capitalism, socialism, and communism, students will record the definitions of these terms citing at least two different sources for each idea.
4. At the end of a course of study on non-Western cultures, students will, on the average in posttest, increase the recall of dates, names, and places by at least 50 percent over pretest survey scores.

5. On completing a reading of selections from the Federalist Papers, students will draw lots for one section and read it out loud to the class, stopping to define terms as questions arise.

6. Using a set of directions to research a bibliography for an essay on the American presidency, students will spend at least two hours in the library assembling an accurate list of twelve or more books, articles, and news sources.

Note that knowledge objectives are usually quite specific and demand relatively little in the way of critical thought, but they do provide direction for building a rich knowledge base. Questions give students the opportunity to move "beyond the data given" to higher objectives that call for reflection and value judgment.

TO DO

Select a topic of interest to you and make a list of ten "facts" you think students should know. If you cut this list down, how would you set priorities?

Reflective Objectives.   Reflective objectives are used to promote critical intelligence and lead students to analyze and apply alternative definitions, explanations, and theories to their knowledge, or draw these out of the data. The objectives call for analysis, application, and synthesis rather than simply recall or comprehension. Knowledge is a necessary, but insufficient part of fulfilling a reflective objective.

Reflective objectives may require a variety of tasks, from giving relatively simple explanations to formulating high-level generalizations about human behavior. Typically, key words used in developing reflective objectives include the following:

compare	decide	predict
contrast	analyze	conceptualize
hypothesize	generalize	distinguish
interpret	rule	summarize
translate	detect	infer
judge	question	apply
evaluate	conclude	imagine
extrapolate	interpolate	estimate
debate	negotiate	support
prove	criticize	dramatize

The following are examples of reflectively oriented behavioral objectives:

1. While reading selected portions of Jean-Jacques Rousseau's *Social Contract*, students will define the difference between the author's concept of "The General Will" and "The Particular Will" in their own words until there is a general consensus about the meaning.

2. On completion of a semester's study in world history, students will apply their knowledge of the American, French, Russian, and Chinese revolu-

tions to Crane Brinton's theory in *The Anatomy of Revolution*, deciding whether the author's interpretation has been proven or disproven (for the most part) by their own investigation.

3. Based on at least a half-dozen case studies about race relations in the United States, students will evolve and test hypotheses about the underlying factors that promote or inhibit prejudice.

4. Role-playing in a computer simulation game that mimics international diplomatic bargaining between great political powers over a period of two weeks, students will develop hypotheses and generalizations about the difficulties and triumphs in reaching mutually agreeable compromises on issues between competing national interests.

5. Using four autobiographies and four novels by Asian authors as the basis for insights into non-Western cultures, students will compare and contrast their view of Asia on a written pretest and posttest.

6. Reacting to current events in which news reports describe civil unrest and conflict (in Eastern Europe), students will evaluate at least three broadcasts, separating as best they can "fact" from opinion using a content analysis scheme to check for biased language and internal consistency.

Reflective objectives demand skills of reasoning and problem solving by students, with evidence used to support or reject theories. The evidence itself is open to questions about bias, accuracy, and completeness. To achieve reflective objectives you must allow time for the students to find problems, consider alternatives, reach conclusions, and test generalizations over and over again against new data and new criteria. At the heart of reflection lies a sense of inquiry and questioning, and a predisposition to skepticism; there is doubt that conclusions are ever final and trustworthy. Objectives that call for reflection are a natural step up from the didactic, providing a platform above which philosophies and viewpoints will be examined.

TO DO

> Write three reflective objectives for a unit on either Greece and Rome or China. Of these three objectives which, if any, would you say is more important than the others? Why?

Affective Objectives.   Affective objectives are defined here as those that develop questions of feeling, of commitment, and of worth on a subject or issue. Affective values cover the entire gamut of commitment from vague feelings of "liking or disliking" to high-level philosophic judgments about good and evil. Ultimately, all values involve a charge of positive and negative emotions that implicitly or explicitly support or oppose an idea or viewpoint. Proof of one's position must rest on assumptions, a rationale, and evidence, but there is always room for doubt and there are always alternatives available even in a well-developed justification.

Awareness, feelings, and opinions represent lower level affective states, whereas reasoned choices, priorities, positions taken, and moral judgments represent the higher ground. Although value objectives promote student decisions, simply stating which choices are available on a given issue does not insure that students will come to grips in a personal way with ethical, moral, or policy problems. You must request reasons for their decisions and build an atmosphere of tolerance for alternative viewpoints for a deeper analysis to occur. Thus, affective objectives are written for developing reasoned opinions, viewpoints, and stands based on the study and analysis of controversies. Certain key words and phrases, usually indicating judgment—approval or disapproval—characterize affective objectives, including the following:

assess	appreciate	beneficial
good	depreciate	harmful
bad/evil	believe/believe in	encourage
best	ought/ought not	discourage
better	justify	foster
worse	judge	inhibit
worst	decide	accept
sympathy	support	reject
empathy	should/should not	like/love
right	preference	dislike/hate
wrong		

The following assortment of affective objectives is presented as a sample of the types you might write in behavioral format for your lessons, units, and course plans:

1. After reading a novel about an anti-Semitic incident, students will discuss the causes and consequences of prejudice for both victims and victimizers.

2. Given biographical and policy information about two leading candidates in a local or national election, students will publicly express and defend their opinions of each during two class periods based on the politicians' qualifications, proposals, image, and external criteria.

3. While considering the policies of the Reconstruction period in the United States through Northern and Southern viewpoints, students will assess whether the policies and laws of the Radical Republicans were of benefit to the nation as a whole.

4. Using a Milton Friedman *Free to Choose* videotape on health care as a springboard for discussion, students will listen to, analyze, and judge arguments for and against government intervention in the field of health care, deciding on an economic policy they can defend as most reasonable.

5. Completing a month-long unit on the Enlightenment, French Revolution, and Napoleonic eras using texts and original sources, students will form court panels and select prosecutors, defense attorneys, and judges, placing on trial Louis XIV, Louis XVI, and Napoleon according to criteria—of their own invention—and research.

6. Reviewing several different concepts of justice, Western and non-Western, students will compare and contrast these concepts as they work to refine a definition of justice that they see as promoting the most good and least harm.

Affective objectives call into play students' judgmental skills, which can range from an awareness of personal preferences to defensible ethical positions with universal applications, such as those on ecology, defense, or poverty. In a sense, deciding what is approved of or disapproved of is a first step toward developing a viewpoint supported by reasons. Eventually a set of consistent philosophical or moral rules is created to guide daily decisions and actions. Loftier goals are, of course, not necessarily attained by all or even most students, or by us for that matter, but such goals give purpose and direction to studies as ideals to strive toward. Your purpose is to help students become aware of their own biases, choices, and preferences, to review these in the light of different viewpoints and rationales, and to help students integrate personal, social, and universal values into a coherent, meaningful whole.

LET'S DECIDE

> Which values do we want students to consider? With the assistance and advice of several classmates or colleagues, select five values or beliefs (e.g., justice) and build this into objectives for at least three different units. Are you more comfortable writing objectives from a value or from a topic? Why?

Conclusions About Objectives

Value or affective objectives draw on a reflective process, just as reflection depends on a base of information. All three types of goals are intertwined into a whole, each aiming for somewhat different but related outcomes. Within each lesson, unit, or course, there usually is, and ought to be, room for one or more didactic, reflective, and affective goals. Almost all data suggest multiple inferences (hence, objectives to match), some concerning the data themselves, some dealing with contrasting interpretations, and others fixed on moral or ethical issues. For example, wars, a regular part of most social studies courses, can be easily discussed in terms of each of the different types of objectives. World War II must be discussed with a knowledge of events, with analyses of the short- and long-range developments that precipitated conflict, and with ethical consideration of its atomic conclusion and the beginning of the Cold War. Because most topics contain within them the potential for knowledge accumulation, for reflection about explanations, and for position taking on ethical questions, it follows that each lesson should be planned in terms of didactic, reflective, and affective objectives.

TO DO

> Make a list of at least five topics you would like to teach as part of a world or American studies course, for example, the Mexican Revolution of 1911, Industrialization in eighteenth- and nineteenth-century Europe, The Kingdom of Songhay in Africa, the Development of Buddhism in Asia, the women's rights movement in nineteenth-century America.
>
> Prepare a didactic, reflective, and affective objective for each topic, and for a topic of your own choice if you so desire. Share your objectives with another person.

PLANNING A CIVIL WAR UNIT

Setting Objectives

Perhaps the first thing that springs to mind about your students is that they need to have the facts about the U.S. Civil War. So, you, the teacher, turn to references about the Civil War and you discover that there are far too many bits and pieces of information to learn and that many of these are connected to particular interpretations of the causes and consequences of the war. Furthermore, some of the more recent books by historians and social scientists seem to wholly reinterpret the event, often offering conflicting theories to explain the same events.[4] Finally, many authors dealing with Civil War topics raise difficult and disturbing value questions, particularly about slavery and race relations, attacking the messages and meaning of both primary and secondary sources.[5]

To give youngsters a sense of the richness of both data and theories, you decide on several objectives, starting with the informational and progressing to the interpretational and judgmental; written in a behavioral format, these objectives take the following form:

1. Given a list of the most important names, dates, and places of the U.S. Civil War, students will be able to identify correctly at least 50 percent more of these items on a posttest than they did on a pretest.

2. After reading at least three different narratives covering the prewar period, students will compare and contrast the explanations of causes offered, drawing their own conclusions about which factors were most important.

3. Through an in-depth discussion of slavery from original sources, slave and free, Northern, Southern, and foreign, students will develop an overview of the different feelings, pro and con, about the institution and the reasons and emotions underlying each position.

4. By reading, discussing, and analyzing an exchange of letters between a slave owner and a runaway slave, students will decide which party is on the higher moral ground.

5. Serving on a panel of Supreme Court justices, each of whom has been given a biography or resume that reflects the pre-Civil War era, students will research the different positions for or against the plaintiff in the Dred Scott case and render a written decision after hearing testimony from witnesses and attorneys, while a second panel retries the case from a present-day perspective.

6. Subsequent to the trial, students will consider the principles of "equal justice for all" and "equality under the law" in modern contexts with a view to determining whether those principles are followed during the present and examining the consequences of meeting or denying the ideal.

A variety of materials is needed for this range of objectives to fulfill your didactic, reflective, and affective goals, including a mix of original sources, fact sheets of names and places, conflicting interpretations of the events, and perhaps a few philosophical excerpts dealing with conflict and abolitionism.

TO DO

> Add two goals of your own to those already listed. Are any of the goals not to your liking? If they are not, why?

The Civil War produced a great deal of folklore, song, and story before it ended. Much of this material was written or handed down by oral traditions. The following camp song and a poem, from sources collected just after the war, are characteristic of the feelings people had about the event:

The Song of the Camps

Far away in the piny woods, Where the dews fall heavy and damp,
A soldier sat by the smouldering fire,
    And sang the song of the camp.

"It is not to be weary and worn,
    It is not to feel hunger and thirst,
It is not the forced march, nor the terrible fight,
    That seems to the soldier the worst;

"But to sit through the comfortless hours,—
    The lonely, dull hours that will come,—
With his head in his hands, and his eyes on the fire,
    And his thoughts on visions of home;

"To wonder how fares it with those
    Who mingled so late with his life,—
Is it well with my little children three?
    Is it well with my sickly wife?

"This night-air is chill, to be sure,
    But logs lie in plenty around;
How is it with them where wood is so dear,
    And the cash for it hard to be found?

"O, that north air cuts bitterly keen,
    And the ground is hard as a stone;
It would comfort me just to know that they sit
    By a fire as warm as my own.

"And have they enough to eat?
    My lads are growing boys,
And my girl is a little tender thing,
    With her mother's smile and voice.

"My wife she should have her tea,
    Or maybe a sup of beer;
It went to my heart to look on her face,
    So white, with a smile and a tear.

"Her form it is weak and thin,—
    She would gladly work if she could,—
But how can a woman have daily strength
    Who wants for daily food?

"My oldest boy he can cut wood,
    And Johnny can carry it in;
But then, how frozen their feet must be
    If their shoes are worn and thin!

"I hope they don't cry with the cold—
    Are there tears in my little girl's eyes?
O God! say peace! to these choking fears,
    These fears in my heart that rise.

"Many rich folks are round them, I know,
    And their hearts are not hard nor cold;
They would give to my wife if they only knew,
    And my little one three years old.

"They would go, like God's angels fair,
    And enter the lowly door,
And make the sorrowful glad with gifts
    From their abundant store.

"In this blessed Christmas-time,
    When the great gift came to men,
They would show, by their gentle and generous deeds
    How He cometh in hearts again.

"And my sickly, patient wife,
    And my little children three,
Would be kindly warmed and fed and clothed
    As part of Christ's family.

"Well, I leave it all with God,
    For my sight is short and dim;
He cares for the falling sparrow;
    My dear ones are safe with Him."

So the soldier watched through the night,
    Through the dew-fall, heavy and damp;
And as he sat by the smouldering fire,
    He sang the song of the camp.*

The Dead Drummer Boy

MIDST tangled roots that lined the wild ravine,
    Where the fierce fight raged hottest through the day,
And where the dead in scattered heaps were seen,
Amid the darkling forest's shade and sheen,
    Speechless in death he lay.

The setting sun, which glanced athwart the place
    In slanting lines, like amber-tinted rain,
Fell sidewise on the drummer's upturned face,
Where Death had left his gory finger's trace
    In one bright crimson stain

No more his hand the fierce tattoo shall beat,
    The shrill reveille, or the long roll's call,
Or sound the charges, when, in smoke and heat
Of fiery onset, foe with foe shall meet,
    And gallant men shall fall.

Yet may be in some happy home, that one,
    A mother, reading from the list of dead,
Shall chance to view the name of her dead son,
And move her lips to say, "God's will be done!"
    And bow in grief her head.

But more than this what tongue shall tell his story?
    Perhaps his boyish longings were for fame.
He lived, he died; and so memento mori.
Enough if on the page of War and Glory
    Some hand has writ his name.†

In the camp song, what is the soldier really unhappy about? What are his most deeply felt worries? What are his immediate worries for himself? Are all soldiers faced with the same problems? Did the Civil War produce especially great difficulties for the common soldiers and ordinary citizens? Why or why not?

What attitudes are expressed by the poet in the "Dead Drummer Boy"? Why is the soldier looking down at a boy? What was the boy doing on the field of battle? How would you describe the mood of the poem? What fears and emotions are given expression?

---

*"The Song of the Camps," in *The Civil War in Song and Story, 1860–1865*, collected and arranged by Frank Moore (New York: P. F. Collier, 1882), p. 525.

†"The Dead Drummer Boy," in *The Civil War in Song and Story, 1860–1865*, collected and arranged by Frank Moore (New York: P. F. Collier, 1882), p. 51.

Choosing a Strategy

The overall strategy stresses a mystery—why the U.S. Civil War moved from a phase of political negotiation and compromise to one of open warfare between people of the same nation, indeed, even between members of the same families. Slave ownership is discussed in detail with statistics throwing doubt on the slavery issues because relatively few citizens even in the deep South owned slaves. Within the overall strategy, other strategies are employed. Data-gathering techniques are used when dealing with the accumulation of historical events and personalities that played a role in cementing the conflict. A frame-of-reference approach guides the treatment of different viewpoints on slavery. Comparison and contrast is used to analyze the alternative theories advanced to explain the causes and consequence of the war. Drama building is accomplished through the choice of powerful original sources, which are used to further the process of making judgments about the veracity of witnesses, the validity of interpretations, and the ethical strengths or weaknesses of those attacking or defending slavery as a system.

Throughout, your major strategy is still that of mystery, as you work toward a satisfying explanation of the Civil War. As the students absorb different bits and pieces of evidence and theory, ask them to generalize or hypothesize about the causes of civil conflict as a concept of human behavior. Encourage them to create tentative proposals about human action that can be applied to successive examples in history, past or present, of civil wars. Note that the mystery device proposed as an overall strategy is close to teaching traditions (i.e., "causes of the Civil War" lessons) with several twists that make the program more interesting, demanding, and conducive to critical thought by students.

SAMPLE LESSON PLAN

The book order on the French Revolution did not arrive. You are starting that unit tomorrow. You have not even had the chance to call the book company and find out the reason for the delay. A few day's grace is what you need, but how can you accomplish this at the last minute and still do a worthwhile lesson? Aha! A film. You go to the video store next morning and rent a film for discussion: in the foreign category is *Danton*, an excellent film with subtitles starring Gerard Depardieu; in the domestic category, you can always go with the old version of *A Tale of Two Cities*, starring Ronald Coleman, or maybe the classic film *Napoleon* by Abel Gance. Rent two or three. Why not, it's such a good subject!

Other strategies could also have been employed: The Civil War in the United States lends itself beautifully to a drama approach using media and literature, or to a frame-of-reference strategy using autobiographies and biographies. A controversial issues design could also work, calling attention to the many ethical and moral questions posed by the war, government policy, economics, race relations, slavery, the Bill of Rights, and the question of human dignity.

If one strategy is paramount, the others will suffer relative neglect. Some questions will rise to the forefront of discussion and others will decline in importance. Unfortunately, you cannot accomplish all that is desired and there must, therefore, be a trade-off among strategies. Your involvement, the questions posed, and the raw material will shape students' thinking and channel it into a mystery or an issues direction. Whereas much can be done with both dimensions, you should consider how easily a lesson or a unit can get away from you if you try to do too much at once. The more you reinforce a strategy, the sooner students will demonstrate an ability to discuss and debate the causes of the Civil War freely. Much depends on what you want to accomplish in terms of your objectives and which strategy is given top priority over the others.

TO DO

> You could easily teach about the Civil War using a different strategy, couldn't you? Redevelop the entire strategy from a values or affective viewpoint. What would change and what would remain the same?

Daily Lessons: A Unit in the Curriculum

Because the overall strategy for this unit is directed at solving the mystery of civil conflict, it should probably contain a sampling from the following categories of data:

1. One Class Period—pretest of students' familiarity with important names, dates, and places about the U.S. Civil War, including pretest questions that probe students' stereotypes concerning causes of the war: slavery, divergent cultures, economic expansion, and so on (to set up a baseline for later comparison).

2. One Class Period—major chronological events before, during, and after the U.S. Civil War, with a map of key events (to build a base of evidence and familiarity with people and actions).

3. Three or Four Class Periods—contemporary accounts of the North and South, and of slavery, culture, and economics by Northerners, Southerners, foreigners, slaves, and slave owners (to create an awareness and understanding of the contrasting attitudes toward the institutions and issues of the nations's two sections).

4. Two Class Periods—statistics, where available, covering the economic structures of the North and the South, armed forces, numbers of slaves, slave owners, and free Blacks (to encourage analysis of the evidence leading to a test of the theory that slavery alone was the key or sole issue in producing conflict).

5. Two Class Periods—Civil War photographs, pictures of people of the times, famous Matthew P. Brady photos of the death and destruction characteristic of the battlefield, of "brother fighting brother" (to create a sense of

drama and feeling for the war's participants and to set the stage for raising ethical issues about conflict).

6. Two or Three Class Periods—several brief alternative interpretations of the causes of the Civil War by scholars in the field, and at least two or three brief excerpts from U.S. and/or foreign viewpoints (to demonstrate that the same evidence may suggest different theories to those who have studied the problem, setting the stage for students to decide for themselves which is the "best" or most reasonable explanation).

7. One or Two Class Periods—a few excerpts from philosophers and/or social scientists who theorize about justice and social interactions, offering different views of stable and unstable, just and unjust, human relationships (to use as springboards for discussing slavery and warfare as ethical issues, e.g., does conflict resolve problems? Can an unjust state be stable? How can we define justice and dignity? Which is more important—economic rights, states' rights, or freedom and national unity?).

8. One or Two Class Periods—news accounts, information flashes on recent or current civil conflicts, such as in Yugoslavia, Nigeria, Cambodia, or North Ireland (to show the persistence of civil problems; the persistence of questions of rights, justice, and human dignity).

9. One Class Period—panel discussion (with several students playing roles in a past time and several students acting as present-day newspaper or TV reporters, each of whom must review and comment on and evaluate some mystery of the U.S. Civil War (to recapitulate the previous data aiming at building judgments that the group will evaluate in trying to settle on a best consensus interpretation of the whole).

10. One Class Period—posttest of students' grasp of the basic information and of their acceptance, rejection, or revision of previously expressed conceptions "explaining" the Civil War and Reconstruction periods (to assess the degree to which knowledge and understanding of the Civil War period and of historical thinking have increased, decreased, or grown more confused).

LET'S DECIDE

With several others, decide to add one or two new lessons to the overall plan. Are there any missing features that you think should be filled in? Should any be omitted? Write one or two additions with your group and share these with other groups.

Expectations: Planning for Evaluation

Expectations for student growth may be reasonably optimistic given the choice of materials, the teaching plan, questions posed, and the amount of time and attention given to discussion and student participation. Students will have had the opportunity to analyze, discuss, and evaluate a wide variety of material about the U.S. Civil War. Keep in mind, however, that the data used are far less than what is available, and there are gaps in both the information given and the theories presented. Nevertheless, for secondary students, you can be satisfied that they have a structure from which to view the Civil War period and its aftermath. They also have a framework for discussing civil conflict in general from both a social scientific/behavioral and from a philosophical/ethical standpoint. Furthermore, students have had the opportunity to think about and make decisions concerning present-day issues embedded in American history. If pretest–posttest results show satisfactory growth by students and participation was high, you may consider yourself as having reached satisfactory levels of achievement.

TO DO

Write a twenty-item multiple choice test for a Civil War unit that could be used as both a pre- and a postmeasure of student achievement. Gear questions to the top issues and events. Add at least two essay questions that raise problems about slavery in the United States. Decide how you will judge students' answers to these essay topics. Set up clear and precise criteria.

A Sample Lesson on Civil War Issues

Looking through both original and secondary sources is a vital part of planning any secondary school unit, and you should make yourself familiar with a variety of different materials that contain the evidence you want students to consider. Students may contribute to the storehouse of knowledge through their own research, but you must build the framework for them unless they have had previous experience carrying out historiographical inquiry.

The U.S. Civil War, though an "old chestnut" of a topic in the social studies, offers us far too much data to deal with easily. In addition, there are many built-in problems because much of the information and many accounts are biased from a Northern or Southern point of view, sometimes overtly and at other times very subtly. Therefore, you should review and balance sources to adjust for divergent points of view, both to present a fair sample of opinion and to encourage critical thinking about which knowledge is trustworthy.

Art, music, and literature should be regarded as potential bases for lessons as well as documents, biographies, and narrative histories. For the U.S. Civil War period, a much studied event, there is a wealth of material from which to choose. One such example of a lesson is based on two letters between a slave owner, Mrs. Sarah Logue of Tennessee, and her runaway slave, the Reverend J. W. Loguen, now of Syracuse, New York. Mrs. Logue's letter was dated February 29, 1860, and the Reverend Loguen's reply was written March 28, 1860.

Two Letters: An Exchange Between Slave and Slave-Owner (1860)

[a] The Slaveholder's Letter

To Jarm: I now take my pen to write you a few lines, to let you know how we all are. I am a cripple, but I am still able to get about. The rest of the family are all well. Cherry is as well as common. I write you these lines to let you know the situation we are in—partly in consequence of your running away and stealing Old Rock, our fine mare. Though we got the mare back, she never was worth much after you took her; and, as I now stand in need of some funds I have determined to sell you, and I have had an offer for you, but did not see fit to take it. If you will send me one thousand dollars, and pay for the old mare, I will give up all claim I have on you. Write to me as soon as you get these lines, and let me know if you will accept my proposition. In consequence of your running away, we had to sell Abe and Ann and twelve acres of land; and I want you to send me the money, that I may be able to redeem the land that you was the cause of our selling, and on receipt of the above-named sum of money, I will send you your bill of sale. If you do not comply with my request, I will sell you to some one else, and you may rest assured that the time is not far distant when things will be change with you. Write to me as soon as you get these lines. Direct your letter to Bigbyville, Maury County, Tennessee. You had better comply with my request.

I understand that you are a preacher. As the Southern people are so bad you had better come and preach to your old acquaintances. I would like to know if you read your Bible. If so, can you tell what will become of the thief if he does not repent? I deem it unnecessary to say much more at present. A word to the wise is sufficient. You know where the liar has his part. You know that we reared you as we reared our own children: that you was never abased and that shortly before you ran away, when your master asked if you would like to be sold, you said you would not leave him to go with anybody.

[b] The Slave's Letter

Mrs. Sarah Logue: Your letter of the 20th of February is duly received, and I thank you for it. It is a long time since I heard from my poor old mother, and I am glad to know that she is yet alive, and, as you say, "as well as common." What this means, I don't know. I wish you had said more about her.

You are a woman; but, had you a woman's heart, you never could have in-sulted a brother by telling him you sold his only remaining brother and sister, because he put himself beyond your power to convert him into money.

You sold my brother and sister, Abe and Ann, and twelve acres of land, you say, because I ran away. Now you have the unutterable meanness to ask me to return and be your miserable chattel, or in lieu thereof, send you $1000 to en-able you to redeem the land, but not to redeem my poor brother and sister! If I were to send you money, it would be to get my brother and sister, and not that you should get land. You say you are a cripple, and doubtless you say it to stir my pity, for you knew I was susceptible in that direction. I do pity you from the bottom of my heart. Nevertheless, I am indignant beyond the power of words to express, that you should be so sunken and cruel as to tear the hearts I love so much all in pieces; that you should be willing to impale and crucify us all, out of compassion for your poor foot or leg. Wretched woman! Be it known to you that I value my freedom, to say nothing of my mother, brothers and sis-ters, more than your whole body; more, indeed, than my own life; more than all the lives of all the slaveholders and tyrants under heaven.

You say you have offers to buy me, and that you shall sell me if I do not send you a 1000 dollars, and in the same breath and almost in the same sentence, you say "You know we raised you as we did our own children." Woman, did you raise your own children for the market? Did you raise them for the whip-ping-post? Did you raise them to be driven off, bound to a coffle in chains? Where are my poor bleeding brothers and sisters? Can you tell? Who was it that sent them off into sugar and cotton fields, to be kicked and cuffed, and whipped, and to groan and die; and where no kin can hear their groans, or at-tend and sympathize at their dying bed, or follow in their funeral? Wretched woman! Do you say you did not do it? Then I reply, your husband did, and you approved the deed—and the very letter you sent me shows that your heart approves it all. Shame on you!

But, by the way, where is your husband? You don't speak of him. I infer, there-fore, that he is dead; that he has gone to his great account, with all his sins against my poor family upon his head. Poor man! Gone to meet the spirits of my poor, outraged and murdered people, in a world where Liberty and Jus-tice are Masters.

But you say I am a thief, because I took the old mare along with me. Have you got to learn that I had a better right to the old mare, as you call her, than Mannasseth Logue had to me. Is it a greater sin for me to steal his horse, than it was for him to rob my mother's cradle, and steal me? If he and you infer that I forfeit all my rights to you, shall I not infer that you forfeit all your rights to me? Have you got to learn that human rights are mutual and reciprocal, and if you take my liberty and life, you forfeit your own liberty and life? Before God and high heaven, is there a law for one man which is not a law for every other man?

If you or any other speculator on my body and rights, wish to know how I regard my rights, they need but come here, and lay their hands on me to enslave me. Did you think to terrify me by presenting the alternative to give my money to you, or give my body to slavery? Then let me say to you, that I meet the proposition with unutterable scorn and contempt. The proposition is an outrage and an insult. I will not budge one hair's breadth. I will not breathe a shorter breath, even to save me from your persecutions. I stand among a free people, who I thank God, sympathize with my rights, and the rights of mankind; and if your emissaries and vendors come here to re-enslave me, and escape the unshrinking vigor of my own right arm, I trust my strong and brave friends, in this city and State, will be my rescuers and avengers.[6]

After reading these two letters you decide to use them in class to personalize the slavery issue and to raise ethical issues. Your behavioral objectives for the two letters could be the following:

1. Students will review the slavery issues.
2. Students will discuss slavery through the eyes of a runaway slave and a slaveholder.
3. Students will develop arguments, pro and con, on both sides.
4. Students will decide on their own view of slavery in the context of human rights.
5. Students will compare the institution of slavery in the United States with other events and institutions such as South African apartheid and the Holocaust.
6. Students will identify and define their own view of human rights.

Given these objectives, you decide that the letters call for comparison—at least as a beginning:

Strategy (Compare and Contrast).   Ask two students with dramatic abilities to read aloud Mrs. Logue's letter to the Reverend Loguen and then his reply. Meanwhile, ask students to take notes on the letters as each reader proceeds, especially the arguments each presented: Mrs. Logue makes the issue one of property and personal hardship while the Reverend Loguen makes it one of freedom and civil rights. Provoke discussion by asking some students to defend Mrs. Logue while others defend the Reverend Loguen. Develop thought-provoking questions to stimulate discussion, such as the following:

1. Why does Mrs. Logue want $1,000?
2. Why won't Reverend Loguen give her the $1,000?
3. What has Mrs. Logue done to Mr. Loguen's family? Why?
4. Why does Mrs. Logue accuse him of being a thief? Is he a thief in your view? Is he a thief in his own view? Why or why not?
5. Who is right here and who is wrong? And why? What would you have done if you were Mrs. Logue? How about if you were the Reverend Loguen? Who deserves sympathy: both, neither, one or the other? Why?
6. Have human rights abuses been committed here? Is the situation like those you have read about in South Africa? Is it like in Europe during the Holocaust?

7. Which rights do you think Mr. Loguen, and all other people, were and are entitled to and why? Give examples and defend your view.

Conclusion.   Allow one or two periods for a thorough debriefing or review of your Civil War unit in which students are asked to judge which materials they found most or least stimulating, and what they see as the overall learning result on this topic. Where do they feel they received too much data? Too little? Too many questions or too few? Too much theory or too little? Do they believe that their understanding of the event has deepened, that their attitudes have changed toward the participants, or that they have reevaluated heroes and villains? Ask for suggestions to extend or cut your presentation of the Civil War and keep a record of the comments in your log book.

SAMPLE LESSON PLAN

Take a trip to the library and add U.S. Civil War materials to your resource list. Supplement your repertory with at least four or five new collections of primary resources and at least three or four historical and/or social scientific reinterpretations of events. Decide which of the primary documents and which of the revisionist theories you want to share with students.

Some Resources for a Civil War Lesson

Interesting sources to use on the Civil War period are plentiful and provocative, including the following:

Blesser, Carol, ed. *Secret and Sacred, The Diaries of James Henry Itammond, A Southern Slave-holder.* New York: Oxford University Press, 1989.

Commager, Henry S., ed. *The Blue and the Gray: The Story of the Civil War as Told by Participants.* 2 vols. New York: New American Library, 1973.

Davis, Kenneth. *Don't Know Much About the Civil War: Everything You Need to Know About America's Greatest Conflict but Never Learned.* New York: Morrow, 1996.

De Forest, John W. *Miss Ravenal's Change from Secession to Loyalty.* Washington, DC: Reprint Services, 1988 (reprint of 1867 edition).

Douglass, Frederick. *The Frederick Douglass Papers: Speeches, Debates, Interviews, 1855–1863.* New Haven, CT: Yale University Press, 1986.

Foner, Eric, and Olivia Mahoney. *America's Reconstruction: People and Politics after the Civil War.* New York: Harper/Collins, 1995.

Foote, Shelby. *The Civil War: A Narrative.* 3 vols. New York: Random House, 1986.

Freedman, Russell. *Lincoln: A Photo Biography.* London and New York: Ticknor & Fields, 1987.

Genovese, Eugene D., *Roll, Jordan, Roll: The World the Slaves Made.* New York: Random House, 1976.

Harwell, Richard B., ed. *The Union Reader.* White Plains, NY: Longman, 1958.

Horton, Bobby. *Music and Memories of the Civil War.* (VHS cassette, 63 minutes) Alabama Center for Public Televison. New York: PBS, 1995.

Lucent Staff Writers. *Life in the North During the Civil War: The Way People Live. & Life in the South During the Civil War: The Way People Live.* New York: Lucent Press, 1997.

McPherson, James M. *Battle Cry of Freedom: The Civil War Era.* New York: Oxford University Press, 1988.

McPherson, James M. *His Name Was Lincoln: A Multimedia Biography* (2 CD-ROMs, with teacher guides). New York: Sunburst Communications, 1996.

Meltzer, Milton. *Voices from the Civil War.* New York: Thomas Y. Crowell, 1989.

Meredith, Roy. *World of Matthew Brady.* New York: Crown Publishers, 1989.

Meredith, Roy, ed. *Mr. Lincoln's Camera Man: Matthew B. Brady*. New York: Dover Press, 1974.

Murphy, Jim. *The Boys' War: Confederate and Union Soldiers Talk About the Civil War*. New York: Clarion Press, 1990.

Reilly, N. S., ed. *Civil War Maps*. Chicago: Newberry Library, 1987.

Sandburg, Carl. *Abraham Lincoln: The Prairie Years and the War Years*. New York: Harcourt Brace Jovanovich, 1974.

Ward, Geoffrey et al. *The Civil War: An Illustrated History*. New York: Knopf, 1990.

Wiley, Bell Irwin. *Life of Johnny Reb. Life of Bill Yank*. Baton Rouge, LA: Louisiana State University Press, 1971.

SUMMARY

Objectives were used to help you organize and plan for instruction, choose curriculum materials, design a setting, and select the type of strategies you want for your classroom. The division of objectives into didactic, reflective, and affective orientations serve to differentiate between levels of accomplishment and student outcomes. In this chapter, the U.S. Civil War was used as an example for a secondary unit construction. Research on U.S. Civil War documentary sources formed the basis for your presentation and the subsequent discussion by your students. Materials were chosen for suitability, given student maturity and reading levels. A mystery strategy focusing on causes was the major approach to the subject and made use of a number of formats, including role-play and debate. Because goals imply ends, informal and formal evaluation was built into the unit, taking into account the material studied, your methods of presentation, and the achievement levels expected of students.

So, in the best spirit of script writing, keep a checklist of elements for any unit you create:

1. Did you set clear objectives?
2. Did you design a pretest and posttest?
3. Did you use a variety of sources?
4. Did you include "interest provokers" that give a human face to the materials?
5. Did you analyze problems and inconsistencies—discuss the validity/reliability of data?
6. Did you build active participation by a wide array of students?
7. Did you utilize varied group dynamics?
8. Did you relate past events to current events?
9. Did you discuss original sources versus textbook accounts?
10. Did you treat different viewpoints fairly?
11. Did you provide the opportunity to theorize: going beyond the data given?
12. Did you discuss ethical/moral problems and issues?

TO DO

Using your newfound skills of writing behavioral objectives, develop didactic, reflective, and affective objectives for several new units of your own choosing. Once your objectives are established, select materials and a strategy, develop a list of daily lessons, and design evaluation tools for assessing student progress. Do a "start-to-finish" job on the topics you have chosen that is so complete you feel confident enough to walk into your class and begin instruction immediately. We suggest a variety of topics: from U.S. history, Western expansion, the

Monroe Doctrine, or the Great Depression; from World studies, the development of modern India, the Byzantine Empire and the Ottoman Turks, or political and racial conflict in South Africa. Remember to use a wide variety of strategies and sources for your unit: art, music, literature, film, history, and technological invention.

NOTES

1. Robert Mager, *Preparing Instructional Objectives*, 2nd ed. (Palo Alto, CA: Fearon Press, 1975).
2. E. J. Furst, "Bloom's Taxonomy of Educational Objectives for the Cognitive Domain: Philosophical and Educational Issues," *Review of Educational Research*, 51 (1981): 441–59.
3. C. Clark and R. Yinger, "Teacher Planning," in *Talks to Teachers*, ed. D. Berliner and B. Rosenshine (New York: Random House, 1988), pp. 342–65.
4. Eric Foner, *Reconstruction: America's Unfinished Revolution* (New York: Harper & Row, 1988).
5. Dudley Taylor Cornish, *The Sable Arm: Black Troops in the Union Army 1861–1865* (Topeka: University of Kansas Press, 1984).
6. "Two Letters: An Exchange between Slave and Slave-Owner," *The Liberator*, 17 April 1860.

FOR FURTHER STUDY: PLANNING A UNIT FROM START TO FINISH

Beyer, B. *Practical Strategies for the Teaching of Thinking*. Boston: Allyn & Bacon, 1987.

Bloom, B. S. et al. *Taxonomy of Educational Objectives: Handbook I, The Cognitive Domain*. New York: David McKay, 1956.

Dillon, J. T. *Personal Teaching, Efforts to Combine Personal Love and Professional Skill in the Classroom*. Lanham, MD: University Press of America, 1990.

Grabe, M., and C. Grabe. *Integrating Technology for Meaningful Learning*. 2nd ed. Boston: Houghton Mifflin, 1999.

Kallison, J. M. "Effects of Lesson Organization on Achievement." *American Educational Research Journal* 23, no. 2 (1986): 337–47.

Krathwohl, D. R., B. S. Bloom, and B. B. Masia. *Taxonomy of Educational Objectives: Handbook II, The Affective Domain*. New York: David McKay, 1964.

Mager, R. F. *Preparing Instructional Objectives*. 2nd ed. Belmont, CA: Fearon Press, 1975.

Orlich, D. C. et al. *Teaching Strategies: A Guide to Better Instruction*. 3rd ed. Lexington, MA: Heath, 1990.

Ornstein, Allan C. *Strategies for Effective Teaching*. 2nd ed. Dubuque, IA: Brown & Benchmark, 1995.

Posner, George J. *Analyzing the Curriculum*, 2nd ed. New York: McGraw-Hill, 1995.

Powell, M., and J. Solity. *Teachers in Control: Cracking the Code*. London: Routledge, 1990.

Singer, A. J. *Social Studies for Secondary Schools: Teaching to Learn, Learning to Teach*. Mahwah, NJ: Lawrence Erlbaum Associates, 1997.

Steinberg, S. R., and J. Kincheloe. *Students as Researchers: Creating Classrooms that Matter*. Levittown, PA: Falmer Press, 1998.

Walker, D., and J. F. Soltis. *Curriculum and Aims*. New York: Teacher's College Press, 1986.

CHAPTER 8

Evaluation in Social Studies

Don't judge students by what they say or write, but by why they said it!
—Nineteenth-century proverb

OVERVIEW OF CONTENTS

Main Ideas

The Evaluation Process

> The Purposes of Evaluation
> The Types of Evaluation
> Authentic Assessment/Portfolio Construction

Issues in Evaluation

> Reliability and Validity
> Informal Assessment: Dialogue and Discussion
> Pretests and Correlated Surveys
> Giving Final Grades

Designing Tests

> Information-Based Questions
> Document-Based Questions
> Perception-Based Questions

Measuring Student Feelings and Viewpoints

> Student Interest Inventories
> Checklists

Teacher and Course Evaluation

Summary

Author Note

Notes

For Further Study: Evaluation in Social Studies

Addendum: Test Publishers and Distributors

MAIN IDEAS

Feedback on student learning and student opinion is a critically important feature of social studies instruction. Evaluation standards reflect your goals and set levels for student performance. This chapter examines testing and attitude measurement of three types of instruments: those designed to assess didactive goals, those for reflective goals, and those for affective goals. Cognitive testing evaluates student knowledge, basically data or facts; items to accomplish this are termed *information-based questions* (IBQs). Test items that call on students to reason about, interpret, and infer answers from evidence and source material are termed *document-based questions* (DBQs). And, surveys that seek expressions of students' attitudes about social studies, historical figures, controversial issues, or their views of themselves are called *perception-based questions* (PBQs). It is argued here that the vast majority of teacher-made or standardized test questions—whether short answer, multiple choice, or essay—fall into one of these three categories (IBQs, DBQs, and PBQs).

Recently, there is a movement to mix categories in a "portfolio" that provides a demonstration of a broad range of student work that expresses many different skills and talents. Portfolio collections are often called "authentic" or "performance" assessment instruments because the contents reflect what a student's production really looks like rather than their inferred performance on a test. How evaluation instruments are used depends on the teacher, the subject, and official school or state requirements and may involve formative (ongoing) or summative (concluding) testing. Test or survey or portfolio results are discussed as tools to diagnose student and class development and to help teachers arrive at judgments concerning students' levels of achievement for assigned grades.

THE EVALUATION PROCESS

The Purposes of Evaluation

Every day of teaching you must make decisions about student progress and student attitudes. Did Jimmy really have a breakthrough into high-level analysis in our conversation today? Did Matilda wreck her test of Civil War facts because she did not study, or did not feel well? Should José receive the benefit of the doubt for a higher grade because of the rapid rate at which he progressed, even though he is not completely up to standard? Should Mai-lin be given a lower grade on her essay about World War I because her English was poor, even though most of her facts were correct? These are the little problems of evaluation that often make teaching social studies a complex and difficult task.

Evaluation is the organized way in which we gather and interpret evidence to decide how well or how poorly our students are meeting the objectives that have been set for them. In this sense, evaluation is a broad and inclusive concept that encompasses *measurement, testing, opinion polling,* and *self-assessment.* Measurement represents numerically how much or how well someone has absorbed an input involving knowledge, skills, or attitudes. Precise scores are used to express the degree to which students hold a particular belief or the amount of facts they have recalled on a test. Testing, a part of measurement, is a way of sampling behavior so you can estimate someone's abilities and information. Polling (survey research techniques and self-reports) is a way of estimating the strength or weakness of someone's perceptions, values, and feelings about people, events, and issues. Testing and survey research both sample behaviors, but in different areas; the former is largely for didactic and reflective abilities, and the latter is usually for affective expression.

The whole process of evaluation is designed to give you insight into student learning. Thus, evaluation incorporates a wide range of techniques and devices—from formal standardized tests to informal observation and intuition about a student's capabilities. You may also ask students to produce many different kinds of work, written, drawn, acted, and spoken, which they will add to an ongoing "portfolio" of production that you can evaluate as the semester moves along and at its conclusion. Howard Gardner points out that it is important to vary assignments and assessments so more than one of a student's many "multiple intelligences" are allowed to come into play.[1] Eventually, you will use all the data collected to judge a student's overall performance. The more information you have and the greater its variety, the better your judgment will be, both for everyday performance and for overall outcomes.

Ideally, evaluation should be closely tied to the curriculum, your instructional techniques, and your overall course goals. First, the goals must be decided on: Which learning and attitudes are most desirable? Second, find out what students know and believe before you begin instruction: Do students already understand the material you intend to teach? Third, design your curriculum and methodologies to match your goals: Are you using student feedback to monitor progress, to readjust schedules and assignments, and to judge the level of students' understanding? Fourth, prepare a summative test or survey that reflects your original goals, your ongoing analysis of student performance, and the material you taught: Does the final product or examination pull together a fair sample of what was presented? For the best results, goals, curriculum, methods, and tests should match one another closely because this ensures students a fair test of their knowledge and development, and provides you with a reasonably good sample of their behavior. This sample should include a variety of skills, such as test-taking, map-making, narrative and argumentative writing, and so on. A defensible and meaningful grade or judgment is the final product of the evaluation process described in this introduction.

Although assessment provides you with valuable diagnostic information, it also helps you judge a student's output or product, usually at the end of a course of study. Although many of us abhor (and others enjoy) assigning grades, it has become an important, everyday part of school life. Parents, students, and school officials all support a system of examination and evaluation. In fact, the 1980s and early 1990s have seen a trend toward ever-greater reliance on standards of achievement, and standardized tests. However, testing is frequently misapplied; diagnosis is often confused with judgment, and results are often taken too seriously. Nevertheless, testing is an integral part of teaching and must be used as carefully as possible to assure a fair result for students and an honest evaluation of your effectiveness as a teacher.

The Types of Evaluation

Evaluation in secondary social studies conforms to the principles and procedures that apply to education in general. To understand and use modern assessment techniques, you must know the meaning of a variety of commonly used technical terms. For example, cognitive tests are usually distinguished by their purpose and reference points: Is the aim to measure knowledge or thinking skills against a set standard, a personal goal, or a group mean?

Most evaluation is designed to measure learning goals in terms of *cognition*, or knowledge of facts and skill at reasoning from lower to higher levels. Social studies tests, for example, typically seek to assess growth in knowledge of world history, ability to apply economic concepts to new data, or skill in writing an argument defending or attacking a controversial position. However, there are also facets of social studies for which affective measures are most appropriate—

measures of attitude, opinion, and self-perception. These are generally viewed as psychological instruments that follow rules different from tests used to assess cognitive outcomes.

Attitudes, for instance, are products of perceptions about the world or the self, which can be scaled (ranked) according to their emotional strength or weakness on a given topic or issue. Cognitive examinations measure factual knowledge and analytical skills that can usually be judged as correct or incorrect, better or worse, but that are ultimately based on research and established criteria for logic. Thus, the two major branches of evaluation divide along the lines of goals and methods. The didactic and reflective branch is oriented toward assessing factual knowledge and reasoning ability, and the affective branch is oriented toward diagnosing attitudes, opinions, and self-image. There are also "gray areas" in social studies testing when questions are difficult to classify, particularly those involving judgmental skills. Because judgment incorporates both cognitive and affective components, perceptions and knowledge may influence student answers, making teacher assessment more difficult.

There are several ways to classify evaluation methods, but most deal with two concepts basic to the analysis of performance: *centrality* and *quality*. Centrality is usually used to discuss what constitutes the "normal," or average, achievement levels of students. It can also apply to interests, attitudes, and opinions insofar as these represent widely held views. Quality is often used as a metaphor for high-level achievements. Cronbach labeled these two ideas *maximum performance* and *typical performance*.[2] Both are vital elements in the evaluation process because knowledge of the typical, average, or central gives you insight into what to expect from most of your students. Quality, or "maximum," measures demonstrate the upper limits of knowledge, ability, and skill, or the unusual nature of opinions and values (two or more standard deviations from the mean).

WHAT DO YOU THINK?

TEST TERMINOLOGY

Standardized or Informal Tests/Polls: Standardized tests or surveys are constructed by experts and subjected to one or more field tests; informal tests or polls are those created by a teacher and/or a team of students.

Group or Individual Tests/Polls: Often, tests or polls are administered on a case-by-case basis (e.g., a personal interview), whereas others, more commonly, are given to groups.

Survey Tests or Mastery Tests: Usually, survey tests (whether didactic, reflective, or affective) are norm-referenced, seeking "typical" results or averages; on the other side, mastery examinations usually are criterion-referenced and seek to measure specific skills against established criteria.

Selection or Supply Tests: Selection tests or polls ask students to choose from ready-made alternative answers, and "supply" tests, such as fill-ins or essays, require students to provide the answers.

Power or Speed Tests: Power questions (usually reflective in nature) provide students with enough time to reach their highest level of performance and speed tests place students under specific time pressures to finish their work.

Objective or Subjective Tests: Objective simply means that, because answers are previously established, an examination is scored the same for all; in contrast, with subjective tests the reader's or evaluator's opinion determines the final score or grade.

Product or Performance Tests: Product or performance work means that a student must complete written, artistic, or active/oral presentations in a form, package, or portfolio that can be judged against set or established criteria (rubrics), or in comparison with the work of others in a class or group.

Questions:
1. Based on these definitions, what purposes do tests serve?
2. Why have different types of tests been developed?
3. Which skills do tests test?
4. In what ways are polls and surveys like or unlike cognitive tests? Why have many tests been field tested for use on a national basis?
5. When might you want a student to complete an oral examination, or present you with a portfolio of their work? Would such material be easy or difficult to judge in comparison to "objective" or multiple choice tests?

When you set arbitrary standards for passing a test (even if this is a minimum figure), such as 75 percent, you are in effect evaluating a maximum performance. If you assess scores in terms of averages, these serve as measures of the "typical" result. This might also be called an average, or usual, performance. A maximum holds students to a set standard, and a normal curve measures individual performance against the typical distribution of group scores. Neither type of evaluation is necessarily correct or incorrect. Each has a place in a social studies classroom depending on your goals and your diagnosis of audience skills and capabilities.

Authentic Assessment/Portfolio Construction

Standardized methods, however, give only a broad picture of a student's productivity—whereas "authentic" assessments and portfolio concepts provide a detailed personal review for each learner. An authentic assessment (so-called because it reflects the actual, ongoing activities of a learner), requires that you develop a series of related assignments and exercises that students must complete, each of which calls on them to express or demonstrate the knowledge and different skills that they possess in social studies. The goal for authentic or portfolio assessment is to obtain a picture of "the whole child or young person," not simply the student's test performance on a paper- and pencil-examination[3] (see portfolio example in the appendix).

Because the child or young person is growing, changing, and absorbing new ideas, the portfolio assessment should give teachers the opportunity to judge the amount and quality of student development. Portfolios are formative measures based on criteria set by you and your students, a committee, your school, or by any of the national subject matter standards that have been created for history, geography, civics, and economics. A well-designed portfolio assessment should (a) be purposeful, systematic, and meaningful; (b) promote student selection and judgment of products; (c) permit input from parents, teachers, and administrators; (d) reflect daily assignments and activities; (e) accumulate over a long period of time; (f). encourage revision and rethinking of contents; and (g) include many different media in a variety of forms.

As you can gather, portfolio or authentic assessment takes a broad view of human development and focuses on growth over time, with participation by the learner in setting standards for judgment. There is no "rush to judgment" by you or anyone else, because students may select their best work for inclusion in their final portfolio, tidying up and revising any products they see as weak or unpresentable before submitting the total package for a mark or grade. This is very different from a quick quiz or a standardized test, and tells you a great deal more about what is going on in a student's mind than number scores alone. The contents of the portfolio can include anything and everything that you believe will reveal evidence of student progress or lack of development. Portfolios in social studies, much like those in art (from which the concept is borrowed), might include notes, reflective writing, arguments and essays, peer reviews, videotapes, photographs, paintings and drawings, musical or audio tapes, descriptions, rough drafts of unfinished work, diagrams, graphs, and charts, group products, and computer-generated materials.[4] As much as possible, all items selected for inclusion in the portfolio should be "authentically" that of students, and their group. Copied or plagiarized materials have no place, unless clearly used or reinterpreted by the student for a reason. With this wealth of productivity to choose from, the portfolio permits continuous diagnosis by you, and the pupil, of how far and how deeply this student has progressed in the subject you are presenting.

Quality in a "portfoliio classroom" is always measured against established criteria that are shared with students. Students are allowed to choose their own projects and review their own performances before submitting final projects, or selections from their production, to the teacher or committee for evaluation. Projects should include a sample of long- and short-term work and a variety of expression (i.e., oral, written, drawn, or constructed). In addition, experiences with portfolios often produce more critical minded students, who often turn into "harder graders" than their teachers. Although "typical-ness" is frequently hard to ascertain in an authentic assessment situation, quality is easier to measure than most teachers think because work is continuously evaluated by the student, classmates, teachers, and other critics set against agreed-on criteria or rubrics. For example, a set of rubrics would specify high, medium, and poor performances in history. These might involve such standards as (a) understanding cause and effect, (b) drawing inferences from primary sources, and (c) comparing and/or contrasting primary with secondary sources.

High Quality Performance. Knowledge of history is extensive and students can draw historical inferences using both primary and secondary sources; students can consistently judge reliable and unreliable historical witnesses; students can regularly point out cause and effect relations in events; students can develop a project, such as a travel brochure, that accurately and imaginatively reflects research on a time period and place using both primary and secondary sources.

Medium Quality Performance. Knowledge of history is considerable and students can support ideas with texts and sources, sometimes drawing inferences and judgments; students usually tell reliable and unreliable witnesses apart; students understand cause and effect relations most of the time; students can develop a project that uses either primary or secondary sources, such as constructing a "newspaper from the past" of modest length.

Low Quality Performance. Knowledge of history is limited and student knowledge is factual in nature rather than inferential; students can understand the concept of bias and reliability, but sometimes confuse primary and secondary sources; students can partially interpret original sources, but usually are more comfortable taking notes from history textbooks using the text as a guide to events; students are capable of a small-scale project, such as creating a postcard from the past.

In line with measures of typicality and quality, there are three main ways of using results to understand student outcomes on tests, products, and surveys. One way is to relate the individual's actions to those of a researched group: Elliot's map interpretations were better than those of 80 percent of his classmates. This type is a norm-referenced test because it is a measure of someone's performance relative to a known group. A second way to interpret evaluation results is by specifying which actions match a criterion for success. This is a criterion- or objective-referenced test: Melanie correctly identified eighteen of twenty nations on an outline map, with twenty the maximum possible score. A third way involves measuring a student's own performance against a previous one. Assessing growth and change is the goal for personal measures. For instance, you and the student could compare three attempts at drawing a map of the world from memory, or contrast written arguments for or against a public issue from the beginning, middle, and end of the school year. In the first type, performance is judged against a "normal," or "typical," result that we actually know about based on previous measures of other student groups. In the second type, performance is measured against a specific teaching objective, a criterion or rubric for success. In the third type, productivity is measured against a baseline set by the student's earlier, or ongoing, performance.

Whatever goals are assessed—didactic, reflective, or affective—results can be interpreted either from a norm-referenced or a criterion-referenced viewpoint, often with quite different conclusions. Therefore, your overall course objectives are a key element in any assessment scheme. Your objectives, general or specific, may apply to the group as a whole and to each individual within it.

A third concept of evaluation rests on function rather than form, that is, the use to which a survey or test is directed in a classroom. Benjamin Bloom and colleagues suggest that there are several major uses for evaluation, for example, (a) placement (early judgment for intake); (b) formative (ongoing judgment), including diagnostic and appraisal; and (c) summative (final decisions for grading and evaluation of performance).[5] In brief, tests and surveys or self-reports can be used to judge the level at which students are operating before they are placed in a new setting or program. Knowing an individual's predisposition, interests, and mastery of a body of material are key to understanding which tasks are needed in a learning sequence. Placement procedures might involve assessing personality type, determining individual learning style, or finding out how much a student already knows about U.S. history. Assessment could be conducted through teacher-made pretests, formal standardized aptitude tests, cognitive mapping or semantic webbing, surveys of feelings about a subject, your own observations, a final portfolio of student work, or a combination of the aforementioned.

Formative evaluation refers to tests used to acquire feedback from students about their ongoing work and attitude development. Formative testing is usually designed to examine small increments within a larger scheme, providing a demonstration of student performance so you can adjust your program. Quizzes might show that students need more or less data on a topic, higher or lower levels of inquiry, or a faster or slower pace of instruction. If a portfolio is being accumulated, then each essay could be compared with the previous one to discern any improvements in style, reasoning, or analysis of primary sources. A test on economics, for instance, might show widespread misunderstanding of the comparative advantage concept, implying the need for review and application; a test on Civil War facts could show virtually complete absorption of the material, indicating that you should move on to the Reconstruction unit that follows. Thus, there are different ways to think about evaluation, and special terms for discussing testing and attitudes. Using our three-category conception of instruction and assessment, Figure 8.1 summarizes ways in which different aspects of assessment intersect.

Figure 8.1 shows how evaluation goals intersect with the didactic, reflective, and affective dimensions. Assessment can take place at all levels as both an ongoing and end-of-course process. Students may be measured against absolute standards or against averages derived from "normal" performance. The greater the variety of testing, the broader and more comprehensive will be your picture of both the individuals in your classes and groups as a whole.

WHAT DO YOU THINK?

Which types of tests have you taken or given recently: norm-referenced or criterion-referenced; maximum or typical; summative or formative? What, in your opinion, are the advantages and disadvantages of each type? Which standards would you favor in your own classroom: those based on absolute levels, such as 75 percent to pass, or those based on a normal curve, where student performances set the average? What if your class usually achieves a mean of 50 percent or 60 percent? Is this acceptable? Why or why not? What if your standard of 75 percent is achieved by only half the group on any one test? How will your answers change (if at all) when 80 percent of your class scores 90 percent or better? Will you give those below 90 percent C's and D's? Why or why not? Write a policy for giving grades to which you will personally subscribe.

ISSUES IN EVALUATION

We are faced with serious problems each time we attempt to judge student progress or the quality of student work either in groups or as individuals. Testing, diagnosing, or surveying students' knowledge, understanding, and/or values is a fine art often distorted by problems of evaluation. This section discusses some of these problems that concern questions of validity and reliability, informal teacher

	TYPE OF EVALUATION	
	Formative	Summative
Evaluation Levels	DIDACTIC REFLECTIVE AFFECTIVE	DIDACTIC REFLECTIVE AFFECTIVE
Evaluation Purpose		
Diagnosis of Learning		
Assignment of Grades and/or Scores	Criterion-Referenced Norm-Referenced	

Figure 8.1 The structure of evaluation.

testing and observation, measuring the quality of student work, and formal standardized testing.

Reliability and Validity

From one time to the next, measurement instruments should yield similar results. This is termed *test reliability* and it will enable us to compare findings in a meaningful way. If results vary widely, there can be a problem of low reliability. Using different tests and diagnostic tools at different times during a course will diminish the extent to which scores can be justifiably compared to each other. Reliability is usually enhanced when a teacher uses matched pre- and posttests to measure cognitive changes, or employs correlated forms of the same survey to judge shifts in opinion or behavioral development. However, rigorous controlled testing does not reflect a student's many different abilities and talents in the way exhibited by an authentic assessment portfolio of work. Thus, a dilemma exists for you in choosing between self-expression and standardization, measuring growth and measuring achievement. I believe this dilemma can be resolved by asking students to do a variety of related tasks, which though judged in different ways add up to a more complete and realistic picture of ability and accomplishment than test scores alone. Keep in mind, too, that a portfolio of projects and student work can include traditional tests and essays as well as artwork, oral history, cartoons, or museum projects.

A second critical problem arises out of the match among educational objectives, treatment (what is taught), and test instruments. In other words, we need to ask if we are measuring what we really want to measure. This is termed *test validity*. More frequently than we would care to admit, tests may measure experiences and/or knowledge that students have not had. Tests may also be written in a way that differs partially or substantially from the assessment goals. For example, a teacher or test-maker may decide to measure thinking skills, but then may construct a test that on careful review, contains mostly items that require the recall of information rather than comprehension, inference, or analysis. This is a quintessential validity problem: The goals and the content of the test do not match each other, therefore the test results lead to incorrect conclusions.

TO DO

Review dictionary definitions of reliability and validity. Compare these definitions to those offered in a test and measurement textbook. Do the definitions differ substantially, or are they similar? Define *validity* and *reliability* in your terms.

Informal Assessment: Dialogue and Discussion

Informal assessment is the ongoing process of observation by which you try to find out what students know and how they feel. The focus is on their current capabilities and the attitudes and values that characterize their outlook. Evaluation in this sense is continuing because it is a way of establishing benchmarks, points at which students show they have achieved a new, higher plateau of learning. Based on responses to your classroom questions, you can make important decisions about what the future pace of instruction should be, which materials to assign, and what level of difficulty is next in the sequence of events. Frequent questioning matched by a high response level also improves achievement levels.[6]

In an authentic assessment program, you might ask students to record their questions or answers in a log for future reflection, adding these to their portfolios for later consideration. Using evaluation diagnostically helps you know "where students are at" in achieving classroom goals; you can miss this if you use tests only to measure expected outcomes. So, ask!

For example, if a teacher judges students against a set standard of 75 percent for passing, slow students who have made great progress from a low base but have not achieved 75 percent will certainly fail. The notion that testing comes after a given unit of work is dangerous for a number of reasons. First, we have no idea of the students' starting point and thus cannot accurately assess their progress. Second, if the goals are set low or too high, then students will seem brighter or slower than they really are. Third, individual strengths and weaknesses will be obscured by a group mean or norm that may conceal serious problems within groups or for individuals in the class. Therefore, regular diagnosis of progress in an informal as well as formal manner is vital to an accurate view of students' individual strengths and weaknesses, and to their place in a group.

WHAT DO YOU THINK?

Would verbal feedback be a way of judging student growth on an informal basis? How much do you think verbal comments reveal about students' thinking levels? How much or how little would you trust verbal reasoning as a guide to student progress? What could students say to you during a lesson that would show insight or lack of understanding? Give two examples.

Diagnosis may be nothing simpler than your close scrutiny of early discussions on a topic. You can get a pretty good sense of students' comprehension and analytic ability by tracking the level of student thinking through questions and answers. Questions, directions, and the use of student ideas through redirection and paraphrase will usually elicit enough feedback for you to decide how to proceed. For instance, if a unit on foreign policy is underway, a preliminary discussion with a class may reveal that ten or twelve of the students cannot define the concept of foreign policy in their own words. Many others are silent. Such poor reactions indicate that you must backtrack to the comprehension level and define basic terms. Or, if a number of students seem unable to use new evidence about Eastern Europe to test a theory of conflict and cooperation, then a practice session on application is in order. You might demonstrate through an example how to use evidence to build or critique a hypothesis, theory, or generalization. Their early, midterm, and concluding attempts at developing a theory might be saved and noted as a measure of growth, checked first by peers and later by you.

TO DO

Design your own list of comments and reasons students give verbally that lead you to judge their comprehension as high or low. Create your own rating scale for student insights. Will you give a higher rating for information, definitions, concepts, or generalizations? Why? Ask students to submit their own rating scales, or their own "rubrics," and organize an exchange of rating systems or rubrics in class using several anonymous products, papers, or essays as test cases for students to evaluate.

Pretests and Correlated Surveys

A second, vital link in a diagnostic approach would be to develop a pretest or premeasure that could also serve as a posttest of information and/or attitudes on a social studies subject. The pretest could take the form of a cognitive map, a checklist, a questionnaire, drawings, a quiz, or an information test. If the next month or so will be spent studying Latin America, then you could offer students a blank map of that continent showing political boundaries and ask them to write in the names of all the countries they can identify in a span of three minutes. Student helpers could then tabulate the results, counting accurate and inaccurate identifications for each country, and compare the students' "mental" map of Latin America to an up-to-date wall map or handout of the correct political geography. (This could be done for any country or region.) Toward the end of the unit, the same test could be given a second time (and a third time still later) to discover whether the range and accuracy of students' identifications have improved significantly.

Attitudes can also be diagnosed through survey research-style instruments in which students are asked whether they think they will find (and later, whether they did find) a topic worthy of future study. Students might be polled concerning which aspects of a subject they would like to study in greater or lesser depth and for what reasons. They might feel they already know a great deal about the U.S. Constitution and prefer to go into greater depth on the Panama Canal. A preference poll offers insights into student interests and creates links to the students by showing them that you take their views seriously. You are demonstrating that you wish to know more about students' views before you plan your next unit or decide on which books to assign.

SAMPLE LESSON PLAN

Coffee spilled all over your test ... Noooooooooo! What can you do while the tests are drying out (if they do)? How about an essay instead of all those multiple choice questions you had planned on the history of India? The students saw the film *Gandhi* and read some of his speeches, so why not put this to good use by asking them to write about his role in creating an independent nation. Was Gandhi a great leader in theory, or in practice, or in both aspects? How do you define a great leader? Would you defend your definition as good for all times and places, or only for the India of Gandhi? What would he say about your definition? Would he approve or disapprove? Why?

Measures of satisfaction or agreement can also be used to check on the strength or weakness of student interest in a topic or identification with a position or feeling. Likert-type scales, named after their creator Dr. Rensis Likert, arrange responses on a continuum ranging from a high degree of agreement (or satisfaction) to high degree of disagreement with a neutral point midway:[4] Strongly Agree (SA), Agree (A), Undecided or Don't Know (U), Disagree (D), or Strongly Disagree (SD). Students are asked to answer a series of survey questions, checking the response they wish, using the agree–disagree format. You could design your own survey of their views on the U.S. Bill of Rights by asking the following questions:

Bill of Rights Opinion Poll

1. The Bill of Rights is familiar to me and I can explain most of its content.
SA __ A __ U __ D __ SD __
2. The Bill of Rights is the most interesting part of the U.S. Constitution.
SA __ A __ U __ D __ SD __
3. The Bill of Rights is just on paper; it doesn't tell what's really happening.
SA __ A __ U __ D __ SD __
4. The Bill of Rights should be understocd by all Americans.
SA __ A __ U __ D __ SD __
5. The Bill of Rights is part of the Constitution I want to know more about.
SA __ A __ U __ D __ SD __

First, you could calculate the percentage of students choosing each response to an item, and then compute the averages for each response to discover any trends in student thinking. Students should present their results to the class in a table or graph. This presentation provides you with feedback about how students perceive the Bill of Rights and fosters useful research skills as well.

Giving Final Grades

Grades and scores may be based on personal growth, class norms, or absolute standards for achievement. Whichever standard is decided on, you should be as consistent as possible with your students.

Unless you explain beforehand what you are going to do, switching from one approach to another confuses and seems unfair to students. Grading on a curve is probably fairer to students because it is based on their own performance, with the class setting the mean. However, studies have shown that absolute standards tend to produce greater achievement, at least for the better performing social studies students.[8] On the other hand, those who are doing poorly and need more assistance often give up altogether when there is a strict criterion for success. Perhaps less able students need a "personal" growth standard that sets successive benchmarks for them to reach. In effect, this allows students to assess their own learning, comparing their output against a beginning baseline. Thus, much depends on the type of class you have and your goals for them. Grading has a direct effect on motivation, so it is probably best to assess students against themselves and their group norm. Whenever possible, you should give slower students the benefit of the doubt on a grade and watch the effect. If positive, as expected, then your standards and/or norms can safely rise. If negative, then you have reinforced one student on one occasion, which will not have much overall impact on group work averages over a semester or year.

Cooperative learning for tests is an excellent way to promote prosocial behavior and strengthen the review process. Students working together tend to reinforce each other and understand the material better, particularly if rewards are based on the total performance of all individual members.[9]

Giving or receiving explanations is a key factor in promoting deeper learning. More interaction with peers also produces higher levels of self-confidence and lower test anxiety.

Formative and summative grades should also reflect effort on a wide mix of measures: classroom questions, true–false quizzes, oral presentations, projects, multiple-choice tests, and essays. Variety allows students with different strengths and weaknesses the opportunity to perform better on some measures and worse on others; eventually everyone has a roughly equal chance to succeed or fail. In a way, authentic assessment seeks to create a broad measure of observations, performance samples, and tests, combined into a cumulative record unique to each student.[10]

Overall, grades should reward insight, cooperation, and care rather than quantity. Special encouragement should be given to those who are willing to move from surface to deeper thinking on a topic, whatever form this may take.[11] You can promote student interest by choosing topics that have appeal, introducing lessons in a thought-provoking manner, and setting standards that highly value reflective and affective over didactic responses.

When grading time arrives, you should always be a bit wary of the numerical results and, when warranted, be a bit generous in scoring. Evaluation of student work must eventually yield a social studies grade. Daily, weekly, and monthly performance should add up to a summative judgment that accurately reflects a students' work and ability. Tests for diagnostic or grading purposes should measure students' growth from an established pretest baseline. Results may be set against class norms or precise passing standards. Sometimes you may use formal, standardized test instruments; at other times, you may use teacher made tests. Classroom observations of students' verbal feedback should also play a part in your final judgment.

Whether evaluation is standardized or teacher made, summative or formative, it is nearly always tied to the diagnostic or grading objectives that shaped your social studies program. Therefore, you should clearly distinguish for students those tests and portfolio selections that will be graded from those used for diagnostic or self-assessment purposes. Test performance is also tied to your methods and materials of instruction. Ideally, your goals and concepts, data and questions, tests and surveys, should be closely related to your grading criteria. And these criteria should have been made explicit to students at the beginning of their course of study. The final must fairly reflect the curriculum that was taught. Otherwise, you are asking students to recall and define items with which they may be unfamiliar. In addition, if a summative test is geared to a much earlier stage of study, students may have forgotten the details they once knew, yielding an inaccurate picture of their abilities. Thus, your final test should include a *balanced selection* of key questions based on memorized data and new examples, with adequate time for review and reflection.

TO DO

How much faith do you place in knowledge tests? How about teacher-made tests? What about opinion polls? What circumstances increase your respect for a test or poll? What circumstances reduce your estimate of test reliability or validity? Write a brief two- or three-paragraph essay stating your views on testing, and on how seriously scores should be taken. Would you base students' grades entirely on their scores or averages? Why or why not? Would you include credit for active participation? Why or why not? If so, how much? Save your essay for rereading as you complete this chapter.

DESIGNING TESTS

Information-Based Questions. The test questions with which we are most familiar are designed to elicit what a student knows in terms of data. These data recall kinds of questions are almost always convergent, cognitive, and didactic, implying that answers are either correct or incorrect. Students usually get the answers from reading textbooks and listening to classroom lectures. Information-based inquiries are also the easiest to compose for a classroom test, requiring relatively little effort; they may be objectively graded because they tap few of the complexities that characterize higher level thinking. Particularly if you administer a pretest before a unit of instruction and a posttest afterward, you will have a reasonable sample of the state of student knowledge in your classroom—assuming that your test, instructional goals, and curriculum materials match one another and the audience's ability level. Even with excellent information-based questions, however, you will not be able to diagnose or assess the level of student understanding or affect in your course. Typically, information-based questions (IBQs) are presented as paper-and-pencil tests in a matching, true–false, fill-in, or multiple choice format supplemented by ongoing recall questions during daily lessons. Samples of each type of IBQ test item are offered in the following sections.

Short-Answer Tests.   Paper-and-pencil tests are designed primarily to assess students' recall of information skills. Published, standardized tests are often given only at the conclusion of a lengthy sequence of instruction, but they can and should be used on a pretest–posttest basis, as well as to provide for comparisons over time. Short answer or multiple choice tests are very popular because of the ease of scoring, their reliability, and their direct tie-in to textbooks. A great many textbook series provide tests after each unit and at the end of the book, although these tests may vary greatly in quality. Typically, short answer questions leave students a blank space to fill in or they provide a few answers from which students choose the right one to place in an open space or on an answer key. Several such items from a unit on Rome are offered as examples of the fill-in-the-blank type of test question:

1. The representatives of the Plebians in Republican Rome were called
   _____ .

2. The representatives of the Patricians in Republican Rome were called
   _____ .

3. When the Roman Republic collapsed after the assassination of Julius Caesar, there was a period of civil war followed by a new leader who was titled _____ .

Note that each blank asks for specific terms or names, which students presumably discussed in class or read about in their textbooks. Short answer questions are easy for you to invent, but their limitations must be kept firmly in mind. Students are placed in the position of either knowing or not knowing, and must repeat the key words exactly as taught.

Matching.   Matching items also seek mainly recall of information, but they can demand a slightly higher level of thinking from students by emphasizing elimination strategies. To work well, the matching list should not be overly long and should hold to the same categories on both sides or columns of information. The overall difficulty level may be increased by offering a longer list of matching items or by presenting some that are indirectly rather than directly related to each other. The matching format is also relatively easy for you to prepare and grade, but it does not give a great deal of insight into student reasoning processes.

The following are some examples of matching items on Roman history:

1. Patriarch	a. the father or head of the family
2. Monogamy	b. the son or inheritor
3. Tribune	c. judges the laws of the country
4. Consul	d. creates laws for the country
5. Polygamy	e. decides on what laws are best
6. Plebian	f. marriage to more than one wife
	g. one husband and one wife in a marriage

Notice that more responses (seven) are offered than possible matches. This makes elimination more difficult and causes students to compare and contrast possible answers before choosing one.

True–False. True–false items are fairly cut and dry in their approach to knowledge, usually taking the form of a series of statements that students must evaluate as either correct or incorrect. Statements are almost always factual in nature, formulated on the assumption that the knowledge described has been properly validated and is not open to question. (Of course, this may or may not be true because distinctions may become invalid as student knowledge deepens.)

True–false tests are easy to score but probably more difficult to prepare than one might think; great care must be taken not to give the answers away with qualifiers, such as *all*, *none*, *some*, *few*, or *many*. Furthermore, students can often guess their way through many of the items by the process of deductive or syllogistic reasoning. True–false items can be made much more exciting if you introduce the concept of probabilities, that is, some answers are more likely to be true or false than others. For instance, conclusions that are neither completely true nor completely false may be offered, asking students to categorize these as generally true, sometimes true, or seldom true. Students could be asked to identify and judge items using these more discriminating classifications, thus converting the lowly true–false item into a vehicle for somewhat more elegant responses requiring a higher degree of understanding.

Here are some examples of standard true–false items from a teacher-made test on traditional China:

Directions: Mark T for True or F for False in each blank provided.

_____1. The Great Wall of China was constructed during the Ch'in Dynasty.

_____2. The Han Dynasty was a period of constant warfare and dissension.

_____3. Confucius believed that under no circumstances should young people argue with their elders.

_____4. Confucius, though very influential in China, was not able to convince any of the rulers of his time to adopt his ideas.

_____5. Chinese language reform, the pinyin system, involves using Chinese characters for a new alphabet.

To answer these questions students must have stored the knowledge you want them to have about China and be able to recall it. For example, Item 3 is probably true, although it is stated as an absolute, "under no circumstances," which may be changed after careful study of Confucius's writings. Item 4 is true because it is supported by available records of the time, whereas Item 5 is most likely untrue because language reform in China uses Latin letters, not characters, to express Chinese sounds.

Although memory is the key element in successful responses to true–false quizzes, reading and definition can also play an important role. Much depends on the way items are written and what was taught in class on the subject. Thus, a true–false format can be used to evaluate mainly didactic and some reflective goals.

Multiple Choice. Multiple choice items are among the most flexible of test formats and, contrary to popular opinion, can be used to measure virtually every level of didactic and reflective thought. The types of multiple choice questions posed to students depend on your goals and your skills as an item writer. Multiple choice items need not be limited to assessing student knowledge, but can easily be adapted to measure reflective and affective goals, such as application, analysis, synthesis, and judgment. True, items that seek to measure thinking skills are probably more difficult and time consuming to write than those that test recall of facts. However, reflective questions may be worth the extra effort because multiple choice results are easy to score, allow comparisons among student responses, and permit detailed analysis of each item and the test as a whole in terms of averages and standard deviations.

Multiple choice responses can also be recorded on special sheets designed for easy scoring and may be read by an electronic scanner that totals up the results, indicating which questions were answered correctly or incorrectly. Numerous computer programs are available to assist you in creating and storing test items on different subjects. Programs are also available to provide statistical analyses using the normal curve as a basis for diagnosing student performance. In fact, you may want to use multiple choice results to grade on the curve. As in other types of evaluation questions, multiple choice items may be well or poorly written. Items should be field tested several times before you adopt them for your standard repertory. New questions should be given to several classes and the answers carefully analyzed for signs of misunderstanding, such as very low or very high percentages of correct responses.

Experts suggest a format and structure for writing multiple choice items that usually consists of a stem and three to five responses.[12] The stem is the question portion that requests one or more correct or "most reasonable" answers from a set of alternatives. The responses are usually presented in sets of three, four, or five choices, one or two of which are designated as correct or best. Often three illogical answers, the *distractors*, are wrong, and the one logical answer, the *key*, is correct. An example of a didactic IBQ, four-response item is given here (an asterisk indicates the correct response):

Stem: What is the capital of Botswana?

Responses: 1. Pretoria
                        2. Gaborone *(key)
                        3. Cairo
                        4. Ouagadougou

In this geography example, assuming students have done their homework on Africa, Cairo should be a far-fetched choice because it is quite distant from Botswana, which is sub-Saharan in location. Ouagadougou is somewhat closer but in West Africa, and Pretoria is very close and thus the most difficult of the distractors.

In addition to knowledge of specific facts, IBQs may also ask for knowledge of political procedures or principles:

Which of the following principles guided the framers of the U.S. Constitution in choosing a government with three branches?

    a. the need for separate meeting places

*b. the need for checks and balances among powers

c. the need for reverence for the law

d. the need for expertise in law, legislation, and leadership

Again, note that two of the answers, (a) and (c), are improbable or irrelevant, and (d) is an excellent principle that does apply to American politics. However, expertise was not the main idea expressed by the founding fathers as their rationale for a three-part system of government. So that leaves checks and balances, (b), as the correct selection.

Good distractors are vital to successful multiple choice items in social studies tests because they differentiate between those students who do or do not understand the material. If distractors are too illogical, then the right answer will be much easier to select; if the distractors are too much alike, then the right answer will be too difficult to select. Therefore, distractors are often designed to fit a continuum, one being obviously wrong, a second being almost as good a choice as the correct answer, and a third somewhere in between.[13]

Multiple choice questions may be used effectively to test students' information bases, including knowledge of specific facts, principles and rules, and procedures and methods. Nearly all student knowledge for testing comes from memory storage based on your instruction and student reading and at most requires a degree of comprehension; it does not, however, call on higher level reasoning skills.

Conclusions.   Information-based questions are designed to measure the extent rather than the depth of a student's knowledge. Because IBQs ask mainly for recall of data, questions tend to be brief and answers even briefer, with a premium usually placed on speed and correctness of responses. True–false, short answer, and multiple choice formats are typical of information-based examinations in combination with classroom recitation. Because choices are clear between correct and incorrect answers (whether or not students see this), test construction, administration, and scoring are accomplished with relative ease.

Document-Based Questions

Document- or evidence-based questions (DBQs) seek to assess students' reflective skills and reasoning ability. DBQs are designed to promote the largely cognitive skills of application, analysis, and synthesis for both convergent and divergent problem solving. Questions that ask students to deal with reading documents and viewing art and artifacts require problem-solving strategies. A DBQ cannot be answered on the basis of knowledge alone, although some knowledge may be very useful for understanding definitions and interpreting clues. Each DBQ provides or is drawn from information presented on the examination; this may consist of a historical document, quotation, graph, chart, photograph, painting, song, or research report.

Answers must be developed from the application of reasoning skills to this new or partially new material. Choices must be made among alternative responses. Unlike IBQs, responses involving reasoning offer a much wider range of alternatives, none of which is specifically or clearly right or wrong. The standard for a good answer to a document-based question is reasonability—the argument or response that makes the most sense given the data and/or the best logic.

Thus, higher level thinking must be assessed differently from recall of information; it generally requires tests in the form of multiple choice, essay, and oral examinations. DBQs are more difficult to write than "fact" questions and require more subjective grading, but they do evaluate richer and deeper levels of student understanding, such as how and why students have drawn conclusions rather than what they know.

RESEARCH REPORT

Using Bloom's taxonomy as a rough framework for coding 8,800 test questions developed by teachers in twelve grade and subject combinations (mostly upper elementary through high school), researchers estimated that approximately four fifths of all questions were at the recall level, the lowest of the six levels.* The social studies test items within this pool were, on the whole, more oriented toward recall of information than were mathematics and language questions; oddly enough, these were characterized by greater proportions of higher level queries. Teacher emphasis on recall questions has been explained by poor training in measurement, the difficulty of writing questions aimed at evaluating higher level problem-solving skills, and fear that more open-ended items will promote student confusion and anxiety, and increase failure rates.[†]

---

*M. Fleming and B. Chambers, "Teacher-Made Tests: Windows on the Classroom," in *New Directions for Testing and Measurement*, vol. 19, *Testing in the Schools*, ed. W. E. Hathaway (San Francisco: Jossey-Bass, 1983).
[†]William Doyle, "Classroom Organization and Management," in *Handbook of Research on Teaching*, 3rd ed., ed. M. C. Wittrock (New York: MacMillan, 1986), pp. 392–431.

Teacher Questions and Oral Tests.   Students' questions and answers are valuable sources for evaluation. What students say indicates the extent and depth of their knowledge, and sometimes their feelings, about a topic. Unlike writing, the more they say and the lengthier the exchanges (up to a point of course), the better your sample of their thinking for both diagnosis and judgment. Research suggests that frequent questioning in class by the teacher is generally related to improved academic achievement of students, particularly when there is a high proportion of student responses.[14] To promote frequent higher level feedback, ask many probing questions and allow students enough time to think through their answers.

If you have a good memory, you may keep track of the quality and frequency of student responses as you move through the course. If your memory is crowded with other business, you may want to keep a diary or log of response levels and frequencies or leave space for notes in your grade book. You might also build a checklist into your grading procedures on which you can record examples of students' thinking styles, for example:

Response Levels   *Respondents*

High: Makes and defends judgments. Hypothesizes about causes   Mary Jones
and theories for events; draws inferences and conclusions.

Medium: Offers reasons for statements; analyzes underlying mo-   John Smith
tives for actions. Understands and applies concepts and definitions.

Low: Accurately recalls or offers information on a subject. Presents
a list of names, dates, or places.

A bookkeeping device of this type, a *log*, would be an aid to your overall evaluation of individuals and of the course as a whole. You may also build verbal feedback into your programs as speeches, role-plays, or oral tests. Students could be called on to do a bit of public speaking on a social studies topic to demonstrate their knowledge and skill at putting ideas together. As an example, you might ask each student to prepare and present the answer to a reflective question as a short speech, or perhaps reenact a speech by a famous person (e.g., Daniel Webster or Abraham Lincoln).

LET'S DECIDE

1. Design an oral examination with a group of students on a critical issue, such as the bombing of Hiroshima and Nagasaki or the Cuban missile crisis. Stress public speaking skills.
2. Ask students to develop and submit in writing the list of questions they would like to see answered in class. Direct them to set up their own interview procedure with a checklist that distinguishes between better and worse answers, resulting in a grade for each speaker. They'll love it!

Questions for Complex Reasoning. With relatively simple multiple choice, best answer formats, many variations can be created to test reflective thinking, including missing answers (excluding a key factor), "two-best" answers, one "best" or the one "worst" answer, or a single worst answer, that is, the only answer that is wrong out of the four or five choices. More creative questions can be developed by supplying students with documentary, graphic, or text materials on the test itself. In other words, students can be given new data to interpret as part of their test, data drawn from the studies they have completed at home or in class. Or, you may present data that is analogous to or an extension of the work with which the students have grown familiar, pushing them to apply past learning to new situations.

When developing best answer items, you should make clear to the respondents that although many of the responses are reasonable in some sense, only one is best in the light of the evidence or through logical inference. In the item that follows, the same basic concept is handled in two ways: Which do you think promotes more reasoning for the reader, Type 1 or Type 2?

Correct-Answer Format

The capital of a country is a location that serves as

1. the cultural center.
2. the economic center.
*3. the government center.
4. the population center.

Best-Answer Format

The main reason for choosing a location as the capital of a country is probably

1. the need for a home by the leader.
*2. the need for a political center.
3. the need for a national symbol.
4. the need for a geographic heart.

Note that each stem and the accompanying distractors in the two formats are quite different in intent and phrasing. The correct answer set aims at assessing knowledge; the best answer set seeks comprehension and application. Phraseology is also dissimilar, with the best answer format asking for the main reason rather than the one right bit of data. None of the best answer distractors is "wrong," but offers a more or less logical choice.

Challenging questions can also be created from charts, graphs, quotations, pictures, and documents. Readings and visuals may be reproduced on the test itself. Varying difficulty can be introduced by selection of lengthier and more complex readings for interpretation. A complex multiple choice example could be created in conjunction with a U.S. government census chart showing voter participation in presidential and congressional elections over the last thirty years (see Figure 8.2). A wide range of items could be generated from this chart because it is rich in meaning and amenable to many interpretations. Consider these examples.

1. This voter turnout chart demonstrates that voters have been least interested in presidential elections in the following sets of years:
   a. 1938 to 1950

   b. 1924 to 1936
 *c. 1972 to 1984
   d. 1954 to 1966
2. Based on the turnout chart, the level (%) of participation in presidential elections since 1948 has
   a. declined for almost every election.
   b. risen for almost every election.
 *c. declined for most, but not all elections.
   d. risen or declined from one election to the next.
3. If you compare the voter turnout for presidential elections with the turnout for congressional elections for 1924 through 1984, you would probably conclude that when both elections occur simultaneously
   a. a congressional election pulls up the vote for president.
   b. a presidential election pulls down the vote for the congressional election.

	1980	1982	1984	1986	1988	1990	1992	1994	1996
Congressional Turnout	48%	38%	48%	34%	45%	33%	51%	36%	50%
Presidential Turnout	53%		53%		50%		55%		49%

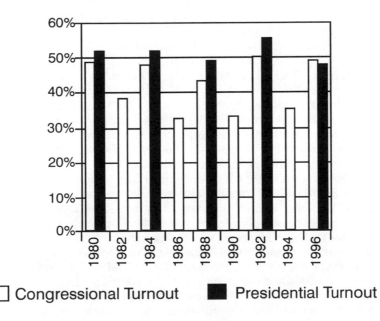

☐ Congressional Turnout   ■ Presidential Turnout

Figure 8.2   Voter turnout in presidential and congressional elections.
SOURCE: Based on *Who Votes and Why?* Taft Institute, 1988; and Bureau of Labor and Voting Statistics, 1997.

    c. a congressional election pulls down the vote for president.
  *d. a presidential election pulls up the vote for the congressional election.
  4. Based on your overall reading of voter turnout over a sixty-year period, you might logically conclude that a majority of Americans are
    a. equally interested in local and national politics.
    b. more interested in local than national politics.
  *c. more interested in national than local politics.
    d. less interested in national than local politics.

All four questions demand graph interpretation skills in which the student discriminates between less and more reasonable answers based on the data at hand. For question 1, answer (b) is clearly a poor choice, whereas two of the four answers, (a) and (d), are reasonable to some extent. Only one, (c), closely follows from the data, which demonstrate a consistently low level in voting throughout the period. Both the declines and levels of improvement cannot, however, be described as rising or falling from one election to the next because this would create a jagged pattern. The one shown is relatively smooth.

Question 3 asks for a comparison between the patterns in the presidential and congressional elections as a step toward drawing a conclusion about voter behavior. Both application and analysis come into play in a student's answer, with (a) and (b) representing misreadings of the chart, and (c) and (d) appearing as reasonable inferences. However, there is no evidence to show that congressional elections pull down presidential turnouts, whereas presidential elections always indicate higher local participation. Thus, (d) is the most logical selection for the student who pays close attention to the data.

Question 4 pushes students a bit further into the realm of generalization from data that have already been carefully analyzed. They must link a concept of local and national politics with congressional and presidential elections. From this they can infer American behavior patterns in which signs point to greater interest in national than local affairs, if you assume that the office of president represents the pinnacle of voter concern. Choices (b) and (d) are reflections of each other and not supported by the evidence, and (a) is a distractor that is reasonable if you consider presidential years and disregard off-year congressional elections. Thus (c) is left as the best fit for the data and thus the most reasonable answer.

Test items measuring higher level document-based objectives may be designed and written for the classroom on a regular basis, although these are somewhat more difficult to invent on your own than information-based questions. Great care must be taken in selecting artifacts and reading materials for student analysis and response. Nevertheless, it is worth the trouble to write or purchase ready-made sets of more complex and demanding questions because these encourage critical thinking of a high order in students, and tie in with stated reflective goals. Standardized tests are also available for purchase through textbook companies and professional agencies for many subjects, ranging from U.S. history through economics. Particularly well developed economic reasoning tests are available for the middle and senior high schools.[15] Some excellent geography examinations are offered by the National Council for Geographic Education.[16] In addition, if you regularly practice writing and administering document-based questions, your skill and experience will increase markedly and the questions will become easier for you to create. Remember to save your test items; file standardized tests in a test bank for the different courses you teach and swap items with colleagues to make your life easier and to improve your tests.

Some rules to follow in constructing DBQs might include the following:

  1. Match tests with reflective course objectives.

2. Design questions that humanely reflect the state of student knowledge and skill.
3. Prepare questions drawn from what you taught in the course.
4. Insert new (but analogous) questions to promote critical thinking and application skills.
5. Choose pictures and readings that are dramatic, puzzling, and interesting.
6. Keep introductory evidence brief so students can retain or easily glance at it in deciding on answers.
7. Place most of the question in the stem portion and keep the distractors and answers relatively brief.
8. Check questions, stems, and alternatives to make sure you are not leading students, or that there is a single correct answer built in.
9. Keep choice categories homogeneous, standard, and mutually exclusive: the format for responses should be identical throughout a set of questions, and categories should be distinct (e.g., a statement supports or contradicts a theory, or is irrelevant to it).
10. Try out new items with at least one group you are teaching and subject their responses to item analysis. If responses range all over the different choices, are very inconsistent, or are consistently unreasonable alternatives, then discuss the item with students and revise or discard it. Save successful items for which most students select the logical choice, the next highest number choose the major distractor, and the fewest choose the incorrect or illogical responses.[17] With practice, you can develop your own battery of test items for the major courses—world history, U.S. history, economics, and government.

SAMPLE LESSON/TEST PLANS

1. Using a multiple choice, best answer format, write a series of at least six related document-based items on portions of George Washington's "Farewell Address." Increase the difficulty level of each question, beginning with comprehension and analysis and concluding with a judgment question calling for students to draw conclusions from the source.

2. Select a famous European painting or sculpture, such as Picasso's *Guernica* or Rodin's *The Thinker*, and devise at least three higher order multiple choice questions that require students to compare and contrast or draw inferences about society and politics.

3. Choose a graph or chart that you believe illustrates valuable data, such as Japanese and American economic growth or savings rates in the 1950s and the 1980s. Create at least four questions that ask students to use the graph's statistics as a basis for analyzing economic trends.

4. Research secondary-level standardized tests in at least two subjects, such as world studies and geography. Critically evaluate the questions in each, according to level (lower or higher), and calculate the percentage of each type on the test. Are there enough higher level items for students?

5. Direct students to respond to a set of your items and analyze the results together, noting percentages of correct and incorrect choices. Be prepared for criticism and revise your items to the students' and to your own satisfaction.

Essay Tests. Writing Skills in the Social Studies. Generally, essay tests give you greater opportunity to elicit reflective and affective responses from students than do other formats. If we use the ability to develop a full line of reasoning as a criterion, then essay questions are by far the best vehicles by which to assess students.

However, there are problems that arise with essay tests: variability of response (how do you judge the quality of a response in comparison to criteria or to responses of other students?), meaning and message (will each reader interpret the assignment in a similar way?), and the assignment itself (is the problem clear or ambiguous?). Thus, although the essay allows a great deal of freedom and flexibility for respondents in terms of length, complexity, and degree of creativity, there are problems of interpretation and standardization for you. An essay format does not by itself guarantee reflection because the directions may ask for what is essentially recall or a listing of information or conclusions. We have all seen essay questions that are really no different from matching or fill-in items except that full sentences are required as responses. On the other hand, essay examinations may be highly creative and exceedingly difficult. You may require that students interpret and synthesize large amounts of data, develop a logical argument, or speculate creatively about the future.

Compounding the problems of assessing the content and reasoning in an essay is your inevitable reaction to the way the language is used. Poorly written but thoughtful essays are often graded lower than less thoughtful but well-written essays. There is always a conflict between teachers who want to encourage good writing and those who seek to test knowledge of subject matter. Because of these problems, it is very important that you make your criteria for assessment clear to students indicating how much content or evidence is expected, which data will be valued, the type of reasoning process that will be expected (argument, narrative, creative, etc.), and how much language will count as part of the total grade. If criteria are established early in the semester for essay questions, and if frequent practice and feedback characterize your teaching style, then student writing and thinking skills are likely to be strengthened over the period of your course. Conversely, the more ambiguous the criteria and the poorer your feedback, the less students' skills will improve.

Despite problems, essays should be a regular and integral part of social studies coursework and evaluation. Ideally, a typical unit or course should contain a mixture of essay questions: short or long, with definite word limits, and open-ended or creative. Reliance on one type of essay test penalizes some students while rewarding others who have the knowledge or skills that best fit that particular type of test. Tests and papers of different essay sizes help students learn to use a broad range of abilities. An example of essay questions aimed mainly at assessing comprehension might include the following:

1. Explain three key causes for the Civil War in complete sentences in your own words (no more than 250 words in all).
2. Describe the reasons for including the Bill of Rights in the U.S. Constitution (no more than 2 pages).

Essay questions may also help you assess students' higher level reflective skills of a general or specific nature; the following are examples of such questions:

1. Compare Athens and Sparta telling how they were similar or different in terms of political, social, and economic factors.
2. Explain why you think the Soviets and the Americans will or will not and should or should not relax tensions between them into the twenty-first century.

The construction and grading of essay questions can be enhanced if you establish criteria for success that both you and your students can use to interpret and judge results. Using an essay about Third World development as a case in point, we propose the following rules for essay writing in social studies.

Recapitulate the Goals You Want to Assess. To judge how well students have understood the economic, social, and political problems that many Third World countries share, define the specific goals that you want students to achieve:

    a. to collect relevant statistics about per capita income and technological capability of ten selected nations;

    b. to understand that lack of technology combined with narrow, one-crop economies leave Third World nations vulnerable to changes in world markets;

    c. to analyze and synthesize the reasons for political instability: frequent changes in government, limited technology, and military rule; and

    d. to decide what remedies are best—from foreign aid, investment, and sanctions to revolution—for solving the technological, social, and political problems of Third World nations.

Provide Detail and Direction in the Essay Question. Rewrite the essay question by presenting data as part of the question itself, or by referring directly to examples and cases from the curriculum. Prepare students for the essay by asking them to submit questions they would like to see answered or questions they believe would make people think. For instance, the original question could be reformulated into a more specific problem:

> The average per capita income of nations classified as Third World is under $500 a year. Most Third World countries use very low levels of energy and have few roads, rails, or air and communication networks. How would these problems affect future political and social development? Choose three nations with which you are familiar and write an essay of five hundred words or less discussing whether the political situation of each is related to its economic problems. Save about fifty words or so at the end for your own judgment of the causes for these problems.

Specify Size, Structure, Time Allotment, and Grading Standards for an Essay. Ask students to write an essay of between four and five hundred words in a specified time, such as one forty-minute period. If you want special features, request them specifically. These could include a conclusion, an expression of opinion, or a defense or attack of a hypothesis. Indicate which points will be considered most valuable and provide at least a few clues about how the essay will be graded. Identification of relationships, such as cause and effect, or judgments about low- and high-ranking problems will be highly prized and likely to receive more points than general theories or vague reasons.

    Make clear that points will also be given for accurate information. If students correctly identify three countries, their political leaders, and the economic situation in each, their scores will increase by ten, twenty, or thirty. Those who tie together the three examples into an overall generalization and judgment will receive still higher point totals. This information helps students know where to invest their greatest energies for the highest possible return.

Analyze the Answers. Answers should fit the goals that you laid down previously (four in this case). These can be used as a basis for evaluating essays in a somewhat more objective fashion than is usually possible. In the example given on the Third World, five criteria may be used to interpret students' writing:

    a. supplies accurate statistics and other data about Third World countries,

b. draws connections between local economic problems and world markets,
c. presents clear and specific reasons for political changes,
d. offers at least one major generalization or hypothesis that summarizes common problems, and
e. recommends one or two best solutions to ameliorate the situation.

Up to 20 points can be given for each criterion that is met up to a total of 100, with a bonus perhaps added for quality writing:

uses data = 20 points

draws connections = 20 points

presents reasons = 20 points

develops hypothesis = 20 points

offers recommendations = 20 points

writes well = 10 points

Maximum Points = 110 points

By looking at the essays in part and as wholes, you will be able to identify patterns of excellence or misunderstanding among students, as well as decide on an overall evaluation of each pupil's work compared to either publicly understood standards or to class norms.

Perception-Based Questions

Perception-based questions (PBQs) are concerned with the affective realm, how students feel about or view themselves, events, or issues, and their reasons for these attitudes. Affect may range from low-level awareness of feelings about one's self-image to sophisticated defenses of value positions. Psychological assessments of self-confidence and survey research polls of public opinion fall within the PBQ category because all assess how people see their world rather than objectively calculate the amount of verifiable information someone possesses. Generally, PBQs focus on three different areas: psychological, attitudinal, and self-evaluative.

First, self-perception and feelings about social roles are often measured with psychological types of instruments, such as thematic apperception tests, student interest inventories, and self-reports. Second, the purpose of the measurement is to learn about a person's attitudes toward school, society, politics, and social issues by use of scales of agreement or satisfaction. These include typical Gallup or Roper surveys and polls. Third, perception may involve judgments about quality or educational experience covering lessons, units, courses, workshops, and teachers. Thus, perception-based questions deal with subjective opinions, feelings, and viewpoints; they are used to learn more about individual responses and group reactions to experiences in a systematic way that can guide your classroom planning.

MEASURING STUDENT FEELINGS AND VIEWPOINTS

Student expressions of feelings, interests, and values show how they view themselves and their educational milieu. For affective goals, the focus of evaluation is on opinions, issues, and self-reports that express positive and negative feelings. Although we are drawing distinctions between the affective, reflective, and didactic for pedagogical and analytical purposes, almost any expression of feeling or judgment is based on experience, knowledge, and reflection as well as preference and perception. What makes affective evaluation different is the emphasis on opinions and values that do not fit a "right or wrong" assessment mold.

Values are at the very heart of social studies instruction although they are rarely diagnosed by students or teachers for either informational or decision-making purposes. Decisions on the most important questions that we face are almost always based on a mixture of facts and feelings, empiricism and phenomenology, reality and perception.

By bringing the assessment of affective objectives into the open, you make the expression of opinion legitimate and you can diagnose important attitudinal changes with the assistance of your students. Studying students' feelings and attitudes should be part of normal routine, as should student feedback on your methods and materials of instruction. There is every reason to include maturing middle and secondary school students in the process of reviewing their own educational experience. For example, students can learn how to conduct a survey in a careful, scientific manner by polling reactions to your course of study. Simultaneously, this activity will improve their inquiry writing and mathematical skills.

There are dozens of interesting ways to learn student attitudes and values, to teach students how to conduct survey research, and to offer students the opportunity to review their class experience. Central to the assessment of affective goals is the problem of perception. At the heart of perception is the private world of the individual from whose opinions or views we infer deeper beliefs and motives. Individual attitudes are often difficult to judge or unrepresentative; this is why peer appraisal and self-report surveys have been developed for groups and sample populations. Precise statistical procedures and techniques have been created for sampling that represents mainstream opinion and for analyzing self-reports. Among these techniques are informal observation, self-reports, attitude scales, peer appraisal, checklists, course evaluations and tests of imagination, creativity, and problem-solving style. Of course, all such polling is subject to errors, depending on the quality of the sample and the design of the survey instrument.

Student Interest Inventories

If you want to learn more about students' interests and attitudes, why not ask them? One way of doing this is to hand out survey forms from time to time that ask students to report their feelings and attitudes on subjects and issues that will be or have been discussed. You may develop an attitude inventory of your own or choose one from among the many that are available commercially through publishers and testing corporations.

Student feedback could be gathered from a straightforward interest questionnaire. You might present one like the following before beginning a unit on industrialization:

1. What topics on industrialization would you like to see included in our U.S. history course?
2. What topics do you feel are already familiar to you and do not need to be discussed?
3. Do you see industrialization or technology as important or unimportant topics? Why?

You might like to preface a new work you are writing with a survey of student feelings toward social studies in general. Asking for their advice could aid your planning and help you avoid or shorten unpopular or already understood topics. Seeking student advice also demonstrates your respect for their views and opinions. You might ask questions such as the following:

1. Which subjects do you like best? Which do you like least? Why?
2. In which subjects do you see yourself doing your best work? Does your best work include social studies? Why or why not? Explain.
3. How might social studies topics or teaching be made more interesting to you? Please offer a few suggestions for future activities, subjects, or lessons.

WHAT DO YOU THINK?

What areas of classroom life do you think would lend themselves to attitudinal studies or psychological testing? Would you be willing to assist students in preparing an evaluation of your course? Why or why not?

Checklists

A checklist offers students a series of statements about themselves or the class with which they can agree or disagree. A checklist may also provide students with the opportunity to think about how they are doing without worrying about your formal evaluation. You may let them assess past assignments anonymously, expressing what they really did or did not like about your methods and materials of instruction. Naturally, you must be willing to stand up to this criticism. And you must be ready to make the changes, to the degree practicable, suggested by your students or risk loss of credibility.

The following are a few examples of a student checklist:

Key: 1 = Always; 2 = Frequently; 3 = Sometimes; 4 = Hardly Ever
Please circle the one choice that applies in each column.

At the beginning of the course	Toward the middle of the course	During the final portion of the course
I make regular contributions to class discussions		
1 2 3 4	1 2 3 4	1 2 3 4
I look up answers on my own from many sources		
1 2 3 4	1 2 3 4	1 2 3 4
I listen carefully to classmates' views and opinions		
1 2 3 4	1 2 3 4	1 2 3 4

Reactions to this checklist will allow students to review their own activities in social studies and apply these to the goals set for improving participation.

TO DO

Develop a checklist of your own for students on a topic you would like to teach. What will you ask your critics to judge about a unit? What would you like to know about their interests and motivations? What would you avoid asking? Why? If you are having students develop portfolios of their work, which cognitive and which affective measures would you include? Why?

TEACHER AND COURSE EVALUATION

Attitudes toward you or toward the course you are teaching provide valuable insight into student motivation, which was discussed earlier as a crucial part of successful achievement. After all, didactic and reflective growth is related to the state of students' feelings about themselves and attitudes toward teacher and school. You are a vital link in the learning chain, so why not find out how you're doing? The greater the students' motivation to learn, the higher will be the level of achievement in social studies, or in general for that matter.[18] Thus, how students see their teacher and the subject matter is a key part of learning. Student judgments are best made anonymously, with results treated as group data, averages calculated, and trends identified. As with other perception-based questions, a variety of methods can be used to study student reactions (or your self-evaluation). These methods include checklists, attitudinal surveys, and many psychological instruments, including the semantic differential form, an example of which is discussed here as a tool for teacher evaluation.

The *semantic differential* is a psychological test designed to give insight into the way people view themselves or others in a social role. This attitudinal tool is borrowed from psychological research and is particularly well suited to bringing judgments and cultural conditioning to the surface. Respondents are usually given a list of opposite qualities or characteristics to react to, such as poor/rich, weak/strong, sensitive/unfeeling. These terms are arranged along a scale that respondents must mark at the point that best fits their personal reactions to a given subject, such as "my teacher" or "my classmates."

One such form, developed by Tuckman and widely used for teacher evaluation, is presented in Figure 8.3 as an example.[19] Note that seven degrees of feeling are built into the scoring, three points in the direction of one pole and three in the direction of the opposite pole, with a midpoint representing a neutral attitude.

WHAT DO YOU THINK?

The semantic differential form that follows asks the reactor to characterize or assess a teacher (or it could be a student) by a series of opposites (e.g., "disorganized" versus "organized," "lively" versus "lifeless," or "traditional" versus "original"). A basic assumption is that all respondents will share an understanding of the concepts used to define opposites, although each will react in their own way. Class opinion, taken as an average (see Figure 8.4) should demonstrate both a range of feeling about the "teacher" and a central core of judgment represented by group means. Whichever approach you use to assess your programs or yourself, keep an open mind to others' attitudes and perceptions about your methods and curriculum, and listen to your own intuitive feelings about student affect and performance. Awareness and understanding of perceptions is at the very heart of affective evaluation.

SUMMARY

After a brief discussion of evaluation, three major areas of test and survey questions were identified: those that are information based (IBQs), document based

Person Observed _____   Observer _____

Date _____

TUCKMAN TEACHER FEEDBACK FORM (STUDENT EDITION)

MY TEACHER IS

	1 2 3 4 5 6 7	
1 DISORGANIZED	① ② ③ ④ ⑤ ⑥ ⑦	ORGANIZED
2 CLEAR	① ② ③ ④ ⑤ ⑥ ⑦	UNCLEAR
3 AGGRESSIVE	① ② ③ ④ ⑤ ⑥ ⑦	SOFT-SPOKEN
4 CONFIDENT	① ② ③ ④ ⑤ ⑥ ⑦	UNCERTAIN
5 COMMONPLACE	① ② ③ ④ ⑤ ⑥ ⑦	CLEVER
6 CREATIVE	① ② ③ ④ ⑤ ⑥ ⑦	ORDINARY
7 OLD FASHIONED	① ② ③ ④ ⑤ ⑥ ⑦	MODERN
8 LIKEABLE	① ② ③ ④ ⑤ ⑥ ⑦	"STUCK UP"
9 EXCITING	① ② ③ ④ ⑤ ⑥ ⑦	BORING
10 SENSITIVE	① ② ③ ④ ⑤ ⑥ ⑦	ROUGH
11 LIVELY	① ② ③ ④ ⑤ ⑥ ⑦	LIFELESS
12 ACCEPTS PEOPLE	① ② ③ ④ ⑤ ⑥ ⑦	CRITICAL
13 SNOBBY	① ② ③ ④ ⑤ ⑥ ⑦	MODEST
14 CONFUSED	① ② ③ ④ ⑤ ⑥ ⑦	ORDERLY
15 STRICT	① ② ③ ④ ⑤ ⑥ ⑦	LENIENT
16 IN CONTROL	① ② ③ ④ ⑤ ⑥ ⑦	ON THE RUN
17 TRADITIONAL	① ② ③ ④ ⑤ ⑥ ⑦	ORIGINAL
18 WARM	① ② ③ ④ ⑤ ⑥ ⑦	COLD
19 RUDE	① ② ③ ④ ⑤ ⑥ ⑦	POLITE
20 WITHDRAWN	① ② ③ ④ ⑤ ⑥ ⑦	OUTGOING
21 EASYGOING	① ② ③ ④ ⑤ ⑥ ⑦	DEMANDING
22 OUTSPOKEN	① ② ③ ④ ⑤ ⑥ ⑦	SHY
23 UNCHANGEABLE	① ② ③ ④ ⑤ ⑥ ⑦	FLEXIBLE
24 QUIET	① ② ③ ④ ⑤ ⑥ ⑦	BUBBLY
25 AWARE	① ② ③ ④ ⑤ ⑥ ⑦	FORGETFUL
26 "NEW IDEAS"	① ② ③ ④ ⑤ ⑥ ⑦	SAME OLD THING
27 IMPATIENT	① ② ③ ④ ⑤ ⑥ ⑦	PATIENT
28 UNCARING	① ② ③ ④ ⑤ ⑥ ⑦	CARING
29 DEPENDENT	① ② ③ ④ ⑤ ⑥ ⑦	INDEPENDENT
30 UNPLANNED	① ② ③ ④ ⑤ ⑥ ⑦	EFFICIENT

Figure 8.3   A sample semantic differential.
SOURCE: Bruce W. Tuckman, *Conducting Educational Research,* 3rd ed. (New York: Harcourt Brace Jovanovich, 1988) Reprinted by permission of the author.

Person Observed _____   Observer _____

Date _____

TUCKMAN TEACHER FEEDBACK FORM SUMMARY SHEET

A. ITEM SCORING INSTRUCTIONS

    I. Each response choice on the answer sheet contains one of the numbers 1-2-3-4-5-6-7.
    This gives a number value to each of the seven spaces between the 30 pairs of objectives.

    II. Determine the number value for the first pair. Disorganized–Organized. Write it into the formula given below on the appropriate line under Item I.
    For example, if the student darkened in the first space next to "Organized" in Item I, then write the number 7 on the dash under Item I in the summary formula below.

    III. Do the same for each of the 30 items. Plug each value into the formula.

    IV. Compute the score for each of the 5 dimensions in the Summary formula.

B. SUMMARY FORMULA AND SCORE FOR THE FIVE DIMENSIONS

    I. *Organized Demeanor*

      Item   Item   Item   Item   Item   Item   Item

      $((1 + 14 + 30) - (2 + 4 + 16 + 25) + 25) + .42$

    II. *Dynamism*

      Item   Item   Item   Item   Item

      $((20 + 24) \quad - (3 + 11 + 22) + 19) + .30$

    III. *Flexibility*

      Item   Item   Item   Item

      $((15 + 23) - (10 + 21) + 12) + .24$

    IV. *Warmth and Acceptance*

      Item   Item   Item   Item   Item   Item   Item

      $((13 + 19 + 27 + 28) - (8 + 12 + 18) + 17) + .42$

    V. *Creativity*

      Item   Item   Item   Item   Item   Item

      $((5 + 7 + 17) - (6 + 9 + 26) + 18) + .36$

Figure 8.4 Scoring the semantic differential.
SOURCE: Bruce W. Tuckman, *Conducting Educational Research*, 3rd ed. (New York: Harcourt Brace Jovanovich, 1988) Reprinted by permission of the author.

(DBQs), and perception based (PBQs). Each type conforms to the didactic, reflective, and affective goals of social studies instruction, your choice of which will determine the kinds of questions you will ask and the response you expect of students.

Information-based evaluation is concerned with recall of facts and definitions, that is, cognitive testing for knowledge that relies on formats such as short answer quizzes, matching tests, or true–false and multiple choice examinations. IBQ testing is usually criterion referenced, that is, measured against set standards supplied by you, students, the school, or a testing agency.

Document- or evidence-based evaluation (DBQ) measures reasoning and inference abilities rather than recall and comprehension; questions drawn from material built into an examination demand analysis, application, synthesis, and/or judgment to answer. Multiple choice formats and essay writing are the principal means for testing higher order skills and abilities. Essays probably allow for more divergent thinking than do the other test types, but they suffer from subjectivity in the evaluation process. All types of products and tests may be incorporated into a student portfolio for presentation at the conclusion of a course or program.

Perception-based evaluation covers all types of affective questions in which students or teachers express their views, feelings, and judgments about events, issues, or classroom activities. Checklists, surveys, interviews, opinion polls, differential polls, and essays may be employed to probe feelings and values. Surveys and opinion polls tend to dominate attitude measurement because of their easy administration and scoring. Almost all affective evaluation is norm referenced, that is, measured against group averages.

We concluded with suggestions for you, the teacher, to encourage students in designing and writing their own surveys of opinion or course evaluations using either published or class-created review forms. An argument was made for evaluation based on carefully defined goals accompanied by regular and consistent formative (ongoing) measures of student development as well as the usual summative testing in the form of finals.

Evaluation ought to be seen as a vital part of the teaching process because it affords teacher and students feedback on the level and amount of their achievement measured against classroom goals. These goals can be didactic, reflective, and/or affective. From such feedback, students and teacher form judgments about how well or how poorly they are performing, and which learning areas need the least or most improvement. Usually, the better the quality of evaluation, the more specific the actions that can be taken for long-term, future achievement. Authentic/portfolio assessment was discussed and described as a means for getting the "big picture" for a student's performance, and for contributing significantly in measuring growth and change over time. Thus, evaluation is a continuing process of both diagnosis and judgment, spurring students to change their study habits or attitudes, redouble work efforts, or seek additional resources to promote learning.

Finally, heed a word of caution. Although tests and surveys are useful, probably necessary, and most likely unavoidable given present trends in social studies (and all) education, assessment as a set of procedures and tools can at best produce a result that represents only the tip of the iceberg of student knowledge, reasoning, and values. Each self-report, test score, portfolio presentation, or observation can only approximate the true internal state of a student. Variations in test reliability, student health, teaching methods, and a multitude of other factors may lead to accurate or erroneous interpretation of a students' real strengths and weaknesses. We as teachers need to learn what is happening to our students through a variety of evaluation techniques for diagnostic or grading goals, or through authentic assessment procedures, but we must allow our own compassion and judgment to play a part in all our decisions.

TO DO

1. Write a twenty-item multiple choice test using only DBQs (document-based questions) drawn primarily from world studies readings and statistics. Predict student performance on each item: degree of success, percentage of correct responses, difficulty or ease in answering, and so on. Administer the test to your class and analyze the response patterns. Were your predictions correct? Why or why not? Did you prepare students to deal with this type of examination? Be fair!

2. Assist students in preparing an opinion poll on the power of the U.S. presidency compared with that of the Congress and Supreme Court. Use a scale of agreement or disagreement with a range of positive and negative statements about the three branches of government. Offer students previous surveys and polls of political attitudes to adapt for their own purposes. Select a sample and collect the responses. Use a computer, item-analysis program, if possible, to organize the results. What were the averages for each question, the standard deviation from the norm? Were any results significantly different from chance? Why? In general, how would you and the students characterize the flow of opinion? Was it positive or negative? For what reasons?

3. Prepare an identification pretest and posttest on geography, perhaps for Asia, Africa, or Latin America. Ask students to identify the nations on a blank map. Then tally the results for each student and the class as a whole. Next, offer instruction for two weeks on the continent in question providing details about each nation's life style, living standards, weather, and topography. Repeat your identification IBQ test. Did the students improve individually and as a group? Why or why not?

4. Select a teacher or course evaluation form from among those published for the purpose and ask students to respond to the questionnaire anonymously. Leave space at the end for suggestions and criticisms in writing. Did most enjoy the program or disapprove of it? For which reasons? How do you feel about subjecting yourself to an evaluation by students? Do you trust the results? Why?

5. Select a course and level you would like to teach: seventh- or eighth-grade U.S. history, civics/problems of democracy/government, world studies, or high school economics. Second, write a set of goals for the course that includes didactic, reflective, and affective dimensions in roughly equal proportions to each other. (Which goal[s] will be your highest priority?) Third, design a complete evaluation program for your students encompassing information-based questions, document-based questions, and perception-based questions. Select or design items for each area and decide how and when you will ask students to respond. Are you planning to administer pretests and posttests of student knowledge and understanding of the material, or student attitudes toward you and the subject? Will you offer students the opportunity to review the program two or three times during the semester? Are you going to give a few major tests, unit by unit, many short quizzes, or a mixture of the two approaches?

6. Design an authentic assessment program for a global studies or world history course at your school. Provide students with examples of the rubrics or criteria for a successful portfolio of work and include assignments that involve many of the students' "multiple intelligences," (i.e., visual, verbal, and writ-

ten). Make sure that a there is a wide variety of tasks that contribute to an over-all judgment.

NOTES

1. Howard Gardner, *Frames of Mind: The Theory of Multiple Intelligences* (New York: Basic Books, Tenth Anniversary Edition, 1993).
2. Lee Cronbach, *Essentials of Psychological Testing*, 5th ed. (New York: Harper & Row, 1989).
3. Alan A. De Fina, *Portfolio Assessment: Getting Started* (New York: Scholastic Books, 1992).
4. Diane Hart, *Authentic Assessment: A Handbook for Educators* (Reading, MA: Addison-Wesley, 1994).
5. Benjamin S. Bloom, G. F. Madaus, and J. T. Hastings, *Evaluation to Improve Learning* (New York: McGraw-Hill, 1981).
6. B. Rosenshine and R. Stevens, "Teaching Functions," in *Handbook of Research on Teaching*, 3rd ed., ed. M. Wittrock (New York: Macmillan, 1986), pp. 376–91.
7. Rensis Likert, *Human Organization: Its Management and Value* (New York: McGraw-Hill, 1967), pp. 39–43.
8. G. Natriello, "The Impact of Evaluation Processes on Students," *Educational Psychologist*, 22 (1987): 155–75.
9. D. W. Johnson, R. T. Johnson, and L. Scott, "Instructional Goal Structure: Cooperative, Competitive, or Individualistic," *Review of Educational Research*, 44 (1974): 213–40.
10. Diane Hart, "Where Are We Heading: Authentic Assessment," in *Authentic Assessment: A Handbook for Educators* (Reading, MA: Addison-Wesley, 1994), pp.9–14.
11. F. Martin and R. Saljo, "On Qualitative Differences in Learning: Two Outcomes as a Function of the Learner's Conception of the Task," *British Journal of Educational Psychology*, 46 (1976): 115–27.
12. Educational Testing Service, *Multiple-Choice Questions: A Closer Look* (Princeton, NJ: Educational Testing Service, 1973).
13. Norman E. Gronlund, *Constructing Achievement Tests* (Englewood Cliffs, NJ: Prentice-Hall, 1982).
14. R. J. Hamilton, "A Framework for the Evaluation of the Effectiveness of Adjunct Questions and Objectives," *Review of Educational Research*, 55 (1985): 47–85.
15. John C. Soper and William B. Walstad, *Test of Economic Literacy, Form A and B* (New York: Joint Council on Economic Education, 1986, 1987).
16. National Council for Geographic Education Test Development Committee, *Competency-Based Geography Test, Secondary Level, Intermediate School Level* (Macomb, IL: National Council for Geographic Education, Western Illinois University, 1983).
17. Norman Gronlund, *Measurement and Evaluation in Teaching*, 5th ed. (New York: Macmillan, 1985), pp. 193–213.
18. S. C. Erickson, "Private Measures of Good Teaching," *Teaching of Psychology*, 10 (1983): 133–36.
19. B. W. Tuckman and D. S. Yates, "Evaluating the Student Feedback Strategy for Changing Teacher Style," *Journal of Educational Research*, 74 (1980): 74–77.

FOR FURTHER STUDY: EVALUATION IN SOCIAL STUDIES

Allen, D., ed. *Assessing Student Learning*. New York: Teachers College Press, 1999.

Archbald, D. A., and F. M. Newmann. *Beyond Standardized Testing: Assessing Authentic Academic Achievement in the Secondary School*. Reston, VA: National Association of Secondary School Principals, 1988.

Bloom, B. S., J. T. Hastings, and G. F. Madaus. *Handbook of Formative and Summative Evaluation of Student Learning*. New York: McGraw-Hill, 1971.

Driscoll, M. P. "The Relationship Between Grading Standards and Achievement: A New Perspective." *Journal of Research and Development in Education*, 19, no. 3 (1989): 13–17.

Fraenkel, J. *Helping Students to Think and Value*. Englewood Cliffs, NJ: Prentice-Hall, 1980.

Gronlund, N., and R. L. Linn. *Measurement and Evaluation in Teaching*. 6th ed. New York: Macmillan, 1990.

Haladyna, Thomas M. *Writing Test Items to Evaluate Higher Order Thinking*. Needham Heights, MA: Allyn & Bacon, 1997.

Hart, Diane. *Authentic Assessment: A Handbook for Educators*. Reading, MA: Addison-Wesley, 1994.

Morse, H. T., and G. H. McCune. *Selected Items for the Testing of Study Skills and Critical Thinking*. Washington, DC: National Council for the Social Studies, 1973.

National Education Association. *Student Portfolios.*

NEA Teacher-to-Teacher Books. Washington, DC: National Education Association, 1993.

Persky, H. R. et al. *NAEP 1994 Geography Report Card: Findings from the National Assessment for Educational Progress*. Prepared by the National Center for Educational Statistics and the Educational Testing Service. Washington, DC: Office of Education, 1996.

Natriello, G., and S. M. Dornbusch. *Teacher Evaluative Standards and Student Effort*. New York: Longman, 1984.

Perrone, V., ed. *Expanding Student Assessment*. Alexandria, VA: Association of Supervision and Curriculum Development, 1991.

Popham, W. J. *Modern Educational Measurement*. Englewood Cliffs, NJ: Prentice-Hall, 1990.

Sudman, S., and N. M. Bradburn. *Asking Questions: A Practical Guide to Questionnaire Design*. San Francisco, CA: Jossey-Bass, 1982.

Tuckman, B. W. *Testing for Teachers*. San Diego: Harcourt Brace Jovanovich, 1988.

ADDENDUM: TEST PUBLISHERS AND DISTRIBUTORS

All test publishers and distributors will provide catalogues of their current tests. The names and addresses of other test publishers and distributors can be obtained from the latest volume of the *Mental Measurements Yearbook*, which should also be consulted for current addresses and Internet sites.

American Guidance Service, Inc.
4201 Woodland Rd.
Circle Pines, MN 55014
800-328-2560

American College Testing
P.O. Box 168
2201 W. Dodge
Iowa City, IA 52243-0168
800-498-6065

The College Board
45 Columbus Avenue
New York, NY 10023-6992
212-713-8060

Consulting Psychologists Press, Inc.
3803 E. Bayshore Road
Palo Alto, CA 94303
800-255-1036

Creative Learning Press Inc.
P.O. Box 320
Mansfield Center, CT 06520
203-429-8118

Critical Thinking Press & Software
P.O. Box 448
Pacific Grove, CA 93950
800-458-4849

CTB/McGraw-Hill
Del Monte Research Park
20 Ryan Ranch Rd.
Monterey, CA 93940

Educational Testing Service
P.O. Box 6155
Rosedale Road
Princeton, NJ 08540
609-951-1691

Examgen, Inc.
Data Bases for Teachers
1201 East Fayette St.
Syracuse, NY 13210
800-736-8172

Institute for Personality and Ability Training
P.O. Box 1188
1801 Woodfield Drive
Champaign, IL 61824-1188
217-352-4739

Objectives and Items Co-op
School of Education
413 Hills House North
University of Massachusetts
Amherst, MA 01002

National Assessment of Educational Progress (NAEP)
Office of Educational Research and Improvement
U.S. Department of Education: National Library of Education
555 New Jersey Avenue, NW
Washington, DC 20208-5641
800-424-1616 or 202-219-1651

Psychologics and Educators
P.O. Box 513
Chesterfield, MO 63006
314-536-2366

Psychological Corporation (Division of Harcourt Brace)
Harcourt, Brace Educational Measurement
555 Academic Court
San Antonio, TX 78204
800-228-0752
Riverside Publishing Company
8420 Bryn Mawr Drive
Chicago, IL 60631-3476
800-767-8378

Scholastic Testing Service
P.O. Box 1056
480 Meyer Road
Bensenville, IL 60106-1617
800-642-6787

India Guide Book

Ινδια Γυιδε Βοοκ

Cindy Wang
Global Studies/ English
Ms. Damato, English
Ms. DeFreitas, Social Studies

*Many thanks to Cindy Wang and her teachers, Ms. Damato and Ms. DeFreitas, for allowing us to reproduce portfolio work from Newtown High School.

Dear Journal:

Today, Yleana and I planned to work on our projects together. So we decided to go to the temples. At first we were going to the Islamic ...que but then when we got on her aunt's car, they decided to go to ...Hindu Temple on Corona Avenue since it was closer.

"We got off the car and walked in. I was...(I can't seem to find the word for it) um..scared Yes! scared is the word. Even though I am a ...hist and Buddhism came from Hinduism, I was still scared. I mean, ...different can they get. Anyway, when we walked in, we realized we had to take off our shoes. I didn't understand why but I still had to do it right? So then, there we were walking inside, holding the letter, wondering to whom should we show it to. Finally we saw this person, ...earing an orange outfit. We showed the letter to him but then he ...ted to us another guy and that other guy pointed to us another person. This man took the letter and read it. He said that "You want to ...ok around or do you want me to explain?" We said "Can you please ...ow us around and explain to us what these Gods are all about?" He ...more than happy to do it.

He walked us out to the front again. He explained that ...inute that we step into the door, we enter the place of worship. He also explained the religion Hinduism. Hinduism was known as *Sanatan Dharma* → (internal ...religion) before. And this temple is build according to the holy book.

Then we walked to the second door, it was like a reddish gate. He ...ved us a bell that was hanging from the ceiling. He said that ...everybody rings the bell before they walk in, it's like the symbol of calling ...elf. Then we entered the big room that was full of "Gods". Before he ...

...go on, Yleana asked him why do people have to take off their ...hoes? He answered that hats and shoes are taken off to show purity. ...ome people even washes their hand before coming in. It is like a symbol ...urity.

He took us to this room. It's was like a fountain and some picture ...sculpture of Gods. I read a sign that said "Do not break a coconut in ...oom". I was going to ask him what this meant but I didn't for some ...rea...n. He went on speaking. He explained that in Hinduism there is only ...one...super power", where the power came from, the supreme. He said ...th...people can not see the supreme. A person cannot worship ...something that they can't see. So people made up these different types of Gods. "It's like, pretending you don't know what the heart looks like, and I tell you the heart looks like this, looks like that. And other people

...lls you the heart looks like this. You will soon have an image, of what ...ou thi...the heart looks like. That is how people came up with all these Gods. ...it there...ly a super...r b...t s...power ...iffere...rm... "He...look us...t e roo...Ylean asked him. Why ...here...ny...or else...ods. H...said "Y...see, a...from th ...ance...p...ask...whe...t y m...or el... ...ants from ... ...answer will be...'s Gods' creation. So the monkey or the elephant will be a form of God too. He then showed us these different figures that were displayed one next to another. The first one he showed us was called "Santoshi Maa" (Maa means mother), people who worship this Goddess believes that perfect satisfaction is all they need. When they are satisfied, then nothing else really matters. Next was the "Gagatri Mata" (Mata also means mother), this Goddess is the Goddess of perfect inte ligence. People who worship Her believes' that if you are smart, then nothing else matters. Next was the "Sarwati Maa". She represents perfect education. the same thing goes with people who worships Her, they believe that education is the most important. If you have education, then nothing else matters. Then he showed us the "Bhagran Parswanath" this represents kindness. If you are kind, then nothing else is important.

He walked us across the room to show us more forms of Gods and Goddesses. The next thing he showed us was Varunder, this is the Goddess of Sea, this meant since the sea looks endless, this Goddess is like it. He then explained to us that the system is like a pyramid. The top is the Supreme, then it is divided into three branches. These three Gods are Chief Gods. One of the three is the Lord Bramha, this God takes care of the beginning. For example he plants the seed. He is the beginning, if he doesn't plant the seed, then where will the plant come from. Then there is Lord Bishnu, he takes care of nourishment or maintenance. For example, when Lord Bramha plants the seed, who will take care of the watering and all the others? Lord Bishnu takes care of the watering and everything else. Then the last of the three is Lord Mahesh. That is the God of Destruction. For example, this God destroys the plant which turns the plant back to dust. Well, I guess we had learn more than what we expected, before we left, we asked him if we can get a few photos of the Gods or Goddesses. He gave us the Santoshi Maa, Lord Mahesh, Gagatri Mata, the monkey God and finally Lord Bishnu. This man was very nice. He made some jokes and made us laugh. He said it was a honor to show us their religion. And the last thing I did before leaving was of course put my shoes back on, kind of put my hands together and nodded my head to show respect to the Gods and Goddesses, and take a photo of the place. That was about it. I had fun though, like always.

PART FOUR

Teaching the Social Studies Curriculum

CHAPTER 9

Teaching World/ Global Studies

East meets West, fifteenth century. How does the artist see each group?
Who, in your opinion is portrayed more realistically, more sympathetically?

SOURCE: Illumination from "Le Livre des Marveilles du Monde." The Pierpont Morgan Library, New York. M. 461, f. 25.

OVERVIEW OF CONTENTS

Main Ideas _____

Setting Goals _____

      Didactic Goals
      Reflective Goals
      Affective Goals

Designing a Program _____

      The Western History Approach
      Alternative Approaches
      An Integrative World or Global History Approach

Key Questions for Teaching World Studies _____

Summary _____

Notes _____

For Further Study: Teaching World Studies _____

MAIN IDEAS

Ten or twenty years ago, world studies was easy to plan and to teach. The dominant goal was to impart to students information about the history of Western Europe; other regions and cultures were mentioned briefly, if at all, and usually from a Western or Eurocentric perspective. There was little consciousness that every people and culture have their own views of history. As a teaching plan, chronology was the rule; world history was typically defined as a series of set pieces beginning with Greece and Rome, progressing through the Middle Ages and the Renaissance, and concluding with World War I, World War II, or—with great luck—the present.

Since those relatively simple days, the world—and world studies—has changed, and so has history. World studies can no longer be taught from a purely Eurocentric or ethnocentric approach.[1] East and west, north and south, have done more than just meet; each is interdependent with the other, resulting in a closer and more sensitive world.

This chapter offers alternative approaches to world studies. You may choose the one most suitable to the goals developed for a school or class, or you may invent a plan that takes into account the particular needs of your own students as well as your responsibility for presenting a balanced view of our changing world.

SETTING GOALS

The goals chosen for a course set its direction, organize its content, and promote different levels of learning. Within world studies/world history, three basic structures guide course development: *theme*, *chronology*, and *place*. Thematic units are usually built around general concepts such as revolution or technological change; chronological units follow a time frame; and a place structure organizes units around area studies such as Africa, Asia, or Latin America. Goal choices should specify the level at which you want students to operate and the way in which you wish to structure the content (see Table 9.1).

TABLE 9.1 Goals for World Studies

Specify Level	Specify Organization		
	Theme	Chronology	Place
Didactic	X	X	X
Reflective	X	X	X
Affective	X	X	X

Didactic Goals

World studies naturally demands a great deal of knowledge—an amount that is nearly impossible to contemplate, let alone teach. Nevertheless, teachers try to cover the facts as well as they can, often consciously or unconsciously offering students a highly selective list of cases and interpretations drawn from the vast pool available.[2] In planning a program, you should acknowledge frankly the need for selection. In particular, avoid didactic goals that are vague, value laden, and general. The following are three examples of ineffective didactic goals:

1. Students will know more about the world. (This goal does not specify what students will know.)
2. Students will understand the sweep and grandeur of Western civilization. (This predisposes students to accept values and judgments that they should decide on for themselves.)
3. Students will comprehend how Western civilization became unique in comparison with others. (This implies that differences exist without searching for similarities and offers no concepts on which to develop either variations or commonalities across civilizations.)

More effective didactic, or informational, world studies goals focus on the themes, concepts, and ideas you want students to acquire; these should be limited in scope and number. Most world studies programs require students to be familiar with the major periods of Western history and with major cultural landmarks. Improved didactic goals for world studies might look like this:

1. Students will accurately describe a major period of Western history from Ancient Greece to the Age of Technology.
2. Students will correctly identify outstanding philosophies, writers, and political leaders from three Western and three non-Western cultures.
3. Students will be able to divide the world into specific regions and distinguish among their physical characteristics and human populations.

Compared with the first set, these goals, though far from perfect, give you and your students a more concrete notion of what they are supposed to know and be able to do. They also provide insight into the direction and content of the program as a whole. The first goal alerts students to chronological periods in Western history, the second goal asks that students learn about important people ("idea" people and government leaders), and the third goal requires students to have a thorough knowledge of landforms and peoples in the different world regions. Although your first didactic goals may be vague and general, you can refine these until you have developed more specific objectives and finally settle on an outline that defines the precise topics, facts, and areas to be studied and the amount of time to be devoted to each.

RESEARCH REPORT

In the mid-1970s, an extensive national sample of U.S. adolescents was taken to measure their knowledge of American and international affairs. The adolescents of eight other nations were tested as well. Predictably, U.S. students knew far less about international topics than about the United States. More interesting, perhaps, was the discovery that American students scored lower, on the average, than did comparable adolescents surveyed in almost every other nation.

SOURCE: J. Torney, A. M. Oppenheim, and R. Farnen, *Civic Education in Ten Nations: An Empirical Study*, a report on the International Association for Evaluation of Educational Attainments (IEA) Civic Education Survey (New York: Wiley, 1975). A shorter report on some key findings is contained in J. Torney, "The International Knowledge and Attitudes of Adolescents in Nine Countries: The IEA Civic Education Survey," *International Journal of Political Education*, 1 (1977): 3–20.

Reflective Goals

There are two kinds of reflective goals in world studies: those designed to foster understanding of causes and influences through analysis and those designed to develop skills of historical and social scientific inquiry. As with didactic goals, there are far too many possible reflective goals for a world studies program, so you must exercise caution and selectivity. Again, you may begin with general goal statements, such as the following:

1. Students will appreciate the contributions of Western societies to the world.
2. Students will understand why technology is the key to history.
3. Students will learn how to think like a historian or social scientist in viewing past events.

These three examples are a beginning, but they leave out the specifics of what is to be studied, how the material will be studied, and which thinking processes students will be asked to apply to the data. "Appreciate," for instance, might mean nothing more than recalling a list of facts, or as much as being able to describe and analyze those Western ideas that appear to have had widespread impact on the everyday affairs of large populations. The second goal assumes an answer (that technology is the key to history) and does not allow students to develop alternative theories. The third goal seeks to develop historiographic or social scientific thinking in students, but does not give an example of exactly which tools of investigation will be stressed.

After more deliberation, you might reshape the three goals into statements with greater behavioral precision:

1. Students will describe and explain at least three inventions, ideas, or skills from five different societies, Western and non-Western, that they

consider contributions to most or all people in the present-day world, and defend their choices with reasons and evidence.

2. Students will examine cultural growth, change, or decline, drawing connections between the economic development and political stability of each, deciding which factor is more important for a "successful" culture (as defined by students).

3. Students will interpret and apply primary sources such as statistics, autobiographies, and public documents of the time to test two or more competing theories of historical "progress" (in excerpted form) offered by scholars in the field, concluding with written judgments about which they would adopt as their own view.

Note that the aforementioned goals still lack specifics—names, dates, theories, primary sources, and so forth—but they provide far more direction than the previous set. The first goal asks students to move from description and analysis to evaluation, not only being able to list contributions but also to defend their choices as good ones. The second goal asks students to consider key or leading ideas (in this case growth, change, and decline) and to compare and contrast these in political and economic terms. The third goal asks student to "think like historians" but not in those terms; rather, it calls on them to use reading and research skills to check the bases on which historians' explanations rest. In short, all three of the expanded, more specific reflective goals (bordering now on what teachers call learning objectives) require student application and interpretation, with a stress on decision making and problem solving rather than the storage and retrieval of information.

Affective Goals

World studies programs also seek to develop affective goals that raise problems of ethical choice and decisions for action.[3] Helping students to decide issues or formulate value positions without forcing them to adopt any specific viewpoint is difficult but worthwhile. Your job is to prepare affective goals that support independent judgment and raise issues but do not easily solve world studies problems.

Affective goals in world studies frequently deal with the way in which students and teachers see other cultures, times, and places. Many world studies programs include aims such as "building sensitivity to other cultures," "seeing ourselves through others' perspectives," "evolving open-mindedness or empathy for other cultures," and "building cross-cultural awareness." All of these phrases share a common commitment to diminishing the prejudice and bias that often seem inherent in the contact among different cultures and societies, and to allowing students to view those unlike themselves as fully human subjects for whom feelings and understandings can be evoked. Affective goals in world studies also frequently encourage students to take positions on issues, especially in the area of international relations. These issues can range from foreign policy to trade and aid, typically centering on such topics as world hunger, human rights, environmental protection, and energy exploitation or conservation.

Typical preliminary, general affective goals are the following:

1. Students will show growing sensitivity to bias directed at others.
2. Students will understand the advantages of democratic ideals and practices.
3. Students will be able to take a stand on foreign affairs.

Sensitivity is not defined in the first goal, nor is it clear how students will demonstrate their increasing awareness of the existence of bias. Defending democratic ideals certainly appears to be a worthy goal, but it presupposes that only democratic ideals as we know them are desirable, without giving students the chance to test these against the realities of relations among nations. Finally, taking a stand is always a useful goal in the social studies, and certainly in world affairs, but nothing in the statement suggests how that stand will be created, from what sources, or to what effect. The addition of the following specific procedures clarifies these goals and makes them more useful to students and teachers alike.

1. Students will develop a list of key words and behaviors that indicate bias and prejudice by one person or people against another (based on a series of case studies—historical events—in which different groups came into contact) and apply their list to two or three present-day examples, deciding in which, if any, of the situations suspicions of bias can be justified.

2. Students will review the United Nations Charter on Human Rights debating which rights they would and which they would not be willing to defend as universal. They will present their arguments in an orderly, organized way and listen carefully to the arguments of those who disagree.

3. Students will collect, analyze, and summarize evidence on a world problem (e.g., human rights, self-determination, the environment, helping others, international trade, and race or ethnic prejudice) as the basis for taking and defending a position, pro or con, on a current proposal for a solution.

These more elaborate goals suggest what students will study, which skills they will be asked to employ, and what kinds of outcomes are sought (e.g., being able to hold and defend a position on a specific issue they have researched). All three examples share a commitment both to amassing evidence for or against an issue and to deciding where the student wants to be in an argument. Actions supporting these goals might include having students raise money for a worthy organization; participate in a protest march on an issue; write a letter to a local, state, or national politician; or perhaps send an editorial to a newspaper. Whatever choices are made, affective goals in world studies guide your development of the course and frame the kinds of skills and sensitivities the curriculum and instructional process will build into the year's work and discussion.

TO DO

Let's say that you are asked to create a unit on one of the following:

family in different cultures

political leadership

social class and caste

cultural contact and conflict

Write a set of at least five didactic, reflective, and affective goals for one of these four world history/global studies units using the behavioral form discussed in this section. As you develop each goal, think about answering the questions that follow:

What would you want students to learn about the topic? Which facts, and which sorts of data might you convey to them? How would you present the unit? Which problems and issues should be raised?

How will you arrange the materials to promote critical and creative thinking about causes and consequences? What kinds of ethical and moral questions arise from the examples presented? Which controversies do you think students need to consider? Offer reasons for your choice of goals and procedures, explaining clearly what you hope to accomplish overall.

DESIGNING A PROGRAM

As we suggested earlier, world studies programs are typically organized in three major ways: by themes, by chronology, or by place.[4]

Thematic approaches usually stress a single focus around which materials are organized (e.g., cultural achievements, international relations, or political power), but multiple themes or concepts can be used as organizing ideas under which events and peoples from many different times and places can be studied. A single theme for a course usually implies a developmental view of events, whereas multiple themes set up a comparative framework; for instance, using the idea of revolution as a concept for side-by-side case studies of the American, French, Russian, Chinese, and Mexican revolutions will lead to student hypotheses about the concept of revolution.

Chronological approaches usually begin at some starting point in the past and work forward, although occasionally courses begin with an aspect of the present and work backward. A starting point in the past inevitably encourages students to focus on the way events and people develop in historical perspective, whereas a present-day beginning leads students to think about the roots of current ideas and actions. Time is a key perspective of both approaches.

World studies programs organized around the idea of *place* usually focus on regions, cultural heartlands, or the historical uniqueness of particular areas. Often, world studies programs introduce geographic concepts followed by units on Africa, Asia, the Middle East, Europe, the Americas, and perhaps Oceania. Manageability is provided by selected case studies from each area that either are directly compared to each other or are followed in time from their historical beginnings to the present.

The three organizing principles—theme, time, and place—yield very different world studies courses if followed rigorously. Often, however, the three approaches are used to develop a program divided into large themes presented chronologically, or a chronologically oriented program that offers flashbacks and "fast forwards" for comparison and contrast. The permutations and combinations are many and varied, all seeking to solve the problem of integrating vast amounts of data from very different histories into a defensible, unified whole. The primary "fused" approach is historical, and this is the dominant approach to world studies overall.

RESEARCH REPORT

In 1981, the Educational Testing Service sponsored a study, "Survey of Global Awareness," of college students, followed two years later by a less elaborate version for secondary school students. With twenty-eight knowledge items from the earlier study and a ten-item "global concern scale," approximately fifteen hundred students in nine states were surveyed regarding their information about and attitudes toward world affairs. The study's aim was to assess the awareness levels of students who had or had not experienced a global program. Results demonstrated that not all programs were equally successful. Most successful were those aimed at brighter students and those that sponsored teacher training in international issues. Least successful were newly created courses, those taught in a traditional manner, and those that could be characterized as regional, or one area, studies.

SOURCE: J. Torney-Purta, *Predictors of Global Awareness and Global Concern in Secondary School Students* (Columbus: Ohio University, Mershon Center, 1985). (A report of the use of a twenty-eight-item knowledge test and a ten-item attitudinal survey derived from the ETS survey with secondary school students in nine states.)

The Western History Approach

World studies programs are relative newcomers to social studies. Western history, with a stress on both the Western and the history aspects, has been the major social studies course available in junior or senior high school for several decades.

Only since World War II has serious national attention been given to the study of non-Western history and culture—an attention resulting eventually in calls for a fully integrated world studies course. A number of attempts have been made to create a global history or world cultures program that integrates east and west, north and south, but no widely popular or entirely defensible solutions have yet emerged.

In contrast to the problems of developing a curriculum of world studies courses, most Western history and/or European history courses rest on a well-organized structure and clearly defined body of information. Typically, Western history is presented as a series of chronological periods, each with a distinct character and set of ideas that have contributed to succeeding stages. The course is usually taught as though Western civilization is following a developmental path of its own, no more than marginally influenced by other regions and cultures. Each time period is presented with its own cast of characters and major events, causes, and consequences, although there are historical schools that would consider either an "outstanding people" or a "causes" approach unacceptable.[5]

Most Western history programs are Eurocentric, meaning that they are organized from a European or American point of view—America being seen as part of the European tradition. This approach ignores the concerns of those whose history is being analyzed.[6] For example, the growth of Islam is often presented almost entirely by the way it affected Western nations. It is rare that more than a few pages are given to important events in Islam, such as the rise of the Ottoman empire. Western civilization programs typically begin with ancient Greece and Rome (and sometimes with the Hebrews), shown as the foundations of Western tradition. Prehistory and the complexities of cultural diffusion that existed even in the periods studied are often overlooked. Indeed, history itself is organized into "ages" or "periods" that imply a steady, linear sequence in Western history. Despite these flaws, however, Western history courses persist and are defended on the grounds that students need to understand their own nation's background and cultural heritage. Course organization is quite predictable. Typical Western history courses cover the following major topics:

A. The Foundations of Civilization
   1. Human Prehistory
   2. Cradles of Civilization
   3. Greek Civilization
   4. Roman Civilization
   5. The Development of Feudalism

B. Restoration and Continuity
   1. The Renaissance
   2. The Reformation
   3. The Age of Discovery
   4. Age of Religious Wars
   5. England and France in the Seventeenth and Eighteenth Centuries
C. The Age of Revolution
   1. The American Revolution
   2. The French Revolution
   3. Napoleon and the Empire
   4. Temporary Restoration
   5. Revolution of 1830
   6. Revolution of 1848
   7. Industrialization
D. Age of Nationalism
   1. Italian Unification
   2. German Union
   3. The Hapsburg Empire
   4. Russia—Change and Emancipation
   5. British and French Imperialism
   6. Ideologies and Social Movements
   7. Alliances and Ententes
   8. World War I
   9. The Peaceful 1920s
   10. World Depression
   11. Rise of Dictators
E. World War II
   1. Preludes
   2. War Breaks Out
   3. The Holocaust
   4. Defeats
   5. Peace and the United Nations
F. Age of Internationalism
   1. Europe Caught between Soviet–U.S. Rivalry: The Cold War
   2. Decolonization of the Third World
   3. Decline of Colonial Powers
   4. Rise of Asian Industrial Powers
   5. Fragmentation of the Communist Countries
   6. Conflicts in the Middle East
   7. Détente: The Soviet Union Crumbles
   8. First, Second, and Third World: Dependence and Interdependence
   9. American Hegemony and the Rise of World Capitalism
   10. A postmodern condition?

Western history courses provide students with solid grounding in the line of history that runs from the Cro-Magnon cave artists to modern times. The program is plotted in terms of events and ideas (e.g., Greek philosophy, Hebrew monotheism, and the birth of Christianity) as foundations for understanding the Middle Ages and the Renaissance, which in turn lay the groundwork for the nationalism, revolution, imperialism, and wars of the eighteenth, nineteenth, and twentieth centuries. Proponents of teaching Western history to U.S. students argue that they need this material because the symbols, ideas, and ideals of U.S. culture have grown from these roots.

WHAT DO YOU THINK?

1. How would you expand the list of topics for a world studies program, especially if you were working on a sensitive topic like Islam? The following is a piece of the Western history outline dealing with the Age of Feudalism, and Threats from the Outside, one of which is the force of Islam. Assuming you wanted to give fair treatment to Muslims vis-à-vis Europeans, how would you change or rearrange these topics? Would you ask students to read portions of the Koran? Would you offer students Muslim views of Christians and Crusaders? How much time would you take away from Europe if you had only three weeks for instruction? What choices need to be made to give students a balanced view of the time period?

    B. The Age of Feudalism
        1. The Growth of Christianity
        2. Threats to Europe From "Outside"

2. Expand the brief outline of Western history given. Revise it in a way that is fair to others (e.g., Arabs, Turks, or Jews) and diminishes student stereotypes of both European and non-European peoples and time periods (e.g., the Dark Ages or Colonialism).

Criticism. Western history courses are open to serious criticism, much of which arises from the growing acknowledgment that we live in a shrinking global community. Immigration westward from the east and south has altered the U.S. population mix significantly. There is a growing recognition that many peoples, cultures, and critical events have been seriously neglected and a new cry has been raised to replace the Western history model in social studies with world or global studies programs. At the very least, critics ask that Western courses be expanded to include more comparative examples from other cultures, or that a parallel non-Western studies program be offered in tandem.

    Educators who believe that we are moving closer and closer to a one-world community argue that Western history programs give students a biased and isolated view of both the past and the present. They argue that cultures have nearly always traded, traveled, borrowed, and combined with each other and that Western history courses do not take adequate account of cultural diffusion. In addition, critics point out that the course itself is often extremely narrow in focus, concentrating mainly on a chronology of major political and technological growth and slighting cultural and social issues. Most courses focus primarily on only a few European countries (France, England, Italy, Germany, and the Soviet Union) with scant reference to Eastern Europe, the Iberian peninsula, or the Middle East and Greece beyond ancient times. Finally, critics argue that Western history courses reflect scholarship that is largely the product of a White, male, Christian conqueror's point of view—one that ignores or slights women, non-Whites, non-Christians, the poor and less fortunate, minorities, and the conquered. To understand these arguments, you need only review a representative Western history outline. Few women or minorities are mentioned; the conquered rarely have the opportunity to describe their views and feelings; and competing cultures are treated as peripheral to the main events in the West, even though some groups (e.g., the Byzantines, the Turks, and the Persians) threatened or influenced Europe for centuries.

Defense.   Attacks on the role of Western history in the curriculum have been met with equally vehement defenses, such as the one mounted by the members of the Bradley Commission on History in Schools. This group argues strongly in favor of retaining a focus on European traditions, emphasizing history over the social sciences, and reinforcing students' identification with a common heritage of Western ideas and symbols.[8] The core of the defense is the notion that the United States is largely a product of Western historical development and that all students need to understand that development, whatever their own backgrounds. Many of those who defend the importance of teaching students about the rise of the West nevertheless are displeased with the way they see the course taught, preferring, especially at the secondary level, discussions of great works of literature, philosophy, and art to textbook narratives and lectures. Real familiarity with Western history, they argue, can emerge only from firsthand study of the most influential key works, from the Bible and Plato through Machiavelli and Descartes to John Stuart Mill and Rousseau. They contend that through such study, methodological as well as course content issues are raised.

Powerful arguments for Western history or European studies, then, are countered by equally intense and well-grounded arguments for world or global approaches. The two, of course, are not necessarily incompatible. But a number of problems must be resolved in fusing them into a single, coherent world studies program. Most global history or world studies programs are piecemeal collections of Western and non-Western time periods, famous personalities, and cultural contributions. Often non-Western units are simply added to Western or European history courses without any real concordance of events and personalities. Courses stress points of contact—an East meets West or North meets South perspective—but difficult choices must still be made about what to teach among materials that remain unfamiliar for many teachers. The difficulties are compounded because there is little direct linkage among time periods across cultures; the Middle Ages in European history, for example, have no relevance for African or Chinese history.

SAMPLE LESSON PLAN

> As you walk down the school hall, you notice the print of a famous painting. It is just what you need for your Renaissance unit, so you ask the office if you can take it down for the day and discuss the style and subjects with your students. The painting actually awakens student memories of other artworks, and they supply more examples by citing the *Mona Lisa*, *David*, *The Creation*, and *The Last Supper* during the class discussion. ... What a success!

World studies embraces so much material that neither teachers nor students have time to absorb more than a modest amount in the course of a normal year. Selections must be made that do not always seem reasonable to students. As the demand to teach more information grows, teachers tend to use instructional techniques that speed up the transfer of that information (i.e., lectures, textbook assignments, and homework) in a program that would be better served by involvement, discussion, and understanding of what are frequently confusing and unfamiliar ideas and events. A teacher who wants students to know and understand Buddhism or Confucianism but rushes through the "facts" of Chinese history or severely condenses the Buddha's main ideas loses the chance for comparing and contrasting, or lingering over complex and thought-provoking ideas that have influenced millions of people for thousands of years. That teacher is left with a "cover versus understand" dilemma that can be resolved only by relatively unsatisfactory compromises. Within the emerging field of world studies, some alternative approaches to instruction have been developed to address this problem.

Alternative Approaches

As yet, there is no universally accepted structure for teaching world studies in the social studies curriculum, but there is progress and movement. Many trial runs are underway that offer a variety of conceptions from which to choose.

Four major themes have emerged: a *geographic* approach, which stresses human and physical interactions among the world's regions and climates; an *international relations* approach, which stresses the relations between and among the political systems of the world; a *cross-cultural* approach, which invites comparisons among cultures that have evolved different (or similar) solutions to fundamental human problems; and an *integrated* or *global history* approach, which focuses on social, economic, and political change working toward increasing global interdependence.

Within each of these approaches, teachers can make other choices as well. The three organizing principles outlined at the beginning of this chapter—theme, chronology, and place—can structure any of these alternative approaches. You might want to work backward from current events, or focus on issues such as human rights, or recombine historical topics into conceptual areas like social systems, cultural diffusion, or the environment.

A Geographic Approach (Regional Studies).   World studies programs can stress the variation and development of place and location framing everything in a spatial rather than a historical perspective.[9] If you choose this route, introduce students to places by discussing the relation of sites to other factors such as resources or trade routes. Focus on where innovations began and how they spread, where cities or agriculture first developed, and how new technologies were disseminated. Move on to discuss why the same ideas and institutions took different forms in different locales and regions, viewing variation on a local, national, regional, or worldwide basis. This geographic or regional approach to world studies invites comparisons of cities, technology, culture, and political systems, and raises questions about why some people have achieved great wealth and influence while others cope poorly with their environments and eke out only a subsistence living.

Introduce students to physical and human regions as defined by historical and geographical research, usually along cultural or physical lines (such as those that delineate Europe, Asia, Africa, and the Middle East). Ask them to use data to analyze and discuss the ways in which peoples and ecosystems have interacted on local, national, regional, and worldwide bases to create distinct cultures. National development, its causes and consequences, is one key concept that holds together the threads of the course because this is a major problem confronting the modern world. Rich and poor nations are increasingly interdependent economically and ecologically, sharing a world where economic development brings prosperity to some people but often havoc and destruction to the environment, which is a tough value dilemma for students to wrestle with throughout the course.

SAMPLE LESSON PLAN

Not another day for review, say the students. Dull, boring, ugh! They suggest that they will do their own review in the form of the game of *Jeopardy*, with items rated by difficulty, 100 to 400 points, set up by categories of famous people, events, inventions, and places. The students reorganize the room and play the game during which they review all of your materials on Africa. The winner surprises you with her knowledge. The class seems well prepared for the examination, and they had a lot of fun as well. So, be happy and let them take over again.

A world geography (i.e., regional) approach to social studies might include the following topics:

A. Spatial Relations
   1. Definitions of Geographic Terms
      a. land use/activity patterns
      b. topography
      c. location and place
      d. cultural variation
   2. Regionalization
      a. functional regions (linkages through trade, travel, and communication, etc.)
      b. physical regions
      c. human regions
   3. Physical Geography
      a. climate zones
      b. land forms
      c. natural resources
      d. human–land interaction
   4. Human Geography
      a. population distribution
      b. geographical heartlands
      c. cultural diffusion
      d. political conflict
   5. Functional Regions
      a. international trade
      b. political alliances
      c. migration patterns
      d. cross-national and international organizations
   6. Development Patterns: Theories of Social/Political Stability
      a. economic growth
      b. demographic change
      c. social/political stability
      d. technological development

In the geographic approach (of which the previous list represents but one possible format), human–environmental features emerge strongly, as do questions of place and location, change and crisis. Unfortunately, the approach does not provide a very strong historical background for students, nor does it yield a clear picture of periodization for either Western regional or non-Western regional history. Nevertheless, if your goals are to build student understanding of the earth's features and how people have developed in different regions, the geographic approach is excellent.

LET'S DECIDE

The idea of place gives world studies quite a different perspective from that of theme or chronology, yet the latter are important as well. If you and several colleagues or classmates follow a place or regional structure for teaching world history, how would you and the group select content for the different regions—by theme, by time, or by country? Would your Africa unit begin with a study of its culture, its prehistory, or a case study of several nations such as Egypt, Kenya, and Nigeria? Would it make a difference to you and your students how the course is organized?

How would you solve conceptual problems if you decide to teach by countries? For example, are China, Japan, and India comparable to Africa south of the Sahara? Is Central America a place in the same sense as France and England? Your group choices!

REGIONAL CASE STUDIES (e.g., three selections from each area)
1. Africa
    a.
    b.
    c.
2. Asia
    a.
    b.
    c.
3. Europe
    a.
    b.
    c.
4. The Middle East
    a.
    b.
    c.
5. The Americas
    a.
    b.
    c.
6. Oceania (Australasia) and the polar regions
    a.
    b.
    c.

An International Relations Approach.   An international relations approach to world studies stresses issues that grow out of the political relationships among people, groups, agencies, institutions, nations, and worldwide organizations throughout history. Generally, an international focus works best if the course begins with or stresses the present and works back to the causes and underpinnings of current events.[10] The increasingly connected current events of our time as reported in the media help to justify an international approach to a global studies program. Each day, the media report a wide range of developments in trade, world debt, political diplomacy, human rights, and popular music to demonstrate the influence people and nations have on others, with distance often less important than political and economic factors.

In addition, students need to be introduced to foreign affairs concepts and to the tools and ideas used by political and social scientists. Through the issues you select, you can involve students in debates, discussions, and activities. This can be citizenship education with special attention to tensions between local/national citizen concerns and world concerns: Are the interests of my nation the same as those of the region or world as a whole? If not, then what, if anything, can be done to satisfy as fairly as possible the needs of all?

Global citizenship discussions help students to understand their own individual place in the international system and the role that their nation plays as an actor, for better or worse. Past and present events can be seen as part of a worldwide set of power relations where all of us have a role, with students interpreting events through a series of policy "futures."[11] Such an active understanding of global policy and its effects will, in turn, enable students to take stands on the vital issues of the time.

Course topics for a world studies program organized from a foreign policy or international point of view might include all or some of the following:

A. An International Political Approach
   1. International Relations
      a. power: war and diplomacy
      b. wealth: trade and investment
      c. information: travel and communication
      d. policy: alliances and enmities
   2. Ideology
      a. capitalism
      b. socialism
      c. Marxism
      d. mixed forms
   3. Key Points of Conflict
      a. east–west
      b. north–south
      c. interregional
      d. intraregional
B. The Big Issues
   1. The International System
      a. world as a system
      b. emergence of one-world system
      c. U.S. role: trade and aid
      d. distribution of income and resources
      e. sovereignty and intervention
   2. Actors in the System
      a. states and empires
      b. multinational corporations
      c. international organizations
      d. groups and special interests
      e. local grassroots movements
C. Security Among States and People
   1. Global Interdependence and Control
      a. national defense systems
      b. regional alliances
      c. international peacekeeping
   2. The Challenge of Development
      a. inequality between states
      b. new technologies
      c. political stability
      d. economic development
      e. environmental challenges

As with all outlines in these chapters, this is only one of a variety of structures that can be used. It is intended to suggest possibilities rather than to serve as a final course description.

WHAT DO YOU THINK?

How far back in time could an international relations approach be used to teach world history? It could be used to study the nineteenth century, surely! And it could go back to the eighteenth, seventeenth, sixteenth, and fifteenth centuries as well. Some scholars such as Immanuel Wallerstein, in *The Modern World System*, assert that the entire planet has been drawing together into a single economic and political system since the Renaissance in Europe.

Using this idea, could you design a global course in which all of the traditional topics of the Western approach are matched with analogies, similar cases from Asia, Africa, and the Middle East? What diplomatic initiatives would the Chinese of the sixteenth century have to employ to compete with Europe? Why did some nations, like Japan, choose not to compete for hundreds of years and then suddenly emerge as a world power? Why did Turkey, a great world power in the sixteenth, seventeenth, and eighteenth centuries, decline so much in the nineteenth and twentieth centuries?

Develop an international relations/world history course for one century—say the sixteenth—remembering to keep a balance between East and West in choosing examples and case studies.

A Cross-Cultural Approach.   Cross-cultural approaches are organized around concepts or themes that invite immediate and direct comparisons of institutions, traditions, customs, ideas, literature, art, and music. Themes may be political, social, economic, aesthetic, philosophical, and geographic or environmental. The cross-cultural approach is ideally suited to help students understand that many common problems have been solved quite differently by people around the globe.[12] Further, a cross-cultural view encourages students to look at developments from the perspective of other cultures as well as their own. "Strange and exotic" customs take on new meaning through comparison with more familiar ideas and practices, and familiar customs frequently benefit from the comparison and can be viewed in a new light. You might ask students to compare the American nuclear family with the extended family common to the Muslim Middle East; students may perceive advantages in the large networks of relatives, and they may also begin to understand the origins and rationale for polygamy and purdah (the practice among Muslim women of wearing veils in public) in Saudi Arabia and other places, even if they disagree with such practices.

The cross-cultural framework can also yield a deeper understanding of the relation between repressive and authoritarian governments and serious social and economic difficulties. By studying relatively wealthy and poor societies side by side, students can begin to develop their own theories of political development in which they see the correlation between juntas or dictatorships and weak economies and political or ethnic hatred, and between democracies and relative wealth, strong beliefs in the rule of law, and histories of political compromise. You can ask students to check and recheck hypotheses as they encounter new cases and examples.

Within the cultural themes mentioned, data may be arranged with or without reference to chronology, and with or without reference to place. In other words, theme is usually predominant over other organizing ideas and controls the examples. The ancient Greeks of the *Odyssey* and *Iliad* may be seen as a certain type of society for which the Vikings provide a useful analog. Both societies were characterized by seafarers, warriors, polytheists, poets, and storytellers. A cross-cultural view of Viking and ancient Greek societies would provide students with more insights into how cultures develop than would the study of their respective differences, despite the fact that they are separated by fifteen hundred years. A thematic organization looks more toward comparing many societies than it does toward examining immediate contexts or time periods. The big question is whether or not a comparison works in producing useful, productive, and valid generalizations about two or more cultures.

Although the thematic arrangement for global/world studies is infrequently followed for an entire course, you can use it as part of another structure by introducing numerous examples or cases representing the same category for comparison and contrast. These categories can range from the very broad, like political and social systems, to somewhat more specific ideas, such as leadership, class and caste, or family. Use data that relate to the theme and promote hypothesis development about a class of events, products, or ideas. The cross-cultural approach is most open to including art, music, and literature in the social sciences and history.

General themes or concepts that might be used to organize a world studies course include the following:

A. Political System
  1. Leadership
      a. democracy (republic)
      b. dictatorship
      c. military rule
      d. one-party rule
      e. aristocracy (oligarchy)
  2. Traditions and Values
      a. stable forms
      b. unstable forms
  3. Participation Levels
      a. education
      b. income
      c. class and caste
B. Economic Development
  1. Type of Economy
      a. traditional
      b. market
      c. command
  2. Technological Level
      a. underdeveloped
      b. developing
      c. developed
  3. Technological Innovation
      a. invention
      b. application
      c. diffusion
C. Social Structure
  1. Social System
      a. egalitarian
      b. class systems
      c. caste systems
  2. Social Change
      a. development
      b. stagnation
      c. regression
D. Belief and Value Patterns
  1. Thought Systems
      a. religious

      b. philosophical
      c. ideological
    2. Distribution and Impact
      a. geographic spread
      b. length of change
  E. Cultural Creativity
    1. Modes of Expression
      a. language, literature, and learning
      b. the fine arts and music
      c. ideas and styles
    2. Diffusion Networks
      a. adoption
      b. adaptation
      c. conflict

A comparative-thematic structure like the one outlined here encourages imaginative leaps in thinking and the generation and testing of hypotheses about large categories of undeniably important events in human history. The discovery of parallel cases and/or dramatic contrasts for students is what makes this approach exciting and interesting. From this type of course structure your students should develop a strong sense of why and how human behavior shapes and is shaped by political, social, cultural, economic, emotional, and aesthetic needs. Students are often excited by testing a theory about why free enterprise systems develop in one set of circumstances while a different set of circumstances produces state-controlled economies. The major problem in this approach is that students develop relatively little insight concerning the way historical tradition evolves from ancient roots and traditions. A thematic structure does yield a good sense of past and present-day events and problems but is based more on a conceptual understanding of a slice of human behavior than on either geographic influences or temporal sequences.

TO DO

The outline that follows suggests a "shorthand" history of the world from an anthropological and technological perspective. Changing economic and technological patterns dominate each step in a chronological story that moves from hunting and gathering to international trade and communication. Isn't a great deal left out? Isn't the perspective still really based on a Eurocentric view of the world? Aren't cultural products in the literary and artistic sense largely omitted? And where are the "great ideas" of religion and philosophy that still influence daily life on much, if not most, of our planet?

  A. Cultural Diversity and Integration
    1. The Development of Cultural Patterns
      a. hunting and gathering—tool use
      b. agricultural revolution—farming
      c. urbanization
    2. Trade and Travel
      a. local
      b. regional
      c. worldwide
    3. Time Periods/Historical Eras
      a. age of empires

    b. age of discovery and imperialism
    c. industrialization and nationalism
    d. the world wars and the spread of technology
    e. the global system and the "First," "Second," and "Third" cultures
       of the world
4. Internationalization
    a. war and peace issues
    b. environmental issues
    c. information and communication issues
    d. allocation of resources issues

Can you correct the outline and improve on it? Can you change it to omit all trace of bias? Where would you fit the history of Latin America and Africa into this outline?

Rewrite the capsule outline from (a) a non-Western perspective, for example, China, the Middle East, or India; (b) a religious and philosophical perspective, stressing great moral, ethical, and religious thinkers—from Confucius to Gandhi; (c) an artistic perspective, emphasizing great masterpieces of art, music, and literature across cultures; and (d) a perspective of your own as the basis for developing the world studies program on a thematic cross-cultural basis.

An Integrative World or Global History Approach

Instruction that takes an integrative world or global history approach seeks to survey the earth's development in time and space, relating the events in one culture or region to those of other cultures and regions. A single theme (e.g., cultural diffusion, political interaction, or economic exchange) may dominate the curriculum, or you might focus on more than one theme with each time period or region. Clearly, the integrated course is the most challenging to prepare, to teach, and to conceptualize, but it is the most potentially useful in understanding the world's history and also the most intellectually provocative. It pulls together theories, events, personalities, and peoples in ways most students or teachers have not examined before. Risks are involved because some comparisons might yield little interest, whereas others could present many fascinating avenues for investigation.

Even if Western history is the target, a global approach can offer new insights by juxtaposing cases and examples that have influenced the West. As an example, the inclusion of better materials on the rise of Islamic culture during the so-called European Middle Ages raises interesting questions about comparative lifestyles as it demonstrates a very strong diffusion of ideas in science, the arts, and philosophy from East to West rather than the other way round. The contribution of Muslim societies to European culture is, of course, nothing new, but it is rarely emphasized when the course is taught from a narrow Western perspective. As students broaden their perspectives on the world, they find new ideas and connections for study and discussion, and both students and teachers may conclude that interaction in previous eras was undoubtedly greater than is commonly assumed. Networks of trade, aid, and borrowing provided a framework for modern development, even when groups and societies were (or are) in a state of conflict and expressed mutual hostility toward one another.

Many school systems offer two-year world/Western history programs that may still be inadequate to the task but are better than only a single year of instruction. The key to a sensible and meaningful course of study is in two decisions that you must make: Which theme(s) will provide a central focus by which to integrate the vast quantity of material to be discussed? And, what cases or events will be selected out of all those available? Programs often flounder in confusion because they attempt the impossible: a too-brief coverage of all eras and cultures. The usual result is that students memorize disparate facts, strange names, and peculiar, unrelated events from around the world. Without a central theme, the global approach will not make sense to students, who will drown in a sea of details.

By focusing on selected time periods and a few themes, you can build a comparative framework for students that may be expanded to other cultures and time periods, although a certain amount of data will be lost in the process. A world history course that integrates many aspects of human society usually does not lack data; rather, it lacks a conception. Whatever overall conception is used, serious questions will still arise about slighting certain cultures in favor of others, distorting one region's history from the point of view of another, and separating reliable from unreliable evidence and sources.

RESEARCH REPORT

Based on interviews, case studies, and observational data, Bay Area teachers and students were surveyed concerning their knowledge of international economics and peace/conflict issues. The "Study of Stanford and the Schools," conducted in the mid-1980s, demonstrated that the more knowledgeable students were those who felt most free to express opinions in class contrary to those of the instructor, and those who felt least free to voice their opinions also demonstrated the lowest scores on international economics and peace/conflict items.

SOURCE: J. Torney-Purtz and D. Landsdale, "Classroom Climate and Process in International Studies: Qualitative and Quantitative Data from the American Schools and the World Project," paper delivered at the American Educational Research Association, San Francisco, 1986. It assesses the results of data gathered as part of the study on Stanford and the school.

Conceptual organizing themes are readily available. Contact among societies or the diffusion of ideas and inventions could serve as your guide to choosing periods and cultures. You would select only those times and places that illustrate the effects of contact, positive or negative; and you might achieve balance by drawing a case study from each cultural region: Africa, Asia, the Middle East, Europe, and the Americas. The rise and fall of empires is another potential organizing theme through which you can demonstrate political growth and variety, surges and declines in international contacts, and the problem of accommodating both freedom and political stability as basic human desires.

At present, numerous outlines exist for integrative approaches, all of which are experimental and subject to revision as our research and experience in teaching a "world view" of history deepens and broadens. Although some fear this lack of structure, many view it as an invitation for trial and innovation.

SAMPLE LESSON PLANS

Integrating histories is not as easy as it looks: What would the European Middle Ages or feudal period correspond to in China or the Middle East? Was there a frontier in African history as there was in North America? What would world history look like through the eyes of a Chinese emperor? Can valid comparisons be made among European, Indian, and Native American myths and epics? What about all epics? What perspectives would help in bringing disparate histories and cultures together? Prepare an outline integrating two or more cultures on the basis of the following:

    a. great personalities
    b. broad social movements
    c. diffusion of ideas
    d. diseases and medical innovations
    e. technological inventions
    f. trade and commerce
    g. population changes and pressures

KEY QUESTIONS FOR TEACHING WORLD STUDIES

The complexities and the variety of world and Western studies programs place them among the most interesting and worthwhile courses social studies programs can offer. A number of key questions and common themes emerge from the conflicting views on how to teach the course and what should be included or excluded in the content. These questions provide methods and viewpoints from which to study the history of all cultures that have contributed to human history in as fair a manner as possible.[13]

SAMPLE LESSON PLAN

A different view of the Cold War might result from focusing on the development of weapons systems in the United States and the Soviet Union. Given the data presented in this chart, what conclusions would you draw? See Figure 9.2 on the following page.

SOURCE: Sam Keen, *Faces of the Enemy* (San Francisco: Harper & Row, 1986). Reprinted by permission.

Listed here are elements that could provide an organizing framework for global study:

Interdependence: how and why events and peoples are linked with each other and their environments.

Development: how and why cultures and societies have forged ahead or have fallen back economically and technologically.

Change: how and why different social, economic, and political systems have evolved.

Conflict and Cooperation: how and why people have sometimes shown hostility toward each other and worked together in peace at other times.

Cultural Diffusion: how and why historians and social scientists have created techniques and methods to analyze critically and to compare historical events and human behavior.

Diversity and Universality: how and why individuals, groups, and peoples have created distinct lifestyles and societies to solve problems of security, well-being, making a living, organization, and creativity.

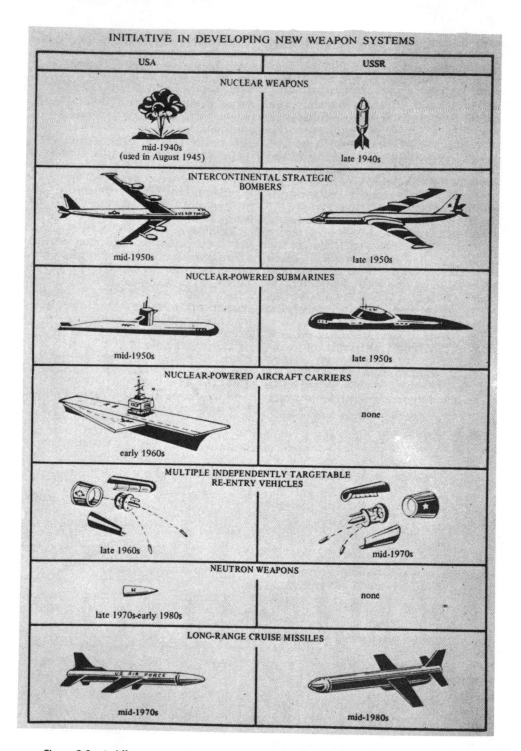

INITIATIVE IN DEVELOPING NEW WEAPON SYSTEMS

USA	USSR
NUCLEAR WEAPONS	
mid-1940s (used in August 1945)	late 1940s
INTERCONTINENTAL STRATEGIC BOMBERS	
mid-1950s	late 1950s
NUCLEAR-POWERED SUBMARINES	
mid-1950s	late 1950s
NUCLEAR-POWERED AIRCRAFT CARRIERS	
early 1960s	none
MULTIPLE INDEPENDENTLY TARGETABLE RE-ENTRY VEHICLES	
late 1960s	mid-1970s
NEUTRON WEAPONS	
late 1970s-early 1980s	none
LONG-RANGE CRUISE MISSILES	
mid-1970s	mid-1980s

Figure 9.2   A different view of the Cold War might result from focusing on the development of weapons systems in the United States and the USSR. Given the data presented in this chart, what conclusions would you draw?
SOURCE: Sam Keen, *Faces of the Enemy*. San Francisco: Harper & Row, 1986. Reprinted by permission.

The Bradley Commission on History in Schools suggests a similar list of themes that its members consider basic to all history: (a) civilization; (b) human interaction with the environment; (c) values, beliefs, political ideas, and institutions; (d) conflict and cooperation; (e) comparative history; and (f) patterns of social and political interaction.[14]

LET'S DECIDE

With at least two colleagues or classmates, develop one or two of the themes suggested, for example, political ideas or patterns of social and political interaction by using old and new films that have a common cross-cultural and literary theme. These might include titles such as the following: *The Last Emperor* (1987), which is the story of Pu Yi, last Manchu royal ruler; *Metropolis* (1926), which portrays workers versus managers in a futuristic city; *Shogun* (1980 TV series), in which a British sailor meets Samurai warriors; *Reds*, in which John Reed witnesses the Russian Revolution (1981); *Cabaret* (1973), which shows decadence and oppression in pre-WW II Germany; *Beyond Rangoon* (1995), which depicts military repression in modern Myanmar (Burma); *A World Apart* (1988), which is the story of a mother and daughter facing problems of Apartheid in South Africa; *Amistad* (1997), which details a revolt on a slave ship headed for the Americas; or *Gandhi* (1982), which is the story of the epic struggle for freedom and independence in India.

SUMMARY

World studies/world history is a complex and demanding course to design, prepare, and teach. You can develop goals on the didactic, reflective, and affective levels that require students to acquire knowledge, to build understanding, and to raise ethical questions about the world's peoples and events. A well-balanced program could ask students to collect information about diverse cultures, reflect on the reasons for differences and similarities among social groups, and make choices among policies and actions that affect the world's environment and population.

World studies/history courses have grown out of Western history programs that have usually been Eurocentric in perspective, viewing history only in relation to American or Western events. Traditional topics range from ancient Greece and Rome to the Medieval and Renaissance periods and on to the French Revolution and World Wars I and II. In response to a growing demand for the study of non-Western cultures, alternatives to this largely chronological Western European organization have evolved. Global studies programs attempt to present elements of all major areas and cultures to students. Among alternative approaches are those that unite and compare cultures through themes, time, and place. Examples of world programs have included those emphasizing area or regional studies, cross-cultural concepts, international relations, or some combination of these designs. All share a commitment to the same key concepts of interdependence, economic development, social change, diffusion, perspective, and universality.

TO DO

Every culture has had its view of the world, often in startlingly different forms and frequently placing themselves at the geographic center. It seems that most people have great difficulty imagining the world from any but their own point of view. Likewise, social studies teachers often have trouble imagining the world history course from anything but a Western point of view. To correct this situation, you are invited to take action in researching two areas that could use some attention.

Collect at least a half-dozen maps of the world from different nations (e.g., China, Japan, Nigeria, Brazil, Israel, or Iran). Is their depiction of the earth realistic? Is each country at the physical center? Do any of the maps view the world from the European perspective? Discuss why maps and worldviews may differ. Raise questions about the widespread use of the Mercator projection in English-speaking nations. Are there any objections to the Mercator projection? Are there alternative projections? Are there any geographic projections that are entirely fair and unbiased to all sections of the globe? Why or why not?

Select a commonly taught topic such as one of the following: ancient Greece, imperial Rome, the Renaissance in Italy, the American Revolution, World War II, or the Cold War.

Search out at least one competing view of the time, possibly a Persian perspective on Greece or a Muslim description of Renaissance Italy. Treat the event from more than one standpoint, that is, fit and refit the topic you have chosen into a chronological, cross-cultural, thematic, and international relations framework. Do the key questions you might ask change or remain the same? Are the same ideas suggested by each framework or do interpretations and concepts change? What are the advantages and disadvantages of each of the different organizations for world studies?

Share your conclusions with others. Decide which framework is best. Discuss and list the didactic, reflective, and affective questions that are most important for the topic you selected, no matter what perspective or framework is employed.

NOTES

1. Paul Robinson and Joseph M. Kirman, "From Monopoly to Dominance," in *Social Studies and Social Sciences: A Fifty Year Perspective*, Bulletin No. 78, ed. Stanley P. Wronski and Donald H. Bragaw (Washington, DC: National Council for the Social Studies, 1986), pp. 15–28.
2. Arno Bellack, "What Knowledge Is of Most Worth?", in *Curriculum Development*, ed. Donald E. Orlosky and B. Othanel Smith (Chicago: Rand McNally, 1978), pp. 212–19.
3. Douglas D. Alder and Matthew T. Downey, "Problem Areas in the History Curriculum," in *History in the Schools*, Bulletin No. 74, ed. Matthew T. Downey (Washington, DC: National Council for the Social Studies, 1985), pp. 114–23.
4. Robert B. Woyach and Richard C. Remy, *Approaches to World Studies* (Needham Heights, MA: Allyn & Bacon, 1989).
5. Gilbert Allardyce, "The Rise and Fall of the Western Civilization Course," *American Historical Review*, 87, no. 3 (June 1982): 695–743. (Includes responses.)
6. Amin Samir, *Eurocentrism* (New York: Monthly Review Press, 1989).
7. Richard C. Remy and Robert B. Woyach, *Strengthening High School World Studies Courses: Conference Report* (Columbus: Ohio University, Mershon Center, Citizenship Development for a Global Age Program, 1984).
8. Bradley Commission on History in Schools, *Building a Curriculum History: Guidelines for Teaching History in Schools* (Washington, DC: Educational Excellence Network, 1988).
9. S. J. Natoli and A. R. Bond, *Geography in Internationalizing the Undergraduate Curriculum* (Washington, DC: Association of American Geographers, 1985).

10. Richard C. Remy et al., *International Learning and International Education in a Global Age*, Bulletin No. 47 (Washington, DC: National Council for the Social Studies, 1975).
11. Center for Foreign Policy Development/Choices for the Twenty-First Century Project, *Keeping the Peace in an Age of Conflict: Debating the U.S. Role* (Providence, RI: Brown University, 1994).
12. Philip D. Curtin, *Cross-Cultural Trade in World History* (Cambridge: Cambridge University Press, 1984). (Excellent study of trade in global perspective.)
13. Merry Merryfield, "Pedagogy for Global Perspectives in Education: Studies of Teachers' Thinking and Practice," in *Theory and Research in Social Education*, 26, no. 3 (Summer 1998): 342–379.
14. Bradley Commission, *Building a Curriculum History*, pp. 10–11.

FOR FURTHER STUDY: TEACHING WORLD STUDIES

Anderson, L. *Schooling for Citizenship in a Global Age: An Exploration of the Meaning and Significance of Global Education*. Bloomington, IN: Social Studies Development Center 1979.

Barber, B. R. "Jihad vs McWorld," *Atlantic Monthly* (March 1992): 53–55, 58–63.

Berggren, P., with the editors. *Teaching with the Norton Anthology: World Masterpieces. A Guide for Instructors*. New York: W. W. Norton, 1997.

Braudel, F. *Civilization and Capitalism, Fifteenth–Eighteenth Century*. Vol. 1, *The Structures of Everyday Life*. Vol. 2, *The Wheels of Commerce*. Vol. 3, *The Perspective of the World*. New York: Harper & Row, 1979, 1981, 1984.

Center for Foreign Policy Development/Choices Education Project. Thomas J. Watson Jr. (multiple units for schools and colleges on international topics, 1991–1997) The Institute for International Studies at Brown University, Box 1948, Providence, RI 02912.

Contreras, G., ed. *Latin American Culture Studies: Information and Materials for Teaching about Latin America*. Austin: University of Texas Institute of Latin American Studies, 1987.

Facts on File Regional History Series:
  Diagram Group
  African History on File, 1994
  Diagram Group
  Asian History on File, 1995
  Diagram Group
  European History on File, 1996
  Chapman, V. L. & Lindroth, D. eds.
  Latin American History on File, 1996
  New York, NY: Facts on File, Inc. 10001-2006
  World Literature Today
  Norman, OK: University of Oklahoma

Goodlad, J. L. "The Learner at the World's Center." *Social Education*, 50, no. 10 (1986): 424–36.

Hanvey, B. *An Attainable Global Perspective*. New York: Center for Global Perspectives, 1978.

Hein, H. *The Exploratorium: The Museum as a Laboratory*. Washington, DC: Smithsonian Institution Press, 1990.

Hibbert, C. *Cities and Civilizations*. New York: Welcome Rain (distributed by Stewart, Tabori, & Chang), 1996.

Kneip, W. M., ed. *Next Steps in Global Education: A Handbook for Curriculum Development*. New York: American Forum, 1987.

Kobrin, D. *Beyond the Textbook: Teaching History Using Documents and Primary Sources*. Portsmouth, NH: Heinemann, 1996.

Leinwand, G. *Teaching of World History*. Bulletin No. 54. Washington, DC: National Council for the Social Studies, 1978.

Lund, M. *Preventing and Mitigating Violent Conflicts: A Guide for Practitioners*. Washington, DC: U.S. Institute for Peace Press, 1996.

Merryfield, M. *Teaching About the World: Teacher Education Programs with a Global Perspective*. Columbus, OH: Ohio State University, Mershon Center, 1990.

Merryfield, M., E. Jarchow, and S. Pickert. *Preparing Teachers to Teach Global Perspectives*. Thousand Oaks, CA: Corwin Press, 1997.

Organization of American Historians. *Restoring Women to History: Teaching Packets for Integrating Women's History into Courses on Africa, Asia, Latin America and the Caribbean, and the Middle East*. Bloomington, IN: Organization of American Historians, 1990.

Roupp, H., ed. *Teaching World History: A Resource Book*. Armonk, NY: A. E. Sharpe, 1997.

Spier, F. *The Structure of Big History: From the Big Bang until Today*. Amsterdam: Amsterdam University Press, 1996.

World Literature Today. Norman, OK: University of Oklahoma.

Woyach, R. B, and R. C. Remy, eds. *Approaches to World Studies: A Handbook for Curriculum Planners*. Boston: Allyn & Bacon, 1989.

CHAPTER 10

Teaching U.S. History and American Studies

Figure 10.1   Queries: What is this march all about? Why was it necessary for citizens to organize a protest? Is the action shown typical of events in American history? Why or why not?
SOURCE: National Archives and Records Service, *The American Image* (New York: Pantheon Books, 1979).

OVERVIEW OF CONTENTS

Main Ideas ⎯⎯⎯⎯⎯⎯⎯⎯⎯⎯⎯⎯⎯⎯⎯⎯⎯⎯⎯⎯⎯⎯⎯⎯⎯⎯⎯⎯

Setting Goals ⎯⎯⎯⎯⎯⎯⎯⎯⎯⎯⎯⎯⎯⎯⎯⎯⎯⎯⎯⎯⎯⎯⎯⎯⎯⎯

       Didactic Goals
       Reflective Goals
       Affective Goals

Designing a Program ⎯⎯⎯⎯⎯⎯⎯⎯⎯⎯⎯⎯⎯⎯⎯⎯⎯⎯⎯⎯⎯⎯

       The Chronological-Topical Approach
       Alternative Approaches
       An Integrative Worldview Approach

Key Questions for Teaching American Studies ⎯⎯⎯⎯⎯⎯⎯⎯⎯⎯⎯⎯⎯

Summary ⎯⎯⎯⎯⎯⎯⎯⎯⎯⎯⎯⎯⎯⎯⎯⎯⎯⎯⎯⎯⎯⎯⎯⎯⎯⎯⎯

Notes ⎯⎯⎯⎯⎯⎯⎯⎯⎯⎯⎯⎯⎯⎯⎯⎯⎯⎯⎯⎯⎯⎯⎯⎯⎯⎯⎯⎯⎯

For Further Study: Teaching U.S. History or American Studies ⎯⎯⎯⎯⎯⎯⎯

MAIN IDEAS

American history has been a mainstay of the social studies for about one hundred years, reflecting the deep-seated need of a people to understand their own past. Although open to interpretations and subject to periods of scholarly theorizing and controversy, the teaching of American history has changed very little over the last four or five decades except for the addition of new information to bring the subject up-to-date. New directions for teaching U.S. history and new materials have been proposed from time to time, but the course is usually taught along chronological lines covering a series of time-honored topics. Within this chapter, the basic outline of secondary school American history teaching is discussed with particular attention to criticisms and defenses of existing historical content and instructional methods.

SETTING GOALS

Didactic Goals

Didactic goals stress the acquisition of knowledge and the ability of students to absorb the facts deemed vital to understanding American historical development and for building cultural identity. In U.S. history, didactic goals usually focus on famous personalities and events, demanding that students collect a repertory of names, dates, places, periods, and definitions that will serve as building blocks in the creation of an overall framework for national growth and development. Typically, didactic goals would require students to complete one or more of the following tasks:

1. To describe the important cultural, political, and social characteristics of pre-Columbian societies.
2. To relate accurately the story of European contact with the new world and subsequent colonial settlement.

3. To distinguish between the different European cultures occupying North and South America, with special attention to the details of colonization in North America by people of largely English descent.

4. To identify the key elements in the process by which the American colonies established their own nation through revolution, the Declaration of Independence, the Articles of Confederation, and later, the Constitution and the Bill of Rights.

5. To be able to describe the chain of major periods in U.S. history, which have led to the growth and integration of large territories and diverse peoples into a single national unit.

6. To recognize important personalities who have contributed to the evolution of American society, culture, economy, and politics.

7. To list the major issues and debates that have influenced U.S. history from time to time, accurately associating the issues with the historical context and personalities to which they were (or are) related.

8. To place U.S. history within the larger geographical, ecological, and cultural setting of North American patterns, including the identification of key Canadian and Mexican/Central American events as these relate to U.S. history and vice versa.

Note that these didactic goals call on students to incorporate a knowledge of North America into their picture of U.S. history and to build recognition of issues and periods, as well as the specific names, dates, and places that make up a study of any nation's history. Knowledge acquired in pursuit of didactic goals can and should be used as a basis for further inquiry of a reflective and affective kind, a discussion of which follows.

TO DO

Choose one of the aforementioned goals, 1 through 8, and immediately perform the task! Check your own information base in response to one of the goals, to all if you have time. Are there any areas in which you need to do reading and research in U.S. history?

Reflective Goals

Reflective goals center on the thinking process and require students to analyze ideas and apply these to case studies and evidence about the American past and present. Objectives that require thinking skills and critical approaches often ask students to interpret the data they have accumulated, debate alternative explanations and theories, compare primary and secondary sources of evidence, and develop generalizations that illuminate whole classes of events. Reflective goals complement the didactic ones by encouraging students to go beyond the data presented to the realm of hypothesizing and theorizing about the factors that have played and still play key roles in U.S. history. Concepts such as foreign policy, conflict, assimilation and acculturation, technological change, social studies, and political power are frequently used as the focal points for writing reflective objectives and goals for American studies courses and programs.

Examples of reflective goals constructed in a behavioral format for students may incorporate the following:

1. To identify and analyze the causes and consequences of social and religious movements in the United States.

2. To apply the U.S. Constitution and Bill of Rights to past and present examples of issues that affect basic freedoms in the United States, analyzing and debating the judicial interpretations as a step toward deciding which decision(s) are best.

3. To promote a comparison and contrast of primary accounts and secondary interpretations of key historical events and decisions such as the American Revolution, the adoption of the Constitution, the Monroe Doctrine, the Civil War, and others.

4. To encourage the viewing of American history from different frames of reference as a way of understanding events through insider and outsider or detractor and supporter perspectives, thus demonstrating the range of opinion and interpretation that exists on issues in American history, such as the accounts of minorities, women, native peoples, enemies, visitors, and those of lesser status.

5. To discuss and evaluate critically the way in which historians and social scientists draw conclusions in their scholarly writings and in textbooks, testing their ideas against empirical and logical standards.

6. To become involved in historical studies through a wide variety of dynamic techniques that include role-play, simulation, committee work, research, debate, mock elections/trials, and other devices that excite interest and sustain inquiry.

7. To reevaluate, using the work of historians and social scientists, some of the commonly accepted interpretations of American institutions and values such as those concerning slavery, or relations with neighboring states, foreign policy initiatives, and interactions between labor and management.

8. To build an overall interpretation of the course of American history that explains the behavior and values of its citizens and main actors in a way that is supported by the evidence.

Thus, to satisfy reflective goals, students must use the knowledge they have acquired to draw inferences about history and to subject to critical examination the conclusions others have drawn from the available records. Central to reflective goals are the processes of student decision making and problem solving based on careful study of selected problems and data. From this study, students should learn not only how to derive conclusions but also how to formulate and test hypotheses. No longer should they or you be content with accuracy and breadth of information. Now, with reflective goals, a new layer of learning has been added that demands analysis, application, and synthesis with an emphasis on defining, using, and testing concepts. Knowledge is used to help students verify interpretations of U.S. history and to develop an overall framework through which both past and present events can be filtered. Reflection assists them to understand people and events, to develop their own views of past and present, and finally to judge critically the interpretations of experts and authorities. Instead of remaining a collection of information about dates, places, and peoples, American history becomes part of a larger and more meaningful picture of human behavior and global change.

TO DO

Select a reflective goal, 1 through 8, and plan a lesson according to the direction given. Choose materials, decide on a method of instruction, go to the library or other resources for data, and develop a list of questions to ask. Write two versions of your lesson, one for advanced students and one for a class of poor readers.

Affective Goals

The aim of affective goals is to develop students' judgmental and decision-making capacities on American history topics. Objectives stress the identification, formulation, examination, and defense of opinions, values, and policies. Based on accumulated data that they have analyzed and interpreted, students are asked questions that require them to choose between alternatives representing different ethical, moral, and philosophical positions. The essence of affective activities in U.S. history classes would be in developing judgments and taking sides in debates on the issues that have been and still are important elements of American life. The examination of value positions is but one possible affective goal leading to choice. Without choice by students, the goal would at best be only partially fulfilled; the pupils could elect to stop with a simple understanding of the schools of thought on an issue, without themselves making a decision about which side to support and why they want to support it. A fully developed set of affective goals would encourage students to be able to outline the different ideas and views on a topic, explain the grounds on which each view rests, and defend a choice of their own—for their own reasons.

Affective goals include developing judgments, controversies, issues, debates, and public policies on topics such as evaluations of presidential administrations, the extent (or limits) of a free press, or the rights and roles that should be accorded women in U.S. society. In line with the concept of student choice, affective goals are usually expressed in words and phrases that ask for a moral decision or imply that a value is involved; such terms include right, wrong, best, worst, ought to, should be, judge, and evaluate. Responses from students may range from opinions to fully formulated defenses of a viewpoint, with the teacher encouraging the refinement of positions.

Examples of affective goals covering a variety of activities could include requests for the students to do the following:

1. Identify and rank in order of importance the different positions that exist on the constitutional guarantee against search and seizure, for example, whether it should extend to drug testing for people in sensitive jobs.

2. Evaluate the leadership records of five U.S. presidents by developing criteria for quality and applying these to each administration giving each a score for performance.

3. Read, examine, and debate the arguments—pro and con—on gun control concluding with a vote on which side to support.

4. Discuss the nature and roots of prejudice with reference to important eras in U.S. history, deciding whether actions that were taken could or could

not be defended on an ethical basis, for example, treatment of native populations, slavery and segregation in the pre- and post-Civil War South, and
the struggles between management and labor during the late nineteenth-
and early twentieth-century period of industrialization.

5. Look at events, perhaps the Battle of the Little Big Horn, from the point
of view of others, especially ordinary witnesses rather than leaders. These
could be outsiders, dissidents, and the unpopular. Develop empathy for
their feelings and values on an issue or event.

6. Develop, through role-play, an understanding of and feelings for vital
decisions taken by leaders, particularly choices that were controversial,
such as the decision to start a "police action" in Korea that began the Korean
War, followed by a judgment about whether the choice was right.

7. Compare, contrast, and critically evaluate historians/social scientists'
judgments on U.S. personalities, events, and institutions, such as the power
of the American president—too little or too much? Students should develop their own views on the subject.

8. Identify, analyze, and agree or disagree with the views expressed in
American artistic, musical, and literary works on the subject of social status,
war, race relations, work, beauty, or individualism. Use sources that include
popular and folk songs, short stories and novels, advertisement, paintings,
and films.

9. Reorganize the major arguments between those advocating environmental protection and those advocating economic development, leading to
a statement of a policy that can be defended adequately as best serving the
interests of the whole society.

Affective goals, then, deal with the growth in students' decision-making
ability on all questions and problems for which real choice is possible—from daily
consumer economics to morality in public controversies. Goals that promote
value analysis and choice may begin with role-playing and empathy building for
viewpoints not previously considered by students or teachers. The same plans
may conclude with the creation of well-formulated philosophical positions on a
particular issue. Intelligent and carefully considered choice is the common de-
nominator running through affective goals, plans, activities, and outcomes in
U.S. history classes, with decisions expressed through voting, debate, discussion,
role-play, writing, and even art, music, and poetry.

Indecision, abstention, and waffling must also be respected as part of the
process of affective reasoning because students need time to find a position or argument that suits their own backgrounds, interests, and beliefs. It is also conceivable that many students may find themselves paralyzed by a dilemma because of
conflicting values; they may be unable to accept compromise or reject a position.
Some political scientists argue that nonparticipation is perfectly acceptable in a
democracy and that noncommittal citizens may be both logical and helpful in de-
laying action. Their contention is that inaction allows everyone time to consider
issues, thus reducing tension.

In promoting affective goals, teachers must remember that philosophical
reasoning and value formation are complex processes that cannot be rushed if
students, particularly adolescents, are to work out and defend attitudes that are
truly their own. Goals may not be achieved unless time and attention are allotted
in classroom discussions to expressions of apathy, powerlessness, anomie, and
alienation, as well as to arguments for good citizenship and moral responsibility,
with the burden of choice resting on the students. In terms of long-range affective
growth, the more data and debate are incorporated into a decision, the better it is

likely to be and the more firmly it will be held as a long-term commitment. Therefore, affective goals should be viewed as both short- and long-run processes in which quick emotional reactions and daily opinions on topics, problems, and issues slowly develop into deeper, firmer, and more well-reasoned convictions that students can express in public with greater skill and ease.

TO DO

1. Choose an issue possessing a strong controversial or affective component. Quickly outline the main positions on the issue and discuss whether it will promote student debate: Is it too weak to develop interest, or does it arouse such strong emotions that rational discussion will be difficult? Can you accurately predict student reaction without any trial runs in the classroom?

2. Given the examples of affective goals, 1 through 9, write a tenth one of your own for a class you intend to teach, making certain that you specify your purpose, identify materials, provide for student outcomes, and pinpoint your method of technique for presentation. Try it out on a group of secondary school students. Do you think your objective will motivate them to participate? Why or why not?

DESIGNING A PROGRAM

U.S. history is at the same time a difficult and an easy course to teach at the secondary level. Much depends on whether you are satisfied with the dominant chronological-topical approach, which usually emphasizes broad coverage. You may want to promote different viewpoints and new scholarship, an approach that emphasizes greater depth. As in all other courses, there is the problem of trying to deal with too much material in too little time for an audience of young adults whose backgrounds, skills, and knowledge levels vary greatly. In addition, U.S. history courses often exhibit serious problems of distortion and bias, in which the point of view of the victor or dominant culture tends to obscure the way events are seen by the conquered and the minority. It is almost impossible for authors of American history materials, either through omission or commission, to avoid offending some political or social group in the society. Further, U.S. history is often perceived as isolated from that of the rest of the world. Even America's geographical neighbors, Canada and Mexico, are given little attention, leaving students with very slight knowledge of the two nations that share lengthy common borders and trade relations with the United States.

This section of presents an overview of the most common approach to American history and offers examples of possible alternative conceptions that you might like to employ on a trial basis. The dominant or most common approach is one in which standard topics, usually time periods, in North American history are presented chronologically from early Native American and European settlement to the present, stressing largely political and legal events over cultural or socioeconomic interpretations. Alternative conceptions may involve teaching the course backward from the present to the past; stressing economic, social, or cultural rather than political development; placing the United States in a global context; or considering history from a thematic structure that redivides or reinterprets time into broad units on technological change, social movements, political development, and cultural contributions. Finally, whatever the organization of the program, it can be enriched by incorporating minority views and documents into the usual topics; by infusing art, music, and literature of the times; and by presenting for discussion new and innovative historical and social science interpretations of past and present events.

RESEARCH REPORT

STUDENT OPINION OF U.S. HISTORY IN THE EARLY 1970s

In a national, but unrepresentative, sample of largely middle-class college-bound White seniors conducted in 1971, researchers found that most of these students were critical of history and civics courses and preferred methods and materials different from their usual classroom experiences. For example, 66 percent of the students felt that most U.S. history and civics courses discussed legal rules rather than how people actually behave politically. They also saw courses as going over material they already knew, and many (90 percent) suggested that more attention should be given to uses of war and peace and race relations (82 percent). More debates in school and more participation in class government were requested by 51 percent and 45 percent of the sample, respectively. As Figure 10.2 shows, U.S. history was the lowest rated course of all in terms of new knowledge.

Courses seem to vary in terms of how much *new knowledge* students learn from them. Listed below are some courses commonly taught in high school. For each course you have taken (or are now taking) indicate how much *new knowledge you learned.* (New knowledge means knowledge you had not learned before in other courses or from other sources such as parents, TV, or books and articles you had read on your own.)

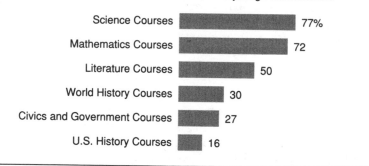

% Almost Everything I Learned New

Science Courses	77%
Mathematics Courses	72
Literature Courses	50
World History Courses	30
Civics and Government Courses	27
U.S. History Courses	16

N's range from 1273 to 1430

Figure 10.2   Amount of new knowledge in civics and government courses compared to other courses.
SOURCE: Richard C. Remy, "High School Seniors' Attitudes Toward Civics and Government Instruction," *Social Education* (Oct. 1972). Copyright © 1972 by the National Council for the Social Studies. Reprinted by permission.

Changing a U.S. history course can be quite difficult because of the almost universal expectation that a standard set of topics will be covered. How can portions of the Civil War or Jacksonian democracy be omitted from the curriculum? Even though secondary students have reported boredom with U.S. history; testmakers, parents, teachers, and the society as a whole expect certain types of knowledge from young people about American history, the Bill of Rights, and the Constitution. Therefore, the easiest way to make changes designed to spark interest in a tightly bound course of study is through internal redesign. New and different points of view, issues of gender and race, and engaging primary sources can be used to enrich traditional topics, meet long-standing criticisms, and provide a fertile base for student argument. The immense body of facts to be covered can be efficiently dealt with by the use of data sheets giving students a precise list of terms, names, dates, places, and events they must know for examinations but that will not serve as objects of classroom discussion. The computer, if available, in the classroom, can be used an encyclopedic resource to call on, saving time for all, and lessening the need to memorize details. In a freer atmosphere, you can experiment with more unusual forms of U.S. history (e.g., themes like war and peace, or social movements), drawing together examples from the entire range of the nation's past rather than addressing it chronologically.

Pressure has been growing for several decades to incorporate accounts of women, minorities, and ethnic groups in the curriculum. This is often termed "social" history because the emphasis is more on the lives of ordinary people and social movements than elites. Innovation is also supported by reformulations of history by scholars who offer new, sometimes disturbing, views of historical figures and events. An example of a historical reformulation is the widely accepted rethinking of the Lincoln presidency as focused primarily on preserving the union rather than in freeing the slaves. Similarly, arguments are increasing for women to be moved out of the "contributions" and "great women" categories and integrated with "male" U.S. history.[1] Especially in giving neglected people and groups a greater share of the curriculum, you should be able to make important changes in a typical U.S. history course, even when these fall short of a thorough overhaul of the content and design. The role of women in U.S. history is still a much neglected area calling for improvement in terms of both time period and social issues.[2]

The Chronological-Topical Approach

The chronological-topical approach to teaching U.S. history developed over the last hundred years and has become virtually the standard at both the junior and senior high school levels with remarkably little variation in content or structure. Widespread use of nationally distributed textbooks has helped to homogenize the program so that it covers a limited set of prescribed time periods familiar to all social studies students and teachers.

The following is a typical outline of topics:

A. Native Americans and Europeans (1450–1763)
    a. prehistory—North America
    b. prehistory—Central and South America
  1. Contact: Europeans and Native Americans
    a. conflict and cooperation of peoples
    b. contributions and problems
    c. impact and cultural diffusion
B. Colonizing the Americas (1620–1750)
  1. The Slave Trade
  2. Servitude and Indenture
  3. Merchants and Planters
C. England's Colonies Grow (1750–1775)
  1. Economic Development and Mercantilism
  2. Taxation and Representation
  3. Tensions among Settlers
D. The American Revolution (1775–1783)
  1. Declaration of Independence

2. Articles of Confederation
3. U.S. Constitution and the Bill of Rights
   a. separation of powers
   b. branches of government
   c. state and federal organization
   d. checks and balances
E. The New Nation (1789–1845)
  1. The Federalists
  2. Growth and Expansion Under Jefferson
  3. War of 1812
  4. The Monroe Doctrine
  5. Jacksonian Democracy Promotes Greater Involvement
F. Rise of Sectionalism (1820–1865)
  1. Northern States Develop Industry
  2. Southern States Create an Agricultural System
   a. cotton
   b. tobacco
   c. slavery
  3. The Westward Movement
   a. the Oregon Trail
   b. Lone Republic of Texas
   c. War with Mexico
   d. California Gold Rush
  4. Reform Movements
   a. public education
   b. women's suffrage
   c. abolition of slavery
   d. greater democracy
  5. Tensions Between the North and South
   a. keeping a balance
   b. Compromise of 1850
   c. Dred Scott Decision
  6. Secession and Civil War
   a. North and South mobilize
   b. war breaks out
   c. the Lincoln presidency
   d. the South collapses after four years
G. Reconstruction (1865–1897)
  1. The Radical Republicans and Their Programs
   a. slaves granted freedom and full rights
   b. southern White resistance
   c. government power restored to Whites
   d. disenfranchisement of Black people: the "Jim Crow" era
H. The Rise of Industrialism
  1. Development of Big Business
   a. transportation and communication networks set in place
   b. corporations founded
   c. tycoons create financial empires
  2. Agriculture Is Transformed
   a. resistance to innovation
   b. trend toward large, mechanized farms
   c. farmers organize: the grange
   d. the Wild West as a last frontier
  3. Rise of Labor Unions
   a. workers face low wages and long hours

       b. exploitation of immigrants and children in the labor force

       c. workers organize

       d. job action—strikes—are carried out

    4. Immigration

       a. pattern shifts from western and northern to southern and eastern Europe

       b. assimilation and resistance

       c. the melting pot

    5. Urbanization

       a. growth of big cities

       b. concentration of labor and capital

       c. political machines develop

       d. poverty, crowding, and crime

    6. Reform movements

       a. progressivism

       b. Theodore Roosevelt and the "Square Deal"

       c. conservation of land and resources

       d. social welfare and social consciousness

       e. education and recreation

       f. women's suffrage movement

I.   World Power (1898–1920)

    1. Expansion

       a. Spanish-American War

       b. intervention in the Caribbean and Mexico

       c. "The March of the Flag"

    2. World War I

       a. isolationism

       b. neutrality

       c. mobilization

       d. victory

       e. League of Nations—repudiation

    3. The "Roaring Twenties"

       a. prosperity and social change

       b. technological innovation

       c. decline of unionism

       d. Republican leadership

    4. The Great Depression

       a. the crash of 1929

       b. the New Deal—Democrats take control

       c. recovery measures

    5. World War II

       a. Japanese expansion—Pearl Harbor

       b. German expansion—Hitler attacks England

       c. alliances and battles

       d. peace: defeat of Axis powers, use of atomic bomb

J.   World Leadership (1945–present)

    1. The United Nations

    2. The Cold War/U.S.—Soviet Rivalry

       a. communist takeover of China

       b. war in Korea

       c. war in Vietnam

       d. détente/glasnost—Gorbachev leads USSR

       e. the Berlin Wall falls: end of the Cold War?

       f. war with Iraq

    3. Domestic Initiatives

a. civil rights movement
b. improvement of educational opportunities
c. war on poverty
d. return to conservativism
4. Economic Growth and Economic Problems
    a. Japan and Germany rebuilt
    b. decline of U.S. industry
    c. rise of a service economy
    d. international finance
    e. the oil cartel and inflation
5. A Shrinking World
    a. shifting power blocs
    b. new ties to China and the USSR
    c. retreat from social support system
    d. interdependence of domestic and foreign trade
    e. financing the Third World
    f. conservation and crime (drug) problems in the 1980s and beyond
6. The Future
    a. globalization
    b. economic interdependence
    c. age of communications
    d. postmodernism in the arts and social relations

LET'S DECIDE

Working as a group of several people, collect three or more textbooks: one or two of a recent printing, one or two about twenty years old, and another one or two examples forty years old or more, if available. Compare how each organizes the topics on the New World peoples, such as colonization, the Revolution, and Civil War. How much attention is given to Native Americans? Are Native Americans treated from their own viewpoint or only from a European stand? What sort of treatment are the "loyalists" given in the texts as compared to the "patriots" or revolutionaries? How much space is allotted to slavery and social issues? Are the books all pretty much alike or different in discussing the Civil War? Are causes of the war clearly identified? Which cause or causes are given top billing? Why? As a group, do you agree with or like the presentations? Could you design one that is better? Fairer? More thought-provoking? How?

Note that the chronological-topical approach tends to focus on significant political and legal events such as laws, institutions, rules, presidents, wars, and foreign policy with a touch of economics here and there and some attention to social conflict in certain periods such as Reconstruction. Culture and social structure are generally left out.

Criticism.   U.S. history and American studies textbooks have come under fire from a variety of critics, each of whom represents a particular point of view, liberal or conservative, academic or popular. Frances Fitzgerald, in a much-quoted book, studied texts from the 1880s through 1970s and found that the content and outlook shifted dramatically from period to period, nearly always in the direction of prevailing norms: more activist and socially concerned in the 1930s and less so in the 1920s; more conscious of the "Communist menace" during the 1950s and early 1960s and less so in the 1970s.[3] By implication, the "hard facts" of history seem easily influenced by political, social, and economic conditions of the time. A second set of critics, well represented by Diane Ravitch and Chester Finn, are very disturbed by what they view as lack of accurate information in history texts and by students' lack of knowledge about the heroes, heroines, and traditions of U.S. history.[4] They want good, traditional history for students presented in lively, personal narratives. Following the Ravitch point of view, Sewall conducts an extensive review of American history textbooks asking questions such as these:

> Are American history textbooks likely to make history come alive for students, giving them a vivid and inspiring sense of their origins? Are these books well written? Do they overwhelm with names, dates, facts, and concepts presented in a pedantic fashion? Do attempts to satisfy textbook clienteles with clashing opinions create narratives that strain credibility?[5]

From this approach, it seems that U.S. history should be lively and "inspiring" but not too critical. In this view, offering confusing and conflicting opinions of a person or event may be more than impressionable adolescents can handle! Results of the review generally indicate that most widely used textbooks fall far short of being well written. They are dry, dull, and lifeless for the most part, many failing to offer either a critical or a warm and ego-building view of the past.[6]

Countering this argument for more and better historical literacy in the schools, social studies leaders have argued that continuing to stress the study of military heroes, treatymakers, and statespeople does a disservice to both modern historians and to the social studies teachers who have "turned their attention to such new topics as social history, including the history of families and communities, minorities, and women."[7] From this point of view, U.S. history needs to be updated and revised to give greater attention to neglected groups and figures, especially those who are not White, European, male, political leaders, or conquerors. Clarity and accuracy are probably more important than literary quality or "uplift." The goals of American history textbooks are basically conservative and socializing. This condition is underscored by a philosophical analysis in which Barth and Shermis ask why texts have so many problems that have been debated for so long with so little apparent change. They look at two sets of 20 texts each—one from 1874 to 1927 and a second from 1960 to 1980—and find that content is for the most part identical, with a pattern of emphasis on "celebration" and patriotism. Issues and problems are suppressed, distorted, or missing from events that most historians have reported as deeply divisive and sometimes violent.[8] Although interpretations have shifted, the basic topics, structure, and content have remained nearly the same over a period of a hundred years or more. Barth and Shermis explain this phenomenon as follows:

> In brief, the conception of social studies as the social sciences fitted neatly with the imperatives of the culture. The notion that one could translate the findings of social scientists into something appropriate while at the same time leaving the essential structure of society unchanged must have been a source of comfort and encouragement to all concerned. Let us elaborate on this theme.
>
> What had been a fairly undisguised celebration of society with only the external trappings of scholarship—that is to say, the typical 19th century U.S. history and civics text—lent itself to being transmuted into a 20th century social science text. What had been celebration of a divine origin, a great destiny, heroic leaders and a steadily improving society was not essentially altered by the addition of 19th century Positivism. With but very little change it was possible to superimpose the language and assumptions of 19th century social science on 20th century textbooks to create a basically unaltered textbook.
>
> Furthermore, the self-confidence, indeed certitude, of a social science was itself a source of comfort. What could have been more comforting than know-

ing that the information students were required to learn had received the blessings of scientists? If "science" had transformed a primitive and agrarian pre-Civil War America into the industrial juggernaut that it was fast becoming, why could not the same "science" address itself to "social" problems?[9]

Thus, philosophical and historical issues join those of content, style, and interpretation.

Finally, the way presentations are made in texts has become an issue. Students' comprehension of what they read in textbooks is often inhibited when their understanding of events and especially relationships is vague or nonexistent. Understanding why something happened or what motivated people to act is very helpful to learners in remembering narrative and in building connections between events.[10] Students who collected facts into lists and classified information by categories easily and quickly forgot the bulk of what they learned and those for whom a mental model or framework of understanding was supplied retained a far larger proportion of the data.[11] Thus, texts need to be organized in a way that promotes memory and understanding as well as higher thinking processes—qualities lacking in many publications.

An account of the end of the Vietnam War may serve as an example of textual distortion:

> On January 27, 1973, a peace agreement was signed. The agreement called for a cease fire and a return by North Vietnam of several hundred American prisoners of war. It also said all remaining forces would leave Vietnam.... In April 1975, the Communists took control of Saigon, and the war was over. Many Americans wondered whether the United States had truly achieved "peace with honor."[12]

Does a student really have any idea of the causes of the Vietnam War from these sentences? Is there any clear indication that the United States won or lost the war? Critical analysis would indicate that this nation was lost because it was withdrawing and returning property. It is interesting that no mention is made of Americans returning prisoners to the Vietnamese or of the mass exodus of South Vietnam supporters when the Communists took Saigon. The tone is almost neutral except for the question of "peace with honor," the intention of which is unclear. Is it to arouse pity, patriotic anger, support, a continuation of war, or to question the specifics of the settlement?

In addition, when women and minorities are worked into historical accounts, they are often given very little space compared with that given to men and dominant groups. Women and minorities are often treated in an isolated manner that is unconnected to the total narrative flow. Further, those women and minorities who are included in the text seem to serve as tokens, perhaps to appease groups critical of the school curriculum. Generally, only very well-known and famous women and minority figures like Martin Luther King, Jr., or Susan B. Anthony are included; key contributions of many others deemed too unimportant to include are ignored.

RESEARCH REPORT

In an initial content analysis of leading textbook presentations of the period leading to the American Revolution, Beck and McKeown distinguish between "presenting events" and "providing for an understanding of … events." Using four elementary and four intermediate grade books as vehicles for analysis, they find that key issues such as the intolerable acts, the Boston Tea Party, and the conflict at Lexington and Concord are offered in a way that avoids linkages altogether or discusses causes and issues indirectly. Major problems are frequently left unstated or obscured by the presentation. "The approach the texts take is one of merely giving information rather than engineering it to bring about understanding," according to the authors, who argue that the texts did not help young learners to "develop a sense of history."

SOURCE: Isabel L. Beck and Margaret C. McKeown, "Toward Meaningful Accounts in History Texts for Young Learners," *Educational Researcher* 17, no. 6 (Aug./Sept. 1988): 31–39.

Last, a great deal of discontent has been directed at the way American history is taught to students: as a rigidly organized, rather dense, body of facts to be covered (i.e., memorized) rather than discussed, analyzed, and debated.[13] Courses organized chronologically around dates, names, and places do not encourage students to develop themes or to debate the merits of issues that have frequently arisen throughout American history. Pressures on teachers to stuff students full of the required information allow insufficient inquiry to give meaning (identifying causes and explanations) to the events and personalities they have learned. In effect, a preoccupation with coverage leads to a shallow and easily forgettable version of U.S. history. Students retain mainly the highlights of history that are reinforced by society and absorbed, if not understood. In my opinion, secondary and intermediate level U.S. history has reached a stage of canonization into which it is very difficult, if not impossible, to promote change. Unfortunately, a consequence of canonization is a closing of tradition and a strong sense of staleness.

Defense.   Those who have helped to formulate and sustain the chronological approach to the teaching of U.S. history support the typical program, arguing that the organization itself does not preclude more attention to debating the issues, to the role of women and minorities, or to recognizing and counteracting hidden biases and prejudices in the textbook narratives.[14] Defenders of traditional U.S. history courses contend that such problems depend as much on a teacher's methodology as on the material itself. The dominant view is that students need a standardized approach to the course that is easily recognizable and follows the developmental path of U.S. history. This approach is seen as giving students a grasp of the major events and personalities that have shaped the nation's destiny. One advantage of a standardized approach is its interchangeability and portability, implying that students can move all over the country, easily reentering the course, each part of which proceeds in sequence and provides an agreed on list of fundamentals that everyone should be prepared to know for testing and as part of the common culture.[15] These basics, it is argued, provide students with a high degree of cultural literacy so they and others can communicate with one another about the important features, periods, and leaders in the history of the Americas. The inclusion of great quantities of new materials, new figures of prominence, or new theories must proceed carefully so as not to confuse students or expand the information base to too great a size, particularly with data that may not be of lasting value.

SAMPLE LESSON PLAN

Why were immigrants stopped on Ellis Island? Why were so many coming to America? Why did they all have to be checked out? What role did immigrants play in the United States historically? Do they still come?

Figure 10.3 An Ellis Island scene: First entry point for millions of European immigrants in the late nineteenth and early twentieth centuries.
SOURCE: Sy Seidman, "Ellis Island New York Line Inspection of Arriving Aliens," *Records of the Public Health Service* (990-G-885), 1927.

The dominant approach to American history has evolved over decades of revision and refinement by educators, historians, and textbook companies to reflect those topics that are considered basic and most important to the common culture, omitting or ignoring issues of lesser importance or relegating these to brief mentions or footnotes in the overall narrative. The argument is put forward that the chronological approach gives students a sense of the way the United States grew, from its colonial origins to its present role as a great world power, by presenting the key leaders and the political and economic events and changes that contributed to its rise to power over the last several centuries.

SAMPLE LESSON PLAN

Which states were the most populous in 1790? Which were the least populous? Where was slavery a big part of the economic system and where was it a small part? What was the ratio of men to women in the big states? What was the ratio of slaves to total population? Which states were probably the most politically powerful? Why? Who do you think are "all other free persons"?

Districts	Free white Males of 16 years and upwards, including heads of families.	Free white Males under sixteen years.	Free white Females, including heads of families.	All other free persons.	Slaves.	Total.
Vermont	22435	22328	40505	255	16	85539
New Hampshire	36086	34851	70160	630	158	141885
Maine	24384	24748	46870	538	None	96540
Massachusetts	95453	87289	190582	5463	None	378787
Rhode Island	16019	15799	32652	3407	948	68825
Connecticut	60523	54403	117448	2808	2764	237946
New York	83700	78122	152320	4654	21324	340120
New Jersey	45251	41416	83287	2762	11423	184139
Pennsylvania	110788	106948	206363	6537	3737	434373
Delaware	11783	12143	22384	3899	8887	59094
Maryland	55915	51339	101395	8043	103036	319728
Virginia	110936	116135	215046	12866	292627	747610
Kentucky	15154	17057	28922	114	12430	73677
N. Carolina	69988	77506	140710	4975	100572	393751
S. Carolina	35576	37722	66880	1801	107094	249073
Georgia	13103	14044	25739	398	29264	82548
	807094	791850	1541263	59150	694280	3893635

Total number of Inhabitants of the United States exclusive of S. Western and N. Territory.	Free white Males of 21 years and upwards.	Free Males under 21 years of age.	Free white Females	All other persons.	Slaves.	Total.
S.W. Territory	6271	10277	15365	361	3417	35691
N. Territory	—	—	—	—	—	—

Figure 10.4   Summary data from the 1790 Census.
SOURCE: U.S. Bureau of the Census, *1990 Census of Population and Housing. Census Project: 1990* (Washington, DC: U.S. Government Printing Office, 1988).

On the issue of national chauvinism (bias in favor of the United States), defenders of standard U.S. history courses tend to believe that young adults should be taught a balanced, but basically uplifting, version of their history because this will foster good citizenship and result in pride in self and country. Courses are also seen as promoting participation in political affairs as students approach and then reach voting age.

Although both critics and defenders agree that secondary school students are capable of understanding and debating many of the more controversial and even ignoble actions in American studies, they disagree on the degree to which heroes should be debunked, believing that examples portraying the U.S. government in a poor light should be added with great care to the student diet. On the other side, critics see incidents that reflect negatively on the government or dominant groups (e.g., President Jackson's removal of the Cherokees from their homeland, Jim Crow laws, the Teapot Dome Scandal) as humanizing history rather than destroying students' feelings for their country, because these episodes provide material for honest debate. They argue that, for junior high school, issues should be debated frequently and that for senior high school, there should be a regular reexamination of national decisions and heroes, resulting in a more balanced view of history. Defenders usually view this approach as perhaps too bold, and worry about creating cynicism and apathy.

Thus, U.S. history courses are frequently subject to pushes and pulls from both the "critical" and the "socialization" factions. Results are present-day textbooks and courses that try to achieve a balanced presentation of a history through bland and neutral portraits of characters, events, and decisions. Multiple interpretations, philosophical debate, and ethical examinations of political, social, and economic decisions tend to be avoided or suppressed in favor of chronological, factual narratives.

SAMPLE LESSON PLAN

JOHN HENRY

When John Henry was a little baby
Sitting on his pappy's knee
He grabbed a hammer and a little piece of steel,
Said, "This hammer'll be the death of me, Lord, Lord,
This hammer'll be the death of me."

Now the captain said to John Henry,
"I'm gonna bring that steam drill around,
I'm gonna take that steam drill out on the job,
I'm gonna whop that steel on down, Lord, Lord,
Gonna whop that steel on down."

John Henry told his captain,
"A man ain't nothing but a man,
But before I'll let that steam drill beat me down
I'll die with my hammer in my hand, Lord, Lord,
I'll die with my hammer in my hand."

John Henry hammered on the mountain
Till his hammer was striking fire.
He drove so hard he broke his poor heart,
Then he laid down his hammer and he died, Lord, Lord,
He laid down his hammer and he died.

They took John Henry to the graveyard,
And they buried him in the sand,

> And every locomotive comes rolling by
> Says, "There lies a steel-driving man, Lord, Lord,
> There lies a steel-driving man."*
>
> What is the main point of "John Henry"? Why does he challenge the steam drill? Why does John Henry outdo the drill but die? What does John Henry symbolize and why do you think the song was written in the late nineteenth century?
>
> ---
>
> *Richard B. Morris, ed., *The American Worker* (Washington, DC: U.S. Government Printing Office, 1976), p. 101.

Alternative Approaches

The Counterchronological Approach. U.S. history can be viewed in a new light if it is taught from a modern or present-day perspective looking back to past events. Beginning with the present is an effective way of demonstrating to students the relation that exists between past and present events and can serve as an antidote to the forward chronological approach, which makes students cover large quantities of material before they can draw connections between past historical eras and our own. Jumping back into time from the present encourages a search for historical elements common to or very different in the two time periods (e.g., a current "free speech" or "search and seizure" case could be compared with one or more of historical importance such as *Mapp v. Ohio*, 1961, or *New Jersey v. T.L.O.*, 1985. Students could compare political events such as the formation of the United Nations after World War II and the creation of the League of Nations after World War I, considering the problems and benefits of each institution. They might conclude with a discussion of the current status of the United Nations and other international political, social, and economic agencies as they relate to the United States.

Working from current events to past history lets students see development patterns in brief segments of U.S. history, rather than being confronted with long sequences of chronological events. Students can thus compare the present with past historical periods and build a folder of case studies without delay. Teachers can work backward in the text, or move back and forth as the opportunity presents itself, using current events as a springboard for discussing related historical events and decisions.

WHAT DO YOU THINK?

> Take a present day-problem and trace it back in time to locate its origins and causes. For instance, why does the United States have a relatively high rate of violent crime? Is this high rate related to past history? Is it related to the right to bear arms? How about to the Wild West? Is current behavior a new development?

Why does the U.S. government often support conservative or even dictatorial regimes against revolutionaries or rebels, for example, in Central America or Africa? Is this a new policy? Does it square with the ideals of the American Revolution? Choose cases from at least six past presidents of the early and late nineteenth and twentieth centuries, comparing the types of governments they supported in Latin America. Can you explain the policies they followed? How so?

Thematic/Conceptual Approach. A thematic or conceptual approach to U.S. history is a second alternative for organizing a course. This approach is based on major ideas rather than on time periods. In this approach, information on events, cases, and personalities is reorganized, wholly or in part, to center on a few powerful ideas that give students a focus for questions and for hypotheses about the American past and present. Central ideas may include economic growth and decline, political power, social change, and cultural expression. Political power, for example, is a theme through which students might compare and contrast 10 significant elections in American history. They might identify the issues, discuss voter sentiment, and develop hypotheses about which policies and personalities had the greatest or least appeal under a given set of economic and social conditions. Administrations could be evaluated at the conclusion of or during a unit on political power. Students could draw conclusions about which components of the political system work best and which appear subject to corruption and abuse. The political power concept could also be subdivided into smaller themes that would serve as organizers for cases and examples, for instance, a war and peace theme. Key conflicts (including the Revolutionary War, the War of 1812, the Civil War, World Wars I and II, and the Korean and Vietnam wars) might be profitably compared side by side as a means for developing hypotheses about the causes, conditions, and eventual resolutions of U.S. conflicts, both domestic and international. Grouping conflicts together under the same theme heading would not provide a sequential presentation of history but would offer the chance for students to engage in meaningful analysis and synthesis of a class of events.

Generally, the thematic approach is one in which a concept is applied to a class of events for the purpose of promoting higher order student reasoning and theorizing about cause and effect in history. It also helps to focus on the key factors that produce or inhibit violent and peaceful human behavior patterns. A theme or concept acts as a lens through which related events are defined, analyzed, redefined, tested, and put together into an overall framework or theory for understanding new examples. Thematic units can be arranged inductively by first providing students with the case studies from which a concept or theory can be derived, or deductively, by providing a theme or major idea that is then applied to a set of cases that meet definitional criteria. Thus, the thematic organization is very different from the chronological or the reverse-chronological because comparative and contrastive groupings of events are favored over time sequences. Themes might include the following:

exploration

settlement

adaptation

conflict

leadership

technology

cultural diffusion

social movements

trade and aid

foreign policy

political participation

cooperation

With the themes approach, a sense of temporal development is far less important than a sense of pattern in human actions. Generalizations based on comparable data samples would be a major classroom goal if a conceptual approach were utilized for American history.

TO DO

Review a typical U.S. history program and reorganize it into themes. Will your major focus be on big political events dominated by "important people" or on social history with a focus on the lives of "ordinary" people? Choose wars or social movements and bring together examples from each major period for side-by-side comparison. Do American social movements in the eighteenth, nineteenth, and twentieth centuries share any goals, methods, and results, or is each unique to its era? Do problems of race and gender persist? Does each time period promote or inhibit change? Can you find examples of important movements or social reformers who were left out of the typical outline? Select a reformer and movement you think is deserving of better treatment and make a written case for its inclusion in your own outline.

An Issues-Centered Approach.   Similar to the thematic approach is an issues-centered approach to U.S. history, which presents a third alternative structure for the subject. Controversial issues and social problems can be used as the main focal points for the commonly taught American history sequence, with examples relating to debatable questions rather than content: (a) Should the United States have dropped the atomic bomb on Hiroshima and Nagasaki? (b) Should the Radical Republicans have treated White Southerners more generously? (c) Should the president have been given so much power by the U.S. Constitution? Unlike the more analytical, social science themes, an issue-centered approach would use content as evidence to prove or disprove arguments within a controversy. The main goal of an issue-centered course would be to involve students in a decision-making process about historical events.[16] U.S. history lends itself well to an issues approach because many of the value conflicts within American culture have persisted in different forms and styles since the foundation of the nation and the formation of the states in a federal system under the Constitution.

In a sense, controversial issues serve much the same function as themes, except that the process of creating and testing generalizations about history is overshadowed by the process of formulating and defending positions on key questions and problems that have characterized many, if not most, periods in U.S. history. Discussion of issues helps students consider U.S. history as an ongoing dialogue in historical writing and rewriting rather than as a finished product, treating "history as contested turf".[17] Issues also promote consideration of ethical beliefs, presenting many opportunities for students to examine values. Affective goals and processes are likely to be much more prominent in an issues-centered U.S. history course than they would be in either traditional or thematic approaches, although value problems could certainly be worked into chronological and thematic approaches.

Examples of important issues in American history, around which an entire course could be developed include the following:

1. Controversies about equity, which incorporate problems of racism, sexism, poverty, and equal opportunity.
2. Controversies about rights, which incorporate problems of freedom of speech, press, assembly, and religion.
3. Controversies about justice, which incorporate debates about search and seizure, fair and speedy trial, and public safety.

4. Controversies about government integrity, which incorporate problems of treason, rational defense, corruption, secrecy, and war powers.

5. Controversies about the system of political checks and balances that incorporate debates about authority, public initiative, participation or empowerment, civil law, and interest groups.

6. Controversies about personal happiness and the realization of potential that incorporate debates about identity, education, and philosophy of life, lifestyle, and morality.

You can apply one or all of these sets of issues to virtually any period of U.S. history because they are an integral part of the culture as it now exists and as it has evolved from the colonial period. The issues approach would tie in closely with legal and value problems, which are easily identified in American history programs but frequently given little attention in a chronological structure. Certain eras are richer in issues than others, but numerous issues can be found in all the conventional junior and senior high school units of study. For instance, the constitutional period might easily support debates about power, leadership, government organization, citizen rights and responsibilities, or equity and racism while the 1960s and 1970s continue to suggest numerous economic, social, and governmental problems, none of which have been completely or satisfactorily solved to date by the courts, the political system, or private individual action.

WHAT DO YOU THINK?

1. What do you think makes for a good argument or debate in U.S. history? Are old issues as good as new ones, or better? Is it easier to talk about a past problem or one that is current? Write a brief essay on these questions and share it with your peers. Is there agreement on the concept of an issue? Is an issue properly defined if all the arguments point to a single solution?

2. Which specific and general issue seems to have broad application to two or more periods of U.S. history? Select an issue that you think carries across at least a one hundred-year span and write questions or debate topics for your students to argue in class.

An Integrative Worldview Approach

An integrative approach to U.S. history is one that places the evolution of the Americas in a global setting.[18] The central notion of an integrative approach is that the history and culture of the United States should be viewed as one evolving part of worldwide changes in population, migration, technological change, philosophical attitude, and cultural diffusion. This approach sets U.S. history into a cross-cultural perspective linking domestic developments to worldwide changes. The United States becomes a single component in a complex web of changing ideas and conditions that emanate from within the region, as well as from Europe, Asia, Africa, and the Middle East, and that impact on one another with varying, and sometimes surprising and unforeseen, results.

An integrative structure incorporates many historical, social, ecological, and cultural factors into U.S. history in an effort to give students a holistic view of the earth's evolution and the role of humankind within it. For example, settlement of the New World could be reconceptualized as a meeting of native and European peoples with equal weight given to both. The Monroe Doctrine might be presented from both the South American and the North American perspective.

An integrative worldview of U.S. history would probably be less ethnocentric and more international in feel than any of the other plans discussed so far, but it would consequently provide less attention to the United States as a unique, separate entity for study.

WHAT DO YOU THINK?

Here, you have been working like a dog to acquire pictures and statistics on immigration to the United States, and you just discovered that five of your own students are recent arrivals on our shores. They are a bit shy, but so are most of the other students as well, and they could use some exposure to public speaking. So, you ask them to serve as a panel and talk about their experiences leaving their homeland to settle in, or visit, the United States. What, you might ask, was most difficult about leaving? What do you miss most? What do you like most about your new land? Why have you resettled? Do you expect to stay or to return home? How have you adjusted to American culture and customs? Have there been any difficulties? Has it been an enjoyable experience?

The integration of the United States into the stream of world history could follow a chronological or a thematic sequence, with the teacher referring to global events at each point in the course, especially when new ideas and technological changes have been adopted from or diffused to other parts of the world. The Industrial Revolution, for example, would become part of the movement to industrialize Europe and develop capitalism as a worldwide economic system. The women's suffrage movement would be viewed in a context of deep social and economic changes throughout Europe and the Americas in the direction of greater freedom and equity for women and minorities. American foreign policy could be viewed from several perspectives (e.g., as a tool for protecting national security or as a means of global domination) giving students the opportunity to judge past and present decisions in a global context.[19]

Given the conventional nature of most U.S. history courses and the relative lack of integrative courses of study, a global approach to American studies would probably work best as an introductory or concluding segment of a traditional course. This suggestion notwithstanding, a full-length integrative approach could result in a provocative and conceptually powerful American studies program that would encourage students to look at their mother country from a new and different perspective, one that joins U.S. history to that of the planet as a whole and all of its varied groups and cultural traditions. Multiethnic education would assume a new meaning within an integrative framework and American culture could be viewed as a dynamic and creative entity contributing to the global economic and social system while receiving ideas, goods, and institutions from it.

TO DO

Apply the concept of cultural diffusion to one period of U.S. history, for example, early settlement by Europeans, or the immigration waves of the 1880s, 1890s, or perhaps the present. Identify at least five instances in which American ideas, techniques, and institutions have influenced the outside world and at least five instances in which outside ideas, techniques, and institutions have influenced Americans. Is it possible to separate outside from internal inventions and creations? What are internal ideas based on?

Is it possible to find American practices that would be familiar to most of the world (e.g., rock and roll music, multinational corporations) or outside ideas that have affected the United States and much of the world as well (e.g., European classical music or the idea of a Bill of Rights)? Choose two ideas of your own to pursue and trace the lines of influence back and forth to the United States on a map of the world.

KEY QUESTIONS FOR TEACHING AMERICAN STUDIES

Although there are many designs for American studies programs, most educators would agree that certain key issues and questions should be engaged in any course. Key questions are those that can be posed throughout a U.S. history course rather than being limited to a particular era or controversy. American culture almost from its inception brought with it problems that remain to this day, such as where to draw the line between church and state or how to promote equality before the law while combating the effects of racism. In short, key questions should be powerful devices that you can use to stimulate discussion on almost any period of U.S. history.

A suggested list of questions for American studies/U.S. history courses follows:

Security: To what extent should the United States arm and protect itself against other nations? For what reasons should a democracy intervene in or remain aloof from the affairs of other nations?

Freedom: How shall freedom be defined in American culture? What ought to be the limits, if any, on press, assembly, and speech?

Equality: What does "being equal" mean to Americans—economic, social, legal, political, or educational parity? Where can and should equality be achieved and which areas of life should remain competitive and stratified?

Justice: What concepts of fairness and moral righteousness should prevail in social customs and in formal laws? Is justice important to our system? How should justice be applied to criminal and civil cases?

Growth: Why has U.S. society become wealthy and powerful and how is the wealth distributed and used? Which purposes are held in high esteem and which in low esteem?

Competition and Cooperation: How much competition or cooperation should be encouraged in U.S. society? How much laissez-faire effort versus government control and guidance should there be? Which areas of life should be considered public and which private?

Identity and Diversity: Has the United States evolved into a multicultural, pluralistic society? To what degree have newcomers, minorities, women, and ethnic groups been integrated into the social fabric of the nation? To what degree has integration been resisted, and why? Who is an American? How does the American see others: positively or negatively, fairly or from a biased perspective?

You are, of course, invited to add your own key questions to those already described, and you are encouraged to apply them to your daily lessons. Similar conceptions of the basic problems of American history are offered by the Bradley Commission on History in Schools (National Center for History in Schools), underscoring the importance of questions on freedom, justice, democracy, economic opportunity, and relations with other states for U.S. history programs.[20] Although the United States has experienced profound social, economic, and political changes over the last two hundred years or so, certain issues keep coming back because these are built into the basic values of the people. You can and should use these values as a basis for discussion, debate, and decision making among your secondary school students.

SUMMARY

U.S. history and American studies at the secondary level generally follow a chronological structure, the content of which is predominantly political and economic, often with a strong dose of patriotic values. The traditional American history program begins with European settlement and follows a relatively ethnocentric perspective throughout, stressing the American view of others without much attention to external influences. Research indicates that most courses stress dramatic political and military events to the detriment of social and cultural history, slighting women, minorities, and unpopular causes and movements.[21] Since the 1960s, there has been a consistent and noticeable effort to bring the curriculum into balance by correcting for race, gender, and ethnicity, although this usually follows a traditional formula stressing successes, contributions, and progress.[22] Much of U.S. history is presented as a relatively unconnected series of facts leading to low levels of student understanding and a feeling, among senior high school students, that the program has little to offer that is new or intellectually provocative.

Alternative designs are available, including a thematic approach in which events and people are regrouped under broad units that compare classes of events such as conflicts, freedoms, and immigration patterns. Another possible structure is one that focuses on issues and controversies that have persisted throughout much of U.S. history, such as those involving equal treatment for women, racism, laissez-faire capitalism (free enterprise), and unionism. A third approach would place American history in a world setting, seeking points in the course of events at which important exchanges of ideas, peoples, and institutions took place.

On the whole, although alternatives are increasingly available, most courses follow the traditional model that is, of course, open to change in topics if not in structure. The field of history provides a fertile base of ideas from which to choose readings, documents, resources, and narratives about social and cultural history. Finally, key issues about power, justice, equality, and freedom run throughout any program in American history. These can serve as focal points from which you can develop reflective and affective goals. Exploring these issues should also supply students with the basic information they need to reach the didactic goals of knowing the key events and personalities of the American dream.

TO DO

1. Write your own didactic, reflective, and affective goals for a unit on Soviet–U.S. relations in the 1980s and 1990s.
2. Create a course outline for U.S. history that builds student awareness of outstanding cultural and social figures as well as political and military leaders.
3. Build a unit on the Reconstruction period from primary sources: White Southerners and Northerners, foreigners, and Blacks. Compare that period to the most recent thirty years of history in South Africa.

4. Develop a unit for students, including firsthand and secondary sources on the Vietnam War. Conclude with an exercise directing them to write their own fair and balanced history of that conflict.

5. Read the work of at least three historians and/or social scientists who offer new interpretations of frequently taught events in U.S. history, using their interpretations to guide your preparation of materials. Look especially for historians who provide guidance on women's history, the life of minorities, and social movements.

6. Identify respondents from whom you can collect oral history material on an important event such as World War II, President Kennedy's assassination, or a noteworthy labor strike. Fashion these materials into a presentation that will be part of an American history topic.

7. Write five highly provocative questions on any issue of your choice in American history and try it out on a group of students noting the level, length, and number of ideas and questions your inquiries generate.

8. Prepare a multiple choice test on the civil rights movement consisting of ten items, all of which are designed to measure understanding, application, analysis, and synthesis, in other words, higher level thought processes. Use original documents, autobiographies, songs, and cartoons as the evidence or bases for your items. For example, write several items using Martin Luther King, Jr.'s, "Letter from a Birmingham Jail" as a reading students will be asked to interpret.

9. Prepare a test or diagnostic instrument that will assess (a) what students know about different areas of U.S. history; (b) how great or small is their skill at interpreting events, especially linking causes and actions to consequences and changes; and (c) how they feel about the events they are studying and the course they are taking.

You could approach the assessment of affective change through a formal survey research instrument that asks for student viewpoints and beliefs. Because you want to determine whether there are changes in student attitude on a number of issues, and whether these changes are positive or negative, any questionnaire used to measure attitude should be given at least twice: once before the issue has been taught or discussed, and once afterward. In a section on the death penalty, a survey of students' feelings about this topic might precede a debate on capital punishment. The survey should be done a second time, after the debate. You could then compare class averages for the two administrations to learn whether there had been any significant shift of opinion. A survey could also be longitudinal, stretching over an entire year. In this case, student reactions to a list of issues should be collected three or four times during the year and the results compared and evaluated, perhaps by the students themselves as part of their class work. Finally, attitudes toward the entire presentation—the teachers' methods and the materials used in the U.S. history course—could be surveyed and the results used as a classroom planning guide. A survey of this type could ask students whether they are stimulated or bored by the textbook, simulations, assignments, and discussions. It might also ask them for suggestions on how to supplement or alter the program.

Junior and senior high school students are quite capable of providing astute judgments of their courses. Typical questions could explore whether students are satisfied with the course content, have learned anything new on a number of topics, and have developed a more or less positive image of their country as a result of their study. Response choices could be arranged in a scale form ranging from "strongly agree" to "strongly disagree." Scaled responses can be easily coded, summarized, and interpreted, particularly with the aid of a computer program designed to tabulate survey results.

NOTES

1. Gerda Lerner, ed., *The Female Experience in America* (Indianapolis, IN: Bobbs-Merrill, 1976).
2. Frances Fitzgerald, *America Revised* (New York: Vintage, 1979).
3. Nell Noddings, "Social Studies and Feminism" in *The Social Studies Curriculum: Purposes, Problems, and Possibilities*, ed. E. W. Ross (Albany, NY: State University of New York Press, 1997).
4. Diane Ravitch and Chester E. Finn, *What Do Our Seventeen Year Olds Know? A Report on the First National Assessment of History and Literature* (New York: Harper & Row, 1987).
5. Gilbert Sewall, "Literacy Lackluster: The Unhappy State of American History Textbooks," *American Educator* (Spring 1988): 37.
6. Gilbert Sewall, *American History Textbooks: An Assessment of Quality* (New York: Educational Excellence Network, 1987).
7. Theodore Kaltsounis, "A Critique of Gilbert T. Sewall's American History Textbooks," *Social Education* (April/May 1988): 252–53.
8. James L. Barth and Samuel Shermis, "Nineteenth Century Origins of the Social Studies Movement: Understanding the Continuity Between Older and Contemporary Civic and U.S. History Textbooks," *Theory and Research in Social Education*, no. 3 (Fall 1980): 29–50.
9. Ibid., p. 46.
10. J. B. Black and H. Bean, "Casual Coherence and Memory for Events in Narratives," *Journal of Verbal Learning and Verbal Behavior,* 20 (1981): 267–75.
11. A. L. Brown et al., "Learning, Remembering and Understanding," in *Handbook of Child Psychology: Cognitive Development*, vol. 3, eds. John H. Flavell and Ellen M. Markman (New York: Wiley, 1983), pp. 77–166.
12. James J. Rowls and Phillip Weeks, *Land of Liberty* (New York: Holt, Rinehart & Winston, 1985), p. 436.
13. O. Hallden, "Learning History," *Oxford Review of Education,* 12 (1986): 53–66.
14. Mary Kay Tetreault, "Integrating Women's History: The Case of United States History High School Textbooks," *The History Teacher* 19, no. 2 (Feb. 1986): 211–62.
15. E. D. Hirsch, Jr., *Cultural Literacy: What Energy American Needs to Know* (Boston: Houghton Mifflin, 1987).
16. Shirley J. Engle, "Proposals for a Typical Issue-centered Curriculum," *Social Studies,* 80, no. 5 (Sept./Oct. 1989): 187–91.
17. Thomas Quinn, "History as Contested Turf," in *The Ford Foundation Report* (New York: Ford Foundation, Winter 1993): pp. 1–4.
18. Robert Woyach et al., *Bringing a Global Perspective to American History* (Columbus: Ohio State University, Mershon Center, 1983).
19. Stuart A. McAninch, "Cold War Paradigms and the Post-War High School History Curriculum," *Theory and Research in Social Education*, 23, no. 1 (Winter 1995): 34–51.
20. Bradley Commission on History in Schools, *Building a Curriculum History: Guidelines for Teaching History in Schools* (Washington, DC: Educational Excellence Network, 1988).
21. Sheila M. Rothman, *Woman's Proper Place: A History of Changing Ideals and Practices, 1870 to the Present* (New York: Basic Books, 1978).
22. L. Tiedt and I. M. Tiedt, *Multicultural Teaching* (Boston: Allyn & Bacon, 1986).

FOR FURTHER STUDY: TEACHING U.S. HISTORY AND AMERICAN STUDIES

Bradley Commission on History in Schools. *Building a History Curriculum: Guidelines for Teaching History in Schools*. Washington, DC: Educational Excellence Network, 1988.

Burns, Ken, producer, Stephen Ives, producer/director with co-writer Dayton Duncan & others. *The West* (nine videotapes with comprehensive curriculum package/audio, indiex, posters, etc.) Alexandria, VA: PBS Video, 1996.

Cartwright, William H., and R. L. Watson, Jr., eds. *The Reinterpretation of American History and Culture*. Washington, DC: National Council for the Social Studies, 1973.

Council on Interracial Books. *Stereotypes, Distortions, and Omissions in U.S. History Textbooks*. New York: Council on Interracial Books for Children, 1977.

Davidson, J. W., and M. H. Lytle. *After the Fact: The Art of Historical Detection*. New York: Knopf, 1982.

Downey, M. T., ed. *History in the Schools*. Washington, DC: National Council for the Social Studies, 1985.

Foner, E., and O. Mahoney, *America's Reconstruction*. New York: HarperCollins, 1995.

Husbands, C. *What is Teaching History? Language, Ideas, and Meaning in Learning About the Past*. Buckingham, UK: Open University Press, 1996.

Kownslar, A. O., ed. *Teaching American History: The Quest for Relevancy*. Washington, DC: National Council for the Social Studies, 1974.

London, H. I., and A. L. Weeks. *Myths That Rule America*. White Plains, NY: Longman, 1981.

O'Connor, J. E. *Teaching History with Film and Television*. Washington, DC: American Historical Association, 1987.

Reif, J. A. *Structuring the Past: The Use of Computers in History*. Washington, DC: American Historical Association, 1991.

Rosenzwieg, R., S. Brier, and Josh Brown. *Who Built America: From the Centennial Celebration of 1876 to the Great War of 1914*. New York: CD-ROM by Voyager, Inc., 1993, 1994.

Ross, E. W. *The Social Studies Curriculum: Purposes, Problems, and Possibilities*. Albany, NY: State University of New York Press, 1997.

Smith, C., exec. ed. *American Historical Images on File*. New York: Facts on File (many titles):1988–91.

Virtual Archives of American History. *American Impressions* (CD-ROM). Vols. I and II. New York: HarperCollins Interactive, 1995.

Weatherford, J. *Indian Givers: How the Indians of the Americas Transformed the World*. New York: Fawcett, 1988.

Weitzman, David. *My Backyard History*. Boston: Little, Brown, 1975.

Wineburg, S. S., and S. Wilson. "Models of Wisdom in the Teaching of History." *Phi Delta Kappan* 70, no. 1(1988): 50–58.

CHAPTER 11

Teaching U.S. Government and Civics

It is to be remembered, that if Princes have Law and Authority on their sides, the People on theirs may have Nature, which is a formidable Adversary; Duty, Justice, Religion, nay, even Humane Prudence too, biddeth the People suffer any thing rather than resist; but uncorrected Nature, where e're it feels the smart will run to the nearest Remedy. Mens Passions in this Case are to be consider'd as well as their Duty, let it be never so strongly enforc'd, for if their Passions are provok'd, they being as much a part of us as our Limbs, they Lead Men into a short way of Arguing, that admitteth no distinction, and from the foundation of Self-Defence they will draw Inferences that will have miserable effects upon the quiet of a Government.

Our Trimmer therefore dreads a general discontent, because he thinketh it differeth from a Rebellion, only as a Spotted Fever doth from the Plague, the same Species under a lower degree of Malignity; it worketh several ways; sometimes like a slow Poyson that hath its Effects at a great distance from the time it was given, sometimes like dry Flax prepared to catch at the first Fire, or like Seed in the ground ready to sprout upon the first Shower; in every shape tis fatal, and our Trimmer thinketh no pains or precaution can be so great as to prevent it.

In short he thinketh himself in the right, grounding his Opinion upon that Truth, which equally hateth to be under the Oppressions of wrangling Sophistry of the one hand, or the short dictates of mistaken Authority on the other.

Our Trimmer adoreth the Goddess Truth, tho' in all Ages she hath been scurvily used, as well as those that Worshipped her; tis of late become such a ruining Virtue, that Mankind seemeth to be agreed to commend and avoid it; yet the want of Practice which Repealeth the other Laws, hath no influence upon the Law of Truth, because it hath root in Heaven, and an Intrinsick value in it self, that can never be impaired; she sheweth her Greatness in this, that he Enemies even when they are successful are asham'd to own it; nothing but powerful Truth hath the preprogative of Triumphing, not only after Victories, but in spite of them, and to put Conquest her self out of Countenance; she may be kept under and supprest, but her Dignity still remaineth with her, even when she is in Chains....

—Walter Raleigh, ed., The Complete Works of George Savile, First Marquess of Halifax

OVERVIEW OF CONTENTS

Main Ideas

Setting Goals

    Didactic Goals
    Reflective Goals
    Affective Goals

Designing the Program

    The Operational Approach

Alternative Approaches

Key Questions for Teaching U.S. Government _____

Summary _____

Notes _____

For Further Study: Teaching U.S. Government _____

MAIN IDEAS

What should be the goals, form, content, and title of a course on government? Should the main focus be on facts or ideas or values? Should the program as a whole be organized around descriptions of government roles and institutions, discussions of political issues, in-depth study of participation, or careful application of political systems theory? Should a U.S. civics course include data about other nations' political systems, international agencies, or aid issues? You will be asked to consider how government can be taught to increase student interest in politics and eventually create more aware, active, involved citizens rather than citizens who are apathetic and cynical. You will be assisted in selecting a form, sequence, and content for a civics or democracy course, that is, a plan that you think will best achieve growth in student knowledge, understanding, and values.

SETTING GOALS

Secondary social studies sequences usually include a course on government, civics, or problems of democracy as part of student requirements for graduation. A somewhat newer label for the program is "Participation in Democracy." Unlike some of the other formula standards in the field, the government course can vary greatly in design, content, and conception. There appear to be at least two major views of the course. One stresses a political science study of the structure and function of government.[1] A second emphasizes past and current social and political problems. Both major conceptions justify their approach as contributing to positive citizen values that young people will acquire through knowledge about the formal mechanisms of government and/or through active debate of current social problems. Many teachers often mix modes by switching from "government" to "problems" within the same program.

Most textbooks and social studies materials tend to support either the formal political or the social values approach. Relatively little concern is shown for personal decision making by students, or for applying democratic principles to school life, although this has changed somewhat over the past two decades.[2] A comprehensive and all-inclusive set of standards for civics and government has been developed that provides "organizing questions," goals, and content guidelines for almost any course that could be created for K–12.[3] The national standards for civics and government, although not a curriculum mandated by the U.S. government, contain a wealth of quotes, performance criteria, and suggestions for content, which teachers can use as a valuable resource for planning a secondary or elementary level program.

Finally, there is a serious issue concerning classroom control and simple-minded positivism in teaching about government. Classroom discipline frequently overrides the desire for exciting argumentation and role-play. This situation has been termed *defensive teaching* because control factors prevent schools from involving students in real participatory experiences.[4] We must keep in mind that student government is a training ground for students who will function in a democracy, and that schools need to encourage participation by modeling elections and voting as a minimum for good citizenship training. Given that only about half of all registered voters took to the polls to cast their ballots in the 1996 presidential election, secondary school experiences with government could be a crucial positive influence on future participation.

Most programs stress an inherent commitment to American values, accepting the need for a belief in the political tenets that define daily life. Although a commitment to political values does not necessarily restrict student thinking, the level of specificity can be very important. For example, using civics to promote national defense as a concept may be reasonable, but is arguable when used to justify a particular conflict. In other words, if we value free speech, does that apply to expressing criticism of our country? Or, are we trapped in a "my country right or wrong" position?

Ironically, the instructional style of many civics or government courses works against allowing students the time and freedom to debate controversies and participate in ongoing community politics. Coverage of history and government, especially if it is largely positive and self-congratulatory, is necessary but insufficient to predispose students toward activism and involvement.[5]

Didactic Goals

Didactic or informational objectives for a civics/government program are usually concerned with building formal knowledge about the political system. There is a tendency to ask students to learn *de jure* aspects of politics: how a bill becomes a law, the three branches of U.S. government, and voting procedures. Political behavior, as de facto operations, however, may also be built into any type of government/civics/problems of democracy program. Often the teacher begins with a vague interest in building students' knowledge of government operations leading to goals such as these:

1. Students will know how legislation is passed.
2. Students will be able to identify the branches and functions of the U.S. government.
3. Students will learn more about government and voting.
4. Students will know how local, state, and federal agencies are organized.

Beginning with such general goals, the teacher will soon realize that *learning* is too broad a term to use for planning purposes. The idea of legislation needs to be clarified, and the identification of the parts of government may result in students' knowing nothing more than a set of terms or labels. Therefore, initial goals should be rewritten in behavioral terms to reflect more fully what students will study and what they will be expected to accomplish. Understanding of definitions and terms may be added to the recall process. The same goals can be improved easily by making each more specific and by defining clearly what behaviors are expected of learners:

1. Students will describe the major steps in moving bills from the House and Senate to the executive branch and back again.
2. Students will be able to write a list of the three branches of government (executive, legislative, and judiciary), including the main parts of each.
3. Students will verbalize one or more formal definitions of government and voting.

4. Students will chart on the blackboard the hierarchical structure of local, state, and national agencies of government.

Although characteristic, these four goals should not be viewed as the only ones either possible or desirable. As teachers develop more specifics about a topic, the way it will be taught, and expected student behaviors, they will be able to plan the program and choose materials for study more easily.

The didactic realm, however, is only one part of the whole set of expectations for students studying government and the problems of democracy. Reflective and affective goals are also needed to encourage higher order thinking and decision making in a well-balanced program.

TO DO

Would you teach about international politics in a civics course? If not, write a statement indicating why you would omit this level. If so, write an argument defending the inclusion of a global level. Share your ideas with others. Who wins?

Reflective Goals

Reflective goals are intended to move students to higher cognitive ground than they were on in acquiring information about government. With the established database as a foundation, the aim of reflective goals is to develop student inquiry into the reasons behind political decisions and the use of power. Students will be expected to explore the whole relation between formal, written law and informal, behind-the-scenes practice on many levels: personal, local, state, national, and international. Reflective goals should be written to stress the analysis of human political behavior. Conclusions might serve as guides for a better understanding of political trust, participation in political activities, protest actions, political decisions made by others, and the use and abuse of authority. In general, reflective goals guide students toward building an analytical framework, a set of theories and generalizations about the reasons behind political action or apathy, and the way laws are turned into social policy.

For a government or problems of democracy course, you might begin by formulating expectations for students like the following:

1. Understand how political decisions are made.
2. Discuss ways in which laws are reflected in daily life.
3. Develop a definition of political participation and use it to identify the causes of social activism or apathy.
4. Build sensitivity to media influences on our knowledge and "images" of political leaders, events, and policy debates.

SAMPLE LESSON PLAN

Why did the artist, a contemporary of Washington, portray our first president as rising into the heavens in the arms of two angels? What is the picture meant to convey about the leader?

What has happened to him? Can you interpret this print and develop a lesson plan using it as a basis of discussion about how Washington was seen at the time of his death?

Figure 11.1   Hierarchy of political involvement. Query: According to this concept of participation, who are the most active and who the least? Do you agree?
SOURCE: John J. Barralet, *Sacred to the Memory of Washington*, circa 1800, stipple engraving Historical Society of Pennsylvania, Philadelphia.

Thus, we have set up four goal areas targeted for further development: comprehending the process of political choice, comparing de jure and de facto political behavior, and searching for the factors that make people active or passive citizens. Each of these general goals demands of students a degree of knowledge about political behavior and a grasp of political terminology. Now we can think about filling in the missing elements of our goals: materials, techniques, outcomes, and assessment. As each missing element is identified, the plan for each lesson, unit, and the course as a whole will be correspondingly easier to determine. More specific versions of our goals might look like the following:

1. Using a series of case studies on welfare proposals from the community, state, local, and national levels, students will play roles as legislators who

identify and analyze the issues in each case, deciding which proposals will be cheap or costly and which will be most acceptable to the voters.

2. Students will examine the formal procedures by which a bill becomes law by comparing the legal rules with selected descriptions of the lawmaking process by public officials, lobbyists, and social critics (and maybe novelists, too), developing conclusions about which groups are most important in forming public policy.

3. By brainstorming a definition of political participation (e.g., voting, letter writing, protest, community volunteer service, etc.), students will create their own scale or ranking of political activism, setting priorities for the highest and lowest degrees of participation. (The teacher should ask students to consider whether some forms of participation might be considered negative in certain contexts—bullying opponents, destroying property, and so on—applying conclusions to at least two political events posed as problems during an oral examination.)

4. By building sensitivity to media, including radio, newspapers, journals, television, and films, students will "learn to look" at the techniques, signs, and symbols used to affect, their feelings and attitudes toward politics and decision making. You might suggest that the students collect photographs, posters, and campaign buttons, evaluating which are most effective in communicating either negative or positive images of political leaders and activists, during or in-between campaigns for office. Perhaps the class could form media consultant groups, each of which creates its own ad campaign to promote a personality or issue in which they are interested.

Once rewritten, reflective goals indicate which materials will be used, how students will accomplish each task, and what outcomes are expected. Further, the goals include some form of evaluation, whether formal written and oral examination or informal observation of student feedback during discussion. Other reflective goals may relate to comprehension, analysis, application, and synthesis levels of thinking applied to those topics commonly covered in government, such as the U.S. Constitution, voter participation, Supreme Court decisions, the structure of the American political system, political parties, media management, pressure groups, community affairs, taxation policy, social problems, values and beliefs, and leadership. Although somewhat unwieldy, these behavioral objectives constitute a kind of lesson plan for a unit or course. You are invited to write neater goals of your own to fit your needs and audiences.

TO DO

If students are supposed to analyze issues in their own terms as part of reflective goals, are all of their answers equally acceptable? How much can you, as the teacher, steer students to specific answers? How much should you help them? How much should they think for themselves? Select two examples from a civics or government course, for one of which you believe students will need guidance, but not the other. Write an argument defending or attacking teacher intervention. What would you recommend as a general plan to promote reflective thinking: (a) providing answers, (b) providing guidance, or (c) providing independence? Why?

Affective Goals

Affective objectives are vitally important to any civics, government, or democracy course because the political realm inevitably rests on human judgment and values.[6] Didactic and reflective goals form a basis for the affective, but without the values component, politics turns into a kind of pseudo-neutral compilation of dry facts and definitions about the way government works. Even the phrase "the way government works" begs for criticism because students, and most citizens, snap to attention when they discover news about the government "not" working. Newspapers and television gain more audience attention with stories of political corruption, conflict, and personality clashes than with details of the legislative process. Why then do we, in effect, censor for young adults events that are already known and promote interest? Some argue that the schools' efforts to present only noncontroversial ideals and the "good" side of the American political system offer a distorted perception of reality for students and reinforce rather than counteract cynical, apathetic attitudes.[7]

RESEARCH REPORT

Secondary Students' Attitudes and Knowledge in the Bicentennial Year
During the bicentennial year, 1976, the National Assessment of Educational Progress surveyed a random sample of approximately twenty-five hundred American youth, ages thirteen and seventeen, asking them for information about government and for responses to attitudinal inquiries toward politics and their classroom experiences. Results were divided into four categories: social attitudes, political attitudes, political knowledge, and political education. Students of both age groups generally agreed (88 percent) that they were "always," "often," or "sometimes" encouraged to speak freely and openly in class. Very few (12 percent) replied "never" to this question. Further, about three quarters of both age groups thought that their teachers "usually" respected their views; 69 percent and 72 percent of thirteen- and seventeen-year-olds, respectively, felt that they "sometimes" were asked to "help decide about school affairs."

Despite this relatively positive picture, results on several knowledge and attitude items were rather poor. For example, only 47 percent and 41 percent of the thirteen- and seventeen-year-olds could correctly identify the powers of the United Nations to settle or intervene in conflicts. Correct answers to questions about the Senate, the House of Representatives, and Congress were in the 30 percent to 50 percent range. Fifty-six percent of seventeen-year-olds and only 32 percent of thirteen-year-olds were aware that the number of congressional members varies with state populations. Of the younger group, 44 percent agreed that "a lot of elections are not important enough to vote in"; 32 percent of seventeen-year-olds agreed. It is interesting that African American students indicated more interest in politics, overall, than did Whites; there was very little difference generally between younger and older secondary students on most items, whether of knowledge or attitude, although older students did tend to receive slightly higher scores on knowledge questions.

SOURCE: National Assessment for Educational Progress, *Education for Citizenship: A Bicentennial Survey*, Report No. 07-CS-01 (Denver, CO: National Assessment for Educational Progress, November 1976).

A third major goal set for any government course at the senior or junior high school level should be concerned with policies, values, perceptions, and decision making. Although many view values as "soft" and data as "hard," political scientists would argue that attitudes are quite real in the sense that feelings are a major factor in tilting a political system toward one decision or another. A great deal of research and polling occupies scholars and politicians who take the results quite seriously. Important legislation and great amounts of power often depend on public feeling toward a given problem or issue. Poll results also give insights into how people and groups view an issue, often suggesting alternative solutions to a problem. Students should be familiar with the scientific process of sampling opinion because it is so prevalent in modern society and because attitudes often reflect and influence policy.[8]

Thus, in framing objectives for a democracy or government course, we might begin with the following:

1. Students will use polls to identify major values.
2. Students will develop a tolerance for the viewpoints of other people and groups.
3. Students will debate the different sides on an issue deciding where they personally will take a stand or opt out of the situation.
4. Students will discuss how much or how little they feel a part of the political system and why.

Initial goals focus on different aspects of values and policy and involve decision-making skills. Attitudes are both studied and formed during class activities, although the specifics of curriculum and group dynamics are missing as yet. Tolerance and empathy are built into several goals as desirable general outcomes, but the way in which growth in this area will be measured is left out. Finally, students are asked to analyze and evaluate their own feelings about "the system" and whether they intend to participate in it. Not only are others' viewpoints and the public's attitudes to be debated, but students will also probe their own beliefs and emotional states, such as their feelings of political trust or mistrust, alienation or identification, efficacy or apathy.

Reflecting on our initial efforts to write behavioral objectives for a government or democracy program, we can now add more specific features about content and process to improve planning. The new, improved versions of our original four goals might be these:

1. Students will review a recent Gallup poll of public attitudes foreign aid issues, analyze the testimony of at least three experts, and decide where they stand both as individuals and as a group by trying to reach a consensus for a national policy on foreign aid proposals.
2. Using a pre-lesson survey of peer attitudes toward a public controversy—the death penalty or affirmative action—students will carefully examine and discuss the viewpoint most opposed to their own, administering the same survey a second time to see whether any opinions have been changed or greater empathy has developed for the contrary argument, and to what degree the shift, on average, can be considered significant.
3. Students will take part in a formal debate or mock trial on a civil rights issue using a recent Supreme Court ruling in a discrimination or affirmative action case as a basis for argument. They will prepare and present statements, cross-examinations, and rebuttals that will be rated on a scale of 1 (worst) to 10 (best) by the class voting as a whole.

4. Using a series of case studies on many forms of political participation, such as community action, assisting a campaign, letter writing to officials, voting, taking part in a protest, and abstaining or "fence sitting", students will analyze and evaluate those forms of active or passive response to political problems they see as most or least valuable. They will explain in writing which types of participation they believe to provide the greatest or least sense of belonging to the American political culture, concluding with an exchange and critique of each others' stands on the subject.

These rewritten, expanded goals provide much greater clarity about what the students and the teacher are actually going to accomplish in the classroom. Activities include self-analysis of political values and attitudes, practice with survey research techniques as a prelude to value formation, decision making on international disarmament issues, and the consideration of others' views even when unpopular, perhaps leading to greater tolerance for disagreeable choices.

Throughout the formation of these goals, students are asked to make decisions for themselves based on the study of political behavior, public perception of the issues, and introspection into the beliefs we ourselves hold. Policy formation and value analyses are accompanied at each stage by materials that provide factual data and expert arguments that students may use as a basis for building their own commitments. At all times, students may opt to abstain as well as participate, to remain open or unsure of the stand they find most satisfying for themselves. While the teacher encourages choice and taking a position, lines are left fluid for those students who need more time to think over their own feelings, or who feel they need more information about a problem before they make a decision. Positive and negative aspects of perceptions and political conditions ought to be carefully considered, with decisions left to students. You, however, should seek to develop more comprehensive values for students, such as (a) empathy for others' viewpoints, (b) a commitment to consider arguments before choosing a stand, and (c) a stronger feeling of efficacy—the notion that ordinary individuals can be heard in the political process.

TO DO

Write ten affective goals that you believe should be part of any civics or government program. In your goals, would you try to convince students which values are best or have them develop their own statements? What sorts of goals will create an atmosphere of free and open discussion? Are there any goals that might inhibit discussion. Would you value free and open discussion as important?

While you think these questions over, write the ten affective goals at top speed and share them with a colleague or fellow student. Rate each goal according to its power for promoting (+) or inhibiting (-) the free discussion of ideas. Was it easy or difficult to decide how each one would affect discussion? Why?

DESIGNING A CIVICS PROGRAM

Designs for civics courses vary widely because of different conceptions of their purpose. A few are overtly patriotic, seeking to persuade students to a particular point of view. Social problems dominate some course structures, others offer descriptions of the U.S. government, and a few emphasize a jurisprudential model or a political systems theory.[9]

The "Civics Framework for the 1998 National Assessment of Educational Progress" suggests that civic knowledge can be "embodied" in five powerful questions about political life:

1. What are civic life, politics, and government?
2. What are the foundations of the American political system?
3. How does the government established by the Constitution embody the purposes, values, and principles of American democracy?
4. What is the relation of the United States to other nations and to world affairs?
5. What are the roles of citizens in American democracy?[10]

These five questions could be the focus of one or more course designs for government or civics, particularly if the questions posed are treated as open to a variety of responses and viewpoints. Virtually all courses in government and politics, whatever the title, claim that their content and methods are preparing young adults for entry into the political life of the nation, but few seem to have been very effective in terms of improving the voting record of American citizens, particularly the eighteen- to twenty-five- year-old group, or of promoting public activism.

RESEARCH REPORT

RATING TEXTBOOKS ON GOVERNMENT

A panel of scholars and educators reviewed eighteen junior and senior high school civics and government texts according to set criteria for judging the overall approach, treatment of the Constitution and Bill of Rights, development of controversial issues, and the degree of practice built into the program.

Although a few texts were judged impressive, most were viewed as containing two or more serious shortcomings. Most of the texts were large in size and dull to read, with a stress on institutions rather than politics or peoples. Controversy was generally absent, with 80 percent of the books downplaying conflict, problems, or strains in the system. International politics or comparison with other systems was either totally absent or very sketchy. In general, the critical issue of participation was missing and models to follow were left to the students' imagination. The best feature of most books was their description of branches and processes of government and discussion of the U.S. Constitution, both of which were covered in great detail. However, one reviewer noted that "if these books are representative of how government is being taught, then government is a dead subject."

SOURCE: James D. Carrol et al., *We the People: A Review of U.S. Government and Civics Textbooks* (Washington, DC: People for the American Way, 1981). (Quotation is from p. i.)

The Operational Approach

To generalize about the dominant model in the fragmented and disorganized democracy/civics/government area is difficult; however, most published texts seem to stress the formal operations of the U.S. government more than anything else. Many programs mix modes resulting in an often-confusing amalgam of social problems, participation issues, description, and political theory. A few programs provide data on comparative government or world structures, although this is relatively rare because political science as an evolving discipline has had marginal influence on civics courses.[11]

Most programs usually feature discussions of voting and other forms of participation, emphasizing the formal aspects of American political institutions and legal rules. They purport to prepare citizens to make decisions, but they do so by encouraging them to vote rather than to become analysts of political behavior or current issues.

Typically, topics for an American government, civics, or problems of democracy course include the following:

Major Topics for a Standard Government Course

I.   Political Systems
    A. How Decisions Are Made
    B. Basic Concepts
    C. Comparative Examples

II.   The U.S. Political System
    A. Historical Background
    B. Constitution and Bill of Rights
    C. Federalism
    D. Separation of Powers
    E. Checks and Balances

III.   Executive Branch
    A. Office of President
    B. The White House Staff
    C. The Cabinet and the Federal Bureaucracy

IV.   Legislative Branch
    A. Congress
      1. How a bill becomes a law
      2. Committee powers
      3. Political parties

V.   Judicial Branch
    A. Powers of the Supreme Court
      1. Trial courts
      2. Appeals courts
    B. Setting Precedents: Famous Cases
    C. Interpreting the Constitution and Bill of Rights

VI.   Policy Formation
    A. Social Values and Economic Conditions
    B. Public Opinion
    C. Leadership
    D. Interest Groups
    E. Lobbying
    F. Mass Media

VII.   Elections
    A. Political Participation
      1. Voting patterns
      2. Polling and research
      3. Local and state activism
      4. Causes and group memberships
      5. Protest movements
    B. Political Parties
      1. The two-party system
      2. Organization
      3. Membership
      4. Values and platforms

VIII.   Choosing Leaders
   A. Nomination Procedures
      1. Primaries
      2. Party designation
      3. Independents
   B. Campaigns
      1. Appeals and programs
      2. Finances
      3. Fair and foul
   C. Case Studies
      1. Winning and losing
      2. Mandates
      3. Liberals and conservatives
IX.   World Government/International Affairs
   A. The United Nations
   B. International Agencies
   C. Regional Associations
   D. Alliances and Foreign Policy
   E. Trade and Aid

The aforementioned course provides students with the basics about American government and the election process with a touch of global concerns. There is a heavy concentration on students' being able to identify the parts of government and how these relate to each other in a formal, legal sense. A good deal of what is presented overlaps with American or U.S. history materials but generally without the historical dimension. The emphasis is clearly on the present de jure structure but with considerable attention to the forces that influence decisions (i.e., the voters, media, special interest groups, the economic situation, and party politics).

WHAT DO YOU THINK?

> Form small groups and discuss which areas of government really deserve the most class time—for example, are the three branches worth one third of the course? Why or why not? Is world government or foreign policy worth only one unit? Why or why not?

Criticism.   The formal nature of many civics or government courses has been criticized on the ground that the knowledge provided, at best, gives young people a very narrow view of politics.[12] Left out are personal politics, community experience, volunteer work, and precinct-level door-to-door campaigning. Yet these are the forms of political activity that are realistic training grounds for future leaders and that probably represent areas of interest that people find more involving than voting. Human interaction in face-to-face relationships may also be viewed as a kind of politics, but peer, parent, and institutional relationships are almost entirely absent from most civics courses. Nevertheless, these connections are at the heart of daily political life. By contrast, voting occurs only at occasional designated points in the political process.[13]

Worse yet, some critics argue, although the schools themselves are fertile grounds for political activity and training, particularly for young adults, in most schools this opportunity is totally ignored.[14] Certainly, high school students are cognizant of their emerging roles as citizens and adults in our society and are capable of assuming a great deal more responsibility than they have in the usual student government offices that hold no power. Suggestions for student empowerment range from serving on committees to assist teachers in curriculum planning and on advisory groups to discuss issues with the school administration, to publishing student newspapers and conducting course evaluation surveys and school assessments. Active school participation involving real decision making would reduce students' cynicism about the political process as well as offer teachers firsthand examples of political compromise and the exchange of views.[15]

Also largely missing from the typical government course are analyses of vital social and economic issues that frequently perplex and divide people. These include frank and open discussions about the place of women in politics, the role of minorities, and the part religious groups play in the American system. Women in particular, more than half the population, are often mis- or underrepresented in politics, even on issues dealing directly with gender.[16] In general, critics point out that most secondary school students receive sanitized versions of the political system that are either so boring or so different from reality that their attitudes become more negative than positive as a result of their studies.

Finally, American government courses are accused of viewing the U.S. system in isolation from other systems with which it could be compared, such as European parliamentary democracy, one-party rule, authoritarian regimes, and military juntas. Students have little knowledge of why different systems exist or how these systems may borrow techniques and institutions (as they always have historically) to achieve social and economic goals.[17] For example, most students know only basic information about Mexico and Canada, both of which share long borders and trade heavily with the United States.[18] Just as comparative systems are absent or deemphasized, so too is the worldview, or how the United States fits into the total political scheme as a global power in international affairs.

Thus, the typical government course is attacked on several grounds: (a) formalism, (b) inattention to personal and school politics, (c) lack of emphasis on social problems, (d) too narrow a definition of participation, (e) no comparative framework for types of government, (f) an often biased view that we are "the best," (g) and little or no attention to the position of the United States as a participant in global politics.

Defense.   Standard courses and citizenship competencies are defended on the grounds that students need to know the basics of their government before they can move into more sophisticated issues and problems or understand the international scene.[19] Because there is at present no widely agreed-on framework for teaching about political values and social issues, it is more sensible to stick to government structures, party politics, and the election process. The traditional civics course provides information vital to voting, which is after all a major form of political expression in the United States. After students have absorbed the basics, you can easily supplement each topic with relevant case studies taken from other cultures. Local, state, or national news and supplemental materials can be designed to teach students how to evaluate arguments about social policy.

SAMPLE LESSON PLAN

> You have left your materials on gender issues at home, alas, but this is the topic scheduled for your class today. The students have already discussed the Bill of Rights and the thirteenth amendment, but you need something to capture their interest. What can you use as an example? How about sports? Private clubs? The military? Direct the conversation toward equal rights by asking questions about women serving in combat, or being integrated into baseball teams—professional, pony, and little league. That should get a good discussion going? What do you think?

Because events change so rapidly, the teacher must adapt the basic course structure to current controversies, media reports, and political disputes. Value issues come and go, but basic structures remain in place for long periods of time and are valuable to know and understand. A sense of involvement can be built through school activities, such as student government, mock trials, model United Nations, student review committees, and school newspaper reporting.

Alternative Approaches

Whereas the mainline government or civics course focuses on the mechanics of politics, alternative approaches stress issues, participation, and political science systems analysis. Oddly, issues- and participation-oriented programs are probably more common than those that rest on modern political science.[20] Political scientists may be avid people watchers but they do not pay much professional attention to the social studies, a field that many believe to have citizenship as its central goal.[21]

A Problems- or Issues-Centered Approach.   Political and social controversies lie at the heart of the issues-centered approach to the government course, which is sometimes retitled "problems of democracy" or "crucial issues in democracy." Whatever its name, the content of a "problems" course is usually organized around themes or questions that encourage debate about both long- and short-range controversies. Instead of topical coverage, problems and issues may often be arranged as a series of pro and con debate questions for students to use as guides for developing their own positions. The classroom becomes a public forum for the free expression of views on issues that face society. Students are continually called on to make decisions using evidence and values as sources of defense. Usually, the issues themselves are discussed through advocacy case studies, simulations, or contrasting positions.

Two outstanding experiments with this type of program date back to the 1960s and 1970s: the Harvard Social Studies Project and the Crucial Issues in Government series.[22] Both used small pamphlets to provide students with a sample of the data and the ethical positions that characterized problems of racism, gender, pressure groups, lawsuits, voter apathy, community participation, free speech, and foreign aid. Modest amounts of data in the form of statistics, articles, and editorial cartoons were presented to students as springboards for discussions. The selections represented a fair sample of the common positions on an issue. Activities and questions would stress student choice and position taking rather than teacher domination of the decision-making process. A recent study of an issues-oriented classroom portrays the teacher as the "dilemma-manager" of a robust and lively classroom in which students "reported a more complex, diverse, tentative, and skeptical disposition toward knowledge."[23] Characteristically, an issues-centered approach calls upon the teacher to play a role that balances knowledge with in-depth argument in a situation where there is support for an exchange of views.

An issues course could be composed of units on popular problems that might look like the following:

Major Topics for Problems of Democracy Course

1. The Three Branches: Are They in Balance?
2. The President: Is the Office Too Powerful?
3. Lobbying: Should It Be Controlled for the General Good?
4. Free Speech and Assembly: Where Should the Lines Be Drawn?
5. Participation: Why Should the Voters Care?

6. Political Parties: Are There Any Real Differences?
7. Women and Minorities: Are They Really Equal Before the Law? In Practice and in Theory?
8. Rich, Middle Class, and Poor: How Shall the Wealth Be Distributed?
9. International Human Rights: Should These Be the Standard for All?
10. Foreign Aid: How Much for Guns and How Much for Butter?

Underlying a problems structure is a strong commitment to analyze and weigh the issues by identifying the causes and consequences, costs and benefits of alternative solutions. Questions of justice, freedom, and authority permeate the entire course providing a framework for the separate topics. Many other possibilities could be added to the previous list, such as the disputes over the death penalty, campaign financing, environmental protection, political corruption, and police powers and rights of the accused.

Problems and issues are also a perfect vehicle for employing computer applications to save, analyze, and cross-check databases that justify (or fail to) a political position. For example, homicide rates for states with and without the death penalty could be compared statistically, using a bar graph, to discover whether the death penalty correlates with reduced levels of murder. Rates of participation in elections for different segments of society could be compared to learn which groups vote most or least frequently, and whether activism correlates with class, race, or ethnicity. From the correlations that might be identified, tentative hypotheses could be developed to explain homicide or voting or other social patterns.

SAMPLE LESSON PLAN

Read the story below and answer these questions:
1. What do you think are the facts of the Cantwell case?
2. How thought provoking are the "persisting questions"?
3. Are there questions that you think need to be changed or added? Why?

While you are thinking about the questions provided, decide how you might use the case of Jesse Cantwell to discuss and debate constitutional and social issues with your pupils or with your possible future pupils in the secondary schools.

Create a lesson plan for a government or civics course in which you could apply this "classic" social studies lesson.

THE CASE OF JESSE

Does religious freedom include the right to criticize other faiths? The U.S. Supreme Court faced that question.

Jesse Cantwell trudged heavily down the street, his figure lopsided from the drag of a bulky black suitcase. It contained books, pamphlets, a portable phonograph, and a set of records. Cantwell wore a neat business suit and a felt hat. From outward appearance he might have been just another hardworking salesman. In a way he was. He was a Jehovah's Witness.

Cantwell walked on Cassius Street in New Haven, Conn. The street was heavily populated and full of life—clusters of men in earnest sidewalk conversations, housewives chatting from porch to porch. That was good for a man with calls to make.

Cantwell had spent most of the day going from door to door. First he would ask each person for permission to play a record, which introduced and described a book. If permission was granted, he played the record and asked the person to buy the book. If permission was refused, Cantwell asked for a contribution toward the publication of pamphlets. For each contribution, he gave a pamphlet—on condition that it be read.

His day, he thought, had not been very successful. Some homeowners had taken quick offense at his presentation. There had been more than the usual number of slammed doors. Yet Cantwell felt some consolation. He knew why the day had been difficult. Cassius Street was more than 90 percent Catholic.

Even in the best of circumstances, Cantwell knew, the work of a Jehovah's Witness was not easy. Every Witness who preached the truth of the Bible as faithfully as he should, Cantwell thought, could expect resistance.

He knew this resistance might take the form of ridicule, threats, and even violence. From time to time Witnesses had been beaten or chased through the streets.

What was more, Cantwell knew, was that Witnesses often encountered a wall of restrictive local laws. These laws might forbid uninvited calls at homes, or levy high taxes, or require licenses that were often impossible to obtain.

Opposition arises partly in response to basic beliefs of the Jehovah's Witnesses. Witnesses believe that Satan has ruled the world since 1914. They believe that the world has gotten progressively worse since then and is rapidly moving toward Armageddon. In this great battle, Jehovah (from the Hebrew name for God) is expected to destroy Satan and all other evil. Thereafter, Witnesses say, God will rule a world free of pain, sorrow, and even death.

At their periodic conventions, Witnesses wear badges proclaiming, "God's Kingdom Rules—Is the World's End Near?" Yet, according to Witnesses, only 144,000 persons will go to heaven, there to rule with God as kings for a thousand years.

Witnesses base all their beliefs solely on the Bible. They cite references to both the Old and New Testaments, but their interpretations differ greatly from those of other faiths. For example, Witnesses do not believe in the general immortality of the soul, but say that the soul—except for those of people who will go to Heaven—dies with the body. Witnesses deny the general belief that Jesus died on the cross; they say He was tortured to death at the stake.

Another Witness belief forbids blood transfusions as violating a biblical injunction against "eating blood." Time after time Witnesses have refused to consent to blood transfusions for themselves or for their children, even when the refusal appeared to mean certain death. The courts have generally respected the right of adult Witnesses to refuse; but judges have often ruled that no parent has a right to consign his child to death by refusing blood out of religious conviction.

Because all Witnesses regard themselves as ministers, opposed to taking part in war, they frequently seek to be exempted from military service. Draft disputes have landed hundreds of them in federal prisons. In most other respects, Witnesses have won the right to be considered ministers in the eyes of the law. This was right, thought Jesse Cantwell as he walked down Cassius Street. He was disturbed about some of the incidents of the day. But then, he reflected, God had commanded Jehovah's Witnesses to teach others.

The thought made Cantwell feel somewhat better about the most unfortunate incident of the day. It had occurred when Cantwell stopped two men in the street to ask their permission to play a record for them. Somewhat bemusedly the men had given permission. The record described a book entitled *Enemies* and contained a general attack on all organized religious systems as instruments of Satan and harmful to men. The record singled out the Roman Catholic Church as the most evil.

As the record played, the two men, both Catholics, had looked at one another in astonishment. Then anger had welled up in them, pumping their faces red. Cantwell had been sure that they were going to hit him. But instead one of the men had told him angrily, "You better get off the street before something happens to you." Without hesitation and without a word, Cantwell had picked up his things and left.

Cantwell made a point of never forcing the issue. Throughout the day, he had tried to conduct himself in a quiet, orderly manner. If anything, he thought, he had been more courteous than usual in view of the determined Catholicism he found on Cassius Street.

Nonetheless, the day had not been without its rewards. Cantwell thought he had obtained a few leads—names and addresses of persons showing some interest in the Jehovah's Witnesses. Next week he would call on these people again, this time inviting them to a free Bible lecture.

Cantwell arrived at the spot where he was to meet his father and his brother Russell. They were working on the opposite ends of Cassius Street. Cantwell glanced at his watch and saw that he was early. Rather than stand there, he might as well make one last call, he said to himself.

Cantwell was looking about for a likely looking house when a policeman approached him.

"Are you Jesse Cantwell, a member of an organization called the Jehovah's Witnesses?"

"Yes, I am Jesse Cantwell."

"I think you better come with me."

"May I ask the charge?"

"Inciting a breach of the peace and soliciting funds without a permit."

Jesse Cantwell, his father, and his brother were all arrested. Each was convicted in the New Haven Court of Common Pleas of inciting a breach of the peace and soliciting funds without a permit.

The state law read in part: "No person shall solicit money, services, subscriptions, or any valuable thing for any alleged religious, charitable, or philanthropic cause ... unless such cause shall have been approved by the secretary of the Public Welfare Council."

The State Supreme Court upheld the convictions of all three on the charge of breaking this state law. The court reversed the convictions of Cantwell's father and brother on the breach of the peace charge, and ordered new trials for them. But the court upheld Jesse Cantwell's conviction on that charge specifically because of his contact with the two men for whom he had played the record in the street.

The Cantwells then appealed to the United States Supreme Court, which agreed to hear the case. In a unanimous opinion, the Supreme Court reversed the convictions of the Cantwells.

The Court held that the state law deprived the Cantwells of their liberty. The Court ruled unanimously that "Freedom to adhere to such religious organization or form of worship as the individual may choose cannot be restricted by law."

The Court held that requiring the Cantwells to obtain a certificate as a condition of soliciting support for their religious views was "censorship of religion as a means of determining its right to survive," and a "denial of liberty protected by the First Amendment. ..."

The Court noted that on the day of his arrest Jesse Cantwell "was upon a public street, where he had a right to be, and where he had a right peacefully to impart his views to others. There is no showing that his deportment was noisy, truculent, overbearing, or offensive.... It is not claimed that he intended to insult or affront the hearers.... It is plain that he wished only to interest them in propaganda."

In conclusion, the Court said: "In the realm of religious faith ... sharp differences arise.... The tenets of one man may seem the rankest error to his neighbor. To persuade others to his point of view, the pleader .... at times, resorts to exaggeration, to vilification.... But the people of this nation have ordained in the light of history that, in spite of the probability of excesses and abuses, these liberties are, in the long view, essential to enlightened opinion and right conduct on the part of citizens of a democracy."

Facts of the Case

1. Describe Jesse Cantwell's approach as he went door to door on Cassius Street.
2. Why was Cantwell's task especially difficult?
3. What did Cantwell's recording say about other religions?
4. On what charges was Cantwell arrested?
5. On what grounds did the U.S. Supreme Court set aside the convictions of the Cantwells?

Persisting Questions of Modern Life

1. Evaluating the Decision. Do you agree or disagree with the Supreme Court's general decision in the Cantwell case? Explain. What do you think of the opinion that "exaggeration" and "vilification" are permissible for use in attempts to persuade people of the worth of certain religious views? Explain. Do you think the following statements are permissible or not?

   a. "The ritual of your religion is a stupid, heathen magic show."
   b. "You people only celebrate religious holidays to get out of work."
   c. "You believe in life everlasting because you are too weak-minded to face the hard daily demands of life."
   d. "You're deluded in thinking you are chosen for heaven. We are chosen for heaven."

2. Distinguishing Rights. People sometimes complain that their privacy is invaded by salespeople who bombard them by means of TV, radio, "junk" mail, doorbell-ringing, phone calls, and other ways. Should religious groups be limited in their use of such means to persuade others? Why or why not? Would you agree or disagree with the idea that religious groups should be given reduced rates or special privileges in the use of the following facilities?

   a. TV and radio,
   b. mail,
   c. telephone,
   d. public meeting places such as school auditoriums and town halls,
   e. door-to-door solicitation. Explain your opinions.

SOURCE: *Religious Freedom: Belief, Practice, and the Public Interest*, adapted from the Harvard Social Studies Project by James C. Schott (Boulder, CO: Social Science Education Consortium, 1991), pp. 41–46. Reprinted by permission.

An issues approach is likely to be far more involving and motivating for students than a descriptive government class. The basics of government can be worked into the issues and covered as part of each debate. However, there are drawbacks to controversy because not all issues can be neatly divided into pros and cons. Often, the issue itself is complex and the proposed solutions may involve many distinct positions to evaluate. In spite of the difficulty of splitting issues into neat divisions, student decision making should be an integral part of every lesson. This design for the democracy/civics/government program should be given more serious consideration by social studies teachers.

WHAT DO YOU THINK?

Are there other issues that should be added to the course outline? Make a list of those that are "musts" for discussion. Explain why you feel as you do. Are there any issues you would avoid? Why?

A Political Systems Analysis Approach. A political science approach to government/civics/democracy courses applies the concepts and research methods of the social sciences to the study of human values and behavior. In this approach, emphasis is given to actual political behavior rather than to formal government structures. The causes and consequences of action or inaction are analyzed to determine whether any patterns exist in the way people behave, vote, make demands, assume leadership, and so on. A political science approach might ask such questions as: How do active citizens compare to apathetic citizens in terms of party membership, socioeconomic status, ethnicity, race, education, or sex? The driving interest of a political science approach would be to study the meanings people give to political actions and symbols so as to understand the factors that influence their decisions. Political scientists wish to interpret and compare events. Legal structures and the decision-making apparatus are secondary to the way people apply or evade the rules. Statistics can be used to support a theory, and primary sources, such as eyewitness reports, can serve as the basis for studying different vantage points and value systems.

SAMPLE LESSON PLAN

Look at the chart.
  A. Questions:
    1. How do most people justify their political allegiance?
    2. Have allegiances changed over time? How much? Why do you think people change?
    3. Do most people hold fast to their values or do they alter their preferences easily over time? Why?
  B. Ask your students to explain (anonymously) their allegiances to party or leader. Can you categorize their views into the four-part set presented in this chart?

Level of Conceptualization	1956	1960	1964	1968	1972	1976	1980	1984
Ideologues (a)	12%	19%	27%	26%	22%	21%	22%	22%
Group Benefit (b)	42	31	27	24	27	26	30	27
Nature of Times (c)	24	26	20	29	34	30	31	34
No Issue Content (d)	22	23	26	21	17	24	17	17
	100%	99%	100%	100%	100%	101%	100%	100%

a. These are people who use clearly ideological or issue-based reasoning to describe their orientation to parties or candidates. Only this group really can be termed "issue oriented."

b. Respondents who related themselves to the candidates or parties only by virtue of group identification (e.g., "Democrats favor us poor people") rather than issues or ideological labels are in this group.

c. These individuals referred to the general nature of events to describe their position on parties and candidates (e.g., "It's time for a change" or "we always have war when Democrats are elected") are in this category.

d. In this group are those who could not give any issue-based ideas of any sort to explain their preferences for party or candidates.

SOURCE: Herbert B. Asher, *Presidential Elections and American Politics*, 4th ed. (Chicago: Dorsey, 1988).

During the 1950s and 1960s, value judgments and policy issues were seen as secondary to analysis. Position taking was shunned by the widely accepted systems theory school of political science, which sought objective and universal laws of behavior.[24] More recently, policy analysis has returned to favor, and most political scientists are willing to offer carefully developed normative (value) judgments to provide interpretations of events.

In a systems theory approach to politics, large groups or categories of events are defined and compared. From this analysis, increasingly higher order theories can be formulated to explain large portions of human action. Studies might typically focus on democratic and authoritarian regimes, the path of revolutions and counterrevolutions, the development of centralized and federal state structures, and the building of ideologies and rationales. Concepts are used as tools for interpreting events and testing theories that may relate to situations ranging from the local to the international. Throughout any political science-type of course, there must always be a consciousness of the way an inquiry is being undertaken: its research tools, data sources, possible errors, and real or potential biases. Students are asked to tune in to the methods of the social sciences by adopting a scientific point of view in analyzing human belief and action.[25]

SAMPLE LESSON PLAN

A PROFILE OF THE MORE ACTIVE AND LESS ACTIVE CITIZENRY

More Active	Less Active
More Likely to Vote	Less Likely to Vote
High income	Low income
High occupational status	Low occupational status
College education	Grade school education
Male	Female*
Middle-aged	Young or old
Urban resident	Rural resident‡
Metropolitan area resident	Small town resident
White	Black
Northern state resident	Southern state resident
Resident in competitive party environment	Resident in noncompetitive party environment

Union member	Nonunion member
Homeowner	Renter
Jewish and Catholic	Protestant

Using the previous list, think about the following questions: Why do people of high income take a greater interest in politics? Do memberships help? How does a person's lifestyle influence participation?

*In recent elections, 1996 for example, the gap between male and female turnout has opened a bit more in some races.

‡There is conflicting evidence on the voting participation of rural and urban residents. A study of Illinois voters finds that, contrary to the usual pattern, turnout is much higher in rural areas than in urban areas—despite the fact that rural voters rank lower in education, income, and socioeconomic status. See Alan D. Monroe, "Urbanism and Voter Turnout: A Note on Some Unexpected Findings," *American Journal of Political Science,* 22 (February 1977): 77–78.

SOURCE: William J. Keefe, *Parties, Politics, and Public Policy in America* (New York: Holt, Rinehart & Winston, 1980).

The concepts and methods of political science can be useful investigative tools for interpreting elections, analyzing conflicts, and summarizing patterns of influence. Ideas such as power, socioeconomic status, political socialization, efficacy, authority, community, and choice infuse the vocabulary of a social science approach to government.

A political science approach might contain the following:

Topics for a Political Systems Course

I. Making Decisions as a Citizen of the United States
   A. Personal Factors
   B Social and Economic Factors
   C. Religious and Values Factors
   D. Occupation and Educational Factors
   E. Customs and Traditions

II. Goals and Objectives
   A. Wants and Needs
   B. Organized Demands

III. Forms of Authority: Leadership Positions in the United States
   A. Three Branches of Government
   B. Nongovernment Groups and Organizations
   C. Communities, Local and National
   D. Expertise and Specialists

IV. Political Structures: Comparative Systems
   A. Military Juntas
   B. Representative Systems
   C. One-party States
   D. Theocratic Regimes
   E. Oligarchies
   F. Monarchies

V. Organizations and Groups
   A. Gender
   B. Race
   C. Ethnicity
   D. Family

E. Social Classes
F. Communities
VI.   American Communications: Image Building
A. Face-to-Face Contacts
B. Large Groups
C. Media
D. Symbols and Signs
VII.   Conflict and Conflict Resolution
A. American Political Parties and Elections
B. Pressure and Interest Groups/Campaign Financing
C. Value Differences/Ideologies—Liberals and Conservatives
D. Lobbying and Lobbyists
E. Negotiation, Compromise, and Stalemate
VIII.   The United States in the Modern World System
A. Distribution of Power and Wealth
1. East and West
2. North and South
B. Alliances and foreign policy
1. Hegemony and control
2. Regional and local interests

In this example, which is only one of many possible options, a systems approach concentrates on analytical ideas, fitting issues and controversies into larger, more encompassing categories such as conflict and conflict resolution. The U.S. government is viewed as a case study in politics to be compared and contrasted with other systems from around the world. In this social science perspective, the civics/U.S. government aspects of democracy are viewed from a theoretical perspective that would work equally well for almost any nation-state. Students begin to see the U.S. system as one of many with built-in freedoms that have emerged from English law and custom to be codified in the Constitution and Bill of Rights. The system works because of effective socialization methods (education, media, and leadership) and because of the relative wealth of the nation. Less attention is afforded to citizenship values, patriotism, and historical evolution. Gains are made in global perspective, comparative political structures, and insight into political motivation. Personal decision making is linked directly by political analysis to predictions about how people will act based on their social values and previous performance. The political science approach offers a provocative alternative to the standard, formalized government course.

A Participation or Community Action Approach.   American politics may also be presented to secondary students in the form of a "participation in democracy" format. Participation in democracy or participatory democracy is an approach that stresses activism—firsthand experience in political situations such as internships and field trips. A participation approach seeks exercises designed to bring the students out of the classroom and into the real-life drama of politics. This method shares many goals with the other designs, especially those promoting issues and controversies. The success of this type of presentation depends largely on school support for field-based experience. Also helpful are ties to local organizations, which can provide a steady stream of visitors to the classroom. Participation is an exciting idea, particularly relevant to high school juniors and seniors who will soon vote, but equally applicable to junior high students as a way of bringing abstract ideas and institutions to life.

The possibilities for a participation approach are virtually endless. You could arrange classroom visits by lawyers, lobbyists, politicians, and organizational representatives. You might schedule field trips to courts, political clubs, campaign offices, city hall, or government agency headquarters. Media consultants and newsmakers could be asked to discuss how they choose and present stories about candidates or events.

Students could apply the principles they have learned to mounting a campaign within the school itself, with permission of the authorities. Where possible, arrange cooperative work study programs in which students assist political representatives, lawyers, judges, civil servants, or private organizers in their duties and get a chance to observe political action at firsthand. Of course, there are also dangers involved in close contact, such as losing objectivity for a candidate or issue because you are working to achieve the goals of only one side. Other problems may arise when the experience itself becomes all-consuming, blotting out the curriculum.

To be keen political observers and decision makers, students still need to know the basic rules of government. They will also certainly benefit from some form of system analysis to understand how and why lines of power and influence develop. Thus, participation in democracy requires much the same sense of basics as do the other approaches, but this knowledge is applied directly to life experiences.

In its best sense, a participation approach would offer students an overview of constitutional rules, election procedures, legal precedents, and voting patterns while integrating these into carefully selected practical experiences. For example, a visit to criminal court could yield a sociological picture of the defendants: Are they rich or poor, well or poorly educated, and so on—and why? Theories and rules could then be tested through the observation of de facto behavior. To work well, a participation approach must incorporate regularly spaced field experiences with presentations about formal government operation and political science research on participation, protest, and apathy. The whole game plan or strategy for a participation course would rest on the counterpoint between de jure and de facto politics.

If it is well balanced, a participation approach can yield vital and interesting questions for discussion in classrooms or in the field. These questions would focus on issues of freedom, authority, justice, and conflict that affect every aspect of life. Consider the following sample questions:

Do most people really want to be highly active in politics?

Why might many people be apathetic?

What if most people were very active?

Can decisions be made without support?

Does authority flow only from above, or from below as well?

Can conflicts be settled with a minimum of violence?

If laws are seen as unjust, should people still obey?

Are there laws that may be seen as higher than the political and legal rules laid down in the Constitution or by legislation?

WHAT DO YOU THINK?

1. Holding public and party office 2. Being a candidate for office 3. Soliciting political funds 4. Attending a caucus or a strategy meeting 5. Becoming an active member in a political party 6. Contributing time in a political campaign	Gladiatorial Activities (1 to 5%)
7. Attending a political meeting or rally 8. Making a monetary contribution to a party or candidate 9. Contacting a public official or a political leader	Transitional Activities (5 to 13%)
10. Wearing a button or putting a sticker on the car 11. Attempting to talk another into voting a certain way 12. Initiating a political discussion 13. Voting 14. Exposing oneself to political stimuli	Spectator Activities (15 to 70%)
	Apathetics

Figure 11.2   Hierarchy of political involvement. Query: According to this concept of participation, who are the most active and who the least: Do you agree?
SOURCE: Lester W. Milbrath, *Political Participation: How and Why Do People Get Involved in Politics?* Copyright © 1965 by Houghton Mifflin Company. Used with permission.

Any of these questions could be directed and redirected throughout a course in conjunction with case studies and examples that fit the theme.

The concept of participation itself would be worth several dialogues on the didactic, reflective, and affective levels; that is, what is participation? Why do people participate or choose not to do so? Which forms of participation are most affective for individuals, groups, and society as a whole?

A well-known conception of participation depicts it as ranging from lows, such as voting, to highs, such as running for office (see Figure 11.1). This hierarchy could be used as a springboard for discussing the participation concept.

This hierarchy suggests an activist interpretation of behavior. Teachers and students may well ask whether voting is or is not a low-level form of participation, and whether it should be classified as such. Should protests in groups be seen as an advanced form of participation? Which forms of activism are best for most people most of the time? What sorts of situations should be seen as demanding a more (or less) active approach by citizens? Furthermore, participation might itself be discussed as a good. For example, if pro- and anti-abortion factions are very active in a divided community, what are the consequences? Often, compromises are made and a community lives peacefully, but other times passions bring a level of activism that tears a group apart. A participation program might be thought of as existing on two tracks, the academic and the experimental, with strong connections between both—perhaps like the following example:

Participation in Democracy

Topic Readings and Discussion

I. You as a citizen study your rights and responsibilities, legal and social.
   A. Personal Problems and Self-Confidence
   B. Attitudes Toward Politics
      1. Trust/mistrust
      2. Power/powerlessness (Efficacy)
   C. Sources of Knowledge and Feeling
      1. Peers
      2. Parents
      3. Media (TV, radio, film, newspapers, journals, etc.)
      4. School
II. Defining Participation
   A. Influence
   B. Involvement Levels
   C. Abstention
   D. Leadership
   E. Decision making
   F. Special Interests
III. Sources of Power
   A. Communication, Personal and Media
   B. Socioeconomic Status
   C. Education
   D. Gender, Race, and Ethnicity
   E. Friendships, Families, and Social Networks
   F. Political Parties
IV. Understanding the Political System
   A. United States, Formal Structure
   B. United States, Informal Structure
   C. Global, Formal Structure
   D. Global, Informal Structure
V. Conflict and Cooperation
   A. Conflict Situations
   B. Conflict Resolution
   C. Interests and Values: The Idea of the Common Good
VI. Choosing a Philosophy
   A. Liberal, Moderate, Conservative, Other
   B. Patriotism and Criticism
   C. Winning Versus Playing by the Rules
   D. The "Highest" Human Values

Experiences and Field Activities

I. Design and conduct a poll of student attitudes. Compare findings with those of a Gallup or Roper Poll.

II. Discuss voting with a representative of the League of Women Voters. Take part in a community environmental or zoning controversy. Attend a school board meeting.

III. Go to a nearby political club or university lecture to hear a lecture on voter participation. Ask a political leader to talk about how the power of an elective office would be put to use.

IV. Visit a court, city council, or police station. Invite a legislator to speak to the class. Prepare a panel to question two or more lobbyists. Participate in a model United Nations.

V. Attend and evaluate a debate between two foreign policy specialists or between pro- and anti-environmental spokespersons.

VI. Take part in rallies for a liberal and a conservative cause. Decide which you favor.

A participation design, although sometimes touted as a "new" course structure, can be traced back to much earlier suggestions for socially active programs that involve students in experiences rather than merely in formal study.[26] The example provided earlier can be emulated, altered, or redesigned depending on the students' needs, the teacher's goals, school mandates, and community issues. Whatever its faults, the participation model does provide an alternative to government courses that mainly offer descriptions of the laws and institutions of federal, state, and local authorities.

KEY QUESTIONS FOR TEACHING U.S. GOVERNMENT

There are important questions that cut across all the approaches to teaching about government. These inquiries focus on the central problem of government: deciding how to allocate scarce resources among unlimited political demands. Everyone, even the apathetic, participates in the process of decision making by inputs into the system or by abstention. Negotiation and compromise alter the demands into manageable rules for all to follow. If negotiations cannot provide a satisfactory solution, there is the danger of violence, especially from those whose demands have gone unfulfilled.

A political system with its laws, leaders, and legislators can be seen as a set of institutions created for the purpose of negotiating and channeling social demands constructively. The following are some of the key questions that can be raised in the participation, government, civics, or problems of democracy course:

1. Who gets what, when, where, and how?
2. How is power defined in the system? How is it practiced? Are power and practice the same?
3. Which groups, classes, sections, or parties have greater power than others? Why?
4. What conflicts seem to be part of the political process? Are all solvable? Why or why not?
5. How much authority are people willing to allow their leaders? How much participation is common?
6. Is the government basically one of laws or one of leaders? How can you tell?
7. To what extent is the political system fair or unfair to each citizen and group? How does the majority view what is fair? What are the views of minorities?
8. Does the system as a whole work to meet all or most demands and advance the interests of its citizens, or are there numerous problems? How are demands negotiated and problems handled by the government?
9. Is the system basically respectful or disrespectful of human life?
10. When is a political decision ethical? Give examples.

Although these ten questions are by no means exhaustive, any one or all may be applied to cases and examples that would be common to all government and civics programs. Key questions call on students to develop explanations based on observations and to generate hypotheses that explain human action. For example, students could try to answer tough questions: Why does a law fail to pass Congress? Why may a strongly supported bill fail to change public behavior? Why do different leaders in the same position achieve a great deal or very little? Why are the political systems of nations so different? Why do economic conditions influence politics? Why do traditions and values shape the way people feel about their governments? In politics, interesting questions are easily formulated and lead to a high production of student ideas and judgments. Above all, it is your role to encourage students to initiate and follow through on their own ideas, and to avoid communicating either a sense that all government decisions are good or that all leaders are corrupt, ineffective, and cynical.

SUMMARY

A course in civics and government is commonly required at the junior and senior high school level. Recently, such courses have been recast as problems of democracy and participation in democracy programs. Central to the mission of government courses is giving students an understanding of U.S. federal, state, and local systems, sometimes in a world setting where other governments and the United Nations are included in the curriculum. This understanding can be shallow, fulfilling mainly didactic aims, or deeper, achieving reflective and affective goals. However, it is difficult to see how politics can be studied without arguing positions and taking sides in the ongoing debates that affect our lives. All civics, participation, and government courses face a built-in dilemma—how to balance socialization with criticism. Course goals may stress building a commitment to common core values, such as the Bill of Rights and patriotic beliefs, while simultaneously pressing for independent decision making and full debate of issues. The potential is great for critical challenge of traditional beliefs and strongly held values. You, the teacher, have to build consensus while promoting critical thinking—not an easy task!

Despite polemical problems in which the textbooks may prompt agreement on a number of issues, government can be taught in a variety of ways, ranging from the traditional structural approach to the more flexible issues or participation design. Professional research and analysis suggests that students need far more involvement with government, directly and through role-play and debate, and less instruction on formal organizations. Furthermore, schools themselves can support positive values by including students in school decisions. Politics poses persisting questions for secondary students (who will soon be legal voters) concerning the uses and abuses of power, who makes decisions, how and why allegiances are formed, and which values should be the basis of social and personal life.

TO DO

Participating in a survey or census is a superb way of engaging students in field-based survey research. Through their own polling efforts, they will learn both the methods and pitfalls of finding out what people know about their society and government, and what issues and beliefs they care about. Computer programs designed for compiling, analyzing, and graphically representing survey data could be applied to the student-designed poll thereby achieving two goals simultaneously: extending research skills and putting computer technology into practice.

An example to follow could be The Census Education Project: 1980, 1990, and 2000,* which incorporates "teacher-ready" lessons for students who plan, conduct, analyze, display, and interpret their own local census. Further, students role-play the parts of community planners and market researchers who are preparing government and business plans for the next ten years. The projections drawn by groups of students represent their conclusions about which changes will be significant in our society in the near future.

*The Census Education Project is available from the U.S. Department of Commerce, Bureau of the Census, Office of the Director, Washington, DC 20233. Project materials for the year 2000 are under development.

NOTES

1. Fred M. Newmann, *Education for Citizen Action: Challenge for Secondary Curriculum* (Berkeley, CA: McCutchan, 1975).
2. Walter C. Parker, "Participatory Citizenship: Civics in the Strong Sense," *Social Education*, 53, no. 8 (Oct. 1989): 353–54.
3. Center for Civic Education, *National Standards for Civic and Government*. (Calabasas, CA: Center for Civic Education, 1994).
4. L. M. McNeil, *Contradictions of Control* (New York: Routledge, 1986).
5. R. Pratle, *The Civic Imperative* (New York: Teachers College Press, 1988).
6. Byron Massialas, "The Inevitability of Issue-Centered Discourse in the Classroom," *The Social Studies* 80, no. 5 (Sept./Oct. 1989): 173–76.
7. F. Wirt, "The Uses of Blandness: State, Local and Professional Roles in Citizenship Education," in *Teaching About Federal Democracy*, ed. S. Schechter (Philadelphia: Temple University Press, 1984).
8. D. J. Mueller, *Measuring Social Attitudes* (New York: Columbia University Press, 1986).
9. Thomas L. Dynneson and Richard E. Gross, "An Eclectic Approach to Citizenship: Developmental Stages," *The Social Studies* (Jan./Feb. 1985): 23–27.
10. NAEP Civics Consensus Project, *Civics Framework for the 1998 National Assessment for Educational Progress* (Washington, DC: National Assessment Governing Board, U.S. Department of Education, 1998), pp. ix–xi.
11. James P. Shaver and Richard Knight, "Civics and Government in Citizenship Education," in *The Social Studies and the Social Sciences: A Fifty Year Perspective*, ed. Stanley Wronski and Donald H. Bragaw (Washington, DC: National Council for the Social Studies, 1986), pp. 71–84.
12. Fred Newmann, "Reflective Civic Participation," *Social Education*, 53, no. 6 (Oct. 1989): 357–60.
13. Margaret M. Conway, *Political Participation in the United States* (Washington, DC: Congressional Quarterly, 1985).
14. William D. Coplin, M. K. O'Leary, and J. J. Carroll, *Effective Participation in Government: A Guide to Policy Skills* (Croton-On-Hudson, NY: Policy Studies Associates, 1988).
15. L. Jennings, "Learning about Life: New Focus on Service as a Teaching Tool," *Education Week*, 8, no. 8 (1988).
16. Jane Bernard-Powers, "The 'Woman Question' in Citizenship Education," in *Educating the Democratic Mind*, ed. Walter C. Parker (Albany, NY: SUNY Press, 1996), pp. 287–308.
17. Willard M. Kniep, "Social Studies Within a Global Education," *Social Education* (Oct. 1989): 385, 399–403.
18. The Gallup Organization, *Geography: An International Gallup Survey: A Summary of Findings* (Princeton, NJ: Gallup Inc., 1988).
19. Richard Remy, *Handbook of Basic Citizenship Competencies* (Alexandria, VA: Association for Supervision and Curriculum Development, 1980).
20. Richard E. Gross, "Citizenship Education: Global Challenge for the 1980's," *Social Studies Review* 26, no. 3 (Spring 1987): 47–52.
21. R. Freeman Butts, *The Revival of Civic Learning: A Rationale for Citizenship in American Schools* (Bloomington, IN: Phi Delta Kappa, 1980).
22. Donald W. Oliver and Fred M. Newmann, *Public Issues Series* (Middletown, CT: American Education Publications, 1969–1974).
23. John Allen Rossi, "In-Depth Study in an Issues-Oriented Social Studies Classroom," *Theory and Research in Social Education*, 23, no. 2 (Spring, 1995): 88–120.
24. David Easton, "The New Revolution in Political Science," *American Political Science Review*, 63 (Dec. 1969): 1051–61.
25. Eric , *The New Science of Politics* (Chicago: University of Chicago Press, 1952).
26. Mary A. Hepburn, "Improving Citizenship Education," *The Social Studies*, 71, no. 1 (1980): 8–13.

FOR FURTHER STUDY: TEACHING U.S. GOVERNMENT

Anderson, Lee et al. *The Civics Report Card: 1976–1988*. Princeton, NJ: Educational Testing Service, National Assessment of Educational Progress, 1990.

Belenkey, M. F. et al. *Women's Ways of Knowing: The Development of Self, Voice, and Mind*. New York: Basic Books, 1986.

Boulding, E. *Building a Global Civic Culture: Education for an Interdependent World*. New York: Teacher's College Press, 1988.

Center for Civic Education. *National Standards for Civics and Government*. 2nd ed. Calabasas, CA: Author, 1994.

Coplin, William. *Teaching Policy Studies: What and How*. Reprint. Washington, DC: Center for Policy Studies, University Press of America, 1985.

Glassner, M. I., and H. J. de Blij. *Systematic Political Geography*. New York: Wiley, 1989.

Hearst Report. *The American Public's Knowledge of the U.S. Constitution*. New York: Hearst Corporation, 1987.

Kaltsounis, T., and B. G. Massialas, eds. "Special Section on 'Democratic Citizenship Education.'" *The Social Studies*, 81, no. 5 (Sept./Oct. 1990): 188–218.

Keane, J. *Civil Society: Old Images, New Visions*. Stanford, CA: Stanford University Press, 1998.

Keller, C. W., and D. L. Schillings. *Teaching About the Constitution*. Bulletin No. 80. Washington, DC: National Council for the Social Studies, 1987.

Kennedy, P. *Rise and Fall of the Great Powers*. New York: Random House, 1986.

Lyons, S. R., and T. S. Arrington. *Who Votes and Why*. 3rd ed. New York: Taft Institute for Two Party Government, 1988.

Mathews, D. *Politics for People*. Urbana, IL: University of Illinois Press, 1994.

Parker, W. C., ed. *Educating the Democratic Mind*. Albany, NY: State University of New York Press, 1996.

Quigley, C. N., and Charles Bahmueller, eds. *Civitas: A Framework for Civic Education*. Calabasas, CA: Center for Civic Education, 1991.

Regan, M. et al. *Global Challenge: A Crisis Simulation*. Washington, DC: Congressional Youth Leadership Council, 1996.

Sehr, D. T. *Education for Public Democracy*. Albany: State University of New York Press, 1997.

Yates, M., and J. Youniss, eds. *Roots of Civic Identity: International Perspectives on Community Service and Activism in Youth*. New York: Cambridge University Press, 1999.

Wallerstein, I. *The Modern World System*. 3 vols. London: Methuen, 1974, 1980, 1983.

Waltzer, M. *On Toleration*. New Haven, CT: Yale University Press, 1997.

CHAPTER 12

Old Concerns,
New Directions

Modernity is the transient, the fleeting, the contingent: it is one half of art, the other being the eternal and the immutable.

—Baudelaire, *The Painter of Modern Life* (1863)

OVERVIEW OF CONTENTS

Main Ideas

Economics

Setting Goals
  Didactic Goals
  Reflective Goals
  Affective Goals

The Dominant Model: Micro to Macro

Alternative Approaches
  A Consumer Approach
  An Issues-Centered Approach
  An International Approach

Key Questions for Teaching Economics

New Emphases in Secondary Social Studies
  Multicultural and Multiethnic Studies
  Law-Related Education
  Geographic and Environmental Education
  Peace Education and International Studies
  Globalism

Alternative Social Studies Electives ——————————————————————————

Summary ———————————————————————————————————

Notes ——————————————————————————————————————

For Further Study: Old Concerns, New Directions ————————————————

MAIN IDEAS

At one time, teaching social studies was virtually synonymous with teaching history. Major courses and electives were drawn primarily from European or American topics, and when teachers strayed into theory or policy, it was either in government (as was discussed in the previous chapter) or economics (as is discussed in the first section of this chapter). Over the last two decades, however, secondary level social studies offerings have expanded to include a wide range of social science disciplines separate from or integrated into United States, world, global history, or civics.

A number of reasons account for the changing character of the social studies. Primary among them is the growing recognition that we live in a shrinking, interdependent world, where understanding rather than stereotyping foreign cultures is not simply useful but vital. At home, too, new immigration from Asian and Latin nations has created a mix of students with needs and interests different from those who preceded them. And finally, the social sciences over the last thirty years have produced a massive flow of research that has both borrowed from and influenced the study of history, thereby diminishing the distinctions among subject fields. The "new" social studies—including substantially more material on women, minorities, and cultures beyond North America and Europe, as well as more instruction aimed at educating consumers—now vies with the traditional course material like history for a place in the curriculum.

This chapter first provides an overview of the secondary school economics course, which is frequently found in the social studies curriculum, and then discusses some of the other courses that have joined the curriculum in recent years, including those with a focus on multiculturalism, law and justice, the environment, peace education and conflict resolution, foreign policy or international affairs.

ECONOMICS

This section helps you set goals and plan for a secondary school economics course. Economics invites reasoning and decision making; it is at the same time very practical, with immediate applications to daily life, and highly theoretical, offering concepts intended to explain behavior at a universal level. Recently developed voluntary national standards for teaching economics provide guidelines for a rationale, content, essential reasoning and decision-making skills, and benchmarks for achievements by students. For example, a rationale from the National Council for Economic Education (NCEE) for teaching economic choice making argues that "identifying and systematically comparing alternatives enables people to make more informed decisions and to avoid unforeseen consequences of choices they or others make."[1]

Examples of the twenty voluntary NCEE economic standard includes ideas such as:

1. Productive resources are limited. Therefore people cannot have all the goods and services they want: as a result, they must choose some things and give up others....

4. People respond predictably to positive and negative incentives....

11. Money makes it easier to trade, borrow, save, invest, and compare the value of goods and services....

15. Investment in factories, machinery, new technology, and in the health, education, and training of people can raise future standards of living....[2]

As you can see, the NCEE standards are broad and inclusive, allowing for multiple applications to a variety of classrooms, ranging from a full-length course in economics to specific units in American or global history. Through these national standards (as well as other standards and criteria) for teaching economics, social studies teachers may profitably explore all aspects of economics: from practical knowledge and consumer decision making to market analysis and micro or macroeconomic value choices.

SETTING GOALS

Didactic Goals

Clearly, students must possess data about economics and have at least an elementary understanding of its basic terms and concepts to put the subject to use. For example, the voluntary standards propose such content ideas as:

1. Productive resources are limited....

2. Effective decision making requires comparing the additional costs of alternatives with the additional benefits....

3. Different methods can be used to allocate goods and services....

4. People respond predictably to positive and negative incentives.

Your didactic instructional goals should include the acquisition of information and the adoption of basic economic concepts and terms. Formal objectives might begin with statements like the following:

Students will acquire information about the size, shape, flow, and problems of the local, national, and international economy.

Students will be able to define, both formally and in their own words, key economic terms such as scarcity, opportunity cost, price supply and demand, system, market, profit, competition, and comparative advantage.

Students will be able to describe clearly important economic problems and issues, giving examples and accurately contrasting policy viewpoints or solutions.

RESEARCH REPORT

William B. Walstad and John C. Soper studied 8,200 eleventh- and twelfth-grade students' understanding of economics by administering a nationally normed standardized examination, the Test of Economic Literacy (TEL). Students represented a national sample of those enrolled in social studies, consumer education, and economics courses during the 1986–1987 school year.

Economic literacy was measured by a series of multiple choice questions based on the twenty-two basic concepts outlined by the Joint Council for Economic Education in its master curriculum guides. Findings indicated that social studies students who did not benefit from economics in the curriculum answered an average of 37 percent of the questions correctly. When economics was incorporated into classwork, the average correct score rose to 48 percent, and those enrolled in actual economics courses averaged 52 percent correct. Based on this analysis, the worst levels of understanding were in the areas of international and macroeconomics concepts, and the better levels were in microeconomics. Students in consumer education courses appeared to do no better than the average social studies student who had no economics instruction and did not improve from pretest to posttest, whereas students enrolled in economics courses per se showed significant levels of growth between pretest and posttest. Finally, the study showed that teachers who had themselves studied economics as a separate subject produced much better test results than did those who had little or no formal instruction in the subject.

SOURCE: William B. Walstad and John C. Soper, "A Report Card on the Economic Literacy of US. High School Students," *American Economic Review,* 78, no. 2 (1988): 251–56.

Reflective Goals

Once students have learned the basic language of economics, they need to move to higher levels of operation like applying concepts to case studies and current situations, and connecting ideas with one another. Economics places a premium on deriving rules and applying these to real-world behavior. Using the list of economic terms in the didactic objectives, we can move easily from simple to complex relations, building each idea on the previous one: The problem of scarcity, for example, leads directly to choices; choices create a demand to which suppliers react by setting a price and deciding on production levels; and suppliers' and consumers' decisions in turn lead to consequences for investment and consumption in the economic system as a whole. Building chains of inference is crucial to economic understanding, particularly if conclusions are to be related to daily life.

Most economists use some form of a circular flow model to illustrate the basic patterns of economics (see Figure 12.1). The concepts in the model relate directly to the most mundane of our daily decisions, and each decision in the flow sends a signal through the economy that ultimately results in value added or lost for the individual and/or society as a whole. Reflective objectives based on the circular flow model for economics might include the following:

Students will apply basic economic concepts to personal decisions about buying, selling, and investment.

Students will use basic economic concepts to interpret the problems of society, analyzing the reasons for dislocations or declines, and the rationales underlying suggested solutions.

Students will create and explain their own versions of the circular flow model, demonstrating how household consumption and savings, income, and investment are related to and dependent on the flow of goods and services and on government taxation policies.

TO DO

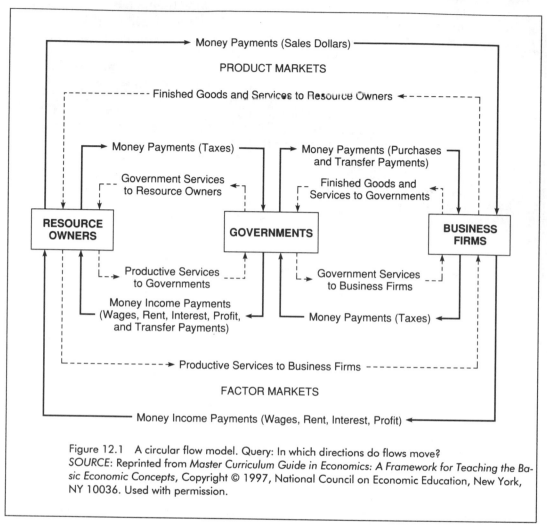

Figure 12.1   A circular flow model. Query: In which directions do flows move?
SOURCE: Reprinted from *Master Curriculum Guide in Economics: A Framework for Teaching the Basic Economic Concepts*, Copyright © 1997, National Council on Economic Education, New York, NY 10036. Used with permission.

Affective Goals

The value component of economics is often termed a *policy decision*, but the underlying reasoning process begins with reflection and proceeds to a choice based on some philosophical rationale. Economics is a policy science, continually struggling to make rational selections between the sometimes conflicting goals of efficiency, equity (justice), productivity (growth), freedom, and stability.[3] Scarcity requires hard choices in a world of potentially unlimited wants and needs; some values stress equity and social welfare, and others stress productivity and efficiency. Economic policy rests on answers to key questions, often formulated in terms of what ought to be as opposed to what actually is at any given time. In a severe recession, for example, should government intervene to provide jobs by keeping inefficient plants in operation, an action that in turn may raise the national debt?

For a secondary economics course, affective objectives might include the following:

Students will apply economic concepts and relations to decide which economic goals they would favor when faced with problems such as inflation, unemployment, poverty, or discrimination.

Students will debate the merits of different economic systems (mixed, directed, and market) in achieving such goals as freedom, efficiency, equity, price stability, and growth.

Students will recognize, discuss, and try to balance economic dilemmas that force choices between ultimate values such as productivity and equity (e.g., as in the Exxon Valdez oil spill, or in the case of affirmative action or quotas).

TO DO

In developing a unit on economics, would you choose to emphasize didactic, reflective, or affective objectives? Do you think your goals would change depending on the topic under discussion? Prepare a set of goals for teaching about:
  a. health care costs and benefits
  b. conservation and production of natural resources
  c. managing daily food shopping
  d. international trade and finance

THE DOMINANT MODEL: MICRO TO MACRO

Most secondary school economics courses follow a well-organized program that moves from micro- to macroeconomic concepts. The course begins with the basic problems of scarcity and choice; moves through price, supply, and demand factors, and aggregate functions of the whole economic structure; and concludes with a look at the world economy and how it works. A one-semester course outline developed by the National Council on Economic Education (EconomicsAmerica) for high school is provided next:

  I. AN INTRODUCTION TO ECONOMICS AND THE BASIC ECONOMIC PROBLEM (2 weeks)
  Major Economic Concepts
    1. Scarcity
    2. Opportunity cost and trade-offs
    3. Productivity
    4. Economic systems
    5. Economic institutions and incentives
    6. Interdependence
  Content
    1. The basic economic problem
       a. Scarce resources, relatively unlimited wants, and the need to make choices.
       b. Human resources, natural resource, and capital goods.
    2. Making choices
       a. All personal, business, and social choices involve opportunity costs and trade-offs;
       b. Making choices involves rational analysis and an orderly approach, such as the following:

(1) State the problem or issue
(2) Determine the personal or board social goals to be attained
(3) Consider the principal alternative means of achieving the goals
(4) Select the economic concepts needed to understand the problem and use them to appraise the merits of each alternative
(5) Decide which alternative best leads to the attainment of the most goals

3. Economic systems and institutions
   a. All societies must answer the questions, "What to produce?" "How to produce?" and "For whom to produce?"
   b. Economic decisions can be made through tradition, command, and market systems
   c. The United States uses a mixed market system
      (1) Description
      (2) Circular flow of income

II. MARKETS, SUPPLY, AND DEMAND (4 weeks)

Major Economic Concepts
1. Markets and prices
2. Supply and demand
3. Exchange

Content
1. Demand
   a. Relation between price and quantity demanded
   b. Determinants of demand
   c. Change in quantity demanded versus change in demand
   d. Elasticity of demand
2. Supply
   a. Relation between price and quantity supplied
   b. Determinants of supply
   c. Change in quantity supplied versus change in supply
   d. Elasticity of supply
3. Equilibrium
   a. Why price and quantity move toward equilibrium
   b. Shifts in supply and demand
   c. Surpluses and shortages
   d. Real-world examples of supply and demand
4. The functions of markets and prices
   a. Information function
   b. Incentive function
   c. Rationing function
5. Exchange

III. BUSINESS, LABOR, AND MARKET STRUCTURE (3 weeks)

Major Economic Concepts
1. Economic institutions and incentives
2. Competition and market structure
3. Income distribution

Content
1. Role of business
   a. Purpose of business
   b. Forms of business ownership
   c. Role of profit system
2. Market structure
   a. Competition and lack of competition
   b. Types of market structure

(1) Perfect competition
(2) Monopolistic competition
(3) Oligopoly
(4) Monopoly
3. Labor and wages
a. The labor force
b. Wage determination
c. Development of the labor movement
d. The government and labor
e. The place and responsibility of unions in the American economy to-day

IV. THE ROLE OF GOVERNMENT (2 weeks)
Economic Concepts
1. Market failures
2. The role of government
Content
1. The scope and purpose of government
a. Correcting market failures
b. Establishing rules
c. Characteristics of public goods
2. Taxation and criteria of a good tax
3. Federal, state, and local government spending
4. Government regulations

V. MACROECONOMICS (5 weeks)
Major Economic Concepts
1. Gross National Product
2. Unemployment
3. Inflation and deflation
4. Aggregate supply
5. Aggregate demand
6. Monetary policy
7. Fiscal policy
8. Money
Content
1. Measuring economic performance
a. Gross National Product (GNP)
b. National Income (NI)
c. Consumer Price Index (CPI)
d. Unemployment rate
e. Constructing and interpreting measurement concepts such as graphs, charts, tables, index numbers, amounts versus rates, ratios, real versus nominal
2. Business cycles, inflation, and unemployment
a. The role of aggregate demand and supply
b. Description of a business cycle
c. Causes of inflation
d. Causes of unemployment and deflation
3. Money and banking
a. Functions of money
b. Functions of the banking system
c. Functions of the Federal Reserve System

VI. THE WORLD ECONOMY (2 weeks)
Major Economic Concepts

1. Absolute and comparative advantage and barriers to trade
2. Exchange rates and the balance of payments
3. International aspects of growth and stability

Content

1. Why nations trade
   a. Absolute and comparative advantage
   b. Benefits of trade
   c. Barriers to trade
2. Analyzing international trade
   a. The balance of trade and the balance of payments
   b. The role of exchange rates
3. The world economy
   a. Economic growth
   b. Economic development and developing nations
   c. Foreign trade and investment
4. Means of managing the economy
   a. Monetary policy
      (1) Goals of monetary policy
      (2) Tools of monetary policy
   b. Fiscal policy
      (1) Automatic stabilizers
      (2) Discretionary stabilizers
      (3) Government deficits and the national debt
5. Alternative approaches to managing the economy
   a. Demand management
   b. Supply management
   c. Monetarism
   d. Rational expectations[4]

A course designed around this kind of outline provides students with a comprehensive introduction to the fundamental ideas of economics.[5] These ideas, the basic tools used to analyze and interpret theory and action, form part of every discussion of economics, whatever the topic—consumer oriented, home economics, career skills, business and finance, or international trade.

Not everyone, however, agrees that the micro-to-macro course outline meets the pressing needs of today's classroom. This approach has been criticized more for what it leaves out than for what it puts in: Some critics contend that students need more practical information that will allow them to make wiser decisions as consumers and investors; other critics argue that the traditional model focuses too much on capitalism and on the American economy, despite increasing evidence that global issues and problems will dominate the future. Most critics would also agree that the standard approach avoids controversial issues, whether practical or theoretical, and provides students with too little insight into current economic debates about policies and values.

In recent years, several alternative approaches have been developed for teaching secondary economics, including consumer, issue-oriented, and international approaches.

ALTERNATIVE APPROACHES

A Consumer Approach

Advocates of consumer-oriented approaches to economics argue that students need to be able to read and understand newspaper and magazine articles on economic issues, to understand basic documents like warranties, leases, and contracts, and to improve the decisions they make about purchases and financial commitments. In short, critics view the standard course as too abstract and theoretical.[6]

WHAT DO YOU THINK?

Figure 12.2   Why did boys do mine work in 1911? What level of education did they probably have? Is child labor permitted now? Why or why not? Develop a lesson plan around this picture that will fit into a U.S. history or civics course in your community.
SOURCE: Lewis Hine, "Breaker Boys Working in Ewen Breaker." Children's Bureau (102-LH-1941).

The consumer approach to teaching economics usually begins with questions of scarcity and price, and decision making plays a significant role. Choice is almost always at the heart of consumer courses, with cases and examples arranged to illustrate economic principles and encourage debate.[7] Courses are often taught practically, providing students with guides for lodging complaints or pursuing grievances against businesses through both government agencies and private means. Most cover some aspects of consumer law; many offer detailed units on how to file a claim in civil court, write a letter of complaint, or build a case against a business.

Consumer courses often include case studies on issues like buying a car, avoiding dangerous food products, or comparison shopping; they appeal to secondary students, nearly all of whom are avid consumers. Properly accomplished, a consumer-oriented economics course can be very exciting, particularly when teachers draw on student interests like baseball cards, clothing, electronic equipment, and so on to demonstrate basic principles of supply and demand, scarcity, and price. Ideally, a consumer course should catch students' interest with "trendy" issues while simultaneously teaching them the major economic concepts through these examples.

Mine in S. Pittston, Pennsylvania. January 10, 1911. A consumer-oriented economics course might include any or all of the following topics:

Scarcity and the consumer. Our social and economic system, income and outflow, consumer rights and responsibilities, decision making.

Using data to make choices. Obtaining and evaluating information, advertising, generic and brand names, research reports and buying guides, government evaluations.

Consumer rights and responsibilities. Consumer protection laws and customs, regulation (and self-regulation) of industry, consumer groups and advocacy.

Case studies. Affording a child, finding and holding a job, managing a budget, the price of energy, credit and borrowing, using a bank, smart shopping.

Government's role in the economy. Taxation and redistribution of wealth, regulations and controls, relation to labor and industry, environmental protection, impact of globalization on the U.S. economy.

Your role in the economy. Short- and long-range goals, making choices and planning (purchases, careers, investments, marriage and family), developing a business, your values and philosophy (free enterprise ideals and social welfare ideals).

This outline is intended to suggest rather than to be comprehensive. Consumer issues provide a virtually inexhaustible source of material, and you may choose to follow current events as a guide, to use classic consumer law cases, to open broad issues that involve costs and environmental concerns, or to focus primarily on personal buying patterns. Many supporters of a more traditional approach to economics contend that consumer programs represent watered-down versions of basic material rather than new or different theoretical designs.[8] Certainly consumer information can be built into the dominant curriculum model to make economic issues more approachable for less able students or those more concerned with making practical choices. Indeed, an economics program could promote all of the aforementioned activities in a format intended both to satisfy consumer needs and to inform students about economics, building in the key concepts that will carry over into other economic discussions as students become increasingly active participants in the political and economic system.

TO DO

> Select a consumer problem—auto insurance rates or the high cost of movie or concert tickets—and develop a lesson that will encourage students to invent strategies. Is refusing to pay an option? How can consumers deal with the effects of their own insatiable demands on prices? What other options are available?

An Issues-Centered Approach

In issues-centered economics courses, economic ideas and theories are presented in a debate-style format that fosters argument about both enduring and short-term controversies. The approach tends to stress affective goals, but ideally neglects neither the reasons behind a controversy nor the data that support alternative points of view. Cooperative learning is a particularly effective strategy in this format, because there are numerous possibilities for panel reports, debates, role-playing, and simulation exercises.

SAMPLE LESSON PLAN

> The Japanese just bought another large U.S. corporation and everyone is talking about how terrible this action is for Americans. But is it terrible? Why have the Japanese been able to invest in the United States? Why has this country allowed them to do so? Can anyone from any nation invest in American industry or property? What are the rules for doing so? Get a debate going on the pros and cons of foreign investment by us, and by foreign investment in us. Define the differences, if any, between these investment patterns? Who benefits and who loses? Then send the students out to research some of the hypotheses they generated in class—and, by the way, you do a little homework too!

At the heart of any issues-centered approach is a commitment to public decision making for the best interests of society as a whole.[9] The process of reaching agreement, or of discovering that agreement may not be possible, produces a sense of economic philosophy that individual decision makers often overlook. Well-informed discussion implies considerable understanding of basic economic concepts, and at least an adequate amount of research and preparation. Students recognize the competition between values like equity and productivity, and among theories of economics such as monetarism, socialism, and Keynesian theory, which generally rank different values as priorities.

WHAT DO YOU THINK?

> Using the information in Table 12.1, answer the following questions:
>> How does each society allocate income?
>> Are the three societies alike or different? In what ways?
>> Which society represents a "fair and just" distribution of income and resources?
>> How can you justify your view?

TABLE 12.1   DISTRIBUTION OF INCOME IN THREE SOCIETIES
(Percentage of Income Received by Each Fifth in 1970)

	Population	Society A	Society B	Society C
Top	20%	58%	20%	38%
Second	20%	30%	20%	26%
Third	20%	8%	20%	18%
Fourth	20%	3%	20%	12%
BOTTOM	20%	1%	20%	6%

Topics that might be included in an issues-centered economics course include the following:

Central economic values. Economic freedom, efficiency, equity, security, full employment, price stability, growth.

Taking a stand. Defining the issue, researching the facts, developing arguments, weighing alternatives, setting priorities, making a choice.

Controversial issues in economics. Public versus private (which services or industries should be run by the government, and which by private interests?), regulation versus laissez faire, monopoly versus free market competition, productivity versus environmental protection, consumers versus producers, labor versus management, public taxation versus individual income, international free trade versus tariffs and barriers.

Evaluating the issues and theories. Private wealth versus the public good, controlling the economy through monetary policy or Keynesian theory, developing an overall economic philosophy.

Again, this list is offered as a model, adaptable to student and teacher needs and open to revision based on historical, political, and economic changes.

An International Approach

Many critics of the traditional micro-to-macro model of economics argue that such courses inevitably spend too much time on the micro issues. These critics see the world moving rapidly in the direction of a single economic system in which a decision in one nation or region can affect less powerful nations all over the globe, international debt management can lead to prosperity or ruin for lenders and borrowers alike, and trade barriers and political decisions can cause havoc in growth and development. A high school economics course, they argue, should begin and end with worldwide issues.

In such a course, the world is seen as a single economic entity in which the various national economies compete, cooperate, or ignore one another to produce a global market structure. Within the world system as a whole, economic development forms a continuum, with varying levels of performance; in fact, the economies of individual nations, command or market, seem less important for the economic future than the overall problems of allocating resources, services, labor, and technology in a world market.

Clearly, this approach to economics brings out understandings that may be passed over in a micro–macro or consumer course. Even an issues-oriented course may lack an integrated perspective through which students comprehend the world as a single system. The international approach raises serious new questions about the fairest, most appropriate, and most productive uses of the earth's resources.

A well-thought out course in global economics may incorporate consumer problems, controversial issues, and basic concepts through current events and case studies. Such a course might include any or all of the following topics:

Developing a cross-cultural perspective on economic systems. Traditional, market, command.

Why people and nations trade. Trade among individuals, trade between countries, specialization incentives and disincentives.

The scope of international trade and aid. Interpreting trade data and aid data, foreign aid and investment, U.S. exports and imports, world trade patterns and assistance networks.

Trade barriers and conflicts. Tariffs, quotas and laws, balance of payments, the positive and negative ripple effect, the United Nations and other treaty and private organizations.

Global markets. Products, systems of production, foreign currencies and foreign exchange, exchange rate fluctuations, international cartels and corporations, advertising and cultural preferences.

World trade issues. Producers and consumers, fair prices and fair profits, environmental exploitation and renewal, wages and profits (labor versus management), "brain drains" and the immigration and emigration of skilled professionals.

Global development and growth. Problems of developing countries, foreign aid (guns or butter?), international debt crisis, rich nations and poor.

Toward a world economic system. Economic integration, the use of natural resources, economic diffusion of goods, services, and ideas.

KEY QUESTIONS FOR TEACHING ECONOMICS

Any discussion of economics must return in some form to a handful of central problems: scarcity, choice, productivity, and values. Decisions about what to produce, how much to save and invest, and how to organize an economic system—whether household or global—may almost always be perceived ultimately as responses to scarcity: There is never enough to go around to satisfy all needs and aspirations. Somewhere, sometime, somehow hard choices must be made about what to give up. Your responsibility as a teacher of economics is to provide your students with a basic understanding of economic issues and concepts so that they can make and interpret these decisions rationally. In spite of the occasional effort by economists to hide value questions beneath a sea of technical rhetoric, the questions and their implied conflicts remain.

A number of resources are available for teaching economics to secondary students; these are listed in Appendix A.

NEW EMPHASES IN SECONDARY SOCIAL STUDIES

Historians and social scientists have grown more sensitive to issues of bias, selection, and cultural conditioning, and they have reexamined the roles of minorities in history from a variety of viewpoints in the last thirty years. Some heroes and heroines have risen in esteem and some have fallen; new movements and trends have been identified as keys to understanding human history, whereas older theories have been under siege and, in some cases, overturned. The deteriorating environment of the planet and the depletion or misuse of natural resources is another issue that has entered the social studies curriculum, and a third area, international and peace studies, has emerged as modern technology shrinks the globe and political events reshape international alliances and political forces.

Many new teaching materials have been designed to correct the neglect of gender, race, religion, ethnicity, and environmental questions in social studies courses that traditionally omitted these issues. Some of these programs and lessons have caught on; others have waxed and waned as educational values changed; still others have already disappeared. The most stable, however, have been integrated into the standard curriculum. These include multicultural and multiethnic studies, law-related education, environmental and geographical studies, and international and peace studies.

Multicultural and Multiethnic Studies

Multicultural education is a fusion of separate topics designed to correct the inequitable attention paid in the traditional curriculum to women and to cultural and racial groups that have been overlooked entirely or whose backgrounds and contributions have been distorted by textbooks and curriculum materials written from the dominant culture's point of view.

An example of the complications that can arise in multicultural discussions occurred when a student teacher introduced the "Palestinian Homeland question" to a junior high school class. She began the session with a brief outline of the Arab–Israeli conflict and recent efforts to establish peace between the contending parties, following this with what were intended to be perfunctory questions covering all notable aspects of the problem. After the sixth or seventh question, one student timidly raised her hand to speak. The teacher recognized the student, who politely pointed out that, from the Palestinian point of view, what the teacher had told the class simply was not true. This girl's friend, also apparently of Palestinian origin, then boldly explained to the class that Arabs are often misrepresented in the United States and what we are told about them is frequently biased. By now, the student teacher was becoming uneasy, but the class was not quite over. As she asked the Arab-Palestinian students to read their texts, two different students raised their hands. They had recently emigrated from Israel and wished to correct some errors made by the Arab informants as well as the teacher. At this point, a full-scale heated discussion ensued—not exactly what the teacher had planned, but a situation much truer to life and to the issues of multiculturalism. By the end of the period, a wonderful debate was under way, and the teacher was learning an important lesson about frame of reference and contrasting viewpoints.

Multicultural topics may be developed into full-length courses or units on a single subject or group (reducing prejudice, e.g., or women in history), or incorporated into a standard U.S. history program, often in units on immigration or industrialization. Curricula for these units present many problems for social studies educators because the issues are sensitive and the approaches to teaching about gender, race, and ethnicity vary greatly.

Debate has developed around the notion of correcting past inequities through revising the "Western" curriculum, which has been characterized often as history from the White, male, wealthy, European-born, conqueror's viewpoint. Those forces who have resisted curriculum revision complain that the revisionists have declared theirs to be "the morally or politically correct" stand, implying that no other is acceptable in academic circles. The accusation of "political correctness" is a code message for clashing interests and philosophies, some liberal and others conservative, some assimilationist and others multicultural or even separatist.

So far, no single view is being enforced by any leaders in authority, whether in schools or universities, and there is solid evidence to show that many serious problems exist in the curriculum, which has been documented as ignoring race,

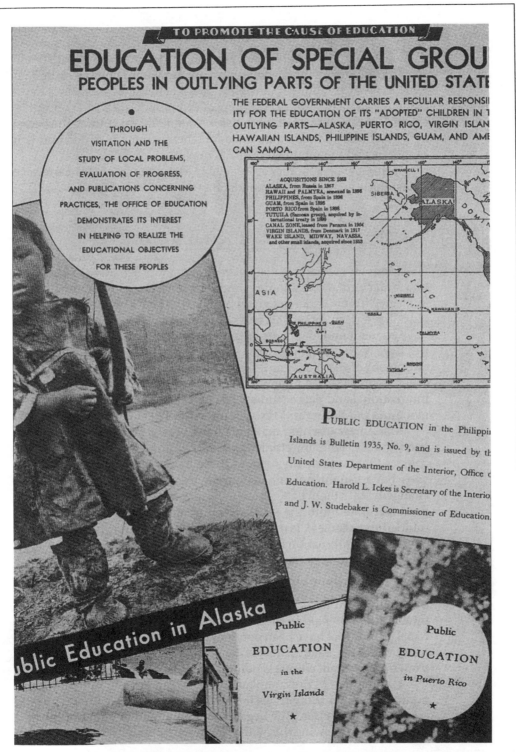

Figure 12.3a
SOURCE: *School Life* (Washington, DC: US. Department of the Interior, Office of Education, February, 1938).

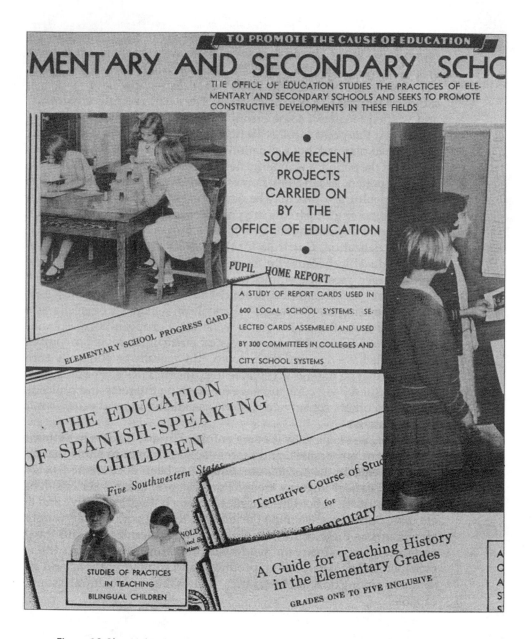

Figure 12.3b Multicultural concerns of an earlier period in U.S. history. Query: How are minorities portrayed in these 1930s government bulletins? Is the view assimilationist or multicultural or pluralistic?
SOURCE: *School Life* (Washington, DC: U.S. Department of the Interior, Office of Education, February, 1938).

ethnicity, class, and gender in many areas of study.[10] Furthermore, there is serious debate in social and literary circles about these issues, among both conservative and liberal thinkers, simply because we must decide how to deal with a wide variety of cultural viewpoints as these come into contact with modernization and the pressures of assimilation to mainstream, worldwide industrial systems.[11] As the world's peoples increasingly share ideas, products, and communications and as migrations continue among dozens of countries, addressing multicultural issues will be inescapable.

Correcting past inequities involves making new decisions about which groups are now to be excluded and that are deserving of more attention. Such decisions are inevitably accompanied by objections, complaints, and renewed cries of bias. Substantial evidence shows that women have been poorly represented in traditional history courses, and African Americans and Native Americans have suffered from negative stereotypes that minimize their roles in and contributions to this society.[12] But the need for fair treatment must be balanced against the problem of whom and what to incorporate into an already overstuffed curriculum.

Four major approaches have been developed to address multicultural instruction: assimilation, cultural pluralism, multiethnicism, and critical pedagogy.

Assimilationists maintain that those who become part of American culture need to learn the dominant Western values and retain their own traditions only to the extent that these traditions do not conflict with their new citizenship. Assimilationists stress the need to teach citizenship and patriotism and to mold a diverse student population into a responsible common citizenry, usually by teaching about the American heritage, its heroes, laws, customs, traditions, and so on.

Cultural pluralists argue in favor of retaining and reinforcing different cultures in the United States. Pluralists advise teachers to adapt their methods and curriculum to their students, rather than the other way around, by including the cultural histories of each group and by matching student learning styles with appropriate strategies and content.[13]

Multiethnicists represent something of a compromise between assimilation and cultural pluralism, suggesting that teachers strive to maintain a balance between the dominant cultural values and individual group traditions.[14] Multiethnic educators often ask teachers to compare group experiences so as to build student tolerance of and respect for different cultures.

Critical pedagogists seek to empower all groups in school so that they may have direct input into the curriculum, a voice and a vote in educational decisions. The critical view is rooted in a liberation ideology that seeks to redress social and educational inequities through active political change.[15]

The relation of multicultural studies to the social studies curriculum is still in a state of flux. Most materials available to teachers still implicitly or explicitly present culture from the majority perspective, providing students with only faint glimpses of minority traditions and little insight into the issues that divide one group from another. Several states, led by New York and California, adopted guidelines or frameworks for approaching multicultural issues during the 1980s. Recommendations for teachers include the following:

> Be particularly attentive to details or clues that indicate bias, distortion, or the omission of important issues, particularly in materials that deal with gender, or with disadvantaged, minority, or "conquered" peoples.

> Use firsthand accounts by members of multicultural groups themselves whenever possible, including autobiographies, novels, position papers, organizational publications, speeches, art, and music to counterbalance contrasting sources.

Design units on gender and minority issues to include both "insider" and "outsider" accounts, primary and secondary sources, so that students have a fair sample of views from which to draw conclusions.

Use outside resources—community members, organizational leaders—to provide students with nonstereotypical representatives of gender and minority groups.

Be willing to talk about the differences and disharmonies that students will inevitably see between social ideals and daily practice, between what people say officially and what they do in private. Use the culturally diverse members of your own class as resources; ask them to draw on personal experiences.

TO DO

Choose one or two popular novels about cross-cultural encounters, assimilation, or cultural identity in the United States and construct a lesson around them. You might consider Piri Thomas's *Down These Mean Streets*, Mario Puzo's *The Fortunate Pilgrim*, Chaim Potok's *The Chosen*, Amy Tan's *The Joy Luck Club*, Maya Angelou's *I Know Why the Caged Bird Sings*, or Oscar Hijuelos's *Mambo Kings Play Songs of Love*. Many others are also available or being written right now for you to try out with your students.

Resources and further readings on multicultural issues can be found in Appendix A.

Law-Related Education

Law-related topics in social studies grew out of the civil rights movement of the 1960s in response to demands for a better understanding of law, the U.S. Constitution, and people's rights. A wide range of projects developed, some specialized and some broadly conceived—all competing for influence on social studies education.[16] The largest and most influential area of study that emerged was constitutional law, with a focus on the Bill of Rights, and lawyers and educators created a variety of casebooks that traced the rule of law from early American and British history to current appellate and Supreme Court decisions.

Many schools now offer courses under the rubrics of constitutional law, law and order, justice studies, and consumer law. These routinely include field trips to courts; classroom visits by judges, lawyers, and police officers; mock trial competitions; and an emphasis on "street law"—those statutes that materially affect the personal rights and interests of young people. Some materials have also been developed for courses on cross-cultural and international topics for use as part of a world studies or global history program. The expectation in all these law-related programs is that, by building familiarity with law and legal reasoning, students will develop a sense of respect for the law that will ultimately help them make better personal decisions and be more active in defending their own rights and those of others. For some, knowledge of and respect for the law is seen as building better character and citizenship at the same time as it expands knowledge.[17]

Thought-provoking units on constitutional law, street law, and citizens' rights are widely available, as are a variety of imaginative law-related simulations and activities. For example, the American Bar Association through its Special Committee on Youth Education for Citizenship has sponsored a wide variety of topics and programs ranging from traditional domestic issues and cases to international and environmental law, providing teaching strategies, case studies, questions, and cutting edge legal problems (e.g., "law in outer space").[18] In some

Figure 12.4   Federal rule in the former Confederate states changed political institutions dramatically. This composite picture shows the radical members of South Carolina's legislature in 1868. During Reconstruction, Blacks were elected to Southern legislatures in numbers not even approached again for more than a century. Why? Create a lesson plan using the official photograph, making sure students observe it carefully for clues about the culture and society of the time. *SOURCE:* South Carolina Library, Columbia, SC.

places, students are able to prepare and argue a constitutional case in a courtroom "mock trial" situation.[19] Role-plays and mock trials are an integral part of law education. The following are several recommended practices for infusing legal and political issues into social studies classrooms:

Present—or use outside experts to present—the legal system as it actually works, and compare this to the ideal laid down by the founders of the republic. Students need to draw their own conclusions, with your guidance, about the degree to which present practices approach the original philosophy, and why differences exist.

Encourage free expression of positions on legal issues, but ask for supporting arguments for both popular and unpopular positions.

Contrast legal reasoning with scientific and commonsense reasoning. Help students find reasons for the differences.

Offer real court cases for students to analyze, with accurate facts and an analysis of relevant laws. Let students come to a decision, and see whether it differs from the actual decision and why.

Present legal materials and cases that have political, social, and economic ramifications for real life—tenant–landlord disputes, property disputes, civil rights cases. Let students draw conclusions about decisions that are best for themselves and/or best for society as a whole.

Encourage discussions of student opinion about the law and law enforcement agencies, including the police. Ask students about the sources of their attitudes (peers, parents, media, experience) and the consequences of these attitudes on their own behavior (schooling, protests, careers, etc.). Organizations, resources, and further reading materials on law-related education can be found in Appendix A.

Geographic and Environmental Education

In the mid-1980s, the National Association of American Geographers (with the aid of a grant from the National Geographic Society) developed a plan to introduce separate geography courses at the secondary level and to infuse key geographic concepts into standard U.S. and global history courses.[20] Geographic "alliances" were set up in most of the states to promote and foster geographic education in the schools and most of these are still in place providing workshops, materials, newsletters, and advice to teachers across the country. From this beginning, a consortium of groups created national geography standards, or "Geography for Life" to serve as a guideline for further application to the schools.[21]

As part of the plan to reestablish the place of geography in the school curriculum, a philosophy of instruction was developed to promote conceptual growth in geographic thinking, rather than simply channel new geographic and environmental information to students. In the plan, five key concepts were identified to focus classroom efforts in teaching geography. These five concepts can be used to analyze environmental, political, and economic issues as potential themes in teaching law, civics, history, and of course, geography itself.

The five geographic themes are:

Location. Absolute location is where a place exists in terms of longitude and latitude; *relative* location is where it exists in relation to other places. Mt. St. Helen's, for example, is a specific place on the map, but it is also part of a mountain range that contains other volcanoes.

Place. Geographers describe places in terms of their physical and human characteristics. The former includes climate and landscape; the latter includes such things as population density and ethnic makeup.

Human–Environment Interactions. People interact with their environments in different ways: Large-scale agricultural activity in the Texas panhandle, for example, did not occur until the invention of circular irrigation systems. Geographers examine how human–environment interactions happen and what consequences they cause.

Movement. People, goods, and ideas are all mobile. Geography helps us understand the nature and effects of movement.

Regions. Regions are areas on the earth's surface that are defined by certain unifying characteristics, sometimes physical and sometimes human. The Rocky Mountains form a physical region; the "corn belt" forms a human region, unified by the choices people have made to grow a particular crop.

These five themes can be used to develop goals, strategies, and lessons for almost any social studies or interdisciplinary history/humanities course because they are flexible and universal. Furthermore, the five themes cast a new light on virtually all ecological or environmental debates, past and present, and help students understand the processes of historical change and human adaptation.[22]

Environmental and ecological issues tend to enter the social studies curriculum when you deal with current events, geography, or, occasionally, politics and economics. Evidence suggests, however, that even in the face of overwhelming ecological crisis, environmental issues are often pushed aside in the effort to cover the standard curriculum. Despite polls indicating that student knowledge of even the most basic geography is sadly lacking, most social studies programs fail to incorporate global geography and environmental issues.[23]

Your goal in environmental or geographic instruction should be to help students see that the environment is complex and that understanding it demands a grasp of a variety of disciplines, including geography, biology, technology, economics, and politics.[24] Environmental issues nearly always draw people in two or more directions at once: Shall we develop our national parks as playgrounds or limit visitation to keep them ecologically pure? Shall we develop much-needed housing, even if that means losing a marshland? Geographic and environmental studies provide an excellent forum for discussing these kinds of trade-offs, which may be very intense in some regions of the world, particularly where climates are harsh, poverty is widespread, and territorial disputes are common.

SAMPLE LESSON PLAN

Radio, television, and newspapers report that war has broken out unexpectedly in X and Y, or Z, and here you are in the middle of a unit on the explorers during the sixteenth century. What should you do? Why not tie in the explorers with a geography lesson featuring the two nations at war? Ask the students to act as explorers themselves and research the topography, vegetation, climate, and population of the conflict area. What will they discover? Why has conflict developed? Is hostility something new to this area?

A number of organizations have developed formal curriculum materials on geography and environmental issues (see Appendix A), and ample information can also be had through news articles, government publications, and advocacy groups. Considerable effort has been made to adapt geographic topics and materials to new technologies, such as computer-assisted instruction using discs, CD-ROM, and laser disc formats.[25] As noted in previous chapters, interesting simulations such as *SimCity*, *SimCity 2000* and *Where in the World Is Carmen San Diego* are available, and comprehensive and colorful electronic atlases such as *3D Atlas* and *Exploring Ancient Cities* are offered for both home and schoolroom usage. Such items may be helpful and well-balanced, but others may be biased or incomplete, and part of your role must be to help students evaluate different positions and note significant omissions, if any. As with instruction in any controversial area, students need to know how to research and assess data and to have ample opportunities for debate. You can strengthen students' recognition of geographic and ecological questions through any of the following activities:

Review a print or electronic atlas checking for accuracy and currency of maps drawn to represent disputed or changing nations and areas (e.g., the former Yugoslavia, or the contested area of Kashmir).

Apply one or more of the five geographic themes to problems in the news such as immigration, forest conservation, pollution, productivity, or population concentration.

Debate issues of "culture shaping environment" versus "environment shaping culture," asking students to accept or reject the proposed dichotomy.

Invite guest speakers from different sides of an environmental issue to discuss their ideas in a debate or panel format.

Have students write to environmental organizations (see Appendix A) for information, which they can then present to the class.

Draw attention to the influence of environment (climate, topography, vegetation) on human settlement patterns, immigration, and territorial conflict.

Link past and current problems, like the effect on water supplies of the creeping desertification of the Sahel region of Africa.

Build a case for a global view of the links between history and geography, population, development patterns, and the current condition of the environment.

Ask students to survey their fellow students about geography, or about the environment and the future of the earth, and to assess their knowledge. Compare their results with those obtained from national surveys on the same issues.

Compare and contrast the positions of different nations on environmental questions—such as U.S. and Canadian interpretations of the acid rain problem, Japanese and American views on whaling, and Brazilian and European views on destruction of the rain forests. Have students sit as a "world court" to decide which side has the best case and which has the worst, and for what reasons.

TO DO

Draw your own "mental map" of the world's biggest trouble spots in two minutes or less, and ask at least two or three classmates or colleagues to do the same. Compare maps, checking off which places are mentioned most frequently and which are mentioned least frequently. Do those places mentioned most often correspond to the latest TV and newspaper accounts of troubled places?

See Appendix A for suggestions for further reading and lists of organizations that can provide instructional resources in the areas of geography and environmental studies.

Peace Education and International Studies

The past several decades have brought numerous initiatives to incorporate more, and more current, materials on foreign affairs and the problems of world peace into the social studies curriculum. Particularly when world political conditions are changing rapidly, students need to understand the geopolitical forces that cause conflict or provide a context for peace. Advocates of a more global and current social studies program tend to argue for one of two approaches: peace advocacy or an analytical social science focus. The former tends to stress issues, and the latter tends to stress cognitive understanding.

Peace advocates hope to use the social studies curriculum to deepen students' understanding of human and political dynamics, as a first step toward building positive attitudes toward worldwide negotiation and diplomacy as a way to resolve conflicts, rather than by violence. Such programs stress not only historical and current issues but also diplomatic role-play, negotiating skills, and openness to other viewpoints.

Social science approaches often stress a morally neutral, analytic view of world issues, asking students to examine and evaluate rather than debate policy. Such programs often include case studies in war and peace to test theories about why people engage in conflict in some situations and work in harmony in others. Many of these programs grow out of or emphasize a foreign policy orientation, or concentrate on international affairs, whether political, economic, or geographic. An example might be the "alternative futures" approach adopted by the Center for Foreign Policy Development at Brown University, in which students play out roles discussing current international problems from a variety of options like "standing up for principle," "keeping our distance," or "protecting our interests".[26]

Within the peace, economic development, foreign affairs, and international education spectrum, a wide range of programs, projects, and curriculum materials is available. Many of these, however, represent positions developed by advocacy groups, so again, your role will include helping your students in data gathering, assessment, and evaluation. Peace and international affairs education, in particular—because it is heavily involved in policy—formulation, often carries a heavy freight of values and philosophical assumptions. Many educators begin from a "problems or issues" base that leads to debate about alternative policies; others begin with a historical and political analysis of human behavior that often fosters theorizing about power relationships.

Most programs in this area are designed to build strong student values in three areas: understanding of and empathy for others, insight into the moral and ethical basis for foreign policy, and commitment to personal action once students determine where their values lie. For example, foreign policy studies promote an understanding of the relations between nations largely through academic study and more recently through simulations and panel discussions. International studies takes a different approach by setting up exchanges between students from different countries, offering on-site visits, long-term reciprocity, and pen-pal programs. For instance, the National Association of Secondary School Principals has created an exchange program for students to pursue, whereas the Center for the International Exchange of Scholars (Fulbright Association) offers teachers summer seminars and workshops in other "host" nations. Teachers have successfully used a number of strategies in supporting the aims of international studies and international relations:

Model United Nations programs, in which students represent individual countries. Such experiences can enhance social and speaking skills as well as research abilities.

Computer simulations, like *The Other Side* from Tom Snyder Productions, in which students conduct diplomatic negotiations with an enemy or competitor.

Presentations by speakers from private aid or peace advocacy organizations such at Greenpeace, New York Public Interest Group, and The Sierra Club.

Discussions of cartoons and caricatures from many different sources that deal with social and political issues using newspapers, journals, and perhaps the recent *Cartoon News: The Current Events Educational Monthly* to promote reflection and argument about domestic and foreign problems.

Adopt-a-country projects, in which students prepare a file and report to the class over a period of time, providing statistics, "human" stories (perhaps from pen-pals), and information on events and history. Invite a consular official from several of these countries to visit the classroom.

Further resources for instruction in international and peace education are listed in Appendix B.

Globalism

Over the past three decades or so, there has been a growing interest in what is sometimes called global education or world studies, and less frequently international education.

In some cases, definitions overlap or supersede international and peace education, but all share a common and very strong concern for "globalizing" American education, placing America and its history in a world context emphasizing how our society is closely linked to the rest of the world politically, economically, and culturally. Some historians argue that the West, including the United States, has always been tied to the rest of the world, but that many have chosen to ignore this fact at certain periods of history for a variety of political reasons. Braudel, for example, points out that "the modes of production are all attached to each other. The most advanced are dependent on the most backward and vice versa ...", and he is writing about the fifteenth to the eighteenth centuries![27] This global view of the past, extended into the present, needs to be transferred into day-to-day educational goals and ideas.

In a seminal essay on educating citizens for a global viewpoint, Robert Hanvey pointed out five key interdisciplinary dimensions that need to be developed:

Perspective consciousness: an awareness and appreciation for other peoples' views of the world and its problems

State of the planet awareness: a deeper understanding of worldwide issues and current events

Cross-cultural awareness: greater familiarity with the key features of other cultures, especially their literature and art, and the similarities and differences between these ideas and images and our own

Systemic awareness: the ability to see 'the world' as a set of systems linking all peoples and nations in patterns of dependence and interdependence

Options for participation: plans for ways in which individuals, like us, can take part in local, national, or international issues that we believe affect us for better or worse.[28]

Few will deny that the world is drawing closer together than it has ever been before, and economic survival and prosperity are more and more the product of trade and aid for both the United States and much of the rest of the world. The familiar arguments for a "one world" economy and political system are probably well-known, with proof available simply by a visit to your local supermarket or department store. However, there are also many problems for education in this area because cultures, including our own, tend to be "local" in their thinking and concentrate on their own affairs, preferring not to worry about others until danger is signaled. This kind of ethnocentric viewpoint seems increasingly out of place because the United States is now 'the' world power and is involved in the business and politics of almost every nation on earth in some way. A second reason we can no longer remain "at home alone" in our thinking is that the world has come to our doorstep, producing cities and towns of great diversity in terms of cultures and populations, customs and languages. The people of the world are on the move! Finally, a third reason for supporting globalism is that Americans, and American culture, are themselves on the move, traveling to distant lands for business, tourism, and education, as well as promoting American products and culture such as automobiles, restaurants, name brands, popular music, art, and literature around the world. Where in the world can Americans travel without meeting up with McDonalds, rock 'n roll music, or Hollywood films? Thus, the arguments for globalism are quite strong, leading to the conclusion that the schools must work harder to promote a more comprehensive and refined view of other places and peoples than is currently the situation.

To regain a sense of belonging to and influencing the world, globalists advocate a number of additions to and improvements for social studies, including (a) an expanded and better integrated world history, world geography, or global studies program in the secondary schools; (b) a more comprehensive economics program in which macroeconomic concepts and world trade patterns are given at least as much attention as microeconomics; (c) more cross-cultural literature and fine arts in both English, humanities, and social studies, particularly "core" courses taught by interdisciplinary teams of teachers; (d) a wider variety of languages to choose from in secondary schools, tied to a cultural and artistic context supported by literature and social studies teachers; and (e) wider attention across the curriculum to world problems or issues particularly those involving economic development and the environment, and human rights.[29]

LET'S DECIDE

Before beginning any discussion of globalism, poll your classmates or pupils about the five top issues or problems they see in the world, asking them to explain why these are so troubling or important to them. Use their reactions to your questions as a basis for planning your global or world history course.

The whole point of globalism is to connect ourselves, as teachers, and our students with what is happening in the rest of the world, or at least part of it in an empathic way, keeping minds open to other points of view and other interpretations of events. Many vital issues and events can only be well understood nowadays through a global perspective, otherwise we may draw the wrong conclusions and support actions that actually lead to rather than resolve a conflict. However, globalism does not mean to imply that our own nation ought to be demeaned or neglected, on the contrary, the greater the connection to, and respect for, other cultures and countries, the more opportunities will develop at home and abroad.[30] Teachers have invented quite a few ways in which to translate the goals of globalism into their everyday classroom activities, and these include:

Regularly reading foreign or ethnic newspapers is one way of obtaining other viewpoints.

Making a list of leaders students feel are the "makers of world history"; as well as making a list of those "great" individuals who have either harmed or benefited the world.

Studying other countries in other countries, or even visiting other countries as part of a school-sponsored trip, with the purpose of meeting the locals, and touring their historical monuments and museums, as well as just having a good time.

Acting out simulation games that emphasize or bring to life world conflicts (e.g., "Starpower" or "The Road Game" for building awareness of conflicts arising from an unequal distribution of wealth, or territorial disputes, respectively).

Organizing a shopping field trip in which students take notes on the labels and origins of a "marketbasket" of products in a typical supermarket or department store.

Tracing or mapping out the entire chain of geographic origins, manufacture, shipment, and assembly of some popular machinery or food product, such as an automobile, a candy bar, or a shirt or dress.

Acting out simulation games that help students think about and consider issues arising from ethnocentrism or racism (e.g., BaFa BaFa, or RaFa RaFa, one for senior high school groups and the latter for junior high groups).

Setting up an electronic database that connects students to other places through the World Wide Web and the Internet.

Selecting timely and "worrisome" public issues that students can study and debate, or investigate and evaluate solutions (e.g., terrorism, trade issues, child labor, conflict resolution negotiations, land or water disputes, and environmental degradation or destruction).

Debating global philosophies and policies about vital issues such as immigration, border controls, business practices, development, and government policies that deal with intervention, cooperation, and/or conflict with other nations and international agencies such as the United Nations.

SAMPLE LESSON PLAN

Cartoons are a very good source of material for lessons, and nearly every paper around the world employs and publishes cartoonists who comment on current affairs or global problems. The figure here is an example of a recent cartoon from abroad that the artist uses to express his views about world trends.

Design a lesson using this cartoon, making sure that you ask a least three or four thought-provoking questions to stimulate discussion. What questions do you think will produce the most interest? Follow up by collecting at least three or four more cartoons on the same or a similar subject that can be compared or contrasted with the one provided here.

SOURCE: *World Press Review*, New York.

ALTERNATIVE SOCIAL STUDIES ELECTIVES

In addition to the standard courses discussed in chapters 10, 11, and 12, and the innovative curricular additions discussed earlier, several other traditional social science disciplines are frequently offered in secondary social studies programs. These are usually offered as electives and occur at various grade levels; they include courses in psychology, anthropology, sociology, geography, and interdisciplinary core courses combining humanities and social studies. Infrequently, electives that were characteristic of the 1960s and 1970s are provided on special topics or issues such as gender (women's studies), race (race relations), media (TV news and film courses), or narrowly focused historical topics (the U.S. Civil War, Non-Western or area studies, e.g., Japan, China, or India, etc.).

RESEARCH REPORT

In 1986, a self-report opinionaire was mailed to a random selection of 1,000 members of the National Council for the Social Studies, asking educators to respond to questions about curricular priorities. For the 345 respondents, history was clearly the top choice (ranked first by about 50 percent), and civics or government was second (receiving about 24 percent of first place votes). Other subjects were ranked in the following order of importance: geography, political science, economics, sociology, psychology, and anthropology.

SOURCE: Rod Farmer, "Social Studies Teachers and the Curriculum: A Report from a National Survey," *Journal of Social Science Research* (University of Georgia) 11, no. 2 (1987): 24–31.

Many of these courses entered the social studies curriculum in the 1960s and 1970s as a result of pressure from various national organizations like the American Psychological Association and the American Sociological Association, which undertook curriculum development projects. Almost all these programs used a college course model adapted for younger students, and all shared a common interest in introducing secondary students to the way social scientists work: how they find evidence, develop hypotheses, and test theories. Observation and statistical surveys were integrated into the classroom, and many programs were designed to let students rediscover principles and tools by reproducing significant studies and experiments. Other electives grow out of "issues-centered" approaches to social studies and echo the minicourses or modular courses created in the 1960s and 1970s that aimed at sparking student interest in specific topics dealing with key or crucial social problems. These have sometimes been updated or reinterpreted to reflect the concerns of the 1990s with immigration, welfare reform, national identity, taxation and budget policies, character education, or political participation and social activism.

Although the social sciences have moved in the 1980s and 1990s toward a sharing of methodologies and an integration of research findings, secondary social studies curricula still tend to present them as separate units. The goal has typically been twofold: to build student skills in using the scientific method, and to disseminate content and research findings in the schools. In the next decade, these courses will no doubt begin to reflect more interdisciplinary concerns, as well as those concerns about values, issues, and philosophic orientations that have been central to social scientists and political activists in recent years and that have called into question some of the basic principles of objectivity and scientific method.

Organizations in a variety of areas can provide instructional resources for teaching the social science disciplines. These are listed in Appendix A.

SUMMARY

From the turbulent 1960s through the 1980s, social studies exhibited a number of new trends toward more emphasis on multiethnic and multicultural topics, law-related education, geography and the environment, and peace and international affairs. Efforts on behalf of these issues have resulted in widespread interest in and implementation of these topics of study, without much depth, however. These topics have, for the most part, been infused into mainstream social studies rather than presented in separate courses. Law studies, for example, are now widely incorporated into U.S. history and civics courses; and world history courses show some renewed emphasis on globalism and international affairs.

Unsettling poll findings about student knowledge in geography, foreign affairs, and politics have been used to promote corrective measures to enrich the social studies curriculum with new materials, methods, and viewpoints. A changing American population has supported movements to redefine the way ethnicity, race, and gender issues are presented in the schools. In particular, a renewed interest in multicultural studies has introduced ways to achieve better integration of other cultures and groups into the standard curriculum, and awareness of multicultural, minority, and gender problems has increased markedly over the past decade. Considerable experimentation is underway to create both materials and teaching approaches that deal honestly with bias, prejudice, and social conflict.

Many social studies innovations of the 1960s returned in new guises in the 1980s, although occasionally diminished in scope or complexity. Some older interests, notably in the social science disciplines, critical thinking, and moral education, have demonstrated renewed vigor, and many signs suggest that the field as a whole is pulling out of a decade or more of relative quiescence in curriculum innovation and methodological experimentation.

LET'S DECIDE

1. Which of the new directions discussed in this chapter do you think are really new? Look up issues of social education and social studies from the 1960s and 1970s to learn whether any topics such as peace education, moral development, multiethnic studies, gender issues, or the social sciences are prominently discussed. What is your verdict on the newness of these "new" directions? How does your verdict compare or contrast with those of another teacher.

2. Choose one of the areas discussed, such as multiethnic/multicultural studies, and collect at least five articles from different sources that seek to define this topic. Read and compare these in order to decide whether the authors define multicultural education in basically the same way or in different terms. Compare your conclusions with a peer or classmate or colleague.

3. Talk with secondary social studies teachers and college professors about new directions they see as significant in this field. Are these the same topics that you have read about or observed in the schools on field trips? Why or why not?

4. Discuss social studies trends, as far as you have experienced them, with friends and classmates, and create a "wish" list of development (materials, ideas, techniques, technology) that you would like to see introduced.

NOTES

1. EconomicsAmerica, *A Guide. Voluntary National Content Standards in Economics: Why and What?* (New York: National Council on Economic Education. 1997).
2. Ibid. p. 4 of foldout guide.
3. Jim Eggert, *What Is Economics?* (Los Altos, CA: William Kaufmann, 1977), pp. 3–12.
4. John S. Morton, chair, et al., "Master Curriculum Guide in Economics," in *Teaching Strategies: High School Economics Courses* (New York: Joint Council for Economic Education, 1985), pp. 173–77.
5. James E. Davis, *Teaching Economics to Young Adolescents: A Research-based Rationale* (San Francisco: Foundation for Teaching Economics, 1987).
6. Kenneth E. Boulding, "What Do We Want from an Economics Textbook?" *Journal of Economic Education* 19, no. 2 (Spring 1988): 129.
7. Judith S. Brenneke, ed., *Consumer Education and Economic Education in the Public Schools* (Washington, DC: U.S. Department of Education, 1981).

8. Lee W. Hansen, "The State of Economic Literacy," in *Perspectives on Economic Education*, ed. Donald Wentworth. (New York: Joint Council on Economic Education, National Council for the Social Studies, and Social Science Education Consortium, 1977).

9. James S. Leming, "Curricular Effectiveness in Moral/Values Education: A Review of Research," *Journal of Moral Education* 19 (1981): 147–62.

10. C. A. Grant and C. E. Sleeter, "Race, Class, and Gender in Educational Research: An Argument for Integrative Analysis," *Review of Educational Research* 56, no. 2 (1986): 195–211.

11. Mario Vargas Llosa, "Question of Conquest," *Harper's Magazine* (Dec. 1990): 45–53.

12. Ricardo L. Garcia, *Teaching in a Pluralistic Society: Concepts, Models, Strategies* (New York: Harper & Row, 1982).

13. Nicholas Appleton, *Cultural Pluralism in Education: Theoretical Foundations* (White Plains, NY: Longman, 1983).

14. James A. Banks, *Multiethnic Education Theory and Practice*, 2nd ed. (Boston: Allyn & Bacon, 1988).

15. Peter McLaren, *Life in Schools* (White Plains, NY: Longman, 1990).

16. R. Ratcliffe et al., *Vital Issues of the U.S. Constitution* (Boston: Houghton Mifflin, 1990).

17. Sheldon Berman, *A Guiding Framework for Character Education. Update on Law-related Education* 20, no.1 (1996): 36–39.

18. *Update on Law Related Education. Special Issue: International Law.* 21, no.1 (Winter 1997): 45–52.

19. The Constitution Works, "The Fourteenth Amendment and Equal Protection of the Laws" Teacher and Student Workbooks: A Student Role-playing Program Based at Historic Sites in New York, Philadelphia, and Albany, NY (New York: The Constitution Works, 1995.)

20. "Guidelines for Geographic Education," Association of American Geographers, 1710 Sixteenth St. NW, Washington, DC 10009, 1984. Adapted in the *New York State Council for the Social Studies Newsletter*, Sept. 1988, p. 4.

21. Geography Standards Education Project, *Geography for Life* (Washington, DC: National Geographic Research & Exploration, 1994).

22. James R. Kimmel, "Using the National Geography Standards and Your Local River to Teach about Environmental Issues." *Journal of Geography*, 2: 66.

23. See, e.g., the Gallup Organization, *Geography: An International Survey* (Princeton, NJ: Gallup, Inc., 1988).

24. Ju Chou and Robert E. Roth, "Exploring the Underlying Constructs of Basic Concepts in Environmental Education," *Journal of Environmental Education*, 26, no. 2 (Winter 1995): 36–43.

25. C. Fitzpatrick, "Teaching Geography with Computers," *Journal of Geography* 92 (4): 156–159.

26. Center for Foreign Policy Development. Choices for the Twenty-first Century, "Keeping the Peace in an Age of Conflict: Debating the U.S. Role." Brown University, P.O. Box 1948, RI 02912. April 1994.

27. F. Braudel, *The Perspective of the World: Civilization and Capitalism, Fifteenth–Eighteenth Century*, vol.3 (New York: Harper & Row, 1979), pp. 70–71.

28. L. Anderson, "A Rationale for Global Education," in *Global Education: From Thought to Action*, ed. Kenneth A. Tye. (Alexandria, VA: 1991 Yearbook of the Association for Supervision and Curriculum Development, 1990), pp. 13–34.

29. R. Hanvey, *An Attainable Global Perspective* (Denver, CO: Center for Teaching International Relations, 1976).

30. M. Merryfield and C. S. White, "Issues-Centered Global Education," in *Handbook on Teaching Social Issues*, Bulletin No. 93, ed. R. W. Evans and D. W. Saxe (Washington DC: National Council for the Social Studies, 1996), pp. 177–187.

FOR FURTHER STUDY: OLD CONCERNS, NEW DIRECTIONS

ABC World Reference. 3D Atlas, Version 1.1. Creative Wonders Electronic Arts/University College London, 1995.

American Bar Association. "The U.S. Constitution: The Original American Dream." In Law Day 1996 Special Issue of *Update on Law-related Education* 20, no. 1 (Winter 1996).

Annual Editions: Global Issues. Dushkin Publishing Group. Published Annually.

Ashbrenner, B. *Still a Nation of Immigrants*. New York: Cobblehill Books, 1993.

Banks, J. *Multiethnic Education: Theory and Practice*. Boston: Allyn & Bacon, 1988.

Banks, J., and C. A. McGee Banks, eds. *Multicultural Education: Issues and Perspectives*. Boston: Allyn & Bacon, 1989.

Carnes, J. "Us and Them: A History of Intolerance in America." In *Teaching Tolerance Magazine*. Montgomery, AL: Southern Poverty Law Center, 1995.

Cartoon News Monthly: The Current Events Educational Monthly. Affiliated with the *New York Times* and Cartoonews International Syndicate. Lurie Academia, Inc., New York: Trump Tower, 10022 (First U.S. edition, Sept. 1996).

Davis, J. E., and J. S. Eckenrod. *Managing World Conflict: A Resource Unit for High Schools*. Washington, DC: U.S. Institute of Peace, 1994.

EconomicsAmerica: National Council on Economic Education/Nebraska Council on Economic Education. *Virtual Economics 1.1, 2.1* (Software Design CD-ROM). Nebraska Council:EconomicsAmerica, 1995, 1997.

Ehman, L., and A. Glenn. *Computer Based Education in the Social Studies*. Bloomington, IN: ERIC Clearinghouse for Social Studies/Social Science Education, 1987.

Fore, J, and H. Hursh. *Global Studies for the 90s*. Denver, CO: Center for Teaching International Relations and Social Science Education Consortium (CIT), 1993.

Giroux, H. *Border Crossings: Cultural Workers and the Politics of Education*. London: Routledge, 1992.

Glassner, M. I. *Political Geography*. 2nd ed. New York: John Wiley & Sons, 1996.

Great Decisions and Great Decisions Activity Book (published each year for classroom use) New York, NY: Foreign Policy Association.

Hahn, C. "Gender and Political Learning." *Theory and Research in Social Education* 24, no. 1 (Winter 1996): 8–35.

Heller, K. *U.S. Response—The Making of U.S. Foreign Policy: A Simulation*. Alexandria, VA: Close Up Publishing, 1990.

Huffman, H. A. *Developing a Character Education Program: One School District's Experience*. Alexandria, VA: The Character Education Partnership/Association for Supervision and Curriculum Development, 1994.

Isaacs, K. *Civics for Democracy, A Journey for Teachers and Students*. Washington, DC: Essential Books, 1992.

Johnson, R. J., P. J. Taylor, and M. J. Watts, eds. *Geographies of Global Change: Remapping the World in the Late Twentieth Century*. Cambridge, MA: Blackwell Publishers, 1995.

Leming, Robert S., and Langdon T. Healy, eds. Resources on Law-related Education. Documentation and Journal Articles in ERIC, 1995. Yearbook No. 2. ERIC Clearinghouse for Social Studies/Social Science Education and the American Bar Association. National Law Related Education Resource Center. Bloomington, IN, 1996.

Lynch, J. *Multicultural Education in a Global Society*. New York: Falmer Press, 1989.

McMahon, E., L. Arbetman, and E. O'Brien. *Street Law: A Course in Practical Law*. St. Paul, MN: West Publishing, 1986.

Merryfield, M., and R. C. Remy, eds. *Teaching About International Conflict and Peace*. Albany, NY: State University of New York Press, 1995.

Parisi, L. S., and R. D. LaRue, Jr. *Global/International Issues and Problems: A Resource Book for Secondary Schools*. Santa Barbara, CA: ABC-CLIO, 1989.

Questar. *Exploring Ancient Cities*. Chicago, IL: Questar, Inc., 1996.

Schug, M. C., and W. B. Walstad. "Teaching and Learning Economics." In *Handbook of Research on Social Studies Teaching and Learning*, ed. James A. Shaver. New York: Macmillan, 1991.

Shaw, J. S., ed. *A Blueprint for Environmental Education*. Boseman, MT: Political Economy Research Center, 1999.

Sleeter, C. E., and C. A. Grant. *Making Choices for Multicultural Education: Five Approaches to Race, Class, and Gender*. Columbus, OH: Merrill, 1988.

Takaki, R., ed. *From Different Shores: Perspectives on Race and Ethnicity in America*. New York: Oxford University Press, 1987.

Thomas, D. C., and M. T. Klare, eds. *Peace and World Order Studies: A Curriculum Guide*. 5th ed. Boulder, CO: Westview Press, 1989.

Turner, M. J., and L. Parisi. *Law in the Classroom*. Boulder, CO: Social Science Education Consortium, 1984.

Walstad, William B., and John C. Soper, eds. *Effective Economic Education in the Schools*. Washington, DC: NEA/Joint Council on Economic Education, 1987.

PART FIVE

Textbooks and Media in the Social Studies

CHAPTER 13

The Role of Textbooks in Social Studies Education

In the European schools the teacher was at the center of the learning process; he lectured, questioned the pupils, and "built up new knowledge in class." In contrast, in the American classroom, "clearly … the master is the textbook." The teacher does not really teach but "acts rather as chairman of a meeting, the object of which is to ascertain whether [the students] have studied for themselves in a textbook."

—Burstall (British educator/U.S. visitor, late nineteenth century)

OVERVIEW OF CONTENTS

Main Ideas

Pervasiveness of Texts in the Social Studies

    Course Dependence

Advantages and Disadvantages of Texts

Advantages

Disadvantages

Overall Evaluation

    Using Textbooks to Meet Different Goals
    Using Texts to Increase Knowledge
    Using Texts to Promote Critical Thinking
    Using Texts to Develop Attitudes

Summary

Notes

For Further Study: The Uses of Textbooks

MAIN IDEAS

Textbooks are in widespread use throughout the educational system at all levels. Often a textbook is more than a bound volume of narrative, including a complete program for the subject with tests, teacher's guide, supplemental readings, and now a videotape or CD-ROM. You may find yourself in a situation in which the text defines both the curriculum and your teaching plan. Many states and communities require a text to be used in the social studies classroom; frequently, a particular text is prescribed for all.

Heavy reliance on a single textbook for civics, U.S., or world history places students at a serious disadvantage because their views are shaped by material that is predigested and summarized. It is often very difficult for a reader to decide how conclusions in the text were reached either in terms of reasoning or by way of evidence. In addition, texts may consciously or unconsciously incorporate biases and distortions into the material students learn, yet present themselves as objective and fair. An example is the criticism that has been directed at textbooks based on race, gender, and ethnicity, both for what is written and for what is left out. Thus, although textbooks are perhaps a necessary classroom convenience, overreliance on them can easily lead to a distorted view of events that may also be dull and uninteresting.

Yet, textbooks can also be used very effectively to promote higher level thinking and the examination of values if you provide students with multiple sources, if you examine critically the content and meaning of what is written, and if you rewrite the material from different points of view. Will you become a captive of your textbook? Or will you find a way to use textbooks to encourage analysis, language development, and critical reading skills?

PERVASIVENESS OF TEXTS IN THE SOCIAL STUDIES

Studies have shown that social studies teachers generally rely on textbooks as the mainstay of their instruction.[1] Virtually no classroom escapes without a required text, which is often out of date.[2] This is true for almost every course taught, from the most common offerings like world or American studies to the less frequent like problems of democracy or multicultural studies.[3] As soon as a new course is required by official state mandate or an old one is revised, publishers are ready to supply the market with one or more textbooks on the subject, varying in scope from review books to elegant, beautifully illustrated narratives.

Social studies is not alone in relying on textbooks; other fields do so as well, but perhaps not in so dependent a fashion. In many English programs, for example, a literature textbook may be assigned, but many teachers often develop reading lists that include novels, poems, plays, and short stories to use in conjunction with the text. Science courses depend more heavily than English programs on textbooks, but they do have the advantage, if taken, of built-in laboratory exercises and hands-on experiments that bring theoretical concepts to life in the classroom.

Most social studies teachers, unfortunately, tend not to view the classroom as a place to design and conduct experiments, although this is certainly both possible and potentially exciting. Nor do social studies teachers consistently draw on "great books" or documentary collections as important sources of evidence for classroom discussions. Indeed, when texts are utilized, usually one is assigned; the entire class must then rely on this secondary source for information without the benefit of any comparative examples for outside verification.

Across the nation, people often remember their social studies teacher assigning readings from a textbook followed by assignments of end-of-chapter questions. The reading and end-of-chapter questions routine is common throughout social studies education, further indicating widespread reliance on textbooks for the basic substance of the program. Source books, historical documents, simulations, the fine arts, literature, role-playing, and other materials and group dynamics techniques are usually regarded as peripheral to the centerpiece—the textbook!

Figure 13.1a   *SOURCE*: "Washington, D.C. Woodrow Wilson High School, White, Algebra Lesson, 1943," Office of War Information, the Library of Congress.

Figure 13.1b   Classroom body language, past and present. Query: Are these classrooms more subject to conformity or creativity, free expression or tight control? Which appears more open and which more closed? How can you tell?
SOURCE: Photograph courtesy of Gerry Gioia, Boys and Girls High School.

RESEARCH REPORT

Numerous research studies have found that half or more of social studies teachers depend on a textbook as their major teaching tool. Superka, Hawke, and Morrissett report that reliance on textbooks is characteristic of the United States as a whole at both the elementary and the secondary level, with this reliance increasing as the grade levels rise.[*] Shaver, Davis, and Helburn report that by far the majority of the textbooks used in social studies classrooms are commercially available, follow a narrative format, and promote recall over higher level thinking skills.[†] Armento concurs with these findings and concludes that textbooks tend to stress breadth or coverage over depth, yielding little insight into the reasons behind conclusions that are presented about various events.[‡] A thorough national survey by the Effective Programs for Innovation in Education (EPIE) Institute, though somewhat dated, found that two thirds or more of classroom time in a typical social studies classroom was devoted to reading, reviewing, and answering questions from commercial textbooks and related printed matter.[§]

---

[*]Douglas P. Superka, Sharryl Hawke, and Irving Morrissett, "The Current and Future Status of the Social Studies," *Social Education* 44 (May 1980): 362–69.
[†]James Shaver, O. L. Davis, and Suzanne Helburn, "The Status of Social Studies Education: Implications from Three NSF Studies," *Social Education* 43, no. 2 (Feb. 1979): 150–53.
[‡]Beverly Armento, "Research on Teaching Social Studies," in *Handbook of Research on Teaching*, 3rd ed., ed. M. C. Wittrock (New York: Macmillan, 1986), pp. 942–51.
[§]EPIE Staff Report on a National Study of the Nature and Quality of Instructional Materials Most Used by Teachers and Learners" (EPIE Report no. 71) (New York: EPIE Institute, 1976).

Nevertheless, as much as textbooks are deplored by some teachers, parents, and experts, they are a fact of life that is accepted by the majority of teachers and supported by a vast array of state requirements; standardized tests; city, county-, or state-mandated courses; and a powerful publishing lobby. That social studies teachers depend so heavily on textbooks is an entrenched feature of a mutually supportive system. Teachers, parents, and state agencies like to have textbooks in every classroom, and publishers generally aim to please this large market.

Course Dependence

The widespread use of textbooks is not the only or perhaps the major problem facing the social studies. Rather, it is the way the textbooks are often used in teacher-centered classrooms that is far more worrisome.[4] Many teachers tend to follow the textbook as their main source of ideas and material without much enrichment or supplementation from other sources.

In addition, the textbook is used as part of a nearly closed system of assignments, reading, discussion, questions, homework, and tests that provide great security but very little imagination. Whereas texts vary widely in format and quality, most share a commitment to providing teachers and students with the factual background deemed necessary by law, tradition, and scholarship. Hence, relatively little attention is given to reasoning, argument, controversy, or group activities unless these are built into the text; although research surveys indicate that this is usually not the case, programs are improving. The exercises at the end of the chapter tend to emphasize students' ability to recall information or at best define terms and comprehend the basic outline of events. Although students do need to know their facts, a steady diet of reading, recitation, and recall can be dull and boring, thus reducing students' opportunities to practice reasoning and creating negative attitudes toward the subject as a whole.

Part of the dependence on textbooks arises out of the teachers' need for quick, easy, readily available materials that can serve multiple uses. Homework assignments in most classrooms are geared specifically to the textbook in use, and test items are drawn from each chapter or in some cases are provided by the publisher as part of a kit for the teacher. Many textbooks offer a manual for use, a test handbook, supplemental activities, and the student narrative itself, which is virtually an integrated system requiring little or no outside planning or research on the part of the instructor. Such a system also ensures, at least theoretically, uniform course outcomes and uniform performance on departmental or standardized tests—if these are required.

Homework and testing are supported by most teachers and parents as positively related to learning and to building student character; homework assignments and test items are revised periodically to reflect new events and theories. Textbook authors do try to keep up with significant changes but encounter many difficult questions on the way: How can a problem be judged significant? Which facts and ideas should be included and which excluded? Where differences in viewpoint are extremely far apart, how can this be communicated to students? How can we be certain that an account is balanced? Because of the need for condensation in a textbook, as in any summary, the reasoning by which the author's conclusions were developed and defended is largely lost. Generally, room exists to report only major conclusions and facts, often without indicating why these are important or what bases of evidence or logic support them. In short, students may memorize the facts and be able to repeat the predigested conclusions in a textbook, but frequently they have no idea why certain names and dates are important or why decisions were made. The connective tissues, the reasoning and process of research, are often missing experiences for students who use texts as their main source of knowledge.

Textbooks reduce complex events and theories to manageable proportions, but they also eliminate much of the opportunity for students to think for themselves, to see how conclusions were drawn, and to make judgments about history (skills viewed as vitally important by most historians).[5] Consequently, students may be passive rather than active in the social studies classroom.

ADVANTAGES AND DISADVANTAGES OF TEXTBOOKS

Whatever problem is created by reliance on textbooks in the social studies, the books are likely to remain an integral part of the educational system. There are clearly advantages for texts to be so much a part of classroom life, but there are also dangers and disadvantages. Arguments for and against reliance on textbooks are reviewed and summarized here. Think about where you stand on the textbook issue as you read the following sections.

Advantages

Textbooks solve a basic problem in the social studies (i.e., that there is far too much to know about the world in which we live and too little time to learn it). It would be far better for each student to consider each important event and person in detail, basing an informed judgment on primary sources, secondary narratives, and well-written scholarly research. But obviously, there is insufficient time for a thorough inquiry into even the highlights of history and the social sciences. Thus, the textbook was born as a device that summarizes large quantities of factual material in much the same way that the *Reader's Digest* condenses literature, and with some of the same problems. Even with textbooks, teachers and students often feel overwhelmed by the amount of material they must learn.

Textbooks are efficient because they usually offer predigested conclusions based on the author's study and research of complex topics. Enormous effort would be required of the student to develop the same conclusion that is readily supplied by the author. Statistics, dates, names, the causes and consequences of events, conflicting interpretations, bibliographic references: All are integrated into a single volume in which the authors and publishers summarize facts and key conclusions in a relatively easy, assimilable, readable format. Students can approach a text more easily than original sources, which may present reading problems, or many scholarly studies, which present statistical and comprehension problems. Furthermore, the history in texts is organized into succinct accounts offered in a vocabulary geared to the average reading ability of a specified grade level in junior or senior high school.

In addition, textbooks serve to integrate the functions of teacher and student through an established, orderly, and well-defined curriculum. The textbook, after all, can be appealed to as a resource at any time, both sides know its contents, and expectations for accomplishment are exact (i.e., so many pages of reading and homework, so many questions at the end of the chapter, and so many items on the final examination). Students are able to predict with a relatively small margin of error where the course is going and what the teacher is likely to assign for homework and on examinations. Teachers and students accept the textbook as reliable and valid in the sense that it represents a compendium of knowledge checked for accuracy by the authors who wrote it and by the publisher's advisers—a function usually performed before a book is marketed to the schools.

Finally, textbooks tend to be safe—theoretically and pedagogically. They are theoretically safe because, by the very process of cross-examining conflicting viewpoints in history and competing social science theories, textbooks, at their best, present carefully balanced interpretations based on evidence that has stood the tests of time and scholarship. Confusion and controversy are largely eliminated or at least suppressed in favor of knowledge that has been judged important and well grounded, knowledge that is worth knowing and can be reviewed for any test in almost any school with good results because it represents a common core of accepted details and ideas.[6]

Pedagogically, textbooks are relatively safe because most of the contents are didactic, presenting mostly facts. This requires a lecture-recitation teaching technique in which the goals are clear and the questions are crisp, with answers that are either right or wrong. Thus, textbooks have a number of advantages that serve them well: manageability, summary power, comprehensibility, readability, and safety. Texts also serve as bridges on many subjects between teachers and students, including homework, method, content, and criteria for assessment. Textbooks help to create a reasonably predictable world for the social studies classroom out of one that can be and probably is actually very confusing, frustrating, and overwhelming in scope and complexity.

Disadvantages

Unfortunately, the very qualities that give value to textbooks also provide a number of problems. Consider the value of a textbook as a compendium or storehouse of knowledge for an enormous field like world history or American studies. Tremendous amounts of data, literature, and theory are available for either world or American studies, and this knowledge is increasing at an exponential rate every day, hour, and year. There is always more to know, it seems, even about a "dead" past. Students, too, are often supportive because this textbook-driven system, as they see it, sets up goals, defines knowledge, measures results based on clear, specific criteria, and follows a precise, predictable calendar.

Thus, we have a teaching system supported by all but a minority of those involved, including significant segments of teachers, parents, students, and administrators. It is a system that is self-contained and efficient, allowing easy grading of student work, quick student recognition of success or failure (based usually on the quantity of knowledge acquired), and parental comprehension of tasks and standards with which they can judge the success or failure of their offspring. Students are spared the great difficulty of dealing with complicated events and people, of interpreting raw data on their own, and of examining the accuracy of eyewitnesses and reporters.

Unfortunately, these students develop a view of the social sciences and history that is largely unreal. Their experience is of a neatly packaged, tightly condensed view of social studies topics that bear little relation to the often convoluted, ambiguous, and antagonistic situations that exist beyond the textbook in which facts cannot be agreed on and issues are endlessly debated without a conclusion. It is the quandaries, dilemmas, and paradoxes that are left out of textbooks in favor of efficiency; product substitutes for the whole process of scientific inquiry.

Add to this concentration of summarized information the relatively easy reading level of many textbooks and you have a narrative that may be so bland, so agreeable, and so monotonous in style that students cannot stay awake reading it. Critics point out that easy is not always good and manageability is not necessarily the same as effectiveness. Perhaps the most difficult problem posed by texts is that they feed into a teacher-learning system that prizes information above all and rewards recall rather than thought of a higher order. By obscuring the way conclusions were developed, by condensing vast subjects into brief capsules, by asking largely didactic questions, and by offering students little or no involvement in the investigative process, textbooks discourage the growth of student reasoning and thinking skills and offer an oversimplified vision of the historical record and its meaning. By its very nature as a secondary source, the social studies textbook tends to gloss over differences in interpretation and issues, losing the flavor of the past that would come from the study of first hand and/or conflicting evidence.

Finally, however much the authors of textbooks seek to write a finely tuned, fair, and well-balanced approach to the standard social studies topics, they invariably permit their own biases and interpretations to slip through, or they omit materials deemed objectionable by some groups but very desirable by other groups. This is especially true on political, gender, and multicultural issues. The influence of political, social, and economic conditions seems inescapable.[7]

A good deal of the controversy about textbooks stems from criticisms of the amount and quality of the attention given to women and minorities, to different racial and ethnic groups, and to the positions of particular religious or political interests. Whether the textbook developers bow to such pressures, rightly or wrongly, the text itself will suffer errors of omission or commission, or both.

Thus, textbooks may be viewed as suffering from a variety of inherent defects. Among these are a tendency to obscure or suppress controversial or emotionally sensitive issues; to homogenize people and time periods in an effort to create a brief, but fair treatment; to reduce complex events to simple explanations; to oversimplify historical problems and theories or to omit these entirely; and to support and encourage an almost wholly didactic set of goals in which "correct" information becomes a major object of study to the exclusion of reflective thinking and affective concerns.

OVERALL EVALUATION

While the debate about the quality of textbooks goes on, teachers are likely to continue relying on them as a major teaching tool. To be fair, given the demands placed on secondary school teachers, few will have the time or inclination to replace the textbook with a system more attuned to reflective or affective goals than to didactic ones.[8] Indeed, the entire educational system from kindergarten through graduate school uses textbooks, nearly all of which suffer from the same disadvantages and advantages that have been discussed. Textbooks serve as a vital resource and point of reference for both students and teachers, adding or trying to incorporate (like this one) a fair-minded review of what is known in a field of study. Bias, distortion, omission, and style are constant and unsolvable problems in any book that purports to cover any subject in its entirely.

A saner view of the material is as a condensation of selected topics based on an assessment of their relative importance to the total amount of knowledge available. As society changes, people may alter their view of what is important and the curriculum will also shift to new emphases or entirely new topics and interpretations. In the social studies, as in all other fields, the curriculum does change, often dramatically, in concert with the values prevalent at the time. Therefore, the problem is not to do away with texts but to use them intelligently and to develop criteria that distinguish between those that are better and those that are worse, given a particular set of goals. Among the major problems to be solved are the creation and selection of more thought-provoking content and questions for texts, and the incorporation of more activities that involve students actively in the learning process, such as role-play, simulation, mock trials, group projects, or writing a newspaper of the time.

RESEARCH REPORT

In an analytical and anecdotal study of American history textbooks published over a hundred-year period, Fitzgerald points out that content is strongly influenced by political, social, and economic changes, resulting in divergent and conflicting interpretations of events at different historical periods in the United States. Within this context of change, however, publishers and authors try to develop products that yield large sales and appeal to a broad spectrum of pressure groups, often resulting in books that are bland and inoffensive but also generally uninteresting to young people.

SOURCE: Frances Fitzgerald, *America Revised* (New York: Vantage Books, 1979).

In addition, teachers should think about how they use textbooks. A "read and answer the questions at the end of the chapter" approach is probably the most monotonous and mind-dulling method, especially if it is a daily classroom feature. Students are frequently confused about the aims and the meaning of the narratives in the texts and about the questions and homework assignments that accompany them. Teachers frequently assume that the material speaks for itself and treat the text as an absolutely accurate, truthful rendition of the subject. The students may not agree!

One solution to the problem of student confusion and boredom is to increase the variety and intensity of involvement in the reading process (i.e., approach the book as material suitable for individual, committee, or group discussion rather than simple recitation, and spend much more time probing and criticizing controversial, vague, or illogical passages). In short, do more work with less material. A solution to the problem of monotony and homogenization in textbooks is to have students analyze critically rather than memorize the material for recall on a test. Interest is heightened when texts are viewed as subject to error, pressures, bias, and distortion rather than as completely verified. Keep in mind that, no matter how objective an author—human after all—tries to be in the social sciences and history, values, preferences, and viewpoints are inevitably expressed.

Each textbook is based on a conception of human action that controls the selection and presentation of content, and there are always at least a few competing conceptions capable of producing different versions of the same event. Although these competing theories may cause frustration and worry to students who want to know the "absolute truth," a variety of viewpoints also creates a much more exciting classroom atmosphere, one far more conducive to student participation and debate than one with a fixed agenda and set answers. The simple device of using two or more textbooks at the same time to compare and contrast accounts on the same topics will change the complexion of a social studies program. Using multiple texts builds student awareness of author's viewpoints and the problem of bias. Frequently calling student attention to the textbook as an authored work helps. Students begin to see the textbook as a piece of writing by real people, with their own agendas, interests, and causes. Adding a sample of "uninterpreted" primary readings will also bolster reflective goals, and a variety of group activities, particularly issues and controversies, will enhance affective aims and concerns.

WHAT DO YOU THINK?

In our time, political speech and writing are largely the defense of the indefensible. Things like the continuance of British rule in India, the Russian purges and deportations, the dropping of the atom bombs on Japan, can indeed be defended, but only by arguments which are too brutal for most people to face, and which do not square with the professed aims of political parties. Thus, political language has to consist largely of euphemism, question-begging, and sheer cloudy vagueness. Defenseless villages are bombarded from the air, the inhabitants driven out into the countryside, the cattle machine-gunned, the huts set on fire with incendiary bullets: this is called pacification. Millions of peasants are robbed of their farms and sent trudging along the roads with no more than they can carry: this is called transfer of population or rectification of frontiers. People are imprisoned for years without trial, or shot in the back of the neck or sent to die of scurvy in Arctic lumber camps: this is called elimination of unreliable elements.*

Questions

1. What is the author's main point?
2. Why does the author believe that "political language has to consist largely of euphemism"?
3. If we take this author seriously, how would we have to teach the social studies? What cautions would we exercise?

*George Orwell, "Politics and the English Language," in *Collected Works* (New York: Harcourt Brace Jovanovich, 1970), p. 11.

USING TEXTBOOKS TO MEET DIFFERENT GOALS

Textbooks, despite much of the criticism directed at them, can be used for many purposes and in many ways that will alter their impact on student learning. Generally, textbooks are viewed by many teachers as supportive of knowledge goals. Students can find the facts they need from a text, but they are asked to do little more with the material. However, narrative textbooks can also enhance reasoning and critical thinking, especially if multiple texts are available on the same subject and if one or more of these volumes includes primary sources and activities to supplement the basic reading material. Furthermore, textbooks, if subjected to critical analysis, can be the basis for discussions of values, philosophies, and viewpoints and how these ideas affect our thinking about the world—past, present, and future.

Using Texts to Increase Knowledge

Textbooks are probably best suited to increasing the quantity of student knowledge. To the extent that factual material has been subjected to verification, the contents of a textbook will provide you and your students with a solid introduction to social studies subjects (e.g., world studies, U.S. history, civics, economics, psychology, or sociology). If well designed, then the textbook can serve as a source of information, a dictionary of terms, and a reference all rolled into one. Given the scope of information and ideas provided, the text provides a basis for planning the course calendar, assigning homework, and developing tests. However, for most students, the knowledge in textbooks is seen as authoritative and, frequently, complete. Whatever subject is in a text becomes the source of student knowledge and the basis of thinking while outside references are omitted or avoided. Thus any mistakes or distortions in the knowledge presented must be accepted at face value because there are few methods for testing validity except for internal criteria.

When knowledge is the major goal, and the contents of a textbook are viewed as factually correct, you and the students still need to think about questions of accuracy and reasonability (e.g., Is the presentation consistent and does it meet normal standards of logic?). When elements of a formal argument or syllogism are left out of a description, when conclusions are stated without premises, or assumptions made that appear unwarranted, then you have an excellent opportunity for a discussion that will clear up confusions and misunderstandings that may have arisen.[9]

You can help students improve their recall and grasp of factual material in texts by using a few simple techniques:

1. Read small portions aloud and ask students to identify key dates, names, and places.
2. Assign only a few pages of reading at a time, directing students to list the five most important terms or definitions or concepts, either in class or at home.
3. Provide a grid or framework of periods, themes, or issues as a bookkeeping device under which students will group facts rather than accumulating information in the form of lists.
4. Assign certain events or famous people or places to one or two students who will "own" this portion of the text and be responsible for that knowledge, standing ready to supply these data to classmates for review and discussion purposes.

Using Texts to Promote Critical Thinking

Textbooks are very adaptable for meeting critical thinking goals if they are viewed as authored and open to question. The inevitable problems of summarizing vast quantities of information lead to omissions of what many people see as vital information, or to biased and distorted presentations of controversial decisions, events, and personalities. Furthermore, textbooks do not usually identify the assumptions, interpretations, and theories they have absorbed from the community, other accounts, or from scholarly research. Whether theories are proven largely true or are highly questionable, they are always useful as springboards for discussion aimed at pointing out the authors' views or for comparing the authors' presentation of the "facts" with their evident bias or overall philosophy.

SAMPLE LESSON PLAN

Compare these statements about the Vietnam War from five popular texts and create a lesson plan around them:

1. "The cost of the war to the United States has been great—more than fifty thousand Americans killed and hundreds of thousands were wounded."*

2. "The cost of the war was almost twenty-five billion dollars a year … almost fifty-six thousand of them [American troops] had been killed."†

3. "The war had taken more than fifty-seven thousand American lives and cost the United States over $100 billion."‡

4. "By the time the United States had withdrawn from South Vietnam, over 56,000 Americans had been killed, more than 300,000 had been wounded, and $150 billion had been spent on the Vietnam conflict. This conflict proved to be one of the costliest in U.S. history."§

5. "Dating from the start of 1961 to the so-called Paris cease-fire in early 1973, the United States lost 46,397 killed in action in Vietnam. They made Vietnam the nation's fourth most costly war.… Another 10,340 died in Vietnam from causes other than combat."[2]

You could hand these five treatments to students without comment or introduction and immediately engage them in a comparison and contrast of the content, meaning, and intent of each passage. Most students will raise issues of accuracy, interpretation, and truth when confronted by different conceptions or "frames" of the same historical event. A few well-chosen questions can guide their analysis: Do the authors agree on the facts? How about on interpretations? Are accounts the same or different? What does each try to cover? Does any leave out what others cover? Is the coverage satisfactory, accurate, or honest?

*Marvin Perry, *A History of the World* (Boston: Houghton Mifflin, 1985), p. 774.
†Bertram L. Linder, Edwin Selzer, and Barry M. Berk, *A World History* (Chicago: Science Research Associates, 1979), p. 667.
‡Burton F. Beers, *World History–Patterns of Civilization* (Englewood Cliffs, NJ: Prentice-Hall, 1983), p. 731.
§Allan O. Kownslar and Terry L. *Smart, People and Our World: A Study of World History* (New York: Holt, Rinehart & Winston, 1981), p. 541.
[2]Sol Holt and John R. O'Connor, *Exploring World History: A Global Approach* (New York: Globe, 1983), p. 299.

The questions in a text that students are expected to answer for homework or recitation can themselves be questioned, and this is particularly productive if the questions lead to a particular answer that contains biases for or against a theory. Separating fact from opinion and theory from evidence is a rewarding way of building students' thinking skills and affords young people the opportunity to discover how chains of evidence lead to conclusions. For a more ambitious program, you can encourage students to develop their own standards for a good conclusion, testing these criteria against a sample conclusions from a few different textbooks.

If two or more textbooks are used on a regular basis in a social studies classroom, you have a ready-made structure for comparing and contrasting different descriptions of the same people and events. Sometimes, it can be profitable and fun to compare accounts of an event in an older and a newer text, each of which may "show off" its historical context (i.e., a 1950s view of the Peoples Republic of China and a 1990s version). Opportunities abound in the use of multiple texts for identifying biases, analyzing the logic of a narrative, defining cause and effect factors, and deciding whether the same causes are assigned to the same effects in competing versions. In addition, the different narratives used may contain subtle distinctions that promote students' language skills through decoding and encoding meanings.

For many events, such as the Vietnam War or the dismantling of apartheid in South Africa or Nixon's Watergate, textual passages from two or three books lined up side by side are very likely to raise both factual problems and issues of interpretation, leading to the identification of different ideologies or philosophies that may permeate the entire account. You can use multiple passages as the basis for a historiography lesson about how we interpret events: (a) What sources of data are reliable and how may these be influenced by cultural perspectives and values? (b) What are the dangers of jumping to conclusions when a story may be incomplete, politically motivated, or based on untrustworthy eyewitnesses? From analysis and discussion, students could be encouraged to identify their own principles for evaluating evidence, to rate eyewitness accounts, to cross-examine conflicting sources, and to test the logic of proposed theories and explanations.

A multitext approach could revitalize interest in otherwise dull, monotonous material and build reflective skills through thought-provoking questions, assignments, and examinations. Whether a single text or multiple texts are used, narrative accounts can be dealt with in a number of ways to increase interest and build a better conceptual framework for students:

1. Students can be subdivided into small groups, each of which is responsible for only a portion of a unit or chapter, reporting conclusions to the whole class after thorough reading and deliberation.

2. Each student may be assigned only a few, perhaps just one, of the many questions that usually follow a chapter or unit, with the student answering that question for the class as a whole.

3. Students may be given a role to play (based on previous cases) and asked to rewrite the text from a new point of view (e.g., minority, ethnic, female, foreign or outside, or as a news or TV reporter).

4. Students may be given a "process" task to perform on a given question or reading, such as testing the material for internal consistency or determining whether assertions are supported with facts and/or reasons.

5. Students may be regularly offered one or more sources outside the textbook as a basis for cross-checking content and conclusions, or they may be asked to seek outside data, primary or secondary, to prove or disprove what they read in their textbook.

Finally, examine the textbooks you will use as carefully as you would an expensive personal purchase for quality craftsmanship and reliable content. Textbooks vary greatly in style, philosophy, and substance, some being better choices for certain purposes than others. Most are basically narrative accounts of a didactic nature, but many texts are more like teaching programs that include regular sprinklings of activities, primary source readings (either within the text or in a supplemental volume), and questions on both lower and higher intellectual levels. Clearly, if you are interested in promoting thinking skills and concept formation, then the latter type of text would be far superior to the predominantly factual account.

Even in states or communities that require a particular text, the same possibilities exist for critical analysis, comparison with other books (excerpted or whole), and enrichment through primary and secondary sources that are copied, read, or taped for classroom use. Increasing demand for more thought-provoking textbook programs has helped to change both the educational market and teachers' and students' expectations about what a textbook is supposed to do. In evaluating a basic social studies text, writing style, a clear educational philosophy, frequent higher level questions, representative original sources, and thought-provoking illustrations might all be part of the criteria for choice, resulting in adoptions that move away from compilation narratives.

Using Texts to Develop Attitudes

Although not specifically designed for the purpose, textbooks can be used to develop attitudes toward social issues and subject matter interests in the social studies. In the hands of a clever teacher, even poorly written and confusing textbook narratives can come alive as a series of value and methodology problems that may surprise and delight students. In fact, poorly designed narratives with factual and theoretical inaccuracies are often the most productive sources of discussion. Comparing two or more texts greatly enhances affective goals aimed at examination of values, beliefs, and philosophical claims.

If our goals are to help students develop greater interest in social topics and more willingness to express and defend their opinions and decisions in public, then a number of techniques and strategies are available to you on a regular basis. First, your own perception of a textbook must change from a didactic one to a view of text material as a source of issues and judgments. If we assume that narratives, however bland, contain hidden values, historical interpretations, biases and distortions as well as authors' opinions, then we are ready to criticize and debate the reading material.

Second, the textbook may be used as a data set that we can research for underlying values and for the importance of topics. Using such simple devices as counting words, phrases, and pages we can measure the topics or people that are "in" or "out" in the text, and those that are treated positively or negatively. Women, minorities, and other cultural groups complain of lack of attention or of *tokenism*—that is, use of only a few examples when many better ones are overlooked.[10] We can also check for an author's consistency by following ideas from their introduction to their conclusion in a text. In this way, it is possible to determine whether the content of the text is consistent or eclectic in approach.

Most students, for instance, have a great deal of trouble understanding the post-Civil War Reconstruction period in U.S. history. The conflicts and politics of the time are usually unclear for them because texts generally gloss over the more brutal aspects of the period. The impeachment of President Andrew Johnson, Lincoln's successor, is portrayed quite differently in history books, depending on an author's political views or bias toward or against the South. Here is one example to decipher.

Led by Thaddeus Stevens, the House of Representatives quickly impeached Johnson on the grounds of "high crimes and misdemeanors." The House bill of particulars, however, was repetitious, vague, and muddled. With Supreme Court Chief Justice Salmon Chase presiding, the Senate sat as a jury and heard the evidence. As seven Republican Senators voted with the Democrats, the Radical Republicans failed by one vote to secure the two thirds majority necessary for conviction.[11]

First, the politics of this trial are glossed over in this passage. On what grounds was Johnson impeached? Impeachment is a very serious charge and if the House bill was so "vague and muddled," then why was the president saved by only one vote? Why did seven Republicans vote with the Democrats? After all, was not Johnson himself a Republican like Lincoln? This is confusing, indeed. Perhaps he should have been thrown out of office. Perhaps there was a solid case against him. But how can the reader be sure?

Given the view of a textbook narrative as a source of values and as a subject for research, experiment with a number of activities designed to analyze contents critically. Focusing on the language used in a text is one way you can call students' attention to values in historical and social science writing. Exercises can be developed around counting adjectives or underlining "hot" and "cold" words, that is, words with positive or negative connotations. Students might conduct their own research study on the degree to which topics are portrayed in a positive, negative, or neutral light in a textbook, either by informally identifying judgments or by counting the number of positive and negative words in a paragraph and setting up a ratio for comparison.[12] The following is an example: "The score is 113 negative phrases and 43 positive phrases with a ratio of about 3 to 1, clearly indicating that the passage is basically negative about the formation of the People's Republic of China."[13]

Word counts and identification of author judgments are particularly effective for dramatic, emotional topics such as wars, rebellions, and revolutions. Political heroes/heroines, international affairs, and images of foreign countries are also fruitful topics to research. Any conflict, cultural perspective, policy issue, or discussion of laws and rights would be excellent as a subject for value analysis.

Another method you can use to call students' attention to underlying values in particular texts is by asking for measures of the space and information devoted to a topic, either comparing two topics within a single text (e.g., how much space is devoted to Germany and to Japan in a discussion of World War II, or how much space is given to the People's Republic of China compared with the Soviet Union), or by comparing two or more treatments of the same topic from different textbooks. In the latter case, the possibilities for discussion are almost endless because multiple excerpts can be taken from different time periods, different publishers, or different nations. For example, Mexican and American narratives about the Mexican War would be interesting to compare in terms of the portrayal in each country of the United States' motivation for conflict and each country's judgments about that war. Pre-Nixon and post-Nixon descriptions of the People's Republic of China would be rich in contrasting value judgments and probably quite different in tone as well.

Middle, junior, senior high, and college text discussions of political participation could form the basis for a group discussion matching ideas to maturational level, that is, students could look at the way authors simplify and sometimes oversimplify topics for different age groups. For example, voting and participation are seen as nearly synonymous with the concept of citizenship in many texts for younger students. Whereas these generally omit reference to conflict and choice, those for older students may give much greater attention to protests or pressure groups as means of participation. Textbook accounts of the causes of the Cold War would serve as an exciting introduction to both the history itself and to analysis of how different stories give differing weight to the key factors contributing to an event of such international significance.

Counting the amount of space devoted to a topic and comparing treatments from different authors, nations, or time periods are techniques that belong to a tradition of social studies research in which textbooks are used as a database for the study of national values and social change. The techniques described here come from this tradition of using exercises and activities for lessons that focus on attitudes and values. Much of the research on textbooks has focused on the manner in which women, minorities, and foreign countries are described in the narratives presented to young people. In brief, textbook analysts have argued that these nationally distributed books represent events and people to millions of students, influencing public images and often serving as the sole knowledge base for school curricula in a given subject.

Furthermore, researchers and critics point out that the contents of textbooks are subject to the historical milieu in which they were written, reflecting prevailing norms and prejudices. A social studies text from World War II or the Korean War period would undoubtedly treat Asia very differently from a current textbook; race relations or women would certainly receive far different treatment now, even by the most conservative authors, than these subjects received in the 1950s or earlier.[14] Thus, textbooks change their content to reflect national concerns and attitudes of the times. Analyzing these changes can serve to focus classroom study and to enhance awareness of how attitudes and values expressed in textbooks change over time. Questions of reliability and validity, consistency and truth are always useful in a social studies discussion and particularly so in discussions of attitudes expressed by textbook authors.[15]

Understanding that textbooks reflect the values of the times in which they were written and contain problems of bias, distortion, selection, and judgment does not necessarily invalidate them or imply that they are useless. You should treat textbooks in much the same way as historical writing and social science theory—open to criticism and revision. It is only when teachers use textbooks as sources of revealed and absolute truth that students accept the knowledge offered without seeking proof and without feeling the need to make their own judgments.

SUMMARY

Textbooks can be very interesting and useful if students are involved with the material, seeking to identify and solve problems, trying to recognize values and theories, and eventually making their own decisions about what to accept or reject as conclusions. Although textbooks are popularly perceived as compilations of facts and are used in a purely didactic way by teachers, these narratives can also be used to support reflective and affective goals. Reflection and the examination of attitudes may be easily stimulated by an overall view of textbook contents as open to question and analysis. This can be achieved in several ways: (a) through comparisons of two or more accounts of the same event; (b) by checking for consistency and logic in reasoning; (c) by asking whether conclusions are supported with appropriate verifiable data; (d) by research into the amount of space devoted to a topic, issue, person, or event; or (e) by investigating the type of language, objective or subjective, used to describe historical periods and personalities. Whereas the textbooks themselves may be of good quality, including much more than basic material and questions in their programs, it is still beneficial to subject all textbooks to some verification, cross-checking them against both primary and secondary sources.

Given the complex issues and sensitive feelings of many groups who have been overlooked or poorly treated by social studies textbooks, and given past acceptance of biased perspectives into standard historical accounts, it is incumbent on you, as teacher, to be aware of and sensitive to problems that may result from reliance on a single source of information. You should share your perceptions of inconsistencies and biases with students, training them to recognize weak and fallacious reasoning or unsupported judgments and viewpoints as part of their general development of thinking skills, using historical and social science methods. Students should be helped to consider the problems inherent in any portrayal of human behavior. Such problems range from factual inaccuracies to unconscious bias and emotionality, to purposeful distortion for political or ideological ends. Your reward for the process of inquiry into textbooks will be students who can make better judgments, draw more reasoned conclusions, read more carefully, and understand why questions must often remain "open" or sometimes even unanswerable.

TO DO

BUILD YOUR OWN TEXTBOOK LESSON

Select a topic that has the potential to evoke differences of opinion and treatment (e.g., the Vietnam War, voter participation, macroeconomic theory, or European imperialism in the nineteenth century). Randomly choose three or four textbooks for the same course (all of which include treatment of the selected topics) and compare the way each text deals with the chosen subject. Copy each relevant portion and survey its contents in terms of space allocated to the topic, expressed or implied causes, positive or negative judgments about people and decisions, and supported or unsupported judgments. Decide whether the authors are pushing particular viewpoints or basically agree on facts and interpretations. Make a list of points on which the different accounts agree and disagree, calculating whether there is more agreement or disagreement on average. Review your findings, separating statements into two categories: factual matters and interpretations. Or count "hot" and "cold" words. Recalculate your counts to determine whether there is better agreement on "facts" or on "interpretations".

Discuss your results with other teachers, polling their views about textbooks (e.g., do they see the textbook narratives as basically truthful or biased; reliable or inconsistent; fair or unfair to sensitive issues and topics; satisfactory as sources of knowledge for students or seriously deficient and in need of supplements). Then answer these questions for yourself: To what degree would you be willing to rely on (a) a single textbook, (b) multiple textbooks, or (c) a textbook program for global history, American studies, civics, or economics as the mainstay of your teaching? Would you treat the contents of any book you used as final and accurate, as open to question, or as a mixture of the two? Why or why not? Decide on your own judgments on textbooks and be ready to defend your views.

NOTES

1. J. Hoetker and W. Ahlbrand, "The Persistence of Recitation," *American Educational Research Journal* 6 (1969): 145–67.
2. Roland G. Thard and Ronald Gallimore, *Rousing Minds to Life* (New York: Cambridge University Press, 1969).
3. James Shaver, O. L. Davis, and Suzanne Helburn, "The Status of Social Studies Education: Implications from Three NSF Studies," *Social Education* 43, no. 2 (Feb. 1979): 150–53.

4. Larry Cuban, *How Teachers Taught: Constancy and Change in American Classrooms, 1890–1980* (White Plains, NY: Longman, 1984).
5. Howard Graves, "Making Sense of History" *World History Bulletin* 11, no. 1 (Spring/Summer 1994): 25–27.
6. Ronald Evans, "The Societal-Problems Approach and the Teaching of History," *Social Education* 53, no. 1 (Jan. 1989): 50–52.
7. Joel Spring, *American Education: An Introduction to Social* and Political Aspects (White Plains, NY: Longman, 1989). (See chaps. 3 and 4.)
8. W. Anderson, "What Teachers Don't Do and Why," *Education Report* 27, no. 3 (Dec. 1984): 3–9.
9. Syllogistic reasoning is a form of logic that sometimes leads to an unwarranted conclusion: All Chinese are sly and cunning. Confucius is Chinese. Therefore, Confucius is sly and cunning.
10. Nell , "Social Studies and Feminism" *Theory and Research in Social Education* 20, no. 3 (1992): 230–241.
11. Allan Singer, "Challenging Gender Bias Through a Transformative High School Social Studies Curriculum," *Theory and Research in Social Education* 23, no. 3 (Summer 1995): pp. 234–259.
12. James Lemert, *Criticizing the Media.* (Newbury Park, CA: Sage Publications, 1989).
13. Irving L. Gordon, *American History*, 2nd ed. (New York: School Publications, 1989), p. 235.
14. Jesus Garcia, "The White Ethnic Experience in *Selected Secondary U.S. History Textbooks*," *Social Studies* 77 (July/Aug. 1986): 169–175.
15. Elizabeth A. Yeager, and O. L. Davis. "Classroom Teachers' Thinking About Historical Texts: An Exploratory Study," 24 no. 2 (Spring 1996): 146–166.

FOR FURTHER STUDY: THE USES OF TEXTBOOKS

American Textbook Council. *History Textbooks, A Standard and Guide: 1994–95 Edition*. New York: Center for Education Studies/American Textbook Council, 1995.
Anyon, J. "Ideology and U.S. History Textbooks." *Harvard Educational Review* 49 (Aug. 1979): 361–85.
Banks, James. "The Canon Debate, Knowledge Construction, and Multicultural Education" *Educational Researcher* 22, no. 5 (1993): 4–14.
Ben-Peretz, M. *Freeing Teachers from the Tyranny of Texts*, Albany, NY: State University of New York, 1990.
Carroll, J. D. et al. *We the People: A Review of U.S. Government Textbooks*. Washington, DC: People for the American Way, 1987.
Davis, O. L., Jr., et al. *Looking at History: A Review of Major U.S. History Textbooks*. Washington, DC: People for the American Way, 1986.
Elliot, D. L., and A. Woodward, eds. *Textbooks and Schooling in the United States*. Eighty-ninth Yearbook of the National Society for the Study of Education. Chicago: University of Chicago Press, 1990.
Fitzgerald, F. *America Revised: History School Books in the Twentieth Century*. Boston: Little, Brown, 1979.
Loewen, J. W. *Lies My Teacher Told Me: Everything Your History Textbook Got Wrong*. New York: The New Press, 1995.
Patton, W. E., ed. *Improving the Use of Social Studies Textbooks* Bulletin No. 64. Washington, DC: National Council for the Social Studies, 1980.
Said, E. Orientalism. New York: Vintage Books, 1979.
Sewall, G. T. *American History Textbooks: An Assessment of Quality*. Washington, DC: Education Excellence Network, 1987.
Smith, G. A., and D. Williams, eds. *Ecological Education in Action: On Weaving Education, Culture, and the Environment*. Albany: State University of New York Press, 1998.
White, J. J. "Searching for Substantial Knowledge in Social Studies Texts." *Theory and Research in Social Education* 16 (1989): 115–40.

CHAPTER 14

The "New Age" of Multimedia: Part I. Reading Words and Images: Print Media and the Fine Arts

The new value placed on the transitory, the elusive, and the ephemeral, the very celebration of dynamism, discloses a longing for an undefiled, immaculate, and stable present.
—Jurgen Habermas, *The Philosophical Discourse of Modernity* (1987)

OVERVIEW OF CONTENTS

Main Ideas _____

Passive and Active Roles in the "Mediated" Social Studies Classroom _____

      Didactic, Reflective, and Affective Roles
      Narrator and Audience
      Media, Meaning, and Message

In The Mind's Eye: Print Media for Social Studies _____

      Fiction and Nonfiction: Literature, News, and Views _____
      Primary Sources
      Literary Sources
      Scholarly Sources
      Current Events/News Sources

Still Life with Meaning: Reading Images From Past and Present _____

      Reality and Imagination
      The Fine Arts
      Photography

Summary _____

Notes _____

For Further Study: Organizing for Instruction _____

MAIN IDEAS

Like some fuzzy "New Age" music, it is often difficult to decide how social studies should adapt to the much-hyped electronic era in which we live. The concept of "media" has been expanded to include a wide array of sources and technologies all competing for space on the classroom shelf. In schools where funds are frequently short and decisions must be made about what to invest in each year, it may be very difficult to decide what to buy and what to use from the many choices available. Furthermore, there is the problem of content. When older media, like print, present knowledge, they are usually organized to inform but may seem boring to a media-saturated young adult. When newer media, like videos and computers, present knowledge, they may be shaped for entertainment rather than reflection. In addition, the newer media have added vast quantities of knowledge and material to the older sources, creating the potential for what I call "information overload." Too much knowledge is being offered and with a speed that may be overwhelming to both the average student and to us teachers.[1] Clearly, there is great classroom potential for the media, but there are also numerous difficulties to overcome. Therefore, the way in which we use media raises a whole host of questions for you, the social studies teacher. A sample of questions about our multimedia world might include the following:

Should traditional teaching materials be supplanted by computer CD-ROM technology?

Is there still a place for reading and lecture? Does the technology change the content?

Should simulations and "edutainment" be an integral part of the curriculum? Or should this "fun stuff" be a supplement only?

Should students learn word and image processing to prepare research reports?

Where do films and documentaries fit into the classroom curriculum? How many times a week should I show a movie, and which ones are most useful?

Are students able to discern media from message, reality from imagination, fact from fiction, history from propaganda?

What should be done with older media like literature and maps? Or newer media like CD-ROM simulations and databases? In developing classroom assignments and activities, what should be the relation between newer and older media forms?

Chapters 14 and 15, which are two parts of the same topic, provide ideas for using media with an overall goal of provoking thought rather than compiling data. The value, motivation, and seductiveness of media are explored within a framework that divides media for social studies into four general categories: print sources; still images, including photographs, paintings, charts, and maps; moving images and sounds; and interactive computer programs. The first part of this chapter concerns words and images drawn from the more traditional "still" media of books and the fine arts. The second part delves into "moving media" represented by newer twentieth-century electronic and film productions, including computer databases and simulations.

Within each group of media, several recurring themes are discussed, including intended audiences, narrator roles, meaning, and message. In addition, the particular capabilities of each type of media are analyzed and debated, with practical suggestions for application to secondary social studies classrooms.

Throughout the chapter, examples are offered to illustrate ways in which media might be used to promote higher order thinking and stimulate student imagination. A bibliography of resources concludes the chapter, keeping in mind that media technology and programs sometimes change very rapidly requiring continuous updating of references.

TO DO

Do you have any favorite historical dramas or films that you use in your classroom, or that you like to watch? If you do, think of two or three examples; if you have not taught yet, then choose two or three that you might like to use. Now decide which of these you consider most trustworthy and closest to the facts, and which you consider most fanciful and farthest from the facts? How do you decide when moviemakers are being "authentic" and faithful to history, and when they are inventing dramatic situations to please a modern audience? Would your rating of a film or drama influence the way your present it to secondary students? How or how not?

PASSIVE AND ACTIVE ROLES IN THE "MEDIATED" SOCIAL STUDIES CLASSROOM

Didactic, Reflective, and Affective Roles

Media invite attention but do not always allow for input from the viewer, listener, or reader. In some instances, analysis is actually diminished or excluded by the emotional nature of the program. Young people, as well as adults, may be drawn into a drama, computer game, or musical event without much demand on their thinking abilities. This is a kind of passive participation, far from an "optimal flow of data" in which the audience may make little or no contribution to the performance.[2] People who are seeking entertainment and have paid a fee are usually interested in enjoyment, conceived largely as a sensual or emotional experience rather than an experience that promotes reflection about ideas. There is, of course, nothing inherently wrong in wishing to be entertained through media, but in a classroom setting there may be confusion between entertainment and educational goals.

RESEARCH REPORT

A review of research of media influence on adolescents by a pediatrician concluded that the media, particularly TV and films, are very influential in subtle ways that promote product demand, commercialization of activities, including sports, and diminish the categories of fiction and nonfiction in adolescent minds. One consequence of this is that many adolescents report "historical images" drawn from TV or Hollywood films rather than historical sources. However, although influential, the media do not seem to have a great deal of direct impact in terms of immediate behavior in that they do not immediately produce spending, violent, or gender-related actions. Rather, the media shape ways of thinking and imagining that have an influence on decisions at later points in time.

SOURCE: Victor Strasburger, *Adolescents and the Media: Medical and Psychological Impact* (Newbury Park, CA: Sage Publications, 1995), pp. 137–49. pp. 137–149.

In a school setting, I would argue that it is educational goals that take priority over entertainment goals. However, entertainment may make a valuable contribution in motivating students to learn content, consider ideas, and practice skills of analysis. The educational and entertainment functions of a lesson must be balanced to serve didactic, reflective, and affective goals. In an age of "docudrama" and "edutainment," this is not always easy but we must try. Particularly in social studies, we must assist students in questioning and reflecting on their media experiences (most especially their film, musical, and computer experiences). Strong drama and striking images may reinforce stereotypes or promote identification with historical times and places, obscuring the evidence on which these were based. Many stories are shrewdly put together by producers and directors to heighten our emotions, or to deliver propaganda, but not necessarily to promote a great deal of critical thinking. For students, the result may be to confuse factual evidence with fictional representation, stereotyping with thoughtfulness. At this point in a student's experience, a more active role is required to really get the full value from media presentations.

TO DO

> Poll your colleagues, asking them how much TV they watch during the week. Which are their favorite programs? Why? Poll at least two groups of secondary school students and ask them the same questions. Tabulate the results and calculate the average amount of TV time spent by each group. What percentage of time is spent over a week watching TV? Which shows are most popular and why? How many of these shows are entertainment and how many are educational? Share your results with others: Are all of the conclusions similar or different?

As teachers, we need to remind students that there are databases and sources that can be used to check out a filmmaker's conception of history, or a game that simulates an historical movement, or a dramatic recreation of the past. We also need to remind students that they need to compare databases with media representations and reflect on the differences and similarities. Further, they need to look into the reasons behind an author's creation, both its overt message and its hidden meanings. The reflective process asks students, with the cooperation and encouragement of their teachers, to collect, compare, and analyze media materials in order to draw conclusions about style, content, and technique, the "semiotics" or signals of communication.[3] We also need to remind students to consider which values are expressed through a media program, how these are being conveyed, and how these affect our own beliefs and attitudes. We all ought to ask ourselves how media have affected the images in our minds and the beliefs we hold about historical events and personalities, for example:

Have the media helped us to feel so happy or so sad that we can scarcely think about why it has influenced us so strongly?

Is the program we all enjoyed true or really a sophisticated piece of propaganda?

Does the program present a balanced or a biased message about an important social problem?

Do we feel offended and upset by what we have heard, seen or played?

Should we do something about the type of media and the type of message we have experienced?

Should we applaud a masterpiece that has touched our deepest emotions and enhanced our most positive values, or worry about its power?

Should we write letters of protest to our local TV or radio station letting them know how offended we are at a recent program, or ignore it as a necessary part of free speech?

By asking questions like these, we can promote didactic, reflective, and affective goals while using and enjoying a wide variety of media in the pursuit of learning. Keep your critical thinking hat on, please!

TO DO

Write a brief essay in which you set up guidelines for interpreting media for a group of American history students. These guidelines should spell out ways in which students can judge the difference between fact and fiction in film. Can they define the difference between a documentary and a Hollywood creation, between a documentary and docudrama, between an oral history recording and an invented theater piece? If you feel really ambitious, select a few problematic films (e.g., *Reds*, *The American Dream*, *Rosie the Riveter*, and *Hoffa*) for the students to watch all or part of and ask them the same questions again.

Narrator and Audience

Two key concepts in understanding media are narrator and audience. As we read, view, or listen to media, many of us lose track of the author or creator and forget all about ourselves as part of an intended or unintended audience. Secondary school students, much like their adult counterparts, frequently suspend judgment when they come into contact with media, particularly well-designed and effective presentations. Enjoyment takes precedence over thoughtfulness on occasion, and the message or meaning of the presentation may be absorbed uncritically. When using media in a social studies classroom, a major way of calling attention to performance goals and meaning is by making the audience conscious of its creators/writers/directors/producers and their roles in designing and authoring the play, film, radio script, or computer program—or whatever the product.

The audience, even when silent and passive, still plays a role in the drama. Audiences soak up experiences, evaluating their knowledge and feelings all the time, even if subconsciously. In an interactive setting, the audience plays a far more conscious role in making decisions, but may lose sight of the narrator by being drawn into the action. So, both passive and active media require varying degrees of reflection about narrator and audience.

WHAT DO YOU THINK?

Some teachers suggest that any media program be preceded by an "advance organizer," or a set of questions that guide note-taking and call attention to events, characters, speeches, sounds, and images as they move along the screen or soundtrack. Do you agree with this concept, or would you prefer to talk about programs after they are completed? Which is preferable: beginning with questions, ending with questions, or both?

Narrator's Role.   The role of narrator/creator is very powerful because the narrator controls both the content of a program or image and the way in which it is presented. In effect, the narrator/author, broadly defined, is the mind(s) shaping audience perception and attitude. Sometimes, narrators create a personal account for their private self, such as a diary, but most often the account or image is created for others. The audience is often a passive participant to the action, interacting by absorbing information, ideas, and values with or without the benefit of judgment. The narrator usually hopes for a positive overall reaction or judgment, but may not permit much independent thinking until after delivering an entire program or performance. Limiting judgment may be a result of the style through which the program is presented, or a consequence of the way the information is selected and managed. Sending large quantities of images, ideas, information, and values at a rapid rate may allow the narrator to capture an audience's view of a person, time, place, or event so that it conforms to their own views, but not necessarily to what historical evidence has to offer. The less knowledge, experience, and commitment an audience has, the more likely they will be drawn to the narrator's conception of the past or present. However, audiences are only partially gullible because members have their own beliefs and feelings, ideas and attitudes against which a story or program must struggle for influence.

RESEARCH REPORT

Beliefs that television presents socially realistic families were found to be directly related to the age and content of programs. High frequencies of entertainment viewing by younger age groups (e.g., cartoons, situation comedies, action and adventure programs) resulted in perceptions of television as more factual; older and less frequent viewers, or viewers of documentaries and news programs, tended to see TV families as invented and less socially realistic. This implies that there is a developmental aspect to TV viewing, as well as different perceptions of content as an influence, specifically along a factual/fantasy spectrum.

SOURCE: A. Dorr, P. Kovaric, and C. Doubleday, "Age and Content Influences on Children's and Adolescents' Perception of the Realism of Television Families," *Journal of Broadcasting and Electronic Media* 34 (1990): 377–97.

Young people still in the process of maturation may be more susceptible to agreeing with a narrator's viewpoint because they do not have much means for questioning their experience. Young people may also reject an experience before giving the narrator the opportunity to send a message to them. Thoughtful consideration of the role of narrator can be easily achieved by providing students with advance organizers in the form of question and study guides, through the give and take of discussion and debate, and by asking them to create their own narratives. The point of raising consciousness or self-consciousness about the role of narrator is to encourage students to develop their own powers of interpretation in relation to others. As students begin to think about narrators, they may see themselves in that role and realize that the story maker is infusing an account with biases, attitudes, emotions, and goals. They may begin to construct their own narration of events, factual or fictional, or both. Information, for better or worse, is edited and filtered through a lens of personal and social values that shape accounts and artistic creations. The sense or awareness of one's role as a creator—whether painter, narrator, photographer, author, inventor, artist, or filmmaker—is exactly what we seek for students in secondary social studies classrooms. A first step toward interpreting media is asking the question, "Who created this product and why?"

LET'S DECIDE

Have you ever seen or shown *The Crucible*, the well-known play about the Salem Witch Trials, as a film, or read it as a play with a group of students? Is the play/film true to history? Why did the playwright, Arthur Miller, decide to use the Puritans as his subject rather than some other topic? And why did he write the drama at the time of the Army/McCarthy hearings in the U.S. Senate? Can we simply apply *The Crucible* to a unit in colonial American history, or can it serve other purposes and raise other questions as well? Discuss this issue with at least three other colleagues and make a note of your decision.

Audience's Role.   The role of audience is a second key concept in approaching and understanding media. Audiences are usually thought of as the consumers of programs and presentations; they are the ones for whom the narrator created a product. An audience can be an individual, a particular group, a large gathering, an assembly, a nation, or even the world. Much depends on the function of the "meeting" and the characteristics of the person or persons in attendance. Some audiences may be seeking a pleasurable experience: satisfaction, entertainment, fun, catharsis. Part may be seeking information and statistics in order to accomplish practical goals. Others may be seeking intellectual stimulation, ideas, and techniques with which they can solve problems. And a number may be seeking personal growth, self-enhancement, and/or a moral vision or uplift of some sort. Every audience reads the signals sent out by communications, but may not be prepared to interpret a program's "semiology," by applying a science or theory of signs and symbols to achieve a deeper understanding.[4]

Many audiences are used to and would prefer to remain relatively passive, absorbing the narrators' or actors' messages while at rest, so to speak. Others would prefer active involvement, making suggestions and shaping both the content and style of a presentation. For example, sports can involve many levels of audience participation from sitting home in front of the TV munching snacks, through applauding, shouting, and advising while attending a live game, to getting out there on the playing field and joining a team as players. The active or passive nature of an audience influences the narrator's creation or product.

Furthermore, the characteristics of an audience also shape the narrator's activities. Audience characteristics include socioeconomic status, social class, and wealth; political and moral beliefs; ethnicity, age, and gender; level of education; and their tastes, customs, preferences, culture, and background history. As you can see, there is quite a bit to determining the size, shape, and features of a narrator's audience. Assumptions, correct or incorrect, may be made on both sides, with narrators constructing media for their image of the intended audience, and the audience constructing an image of what they expect from their narrator, producer, director, artist, or musician.[5] Frequently, age, social class, and economics combine to form a set of expectations such that audiences divide from each other, with some participating in certain media forms that the others will have nothing to do with—by conscious choice. As "old" teachers approaching "young" students, such prejudices can actually be turned around to our favor with surprising effects. For instance, bringing in a currently popular song for students as the basis for a social studies discussion may breach the "generation gap" (if such exists) by including yourself in the student audience. You can also widen the concept of audience by providing students with one of your favorite "old" songs, which can also serve as a springboard for discussing another time and place. Maybe you should not even tell them the song is old! Through media such as songs, especially pairs of old and new, you can share an even exchange in which you can find

out where your students are "coming from" and then you can share where you
are "coming from."

TO DO

Select a current popular song (a student favorite) that you think would make a
great discussion starter. What questions would you ask about it? Now select a
really old song on the same topic as the new one. Think of new questions that
draw analogies between your two selections. Will it work?

Combining Roles.   A last step in thinking about audience and narrator is to put
these two ideas together in considering any work of art, music, literature, history,
or social science. Questions about intended audiences and narrator goals may be
applied to the entire range of media from print materials and paintings through
music and film to computer databases and simulation games. The reason why an
artist painted a picture, as well as the choice of subject, frame, shape, colors, texture, and light, may be important in understanding its effect on us as an audience.
Why a computer programmer chose to incorporate certain kinds of problems, but
not others, in a simulation about moving West in nineteenth century America
raises issues about the game's objectives and the accuracy of its content.

Purpose and style can be important influences on our perceptions. For instance, narrators may control a story, game, or image to a point where everything
is predictable and safe. Audiences can shape a narrator's product so strongly that
it conforms almost totally to their expectations and ideals. Conversely, narrators
may seek to disturb, infuriate, provoke, and stimulate. Audiences may react to
messages and styles by rejecting the proposed values, or by opening their minds
to new attitudes. Some audiences may even encourage new products that break
out of the commonly accepted molds of taste, custom, and tradition. Thus, the
concepts of narrator and audience can be seen as integrated and interactive, a
dyad connected to each other by common goals and methods, woven into a subtle interplay of ideas and shapes, much like the ancient Chinese notion of Yin and
Yang, neither of which can exist without the other in the circle of knowledge and
comprehension.[6]

TO DO

Do you like to stick with tradition or try something new? Get together with a few
classmates and develop your own list of the kinds of media you would like to see
developed for school social studies classes: You pick the courses and topics.

Media, Meaning, and Message   Contrary to Marshal McLuhan's famous dic-
tum that "the medium is the message," this chapter argues that there is always a
message and it may vary greatly from, and even contradict, its method of delivery.[7] In short, the message is not the medium. The media convey messages, some
of them full of meaning, others nearly empty of meaning. A great deal depends
on the purpose or goal of the author/narrator/sponsors of the message. As already
noted, much also depends on the intended audience, real or ideal. For purposes
of our discussion, media may be viewed as conveyors, or delivery systems, for
messages. Messages may be thought of as the information, ideas, images, feelings, and values carried to listeners, viewers, and readers. Meaning ought to be
seen as interactive, with both senders and receivers supplying interpretations,

some often identical, but others sometimes quite different. Meaning may be understood or misinterpreted for many reasons. First, the nature of the message itself is important. For example, informational messages are usually easier to interpret and absorb than messages that require critical thinking. Where to buy pizza can be found in the yellow pages, but no critiques are offered of quality. Furthermore, data and opinions are usually easier to interpret than messages that contain reasoning and deep values. It is easier to choose between "a smoke" or "a snack" without thinking much about long-term consequences of either act. Furthermore, values distort interpretations because of their heavy emotional content, or because of the complexity of sorting out information from reasoning, and reasoning from beliefs. Value-laden messages are, therefore, often most difficult to interpret, and most likely to be misinterpreted by the audience or receiver.

Information in Media.   All messages require interpretation at some level. Messages may be factual or didactic in character, conveying lists, statistics, directories, and references. Even simple lists of facts, dates, names, and places can cause problems in the sense that the audience must have a way of classifying the data in order to store it in long-term memory. Classifying, sorting, organizing, categorizing, and labeling data is a way of giving meaning to what would otherwise be a confusing mass of largely useless information. By the act of classifying, we give meaning to our facts. Of course, classifications can also lead to trouble if the categories are fuzzy, overlap, or contain biases. For instance, the current debate about what is "Western" civilization often focuses on definitions that are either too rigid or too loose. Must we always begin with the ancient Greeks? What of the Hebrews, the Sumerians, the Hittites? Can none of these be considered "Western"? Just what is "Western" and what is "Eastern" or "non-Western"? Thus, one major type of message involves definitions that are frequently given meaning through classifying and categorizing. In effect, data is stored under labels that are definitions or terms that can be applied to new information, but may collapse as new findings come to light or new problems arise.

LET'S DECIDE

Media come with labels people use to define their tastes and identities. Research definitions in music: country and western, rock and roll, soft rock, hard rock, heavy metal, soul, world beat, classical, jazz, blues, and so on. Which of these categories have meaning? Ask a group of students or peers, or both, to define each category and decide on a perfect example of each.

Reflection in Media.   Messages may also be intellectual or "reflective," that is, aimed at our reasoning ability. These messages offer explanations, logic, and evidence that help us understand phenomena, places, people, and events. Although data is still very important, meaning is derived from some type of formal or informal logic through which we begin to understand correlation's, causes, and consequences. We begin to see how events are connected, which steps lead to a conclusion, and which changes produce an effect. For instance, in economics we may learn that low supplies of a product coupled with high demand will cause prices to rise. We can apply this rule to wheat, corn, rice, orange juice, computer chips, basketball tickets, almost anything that happens in a market system. Meaning depends on how well supply and demand are interpreted in relation to price. Note that messages involving reasoning assume that the audience already has a grasp of basic definitions (not always so), and that data is available for interpretation (often absent, biased, or partial). Thus, reflective messages are usually more difficult to interpret than didactic messages, requiring more work by an audience.

TO DO

> Select two advertisements, autos, refrigerators, CD players, and check out the line of reasoning (if any) used to sell the product. Is the appeal to price, efficiency, durability, or other irrational factors? How is meaning conveyed?

Finally, messages might be persuasive and polemical, giving positions on an issue. These messages may be termed 'value," or "affective," messages. Most are charged, either negatively or positively. Affective messages send data, reasons, and values to audiences, intending to change their attitudes toward a given problem or issue that is under discussion within society. These types of messages assist us in understanding which "positions" or "stands" a narrator is taking on a subject, and which arguments and evidence support that view. A sense of meaning grows out of recognition for a narrator's point of view, feelings, and the reasons behind it. Meaning is enhanced if we are able to compare the narrator's point of view with others, and with our own, if we have one; meaning may be diminished if we or the narrator have very strong feelings on a subject, and use technical or ideological language.[8] Strong feelings on either or both sides may block our understanding of the message, or lead to serious misinterpretations. Ideology often leads to expressions and terms that only the "initiated" understand. Folk wisdom has noted that the deepest understanding results from being able to empathize with our enemies. Of course, this is easier said than done, and requires breaking away from thinking in terms of us versus them. Views, however, do not have to be seen as being in opposition. Views may express alternatives, a continuum of opinions and beliefs, or opposition on a subject. Many variations, of which two-sides is just one possibility, may exist in affective messages and how these are received by an audience.

TO DO

> Pick any issue or controversy of interest to you and then seek out examples of what the opposition thinks. Force yourself to study this material, comparing it to the position you favor. Have you changed your attitude toward the other side as a result? When planning a lesson on the topic, will you present both sides fairly, or do you find yourself giving more time and attention to those you favor? Watch out!

Values in Media.   Explicitly or implicitly, affective messages promote decision making by an audience. Messages deeply rooted in social and personal values may present one side of a problem using only selected facts and a narrow line of reasoning to promote a decision. Even the simplest sort of affective message—"Buy this!"—implies a host of underlying facts, reasons, and values.

Values are sent to be received and believed. Sometimes these messages impact positively or negatively on peoples' views of each other as well as how they think about products.[9] Values being expressed may range from advertisements asking you to purchase a product to demands for immediate action as part of an interest group on a serious social issue. Some messages may be informational sales pitches, others may be blatant political propaganda,.simple slogans and common clichés, or carefully polished arguments. For example, a powerful and artistic film can achieve an emotional hold on an audience through a clever combination of images, action, characters, and sounds. To give meaning to affective messages and reach a satisfactory decision, a receiver must be wary of both the narrator's purposes and methods, sorting and weighing facts, judging arguments and emotions. The "facts" offered by a narrator always (can we find time for this?) need to be checked out against other sources. The reasoning employed by the narrator needs to be carefully and critically evaluated for logic and fairness. Public criteria ought to be applied to value messages. Otherwise, our beliefs will be easily swayed by media, and we might wind up jumping to conclusions that collapse at the first argument or test.

Thus, messages may be viewed as didactic, reflective, or affective, or a combination of all three processes. Meaning is conveyed through the messages sent out to an audience, but the audience may project its own interpretation on the message and derive a new meaning from it, one not originally intended. Meaning and message is, therefore, an interactive two-way street, in which both senders and receivers share in constructing interpretations, and these interpretations are seldom neutral. Nearly all media messages, even nonsense, express or imply a message to the audience, and we must teach students how to control, analyze, interpret, and act on each experience. We should also promote constructive criticism of media as a tool for social studies students to employ in shaping the content and methods used by media producers to influence them.

TO DO

Find a newspaper or magazine advertisement that really got your attention, and then consider these questions as you carefully look it over:

What was its purpose? What images is it sending to you, and to the audience? For which audience is it intended? Do you regard the ad as effective or ineffective and why? Does the ad promote "reason" or choice, or does it draw you to it for its image and feeling?

IN THE MIND'S EYE: PRINT MEDIA FOR SOCIAL STUDIES

Fiction and Nonfiction: Literature, News, and Views

Print media are the basic diet of social studies, and of most other subjects as well. Print media includes all types of messages expressed in words on pages that appear in a variety of formats. These formats may include newspapers, journals, magazines, pamphlets, books, and so forth. The reader usually holds the pages and scans them for information, feelings, reasons, and judgments. Some formats encourage more personal involvement and deeper study; others encourage rapid viewing and quick decisions. A traditional approach to what we read has been to distinguish between fiction and nonfiction.[10] Fiction usually encompasses stories, novels, and folktales that are viewed as products of the imagination. The narrator or author is seen as the key inventor of a story that does not require proof. A major goal of fiction is to entertain and engage our interest in storytelling. Nonfiction usually encompasses biographies, autobiographies, news stories, and scholarly studies that are viewed as products of observation, analysis, and research. A major goal is to inform and educate the reader as truthfully as possible about people, places, and events. The author or narrator in the case of nonfiction is seen as a compiler and reporter who must base all conclusions on 'real' sources.

The concepts of fiction and nonfiction are used to determine genres and to classify print media into works of imagination and works of analysis. For the purposes of social studies education, however, this neat and clean distinction tends to cause problems. First, there is the problem of deciding what is real and what is imagined, fact or opinion. A work of imagination, for instance, is a product of a particular time, place, and culture just as much as a work of nonfiction. In modern media, for example, there is a trend to obscure the difference between art and social science by inventing new fusions like "manufactured news" and docudramas.[11] Are these basically reports that are somewhat dramatized or dramas based on factual reporting?

Second, authors or narrators of both fictional and nonfictional works have goals and intentions that shape the content and the message they are trying to convey. In other words, all writers of print media hold values and beliefs about society, and these ideas are expressed in their works whether or not they are acknowledged. Many well-known and beloved novelists, for instance, use their art to promote social causes or to attack social problems. Sometimes messages are hidden, and at other times they are argued forthrightly. Many nonfictional works can also suffer from a heavy infusion of good or bad intentions, such as biographies that seek either to enshrine or satirize a great personality. Social scientists and historians, as serious scholars, generally explain their intentions, methods, and positions to make clear their values from the beginning so a reader will know where they are coming from, and judge their research accordingly. However, the arts and the media may suppress their intentions or biases in favor of subtly communicating social and business messages.[12]

Third, authors/narrators must draw on historical sources for both inspiration and scholarship, for news and for views. These works are supposed to be based on evidence, proof, and verification. We should be able to check details against other sources, to verify or reject the basic information used to develop arguments and interpretations. In some cases, the authors of historical novels may have done as much or better historical research than their professional counterparts, and they may be better at conjuring up an image than a historian. A few may even share their databases with the reader. In other cases, historians or social scientists may write so well, and use such charming similes and metaphors, that interpretations of data become as entertaining and emotionally satisfying as the efforts of their literary cousins. Thus, lines of demarcation between genres blur.

Works of nonfiction are supposed to prove their cases based on identifiable sources of knowledge and logical argument. Fictional works are not usually held to this standard. This is a reason for teaching research skills: Students must understand that good research must be based on references, sources, footnotes, and in short, on a well-developed bibliography of supporting material. Otherwise, why believe what an author says or tells you about. In a work of fiction, by contrast, no such constraints are necessary; history can be made and remade, told and retold, to make a point, dramatize an event, or preach a moral message. However, even a writer of fiction must still follow rules of plausibility, consistency, and context if the work is to make sense.

TO DO

An excellent example of a young adult fiction and nonfiction writer who bases his work on solid historical evidence is Milton Meltzer, author of many works of social history. Ranging across a wide variety of topics and time periods, Meltzer often includes a discussion of sources for students at the conclusion of a book, including works of fiction. Providing primary sources helps raise student consciousness about how interpretations are constructed by an author based on documents and diaries (e.g., the novel *Underground Man*, which is a story about the smuggling of slaves to the North before the Civil War began through an "underground" network.

Select a work of fiction or fact by Meltzer and write your own book review noting its purpose, style, organization, characters, and devotion to historical sources. Be critical!

Within social studies teaching, it seems that the vital difference between fiction and nonfiction is the degree and quality of proof that is offered. Standards or criteria for excellence may vary between literature and social science, between poetry and history. However, any work of art or social science that has a social purpose can be judged on the basis of its devotion to providing solid evidence to back up assertions and conclusions. For social studies, particularly in the case of the historical component, both fiction and nonfiction can be utilized to illustrate the past and bring it to life. Many important facts can be learned from works of fiction, and many important values can be gleaned from works of nonfiction. As teachers we need to build student awareness of author intention and the quality and quantity of research in any work of print media, whether literature or newspaper reporting, poetic or scholarly. The two categories of fiction and nonfiction can be blended together to weave a rich tapestry for students about times and places, simultaneously inviting their interests and their intellects.

WHAT DO YOU THINK?

Does a work of fiction provide historical insights? Do works of imagination and invention offer clues to the values and beliefs of other times and places? Do stories tell something about the time and place and culture that produced them? Make a list of books (i.e., novels, biographies, or autobiographies) you have read that are vivid in your memory. Write down a few reasons why you think these books created strong impressions in your mind.

Primary Sources

Primary sources are historical documents or written accounts narrated by first-hand witnesses (as far as we can tell) to the events described. These works are most often expressed as straightforward narratives (i.e., telling what happened from the observer's point of view). Authors are reporting or commenting on the events of their day, sometimes with an eye to history and at other times simply as a record of events. Words are usually managed primarily to convey a clear, well-organized message to the reader in the form of description and/or argument. There may, of course, be a point of view built into the author's commentary, and this must be taken into account when shaping our own insights. Sources that provide specific details of a person, place, or event that can be cross-checked against others are generally more trustworthy than those from a single eyewitness. In addition, the more consistent, comprehensible, and unbiased the eyewitness's account, the greater the reliability of the description, report, or argument. The author may be "selling" a particular interpretation of events that the reader has to separate from the reported facts. This can be quite difficult if there are no other witnesses available at the time. Thus, teachers can help students "test for truth" based on details, consistency, and author bias.[13] Basic standards of judgment rest on a source's credibility and trustworthiness, in other words, the degree to which an author is reliable (fits with what we know from other sources) and valid (appears logical and reasonable).

Literary Sources

Literary sources are works of imagination—fiction writing if you will—that represent an author's view of people, places, and events. These works of imagination are expressed in a personal artistic style designed to make a point or engender a feeling. Words are usually managed primarily to convey emotions and values through characters, signs, and symbols as well as through descriptions and argument. "Believability" in fictional writing generally arises from the way in which the literature portrays characters, develops plots, and expresses concepts in words.

The consistency of setting, characters, storyline, plot, and words with the author's intentions and artistic style offer a way of assessing works of imagination. The skill with which authors achieve artistic and emotional goals through their story, drama, or poem may be judged by esthetic and storytelling criteria. The words and styles in which the story is told may themselves provide historical information about standards for beauty and insights into what people saw as entertaining or pleasing. In addition to internal criteria, there are external historical criteria that test works of art against other works or precedents, and against the writing standards of a particular time, place, and culture. In the case of historical novels or recreations of the past, there are also questions about faithfulness to sources, and realism in depicting times past.

Scholarly Sources

Scholarly sources are works of research and criticism in which both primary and literary sources are summarized, analyzed, and judged. Authors usually develop hypotheses or theories about people, places, and events based on a thorough review of available evidence, footnoting throughout to support their interpretations. Assumptions are identified as much as possible, and research methods are laid out in detail for the reader to use in judging conclusions. In effect, scholars demonstrate "proof" by publicly displaying both their sources and their techniques or rules for using their data.

Readers are invited to use their judgment throughout a scholarly work by understanding the author's goals and theories, analyzing supporting data, reviewing research methods, and evaluating conclusions based on clearly established criteria. Scholarly works are not often viewed as "pleasure reading" because they require attention to the way in which details support a chain of reasoning on a subject. Research can be complex and sometimes confusing because theory, goals, data, methods, and conclusions must all be factored into the final decision: to accept or reject the scholar's results. But it is through research that we can decide which sources, documents, news reports, and literature are most accurate, trustworthy, believable, beautiful, or emotionally satisfying. Where primary sources draw you into an eyewitness's experience and literature draws you into an imaginative experience, scholarship takes you into the realm of critical thinking by looking for proof and checking the evidence.

Current Events/News Sources

Print news sources are works of "instant" reporting about current events. With worldwide electronic media well-developed, news reports are faster and more efficiently distributed than at any time in history. The author (reporter) may be in the field at the time of the report or at a base of operations when filing the story. News is a form of direct eyewitness document for classroom purposes, but presents some ordinary and some special problems. "Stories" suffer from all of the problems that vex historical documents, including accuracy, corroboration, and bias. But news also presents difficulties that historical documents generally do not. News is fast-moving, developing every day, and often "political," whereas documents may be studied at leisure, researched, checked, and revisited.[14] News is almost instantaneous as we approach the twenty-first century, and may offer little or no clear research basis.

RESEARCH REPORT

A series of five studies of television reporting of political and social news by S. Iyengar demonstrated that commonly used brief sound and image "bites," termed *episodic framing* by the authors, tended to provide low levels of information for viewers while separating issues into very narrow unconnected stories or episodes. The overall TV reporting also seldom offered any deep analysis or solutions to the problems conveyed to those watching. The study concludes by noting that "the present work suggests that television news not only fails as a mirror of political reality, but also operates in a systematic fashion to shape viewers' attributes of responsibility for political affairs in a way that undermines the democratic norm of electoral responsibility."

SOURCE: S. Iyengar, *Is Anyone Responsible?: How Television Frames Political Issues* (Chicago: University of Chicago Press, 1991), pp. 140–41.

Because sources may be unclear or omitted, news reports are difficult to check or analyze, except on the basis of plausibility. Furthermore, news reporters belong to nations and cultures whose attitudes shape their view of the world adding, or filtering out items important to other peoples and places. In teaching a news report, we must ask if the reporter is giving us an accurate list of facts that can be compared to other accounts, and is free from an ideology or prejudiced viewpoint. All people have deeply held convictions and emotions, and these may color their descriptions of events. Interpretations may be shaped by convictions and feelings so that the same set of facts can be reported in very different ways. Sometimes, certain details that may be important are omitted; at other times, certain important details are included. We might also ask if the author's style and wording are affecting our interpretation of events.

All writing, fiction and nonfiction, follows some sort of style, and this attention to words can easily influence our thinking about a person, place, or event. Furthermore, reporters and editors may consciously or subconsciously combine descriptive reports with "loaded" words that make it hard for the reader to separate story from interpretation. Many reporters explain their purposes to readers, but many leave only subtle clues about their views. The "explainers" are usually seen as more trustworthy, particularly in these days of rapid communication. Thus, it is vitally important that you and your students do not take news or current events reports at face value. "All the news that's fit to print" may contain biases, inaccuracies, and hearsay accounts that raise questions about believability. News accounts, like other print media in social studies, must be analyzed and evaluated in much the same manner as documents from the past, but with extra care and attention to content and style.

SAMPLE LESSON PLAN

Find a copy of *World News*, which reprints cartoons and articles from foreign newspapers and journals on current topics. *World News* is particularly useful for looking at events from other perspectives (i.e., seeing the world and ourselves in foreign eyes). Viewpoints can be quite similar to our own or startlingly different, offering students discussion and debate opportunities as well as comparisons with local U.S. newspaper accounts (e.g., a recently translated article).

"A Shock Felt 'Round the World"

LONDON. *The Guardian* (liberal): Anyone who imagines that normal politics will be resumed after Diana's funeral is in for a shock. Like a landscape stilled by lightning, the country revealed by the public response to her death appears sharp and unfamiliar to the eye.... It is not a country that reveres traditional values. Still less does it defer to any authority that seeks to impose them. It has accepted the challenge of modern times, which is the opportunity to invent one's life for oneself, and its corollary, the obligation to show sympathy for those who come to grief through the absence of choice. It sees its own insecurities in the lives of those who have been excluded from the mainstream—gays, ethnic minorities, the homeless.... In mourning the Princess of Wales the country honors the memory of someone whom circumstances forced to author her own life and who went on to claim that freedom for others.

—John Gray

PARIS *Le Monde* (liberal): This tragic death should prompt us to ask ourselves the question: Has our outlook on women and their love lives really changed all that much since the days of Flaubert?.... The media (but also the conversations of very respectable people) take a keener interest in the sexual frolics of a female celebrity because women's love life is subject to scrutiny—as if society enjoyed a guardianship over them ..., as if nothing had changed since the days when everyone in the village know what you were up to.

—Nadia Kouri-Dagher

NEW DELHI *Times of India* (conservative): The prurient interest in the private lives of public personalities like Diana ... is a hunger that feeds on itself, growing more voracious in the process till it consumes the object of its morbid desire. The unseemly and disproportionate publicity that Diana so long tried to flee has caught up with a vengeance to show that even death is no insurance against the invasion of privacy. This is the final twist of the knife.

NAIROBI *East African* (independent weekly): Mainstream news organizations have sought desperately to distance themselves from the rat pack of ruthless snappers who hound and harass celebrities. Their position is an unconvincing one. While they may not send their own staffers on high-speed car chases, many up-market newspapers and magazines do regularly buy and publish celebrity photos, ensuring a continued market for images to assuage the obsession of the public with the lives of the rich and famous.

CAIRO *Al-Ahram Weekly* (semi-official): The suggestion that Diana was murdered by the British secret service to prevent her from marrying an Arab and inflaming British public opinion if, at some time in the future, he were to become the king's stepfather, received considerable credit in Egypt and the rest of the Arab world. Conspiracy theories are common currency in the Arab world, where many people have difficulty accepting that accidents ... can just happen. Of course, no matter how marked the animosity between Mohamed al-Fayed and the British royal family, it is out of the question that it could have prompted a plan to eliminate Dodi in a fashion worthy of Saddam Hussein.

—Salama A. Salama

MADRID *El País* (liberal): Self-monitoring—rather than new legal provisions that might prove ineffective or open cracks in freedom of expression—seems the reasonable way to curb or roll back a trend toward media meddling.... But journalists and the news media for which they work must show that they are ready for it before another senseless accident again turns them into scapegoats.

SOURCE: *World Press Review* (November 1997), p. 14.

Decide on at least three or four lesson plans using this type of world news material with your world or global studies or government or civics classes.

STILL LIFE WITH MEANING: READING IMAGES FROM PAST AND PRESENT

Reality and Imagination

Social studies can be greatly enriched by art and photography to teach about past and present. As defined in this chapter, art may be viewed broadly as including objects, artifacts, maps, charts, graphs, paintings, sculpture, and other "still" nonmoving media. Images or pictures with messages and meanings open up many possibilities for classroom interpretation and discussion.

Images can be very powerful tools to enhance student attention and interest. Pictures are inherently attractive to our sense of sight, and sometimes touch and hearing as well. "Still" images have several advantages, the first of which is that they do not move and can therefore be studied carefully and in great detail. Of course, you need ideas and techniques for making sense of images, but such methods are readily available for classroom use. Second, still images also have the advantage of providing insights into places and cultures that words cannot easily convey. Students can immerse themselves in another time and place through viewing paintings, sculptures, artifacts, and photographs.[15] These pictures put "flesh on the bones" of history and life, offering readers, especially poorer ones, the potential for insights that may be difficult to obtain from written sources. Third, still images have the advantage of being dramatic and colorful in ways that many historical documents and scholarly works are not. Pictures of people, places, and events develop in our minds and those of our students from many sources. Some sources for these pictures in the mind may help our understanding of human behavior, but other sources may promote stereotypes or inaccurate views.

Thus, the very advantages of images also create disadvantages as well. The staticity, power, and drama of images may, if uncritically accepted, influence our interpretations of events and lead to questionable or false conclusions. In some cases, images are so powerful that they have become icons of the past, clichés that we fail to take seriously after time has passed, and need reinterpretation.[16] Therefore, like print media, images must be viewed, understood, analyzed, and interpreted. Interpretations are aided by adding other materials—written, visual, or auditory—to check our conclusions. Visuals can also be compared and contrasted to other images as ways of building hypotheses and strengthening conclusions. In other words, a sample of images can give us a range of evidence to draw from that a single image simply can not provide. Just as we need two or more eyewitnesses to corroborate an event, we also need many images to support an interpretation.

Images may be taken from the works of artists and from the works of photographers. It is easy to think of art as corresponding to fiction writing and photography to non-fiction, but here we encounter several difficult problems. Photography may be just as "artistic" as painting because the creators of both media have their own styles and purposes. Artists and photographers are using reality and precedent as a base, a source of inspiration, giving us a managed report or visual invention of past, present, or future.[17] Either may use the data they collect in ways that are realistic or imaginative, literal or figurative, or a mixture of both. Artista are usually seen as having more freedom to use their imagination than a photographer. But as electronic and photographic technology develop, the potential for imagination grows in both media. A painted or a photographed portrait, for example, may convey how someone looks, but may also be subtly shaded, controlled, colored, and posed to create a particular feeling about the character. The image might suggest social status, personality, or values, giving us clues to interpret. Sometimes, this creation is so clever that we lose consciousness that we are being manipulated by the author/artist for a purpose. Even amateur painters and photographers convey feelings and send messages, whether purposely or inadvertently, through their lenses and drawings.

SAMPLE LESSON PLAN

Photographs can be very striking, but sometimes we forget to ask if they were "natural" or posed for that purpose. Because pictures may lead us to important conclusions about events, the authenticity of a photograph may be a serious issue. In the lesson shown, the curriculum developer has used a photograph from World War I to raise questions about historical evidence. Read this lesson and discuss it with a colleague: Are the teacher's questions thought-provoking? Could the same or similar questions be asked of other pictures and photos? Which are the key problems posed by the curriculum writer? Could you add a new wrinkle of your own to this gory picture.

Figure 14.1   *SOURCE*: Chris Hinton, *What Is Evidence?* (London: John Murray Ltd., 1990).

Therefore, we must employ images carefully—whether painted, sculpted, or photographed—in drawing conclusions about people, times, and places. We must remember, and remind our students to remember, that images were created to serve some purpose, and have probably been shaped, cut, or styled in ways designed to influence our attitudes and conclusions. Art and photography are marvelous ways of enhancing our historical understanding, but must also be viewed as evidence that is open to interpretation and revision. Once we know several methods for thinking about images, we can add these to our storehouse of critical techniques, tying our pictures and photographs to documents and scholarly works in order to build a more complete sense of peoples and places.

Maps, Charts, and Graphs

Maps, charts, and graphs are rich and compact sources of data for social studies. Often, a map or chart may condense a large amount of information into a small space and provide material for numerous student hypotheses and interpretations. Each map, chart, or graph is also a complex visualization representing many observations and a great deal of research. Maps, for example, can communicate enormous amounts of data on one sheet, including settlement patterns, topography, weather, climate, environment, political boundaries, and economics. Social studies students need to be comfortable with maps and charts because these are part of daily life, as well as of academic study. Statistics and maps are frequently offered as evidence in support of assertions, or to attack claims.[18] Increasingly in the modern world, publishers, newspaper columnists, and political leaders employ maps, charts, and graphs to make points with the public. There is an assumption that the public can comprehend a chart used in a presentation, but this may be questionable. Furthermore, charts and graphs, in particular, have an aura of truth about them. A table of figures may be very impressive in an argument, and readily accepted by viewers and readers, without much criticism. This is an important role for social studies instruction: Teach students how to critically read and interpret rich, condensed visual representations, statistics, charts, graphs, tables, figures, and maps.

The very richness and complexity of maps, graphs, and charts is also a problem for many teachers and students because they must make sense of numbers, signs, and symbols to interpret information. The more abstract and symbolic a visual representation is, the longer it takes most students to understand. Conversely, the more realistic and concrete the visual representation, the easier it is to understand. Abstractness versus concreteness can be used as two poles of a sliding scale to predict probable difficulty levels for students. For instance, an "easy" map might contain only topographic information (e.g., mountains, rivers, plains, forests) as shown in a photograph or in lifelike symbols. A "difficult" map might include three, four, or five major factors with political boundaries crossing topographic colors, and weather patterns in isobars running across the face of the landscape. This multifaceted map is very "busy" and may confuse a large percentage of students, particularly those beginning secondary school or those with poor reading skills. To interpret a complex map takes time and attention, but the rewards are great because, in the process, students will extract much information and learn how to read a map, drawing useful conclusions in the process.[19] Hopefully, learning how to read a map will transfer to other maps and charts later on, making the student more comfortable dealing with abstract visual representations of information.

One way of drawing students into the process of interpreting maps and charts is to assist them in constructing a visual representation of their own. You could provide students with statistical information to convert into a table by hand, or you could provide them with the results of a study that they might convert into bar, pie, or line graphs if a computer is convenient. If you are more ambitious, you could ask students to draw their own maps, using an agreed on, common symbol system, key, or legend (as it is called in geography). An aerial photograph of a region, for instance, might serve as the basis for this mapping exercise. At the beginning, students ought to be directed to draw maps that are realistic, with a tree symbol standing for a forest of 20 square miles, and a few snow-capped little mountains standing for a chain. Later these can be shown as green shadings and blue colors. As students engage in this activity they should understand the twin concepts of correspondence and representation: how symbols serve as a metaphors for reality.

SAMPLE LESSON PLAN

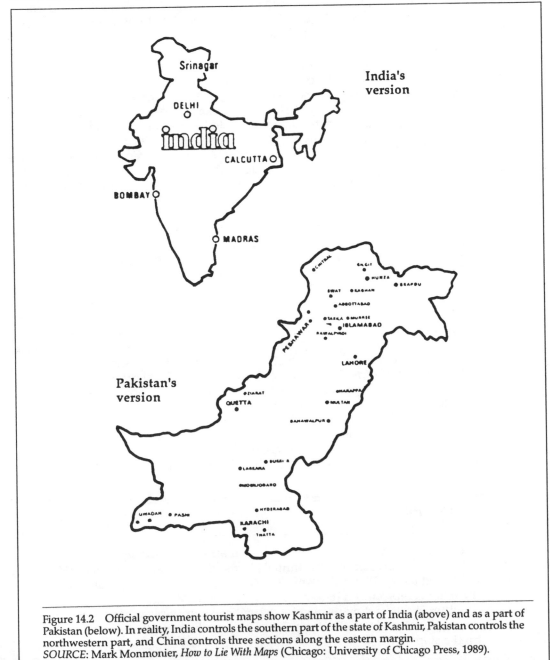

Figure 14.2   Official government tourist maps show Kashmir as a part of India (above) and as a part of Pakistan (below). In reality, India controls the southern part of the state of Kashmir, Pakistan controls the northwestern part, and China controls three sections along the eastern margin.
SOURCE: Mark Monmonier, *How to Lie With Maps* (Chicago: University of Chicago Press, 1989).

Once students have acquired a grasp of the purpose and structure of maps (or charts and graphs and tables), they can move on to more abstract representations. You might, for example, give weather data for a place, and ask them to use symbols to demonstrate rainfall, temperature, and seasonal patterns. Political boundaries, capitals, or voting affiliations could also serve as sources of information for placement on maps, with students following tradition or devising their own methods of representation. Capitals might be depicted as small public buildings, or as circles with stars inside, or as state flags, or whatever reasonable solution students decide on. A major question for teachers is whether or not maps clearly communicate the desired information. Each map, graph, or chart-making exercise ought to strengthen and extend student understanding of these valuable communication devices, and improve their interpretation skills inside and outside the classroom.

A second way of drawing students to the world of mapping and graphing is through controversy. Many students and citizens tend to view statistical presentations and maps as basically correct and factual and because numbers are seen as proof for claims, many people tend not to ask questions when they should.[20] Maps, too, are pretty much accepted "as is," although some may be distorted. Most presentations try to be as faithful to the data as possible, but many take considerable liberties with the presentation. Some map makers manipulate the data to support or enhance a claim to land; others may do so for economic reasons. In effect, these presentations seek to capture your attention using eye-catching representations that are easy to understand but exaggerated. The information may even be basically correct and honest, but the way in which it is shown aims at dramatic effect (e.g., maps printed in strong, bright colors, charts jazzed up with shadow effects, graphs shown as symbolic pies or huge bars). To be fair to both propagandists and artists, there are a good number of students around who need to be awakened!

Other presentations distort the data to suit their own interests, even to the extent of inventing information, or displaying it in a misleading way. These types of presentations are generally propagandistic in nature. Information is provided mainly as a vehicle to get across a point of view, or explain a particular position on an issue. The authors or artists behind such propaganda have an "ax to grind" (i.e., a viewpoint they want readers to adopt). For instance, most advertisers are more interested in persuasion than conveying information. Product and political advertisements are almost automatically suspect, whatever their style, message, and content. Of course, not all advertisements or political campaigns are propaganda; many can be quite informative, with a point of view. To defend against bias, teachers can ask students to rank or rate visuals based on such criteria as honesty, fairness, style, and evidence or reasoning. Involving students in studying, understanding, debating, and criticizing visual representations reinforces their chart, graph, and map reading skills, and teaches them to look for the values and goals that direct even the most objective materials.

WHAT DO YOU THINK?

Many charts and maps are basically informational. An example of very valuable references would be the annual charts of social and economic statistics published by the World Bank or *The State of the World* series. A selection from the latter is reproduced here.

Other charts and maps may be dramatic. An example of drama would be the maps created for the *State of the World Atlas*, which may have a point of view on the statistics.*

Look at the chart below. Which nations spend most on arms? Why? Are the biggest spenders always the most populous or richest countries? Why or why not?

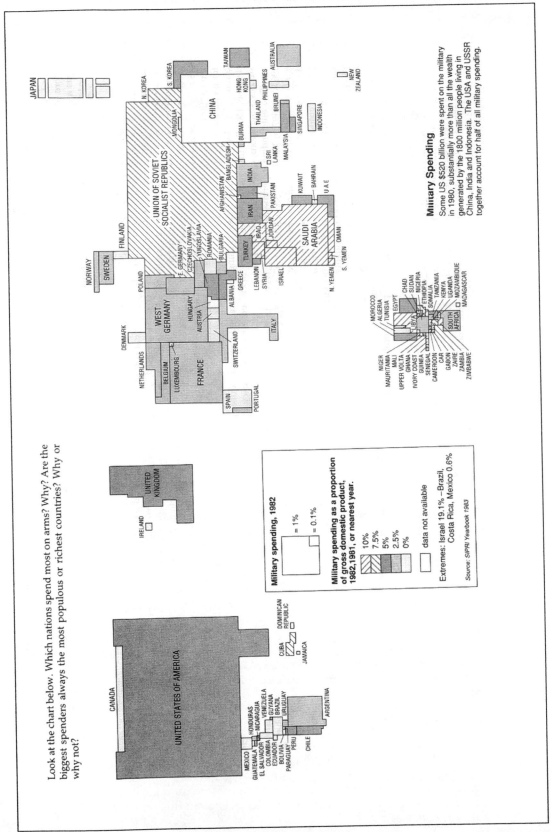

Military Spending

Some US $520 billion were spent on the military in 1980, substantially more than all the wealth generated by the 1800 million people living in China, India and Indonesia. The USA and USSR together account for half of all military spending.

Military spending, 1982

☐ = 1%
▫ = 0.1%

Military spending as a proportion of gross domestic product, 1982, 1981, or nearest year.

- 10%
- 7.5%
- 5%
- 2.5%
- 0%
- ☐ data not available

Extremes: Israel 19.1% – Brazil, Costa Rica, Mexico 0.6%

Source: SIPRI Yearbook 1983

The Fine Arts

The fine arts can be a marvelous addition to a social studies lesson, providing direct historical evidence of a time and place, and visual identification with the past. In other words, paintings, sculptures, artifacts, and decorative pieces can be objects of inquiry in their own right, as well as complement written narratives. A first major value of the fine arts for social studies is its rich depiction of historical figures and peoples from nearly every part of the globe and from nearly every historical period, Paleolithic times to the present. A second major value of the fine arts is as an authentic expression of past and present values, permitting us insights into cultures, personalities, events, social classes, and spiritual beliefs expressed by artists of all types ranging from "folk" craftspeople to the elite personnel of royal courts. A third major value derives from art as artifact: art as an expression of the objects and decorations people used to enhance and embellish their daily lives at home, work, play, or table, giving us intimate knowledge of lifestyles. The rich and famous, the ordinary and average, and sometimes even the poor and humble seem more human to us after getting a look at the way they were represented by artists of the time.

Historical Figures. Paintings of historical figures, for example, are rich sources of insight into past eras. Portraits encourage discussion of personality and artistic style, including pose, dress, ornament, facial expression, placement, mood, and color scheme. Students are also able to put a face to a name, giving historical personalities more meaning and a clearer identity. Art communicates context in ways that words may not be able to accomplish. For instance, it is one thing for a teacher to tell a class about Napoleon Bonaparte's achievements and downfall, but quite another to see paintings of Napoleon as revolutionary (i.e., citizen, general, first consul, and then Emperor). These evoke a style and grandeur that the words alone may not be able to get across to secondary school young people. Agreed?

Depictions of historical figures such as Columbus also sometimes raise questions of authenticity that are worth talking about in these days of instant images.[21] We often take for granted that pictures in books are from the time and place we are studying, but that is not always true. Students who have an appreciation for art and an understanding of styles may be able to detect anachronisms when these appear. For example, nearly every history textbook includes a picture of Christopher Columbus, but none are authentic because they were all painted after his death. Some texts admit to this lack of a contemporary painting of Columbus, whereas others say nothing at all about their sources. Students who want to discover more about how Columbus was portrayed could work together to research historical paintings, collecting examples, carefully recording dates and artists, for contrast or comparison. They might discover that his features and dress vary considerably depending on the artist's origin. Italian, Spanish, German, and other portraits depict Columbus in poses and dress that suit that particular culture's tastes. A study of Columbus portraits, as suggested, would offer an opportunity to discuss the process of historical research as well as the era of European exploration.

SAMPLE LESSON PLAN

Two pictures of Admiral Perry can be used to illustrate the way historical personalities can be represented. One picture is a photograph (Fig. 14.4), and the other is a Japanese artist's idea of Perry's looks (Fig. 14.5). Ask students to compare and contrast the two images, deciding which is most real and which is least real, which is most positive and which is most negative, and which is a product of Perry's own culture and which is from another cultural viewpoint. After discussing these questions, call on volunteers to explain their insights, giving reasons for conclusions.

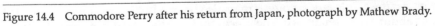
Figure 14.4   Commodore Perry after his return from Japan, photograph by Mathew Brady.

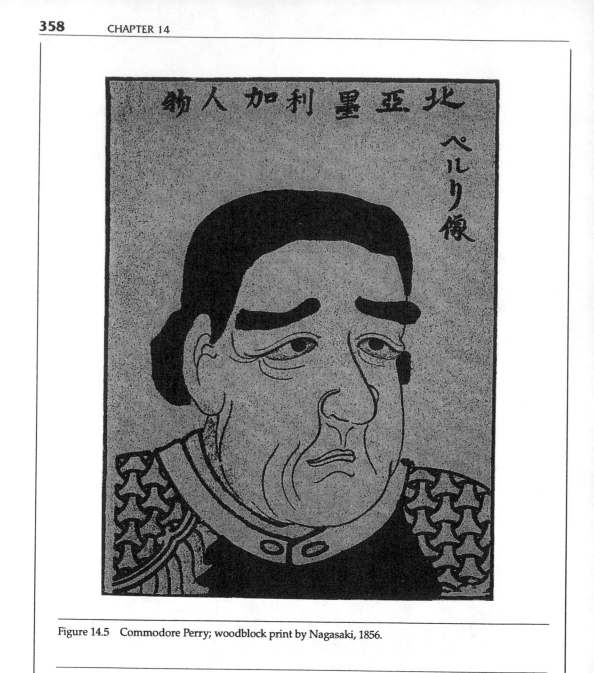

北亞墨利加人物

ペルリ像

Figure 14.5   Commodore Perry; woodblock print by Nagasaki, 1856.

SOURCE: "Discovering the West: Perry's Visit to Japan" (SPICE, 1987).

Art as Artifact.   Many art pieces may also be used as archeological artifacts that tell us about a time and place. The pieces may be discussed from an esthetic point of view involving color, texture, shape, size, structure, and so forth, but also in terms of symbolic meaning, practical function, status, economic well-being, and possibly political and cultural values. Coins, for instance, offer many possibilities for discussion both for their design and their symbolic messages. You could do something as simple as ask students to pull a U.S. quarter out of their pockets and decode all of its signs and symbols. (Do you know the origins of the Eagle image and meaning of the object the eagle is holding in its claws?). You could go future and set up a comparison of several Roman, Medieval, and modern coins, or European and Asian coins, noting similarities and differences in the artistic design and the messages on both sides. You could also look at a wide variety of other artistic products, such as vases and urns (ancient Greek vases make great discussion items), sculptures and statues (Remington's work is an exciting introduction to the Wild West), or arms and armor (Medieval European, Samurai, and Islamic outfits stimulate interesting comparisons). Often, museums and galleries have teacher's guides and packets available for purchase or you can buy slides of the exhibits for classroom use and develop your own teaching plans. Sometimes, large museums offer reproductions of historical pieces, such as ancient Egyptian statues, or Mesopotamian cylinder seals, which if modestly priced, might be useful both as springboards for discussion and for classroom decoration.

Art as Esthetic.   Art and artifacts have an almost unlimited potential for use in the social studies classroom, making for livelier and more colorful discussions.[22] The fine arts offer clues to interpreting a time, place, and style based on materials and design. As still images, the fine arts permit slow and careful analysis and reflection, particularly if paintings form a part of your classroom decor are available as slides, posters, or study prints. Each image can be viewed overall, and in great detail, as the viewer demands, thereby becoming familiar and understandable. If you regularly include artistic works in your lessons, students will become very comfortable with "learning how to look" and will begin to have insights of their own into the meanings and messages of artists, and an appreciation of styles and technical accomplishments. Students may develop a sense of the times from artists' styles and subjects, learning to recognize individual artists' work. As this sense of style grows, students will also be able to date and place a work based on an appreciation of color, texture, subject, technique, goal, and social setting. Art will become a support for the study of social studies, and conversely, social studies will support the enjoyment of art for its own sake.

TO DO

As you wander around (not aimlessly, however) an art or archeological museum, take note of possibilities for American or world history, civics, and economics lessons, and begin your own collection of slides, posters, and reproductions for classroom use.

Photography

Photographs, which have been around only since the late 1800s, much like paintings, communicate information about another time and place to us using real life as the subject. Like paintings, photographs are usually still images that we can analyze slowly and carefully, but record the world rather than imagine it. Photographs can also be art in the sense that the photographer has chosen, shaped, and arranged an image with a purpose, much like an artist decides how to paint a canvas. What makes discussions of photographs different in a social studies classroom is that the photographs are "instant" technological records of people, places, and events, and not the creation of painters or craftspeople. As one of my students put it so aptly, "paintings come out of the artist's head, but photographers show you what's true." Well, this is a good question, isn't it? Can photographs lie? Can paintings be true? How we interpret the evidence from both media is the stuff of many good social studies discussions. Because many of us think about photography as ordinary and true to life, we have a great many possibilities opened up for teaching purposes. Our sometimes naive trust of photographic images may be called into question, raising issues of fact, reason, and value that can carry on through the entire course of study and on into daily life.

First, photographs may be used as sources of information about history, just as you might use an historical document.[23] This type of discussion would focus on quality, visual content, and technological characteristics of the photograph. Whether it is black and white or color, taken in a studio or outdoors, posed or natural, are all clues to its purpose and perhaps its time period. You might consider how the photo was made, what process was used, as well as light and shadow, clarity, and setting. Students also ought to know how to handle and care for their photographs, recording the time and place of its origins. For purposes of finding information in photographs, you might start with family and place, naming those people in the family, or identifying those places we have visited or seen in travel brochures. Encourage the students to think of photographs as valuable historical documents, including their own family and places they have been on vacation. Direct them to bring in family/vacation photos that they or their parents were ready to throw away, and use these for "practice," a next step to interpreting photographs. If time permits, students could construct their own "vacation story" or "family history" from the photographs they find. They may be surprised at how many people and places they do not recognize or are unsure about as time passed. (Alas, the memory is weak, which is exactly why we, as good historians, have to label and care for our photographs!)

Second, photographs can be sources for analysis and interpretation, raising questions about the personal and/or public point of view of the photographer.[24] Photographs as personal expressions may serve esthetic or social goals and photographs as public expressions may serve political or business purposes. Students need to develop sensitivity to a photographer's goals and styles that are often left unexamined. Even the most ordinary of family photos are an expression of the picture taker's and the subject's viewpoint. No two people take exactly the same picture, even at the same time and place. Each of us puts our own "spin" on a subject depending on both how we want to portray them and how we feel about the person or place we are "shooting."

To encourage analysis and comparison of photos, pictures may be organized into "illustrious" and "anonymous" people, with an emphasis on studying portraits, group or individual, from a variety of times, places, and photographers. For instance, old Daguerreotypes from the Matthew Brady collection of the middle and late nineteenth century make a very fine introduction to portrait styles.[25] Portraits can be analyzed for clues to social status, religion, technology, psychology (self-consciousness), attitudes, dress, and cultural values. How people want to appear, and how the photographer presents them, may be in conflict. By careful reading of a photograph, you, the interpreter, may find signals or signs that demonstrate a desire to appear important, or to communicate an emotion. For example, during most of the nineteenth century and early twentieth century, broad smiles and direct eye contact were frowned on as immodest and self-important. Many people were purposely posed in partial profile, looking away from the viewer, averting or lowering their eyes. Photographers shaped these poses based on the prevailing social values of the time. Today's society values shots where everyone appears or is made to appear as happy as possible, and somber three-quarter profiles are regarded as impersonal and dull. But we are still posing and directing people, shaping images to conform to our prevailing customs and sensibilities. Aren't we?

SAMPLE LESSON PLAN

You create your own questions for these photographs.

Figure 14.6   "Home of the Rebel Sharpshooter" is the title of this photograph made by Alexander Gardner at Gettysburg in July, 1863, with the assistance of Timothy O'Sullivan.

Figure 14.7   Following the Battle of Antietam, Gardner took this photograph of Confederate dead along the Hagerstown Pike.

Third, photographs can be used to debate the problem of verification. Because all photographs grow out of an historical context and are taken by "fallible" witnesses, we might ask these questions: Are photographs accurate or biased? Do they have historical value or have they been retouched, faked, or altered to change our view of the past? Whose point of view do pictures reflect?

There are several ways in which issues of verification and bias can be raised using photographs. One is through a study of advertisements; another is through a study of camera work in social settings. Advertisements and social portraits are both usually the products of an informed mind. In a sense, the photographer has a goal in mind before the photograph is taken that shapes the outcome of any resulting image. Of course, the images produced may not always achieve the effect intended, but the artist is trying by design to convey a value and perspective to the viewer. The image-makers in charge of advertisements (whether drawn by an artist, or photographed in a "real" setting) are selling something they hope you will buy. They want you to warm up to an image and part with some money!

By contrast, photographers interested in social or documentary work are using the camera to communicate a sense of approval or criticism, pride or outrage, at what they see in society. This type of photography seeks to shape political and social values by dramatizing problems or by exploiting social issues. For example, Walker Evans or Lewis Hine—both of whom traveled the United States in the 1900s and 1930s, respectively—photographed ordinary people in troubled times portraying their subjects' situation with great skill and sympathy.

These "social" photographers—sometimes subtly, sometimes directly—influenced our view of times and events like the industrial era or the Great Depression. In many cases, both advertisers and social photographers have been so successful at making a visual impression on us that we find it hard to "see" history in any other terms. Thus, photographs have the power to shape our views of social studies, making discussion, argument, and interpretation of these images a necessity in our social studies classrooms.

SUMMARY

This chapter has presented the media as having great potential for social studies classrooms, but not without problems, the most important of which is whether students take an active or a passive role in the learning process. Roles were conceived in different ways: didactic, reflective, and affective; as narrator or audience; and as interpreters of symbols or subjects. First, print media, largely the written word, were defined in terms of fiction and nonfiction with distinctions made between primary documentary sources and secondary scholarship and journalistic and literary reporting. Second, a view was proposed that the categories of fact and fiction are not all that different, with writing often serving the same purposes but in varying styles, or different purposes using styles of presentation that are borrowed from other genre. Examples of problems in teaching were drawn using a wide range of materials, including eyewitness and news reports, historical figures, scholarly sources, the fine arts, and photographs. Whatever the sources or styles involved, teachers are advised to help students increase their awareness of an author's goals, biases, message, and style no matter what the format of the media, print or image, fiction or nonfiction.

NOTES

1. Annabelle Srebeny-Mohammedi, "Forms of Media as Ways of Knowing," in ed. J. Downing, A. Mohammedi, and A. Srebeny- Mohammedi *Questioning the Media*, (Thousand Oaks, CA: Sage Publications, 1990),pp. 42–54.
2. Donald A. Norman, "Experiencing the World," in *Things that Make Us Smart* (Boston: Addison-Wesley, 1993), pp. 19–41.
3. Victor, C. Strasburger, *Adolescents and the Media: Medical and Psychological Impact* (Newbury Park, CA: Sage Publications, 1995).
4. Arthur A. Berger, *Media Analysis Techniques* (Newbury Park, CA: Sage Publications, 1991).
5. Neil Postman, *Technolopoly: The Surrender of Culture to Technology.* (New York: Knopf, 1992).
6. S. Noakes, *Timely Reading: Between Exegesis and Interpretation* (Ithaca, NY: Cornell University Press, 1988), pp. 14–37.
7. Marshall McLuhan, *Understanding Media* (New York: Mentor Books, 1964), pp. 4–17.
8. M. Shrage, *Shared Minds: The New Technologies of Collaboration* (New York: Random House, 1990).
9. S. Steenland, *Unequal Picture: Black, Hispanic, Asian, and Native American Characters on Television* (Washington, DC: National Commission on Working Women, 1989).
10. M. Fabre, *A History of Communications* (New York: Hawthorne Press, 1963).
11. M. Fishman, *Manufacturing the News* (Austin, TX: University of Texas Press, 1980).
12. J. Wolff, *The Social Production of Art* (London and New York: MacMillan, 1981).
13. Gerald Danzer and Mark Newman, *Tuning In: Primary Sources in the Teaching of History* (Chicago: The World History Project/University of Illinois at Chicago, 1991).
14. Neil Postman and Steve Powers, "What Is News?", in *How to Watch TV News* (New York: Penguin, 1992), 13–25.

15. J. Berger, *Ways of Seeing* (New York: , Penguin Books, 1973).

16. Edward Wakin, with Daniel Wakin, *Photos That Made U.S. History*. Vols. I and II. (New York: Walker & Co., 1993).

17. Alan Trachtenberg, *Reading American Photographs: Images as History* (New York: Hill and Wang, Noonday Press, 1994).

18. Les , *America by the Numbers* (Boston: Houghton-Mifflin & Co., 1993).

19. F. M. Shelly, J. C. Archer, F. M. Davidson, and S. D. Brunn, *Political Geography of the United States* (New York: Guilford Press, 1996).

20. John Allen , *A Mathematician Reads the Newspaper* (New York: Basic Books, 1995).

21. James W. , *The Truth about Columbus: A Subversively True Poster Book for a Dubiously Celebratory Occasion* (New York: The New Press, 1992).

22. Joshua C. Taylor, *America as Art* (Washington, DC: National Collection of Fine Arts, 1976).

23. National Archives (intro. by A.), *The American Image: Photographs from the National Archives, 1860–1960* (New York: Pantheon Books, 1979).

24. F. F. , Jr., A. B. Provenzano, and P. A. Zorn, Jr., *Pursuing the Past: Analyzing Pictures and Photographs* (Boston: Addison-Wesley, 1989).

25. George Sullivan, *Mathew Brady: His Life and Photographs* (New York: Cobblehill Books, Dutton, 1994).

FOR FURTHER STUDY: ORGANIZING FOR INSTRUCTION

Aristotle, J. H. Freese, trans. *The "Art" of Rhetoric*. Cambridge, MA: Harvard University Press, 1967.

Bennett, W. L. *News: The Politics of Illusion*. New York: Longman, 1988.

Berger, J. *Ways of Seeing*. London: Penguin Books, 1972.

Boorstin, D. *The Image*. New York: Athenium, 1962.

Ewen, S. *All Consuming Images*. New York: Basic Books, 1988.

Inness, S. A. *Tough Girls: Women Warriors and Wonder Women in Popular Culture*. State College: Universiyt of Pennsylvania Press, 1999.

Jung, C. J. *Man and His Symbols*. New York: Dell, 1968.

Keen, S. *Faces of the Enemy*. New York: Harper & Row, 1987.

Stewart, C. C., and P. Fritzsche, eds. *Imagining the Twentieth Century*. Urbana and Chicago: University of Illinois Press, 1997.

Wald, C. *Myth America: Picturing Women, 1865–1945*. New York: Pantheon Books, 1975.

CHAPTER 15

The "New Age" of Multimedia: Part II. Interpreting Moving Images and Sounds

"I was brought up to be a spectator …. I was raised to be a voyeur."
—John Irving, The World According to Garp, p. 1

OVERVIEW OF CONTENTS

Main Ideas

Film and Music: Words and Actions, Symbols and Emotions

      Film, Live Drama, and Music
      Documentaries, Docudramas, TV News, Oral History, and Home Video

Taking Part in the Action: Interactive Role-Play With Mixed Media

      The Internet and World Wide Web
      Computer Databases
      Entertainments and Edutainments
      Simulation Games: Playing Along With Decision Making

Summary

Notes

For Further Study: Organizing for Instruction

      Books and Materials
      Computer Simulations and CD-ROMS

MAIN IDEAS

Moving images and sound performances are probably the most popular of all media around the world, but these are also a challenge to use effectively in a classroom. Films, videos and musical performances are complex and rapid, offering the viewer/listener thousands, perhaps millions, of images and sounds over the course of an average presentation. Unlike still images, film and music flow continuously, providing a rich experience, but one that is more difficult to analyze and contemplate. Images are often joined by sounds and stories contributing to an overall mood or feeling that changes while you are watching. This combination of media is much more powerful and complicated than dealing with a "still" image. It is a great deal like real life in the sense that time marches on and decisions have to be made without much chance for contemplation.

Movement, whether on a big screen, home TV, or computer screen, invites a kind of audience participation that is mesmerizing and involving, but that may or may not lead to creative or critical interpretation. The attractiveness of these media may increase or deflect thinking as we are pulled into an emotional state evoked by a rich amalgam of story, sound, and image. Thus, we have a highly "motivating" medium for the classroom, but also an overwhelming one that may limit rather than increase opportunities for reflection.

Thus, as teachers who seek to use film, music, and video to stimulate student thinking about social studies topics, we need to plan ahead and consider our choices. There are several ways to accomplish this goal of reflection. First, we ourselves should be familiar with the selection we have made, carefully outlining its contents before we take it into the classroom. As teachers, we should be critical (in the constructive sense) of any moving images or performances that we intend to share with students. We should first develop our own interpretations and judgments and then consult the work of critics or scholars to assist us in our lesson planning. While studying our musical or film choice, we might begin by setting a few "key" goals and deciding on a strategy to use for stimulating student ideas in order to invite a wide range of viewpoints and criticisms about each film, video, or musical.

TO DO

Set a few goals for teaching a war movie like:

Glory
All Quiet on the Western Front
Braveheart
Full Metal Jacket
Apocalypse Now
Sands of Iwo Jima
(or choose one of your own!)

What do you want to accomplish with this film or excerpt?
Are there any peace movies you might like to show? Which one?

Second, while viewing or listening to a movie or musical, we can prepare an "advance organizer" for ourselves and our students to assist us in understanding the program. An advance organizer can be a list of questions to answer, or activities to carry on while following a piece of music or a film. It can also be a reaction sheet on which we ask students to record their emotional state, keep a log of significant statements, or draw sketches of major characters. Key to a successful advance organizer is that it follows along with the action, keeping attention keenly focused on words and actions. Discussions based on student notes and reactions should take place at many intervals during a performance with a summary at the conclusion. Videotapes are a great help to us teachers because these permit rewinding and fast forwarding to review words and actions.

TO DO

> What advance questions will you give students to accompany the film you se-
> lected?
> What will be your key questions? How many will you pose for each set of
> frames? How many questions will pertain to the film as a whole?

Third, a "debriefing," or summary, of student reactions and opinions, theories, and explanations ought to follow all performances. Summary questions
serve to draw students' ideas together in the form of conclusions. Attention
should be paid to didactic, reflective, and affective reactions, with an invitation to
students to talk about their feelings, as well as their insights into a film, drama, or
musical performance. Small study groups might contribute to this debriefing or
summary analysis, venturing their critical opinions of plot, character, and story,
either for a film or live stage performance. As much as practical, students should
develop and defend their own interpretations, with only a little assistance from
you. Evaluations and conclusions might then be written into notebooks for later
use, for example, to compare with historical records, biographies, or other plays
on the same subject or personality, time, or place.

LET'S DECIDE

> Get together with a friend, colleague, or classmate and decide what your sum-
> mary questions would be for the war film you chose? How many questions do
> you need to stimulate responses? Which questions, in your opinion, would be
> the most important in producing ideas and pulling these together for stu-
> dents?

FILM AND MUSIC: WORDS AND ACTIONS, SYMBOLS AND EMOTIONS

What makes film and music so involving to most people is that these media appeal strongly to both mind and emotions, values and situations.[1] Characters in a
film may be posing philosophic questions at the same time that a worrisome crisis
is brewing, all accompanied by stirring music and riveting sound effects. We may
be touched by what we see and hear such that we are moved to tears or to anger.
Often, we are not even sure what the reasons are for our feelings. In films and
music, art is harnessed for both esthetic and emotional purposes, with ideas and
feelings conveyed in an almost magical way. The audience is playing the role of
onlookers peering into very personal dramas, with a chance to be an insider, or
part of "soap" opera.
A noted scholar argues that the power of the media, its ability to mimic, or
even improve on reality, is also a problem because the images, sounds, words,
and action may be shrewdly organized, as art, to convince an audience of values
and beliefs that really require careful discussion—not simple acceptance.[2] In effect, many films, dramas, and musical pieces are forms of sophisticated propaganda promoting or attacking a public issue. As political campaigns have
discovered some time ago, moving images (especially on TV) can be very effective in gaining the attention of voters, with either positive or negative results. I
would argue that it is almost impossible to make a film or write a drama that is
"neutral." Thus, what we are handed is a ready-made teaching device with which
to stir both ideas and emotions. As teachers, we can dissect a film or other perfor-

mance into categories and ask advance questions that will help students to think about the entire performance as both art and message. We can teach students to view films, dramas, and music in terms of words and actions, sounds and symbols, drawing on each to contribute to an understanding of the whole.

Film, Live Drama, and Music

Film, drama, and music usually combine words, story, action, music, and symbols to achieve a total effect. Any work may benefit from different viewpoints for thinking: social, historical, literary, critical, and esthetic. In other words, as a social studies teacher, any work can be discussed in the context of history with a view to figuring out its social meaning. A work may also be viewed as a literary invention, or "construction," that invites us to consider the way language, storyline, and characters are used to influence feelings and attitudes. Artistic styles and social contexts may both be profitably exploited as topics for conversation. If you are in an imaginative mood, why not invite students to play the role of literary or film critics, offering their judgments of a work after they have analyzed its content, style, message, and meaning.

Films. Films are perhaps the most complex and useful media for classroom application. Nearly all media are combined into a film, the purpose and production of which is to draw the viewer into another world, erasing the line between audience and story as much as possible. This is what makes film so intriguing and also so problematic, obscuring the line between fact and fiction.[3] In a very smooth and professional film, viewers, particularly young ones, may forget that the characters are acting (sometimes even true in a documentary) and that someone is directing and editing the words and the action.

Since the advent of inexpensive videotapes, however, we can watch as much or as little of a film as we wish, and we can splice, split, recombine, and eliminate portions to suit our instructional purposes. We can also return to key words or to actions that we think are significant and test our hypotheses. We can compare films and dramas, films and novels, films and historical documents, films and textbooks, or even films and films. Because we are dealing with movement and action, a small thought-provoking portion of a film, play, musical, or video is probably sufficient for a classroom discussion. Two or more brief comparative or contrasting examples would probably be enough for several periods worth of conversation and debate, whereas an entire film would be the equivalent of a book if it were used intensively in a social studies course.

Drama. Dramas, plays, and theater, whether live or recorded, offer most of the motivational advantages of film, and most of the interpretation problems associated with fast-moving dialogue and action. However, the added value of live theater is that students are more conscious (usually) that actresses and actors are carrying out the instructions of a playwright and producer. There is a greater attention, perhaps to the original text by an author than there would be in a film. There is also a greater awareness of the message being advocated in a drama because characters are speaking to you in the words of a writer who is trying to speak with us. An advance organizer for a theater field trip might be to familiarize students with the text and characters of the play before they view the performance. They might approach the theater armed with questions and a sense of direction that will help them interpret the words and action.

Music. Music, musical comedy, opera, music videos, and all forms of sound performance can be a very enjoyable and exciting addition to a social studies classroom. Music is a lovely change of pace from the words that seem to dominate social studies, and may provoke students into thinking about the origins and uses of sounds. Even a purely instrumental (wordless, imageless) presentation has a history and a meaning that might fit into a social studies lesson quite well by conveying a feeling for an historical period, setting a mood for a later discussion. For example, would students confuse a modern classic with a baroque classic? Songs, whether popular, folk, or classical, provide more clues for us to use in our interpretations of the past through the words that accompany the sounds. This gives us two avenues for interpretation and conversation. Musical comedy, opera, or music videos offer a still more complex mix by providing images, symbols, actions, words, and sounds for us to study. Often these mixed productions attempt to integrate many media for an effect, much like a film does, but perhaps without a storyline or a main character. Thus, musical performances offer many avenues for interpretation and the search for meaning. For historical purposes, music allows us insights into the tastes and fashions, activities and attitudes, of other times and places. Just as pictures give us images of a time and place, sounds provide us with a feeling or tone of an era and its people.

TO DO

Research your own list of theater pieces/dramas that might be suitable for teaching social studies. Choose several that could fit easily into an American History course and several that could fit into a World History course. For the avid drama buffs, add several to your list that might fit into an economics or civics course, or an elective of your choice.

SAMPLE LESSON PLAN

Research a list of musical comedies and hit songs (rock, folk, heavy metal, rap, and reggae) that carry messages useful as springboards for class discussion on social, historical, and economic topics. You would be surprised about how many musicals and songs have to do with economics and social status. Take a look out there and see if you can find at least a dozen that carry an economic message of woe or of happiness. Consider an example.

Sixteen Tons*

Now some people say a man's made out of mud,
But a poor man's made out of muscle and blood,
Muscle and blood, skin and bone,
A mind that's weak and a back that's strong.
You load Sixteen tons and what do you get?
You get another day older and deeper in debt.
Saint Peter, don't you call me 'cause I can't go,
I owe my soul to the company store. Well, company store.

I was born one morning when the sun didn't shine,
I picked up my shovel and I walked to the mine.
I loaded sixteen tons of number nine coal.
And the straw boss hollered, "Well, bless my soul!"
I was born one morning in the drizzling rain;
Fighting and trouble is my middle name.
I was raised in the bottoms by a momma hound—
I'm mean as a dog but I'm gentle as a lamb.

If you see me coming, you better step aside;
A lot of men didn't, and a lot of men died.
I got a fist of iron and a fist of steel.
If the right one don't get you then the left one will.

*Words and music by Merle Travis; recorded by Tennessee Ernie Ford.

Documentaries, TV News, Oral History, and Home Video

Much like other moving images, news programs, documentaries, and home videos are usually about real events, past or present. If Hollywood films can be thought of as fiction, then documentaries might be viewed as nonfiction. Documentaries, which are the record of people or events shown in naturalistic ways, are widely accepted as efforts at building an historical memory that we can share with our students. News programs, oral history, documentaries, and home videos seek to create an account of people and events that we can use at a future time. Such records are expected to be as accurate and truthful as possible, using original sources, interviews, and eyewitness accounts. We do not expect imagination and invention to play a big part, although of course all productions have some degree of style.

The modern world being what it is, however, technology increasingly invites creativity and imagination. Audiences do not want to be bored, and producers hope to capture viewers' attention with their production whether the story is true to life or imagined. As a consequence, TV news programs, for example, are carefully managed, stories are compressed and edited, film clips cut and pasted in ways that dramatize events, and overall the viewer winds up with many of the same problems of interpretation and verification that fiction presents.[4] There is a recently minted word, "docudrama," to describe programs that fuse fact and fiction, further thinning the line between story and witness. Fiction might even be easier to use in a classroom than factual or docudrama accounts because we already view stories as invented. We are not expecting "truthful" accounts, as we would from a documentary or news program.

All stories, fact and fiction, are constructed by human beings with attitudes and feelings (albeit in different ways), so we still have to decide how much or how little to believe them. Documentaries, of course, are easier to verify than fictional recreations or totally imagined situations because these can be checked against other evidence. Nevertheless, questions about editing, shaping, and bias should be posed whenever moving images are presented even those that purport to offer witnesses to historical events. Students should be made particularly aware of bias in documentary accounts and TV news because of the management of "facts" and "sources," if these are provided. What is cut out may be more important than what is finally presented. The way events are filmed and reported may grow from a conscious or unconscious prejudice that may blind a producer or director to vitally important issues. The creators may overlook people who others would consider key to understanding events.

Thus, teachers must plan on using TV documentaries and news programs just as carefully as they do Hollywood films, although the key questions are somewhat different.[5] Symbols, characters, plot, and action may be better topics for art films (fiction), but documentaries (fact) may lend themselves more to questions of interviewer bias, eyewitness accuracy, and fairness. Because images, sounds, and storylines are constantly moving and changing, teachers must also keep track of the way in which the program is put together: its order and its dialogue, its mood and its imagery, its style and its goals. As noted before, there is a great deal to pay attention to when images are moving: whether these have a basis in evidence or a basis in literature. Your interpretation can change as a program progresses, and your emotions may be deeply affected.

Documentaries, news programs, even many home videos, seek to touch our souls as well as our minds, contributing to their attraction and entertainment value. But strong programs also ought to make us suspicious.[6] We must always ask ourselves and our students what we really know about the moving image. How do we feel about it? How much has the producer and/or director of the moving image manipulated or influenced our feelings? Is there a "hidden agenda" in the text, in the images, or in the sounds? How about in all of these? Do we need to cross-check our conclusions with historical evidence, with scholarly studies, or with opinions offered from other viewpoints? Do we believe the same ideas after the documentary or has it shaped our views in some way? Do we trust the evidence, or ourselves? Have we enough information to make a reasonable judgment? These are all worthwhile and difficult questions to ask about TV news and historical documentaries presented as moving images in a postmodern world, particularly on the worldwide medium of communication that is television.[7]

SAMPLE LESSON PLAN

Research your own list of documentaries and news programs that would promote classroom discussion of social, political, and economic issues. Find two or three outstanding examples for each category and preview at least two for classroom use.

The following are some examples of documentaries or news programs that may be useful for classroom discussion:

An American Dream (eyewitness accounts of a bitter strike at the Hormel meat packing plant in Wisconsin during the 1970s)

Rosie the Riveter (the story of "Rosies,", or women in World War II who worked in heavy industry because of shortage of "manpower" at home, told through interviews and old newsreel footage)

The War Room (an insider's view, with interviews and home video footage, of the political office and operatives that managed President Clinton's 1992 election)

TAKING PART IN THE ACTION:
INTERACTIVE ROLE-PLAY WITH MIXED MEDIA

Still and moving images presented as pictures or as films, as dramas or as music, invite interpretation and identification from the audience, but usually allow for little or no interaction. As teachers, we must add exercises and activities to any film or set of pictures we want to present. The activities are our inventions, or we borrow them from published sources, but while the moving image is in progress, there is very little direct audience participation. So, for educational purposes, we must intervene and channel student attention by giving directions and asking questions.

With the advent of the computer, particularly since the introduction of CD-ROM technology and Internet (including World Wide Web) capability, we now have available vast new digital resources with which we can interact.[8] Teachers and students can assume active rather than passive roles when dealing with historical or political databases, online conversations, simulations, games, and adventures. Students can participate in choosing sources, playing roles, setting goals, selecting difficulty levels, or immersing themselves in elaborate imagined worlds. In this new cyberworld of the computer, information abounds, and choices are plentiful and fast-moving. The very abundance of data and the strong entertainment values of the computer medium may also overwhelm, leaving us unsure of our direction or choice.

Control, at least partial, of the direction and rate of computer play is frequently in the hands of students, and they really seem to enjoy this feeling of power. Of course, we must keep in mind that any game or simulation has already been prestructured, and we are occupying a creator's world, even if it does allow more choice than usual.

Nevertheless, great opportunities now present themselves for the social studies classroom through computer technology.[9] The following sections suggest ways that teachers may employ several categories of computer products and technologies, specifically historical databases, games or edutainments, and simulations. Each type of resource offers different possibilities, and provides for an interesting change of pace from the usual classroom activities. Any and all of these resources can be integrated into the curriculum or treated as supplements. I personally prefer to integrate computers and their accompanying software into the normal everyday classroom curriculum, if at all possible.

The Internet and World Wide Web

As interactive technologies grow in sophistication and distribution, more and more students and teachers will be able to search electronically for information and news. Most of this search activity is conducted through existing telephone lines by using "browsers" or computer programs that simplify the process of accessing information. Colorful and intuitive programs, such as the popular Netscape, can be purchased and installed on the computer to aid communication and data searches. Furthermore, once a search is complete and valuable information on a topic has been discovered, this material can often be transferred to one's own hard drive by a process called "downloading" and then printed out or manipulated by the learner or teacher for presentation or reporting. Materials can also be sent through online services to others by a process called "uploading," or "attaching files," to messages. Right now, most social studies or historical information seems to be offered at no charge, other than the price of paying your phone or online bill. Therefore, the Internet is a cheap and easy tool to use, boosting its popularity and growth.

Some argue that there are already large, active, "online learning communities" using the "net" for research and for transmitting messages.[10] Internet services are rapidly growing easier to use, although cost can still be a factor, with commercial companies like America Online, Compuserve, and Prodigy offering easy access to the net for either communication or browsing the World Wide Web for games and/or data. In addition to these private firms, there are dozens of public, university, school, and other Internet connections through "servers" that hook up to phone lines so students can access information. At present, there is a good deal of competition between services, but this will probably become more organized as technologies improve and as acceptance grows among educational and business users. Students who have computers with built-in or attached modems for communication with CD-ROM capability can easily learn to access data or send messages on the Internet. For those interested, you can set up your own "home page" or home address on the Internet and offer your ideas and information for others to use, or provide a site so others can communicate with you.

For the social studies, there are already a great deal of resources and services available, and the field is moving very fast, almost too fast to keep track of predictions and current Web addresses may fall into disuse or disappear rapidly. Nevertheless, there are a number of important "sites," or Web addresses, that students and teachers can connect with for historical and social studies data. Even if only one powerful computer is available for your classroom, it could still be utilized imaginatively to teach students "navigation strategies" for finding information.[11] Once navigation is familiar, small selected groups could occupy the machine for a period to find out what they need for a report, research project, or paper, and then turn the computer over to another group. Many students and their families now have computers at home, which in the future will offer teachers great potential for assigning research reports or developing "history fair" or other projects.

Perhaps the best sites (at the time of this writing) deal with American history, current events, and economics, with somewhat fewer addresses providing data about world studies, government, or geographic and social issues topics. For example, there is a tremendous amount of news available, most of it offered through major news services or newspapers if you are teaching current events. There are also quite a lot of economics databases provided on the Internet, many having to do with the stock market. For instance, teachers could play stock market games with students using actual daily movements of stock prices as their guides rather than rely on a cut down simulated version. For American studies there is a rich lode of resources developing or already available, including material on the Civil War era, the Korean War, World War II, and Vietnam. In addition, there are quite a few projects that have classified and collated visual collections, such as the collections of Matthew Brady, Lewis Hine, or other noted photographers. A brief, and probably already changing, sampling of e-mail addresses on the World Wide Web includes providers such as:

About the World Wide Web
  http://www.afcom.com

American Historical Association
  http://www.indiana.edu/chmn/aha

American Memory
  http://lcweb2.loc.gov/amhome.html

Center for History and New Media
  http://web.gmu.edu/chnm

Congressional Record
  http://thomas.loc.gov/

Electronic Text Center
  http://www.lib.virginia.edu/journals/EH/EH.html

The History Channel
  http://www.historychannel.com

Internet
  http://home.mcom.com/assist/about_the_internet.html

MainXChange
  www.mainxchange.com

On-line Museums
  http://www.comlab.ox.ac.uk/archive/other/museums.html

Project Muse
  http://muse:jhu.edu

Social Sciences Data Collection
  http://ssdc.ucsd.edu/

Valley of the Shadow (pre-civil War database)
http://jefferson.village.virginia.edu/vshadow/vshadow.html

Vietnam War
http://www.ionet.net/~uheller/vnbktoc.shtml

This selection provides a guide to a few of the rich resources you and your students may employ for a social studies purpose or goal of your choosing. Many other Web sites and addresses, communications devices, references, and materials are available on and throughout the growing Internet system. This trend will undoubtedly continue to develop rapidly and hopefully will become a widespread public service, with training provided for teachers and schools so they can "log on" to important and useful social science and historical data that would otherwise be difficult to find, unless you were willing to take a trip to another part of the country or world. There is considerable talk of proposals by federal and state governments to subsidize access to the Internet and World Wide Web and support computer purchases by the schools.[12]

If the movement to fund training and equipment comes to pass, then these services will become an integral part of our daily work routines, much as text is now, and will allow teachers to require better research for class or homework than is currently possible. Think of the reports students will write using the very best and latest data that they have acquired through the Internet! And think of the work you will have to do as well in checking it and controlling for rampant plagiarism. But, despite the fact that new technology offers both advantages and problems, the fundamentals of good teaching and quality writing have not changed all that much over the years in social studies education.

Computer Databases

Databases are collections of information made available for student retrieval, either from CD-ROM collections or through the World Wide Web. These databases may be specialized, centered on one topic or period of history, or they may be general and encyclopedic, covering a category of events.[13] Either way, the data may be entered, retrieved, and stored almost at will by the student researcher in any order or quantity given the capacity of your computer hard drive or storage disk. Specific databases might include collections of material on particular events (e.g., the Civil War or Industrial Revolution, historical biographies and autobiographies of famous personalities, compilations of photographs or documents on social history, politics, economics, or statistics). General databases include encyclopedias, dictionaries, and archives that cover many topics and periods, or even strive for comprehensive coverage. Specific databases are often useful for active research by a group or an individual into a specific issue, concept, or historical era, leading eventually to an essay or classroom presentation. Broad-based archives and encyclopedias are probably more useful for individual study and research, providing sources and information to verify theories. Databases, particularly if these are "raw" or left open to interpretation, are marvelous resources for research, but may put off the average student. To be useful in a manageable amount of time, such rich material must be divided into categories and assigned questions, with selected portions used as a basis for student hypothesizing.

As much as possible, I would recommend that advance organizers (yes, those again) research questions be discussed and assigned before students come into contact with a large database. In effect, questions and theory provide direction, an idea of what to look for while scrolling through dozens of facts, documents, and figures. Research questions also lessen the tendency to copy, a great temptation particularly with electronic encyclopedias, where all of the hard work has presumably been done, and the student only needs to repeat it for a good grade! Teachers must make it clear to students that a database should be used as a resource for proving, verifying, and supporting their ideas and theories. Simply repeating or copying a scholar's interpretation or a textbook summary proves very little about a student's ability to interpret and judge information.

TO DO

Conduct a survey of computer catalogs and social studies catalogs to find out how many different kinds of databases are offered for classroom application. Are most on U.S. topics or world topics? Are there very many or relatively few?

A few of the better choices of databases I suggest for social studies instruction include "Visual Archives of American History: Volumes One and Two" and "Who Built America?", both of which offer original sources in the form of photographs, documents, stories, songs, and narrative text with the potential for student interaction and searches.

Entertainments and Edutainments

Let's face it, computer games and moving images are a form of entertainment, particularly to our students. The whole point of this medium is entertainment, that is, to have fun. Some publishers and producers have invented the term edutainment to describe games that they consider to have some educational value, but this is usually small in comparison to the fun value. The real purpose is to create enjoyment, not to stretch the mind or help students finish and improve their homework assignments. (You might have some favorite games as well like *Myst* or *Civilization*, but hopefully not the "smash 'em and crash 'em" pinball type of contest.) Software is available for playing traditional "contest" style games in which players compete with themselves or with others to either top a record or win a match. Such games frequently involve battle lines, racing or flying, or some flirtation with dangerous sports or adventure. Perhaps you are looking for buried treasure, discovering exotic lands, searching for a secret passage, or working to get past barriers and demons, wild creatures, or powerful attackers. Many of these games are violent, raising educational issues about their suitability for students, particularly the young adult set, specifically pubescent males. What are our goals in this area?

For social studies, game formats have been employed to teach history and geography, retaining the adventure or challenge while introducing historical and geographic data to use during play. Two popular choices for edutainment purposes that combine gaming with subject matter include: "Where in the World is Carmen San Diego?" and "Oregon Trail I or II." In "Carmen San Diego," students play the role of detective in tracking down Carmen and other spies as they travel the globe in search of clues. To interpret clues accurately, the student must learn about geographic conditions in different regions to make an educated guess of Carmen's whereabouts. In "Oregon Trail," students take on the role of wagon train managers who must carefully ration supplies in order to get the settlers across the great plains alive. Problems of water and food supplies, Indian raids, and diseases crop up frequently and must be dealt with if the group is to survive the trip. Both games have a rather narrow range of problems to solve, with a limited range of alternatives. Both are probably more appealing to middle school grades than to senior high school students, and *Oregon Trail* has been criticized for its stereotypical portrayal of Native Americans and Frontiers people as always in combat, as well as for its rather unidimensional approach to exploration and settlement of the Western United States.

WHAT DO YOU THINK?

Try out a popular game with students or colleagues in your school's computer laboratory. Take notes on the action and on decisions you have to make. Rate the game: Is it easy to load and play; are there too many or too few directions; how often do you get frustrated with the rules or the format; is it teaching anything worthwhile in terms of knowledge, thinking skills, or values? Is it complex or easy to use? Do the authors leave room for growth and change? Are choices offered for interaction or are players directed to a goal?

Simulation Games: Playing Along With Decision Making

Simulation games for computers are usually elaborate role-play games with a high degree of interaction and decision making for student players. Properly speaking, simulations are more than games because they may involve some of the factors associated with a contest or challenge, plus a sequence of serious decisions using a built-in "realistic" database. A first-rate simulation condenses actual problems into an abstraction that mimics reality. Characteristically, simulations ask players to immerse themselves in one or more roles, or perhaps create a role of their own in order to engage in play. Simulations provide situations in which the problem-solving game is played using historical, political, or economic situations that have challenged people in the past, and that continue into the present. Well-designed simulations promote higher level problem solving on topics that seem familiar to us and speak to "the human condition."

Sometimes, roles in a simulation call on participants to be creators as well as players, managing a limited universe of information while working out solutions to one or more engaging problems. The quality and complexity of problems are keys to a good simulation, and many of the more challenging simulations offer players a variety of alternatives at many levels of difficulty. Some simulations are planned in a series of steps, each one of which contains new and more demanding challenges, pressuring students into maker harder and faster decisions using whatever knowledge they have gathered. Others may be planned as adventure sequences or mysteries, with students interpreting clues while pursuing an overall solution or goal.

Simulations may also come in an entertainment or edutainment style. Entertainment's goal is to give players a sense of fun, a chance to hone their skills, and a feeling of accomplishment in winning. Edutainment may also provide opportunities for winning, but also for skill development, with a major aim of enhancing learning. There is a useful link between fun and learning. What we, as teachers, would really like to have in a computer simulation game are long-term effects on reasoning skills and perspective. To be fair, the art and science of computer simulations is such that a balance is difficult to achieve for designer/authors. Usually, games tend to weigh in on the side of entertainment simply because it sells better. Often it is difficult to tell just what a simulation is all about until playing it for a while. Field testing with students is critical before presentation to a whole group, grade, or program. Some computer simulation games like *Star Wars* or *Prince of Persia* have little point, in my opinion, except to "win" an imaginary battle, whereas others like *SimLife* or *Civilization* may provide weeks or months of "play" in order to solve interesting problems. Quality problems test learner skills and engage them in social and historical decisions that reflect, mimic, and condense real historical,

tion and diplomacy, economic depressions, town planning, political choices, or geographic planning. A model edutainment simulation for social studies classrooms is the *SimCity* series, ranging from the early *SimCity* to the advanced CD-ROM *SimCity 2000*. To play, students must become city planners and mayors all rolled into one, with a mandate to create the most developed city they can dream up while watching their budgets and improving chances for reelection. Creativity is encouraged, but restrained by limited budgets and by popular approval ratings. The city must grow, but many groups have to be pleased in the process, taxes kept relatively low, and crises solved.

Just to make things a little more interesting, unwanted problems appear from time to time to worry the city manager, including floods, quakes, and pollution. If you are really lucky, Godzilla appears out of the bay and runs around town for a while squashing buildings and starting fires. So the student planner/mayors better keep on their toes if they want their city to survive and prosper. In more advanced versions, historical and futuristic scenarios are available, like the bombing of Dresden, or the creation of a pollution-free hi-tech metropolis. There are even secret problems for those who become deeply involved, and terrain kits for those who want to shape their own environments. Based on our criteria for a quality simulation, the *SimCity* series fits quite well because it does mimic the reality of urban development, provides alternative avenues for solutions, and offers a strong sense of play while teaching learners how to make important political and economic decisions.

A sample city from a *SimCity 2000* manual is shown in Figure 15.1.

Figure 15.1   *SOURCE:* Nick Dargahi and Michael Bremer, "Planning—City Design and Scenario Solutions," in *SimCity 2000: Power, Politics, and Planning*, rev. ed. (Rocklin, CA: Prima Publishing, 1995), p. 259. Screen shot courtesy of Maxis, Inc. Copyright © 1995 by Maxis, Inc. All rights reserved.

At present, the field of computer databases and simulations is growing rapidly in the direction of greater flexibility and more complexity. Many products seem applicable to social studies classrooms and offer opportunities for interactive problem solving, which is an important change of pace from textbooks and still images. As computers with CD-ROMs and Internet capability become as widespread as televisions, school demand for, and critical evaluation of, these products will undoubtedly increase.[14]

Right now, databases have an enormous potential to stimulate hypothesizing and research, but most of those published follow a "compilation" format, and allow only modest opportunities for interaction. Encyclopedias on CD-ROM usually try to increase attractiveness by offering visuals, windows, maps, and other resources, but almost no chance to shape or alter the way these are used. Certainly, simulations have a great entertainment and creative value, but where they will go in terms of their educational impact is hard to say at this time. Far more experimentation needs to take place in classrooms, with greater cooperation between programmer/creators and classroom educators to develop materials that are user-friendly, interesting, informative, and fit into tight school schedules. Teachers need to play with some of the simulations themselves in order to see the possibilities or problems that exist for learning social studies. But it is clear that the power of simulations and databases to educate is here; the big questions focus on the purposes for which these products will be created and how they will be used in our classrooms.

TO DO

Collect several current computer magazines, educational reviews, and computer simulations that hold promise for social studies classrooms. Are most of the reviews critical or complimentary? Why? Would your goals in choosing simulations emphasize learning outcomes or entertainment? Which games seem most promising in terms of fitting your goals? Which do not? Choose at least two simulations to experiment with at home and in school before you make your mind up about their quality. Are there any you would build into your courses as regular features each year? Why or why not?

SUMMARY

Images were added to words as springboards for conversation, and as historical resources. Viewed as perhaps a more direct influence on our thinking than words, images were presented as equally problematic in demanding interpretation and careful analysis. The concepts of reality and imagination were applied to still images, most particularly photographs, paintings, maps and graphs, raising issues of authenticity and truthfulness. Photographs, usually accepted as real, could be just as managed as art, which is an issue teachers should raise questions about during classroom discussions of what pictures "prove" in history. The more traditional sources of ideas for lessons: Maps, charts, graphs, photos, and the fine arts were expanded to include computer databases that offer compilations of material for student use. Moving images and sounds, including films, TV shows, music, opera, and other mixed media, were presented as media that greatly enrich social studies classes, providing action, sound, and emotion—a change of pace from the usual formula centered on text. However, it was argued that films and other moving media must be carefully prepared for classroom application because of their power to shape the images in our minds, many of which are quite different from the historical and social evidence available to us. Contrasting film or musical interpretations of the past with original sources is a fine way of introducing questions of truth and interpretation.

This chapter has also presented an overview of the most recent and most mixed media to supplement classroom teaching: computer software in the form of both interactive databases and simulation games. Games and databases can be both educational and entertaining, although entertainment usually wins out over more serious pursuits. Entertainment can be used to stimulate interest and thinking for many students, particularly if shrewdly applied to familiar topics and units. To assist us, a number of examples of valuable and thought-provoking simulations and databases for U.S. and world history were discussed, with suggestions for the social sciences and the arts as well (available as CD-ROMs, disks, or through the resources of the Internet and World Wide Web.[15] In fact, so much is being produced and transmitted that we are in danger of being overwhelmed by an embarrassment of riches, which is why teachers must exercise care and caution in choosing which activities and which media selections will become integral to their 'thoughtful' social studies programs.

NOTES

1. J. Leming, "Rock Music and the Socialization of Moral Values in Early Adolescence," *Youth and Society*, 18: 363–83.
2. Neil Postman, *Technolopoly—The Surrender of Culture to Technology* (New York: Knopf, 1992).
3. Mark C. Carnes, gen. ed., *Past Imperfect: History According to the Movies*, A society of American Historians book (New York: Henry Holt & Co., 1995).
4. S. Ewen, *All Consuming Images* (New York: Basic Books, 1988).
5. K. W. Mielke, "Television in the Social Studies Classroom," *Social Education*, 52, no. 5, (1988): 362–365.
6. W. L. Bennett, *News: The Politics of Illusion* (New York: Longman, 1988).
7. J. A. Brown, *Television "Critical Viewing" Skills Education: Major Media Literacy Projects in the United States and Selected Countries* (Hillsdale, NJ: Lawrence Erlbaum Press, 1991).
8. N. Negroponte, *Being Digital* (New York: Knopf, 1995).
9. K. Sheingold and M. Hadley, *Accomplished Teachers: Integrating Computers into Classroom Practice* (New York: Bank Street College of Education, Center for Technology in Education, 1990).
10. P. H. Martorella, *Interactive Technologies and the Social Studies: Emerging Issues and Applications* (Albany, NY: SUNY Press, 1997), pp. 1–27.
11. A. T. Stull, *Education on the Internet: A Student's Guide* (Upper Saddle River, NJ: Prentice-Hall, 1997), pp. 5–14.
12. U.S. Congress, Office of Technology Assessment, *Teachers and Technology: Making the Connection* (OTA-SHR-616) (Washington, DC: Government Printing Office, 1995).
13. H. Rheingold, *The Virtual Community: Homesteading on the Electronic Frontier* (New York: Addison-Wesley, 1993).
14. B. Cohen, *Social Studies Resources on the Internet: A Guide for Teachers* (Portsmouth, NH: Heinemann, 1997).
15. Ronald L. Pantin, *The Prentice-Hall Directory of Online Social Studies Resources* (Paranus, NJ: Prentice-Hall, 1998).

FOR FURTHER STUDY: ORGANIZING FOR INSTRUCTION

Books and Materials

Association of National Advertisers. *The Role of Advertising in America*. New York: Author, 1988.

Badgikian, B. *The Media Monopoly*. 2nd ed. Boston: Beacon Press, 1987.

Beaver, F. *A History of the Motion Picture*. New York: McGraw-Hill, 1983.

Berger, Arthur A. *Media Analysis Techniques*. Newbury Park, CA: Sage Publications, 1991.

Bissel, J., A. Manning, and V. Rowland. *Cybereducator: The Internet and World Wide Web for K–12 Education*. New York: McGraw-Hill, 1999.

Bordwell, D., and K. Thompson. *Film: An Introduction*. New York: Knopf, 1986.

Carnes, M. C. *Past Imperfect: History According to the Movies*. A Society of American Historians Book. New York: Henry Holt, 1995.

Denzin, Norman K. *The Cinematic Society*. London: Sage Publications, 1995.

Downing, J., A. Mohammadi, and A. Sreberny-Mohammedi, *Questioning the Media: A Critical Introduction*. Newbury Park, CA: Sage Publications, 1990.

Fiske, J,. and J. Hartley, *Reading Television*. London: Methuen, 1978.

MacBeth, Tannis M. *Tuning in to Young Viewers*. Thousand Oaks, CA: Sage Publications. 1996.

Martorella, P. H., ed. *Interactive Technologies and the Social Studies*. Albany, NY: SUNY Press. 1997.

McKibben, Bill. *The Age of Missing Information*. New York: Random House, 1992.

McLuhan, Marshall. *Understanding Media*. New York: Mentor Books, 1964.

Parenti, M. *Inventing Reality: The Politics of Mass Media*. New York: St. Martin's Press, 1986.

Postman, N., and S. Powers. *How to Watch TV News*. New York: Penguin Books, 1992.

Real, Michael. *Exploring Media Culture*. Thousand Oaks, CA: Sage Publications, 1996.

Stull, Andrew. *Education on the Internet*. Upper Saddle River, NJ: Merrill/Prentice-Hall, 1997.

Strasburger, Victor C. *Adolescents and the Media: Medical and Psychological Impact*. Thousand Oaks, CA: Sage Publications, 1995.

Toop, D. *The Rap Attack: African Jive to New York Hip Hop*. Boston: South End, 1984.

Ulanoff, S. *Advertising in America: An Introduction to Persuasive Communication*. New York: Hastings, 1977.

Weibel, K. *Mirror, Mirror: Images of Women Reflected in Popular Culture*. Garden City, NY: Anchor, 1977.

Williamson, J. *Decoding Advertisements*. London: Marion Boyars, 1978.

Winston, B. *Misunderstanding Media*. Cambridge, MA: Harvard University Press, 1986.

Computer Simulations and CD-ROMs

Alpha Centauri. Sid Meier, Microprose, 1999.

American Freedom Library. Western Standard, 1997.

American History Inspirer: The Civil War. Tom Snyder Productions, Grades 5–12, 1997.

Ancient History CD-ROM Series. Cambridge, Grades 4–8, 1998.

Ancient Lands. Microsoft, 1994–95.

Civilization: A Computer Simulation, 1994, and *Civilization II*, 1997, by Sid Meier. Microprose.

Encarta: The Complete Multimedia Encyclopedia, 1996 ed. Microsoft.

NGS Picture Show-Immigration. Washington, DC: National Geographic Society, 1998.

Oregon Trail. MECC, 1991.

SimCity 2000. Maxis, 1995.

SimCity 3000. Maxis, 1999.

Town Government: Decisions, Decisions. Tom Snyder Productions, Grades 5–12, 1997.

Virtual Economics 2.0: An Interactive Center for Economic Education. EconomicsAmerica, Nebraska Council for Economic Education and the National Council for Economic Education, 1995, 1997.

Visual Archives of American History: American Impressions, Vols. 1 and 2. New York: Harper Collins/Interactive, 1995.

We Shall Overcome: The African-American Struggle for Voting Rights, 1963–1965. History Active, 1997.

Where in the World Is Carmen San Diego? and *Where in the USA Is Carmen San Diego?* Broderbund, 1994, 1995.

Who Built America?: From the Centennial Celebration of 1876 to the Great War of 1914. The American Social History Project. Voyager, 1993–94.

PART SIX

Beyond the Social Studies Classroom: Professional Issues and Trends

CHAPTER 16

The Complete Professional

For ongoing professional development for teachers, there must be an environment that encourages creativity and innovation, as well as a means for client-oriented accountability. Time must be provided to review professional practice and to debrief with colleagues. Constructive feedback and developmental/planning sessions are essential to ... success.

—Joseph A. Fernandez

OVERVIEW OF CONTENTS

Main Ideas

Trends and Countertrends

Professional Identity

Professional Organizations
>   The National Council for the Social Studies
>   State and Local Organizations
>   Social Science Discipline Associations
>   Special Interest Groups

Publications for the Social Studies Teacher
>   Major Journals
>   Research Literature
>   Social Science Publications

Other Instructional Resources for Social Studies Teachers

Beyond the Social Studies: Integrating Other Disciplines
>   Art
>   Music
>   Film
>   Media
>   Literature

Science and Technology _____

Summary _____

Notes _____

For Further Study: The Complete Professional _____

MAIN IDEAS

What does it mean to be a professional as a secondary social studies teacher? *Professionalism* means different things to different people, but generally we can agree that it means remaining current in the field in which you teach, in terms of both content knowledge and instructional strategies; taking advantage of opportunities and resources to make yourself a better teacher; and participating in an ongoing process of self-evaluation. This chapter looks at current trends and countertrends in social studies curriculum and instruction, at your professional identity as a social studies teacher, and at the resources available to you for both instruction and professional growth.

TRENDS AND COUNTERTRENDS

The 1980s produced a flood of reports aimed at restructuring schools and building academic excellence. The 1990s have been characterized by a search for standards, criteria, and measures of school success. These 1980s reform reports portrayed education in the United States as having fallen behind education in western Europe and Japan, with an unconscionably high dropout rate and a tragic lack of attention to at-risk students. Although employment levels generally rose throughout the decade, many educators lamented the poor training their students were receiving for careers in an increasingly complex, sophisticated "information age."[1] Demands for basic excellence gave way to "restructuring" proposals for education as a whole or for various aspects of it.

The early 1990s—with a mostly static economy buffeted by budget deficits, low job growth, and corporate "downsizing"—witnessed the development of a spate of voluntary educational standards issued by professional agencies and organizations. Stagnant or declining investment in education during most of the early to mid-1990s across the country seems to be coupled with greater demand for quality and innovation in schools. The ways in which cost-cutting in education will interact with new professional standards for achievement is not clear, but the goals do appear inconsistent.[2] Added to the twin engines of reform and "national" standards is the rapid growth of media and technology, particularly computer science. The mid- to late 1990s have also witnessed a period of sustained economic growth, rapidly rising stock market, and balanced national budget. This economic turnaround has encouraged more experimentation with school and curriculum, such as charter schools and magnet schools accompanied by strong demands for better student performance. Most reformers and most advocates of standards have embraced the idea of universal computer literacy for American students, and although in theory it has been endorsed by the U.S. government, funding has been limited. Groups of historians have shown considerable interest in using new technologies for teaching purposes as well as for research.[3] Nobody knows where all of this will go as the year 2000 arrives, but the pressures to adapt to a changing world economy and to new technology will certainly intensify rather than abate.

Most reform and restructuring plans remained in the planning stages because of declining federal dollar support for education, and because the reformers were far from reflecting a consensus on goals or programs. The social studies curriculum, however, has been restructured in largely conservative ways, with a general return to basic courses in civics, U.S. history, and European or world civilization, and a movement away from the kind of electives and problems and issues courses that had emerged from the turmoil of the 1960s. Minicourses and modules, typically a half or quarter semester in length, have generally disappeared. But that has led to renewed pressure to include in the basic courses more material on gender and cultural issues. Mandated curricula in New York and California, for example, call for the systematic inclusion of gender and multicultural topics, as well as a more global viewpoint in both world and U.S. studies. In the short run, diverse views may struggle for a place in the standard curriculum. In the long run, however, the incorporation of gender and cultural issues in mainstream courses may place those issues more firmly in students' consciousness than would isolated units or minicourses.

The 1980s reform movements often espoused the same broad goals but suggested very different, even mutually exclusive, methods for change. Prominent educators such as Theodore Sizer and John Goodlad criticize schools for their rigidity and conformity, and their stress on content rather than understanding.[4] These critics call for schools to experiment with a variety of time blocks, thematic approaches to subjects, and hands-on experiences for students organized into smaller classes, and to stress reasoning skills, group dynamics, and more decision-making power for teachers in planning both the curriculum and the school day.

A second group of "restructurers," best exemplified by Allan Bloom, E. D. Hirsch, and the "cultural literacy" movement, argue that content, and lots of it, is precisely what students need to succeed.[5] For these critics, one purpose of schooling is to introduce students to classic and enduring (read Western, not World) works of literature, history, and philosophy. They call for a tightening of curriculum restrictions that would leave teachers little room for innovation and decision making.

These two groups share some common concerns. Both would reject textbooks, for example, in favor of intellectual, original material. But shared concerns mask much larger disagreements over educational priorities in general. Deep divisions exist over such issues as teacher improvement and professionalization, curriculum content, the groups in need of more attention (elite or at-risk, bilingual or special education groups), and the techniques and skills teachers will need in years to come. Much of what the reformers argue is based on older movements in American education.[6]

Standards, of which there are many in social studies right now, have been driven by the need to define the field, set goals for student achievement, and reach out to a confused and skeptical public. The different standards, almost one for each historical and social science component of social studies, offer guidelines for teachers to follow in planning and preparing courses. Methods and materials are suggested, and many of the standards demonstrate how the quality of subject matter instruction can be reviewed by local communities. The main organization representing the social studies, the National Council for the Social Studies, has formulated its own general standards inviting states and local communities to model their goals after ten "thematic strands" that encompass history and the social sciences, including:

1. culture
2. time, continuity, and change
3. people, places, and environment
4. individual development and identity

5. individuals, groups, and institutions
6. power, authority, and governance
7. production, distribution, and consumption
8. science, technology, and society
9. global connections
10. civic ideals and practices.[7]

In the social studies during the 1980s and 1990s, conservative thinkers have probably had the most impact. As already suggested, curricula have reverted more to what was common in the 1950s: more required courses, more dependence on textbooks, and more local and state requirements for teacher training, textbook content, and both student and teacher examinations. Despite this return to basic courses, however, countertrends stress international and multicultural and gender studies and a strong reawakening of interest in geography and civics, as well as a renewed examination of current practices for students with special needs (as pointed out in earlier chapters).[8] The standards movement of the 1990s may well provide wide-ranging opportunities for social studies teachers to reinvent parts of the curriculum within the broad constraints of state guidelines. Because of private and public programs pushing reform agendas, teachers may also have more opportunities in the next century to experiment in adapting newer instructional strategies that promote higher order thinking, or new classroom technologies that involve the Internet and CD-ROMs.

PROFESSIONAL IDENTITY

Like most secondary teachers, you are probably a specialist in, and identify fairly strongly with, your subject. For social studies teachers, however, that "subject" is not singular as it is for most secondary teachers. Social studies teachers are generalist-specialists; according to a national survey, most secondary social studies teachers see themselves primarily as social studies generalists rather than specialists in a single discipline like history or economics.[9] Social studies teachers support professional organizations like the National Council for the Social Studies, but they do so in somewhat smaller relative numbers than their colleagues in English or science. The available findings suggest that "activist" professionals make up only a fraction of the total of secondary social studies teachers, and the potential for growth is sizable.[10]

Of course, professional identity is not limited to membership in a professional organization. Another measure may be ongoing participation in seminars, institutes, workshops, and other programs designed to enrich teacher knowledge and upgrade instructional methods and materials. A number of such programs are offered by national and state organizations, notably the National Endowment for the Humanities, Constitutional Rights Foundation, American Social History Project, Center for Civic Education, Taft Institute for Government, and EconomicsAmerica: The National Council for Economic Education, as well as by colleges and universities. See the Appendix A for a resource list of such programs.

TO DO

1. Define what you see as "professionalism" in social studies education. How does, or should, this concept affect behavior? Write a statement listing at least five ways in which you would express your professionalism in or out of the classroom. Share your ideas

> for action with colleagues. Do they agree or disagree with your view of professional identity?
>
> 2. Develop a checklist of opportunities for further study at home or abroad. Inquire about national and international programs, both government and private, offered by local colleges, universities, and boards of education, and outreach opportunities like the Peace Corps, World Church Services, and similar groups.

In general, social studies teachers receive little specific publicity, either positive or negative. However, the 1980s and 1990s brought a series of attacks on textbooks, the teaching of history, and the inadequacy of high school students' knowledge in geography and economics.[11] The Bradley Commission on History in Schools expressed the intention of developing upgraded history programs throughout the country. A review of major social studies textbooks in 1986 found them consistently poor in writing and often factually questionable.[12] A Gallup survey on geography in 1990 commissioned by the National Geographic Society found that American students had a relatively poor sense of place, could not identify important terms, and generally produced a lower average on the survey's test than students of most other nations tested.[13] Attacks have been renewed frequently over the last decade or two, usually directed at what students do not know or how their values and characters are lacking in some way.[14]

Implicit in all this, of course, is a negative evaluation of social studies teachers and of the field as a whole. This negative evaluation is the foundation on which the back to basics movement in social studies curriculum has been built. We should note, however, that most of these surveys emanated from outside the education field rather than from within, usually from commissions, agencies, or business leaders who are not involved in the daily business of managing schools. The clearest need at this point is for a dialogue among critics, reformers, and educators that leads to new ideas and investments in social studies, rather than rushing into rapid changes with short-lived life spans.

WHAT DO YOU THINK?

> 1. If you could design your own award for excellence in social studies instruction, what criteria would you follow? Be specific.
> 2. If you could design your own award for excellence in classroom performance by a social studies student, what criteria would you follow?

PROFESSIONAL ORGANIZATIONS

The National Council for the Social Studies (NCSS) is the single major professional organization to which secondary social studies teachers belong. Based in Washington, DC, this organization represents the interests of social studies groups throughout the country and encompasses a network of regional, state, and local social studies councils and associations. The membership includes all levels from elementary and secondary teachers through supervisors and college faculty.

Many teachers also belong to one of two major teachers' unions: the American Federation of Teachers (AFT) or the National Education Association (NEA). Both speak for teachers' interests in general and there has been some talk of a merger between the two organizations. The AFT is affiliated with the AFL-CIO umbrella organization, whereas the NEA tends to stress teachers' professional roles rather than the functions it performs as negotiator or arbitrator for salary and working conditions. An intense rivalry between the two organizations has gradually given way to a degree of coexistence and cooperation. Members of both groups belong to the NCSS, and the different styles and concerns of the two groups have sometimes led to disagreements about goals and programs within the NCSS. Overall, but not on all issues, the AFT tends to be urban oriented and more attentive to social problems and job stress, and the NEA tends to attract suburban and rural teachers and to favor professional issues over labor conditions.

The National Council for the Social Studies

The NCSS sponsors an annual national convention for social studies teachers, cosponsors regional programs and meetings, and publishes a national journal called *Social Education* and a wide-ranging series of books, pamphlets, and articles. All these activities are designed to help teachers plan lessons, design programs, and keep up with issues that affect the field. NCSS has developed a series of policy statements on censorship, academic freedom, and curriculum, and a code of ethics, which is excerpted in the Research Report on page 000. The organization's policy is decided by a president, officers, and board of trustees elected from the membership, and the day-to-day management is carried out by an executive secretary and staff.

State and Local Organizations

State associations linked to NCSS represent nearly every state in the union. These vary in strength and in aims but generally follow the lead of the parent body in developing conferences, promoting publications, arranging teacher awards, and defending common interests before the state legislature and local communities. Much of the work of state associations is curriculum oriented, especially in terms of establishing course requirements and evaluation standards. State and local associations often argue in favor of more course requirements in the social studies but against the loss of electives and student choices. Over the years, many school districts have developed innovative electives or programs only to find them squeezed out by additional course requirements or budget cuts imposed from the state level.

RESEARCH REPORT

1. It is the ethical responsibility of social studies professionals to set forth, maintain, model, and safeguard standards of instructional competence suited to the achievement of the broad goals of the social studies.
2. It is the ethical responsibility of social studies professionals to provide to every student, insofar as possible, the knowledge, skills, and attitudes necessary to function as an effective citizen.
3. It is the ethical responsibility of social studies professionals to foster the understanding and exercise of the rights guaranteed to all citizens under the Constitution of the United States and of the responsibilities implicit in those rights.
4. It is the ethical responsibility of social studies professionals to cultivate and maintain an instructional environment in which the free contest of ideas is prized.

5. It is the ethical responsibility of social studies professionals to adhere to the highest standards of scholarship in the development, production, distribution, or use of social studies materials.

6. It is the ethical responsibility of social studies professionals to concern themselves with the conditions of the school and community with which they are associated.

SOURCE: *A Code of Ethics for the Social Studies Profession* (Washington, DC: National Council for the Social Studies, 1980).

Local social studies associations are usually built around counties, groups of counties, or urban centers. These organizations are frequently dominated by secondary social studies teachers, who most clearly define themselves as subject specialists; elementary teachers participate in much lesser numbers, and local organizations often work vigorously to bridge this gap.

Local organizations vary greatly in size, range of activities, and effectiveness. Some large cities like Los Angeles, Chicago, and New York have active councils that sponsor annual conferences, develop publications, and conduct a variety of programs; smaller groups typically offer more modest programs. The name, address, and telephone number of any local or regional association should be available to you through the NCSS state or national organization.

Social Science Discipline Associations

In addition to the network of NCSS councils, social studies teachers have a rich base of support from which to choose in particular subject areas. Professional groups like the American Historical Association and the American Geographic Society typically publish one or more journals and often serve as the cutting edge of research and thinking in a given field. These associations are listed in Appendix A. Membership in these kinds of organizations allows you to stay in close touch with the field or fields that interest you most and to keep abreast of current controversies and changes. What is taught in school and what is the basis of scholarly debate in any given field can be quite different, so membership in both NCSS and a discipline association may be vital in allowing you to translate new interpretations from the research world to classroom teaching.

Special Interest Groups

A variety of other organizations offer supportive materials for instruction, information on particular issues, and sometimes programs open to social studies teachers on a long-term or temporary basis. Such organizations may focus on particular countries or cultural regions (the Asia Society), or on a concept like peace education (the War Resisters League), environmental studies (Greenpeace), or foreign affairs (the Foreign Policy Association). Some centers and programs offer valuable opportunities for afterschool or summer study, for both students and teachers. You will find these organizations listed in Appendix A.

PUBLICATIONS FOR THE SOCIAL STUDIES TEACHER

Social studies is rich in resources because it draws from so many different fields for its supply of ideas, methods, and materials. In addition to its own scholarly and organizational base, social studies calls on history, the social sciences, the humanities, and the sciences.

Major Journals

Journals and newsletters are one way of maintaining contact among professionals about the latest materials, issues, theories, and research in a given field. The two major social studies publications are *Social Education*, which represents the interests and concerns of the National Council for the Social Studies and is part of the NCSS membership package, and *Social Studies*, which represents a loose network of administrators, college professors, and secondary and elementary teachers and is supported by the Heldref Foundation (see the Appendix A for addresses for these journals). Both journals cover a wide range of topics and often offer special issues on, for example, the Vietnam War, immigration, or grade-level concerns in the social studies. Both journals also regularly present features for teachers and reports on the latest curricular projects and research in the field.

Research Literature

For those who want to gain more insight into research findings than the social studies journals provide, a number of other important publications are available. The major theoretical journal in the social studies is *Theory and Research in Social Education*, published by NCSS. *Theory and Research* incorporates findings based on observational surveys and experimental studies as well as providing space for debates on controversial issues. A recent issue included articles on "Classroom Teachers' Thinking About Historical Texts" and "Studying Colonization in Eighth Grade."[15]

A more modest but nevertheless useful journal, *Journal of Social Studies Research*, is published by the University of Georgia, and *Social Education* and *Social Studies* offer occasional research sections as well. Social studies researchers occasionally publish articles in one of the three publications of the American Educational Research Association (AERA)—*Review of Educational Research*, *Journal of Educational Research*, and *The Educational Researchers*—but most preliminary work is directed to more specifically focused journals.

Social Science Publications

Each social science professional organization publishes one or more journals that report current research findings. You may find these valuable, particularly if you are offering a special elective or wish to introduce current debates or controversial issues into the classroom. You should also be aware of the wide range of popular publications like *Psychology Today*, *National Geographic*, and *Smithsonian* magazine that address social studies topics, as well as those publications that cater directly to teaching concerns like *Teaching Political Science*, the *Journal of Environmental Education*, *American Anthropology Newsletter* (including tips for teachers), *Senior Economist*, *World Press Review* (articles and excerpts the world's news sources), and the *Magazine of History*. These sources often provide whole articles for discussion, as well as tables, graphs, and pictures to be examined.

OTHER INSTRUCTIONAL RESOURCES FOR SOCIAL STUDIES TEACHERS

Classroom work can be enriched with a wide range of original source materials, outside experts, field trips, and other innovative resources of these kinds. Copies of original source materials for U.S. history and civics classes can be obtained free of charge from a variety of government offices at the federal, state, and local levels. Begin with the National Archives, the Smithsonian, or at the top with the White House; try the various presidential libraries for copies of speeches, memorabilia, and position papers. (See Appendix A for addresses.) Commager and

Morrison's *Documents of American History* is an invaluable classic resource,[16] and similar collections are available for other world regions and time periods as well, including *Roman Civilization* (two volumes), *Through African Eyes* and *Through Middle Eastern Eyes*, Columbia University's *Sources of Eastern Traditions* series, and Benjamin Keen's *Documents of Latin American History*.[17]

Local historical societies often maintain lists of speakers whose knowledge can enliven a classroom; local history can demonstrate how great historical movements of national or international character were reflected in your own town or area. We often overlook our own hometowns as places of historical importance, and yet much can be learned from them: Ask students to design and carry out an oral history project based on older residents in their community, or have them research their town's role in the Revolutionary War, the Civil War, or the Spanish settlement of the southwest.

Not every high school class can visit Williamsburg, Virginia, Sturbridge Village in Massachusetts, or the Alamo in Texas, but virtually every class has some site nearby that is of historical significance—a beautiful old church or synagogue, the site of a revolutionary war or frontier battle, or one of the nation's first steel mills or industrial plants. Let your students discover what sites are important. Sites of national importance like those already mentioned often produce documents and classroom materials. Take advantage of these even if you and your students cannot be there. Plan a simulated trip to the Alamo, with sound effects and slides; let students take the roles of Jim Bowie and Colonel Travis. Check if the stories are authentic and do not forget to include a few Mexican characters like General Santa Ana. Or, work out an itinerary for a trip to China or the Middle East with a list of places to visit and people to talk to when you get there! Have some fun with this assignment.

The primary lesson to understand is that social studies resources are everywhere—often right next door, so to speak—and many of them are free. Take a week of your summer and write letters of inquiry; find out what is available, and then put it to use in your classroom. Or arrange for students to write the letters—they usually enjoy getting mail.

BEYOND THE SOCIAL STUDIES: INTEGRATING OTHER DISCIPLINES

Many superb social studies teaching tools are not social studies tools at all. Because social studies draws from or integrates with other disciplines, including the humanities and the sciences, you may find excellent materials for lessons in other fields. You may want to teach about history through art, about social protest issues through song, about ethical and philosophical issues through classical literature. And you will certainly want to call on resources available to you through technology to teach about development and environmental issues.

Art

Museums offer prime field trip possibilities and frequently provide for the rental or purchase of slides from their own collections or those of other museums. Using slides of architecture, paintings, and sculpture will inevitably bring insights to your students not available from textbook material alone. In addition to museums, private archives can sometimes supply slide collections (although often at some cost) and art history textbooks often have plates that can be reproduced.

Music

Music also provides an extraordinary insight into the circumstances of a given time period—not simply folk music and social protest songs, but opera, gospel, and popular song as well. If your students themselves are willing to perform, all the better. Encourage them to analyze the purpose, meaning, and function of music in history; build a lesson, for example, on national anthems that are designed to build a sense of national identification, or on marches and parade music intended to build enthusiasm for military campaigns, or on social protest songs over the years. Use folk music to show students how cultural styles, forms, and instruments can diverge or converge in different patterns over time and geographic territories. Use topical or campaign songs as a springboard for talking about political issues, or popular songs as indicators of changing class or sexual mores.

Film

Films are democratic by design, easy to assimilate and enjoy, and often a rich source of material for discussion and interpretation. A quick retrospective of scenes from old westerns juxtaposed with a piece from *Little Big Man* or *Dances With Wolves* will open students' eyes to the ways in which movies reinforce or attack stereotypes for a largely uncritical audience. Have students watch *Glory* and then read the letters on which the narrative is based. Let students compare a film treatment of a historical episode, such as *Nixon* or *Braveheart* with primary and secondary accounts, and then ask them to develop their own version of the event based on a comparison of what they have seen and read. With the widespread availability of videotaped movies, you have an almost intoxicating range of possibilities from which to choose.

Literature

Short stories, novels, folktales, poems, and plays all illuminate the time in which they were composed and offer a springboard for the discussion of social, political, and economic issues. Fiction often gives students insights into history that are unobtainable from public documents or narrative history, because these sources often suppress the emotional and dramatic qualities that make literature so compelling. Using literature in the classroom is an instructional strategy that has recently come into its own (see chapters 5, 6, 7, and 8), and resources abound. Comprehensive collections specifically designed for schools have become increasingly available. For example, *Literature: World Masterpieces* moves across time and regions, providing a rich resource of songs, poems, stories and documents for global or world history courses.[18]

In addition to literature per se, numerous works of philosophy represent important changes in thinking and ideology and have had a wide influence on the course of world history. Some philosophers are so important in the development of social thought that they should be part of every social studies program in some form so that students have an opportunity to understand the key ideas that have served as models, and frequently as rationales, for important historical movements. Thinkers whose works could profitably be discussed include Plato, Seneca, St. Augustine, Machiavelli, Ibn Khaldun, Avicenna, Descartes, Locke, Rousseau, Marx, Engels, John Stuart Mill, Ortega y Gasset, Suzuki, Foucault, Confucius, Mo Tzu, and Gandhi. Philosophical writings can be particularly illuminating because they combine historical, literary, and ideological elements in single works. They are also critically important in understanding historical development and intellectual controversies.

Science and Technology

Much of human history concerns the impact of technological change on human economics, culture, and social relations. The argument can be made that scientific literacy is crucial for the public as a whole if it is to make sense of an increasingly technical world. Social studies in particular provides an atmosphere conducive to discussing and evaluating science-related issues, and advocates of interdisciplinary approaches argue for the inclusion of such issues in the curriculum.[19] The movement to develop in students the knowledge and capability to apply scientific concepts to social issues is often called a science/technology/society (STS) approach; this approach has been mainly the work of science educators, but its appeal has broadened over the years to include math and social studies educators as well. The NCSS Science and Society Committee has developed a rationale and guidelines for infusing STS ideas, materials, and issues throughout the social studies curriculum.[20] Science literacy in the social studies demands that students be prepared to keep their minds open to issues and allow time for reflection, resisting quick pro and con judgments about scientific and technological questions. Consider how many modern problems and issues (e.g., birth control, computer literacy, and industrial pollution) have technological aspects, or affect current and future technological changes.

LET'S DECIDE

1. Envision yourself as a social studies teacher in the years 2000 and 2010. What do you see as the most important areas of ongoing concern for you? How will you seek to grow in both knowledge and skill? What kinds of experiences will you pursue—travel, study, reading, further training? Compare your vision of teaching with those of several colleagues or classmates or practicing teachers of social studies.

2. What kind of teacher do you envision yourself being? Do you see yourself making choices between concepts such as active and passive, intellectual and practical, avant-garde and conservative, didactic and reflective, individual and cooperative, meeting content goals and student needs? What are your classmates and colleagues views and how do these compare with your own?

3. Do you see the choices as less clear-cut and more eclectic—a mix of goals and methods designed to suit changing student audiences, social mores, and political atmospheres? Make a list of your choices and share it with colleagues. To which choices do you and others feel most committed? Which do you and others see as least important?

SUMMARY

Two major tenets of professionalism are your continued growth and interest in social studies, and a caring, attentive attitude toward your audience. Professionalism is a commitment to continuously update your knowledge of the social sciences and history, and to keep abreast of changing educational methodology. Professionalism is helping your audience to achieve the didactic, reflective, and affective goals that will produce thoughtful, productive, and ethical people.

The philosopher John Dewey pointed out around the turn of the century that effective teaching represents a balance between subject matter and student learning in which both aspects are woven into a meaningful whole.[21] The students pay attention to the subject while the teacher treats their ideas with interest and respect.

As the experience of teaching grows, you should become an active member of one or more organizations. You should attend conferences, seminars, and summer institutes that deal with topics of interest and will deepen your understanding of people and events in history and literature. Read at least one or two journals regularly. Consider research findings as these apply to teaching. You should use your newfound knowledge to develop materials and lessons of your own unique design and share these with colleagues in your school and at professional meetings and conventions. Seek out the adventure of learning, and do not go stale teaching the same topics in the same way every semester.

Above all, think of your audience as young adults and adults who have ideas to contribute, decisions to make, and problems to contemplate. Build feedback into your programs and take the results seriously as bases from which to improve your choice of subject matter and techniques. Be open-minded, incorporate new technologies, texts, and points of view into your standard fare, whether these are computer games or critical revisions of women's place in the curriculum.[22] Share new ideas, critiques, and difficulties with your audience, demonstrating that knowledge is never completely settled. Above all, bring your audience into the fray, and take them as they are rather than as "idealized" students who should, could, or must perform certain "good" behaviors to be admitted into the halls of power. Be willing to analyze the potential and the deficiencies of your audience, keeping a watchful eye on diagnosing learning problems and a clear mind on seeking instructional improvements.

Make use of a wide variety of resources to enliven your teaching, including drawing from the humanities and the sciences. Employ film, art, music, literature, and other resources to enrich the documents, texts, and historical narratives that form the typical social studies curriculum. Expose yourself to traditions, literatures, and histories from unfamiliar viewpoints (e.g., Muslim, African, Latin American, and Asian sources); select some sources that are countercultural and critical of prevailing ideas, customs, and attitudes. Look at the overlooked, and give the "outsiders" a chance to be heard.

Throughout your teaching career, keep working on a style and method that best suits the educational philosophy you find most comfortable intellectually and most effective for students in achieving didactic, reflective, and affective goals set for social studies education. Set a few goals for building values and character. Ask students to provide suggestions that complement or challenge your own. Invite them to be creative, critical, and philosophical, too. Philosophy is an inherent feature of professionalism because it is from these higher principles that we decide what to teach, how to teach, and why to teach.

NOTES

1. D. Benjamin and D. D. Schneider, "Patterns of Work Experience Among High School Students: Educational Implications," *High School Journal* 66 (Apr./May 1983): 267–75.
2. D. Viadero, "First National Standards Bring Anxiety to Social-Studies Educators," *Education Week* (2 December 1992): 5.
3. A. McMicheal, M. O'Malley, and R. Rosensweig, @147>Historians and the Web: A Guide," *Perspectives: the American Historical Association Newsletter.* Vol.34, no.1 (Jan. 1996): 11–15.
4. Theodore Sizer, *Horace's Compromise* (Boston: Houghton Mifflin, 1984); and John Goodlad, *A Place Called School* (New York: McGraw-Hill, 1984).
5. Allan Bloom, *The Closing of the American Mind* (New York: Simon & Schuster, 1987); and E. D. Hirsch, *Cultural Literacy: What Every American Needs to Know* (Boston: Houghton Mifflin, 1987).
6. Barbara Preisseisen, *Unlearning Lessons: Current and Past Reforms for School Improvement* (Philadelphia: Falmer Press, 1985).
7. National Council for the Social Studies, *Curriculum Standards for Social Studies: Expectations of Excellence.* (Washington, DC: NCSS, 1992).
8. Geography Education Standards Project, *Geography for Life: National Geography Standards 1994.* (Washington, DC: National Geographic, 1994).

9.   Wayne Dumas, Thomas Weible, and Sam Evans, "State Standards for Licensure of Secondary Social Studies Teachers," *Theory and Research in Social Education* 18, no. 1 (Winter 1990): 30–36.

10. S. Sarason, *The Culture of the School and the Problem of Change* (Boston: Allyn & Bacon, 1982).

11. Diane Ravitch and Chester Finn, *What Do Our Seventeen Year Olds Know? A Report on the First National Assessment of History and Literature* (New York: Harper & Row, 1987).

12. O. L. Davis, Jr. et al., *Looking at History: A Review of Major U.S. History Textbooks* (Washington, DC: People for the American Way, 1986).

13. The Gallup Organization, *Geography: An International Gallup Survey* (conducted for National Geographic). Princeton: NJ: Gallup, Inc., 1988.

14. Paul Hill, Lawrence C. Pierce, and James W. Guthrie, *Reinventing Public Education: How Contracting Can Transform America's Schools* (Chicago, IL: University of Chicago Press, 1998).

15. *Theory and Research in Social Education* 24, no. 2 (Spring 1996).

16. Henry Steele Commager and Raymond Muessig, *The Study and Teaching of History* (Columbus, OH: Merrill, 1980).

17. Theodore DeBary, *Sources of Eastern Traditions Series: China, Japan and India*, 2 vols. each (New York: Columbia University Press, 1958). Also see Naphtali Lewis and Meyer Reinhold, eds. *Roman Civilization*, vols. 1–2, 3rd ed. (New York: Columbia University Press, 1990).

18. Ellen Bowler et al., eds. *Prentice-Hall Literature: World Masterpieces*, 4th ed. (Upper Saddle River, NJ: Prentice-Hall, 1996).

19. Faith M. Hickman, John J. Patrick, and Roger W. Bybee, *Science/Technology/Society: A Framework for Curriculum Reform in Secondary School Science and Social Studies* (Boulder, CO: Social Science Education Consortium, 1987).

20. NCSS Science and Society Committee, "Teaching About Science, Technology, and Society in Social Studies: Education for Citizenship in the 21st Century," *Social Education* (Apr./May 1990): 189–93.

21. John Dewey, *New Schools for Old* (New York: Dutton, 1919).

22. Joseph A. Braun, Jr., Phyllis Fernland, and Charles S. White, *Technology in the Social Studies Curriculum* (Wilsonville, OR: Franklin, Beedle & Associates, 1998).

FOR FURTHER STUDY: THE COMPLETE PROFESSIONAL

Banks, J. A., ed. *Multicultural Education: Transformative Knowledge and Action. Historical and Contemporary Perspectives*. New York: Teacher's College Press, 1996.

Clift, R. T., W. R. Houston, and M. Pugach, eds. *Encouraging Reflective Practice in Education: An Analysis of Issues and Programs*. New York: Teacher's College Press, 1990.

Evans, Ronald W., and David Warren Saxe, eds. *Handbook on the Teaching of Social Issues*. Bulletin No. 93. Washington, DC: National Council for Social Studies, 1996.

Kellough, Richard D. *Integrating Language Arts and Social Studies: For Intermediate and Middle School Students*. Englewood Cliffs, NJ: Prentice-Hall, 1996.

Lieberman, A., ed. *Building a Professional Culture in Schools*. New York: Teacher's College Press, 1988.

Massialas, Byron G., and Rodney F. Allen. *Crucial Issues in Teaching Social Studies, K–12*. Belmont, CA: Wadsworth Publishing, 1996.

Nieto, S. *The Light in Their Eyes: Creating Multicultural Learning Communities*. New York: Teachers College Press, 1999.

Onosko, J. "Comparing Teachers' Thinking About Promoting Students' Thinking." *Theory and Research in Social Education* 27, no. 3 (1989): 174–95.

Parker, Walter C. *Renewing the Social Studies Curriculum*. Alexandria, VA: Association for Curriculum and Development, 1991.

Rosenholtz, S. J. *Teachers' Workplace: The Social Organization of Schools*. White Plains, NY: Longman, 1989.

Shaver, James P., ed. *Handbook of Research on Social Studies Teaching and Learning*. New York: MacMillan, 1991.

Spring, J. *Conflicts of Interest: The Politics of American Education*. White Plains, NY: Longman, 1988.

CHAPTER 17

The Future of Social Studies Education

All that is required for this enlightenment is freedom; and particularly the least harmful of all that may be called freedom, namely, the freedom for man to make public use of his reason in all matters. But I hear people clamor on all sides; Don't argue! The officer says: Don't argue, drill! The tax collector: Don't argue, pay! The pastor: Don't argue, believe! ... Here we have restrictions on freedom everywhere. Which restriction is hampering enlightenment, and which does not, or even promotes it? I answer: The public use of a man's reason must be free at all times, and this alone can bring enlightenment among men.

—Immanuel Kant, "What Is Enlightenment?"

OVERVIEW OF CONTENTS

Main Ideas

Professional Issues and Political Cycles

Trends and Prospects

Summary and Recommendations

Notes

For Further Study: The Future of Social Studies Education

MAIN IDEAS

For the past two decades, the social studies has been in a state of retreat and consolidation from the innovation and expansion of the 1960s and early 1970s. At the secondary level, the trend has been toward requiring students to enroll in broad survey courses, particularly U.S. and world studies, with little room left for electives. There has also been a resurgence of interest in civics, geography, history, and democracy courses combined with a lobbying effort to restore Western history to a predominant place in the curriculum. Reformers have proposed and pushed a number of changes during the last decade that have affected school structure and programs, but in a very fragmented way as of this writing. Some reforms have stimulated trends toward smaller, more creative secondary schools, and others have encouraged more rigorous and often more rigid "classical" learning for social studies and other subjects. Since the late 1980s there has been a broad movement to establish national standards for all school subjects that would replace local standards.[1]

During the 1990s, a concerted, but somewhat uncoordinated and confusing effort has been made to establish national standards for social studies, as well as for many of its component subjects (specifically world and U.S. history, geography, civics, and economics). Some of these standards have been proposed by professional organizations such as the National Council for the Social Studies, the American Association of Geographers, and the National Council for Economic Education (EconomicsAmerica), whereas other standards have been sponsored by special projects such as the National Center for History in Schools (U.S. and world history) and the Constitutional Rights Foundation (civics and government). Several of the standards have emphasized overarching goals for social studies, and others have promoted specific content goals. Interestingly, all of the groups sponsoring standards have incorporated statements about building strong thinking and reasoning skills, and examining competing values and beliefs. This struggle for change is still underway and will undoubtedly continue for many years. Some educators have gone so far as to suggest that a national curriculum with agreed on standards should be adopted for the United States as a whole, whereas others vigorously oppose this concept.[2]

WHAT DO YOU THINK?

Do you approve or disapprove of the movement toward state and national standards for social studies? Do you think there should be general standards for the field as a whole, such as those proposed by the National Council for the Social Studies, or many sets of specific standards, such as those for history, geography, economics, and civics?

In contrast to the trend toward more history and civics, greater reliance on textbooks, and course consolidation, there has also been a good deal of research on and promotion of higher order thinking, reflective teaching, and discussing social issues in the social studies.[3] In addition, there have been numerous efforts to integrate ethnic, minority, female, and non-Western data and viewpoints into traditional courses. Which of these trends, if any, will prevail over the others is, of course, speculative, but, for the long haul, a global approach will probably succeed over more Eurocentric traditions; and significant amounts of social and cultural history (as opposed to political and economic) will be infused into American studies.

The incorporation of problem-solving and higher cognitive processes must also be taken seriously even though research shows the field is still dominated by lecture/recitation methods. At least theoretically, the reform movements and the creation of national standards ought to promote more experimentation and better assessment in the nation's schools. However, it is almost impossible to predict whether there will be another period of intellectual ferment and creativity in a field constricted by state and local curriculum guidelines, political mores, funding problems for schools, conservative values, and modest levels of professional activism by teachers. But, as history teaches us, no subject, system, or nation can stay in the same pattern forever!

TO DO

In your own city, town, or district, what have you heard about the movement toward standards? Ask questions of colleagues and educators to find out what their views are about the pressures being exerted on them to adopt new techniques, new tools, and new programs. What has been the view of incorporating improved teaching and learning methods and materials, particularly those stressing higher level thinking or the "multiple intelligences" concept?

PROFESSIONAL ISSUES AND POLITICAL CYCLES

Professional issues in social studies education have focused and are likely to continue to focus on the goals and content of the subject. As reviewed in this book, the goals of this field are by no means settled on by its practitioners. Several strong currents and countercurrents run throughout the curriculum, its instructional methodology, and public mandates for the social studies.

Deeply embedded issues arise from at least two opposing views of the field, one stressing the transmission of factual knowledge along with patriotism and civic pride, and the other stressing active, applied knowledge and critical questioning to create citizens capable of making their own decisions. The twin poles are the transmission or traditional approach versus a more reflective or critical-minded approach. Although these two represent false dichotomies to some extent, each symbolizes for many in our field a philosophy that they hold dear, to the exclusion of the "other side."

Usually, those in favor of tradition, transmission of the past, and civic pride tend to take a more conservative view of the field and see themselves as assisting students to identify with American democracy and Western civilization by providing knowledge of key events in history and by fostering an attitude of national pride and commitment to democratic processes.[4] Often students are viewed as passive acceptors of these ideas and attitudes, although active participation is certainly not precluded by a conservative approach to social studies.

By contrast, those who stress an issues orientation combined with decision making and critical thinking skills often emphasize more recent history, current controversies, and social science approaches toward analyzing human action and belief. Their goal is to encourage students to make up their own minds on the issues and questions before them and mobilize an effort to change the situation. This approach implies a more active student who participates frequently in both class discussion and social action. Unfortunately, this much desired involvement is often honored in the breach by practitioners, however strongly they express goals of "open-mindedness" and "taking a stand" or "expressing values."[5]

There are many variations and combinations in social studies objectives, but an important dividing line separates those who see the subject as a major agent in reinforcing American values and traditions and those who view the subject as a means of fostering independent decision making and social activism.[6]

WHAT DO YOU THINK?

How would you prepare to teach morality and ethics? Would you teach values, or teach about values? Would you uphold traditions critically or uncritically? Would you tell your students about social activism and award it an honorable place in American school culture, or would you leave such choices strictly up to the students and their parents?

Personally, I believe that a great deal depends upon how these two views of the field define their terms and prescribe teacher practices. Deweyians place great value on open-mindedness within a democratic context, and on students interacting with subject matter to draw their own conclusions. More conservative thinkers frankly believe that the schools should indoctrinate children and youth to conform to "proper" values, that is, patriotism, positive work values, good manners, and most recently, excellence of character. More liberal or radical thinkers also press the social studies to direct students' values but in the direction of social justice and community responsibility. All of these competing philosophies demand a commitment to a set of values, some of which do not agree with each other. For instance, many elements of the various national standards demonstrate different philosophical undertones, while trying to combine a broad range of viewpoints and educational objectives. A recent argument in favor of research settling philosophical questions seems to place too much confidence in research and too little confidence in negotiation, implying that there is or could be a consensus on the interpretation of complex educational studies.[7]

The big questions concern how to achieve a balance between the need to guide students and the need to raise questions, between encouraging conformity in some areas and activism in others, and between providing information to absorb, or problems and issues to solve. The difference in the degree to which young people are given the opportunity truly to think for themselves or simply to choose among alternatives is a key, perhaps the key issue in accepting one or another of the major social studies traditions. I would argue that the most useful and acceptable philosophy is the one that allows you and your students the greatest degree of choice and the least amount of distortion and bias.

I have attempted to demonstrate (in what I consider the best Deweyian tradition) that polar opposites need not necessarily be viewed as mutually exclusive. Rather, key elements of each, where these are not in conflict, can be molded into a new approach to teaching social studies that attempts a careful and thoughtful balancing of goals and curriculum. In such instruction, students receive knowledge of the past combined with a critical approach to the knowledge presented, a thorough analysis of selected topics and sufficient time to practice decision-making skills through a variety of group dynamics procedures that could include role-playing, debating, and simulation games. The argument has been made that an effective social studies teacher must incorporate knowledge, reasoning, and value goals into every aspect of the courses that are taught. Didactic, reflective, and affective objectives may be viewed as complementary to and interlocking with one another, to such an extent that the omission of one or another domain from a lesson, unit, course, or program will dramatically weaken the learning that takes place, leaving students with, at best, a partial understanding of history and the social sciences.

It is always necessary to acquire information, but information is not terribly useful by itself, without the benefit of adequate comprehension and synthesis. In other words, you need to teach students facts, but this does not necessarily help them to solve problems. They must learn to organize facts into arguments, and apply facts to claims. Students also must learn to recognize and deal with problems, controversies, issues, and conflicting views and theories. Conflicts and arguments can be understood better if facts are available, but these facts are often marshaled into a sequence that is designed to prove or disprove a conclusion. In reality, two or more competing conclusions may frequently rely on the same facts. At this point confusion begins, and it does not end until students learn to identify assumptions and use, analyze, organize, and judge reasons and arguments.

The problem is not one of fact or opinion, data or argument, but how to combine both in a way that increases students' understanding and builds their reasoning skills and what some have called their "practical competence".[8] Thus, someone who develops an informed opinion or reasoned judgment on a question or issue, past or present, arrives at conclusions on a chain of reasoning based on evidence. Too often, teachers neglect one goal area in favor of another, usually stressing the didactic because passing on information is the easiest aspect of instruction and the one most supported by societal values, textbooks, school testing, and grading procedures.[9] Facts alone, without application to action, principles, or theory, are isolated and sterile, eventually diminishing students' involvement in their studies. Might we ask how students can put their facts to use?

A second area of deep debate and division in the social studies revolves around the role of the social sciences and history in the social studies. Many scholars and much of the public view favorably the notion that the social studies is and should be basically history (or maybe history and geography)—that it has characteristically been so for about a hundred years. Others argue strongly that the social studies represents an integration of history, the humanities, and the social sciences, and really cannot do without any of these subjects as sources of new knowledge and methodology.

There is an active prohistory lobby which sees the field in serious jeopardy within the social studies, although the evidence for a decline in the focus on history seems quite slender.[10] If anything, the decline that exists would appear to be proportionate to the extent of growth of the social sciences, from which historians have felt free to borrow for decades but now object to as school subjects. If anything, over the last two or three decades, there has been a noticeable decline in new or innovative subjects in the social studies, with a national secondary curriculum emerging that consists basically of four subject areas: American studies, world studies, government or problems of democracy (civics), and perhaps economics. Geography has staged a bit of a comeback, but it is still not recognized as a separate course in the school curriculum in most places. Other social sciences and special topics are usually taught as electives when time, interest, and budget allow. Courses on multicultural and multiethnic topics and electives of all types have disappeared to a great extent in the 1980s and 1990s, with a return to large, comprehensive courses into which the other topics have been successfully or unsuccessfully integrated.[11]

Thus, whereas lobbies have arisen for history and for other fields such as geography, seeking to increase and/or upgrade their share of the social studies curriculum, most state or local curricula have been moving toward larger scale secondary level programs that attempt to integrate history and one or more social sciences or humanities. For example, "mainstream" and "minority" history, Western tradition and world studies struggle with a variety of "multicultural" conceptions and formats no one of which has at the present writing taken a dominant position in the field.[12]

Traditional topics and course conceptions, largely chronological, have continued to be taught in most communities at the junior and senior high school levels, with perhaps the most serious incursions of new ideas and materials coming into global or world studies programs that seek to build a comprehensive gestalt of the planet for students, balancing a Eurocentric approach with a geocentric approach. There is also some experimentation with team or 'core' concepts that call for coordinating or integrating social studies and literature courses in secondary schools. It is unlikely, given the overstuffed and overmandated nature of the secondary social studies curriculum in most states, that a history association, any social science association, or any single special interest like civics or law will or should gain more than a marginal increase for their concerns within the overall curriculum. To the extent that any one subject or special interest does gain a place for itself, the victory will probably be ephemeral if the subject matter and its methods are not integrated into the major courses taught by nearly all secondary school teachers.

LET'S DECIDE

Debate, pro and con, these propositions with friends and colleagues:

1. All social studies students must share the same common goals and values.
2. Students must build their own individual visions of societal goals.
3. Every subject within social studies should have its own standards for success.
4. Social studies as a whole should have its own standards for success.
5. History should be the heart and soul of the social studies.
6. Decision making should be the heart and soul of the social studies.
7. Social science should be the heart and soul of the social studies.
8. Develop a "heart and soul" focus of your own to discuss.
9. There should be a national curriculum with the same standards for all students.
10. There should be local control over curriculum, which must reflect the needs and interests of the community.

TRENDS AND PROSPECTS

Based on developments in the 1980s, the social studies has been in what may best be described as a holding pattern. Not only is the intense questioning and debate of the 1960s and 1970s missing, but there has been little in the way of new programs, ideas, or methodologies. If anything, the trend has been toward greater consolidation of secondary school curricula accompanied by a modest return to history as a central focus and a reintroduction of civics and geography in some states in old and new guises. Didactic instruction has probably been bolstered as the curriculum has tightened, even though accompanied by a good deal of talk about reflection.[13]

As stated, most curricula have been reduced to four or five basic courses: American studies; world or global studies; some form of civics, government, or problems of democracy; economics; and a few social science electives such as sociology, psychology, and anthropology. Largely gone are minicourses on selected controversial topics such as crime, lobbying, political protest, women's rights, ethnic studies, or the environment. Many of these controversial social issues have been either subsumed into or smothered by the general programs, particularly American studies. Adding controversies and multicultural topics into standard courses has perhaps increased awareness that gender and diversity are still marginal to the total curriculum.[14] My view is that current courses and textbooks are considerably better than they were twenty years ago, but downplay cultural, ethnic, and gender concerns and viewpoints. Although a great deal of variety and experimentation has been lost because of the trend toward consolidation, there has been a concomitant increase in the integration of specific issues and new historical materials into a more general framework.[15]

Consolidation has also strengthened the trend toward teacher reliance on textbooks at the junior and senior high school levels, with narrative, tests, and supplemental materials often provided by one publisher for a specific course. This reliance on standard textbooks produces greater uniformity in social studies education and makes life easier for most teachers and students, but it also leaves classroom participants as captives of one program or point of view, frequently without their knowing this or being able to correct for it.[16] Of course, some textbooks are better than others, offering original sources to read, pictures to analyze, and a more provocative narrative to discuss. Books that encourage higher level thinking processes and are based on affective and reflective goals are increasingly available, but many others are still dry compilations of facts with relatively little encouragement of debate or discussion.

One of the sturdier trends in social studies education, which began after World War II and was greatly strengthened during the 1960s and 1970s, is the effort to create a truly integrated global or world studies program for secondary school students: one that incorporates East and West, North and South, in a fair and unbiased manner, seeking to give students at least an introduction to the viewpoints of others. The world studies courses that have developed have taken many forms and followed different approaches—from the traditional, chronological Western history structure to those that are thematic, cross-cultural, foreign policy, or economically oriented. In each case, including the Western approach, attempts have been made to incorporate Asian, African, Latin American, and Middle Eastern primary sources and texts, pictures, and cultural artifacts, dates, names, and places into the mainstream narrative of the course.[17]

So far, no fully satisfying integration of elements has been achieved, but there have been notable advances from the purely Eurocentric origins of earlier programs, and there has been sharply increased awareness of the influence of foreign cultures, especially Asian societies, on our own traditions. Latin America, Africa, and the Middle East have probably become far better known to students and teachers than they were in the last few decades, although there is still a great deal of room for growth in familiarity with all non-Western cultures, even the relatively popular Asian group.

Slowly, a worldview has tended to replace a regional view, sometimes with a current events focus on conflict and peace.[18] The trend toward greater interest in and understanding of so-called non-Western societies is likely to grow during the next century, especially given the atmosphere of worldwide political détente; and increased trade between the world and regional powers—particularly the United States, Western Europe, Russia, Japan, East Asia, and the People's Republic of China—which account for the bulk of the world's population and international trade.

Finally, on the much discussed issue of content knowledge versus pedagogy or method, "camps" have developed on both sides. One side stresses the need for subject matter, arguing that thinking can occur only in the context of a topic or concept, such as science, mathematics, or politics. The other side contends that thinking skills can and should be taught as a set of exercises separate from subject matter so students can give their full attention to reasoning strategies.[19] Because subjects are often difficult to define and thinking can take place on both abstract and concrete levels, a rapprochement is likely to develop merging the different views into a reasonable whole. The reason for a merger is that accepting either side as the sole view neglects important aspects of social studies education—knowledge, reasoning, and value goals, all of which are related to and dependent on each other. Whether critical thinking and pedagogic skills can be taught as skills isolated from subject matter is an important issue in some contexts, but is not a very useful question in the social studies because instruction and content must be dealt with together. Teachers—that's us—must also be trained or retrained to teach in "new" ways but also retain a solid knowledge base (i.e., "Although a multi- or interdisciplinary emphasis would be paramount, quality coursework in all of the social science disciplines would still be need.").[20]

If anything, there is far too much knowledge to choose from in a typical curriculum, necessitating difficult choices. Those who opt for subject matter coverage (primarily didactic goals) find that even at their highest speeds they can at best touch only lightly on vital topics and issues in any given course. Whatever methods are used (lecture, discussion, or debate) each expresses a spirit and attitude that informs the content. Theoretically, a lecture could further didactic, reflective, and/or affective goals depending on the teacher's overall plan. A narrow, teacher-directed approach will achieve primarily didactic goals unless you adopt a point of view and stance that emphasizes reflective and/or affective objectives. For instance, South Africa's population, economy, and political parties could be studied without much discussion of the moral issues rising out of the rejected apartheid system, missing the whole point of raising social controversies about life in a multiracial society.

As John Dewey points out, opposing schools of thought may be looking at different elements of the total problem, thereby stressing their antagonisms rather than the search for a solution that solves the educational problems.[21] The debate over content versus pedagogy and coverage versus higher level thinking will probably continue for the next decade at least, but it represents what is probably a false dichotomy rather than an overview of all factors. The real problem is to provide social studies teaching and learning that is exciting, sound, intellectually provocative, meets the needs of the student audience, and is defensible on both practical and philosophical grounds. Students need knowledge, but they also need understanding and will undoubtedly try to convert whatever is taught into meaningful information if they can assimilate it.[22] Perhaps the new "standards" will suggest baselines, benchmarks, rubrics, and goals for us to follow in judging student achievement. In one way or another, value problems and the issue of understanding will not go away in social studies.[23] Teachers of our subject, whatever their methods or philosophies, must come to grips with developing a balanced approach that combines didactic, reflective, and affective components in roughly equal proportions. And we also have many sets of standards to guide our thinking in choosing our methods and materials for instruction.

WHAT DO YOU THINK?

Review the social studies course offerings at your local middle or junior and/or senior high school. How many courses are required and how many electives? Do the offerings conform to the four course patterns of American studies, world history, civics or problems of democracy, and economics? Do you believe this is a sufficiently broad and varied course selection for your students or for yourself? Why or why not? If you agree, write a list of reasons to discuss with your peers. If not, design two or three new courses you would personally want to add to the curriculum. How would you justify the new programs to the school authorities? If they were approved, how would you engage student interest in enrolling? In general, do you find the current courses interesting or boring? In what direction do you think the school's program ought to go? Why?

SUMMARY AND RECOMMENDATIONS

Based on the current state of secondary social studies education, the long-standing problems within the discipline, and our professional needs, I propose a series of recommendations for all of us who teach social studies in the classroom—those teachers who breathe life into the process of social studies education. I urge all teachers to the following action:

1. Become active in professional organizations at the state, local, and national levels, especially the National Council for the Social Studies and its affiliates.

2. Read professional journals (at least one or two) as well as newsletters and magazines, regularly.

3. Take advantage of frequent in-service educational opportunities to broaden and deepen your knowledge and understanding of history and the social sciences—with particular attention to the non-Western world and its cultural products.

4. Try to transmit the past by connecting it to the present, acquiring a deeper and more critical comprehension of traditional topics, without neglecting current events that illuminate our time.

5. Experiment with new approaches and materials, different social sciences such as geography and economics, and especially those that encourage higher level thinking and value analysis of important topics and issues.

6. Incorporate group dynamics and field experiences into teaching in order to create active rather than passive learners and to involve as many students as possible in every lesson.

7. Discuss, examine, argue, debate, and evaluate controversial issues in an atmosphere of tolerance and free speech.

8. Remember that secondary school students are young adults who need recognition and the opportunity to contribute their ideas to the general pool of information in their preparation for daily adult life and their roles as citizens in a democracy.

9. Decrease teacher control by transferring decision making and conclusion drawing to students whenever possible, particularly on those issues that involve values, while reserving the right to challenge statements that demand to be tested.

10. Create new lessons and materials, or reinterpret standard topics, to meet changing student needs and social conditions.

11. Keep abreast as much as possible with scholarly research and experimental conclusions in social studies and related fields.

12. Incorporate regular pre- and posttest evaluation procedures, using both standard and teacher-designed tests that include factual, analytical, and judgmental questions in a variety of formats; replace test items frequently to improve the testing process as a basis for issuing fair grades.

13. Decrease or modify reliance on textbooks, particularly as the sole or major tool of teaching. Supplement assigned books with other tools, including additional texts, original sources, media technology, CD-ROMS and computer simulations, and materials from other disciplines to create a richer and more balanced curriculum as well as to cross-check for bias.

14. Assert your own style and philosophy of teaching, both to students and to colleagues, but remain open to change, improvement, and new policies when these appear soundly conceived, well-defended, and empirically successful.

15. Be prepared to fight for academic freedom, especially when special interests or community prejudices seek to suppress the teaching or discussion of vital issues.

16. Develop and keep somewhere safe your own repertory of "great lessons" and activities, to be continually integrated into your teaching.

17. Listen to student complaints and suggestions. Take seriously students' comments about content, topics, books, and skills they would like to see emphasized or diminished, within the limits of school regulations and course requirements.

18. Read, look, and listen. Promote and expand your own interests in literature, music, art, journalism, media, other cultures, travel, statis-

tics—whatever captures your imagination. Use your interests to enrich your teaching.

19. Consider teaching in a team, core, or integrated approach with other teachers, creating an interdisciplinary approach that combines history and literature, or science and social studies, humanities and world studies, or any other program that pleases you and your colleagues and helps you and your students to view subject matter as an interconnected whole.

20. Always reflect on and revise your goals throughout your teaching career. Question assumptions, test generalizations, allow innovations a fair trial run—just as you would wish your students to do.

TO DO

Write a portrait of yourself as the teacher you expect to be next year, five years from now, and ten years from now. What goals will you pursue? Which subject areas do you foresee as your specialties? Which do you think will be difficult to develop? What subjects do you think are neglected now and need to be developed in the future?

What kind of teaching style do you believe suits you best now and in the future. Will you stress the didactic, reflective, or affective goals and subjects of social studies? Will you build bridges to the humanities, the sciences, to both, or to neither? Why or why not? Which of the reforms that you have read about or experienced do you think will help schools the most? Which reforms would you personally like to implement?

Which courses will you expect to teach and how prepared will you be to present these? Are there areas in which you feel or will feel in need of more education, such as Africa, Asia, Latin America, or perhaps philosophy, literature, and the fine arts? Have your studies so far been adequate?

What accomplishments will you expect of students in your courses? What do you think will be realistic? How will you apply social studies or history or geography or economics or civics standards to your courses? Will students measure up? Do you believe students will deal best with information goals or with critical thinking objectives?

Overall, how to do you see yourself as a teacher in the school setting? What sort of style do you want to create? What do you wish to achieve for your students and for society? What do you think you will actually achieve? What ideals will you pursue despite local problems and lack of adequate resources?

NOTES

1. Diane Ravitch, *National Standards in American Education.* (McGraw-Hill, 1994) and Robert Rothman, *Measuring Up: Standards, Assessment, and School Reform* (San Francisco: Jossey-Bass, 1995).
2. F. Allen Hanson, *Testing Testing: Social Consequences of the Examined Life.* (Berkeley: University of California Press, 1994).
3. Ronald W. Evans and David W. Saxe, *Handbook on Teaching Social Issues,* Bulletin No. 93. (Washington, DC: National Council for the Social Studies, 1996).
4. William J. Bennett and Jeane Kirkpatrick, *History, Geography, and Citizenship: The Teacher's Role* (Washington, DC: Ethics and Public Policy Center, 1986). ERIC ED 283 775.

5. Donald W. Oliver and Fred M. , *Public Issues Series* (Harvard Social Studies Project) (Columbus, OH: Xerox Corp., 1966).

6. Shirley , "Decision-Making: The Heart of Social Studies Instruction," *Social Education* 24 (1960): 301–304, 306.

7. E. D. Hirsch, Jr., "Reality's Revenge: Research and Ideology," *American Educator* 20, no. 3 (Fall 1996): 4–7, 31–46.

8. James A. (Tony) Whitson and William B. Stanley, "The Future of Critical Thinking in Social Studies," in *The Future of Social Studies*, ed. Murry Nelson (Boulder, CO: Social Science Education Consortium, 1994), pp. 25–33.

9. Byron , N. F. Sprague, and Joseph B. Hurst, *Social Issues: Coping in an Age of Crisis* (Englewood Cliffs, NJ: Prentice-Hall, 1975).

10. Thomas Downey, "The Status of History in the Schools," in *History in the Schools*, ed. M. T. Downey (Washington, DC: National Council for the Social Studies, 1984), pp. 11–28.

11. James Banks, "Multicultural Education: Characteristics and Goals," in *Multicultural Education*, ed. J. A. Banks and C. Banks (Boston: Allyn & Bacon, 1987), pp. 19–23.

12. Gilbert , "The Rise and Fall of the Western Civilization Courses," *American Historical Review* 87 (June 1982): 695–725.

13. Larry Cuban, "Persistent Instruction: The High School Classroom, 1900–1980," *Phi Delta* 64 (Oct. 1982): 113–18.

14. James Banks, "Transformative Challenges to the Social Science Disciplines: Implications for Social Studies Teaching and Learning," *Theory and Research in Social Education* 23, no. 1, (Winter 1995): 2–20 (plus reaction letters by Merry Merryfield, Stuart Palonsky, and Geoffrey Milburn, same issue pp. 21–33).

15. Carole Hahn, and Jane Bernard-Powers et al., "Sex Equity in Social Studies," in *Handbook to Achieving Sex Equity Through Education*, ed. Susan S. Klein (Baltimore, MD: Johns Hopkins University Press, 1985), pp. 280–97.

16. Jane T. White, "Searching for Substantial Knowledge in Social Studies Texts," *Theory and Research in Social Education* 16, no. 2 (Spring 1988): 115–41.

17. David M. Seiter, "Teaching World History Today," *Social Education* 53, no. 5 (Sept. 1989): 327–32.

18. Mary M. and Richard C. Remy, *Teaching About International Conflict and Peace* (Albany, NY: SUNY Press, 1995).

19. David Perkins and Salomon, "Are Cognitive Skills Context-Bound?" *Educational Researcher* 18, no. 1 (Jan./Feb. 1989): 16–25.

20. Murry Nelson, "A Social Studies Curriculum for the Future, 'With Malice Toward None …?'" in *The Future of Social Studies* (Boulder, CO: Social Science Education Cosortium, 1994), pp. 61–67.

21. John Dewey, *The Child and the Curriculum* (Chicago: University of Chicago Press, 1902).

22. Eileen P. , David A. Child, and Herbert J. Walberg, "Can Comprehension Be Taught? *Educational Researcher* 17, no. 9 (Dec. 1988): 5–8.

23. Fred Newmann, "Priorities for the Future: Toward a Common Agenda," *Social Education* 50 (1986): 240–50.

FOR FURTHER STUDY: THE FUTURE OF SOCIAL STUDIES EDUCATION

Bloom, A. *The Closing of the American Mind*. New York: Simon & Schuster, 1987.

Bruder, I. "Education and Technology in the 1990s and Beyond: Visions of the Future." *Electronic Learning* 9, no. 4 (1990): 24–30.

Bruner, J. *Actual Minds, Possible Worlds*. Cambridge, MA: Harvard University Press, 1986.

Castells, M., R. Flecha, P. Freire, H. A. Giroux, and P. Willis. *Critical Education in a New Information Age*. Totowa, NJ: Rowan & Littlefield, 1999.

Code, L. *What Can She Know?: Feminist Theory and the Construction of Knowledge*. Ithaca, NY: Cornell University Press, 1991.

Cox, E. *A Truly Civil Society: 1995 Boyer Lectures*. Sydney: Australian Broadcasting Corporation, 1995.

Cuban, L. *How Teachers Are Taught: Constancy and Change in American Classrooms, 1890–1980*. White Plains, NY: Longman, 1984.

Dewey, J. *Democracy and Education: An Introduction to the Philosophy of Education*. New York: MacMillan, 1916.

Gadamer, H. G. *Truth and Method*. New York: Seabury Press, 1975.

Giroux, H., ed. *Postmodernism, Feminism, and Cultural Politics: Redrawing Educational Boundaries*. Albany, NY: SUNY Press, 1991.

Greaves, R. L., R. Zaller, P. V. Cannistraro, and R. Murphey. *Civilizations of the World*. New York: Harper & Row, 1990.

Hahn, Carole. "Gender and Political Learning" *Theory and Research in Social Education* 24, no.1 (Winter 1996): 8–36.

Johnston, W. B., and A. B. Packer. *Workforce 2000: Work and Workers in the Twenty-first Century*. Indianapolis, IN: The Hudson Institute, 1987.

Lerner, G. *The Majority Finds Its Past: Placing Women in History*. New York: Oxford University Press, 1979.

Lyotard, J. F. *The Postmodern Condition: A Report on Knowledge*. Minneapolis, MN: University of Minnesota Press, 1984.

National Center for History in the Schools. *National Standards for World History: Exploring Paths to the Present. Grades 5–12, Expanded Version*. Los Angeles, CA: University of California, 1994.

National Commission on Social Studies. *Charting a Course: Social Studies for the 21st Century*. Washington, DC: National Commission and National Council for the Social Studies, 1989.

Nelson, M. R., ed. *The Future of the Social Studies*. Boulder, CO: Social Science Education Consortium, 1994.

Parker, W. C. *Renewing the Social Studies Curriculum*. Alexandria, VA: Association for Supervision and Curriculum Development, 1991.

Shaver, J., ed. *Handbook of Research on Social Studies Teaching and Learning*. New York: MacMillan, 1991.

Toffler, A. *Future Shock*. New York: Random House, 1970.

Walsh, D., and R. W. Paul. *The Goal of Critical Thinking: From Educational Ideal to Educational Reality*. Washington, DC: American Federation of Teachers, 1987.

Wittgenstein, L. *Philosophical Investigations*. New York: Macmillan, 1985.

Appendix A

Nota Bene: One of my students, enrolled in the student teaching program, once complained that he could not find any ideas for his social studies lessons. I responded in amazement that, if anything, there were so many resources available that it was easy to be overwhelmed! So, the following is a list of organizations, publishers, distributors, agencies, and groups who offer services, publications, and memberships that can provide you with many different kinds of materials and ideas for teaching almost any aspect of social studies.

Where possible, I have given addresses, phone numbers, Web/Internet sites (beginning with www, but omitting http://), and e-mail addresses (where available) for each agency, organization, and association, which hopefully will stay current well after this book is published. However, you should always do a bit of checking on telephone numbers, Internet, and Web sites, so please feel free to add your own addresses and "finds" to the list. Surely, I have missed a few sources that are treasure troves of materials and ideas, so please feel free to build up the list and let me know of any organizations that offer great free or inexpensive materials.

American Anthropological Association
1703 New Hampshire Avenue, NW
Washington, DC 20009
Professional organization of university anthropologists; publishes a journal and sometimes teacher-oriented materials on archeology and cultures.

American Association for State and Local History
530 Church Street, Suite 600
Nashville, TN 37219-2325
615-255-2971
e-mail:aasih@"nashville.net"
www.nashville.net/aaslh
Aims to preserve and encourage the study of local history; publishes a newsletter and a journal, *History News*.

American Bar Association/YEFC 15.3
Special Committee on Youth Education for Citizenship
Update on Law Related Education
541 North Fairbanks Court
Chicago, IL 60611-3314
312-988-5735

Internet: abapubed@abanet.org
Offers a wide variety of materials and news about law-related education activities across the country (through local affiliates and related projects); prints a monthly publication for teachers entitled *Update On Law-Related Education.*

American Federation of Labor/Congress of Industrial Organizations
815 16th Street, NW
Washington, DC 20006
202-637-5000
The parent organization for most American unions provides a great many services, e.g., speakers, and materials for those interested in labor history, such as *Labor's Heritage.*

American Federation of Teachers
555 New Jersey Avenue, NW
Washington, DC 20001
202-879-4400 or 4530
Publishes *American Educator,* sponsors an "Education for Democracy" program, and promotes multicultural and labor education through workshops and free materials.

American Forum for Global Education
120 Wall Street, Suite 2600
New York, NY 10005
212-624-1300
globed120@aol.com
www.globaled.org
Produces a number of publications on world issues, public affairs, and citizenship; and provides a teacher resources catalog.

American Geographical Society
156 Fifth Avenue
New York, NY 10010
An organization that fosters the study of geography.

American Heritage
60 Fifth Avenue
New York, NY 10011
800-624-6283
Well-known national magazine of American history.

American Historical Association
400 A Street, SE
Washington, DC 20003
202-544-2422
web.gmu.edu/chnm/aha
Mainly aims at university-level historians, but also fosters history teaching in the secondary schools through publications and conferences; publishes the *American Historical Review, Perspectives,* newsletter, and a series of pamphlets on historical topics.

American Political Science Association
1527 New Hampshire Avenue, NW
Washington, DC 20036
202-483-2512

Professional organization of college/university political scientists; publishes a monthly journal and provides many teaching materials on politics and civics, some for middle and secondary schools.

American Psychological Association
Office of Educational Affairs
1200 17 Street, NW
Washington, DC 20036
Professional organization of college/university psychologists; publishes a monthly journal and yearbooks, as well as special issues on topics of interest to social studies teachers, particularly those offering a psychology course elective.

American Social History Project
Center for Media/Hunter College
City University of New York
99 Hudson Street, Third Floor
New York, NY 10013
212-966-4248
e-mail: BEynon@aol.com
www.ashp.cuny.edu
Views history from a social point of view; promotes the history of "ordinary people" through books and CD-ROMs, such as the multimedia *Who Built America?*; and publishes a variety of pamphlets for school use at the secondary level on U.S. historical topics.

American Sociological Association
1722 N Street, NW
Washington, DC 20036
Professional organization of college/university sociologists offering annual reviews, a monthly journal, and other publications, some of which would be of interest to secondary teachers, especially those offering a sociology course elective.

Amnesty International
322 Eighth Avenue
New York, NY 10001
212-807-8400
Organization dedicated to assisting the persecuted and the accused around the world, and publisher of newsletters such as *Amnesty Action* and *Student Action*.

Anti-Defamation League
823 United Nations Plaza
New York, NY 10017
212-885-7700 or 490-2525
www.adl.org
Watchdog society working against all forms of bias and bigotry in U.S. society; publishes a number of scholarly and popular materials on racial and religious injustice.

Association for Supervision and Curriculum Development (ASCD)
1250 North Pitt Street
Alexandria, VA 22314-1453
703-549-9110
e-mail:etrc@ascd.org
www.ascd.org

Major organization mainly composed of school administrators and teachers publishing a large number of booklets and materials on educational issues (e.g., *Educational Leadership*) and teacher preparation, including a videotape series about classroom teaching and a yearbook.

Association of American Geographers
1710 16th Street, NW
Washington, DC 20009
212-234-1450
Primarily university-level geographers who sponsor conferences and workshops on the study of geography.

California History-Social Science Project
UCLA
2051 Moore Hall, Box 951521
Los Angeles, CA 90095-1521
310-206-5501
e-mail:glover@gse.ucla
Internet: www.shastalink.k12.ca.us/www/History Project.html
Publishes a journal *Primary Source* and actively promotes the creation of a history-based social studies program in the schools.

Center for Civic Education
5146 Douglas Fir Road
Calabasas, CA 91302-1467
818-591-9321
Internet: center4civ@aol.com
Washington Office
1785 Massachusetts Avenue, NW
Washington, DC 20036-2117
202-265-0529
Internet: www.centereast@aol.com
Develops resources and materials for civic education; publishes a newsletter, *Center Correspondent*, a curriculum guide, *CIVITAS: A Framework for Civic Education*, and a book series for the secondary schools entitled, *We the People*.

Center for Research and Development in Law Related Education (CRADLE)
Wake Forest University School of Law
Box 7206 Reynolda Station
Winston-Salem, NC 27109-7206
Provides studies of law-related education.

Center for Research on Women
Wellesley College
Wellesley, MA 02181
Conducts research on women's issues and gender bias; offers publications and sometimes conferences on current issues.

Center for Responsive Law/Responsive Politics
1320 19th Street, NW
Washington, DC 20036
800-653-2129 or 202-387-8030
Encourages active citizenship through studies of participation, and through pamphlets and materials such as *Civics for Democracy: A Journey for Teachers and Students*.

Children's Book Council (CBC)
568 Broadway, Suite 404
New York, NY 10012
www.CBCbooks.org
Reviews published books from pre-K through eighth grade and publishes a "Notables Children's Trade Books" list for social studies, as well as other fields (e.g., science and literature).

Children's Defense Fund
122 C Street, NW
Washington, DC 20001
A premier social organization that works to defend the interests of children and youth, especially those who are poor and/or minority through lobbying and a series of publications.

Choices for the Twenty-First Century Education Project
Watson Institute for International Studies
Brown University
Box 1948
Providence, RI 02192
401-863-1355
www.brown.edu/Research/Choices/
Publishes secondary teaching materials (reproducible units) on foreign policy issues and historical problems, ranging from *The Role of the U.S. in a Changing World to Ending the War in Japan: Science, Morality, and the Atomic Bomb.*

Church World Service on Global Education
2115 Charles Street
Baltimore, MD 21218
800-456-1310
Offers ideas and resources for teaching about world hunger and other global problems; sponsors World Food Day.

Close Up Foundation
44 Canal Center Plaza
Alexandria, VA 22314-1592
800-CLOSE UP (256-7387), ext. 665
www.closeup.org
Promotes citizenship education through nonpartisan workshops and student field trips to Washington, DC; offers print and media publications on government.

Common Cause
2030 M Street
Washington, DC 20036
75300.3120@compuserve.com
Campaigns for ethical and responsible government; offers a nonpartisan publication of the same name.

Concord Review
P.O.Box 476
Canton, MA 02021
800-331-5007
e-mail:fizhugh@tcr.org

www.tcr.org
Publishes a review presenting studies and reports by middle and high school students.

Constitutional Rights Foundation
601 South Kingsley Drive
Los Angeles, CA 90005
213-487-5590
Offers a monthly newsletter *Bill of Rights in Action*, and a bibliography of teaching materials on legal issues and human rights.

Consumers Union of the United States
101 Truman Avenue
Yonkers, NY 10703-1057
914-378-2000
Noted for research on consumer products; publisher of *Consumer Reports* and *Zillions: Consumer Reports for Kids*.

Council for the Advancement of Citizenship
1724 Massachusetts Avenue, NW
Washington, DC 20036
703-706-3361
An organization devoted to encouraging good citizenship.

Court TV
600 Third Avenue
New York, NY 10016
How to set up your own televised courtroom; transcripts and guides.

C-SPAN
400 N. Capitol St., NW, Suite 650
Washington, DC 20001
202-737-3220
www.c-span.org
A public service offering teaching materials to accompany educational television presentations (e.g., *The Alex de Tocqueville Tour: Exploring Democracy in America*).

Educators for Social Responsibility
23 Garden Street
Cambridge, MA 02138
617-492-1764
esrmain@igc.apc.org
Seeks to encourage activism and promote conflict resolution programs; provides a resource catalog and materials for the classroom, and publishes journals including *Forum* and *Making History*.

Federal Reserve Bank of New York
Education Department
33 Liberty Street
New York, NY 10045
212-720-6130
www.ny.frb.org
Extensive materials are offered in a variety of media for classroom use on the role of the federal reserve in the U.S. economy and on economic topics and issues

ranging from money and banking to trade and taxation.

Feminist Press at CUNY
311 East 94th Street
New York, NY 10128
212-360-6130
Publishes pamphlets and monographs on gender issues and women's history.

Filmic Archives
The Cinema Center
Botsford, CT 06404-0386
800-366-1920
Catalog available: distributor for CD-ROMs, films and videos, documentaries, and TV productions related to history and social studies.

Foreign Policy Association
729 Seventh Avenue
New York, NY 10019
212-764-4050
Conducts workshops, and an annual review of foreign policy, and publishes participatory secondary teaching materials each year, *Great Decisions*.

Foundation for Teaching Economics
550 Kearney Street, Suite 1000
San Francisco, CA 94108
Provides ideas and materials to make economics a more "user-friendly" subject.

Global SchoolNet
P.O.Box 243
Bonita, CA 91908
info@gsn.org
www.gsn.org
Joins teachers and students from around the world.

Greenpeace
1436 U Street, NW
Washington, DC 20009
www.cyberstore.ca/greenpeace/index.html
Active advocacy of environmental issues, supports direct intervention on occasion; publishes a newsletter and journal of the same name.

History Teaching Alliance
Department of History
Western Washington University
Bellingham, WA 98225-9056
360-650-3096
compston@cc.wwu.edu
Serves as a network for teachers, historians, museums, and college faculty interested in historical studies.

Jackdaw Publications
Golden Owl Publishing
P.O. Box 503

Amawalk, NY 10501
800-789-0022
Publishes packets of original documents on a wide range of historical and social topics.

Journal of Social Studies Research
University of Georgia
Athens, GA 30602
Publishes a bimonthly college/university journal with a focus on social studies education.

League of Women Voters
1730 M Street, NW
Washington, DC 20036
202-429-1965
Organization fostering unbiased and impartial discussions of political issues while encouraging voter registration and activism.

Library of Congress
National Digital Library Educational Services, MS-5250
10 First Street, SE
Washington, DC 20540
202-707-5000
www.loc.gov or www.lcweb2.loc.gov/ammem (for American Memory)
Resource for government documents and reports.

Metropolitan Museum of Art
Uris Library and Educational Resources Center
1000 5th Avenue
New York, NY 10028
212-570-3985
Offers a wide range of publications, reproductions, and scholarly studies of art, art history, and culture as well as slide and lecture sets on historical topics such as *Medieval Arms and Armor* and *The Arts of Benin*.

National Archives and Record Administration
Education Division
Washington, DC 20408
202-724-0455 or 202-501-6303
www.nara.gov and The Digital Classroom
Offers an annual workshop and fellowships for students and teachers who want to do archival work in the nation's capital; publishes a newsletter and occasionally documentary collections of historical records with teaching guides.

National Center for History in the Schools
University of California at Los Angeles
404 Hilgard Avenue
Los Angeles, CA 90024-1512
310-794-6740
www/sscnet.ucla.edu/nchs
Authors of the National History Standards.

National Council on Economic Education
The EconomicsAmerica/Economics International Programs

1140 Avenue of the Americas
New York, NY 110036
800-338-1192 or 212 730-1793
www.economicsamerica.org or www.nationalcouncil.org
Promotes economic education through simulations, workshops, courses of
study, pamphlets about current issues, and the CD-ROM collection *Virtual Economics*.

National Council for Geographic Education

16-A Leonard Hall
Indiana University of Pennsylvania
Indiana, PA 15705-1087
Internet: www.ncge.org
editor e-mail: jleib@coss.fsu.edu
A professional geographic educator's organization that publishes the *Journal of
Geography*, as well as many other useful materials and reports, and sponsors an
annual conference.

National Council for History Education

26915 Westlake Road, Suite B-2
Westlake, OH 44145-4656
216-835-1776
Lobbies for history education in schools and U.S. society; publishes curriculum
guidelines and teaching units in U.S. and World history as well as a newsletter
called *History Matters!*

National Council for the Social Studies

3501 Newark Street, NW
Washington, DC 20016-1367
202-966-7840
e-mail: tssp@ncss.org
www.ncss.org/resources
The major organization of social studies teachers of all levels from primary grades
through university level; offers a large array of publications, programs, and yearbooks, as well as hosts major annual national and regional conferences and conventions; publishes and distributes the following journals to members and
nonmembers: *Social Education, Social Studies for the Young Learner, Theory and Research in Social Education, NCSS Newsletter*, and *The Social Studies Professional/News-
letter*.

National Council on Public History

327 Cavanaugh Hall, IUPUI
425 University Blvd.
Indianapolis, IN 46202-5140
garnet.berkeley.edu/~jhurley/ncphpage.html
Publisher of the journal *The Public Historian*, and a newsletter *Public History News*.

National Endowment for the Humanities

1100 Pennsylvania Avenue, NW
Washington, DC 20506
800-NEH-1121 or 202-786-0428
www.neh.fed.us and edsitement.neh.gov/

EDSITEment sites (at edsitement.neh.gov/)

African studies WWW
American verse project
ArchNet (archeological studies)
Columbus and the age of discovery
Detroit Institute of the Arts
The Digital Classroom (National Archives)
Labyrinth: Resources for Medieval Studies
LANIC: Latin American Network Information Center
Native Web (global resources concerning indigenous peoples)
New Deal Network (documents about FDR and Great Depression)
Oyez, oyez, oyez,: A Supreme Court WWW Resource
Perseus Project (maps and texts of the ancient world for students)
SARAI: South Asia Resource Access on the Internet
The Valley of the Shadow (multimedia resources about two Virginia communities divided by the Civil War)

Major grant-giving agency for humanities education with many different programs; offers guidelines for applications, and a journal, *Humanities*; also cosponsors the EDSITEment project, an Internet learning guide for the humanities, along with MCI and the National Trust for the Humanities.

National Geographic Society
Geography Education Program
17 & M Streets, NW
Washington, DC 20036
800-368-2728 202-828-6640
ngsline@aol.com
National Geographic is the main publication of this society, but the organization also offers maps, books, films, videos,
television programs (often with teacher guides), and many other materials suitable for social studies; also sponsors national teacher workshops and state geography alliances.

National History Day
11201 Euclid Avenue
Cleveland, OH 44106
216-421-8803
email:hstryday@aol.com
www.thehistorynet.com/National History Day
Local, state, and national competitions are sponsored
for students culminating in a nationwide judged competition.
National Institute for Citizen Education in the Law (NICEL)
25 E Street, NW, Suite 400
Washington, DC 20001
202-662-9620
Publishes an array of "street law" materials.

National Issues Forums
100 Commons Road
Dayton, OH 45459
800-433-7834
www.journalism.wisc.edu/nif
Hosts public meetings or "forums" for both students and adults on important public concerns. Also publishes pamphlets of different views on issues (e.g., so-

cial security, poverty, health care, international relations, etc.) suitable for classroom debates.

National Organization for Women (NOW)
1000 16th Street, NW Suite 700
Washington, DC 20036
202-331-0066
now@now.org
now.org/now/home.html
Now publishes a magazine and newsletter and raises funds to defend the interests of women.

National Women's History Project
7738 Bell Road
Windsor, CA 95492-8518
707-838-0478
Program focused on revising the standard curriculum to give women fair recognition of their role in history; catalog of resources available on request; research library open to teachers and students.

Organization of American Historians
112 North Bryan Street
Bloomington, IN 47401
812-335-7311
www.indiana.edu/;oah
Historians and history educators group that publishes and distributes a journal for secondary school teachers, the *OAH Magazine of History*, the OAH *Newsletter*, as well as offers other materials for both teachers and college faculty such as the *Journal of American History*.

Organization of History Teachers
St. Louis Park High School
6425 West 33 Street
St. Louis Park, MN 55426
Sponsors teacher workshops and annual conferences linked to the OAH.

PBS Learning Link
1320 Braddock Place
Alexandria, VA 22314
703-739-8464
www.whro-pbs.org/ll/
Offers a listing of public television programs accompanied by lesson plans for school use.

People for the American Way
2000 M Street, NW, Suite 400
Washington, DC 20036
Offers a newsletter, *First Voter*, and studies of U.S. history and civics textbooks, and encourages voter education in secondary schools.

Phi Alpha Delta Law Fraternity
Public Service Center
P.O. Box 3217
Granada Hills, CA 91394-0217

310-368-8103
padscla@aol.com
Law group that distributes information about legal issues and materials for law education.

Research for Better Schools/National Education Service
1821 West 3 Street
P.O. Box 8
Bloomington, IN 47402
812-336-7700 or
1-800733-6786 or
444 North 3 Street
Philadelphia, PA 19123
215-574-9300, Ext. 280
Provides research and advice aimed at dealing with at-risk young people in the schools.

Sierra Club
703 Polk Street
San Francisco, CA 94109
www.sierra.club.org
A leader in the area of environmental causes, which also publishes a catalog of educational materials, videos, slides, and so on, and a free teacher newsletter about environmental issues.

Smithsonian Institution
Office of Elementary and Secondary Education
A & I Building, Room 2283 MRC 444
202-257-1697
www.si.edu
Publishes *Smithsonian Magazine* and curriculum guides for museum activities and field trips.
Anthropology Outreach Office
National Museum of Natural History
NHB 363 MRC 112
National Museum Newsletter for Teachers
Washington, DC 20560
e-mail: kaupp.ann@nmnh.si.edu
Publishes newsletter for teachers, *AnthroNotes*, but also a rich source of publications, historic recordings, and teaching materials through other branches of the Smithsonian, particularly the Museum of American History.

Social Science Education Consortium
P.O. Box 21270
Boulder, CO 80308-4270
303-492-8154
singletl@stripe.colorado.edu
Organization of interdisciplinary faculty in social studies and the social sciences, mostly college and university based, but open to secondary teachers and curriculum specialists; sponsors local workshops and an annual "think tank" conference; publishes a wide range of interdisciplinary materials and studies (e.g., on Japan, The American West, etc.), many of which are designed for grades 7–12.

The Social Studies
Heldref Publications/Helen Dwight Reid Foundation
1319 Eighteenth Street, NW
Washington, DC 20036-1802
202-296-6267 (X213 managing editor)
www.heldref.org
Publishes a number of teacher/administrator-oriented journals, often with suggestions for lessons and book assignments, including *The Social Studies*, a national refereed journal, as well as the *Journal of Environmental Education*, the *Journal of Economic Education*, and the *Journal of Experimental Education*.

Social Studies Development Center
ERIC Clearinghouse for Social Studies/Social Science Education
Indiana University
2805 East 10 Street, Suite 120
Bloomington, IN 47408
800-266-3815 or 812-855-3838
Publishes *The ERIC Review* and *ERIC Digest*, a series of brief articles and bibliographies reviewing a wide variety of social studies topics; provides a free/inexpensive national information system on curriculum and instruction accessible through libraries, Internet, and CD-ROM.

Social Studies School Service
10200 Jefferson Boulevard
P.O. Box 802
Culver City, CA 90232-0802
800-421-4246
SSSService@aol.com
www.socialstudies.com
Distributes a catalog of the largest selection of social studies materials in the country, both published and teacher-made, including subsidiary catalogs on videos, CD-ROMs, for all levels and topics, history and social science, literature and film, from pre-K to university.

Society for History Education
California State University, Long Beach
1250 Bellflower Blvd
Long Beach, CA 90840
310-985-4634 or 310-985-4503
Publishes *The History Teacher* and other materials.

Stanford Program on International and Cross-Cultural Education (SPICE)
Institute for International Studies
Littlefield Center, Room 14C
Stanford University
Stanford, CA 94305-5013
800-578-1114
Spice.sales@forsythe.stanford.edu
Materials on contemporary world issues and world cultures.

Taft Institute for Government at Queens College/City University of New York
Queens College/City University of New York PH 186
Flushing, NY 11367

718-997-5163/64 or 718-997-5489
mkrasner@sover.net
www.qc.edu/Taft/
Conducts civic education workshops promoting active involvement in political affairs; offers a classroom video, *Why Vote?*, and other teacher education materials on citizenship.

Teachers Curriculum Institute
201 Antonio Circle, Suite 105
Mountain View, CA 94040
800-497-6138
Promotes teaching history through imaginative, "hands-on" methods, offers local workshops and conferences, and publishes *History Alive!* through Addison-Wesley.

Teaching History
Emporia State University
Box 4032
Emporia, KS 66801-5087
Reviews history books and offers articles about teaching methods through its magazine.

Tom Snyder Productions
80 Coolidge Hill Road
Watertown, MA 02172-2817
800-342-0236
www.teachtsp.com
Creates and distributes educational simulations in video, disc, and CD-ROM format, many on social studies topics, including the *Decisions, Decisions* series.

United Nations Headquarters (UNESCO, UNICEF)
3 United Nations Plaza
New York, NY 10017
212-963-1234
www.undp.org
UNICEF (212-759-0760)
Materials offered on international and multicultural issues as well as a catalog of gifts and cards aimed at supporting refugees around the world.

U.S. Department of Education
Drug Video Program
Office of Public Affairs
400 Maryland Ave, SW
Washington, DC. 20202
Copies of drug prevention and social programs may also be obtained from the following two government sources:
Schools Without Drugs
Pueblo, CO 81009
National Clearinghouse for Alcohol and Drug Information
P.O. Box 2345
Rockville, MD 20852
Federal drug prevention agencies providing information and advice on dealing with drug-related problems in schools.

U.S. Department of Health and Human Services
Clearinghouse on the Handicapped
Office of Human Development Services
U.S. Government Printing Office
Washington, DC 20401
Also refer to the following government sources:
National Information Center for Handicapped Children and Youth(NICHCY)
P.O. Box 1492
Washington, DC 20013
Office of Civil Rights
Department of Health and Human Services
Room 5146
330 Independence Avenue, SW
Washington, DC 20201
Offices providing information about special students and their needs in the classroom.

U.S. Holocaust Memorial Museum
100 Raoul Wallenberg Place, SW
Washington, DC 20024-2150
www.ushmmm.org
Museum that promotes school and individual visitors to view the exhibit and to conduct research; publishes teaching materials about the Holocaust in Europe during World War II.

U.S. Institute of Peace
1550 M Street, NW, Suite 700
Washington, DC 20005-1708
202-457-1700
usip_requests@usip.org
www.usip.org
Sponsors conferences and exchanges dealing with international relations, and publishes a series of pamphlets and books dealing with foreign policy and international peacemaking.

World History Association
Drexel University
Department of History and Politics
Philadelphia, PA 19104
zinssejp@miamiu.muohio.edu
neal.ctstateeu.edu/history/WHA
Publishes and distributes the *Bulletin of World History*, and the *Journal of World History*.

World Press Review
The Stanley Foundation
P.O. Box 228
Shrub Oak, NY 10588-0228
212-725-2106
Publishes the "Review" as a nonprofit educational service to "foster the international exchange of information," providing a compilation of newspaper and journal articles from around the world on topics of current interest.

Appendix B

SOCIAL STUDIES EDUCATION, SOCIAL SCIENCE, AND HISTORY
"GOOD READS FOR BIG IDEAS"

The following is a list of my recommendations of books and articles, past and recent, for social studies colleagues that have influenced my teaching and thinking, and to which I still return on occasion for some new/old and old/new ideas.

Apple, M. *Ideology and Curriculum*. New York/London: Routledge & Kegan Paul, 1970.

Banks, J. *Teaching Strategies for Ethnic Studies*. 3rd ed. Boston: Allyn & Bacon, 1984.

Banks, J. "The Canon Debate, Knowledge Construction, and Multicultural Education." *Educational Researcher* (June/July 1993): 4–14.

Banks, J. *Educating Citizens in a Multicultural Society*. New York: Teacher's College Press, 1997.

Barr, R. D., J. L. Barth,. and S. S. Shermis. *Defining the Social Studies*. Bulletin 51. Washington, DC: National Council for the Social Studies, 1977.

Braudel, F. *A History of Civilizations*. Trans. by R. Mayne. New York/London: Penguin Books, 1993.

Bruner, J. *The Process of Education*. Cambridge, MA: Harvard University Press, 1960.

Bruner, J. *Acts of Meaning*. Cambridge, MA: Harvard University Press, 1990.

Clarke, J. H., and R. M. Agne. *Interdisciplinary High School Teaching*. Boston: Allyn & Bacon, 1997.

Cuban, Larry. *How Teachers Taught*. New York: Longman, 1984.

Dewey, J. *Democracy and Education: An Introduction to the Philosophy of Education*. New York: MacMillan, 1916.

Dewey, J. *How We Think*. Boston: D. C. Heath, 1933.

Downey, M. T., and L. Levstik. "Teaching and Learning History." in *Handbook of Research on Social Studies Teaching and Learning*, ed. J. P. Shaver, pp. 400–410. New York: MacMillan, 1991.

Engle, S., and A. S. Ochoa. *Education for Democratic Citizenship: Decision-making in the Social Studies*. New York: Teachers College Press, 1988.

Fenton, E. *The New Social Studies*. New York: Holt, Rinehart & Winston, 1967.

Fenton, E. "Reflections on the 'New Social Studies.'" *The Social Studies* 82 (1991): 84–90.

FitzGerald, F. *America Revised: History Textbooks in the Twentieth Century*. Boston: Little, Brown, 1979.

Fraenkel, J. R. *Helping Students to Think and Value: Strategies for Teaching the Social Studies*. 2nd ed. Englewood Cliffs, NJ: Prentice-Hall, 1980.

Freire, P. *Pedagogy of the Oppressed*. New York: Seabury Press, 1970.

Gardner, H. *The Unschooled Mind: How Children Think and How Schools Should Teach*. New York: Basic Books, 1991.

Griffin, A. F. *A Philosophical Approach to the Subject Matter Preparation of Teachers of History*. Dubuque, IA: Kendall/Hunt, 1992.

Hirsch, E. D. *The Schools We Need and Why We Don't Have Them*. New York: Doubleday, 1996.

Hunt, M. P., and L. E. Metcalf. *Teaching High School Social Studies: Problems in Reflective Thinking and Social Understanding*. 2nd ed. New York: Harper & Row, 1968.

Johnson, R. T. and D. W. Johnson, eds. *Structuring Cooperative Learning: Lesson Plans for Teachers*. New Brighton, MN: Interaction, 1984.

Kozol, J. *Amazing Grace: The Lives of Children and the Conscience of a Nation*. New York: Crown Publishers, 1995.

Lowenthal, David. *The Past is a Foreign Country*. Cambridge, UK, and New York: Cambridge University Press, 1985.

Martorella, P. H., ed. *Interactive Technologies and the Social Studies Curriculum: Emerging Issues and Applications*. Albany, NY: SUNY Press, 1997.

Massialas, B., and J. Zevin. *Teaching Creatively*. Malabar, Fl: Kreiger & Sons, 1983.

Mehlinger, H. D. School Reform in the Information Age. *Phi Delta Kappan*, 77 (1996): 400–407.

National Education Goals Report. Washington, DC: U.S. Government Printing Office, 1995.

Noddings, N. Social Studies and Feminism. *Theory and Research in Social Education* 20, no. 3 (Summer 1992): 230–241.

Oliver, D. W., and J. P. Shaver. *Teaching Public Issues in the High School*. Boston: Houghton Mifflin, 1966. Reissued by Utah University Press in 1974.

Postman, N., and C. Weingartner. *Teaching as a Subversive Activity*. New York: Delacorte Press, 1969.

Saxe, D. W. "Social Studies Foundations," *Review of Educational Research*, 62 (1992: 259–277.

Schlesinger, A. M., Jr. *The Disuniting of America: Reflections on a Multicultural Society*. New York: Norton, 1991.

Schmuck, R. A., and P. Schmuck. *Group Process in the Classroom*. 4th ed. Dubuque, IA: W. C. Brown, 1983.

Shaftel, F. R., and G. Shaftel. *Role-playing for Social Values*. Upper Saddle River, NJ: Prentice-Hall, 1982.

Shaver, J. P., O. L. Davis, and S. W. Hepburn. "The Status of Social Studies Education: Impressions from Three NSF Studies." *Social Education*, 39 (1979): 150–53.

Sisk, D. *Creative Teaching of the Gifted*. New York: McGraw-Hill, 1987.

Slavin, R. E. *Cooperative Learning: Theory, Research, and Practice*. Upper Saddle River, NJ: Prentice-Hall, 1990.

Taba, H. *Curriculum Development: theory and Practice*. New York: Harcourt, Brace, & World, 1962.

Tobin, K. The Role of Wait Time in Higher Cognitive Level Learning. *Review of Educational Research*, 57 (1987): 69–95.

Weitzman, D. *My Backyard History*. Boston: Little, Brown, 1975.

Zinn, H. *The Politics of History*. Boston: Beacon Press, 1970.

Index

A

Acceleration, issues in, 54
Adler, Mortimer, 10
Adolescents, as audience, 47–51
Advance organizers, 338, 366
AERA. *see* American Educational Research Association
Affective dimension, 6*f*, 8, 17–18
    definition of, 5
    evaluation of, 184–186
Affective goals, 4
    for economics, 286–287
    and strategy use, 95
    and unit planning, 142, 145–147
    for U. S. government, 259–261
    for U. S. history, 229–231
    for world studies, 203–204
Affective questions, 83–87
    classification of, 83–84
Affective roles, 44–47
    with media, 336–338
AFT. *see* American Federation of Teachers
Ahlbrand, W., 318
Akutagawa, Ryonosuke, 116
Alder, Douglas D., 203
Alexander, Patricia A., 98
Alexander, Thomas, 10
Allardyce, Gilbert, 206
Allen, John, 354
American Anthropological Association, 409
American Association for State and Local History, 409
American Bar Association, Special Committee on Youth Education for Citizenship, 409–410
American College Testing, 193
American Educational Research Association (AERA), 390
American Federation of Labor/Congress of Industrial Organizations, 410

American Federation of Teachers (AFT), 387–388, 410
American Forum for Global Education, 410
American Geographical Society, 410
American Guidance Service, Inc., 193
American Heritage, 410
American Historical Association, 410
American Political Science Association, 410–411
American Psychological Association, 411
American Social History Project, 411
American Sociological Association, 411
American studies. *see* U. S. history
Ames, C., 124
Amnesty International, 411
Analysis questions, 80–81
Anderson, C., 5
Anderson, L., 306
Anderson, W., 324
Angell, Ann, 16
Anthropology, concepts/interests in, 27
Anti-Defamation League, 411
Apple, Michael, 12
Appleton, Nicholas, 299
Application questions, 80
Archer, J. C., 124, 352
Armento, Beverly, 320
Art, 350–351, 355–359
    as artifact, 358–359
    as esthetic, 359
    and social studies instruction, 391
Asher, Herbert B., 272
Assessment. *see also* Evaluation
    informal, 168–169
Assimilationism, 299

Association for Supervision and Curriculum Development, 411–412
Association of American Geographers, 302, 412
At-risk students, as audience, 51–52
Attitudes, development of, textbooks and, 329–330
Audience
of media, 338, 340–341
students as, 39–59
Authentic assessment, 161, 164–166
Avery, P. G., 5

B

Babad, E. Y., 53
Bagley, William, 10
Banks, James A., 299, 400–401
Bardelageor, R., 49
Barralet, John J., 257
Barr, Robert D., 6–8
Barth, James L., 6–9, 237–238
Baudelaire, Charles, 282
Bean, H., 238
Beck, Isabel L., 239–240
Beebe, Steven A., 63–64
Beers, Burton F., 327
Behavioral objectives, 142–147
Belief systems, in social studies, 30–33
Bellack, Arno, 201
Benjamin, D., 384
Bennett, C. I., 56
Bennett, William J., 398
Bennett, W. L., 371
Berger, Arthur A., 340
Berger, J., 350
Berk, Barry M., 327
Berlyne, D. E., 123
Berman, Sheldon, 300
Bernard-Powers, Jane, 265, 401
Bernstein, Richard, 11
Black, J. B., 238
Bloom, Allan, 385
Bloom, Benjamin S., 76, 83, 166
Bogdan, R. C., 53
Bond, A. R., 210
Boulding, K. E., 26, 291
Bowler, Ellen, 395
Bradley Commission on History in Schools, 24–25, 209, 221, 249, 387
Brady, Matthew, 361
Bransford, J. D., 123
Braudel, F., 306
Braun, Joseph A., Jr., 394
Bremer, Michael, 377
Brenneke, Judith S., 292

Briggs, L. J., 99
Brinton, Crane, 105
Brittan, Gordon, 26
Brophy, Jere E., 63
Brown, A. L., 99, 238
Brown, J. A., 371
Brubaker, Dale L., 6, 8
Bruner, Jerome, 11, 123
Brunn, S. D., 352
Budin, Howard, 70
Burstall, 317
Butts, R. Freeman, 266
Bybee, Roger W., 393

C

California History–Social Science Project, 412
Carnes, Mark C., 368
Carrol, James D., 262
Carroll, J. J., 264
Carroll, Lewis, 21
CD-ROMs, 380
Center for Civic Education, 254, 412
Center for Foreign Policy Development, 305
Choices for the Twenty-First Century Projet, 213
Center for Research and Development in Law Related Education, 412
Center for Research on Women, 412
Center for Responsive Law/Responsive Politics, 412
Center for the International Exchange of Scholars, 305
Centrality, in evaluation, 163
Chambers, B., 177
Chance, Paul, 115
Character education, 12
Charts, 352–354
Checklists, 186
Cherryholmes, Cleo, 29
Child, David A., 403
Children's Book Council, 413
Children's Defense Fund, 413
Chi, M. T. H., 98
Choices for the Twenty-First Century Education Project, 413
Chou, Ju, 303
Chronological approaches, 200, 205
Chronological–topical approach, to U. S. history, 233–242
criticism of, 236–239
defense of, 239–242
Church World Service on Global Education, 413
Citizenship education
in social studies, 6

views on, 5
Citizenship transmission approach, 8
Civics. *see* U. S. government
Civil War
resources on, 157–158
unit on, planning, 148–157
Clark, C., 142
Close Up Foundation, 413
Cognitive development, stages of, 49
Cohen, B., 378
The College Board, 193
Commager, Henry Steele, 118, 391
Committees, with controversy strategy, 131–132
Committee work, 63–64
Common Cause, 413
Community action approach, 274–278
Comparison and contrast strategy, 102–107, 106*f*
in Civil War unit, 156–157
problems with, 103–104
teaching techniques for, 104–105
usefulness of, 102–103
Complex reasoning, evaluation of, 178–181
Comprehension questions, 78–79
Computer databases, 374–375
Conceptual approach, to U. S. history, 243–245
Concord Review, 413–414
Concrete stage, of cognitive development, 49
Confucius, 3
Constitutional Rights Foundation, 414
Consulting Psychologists Press, Inc., 193
Consumer approach, 290–292
Consumers Union of the United States, 414
Controversy strategy, 128–135
problems with, 130
teaching techniques for, 130–133
usefulness of, 129–130
Conventional stage, of moral development, 86*t*
Conway, Margaret M., 264
Cooperative learning, 63–64
Coplin, William D., 264
Cornish, Dudley Taylor, 148
Correlated surveys, 170–171
Council for the Advancement of Citizenship, 414
Councils, with controversy strategy, 131–132
Counterchronological approach, to U. S. history, 243

Counts, George S., 12
Course evaluation, 187
Court TV, 414
Cox, Benjamin, 132
Creative Learning Press, Inc., 194
Creative students, as audience, 53–55
Critical pedagogy, 299
Critical Thinking Press & Software, 194
Critical thinking, textbooks and, 326–329
Cronbach, Lee, 163
Cross-cultural approach, 210, 214–216
Crucial Issues in Government series, 266
C-SPAN, 414
CTB/McGraw-Hill, 194
Cuban, Larry, 320, 401
Cultural literacy approach, 10, 385
Cultural pluralism, 299
Current events, sources for, 347–348
Curtin, Philip D., 214

D

Danzer, Gerald, 346
Dargahi, Nick, 377
Databases, 374–375
Data-gathering strategy, 98–102, 100*f*–101*f*
problems with, 99
teaching techniques for, 99–102
usefulness of, 98–99
Davidson, F. M., 352
Davis, James E., 290
Davis, O. C., Jr., 77–78
Davis, O. L., 318, 320, 331
Davis, O. L., Jr., 387
DBQs. *see* Document-based questions
DeBary, Theodore, 391
Debates, with controversy strategy, 131
de Charmes, R., 108
Defensible partiality, 132–133
Defensive teaching, 254–255
De Fina, Alan A., 164
Developmental disabilities, students with, 52–53
Devil's advocates, with controversy strategy, 131
Dewey, John, 11, 27, 32, 60, 123, 393, 403
Didactic dimension, 6*f*, 8, 17–18
definition of, 4
Didactic goals, 4
for economics, 284

and strategy use, 95
and unit planning, 142–144
for U. S. government, 255–256
for U. S. history, 226–227
for world studies, 201–202
Didactic questions, 78–79
Didactic roles, 40–41
with media, 336–338
Dillon, J. T., 42, 47
Distractors, 175
Documentaries, 370–371
Document-based questions (DBQs),
161, 176–184
Dorr, A., 339
Doubleday, C., 339
Downey, Matthew T., 203
Downey, Thomas, 400
Doyle, William, 177
Drama, 368
Drama-building strategy, 107–112
problems with, 108–109
teaching techniques for, 109–110
usefulness of, 107–108
Dumas, Wayne, 386
Dynneson, Thomas L., 261

E

Easton, David, 10, 272
Eclecticism, 7
Economics, 283–295
alternative approaches to,
290–295
concepts/interests in, 27
micro to macro model of,
287–290
patterns in, 285, 286f
questions for, 295
resources on, 312–313
student knowledge of, 284–285
Educational Testing Service, 175,
194, 205
Education of All Handicapped
Children Act (PL 94–142),
53
Educators for Social Responsibility,
414
Edutainment, 375–376
Effective Programs for Innovation
in Education Institute, 320
Eggert, Jim, 286
Emmet, E. R., 32
Engle, Shirley, 15, 245
Entertainment, in social studies in-
struction, 375–376
Environmental education, 302–305
Episodic framing, 348
Erickson, S. C., 187
Essay tests, 181–182

Essentialism, 10
Ethical humanism, 12
Eurocentrism, 200, 206, 296
Evaluation, 160–195
formative, 166
goal selection and, 142
issues in, 167–172
process of, 161–166
purposes of, 161–162
resources on, 193
structure of, 166, 167f
types of, 162–164
unit planning and, 153–154
Evaluation questions, 82–83
Evans, Ronald, 322, 397
Evans, Sam, 386
Ewen, S., 370
Examgen, Inc., 194
Expression, and assessment performance, 218
Extensive curriculum, 10

F

Fabre, M., 344
Farmer, Rod, 310
Farnen, R., 202
Federal Reserve Bank of New York,
414–415
Feminist Press at CUNY, 415
Fenton, Edwin, 23
Ferguson, D. C., 53
Ferguson, P. M., 53
Fernandez, Joseph A., 383
Fernland, Phyllis, 394
Festinger, L., 128
Fiction, in social studies, 344–346
Filmic Archives, 415
Films, 367–371, 392
use in lessons, 151, 221
Final grades, 171–172
Fine arts, 355–359
as artifact, 358–359
as esthetic, 359
Finn, Chester E., 237, 387
Fishman, M., 345
Fitzgerald, Frances, 233, 324
Fitzpatrick, C., 304
Fleming, M., 177
Foner, Eric, 148
Foreign Policy Association, 415
Formal operational stage, of cogni-
tive development, 49
Formative evaluation, 166
Foundation for Teaching Econom-
ics, 415
Frame-of-reference strategy,
116–122
problems with, 117

teaching techniques for, 117–118
usefulness of, 116–117
Freire, Paulo, 12
Fritz, Jean, 109, 112
Fulbright Association, 305
Furst, E. J., 142
Furst, Norma, 42

G

Gagne, Robert M., 99
Gallimore, Ronald, 318
Gall, Meredith, 49–50, 75
Gallup Organization, 265, 303, 387
Games, in instruction, 66–70, 123,
     304, 375–378
Garcia, Jesus, 331
Gardia, Ricardo L., 299
Gardner, Alexander, 361–362
Gardner, Howard, 162
Garner, Ruth, 95
Gearon, John D., 66, 70
Gelman, R., 49
Geographic approach, to world
     studies, 210–212
Geography, 302–305, 400
     concepts/interests in, 27
     resources on, 312–313
Geography Education Standards
     Project, 386
Gerzon, Mark, 121
Gifted and talented students, as au-
     dience, 53–55
Gioia, Gerry, 43, 73–74, 323
Giroux, Henry, 12
Global history approach, 210,
     217–218
Globalism, 306–308
     resources on, 312–313
Global SchoolNet, 415
Global studies. see World studies
Goals
     behavioral, 142–147
     for Civil War unit, 148
     for economics, 284–287
     and evaluation, 183
     setting, 141–147
     and strategy use, 95
     textbooks and, 325–331
     types of, 4
     for U. S. government, 254–261
     for U. S. history, 226–231
     for world studies, 200–204, 201*t*
Goodlad, John, 13, 385
Gordon, Irving L., 330
Grading, 171–172
Grant, C. A., 299
Graphs, 352–354
Graves, Howard, 321

Gray, John, 349
Great Books program, 10
Greenpeace, 415
Gronlund, Norman, 176, 181
Gross, Richard E., 33, 261, 266
Groups
     dynamics of, 61–75
     small, 63–64
Group tests/polls, 163
Guilford, J. B., 76–77
Guthrie, James W., 387

H

Habermas, Jurgen, 11, 334
Hadley, M., 372
Hahn, Carole, 401
Hallden, O., 239
Hamilton, R. J., 143, 177
Hansen, Lee W., 292
Hanson, F. Allen, 397
Hanvey, R., 307
Hare, V., 75
Harmon, Merrill, 12
Harper, G. F., 52
Harris, David, 131
Hart, Diane, 165, 172
Hartoonian, H. M., 31
Harvard Social Studies Project, 266,
     270
Hastings, J. T., 166
Hawke, Sharryl, 320
Hawkins, J. D., 52
Helburn, Suzanne, 318, 320
Hepburn, Mary A., 278
Hertzberg, Hazel, 6
Hickman, Faith M., 393
Hidi, Suzanne, 95, 97
Higher-level skills, teaching strate-
     gies for, 115–139
Hill, Paul, 387
Hine, Lewis, 291
Hinton, Chris, 351
Hirsch, E. D., 385
Hirsch, E. D., Jr., 10, 239, 399
Historical figures, art on, 356
History, 225–252
     resources on, 425–426
     in social studies, 6, 9, 24–25
          decline of, 400
     sources in, 346–348
History Teaching Alliance, 415
Hodges, James, 70
Hoetker, J., 318
Holt, Sol, 327
Holubec, Eduthe Johnson, 46
Home video, 370–371
Hudson, Charles, 121
Hull, K. T., 54

Hunkins, Francis P., 77–78
Hunt, M. P., 12
Hurst, Joseph B., 400
Husserl, E., 116

I

IBQs. *see* Information-based questions
Images, in social studies, 350–363
Inbar, J., 53
Independent projects, groups and, 61–62
Individual tests/polls, 163
Informal assessment, 168–169
Informal tests/polls, 163
Information-based questions (IBQs), 161, 172–173
Information, in media, 342, 348
Institute for Personality and Ability Training, 194
Integrated approach, 210, 217–218
    to U. S. history, 246–248
Intellectual development
    essentialists on, 10
    research on, 13
Intensive curriculum, 10
International approach, to economics, 294–295
International relations approach, 210, 212–213
    chronological span of, 214
International studies, 305–306
    resources on, 312–313
Internet, 372–374
Interviewers, with controversy strategy, 131
Investigative reporters, with controversy strategy, 131
Iran-Nejad, A., 124
Irving, John, 365
Issues-centered approach
    to economics, 293–294
    to U. S. government, 266–271
    to U. S. history, 245–246
Iyengar, S., 348

J

Jackdaw Publications, 415–416
James, William, 140
Jennings, L., 265
Johnson, David W., 46, 64, 171
Johnson, Roger T., 46, 64, 171
Joubert, Joseph, 39
Journal of Social Studies Research, 390, 416
Journals, 390
Judgmental questions, 82–83

Judy, Judith E., 98
Jurisprudence, concepts/interests in, 28

K

Kaltsouis, Theodore, 237
Kammen, Michael, 24
Kant, Immanuel, 396
Keefe, William J., 273
Keen, Sam, 219–220
Kendall, Diane S., 70
Key, 175
Kidron, Michael, 355
Kimmel, James R., 303
Kirkpatrick, Jeane, 398
Kirman, Joseph M., 24, 200
Klauer, K. J., 143
Klausmeier, Herbert, 103–104
Kniep, Willard M., 265
Knight, Richard, 263
Knowledge, textbooks and, 326
Kohlberg, Lawrence, 27, 83
Kounin, J., 40
Kouri-Daher, Nadia, 349
Kovaric, P., 339
Kownslar, Allan O., 327
Krathwohl, David R., 45, 83
Kuhn, A., 26, 28
Kuhn, Thomas, 11

L

Lambert, Karl, 26
Lam, T., 52
Landsdale, D., 218
Law-related education, 300–302
    resources on, 312–313
League of Women Voters, 416
Lecture method, 99
Lemert, James, 330
Leming, James S., 293, 367
Lengel, James G., 12, 15, 70
Lerner, Gerda, 233
Lesson plan
    sample
        on Civil War, 149–151, 154–157
        for Cold War, 219, 220*f*
        on current events, 349–350
        for economics, 293
        for evaluation, 170, 181
        on film use, 151, 221
        with fine art, 356–357
        with frame-of-reference strategy, 121
        on geography, 303
        for globalism, 308
        for integrated global history approach, 218–219

for law-related education, 301
with maps, 353
with music, 369–370
with photographs, 351, 361
for review, 210–211
textbook use in, 327
for U. S. government,
256–257, 265,
267–273
for U. S. history, 239–243
in unit planning, 152–153
Lewis, Naphtali, 391
Library of Congress, 416
Likert, Rensis, 170
Likert-type scales, 170–171
Linder, Bertram L., 327
Lipman, Matthew, 83, 85
Liston, Daniel P., 95
Literary sources, 347
Literature, in social studies, 344–346,
392
Lockwood, Alan, 131
Log, 177
Loguen, J. W., 154–156
Logue, Sarah, 154–155
Lower level skills, teaching strate-
gies for, 97–114

M

MacLeish, J., 99
MacNeil, William, 26
Macroeconomics, 287–290
Madaus, G. F., 166
Madden, R. E. and N. A., 52
Mager, Robert, 142
Maheady, L., 52
Maker, C. J., 55
Maps, 352–354
Martin, F., 172
Martin, Jane Roland, 16
Martorella, P. H., 372
Masia, Bertram B., 83
Massialas, Byron, 128, 132, 259
Masterson, John T., 63–64
Mastery tests, 163
Matching tests, 173–174
Maximum performance, 163
Mayer, R. E., 124
McAninch, Stuart A., 247
McKeown, Margaret C., 239–240
McLaren, Peter, 12, 299
McLuhan, Marshall, 341
McMichael, A., 384
McNeil, L. M., 255
Measurement, 161
Media
influence of, 336–337, 339, 367
information in, 342, 348

message in, 341–343
reflection in, 342–343
role-play with, 371–378
values in, 343–344
Meltzer, Milton, 345
Mercado, C., 56
Merryfield, M., 219, 308
Metacognitive strategies, 98
Metcalf, L. E., 12
Metropolitan Museum of Art, 416
Michaelis, John, 45
Microeconomics, 287–290
Mielke, K. W., 370
Milbrath, Lester W., 276
Minorities
in multicultural curriculum, 296,
299–300
in textbooks, 329
in U.S. history curriculum, 228,
238
in world/global curriculum, 208
Mock trials, 72–73
with controversy strategy, 131
Monmonier, Mark, 353
Moore, Frank, 151
Moral inquiry, 84–85
Moral reasoning, stages of, 86t
Morris, Richard B., 118, 243
Morrissett, Irving, 9, 19, 23, 320
Morton, John S., 290
Movies. *see* Films
Mueller, D. J., 260
Muessig, Raymond, 391
Multiculturalism, 12, 296–300,
297f–298f
and instructional roles, 55–56
resources on, 312–313
Multiethnic studies, 296–300
Multimedia. *see also* Media
active and passive roles with,
336–344, 371–378
movies and sound, 365–380
print and fine arts, 334–364
resources on, 364, 379–380
Multiple choice tests, 175–176
Music, 367–371
and social studies instruction,
391–392
Mystery strategy, 122–128
problems with, 124
teaching techniques for, 124–128
usefulness of, 123–124

N

Nagasaki, 358
Narrator, role of, 338–340
National Archives and Records Ad-
ministration, 225, 360, 416

National Assessment of Educational Progress, 194, 259
  Civics Consensus Project, 262
National Association of Secondary School Principals, 305
National Center for History in the Schools, 416
National Council for Geographic Education, 417
  Test Development Committee, 180
National Council for History Education, 417
National Council for the Social Studies (NCSS), 9, 385–388, 417
  Science and Society Committee, 393
National Council on Economic Education, 283–284, 286, 416–417
National Council on Public History, 417
National Education Association (NEA), 387–388
National Endowment for the Humanities, 417–418
National Geographic Society, 302, 387, 418
National History Day, 418
National Issues Forum, 418–419
National Organization for Women, 419
National Women's History Project, 419
Natoli, S. J., 210
Natriello, G., 171
NCSS. see National Council for the Social Studies
NEA. see National Education Association
Negroponte, N., 371
Nelson, Jack, 11, 45
Nelson, Murry, 402
New Criticism, 11
Newman, F., 50
Newman, Mark, 346
Newmann, Fred, 12, 16, 254, 264, 266, 403
News sources, 347–348
Noakes, S., 341
Noddings, Nell, 237
Norman, Donald A., 336

O

Objectives. see Goals
Objectives and Items Co-op School of Education, 194

Objective tests, 163
O'Connor, John R., 327
Office of War Information, 323
O'Leary, M. K., 264
Oliver, Donald, 12, 44–47, 266, 398
O'Malley, M., 384
Onosko, Joseph J., 16
Operational approach, to U. S. government, 262–266
  criticism of, 264–265
  defense of, 265–266
Opinion polling, 161
Oppenheim, A. M., 202
Opper, H. and S., 49
Oral history, 370–371
Oral tests, 177
Organization, for social studies instruction, 60–91
  resources on, 90–91
Organization of American Historians, 419
Organization of History Teachers, 419
Orwell, George, 325
O'Sullivan, Timothy, 361

P

Panels, with controversy strategy, 131
Pantin, Ronald L., 379
Parker, Walter C., 254
Participation approach, 274–278
Patrick, John J., 393
PBQs. see Perception-based questions
PBS Learning Link, 419
Peace education, 305–306
  resources on, 312–313
Pederson, P. V., 5
People for the American Way, 419
Perception-based questions (PBQs), 161, 184
Perennialism, 10
Performance assessment. see Authentic assessment
Performance tests, 163–164
Perkins, David, 402
Perry, Marvin, 327
Phenomenology, 11
Phi Alpha Delta Law Fraternity, 419–420
Philosophical inquiry, 84–85
Philosophy, in social studies, 30–33
Photographs, 350–351, 359–363
Physical disabilities, students with, 52–53
Piaget, J., 49
Pierce, Lawrence C., 387

resources on, 406–407
goals of, 4
  as bridge between theory and
      practice, 13–16
organization for, 60–91
  resources on, 90–91
problems in, 16
professional issues in, 398–400
recommendations for, 403–405
resources on, 389–391, 409–423,
    425–426
roles in, 40–47
  media and, 336–344
secondary, new emphases in,
    295–308
trends in, 401–403
unit planning in, 140–159
  sample of, 148–157
in U. S. history, 225–252
in world/global studies, 199–223
Social Studies School Service, 421
Society for History Education, 421
Sociology, concepts/interests in, 27
Software, instructional, 70–71, 123,
    304, 306, 380
Soper, John C., 180, 284–285
Sound bites, 348
Special interest groups, 389
Special students, as audience, 51–55
Speed tests, 163
Sprague, N. F., 400
Spring, Joel, 323
Srebeny-Mohammedi, Annabelle,
    335
Stadsklev, Ron, 70
Standardized tests/polls, 163
Standards movement, 384–386,
    396–397
Stanford Program on International
    and Cross-Cultural Educa-
    tion, 421
Stanislavski, Constantin, 40
Stanley, William B., 399
Steenland, S., 343
Stem, 175
Stevens, R., 168
Strasburger, Victor C., 336–337
Strategic knowledge, 98
Strong, W., 132
Student interest inventories,
    185–186
Students
  as audience, 39–59
    resources on, 58–59
  and economics, 284–285
  feelings and viewpoints of, eval-
    uation of, 184–186

and U. S. government, 259
and U. S. history, 232, 232*f*
Stull, A. T., 373
Subjective tests, 163
Subject matter knowledge, 98
Sullivan, George, 360
Sullivan, J. L., 5
Superka, Douglas, 12, 15, 320
Supply tests, 163
Surveys, correlated, 170–171
Survey tests, 163
Synthesis questions, 81–82

T

Taft Institute for Government at
    Queens College/City Uni-
    versity of New York, 179,
    421–422
Task-oriented small group work,
    63–64
Taylor, Joshua C., 359
Teacher(s). *see also* Social studies in-
    struction
  on curricular priorities, 309–310
  evaluation of, 187, 188*f*
  professional identity of, 386–387
  recommendations for, 403–405
  roles of, 39–59, 41*f*, 43*f*
    affective, 44–47
    didactic, 40–41
    reflective, 42–44
    resources on, 58–59
Teachers Curriculum Institute, 422
Teaching History, 422
Teaching strategies, 95–96
  comparison and contrast,
    102–107, 106*f*
  controversy, 128–135
  data-gathering, 98–102, 100*f*–101*f*
  drama-building, 107–112
  frame-of-reference, 116–122
  for higher-level skills, 115–139
  for lower level skills, 97–114
  metacognitive, 98
  mystery, 122–128
  relation of, 136, 137*f*
  resources on, 114, 138–139
Technology, and social studies in-
    struction, 392–393
Test reliability, 168
Tests/testing, 161
  designing, 172–184
    research on, 177
  publishers and distributors of,
    193–195
  terminology in, 163–164

Test validity, 168
Tetreault, Mary Kay, 239
Textbooks, 317–333
    advantages of, 321–322
    dependence on, 320–321
    disadvantages of, 322–323
    evaluation of, 323–325
    on government, usefulness of,
        262
    and objectives, 325–331
    pervasiveness of, 318–321
    resources on, 333
    trends in, 401–402
Thard, Roland G., 318
Thematic approaches, 200, 205
    to U. S. history, 243–245
*Theory and Research in Social Educa-
        tion* (journal), 390
Thomas, J. W., 99
Tiedt, I. M., 249
Tiedt, L., 249
The Time-Line Series, 113
Tobin, Kenneth, 88
Tokenism, 329
Tom Snyder Productions, 422
Torney, J., 202
Torney-Purtz, J., 206, 218
Torrance, E. P., 55
Trachtenberg, Alan, 351
True–false tests, 174–175
Tuckman, B. W., 187–189
TV news, 370–371
Tyler, J. E., 119
Typical performance, 163
    in portfolio assessment, 165–166

u

United Nations Headquarters, 422
Unit planning, 140–159
    resources on, 159
    sample of, 148–157
U. S. Bureau of Labor and Voting
        Statistics, 179
U. S. Bureau of Statistics, 134
U. S. Bureau of the Census, 241, 279
U. S. Congress, Office of Technology
        Assessment, 374
U. S. Department of Education, 422
U. S. Department of Health and Hu-
        man Services, 423
U. S. government, 253–281
    alternative approaches to,
        266–278
    operational approach to, 262–266
    program design for, 261–278
    questions for, 278–279
    resources on, 281
    student knowledge of, 259

U. S. history, 225–252
    alternative approaches to,
        243–246
    chronological–topical approach
        to, 233–242
    program design for, 231–248
    questions for, 248–249
    resources on, 252
    student opinions of, 232, 232f
U. S. Holocaust Memorial Museum,
        423
U. S. Institute of Peace, 423

V

Value inquiry, 84–87
Values clarification, 12
Values, in media, 343–344
Van Sickle, Ronald L., 63
Van Tassel, David D., 23
Vargas Llosa, Mario, 299
Vazquez-Faria, J. A., 56
Viadero, D., 384

W

Wager, W. W., 99
Walberg, Herbert J., 403
Waley, Arthur, 126
Wallerstein, Immanuel, 26, 214
Walstad, William B., 180, 284–285
War or Peace (game), 66–70
Watkin, Daniel, 350
Watkin, Edward, 350
Weeks, Phillip, 238
Weible, Thomas, 386
Weiner, B., 107
Weinstein, C. E., 124
Wesley, Edgar B., 6
Western history approach, 206–210
    criticism of, 208
    defense of, 209–210
Whimbey, Arthur, 43
White, Charles S., 394
White, C. S., 308
White, Jane T., 401
Whitson, James A., 399
Williams, Jo Watts, 6, 8
Wirt, F., 259
Wolff, J., 345
Women
    in multicultural curriculum, 296,
        299–300
    in textbooks, 329
    in U.S. history curriculum, 228,
        238
    in world/global curriculum, 208
World History Association, 423